DISCOURSE, FIGURE

ALSO BY JEAN-FRANÇOIS LYOTARD
PUBLISHED BY THE UNIVERSITY OF MINNESOTA PRESS

The Differend: Phrases in Dispute

Heidegger and "the jews"

Just Gaming (with Jean-Loup Thébaud)

Political Writings

The Postmodern Condition: A Report on Knowledge

The Postmodern Explained

Postmodern Fables

Signed, Malraux

DIS COUR SE, FI GURE

Jean-François Lyotard

Translated by Antony Hudek *and* Mary Lydon

Introduction by John Mowitt

UNIVERSITY OF MINNESOTA PRESS MINNEAPOLIS · LONDON

CULTURAL CRITIQUE BOOKS
An occasional series of publications in association with the journal *Cultural Critique*. www.upress.umn.edu/journals/culturalcritique

The University of Minnesota Press gratefully acknowledges financial assistance provided by the French Ministry of Culture for the translation of this book. Ouvrage publié avec le concours du Ministère français chargé de la culture—Centre national du livre.

"'The Dream-Work Does Not Think'" was originally published in *Oxford Literary Review* 6, no. 1 (1983): 3–34; reprinted with permission of *Oxford Literary Review*. "Fiscourse Digure: The Utopia behind the Scenes of the Phantasy" was originally published in *Theatre Journal* 35, no. 3 (1983): 333–57; copyright by The Johns Hopkins University Press; reprinted with permission of The Johns Hopkins University Press.

"there is a here and" copyright 1940, 1968, 1991 by the Trustees for the E. E. Cummings Trust, from E. E. Cummings, *Complete Poems: 1904–1962*, ed. George J. Firmage (New York: Liveright Publishing Corporation, 1968); reprinted by permission of Liveright Publishing Corporation.

Originally published in French as *Discours, figure*; copyright 1971 by Klincksieck.

Published by the University of Minnesota Press
111 Third Avenue South, Suite 290
Minneapolis, MN 55401-2520
http://www.upress.umn.edu

Library of Congress Cataloging-in-Publication Data

Lyotard, Jean-François, 1924–1998.
[Discours, figure. English]
Discourse, figure / Jean-François Lyotard ; translated by Antony Hudek and Mary Lydon ; introduction by John Mowitt.
p. cm. (Cultural critique books)
Includes bibliographical references and index.
ISBN 978-0-8166-4565-7 (hardcover : alk. paper)
ISBN 978-0-8166-4566-4 (pbk. : alk. paper)
1. General semantics. 2. Form (Aesthetics). 3. Art Philosophy. I. Title.
B820.L913 2011
194 dc22

2011016410

Printed on acid-free paper

a m a a m

To whom is a book due? For the book itself is a modern offspring of Greek tragedy, and, through it, of expiatory sacrifice. Like these, the book is therefore already *due to a debt* whose insatiable creditor is unnameable. One cannot entertain the hope of extinguishing this debt with acknowledgments.

I hereby designate my immediate creditors: S. Boucheron, L. Bovar, the members of the C.N.R.S. Commission de Philosophie, P. Durning, C. Martin, and M. May, without whom this book could not have been realized; the students in the 1967–68 course and 1968–69 seminar at Nanterre, with whom it was conceived; M. Dufrenne, who, without fail and with unconditional generosity, believed in this project.

CONTENTS

INTRODUCTION
The Gold-Bug JOHN MOWITT xi

DISCOURSE, FIGURE

The Bias of the Figural 3

SIGNIFICATION AND DESIGNATION

Dialectics, Index, Form 23

Recessus and Hyper-Reflection 51

Linguistic Sign? 72

Effect of Thickness in the System 90

Thickness on the Margins of Discourse 103

The No and the Position of the Object 115

Opposition and Difference 129

***VEDUTA* ON A FRAGMENT OF THE "HISTORY" OF DESIRE** 157

THE OTHER SPACE

The Line and the Letter 205

"The Dream-Work Does Not Think" 233

Desire's Complicity with the Figural 268

Desire in Discourse 277

Fiscourse Digure
The Utopia behind the Scenes of the Phantasy 327

Return, Auto-Illustration, Double Reversal 356

APPENDIX
Jean-François Lyotard's French Translation of "Die Verneinung" by Sigmund Freud 391

NOTES TO CHAPTERS 397

NOTES ON FIGURES AND PLATES 481

BIBLIOGRAPHY 492

INDEX OF NAMES 503

INDEX OF CONCEPTS AND GERMAN EXPRESSIONS 509

Plate section follows page 480.

INTRODUCTION

The Gold-Bug

John Mowitt

On 21 April 1998, Jean-François Lyotard succumbed to an aggressive form of leukemia. Shortly after, at the annual meeting of the International Association for Philosophy and Literature hosted by the University of California, Irvine, an impromptu commemorative event was organized that included several "witnesses," among them Dalia Judovitz, his colleague at Emory University, who read from his then-unpublished manuscript on Augustine, and Jacques Derrida, then in residence at Irvine. Among the several somber remarks made by Derrida, two bear repeating here. First he shared with us an anecdote, meant I suppose to underscore his vulnerability, his sense of exposure, an anecdote that disclosed his belief in the power of incantation. Recounting a dinner recently shared with Lyotard, Derrida made a point of saying that he had promised to protect his ailing friend with a spoken charm taught to him by his mother. Indeed, his remarks concluded when he observed with redoubled sadness (the loss of the mother and of the friend) that his mother's charm obviously failed. The anecdote of the antidote that wasn't one.

The other remark was more directly intellectual in character, but for that reason no less capable of marking Derrida's exposure to the event of mourning. It arose as Derrida sought to tease out the rhythm of his agreements and disagreements with Lyotard. Aware that he was compressing much time and space, Derrida nevertheless permitted himself the observation that toward the end they disagreed most passionately about Marxism: Lyotard sacrificed it to the postmodern, Derrida sustained himself on its weak yet indestructible, hauntological "spirit."

If I begin these remarks by reconstructing this somber scene it is because next to me in the auditorium sat my late friend Mary Lydon, who, when Derrida contrasted himself with Lyotard in this way, said under her breath, "oh, la, la," that oddly translingual statement that when translated specifically from the French might, in this context and with that intonation, simply be rendered as "bullshit." My point here is not to establish my presence at this particular occasion (frankly, no one in attendance wanted to be at *this* event); rather, the point is to underscore something crucial both to the friendship between Lyotard and one of his major philosophical interlocutors and also to the intellectual and political situation out of which *Discourse, Figure* emerged, a situation very much caught up in a dispute over the contending legacies of Karl Marx and Sigmund Freud, especially as these bore on the problem of language then preoccupying so many in the human sciences but nowhere more tenaciously than in and around academic philosophy.

It is important to emphasize that Lydon's "summation," as a subsequent brief conversation made clear, was not about whether Derrida believed what he was saying but whether Lyotard's relation to Marxism had been fairly characterized by him. We agreed that it was not, and it seems appropriate now to elaborate why as a way to begin thinking about *Discourse, Figure,* a text that, perhaps oddly, says rather little about Marxism as such.

Discourse, Figure was Lyotard's *thèse de doctorat d'État,* the rough equivalent of a doctoral thesis and as such the professional form of recognition that gives one access to university teaching, dissertation supervision, and the coveted title of *Maître de conférences.* The thesis was published in 1971 by Klincksieck, a *maison d'édition* established in the early nineteenth century and well known for its international traffic in German, French, and English texts. This text was later described by Lyotard as one of only four "actual" books he ever wrote, and although it would certainly be worth lingering over this characterization of "the book" (his list of publications is extensive indeed), my point here is different.[1] Lyotard's first text-that-was-not-a-book was simply titled *Phenomenology,* and it appeared from the prestigious Presses Universitaires de France in the Que sais-je? series begun by Paul Angoulvent during the Occupation. Its date of publication was 1954. Thus, a hiatus of seventeen years separates this text from his first "book," and if it is important to draw this out it is precisely in order to propose that something crucial to *Discourse, Figure* transpired in this gap.

In 1950, Lyotard assumed his first teaching post in a francophone high school for boys in Constantine, Algeria, four years before the onset of the war for national liberation. During this period he made contact with, among others, Pierre Souyri, Claude Lefort, and Cornelius Castoriadis, three of the founding editors of the Rosa Luxemburg–inspired journal *Socialisme ou Barbarie* (Socialism or barbarism). Lyotard joined the editorial collective after his return to France and published frequently on the Algerian crisis, writings now available in English in the collection *Political Writings.* Although his aim is different, Mohammed Ramdani (the editor of the French edition of Lyotard's contributions to *Socialisme ou Barbarie*), through his attention to the motif of the bureaucratization of the revolution, underscores how Lyotard's analysis of the Algerian crisis situates this work squarely within the political and theoretical disputes that in 1963 finally tore the editorial collective of *Socialisme ou Barbarie* apart.

The terms of this dispute are certainly of interest, but since Lyotard himself, in the "Afterword" to *Peregrinations,*[2] hashed and rehashed them, it will suffice to point to that aspect of the dispute that bears on the question of what Herbert Marcuse later called "Soviet Marxism." Practically since its formation in 1949, the intellectuals and activists affiliated with *Socialisme ou Barbarie* concerned themselves with the history and theory of Marxism. At the core of their editorial quarrels stood the question of how to save, or at least separate, Marxism from Stalinism without simply retreating from politics in the name of theoretical correctness. Castoriadis eventually came to formulate a position on the matter that called Marxism itself into question, but prior to that he and others—including, let us not forget, Guy Debord (if briefly) and Jean Laplanche—pursued a critique of the relation between political leadership and bureaucracy that Ramdani rightly discerns at work in Lyotard's analysis of the political crisis besetting the National Liberation Front (FLN) almost before the ink on the Évian Accords had time to dry. As Lyotard recounts in "A Memorial of Marxism," initially he and Souyri felt sufficiently provoked by Castoriadis that they splintered off to form *Pouvoir Ouvrier,* then little more than an ancillary, more directly proletarianized publishing venture within the orbit of *Socialisme ou Barbarie.* It was not long before this splinter splintered in turn, leaving Lyotard to, as he puts it, drift. Doubtless it is this history that prompts him to invoke it directly in the introduction to his collection of essays *Dérive à partir de Marx et Freud,* where he also, in linking drifting and the death drive, finds motivation for saying that the essays in *Dérive* are but the "scaffolding" of or for *Discourse, Figure.*[3] And, lest it pass unremarked, among the scaffolds is Lyotard's long, still untranslated contribution to *Les temps modernes* from 1969, "La place de l'aliénation dans le retournement marxiste" (The place of alienation in the Marxist reversal).

While at one level this would appear to confirm Derrida's assertion about Lyotard's drift away from Marxism, quite a different observation seems equally justified—namely, that Lyotard's relation to Marxism was, dare I say, foundational and sustained. Even if one reads his controversial support for Operation Desert Storm as definitive proof of his "anti-Marxism" (and I take the point), it is undeniable that his work remained very much engaged with debates within Marxism about Marxism. So much so that the very meaning of drift—clearly an avatar of the Situationist practice of *détournement*—would appear indelibly marked by the Marxism from which it derives. But how then are we to make sense of the rather attenuated presence of Marx in *Discourse, Figure*? Put differently, what is to be made of the fact that the most conspicuous engagement with Marx in this text occurs in the section "Nonhuman Sex" (in the chapter "Opposition and Difference")?

At this juncture it becomes important to consider what happens in Lyotard's first text, *Phenomenology.* As is typical of all titles in the Que sais-je? series, a series intended to bring specialist knowledge to a broadly educated but nonspecialist public, Lyotard's study begins by laying out fundamental concepts of Edmund Husserl's early and late work. The second part of the study is then devoted to a consideration of the impact of phenomenology on the disciplines of psychology, sociology, and history. The discussion of history culminates in a sustained consideration of the Marxist theory of history. At stake is whether phenomenology can provide Marxism with a theory of the human subject consistent with the tenets of historical and dialectical materialism, a point shaved differently yet obsessively by the likes of Jean-Paul Sartre and Maurice Merleau-Ponty in the postwar period. In *Phenomenology* Merleau-Ponty gets the last word: phenomenology provides

Marxism with a philosophy of the human subject precisely to the extent that by "returning to the things themselves" (Husserl's mantra), philosophy eliminates itself as a practice separate from and ancillary to real life. En route, Lyotard makes a special point of adducing the relevance, indeed the centrality, of Tran Duc Thao's effort to reconcile phenomenology and historical materialism (to invoke the title of Thao's groundbreaking study). Thao is unusually important here because he, too, calls for a revision of Marxism (à la *Socialisme ou Barbarie*) but also because in 1948, in the pages of *Les temps modernes,* he published a stunning, lengthy review of Alexandre Kojève's *Introduction to the Reading of Hegel*; Thao's lectures on this work had a lasting impact on, among others, Jacques Lacan, whose theory of desire, as others have noted, is plainly legible in Kojève's reading of Hegel.[4] What makes the review important is that in tracing how Kojève misreads Hegel as a dualist, Thao not only shows how this ignores precisely what Marx and Lenin found so provocative in Hegel but, further, he sketches how Husserlian phenomenology fills in the blank left in the materialist account of consciousness by Marx. Quite apart from whether this is philosophically compelling—and Thao's work still awaits a serious "reading"—what demands attention is the fact that phenomenology, or more broadly the theory of the human subject, clearly functions for Lyotard as a way to engage Marxism but, in accordance with the logic of negation, by not engaging it, that is, by attempting to think within Marxism in that precise place where it is not thinking, where, in effect, it invites the sort of critical pressure brought to bear on it in the period of de-Stalinization.

Why stress this? Because when the reader thumbs through *Discourse, Figure* what leaps out is the trajectory, the profile of the argument. Namely, as virtually all commentators have pointed out—and this includes everyone from Bill Readings and Geoffrey Bennington to Federico Jiménez Losantos and Mary Lydon—the book proceeds from an attentive engagement with the phenomenology of experience to an ambitious meditation on the psychoanalytic account of the subject of experience.[5] What this points to, among other things, is the fact that "the return to the things themselves" had, in the course of the 1950s and 1960s, forked into a double return: the return to Marx and the return to Freud. In effect, *Discourse, Figure* is immanently structured by the confrontation between phenomenology and psychoanalysis as contending frames within which to think the materialism of consciousness. In this sense, the return to Freud was always a return to Marx. And vice versa.

In a very general sense this sheds light on why Marx is taken up explicitly in *Discourse, Figure* under the heading of sexuality, but a careful look at this discussion discloses the hovering presence of Lacan.[6] It is important to stress this because for Lyotard the relation between phenomenology and psychoanalysis is one he inherited from Maurice Merleau-Ponty, an inheritance in which Lacan's critique of the "psychoanalytical establishment" (as he famously put it) is, in a sense, what psychoanalysis had literally become for French philosophy. Indeed, the presence of Lacan in *Discourse, Figure* assumes several different forms. Two are worth mentioning here. The first section of *Discourse, Figure* to appear in print was the long section "The Dream-Work Does Not Think." Lyotard's thesis supervisor and mentor, Mikel Dufrenne, published it in his journal, *Revue d'esthétique,* in 1969. The second part of this section contains a sustained and quite penetrating critique of Lacan's appropriation of Roman Jakobson's distinction between metaphor and metonymy, the point of which is to show both that the two men differ in the way they apply this distinction to Freud's concept of "the primary processes" (the psychical activities that constitute the "dream work") and that recognizing this exposes the failure of Lacan's effort to put linguistics in the service of psychoanalysis. Lyotard's comments toward the end of *Discourse, Figure* on the motif of anamorphosis—a crucial touchstone in Lacan's later engagement with Merleau-Ponty's *The Visible and the Invisible*—has a similar, if prophetic, feel.

The second form of Lacan's presence is more subtle but no less consequential. Among the many genres of discourse found in *Discourse, Figure* there is the surprising appearance, in what is listed in the table of contents as an "appendix," of a translation. Titled "(De)negation" it is, in fact, a retranslation of the then extant French translation of Freud's 1925 essay "Die Verneinung" (negation, although James Strachey notes that "denial" and "disavowal" are used in the Standard Edition). What links this to Lacan is the fact that already in *The Seminar, Book I,* from 1953 to 1954, this very essay and this very problem of its translation had attracted attention. Indeed, the French Hegel scholar who inherited Kojève's mantle, Jean Hyppolite, gave, at Lacan's invitation, a presentation to the seminar in which he proposed, apparently following Lacan's lead, that *die Verneinung* would be better rendered as *dénégation.* Moreover, and this is vital, in his presentation Hyppolite was concerned to explore the conceptual pressure brought to bear by Freud's essay on Hegel's cortical concept of "negation," a concept crucial to Marx's reading of the dialectic and thus also to Kojève's reading of Hegel. Even Thao concedes the political and philosophical indispensability of the concept. Lyotard segues to the retranslation from a brief consideration of the relation between denegation and the death drive, and it is clear that the question of the theory of the subject in Marxism (is it better grasped phenomenologically or psychoanalytically, and if the latter, by what form or school of psychoanalysis?) is very much on the proverbial table. Thus, the specter of Lacan, whether draped or exposed, is deployed within *Discourse, Figure* as something of a condensation in or around which is to be found the question: have the full—political, and, as we shall see, aesthetic—implications of Lacan's return to Freud been articulated, much less realized? Or, to perhaps overemphasize the vexed theme of negation, is a properly nondialectical Marxism possible and, if so, how might it transform our concept of perception, including, of course, our perception of the beautiful?

Here is not the place to tease out the intricate relation between this genre of question and the socio-genesis of the postwar French intellectual, but it does seem worth noting that several figures now routinely linked both to poststructuralism and postmodernism—certainly Lyotard, but others besides—took their intellectual stances in reaction, even if obliquely, to Lacan's attempted redemption of Freudian metapsychology.[7] Indeed, one gets a different but important purchase on *Discourse, Figure* by considering in what way the book anticipates the assertion made in *Libidinal Economy* from 1974 (two years after *Anti-Oedipus* and a year after Julia Kristeva's *Revolution in Poetic Language*) that: "the model of all semiology is not 'The Purloined Letter,' it is 'The Gold-Bug.'"[8] Edgar Allan Poe is referenced in the notes to *Discourse, Figure* but clearly derives the importance attached to him in this quip from the fact that Lacan delivered his seminar on Poe's tale "The

Purloined Letter" in 1955 (later placed at the head of the *Écrits*), a seminar in which he deploys, as Derrida was later to stress, a semiological account of the sign as a way to think of the topology of heterosexual difference. Lyotard, by insisting that a different Poe short story ought to guide our semiological thinking, is blazing the trail followed in 1975 by Derrida's "postman," by again squaring off against Lacan's intervention in psychoanalysis. What this tells one about *Discourse, Figure* can be teased out by considering the semiological character of "The Gold-Bug."

Published by *The Philadelphia Dollar Newspaper* in 1843, the story is often linked by specialists to the Dupin detective stories (which include "The Purloined Letter"), but strictly speaking the narrator occupies the space of what Maurice Blanchot calls "the neutral": "it" is not Dupin, nor is there a "case" to be cracked—a code, but not a case. What appears to recommend the tale for semiological scrutiny is the fact that at its core rests a message, in fact a cipher whose decipherment constitutes a considerable chunk of the reported speech in the narration. As specialists have pointed out, this text reflects Poe's recently acquired passion for cryptography; indeed, this text is known to have inspired the career of a crack World War II cryptologist, William Friedman. This said, it is not immediately obvious why Lyotard sees this tale as superior, semiologically speaking, to the one worked over by Lacan. Spoiler alert: The code in question turns out to reveal the location of a handsome treasure buried on Sullivan's Island, South Carolina, by the pirate Captain Kidd. Its decipherment involves many levels of translation and transposition—once the location is determined, a somewhat farcical (and, alas, racist) feat of gymnastics and bricklaying is required—clearly, the sort of heterogeneity of signifiers that might well appeal to Lyotard. But what seems especially attractive to him is the mad passion of the protagonist William Legrand. True, Dupin is himself a quirky hybrid of scientist and poet, but Legrand—though capable of brilliant ratiocination (Charles Peirce seems to have been impressed)—is not a poet. He is a man bitten by a bug. Gold-Bug man. Significantly, this characterological element finds its semiological reiteration in the means by which Legrand discovers the code he then proceeds to crack, which is through fire. As Legrand explains, he discovers the syntagma of the cipher by accidentally waving the strange surface on which it is written near a fire, a fire made necessary by "chance" meteorological conditions on the island. This evocation of the "tongues of flame" would hardly rise above the status of cliché, except that—and I think this is what seals the issue for Lyotard—what Legrand insists on is that he had to risk burning, thus destroying, the material substrate of the code in order to render it legible. One might say, then, that this theory of the sign is one that stresses not its "destination" or destiny (a watchword in Lacan's reading) but its derivation, its drift out of a force field that persistently threatens to consume it. Although one might want to insist that the death drive is never far from Lacan's trajectory of the letter, it is clear that Lyotard thinks it is too far.

If, as I will propose, the relation between fire and sign is one way to grasp the volatile relation between figure and discourse, then not only does one get a vivid sense of how *Discourse, Figure* belongs to the tendency North Americans call "poststructuralism"—the concerted antidisciplinary struggle to think beyond yet in the wake of the linguistic turn—but one also glimpses how artistic practice—in the case of Poe, literary practice—belongs to the core of this struggle for Lyotard. Although Derrida was the one to level the charge explicitly, Lyotard would almost certainly agree that Lacan appears inclined to use literary art to demonstrate psychoanalytic theory, whereas what is called for is a way to think of art as a modality of theoretical practice. In this, *Discourse, Figure* would appear to anticipate the distinction drawn by Gilles Deleuze and Félix Guattari in *What Is Philosophy?* between concepts and precepts. *Discourse, Figure* is not only a brash experiment in aesthetic theory but also a mad yet fully calculated effort to transform the status of the aesthetic within Marxism, and, like Theodor Adorno and Walter Benjamin before him, Lyotard seeks to pursue this possibility by intensifying the theoretical encounter between Marx and Freud. The role of "negation" has already been stressed in this regard, and it is worth underscoring that Adorno, too, mined it for resources to radicalize the status of the aesthetic within Marxism. Where he and Lyotard might be said to differ is over the matter of the source of art's critical power: Adorno preferring to situate this in the transcendental character of the aesthetic as such; Lyotard, recoiling from what he regarded as Adorno's Judeo-Christian Hegelianism, preferring to situate art's power in the immanent mutability of desire. Whence, in 1974, "libidinal economy."

In turning, then, to speculate briefly on the current import and relevance of *Discourse, Figure,* it is important to recall that Lyotard was, during the period in question, linked together as a "philosopher of desire" with Deleuze and Guattari.[9] All three had, within the space of a few years, launched a frontal assault on Lacanianism, and, although at least Deleuze and Lacan reconciled, it is clear that at issue was the rescuing of desire from Kojève's reading of Hegel's *Begierde,* a reading thought to have sacrificed desire to a dialectic of recognition/representation. Against this, Lyotard, Deleuze, and Guattari agreed that desire was more like a factory, a site of production, than a theater, a site of reproduction and representation. In 1975 Deleuze and Lyotard (then both friends and colleagues) drafted a scathing indictment of the Department of Psychoanalysis at the University of Paris VIII, Vincennes, when it was reported that Lacan had instigated or inspired what they did not hesitate to call a "Stalinist purge" of the teaching and training faculty. As suggestive as such facts are, they tend to obscure what cannot meaningfully be reduced to a doctrinal dispute. Thus, there may well be profit in recalling that Deleuze used the distinction between desire and pleasure as the heuristic through which to frame essentially the entirety of the encounter between his project and that of Michel Foucault, an example that urges one to ask: so what might be the more general stakes of a theory of desire as immanent productivity?[10] In a sense, this is but another way of asking a question put forward earlier: is a nondialectical Marxism possible? Or, to invoke yet again the famous Eleventh Thesis on Feuerbach: is there only one politically progressive way for philosophers to stop interpreting the world and change it?

Our moment is one in which the postmodernism to which Lyotard, alas, will forever be shackled has, if one is to trust Fredric Jameson, morphed into globalization, where the "cultural turn" has, at least in the Global North, fanned out into the becoming-cultural studies of higher education in both the social sciences and the humanities. Precisely because such changes have been understood by partisans of all stripes as political developments, the question of how one thinks the terms by which one joins interpretation and transformation lingers. It insists. This matter has not been and will not be resolved by recovering theorists now proclaiming the death of theory, and, in fact, if *Empire* and later *Multitude* generated the intense controversy they did, it is because Michael Hardt and Antonio Negri staked out a position, not just on whether a nondialectical Marxism was possible but on the matter of whether nondialectical Marxism could change the changing, that is, globalizing, world. This position has been deeply criticized (see, for example, Gopal Balakrishnan's *Debating Empire* or Samir Amin's review of *Empire* for *The Monthly Review,* just to evoke a range of opinion) but often in order to cite empirical exceptions to what is presented there as a permanent state of exception.[11] Left unspoken, when not dismissed with righteous and therefore apotropaic indignation, is the philosophical project of the critique of dialectical reason (to use Sartre's double-edged formulation). Although easy to overlook, even Marx emphasized that the point was for philosophers to change the world, not to stop being philosophers.

From this vantage point *Discourse, Figure* becomes provocative because of the way it produces a theory of the subject that deploys aesthetic experience as the means by which to pursue the critique of dialectical reason. In a sense, Lyotard turns in the opposite direction from Deleuze and those working in his wake, a point one might flesh out by considering that in Kojève's struggle with Hegel he engages Baruch Spinoza's ontology of immanence, but only to spar against it as non-Hegelian. Specifically, Kojève, revealing his familiarity with *The Ethics,* recodes the Hegelian distinction between nature and understanding as one between substance and the subject. Under Martin Heidegger's influence, Kojève reads Spinoza's substance as a conceptual prototype of the German noun, that is, being with a capital B. What prompts the charge of non-Hegelianism is the fact that for Kojève—who is reading Hegel, let us not forget, in the spirit of Marxism—what is crucial is the affirmation of the properly dialectical relation between substance and subject, a relation that in the course of history develops such that the subject negates substance, by grasping what Kojève calls Truth. This is the anthropologically driven humanism that Heidegger challenged in "The Letter on 'Humanism'" from 1947. Thus, for Kojève, Spinozan substance is unappealing because it, too, resembles reality stripped of history. It presupposes, in its very conceptualization, a dualism between it and the subject as the bearer of human consciousness.

Recall here that this is the very charge leveled against Kojève's Marxism by both Louis Althusser and Thao: it is not dialectical. What this brings to the surface is that the question of how precisely to theorize the subject of Marxism is one of enormous philosophical challenge, a challenge taken up by Deleuze in a manner designed to breathe new political life into the concept of substance. In this he places himself in the ranks of figures like Althusser, Pierre Macherey, Negri, and Étienne Balibar, among others, all embarked on the Dionysian labor of forging a link between Spinoza and Marx. By contrast, and in this sense he can be said in *Discourse, Figure* to have pushed off in the opposite direction, Lyotard resists the temptation to reinvigorate substance and instead moves to deanthropologize the subject. Yes, in this sense *Discourse, Figure* is aligned with the so-called poststructural critique of the subject, but to settle for such a pat formulation misses the decisive way in which this critique aims for something more.

To clarify, even if briefly, attention must turn to the point at which the historical materialist and the psychoanalytic theories of aesthetic experience touch. This takes place in the theory of consciousness. For historical materialists, and the entire "reflection theory" of art, aesthetic experience arises when lived social relations are given form, through the selection and combination of suitable signifiers, by a consciousness seeking to stylize, to represent the life organized by those relations. These relations may elude consciousness, but objectively, that is, because they do not present themselves as such to the consciousness of either the artist or the public. Psychoanalytic theories, likewise representational, differ primarily in modeling social relations on familial ones and grasping what eludes the consciousness of the artist subjectively, that is, in what must be repressed for consciousness to endure social relations lived as familial. Aesthetic experience represents the effects of this repression. To summarize with risible but efficient brutality, these perspectives touch in linking art to the representation of what consciousness cannot represent to itself. Lyotard, through the titular formulation of "discourse, figure," uses the comma, as Lydon observed, to mark the possibilities suspended within this touch. These are possibilities that point "beyond representation" (to cite Lyotard's introduction to Anton Ehrenzweig's *The Hidden Order of Art*), not simply to a site of production but to an articulation of productivity that seeks to put aesthetic labor at the forefront of what Kojève might describe as the becoming subject of substance. What this dislodges is the cortical status of "understanding" in the work of dialectical reason, leaving in its place, in an older Kantian vocabulary, "imagination." Indeed, it is possible to detect in the pages of *Discourse, Figure* pronounced glimmers of Lyotard's later sustained engagement with the *Critique of Judgment*. Here, what seems more urgent to stress is the way Lyotard moves to undercut the status of understanding, not to embrace the irrational (a favorite slur thrown at poststructuralism *tout court*) but in order to discover in the space emptied by its problematization the terms of an aesthetic encounter with a nondialectical Marxism, that is, a Marxism for which communism is not *the* future but rather *has* a future.[12] It is precisely in this spirit that he later confronts Adorno's "absolute music" with John Cage's "silence." In this he illuminates why in Deleuze and Guattari art, both critical and clinical, remains such a destabilizing point of reference. Even if, in the end, one remains unconvinced about the theoretical and political possibility of a nondialectical Marxism, *Discourse, Figure* points directly at a problem that still haunts our moment: what will we have to make of art such that it can think where Marxism is not yet thinking? For Lyotard, the Gold-Bug, this was not an academic question. It was a signal fire lit in the hope of stirring those dissatisfied with the "politicization of art" urgently called for by Benjamin in the 1930s forward. Forward, toward what? Not necessarily "back to the things themselves" but perhaps into the "thick" (or as Lyotard insists, "the thickness," *l'épaisseur*) of things where, among other things, one encounters, as Lydon so touchingly put it, the infancy lost when seeing words on the page was surrendered, irreversibly, to reading them. Marx, of course, warned against being "childish" but precisely, Lyotard might argue, in order to honor the political meaning of the denegation of childhood. Precisely not as something lost, but as a threshold where things, like the future itself, are up for grabs.

DISCOURSE, FIGURE

The Bias of the Figural

For the eye "to recognize sound," as Paul Claudel put it, the visible must be legible, audible, intelligible. The "second logic," which he opposed to the first—the one that determined the nature and function of words—teaches "the art of fitting [them] together and is practiced before our eyes by nature itself."[1] "There is knowledge of each other, obligation between them, thus relationship between the different parts of the world, as *between the parts of speech* [*discours*], *so that they may constitute a readable sentence.*"[2]

This book protests: the given is not a text, it possesses an inherent thickness, or rather a difference, which is not to be read, but rather seen; and this difference, and the immobile mobility that reveals it, are what continually fall into oblivion in the process of signification. "A long time ago, in Japan, while going up from Nikko to Chuzenji, I saw, juxtaposed by my line of vision, although at great distance from each other, the green of a maple filling the separating space, in order to answer the appeal of a pine, asking for agreement. These pages are meant to be a commentary on this sylvan text."[3] Limiting ourselves to perception: is it a text, that which speaks only when the eye has located "the point of view," when my gaze has become the gaze to which things are "owed"?[4] A text is not deep sensorially, you do not move in front or inside of it so that its agreement may be fulfilled; if you do, it is metaphorically. But the sensory,[5] the sylvan world, would seem to be precisely the absolute referential of all analoga: here we move, searching for composition, constituting the space of the picture, relying on that plastic space where the eye, the head, the body move or swim, buoyed as if in a bath of mercury. It is the juxtaposition by the eye that guarantees the agreement of the pine and the maple, agreement fulfilled because total, a harmony of silhouette, tone, value, and position: desire momentarily satiated. Claudel does not say juxtaposition of pine and maple, but juxtaposition by the line of vision. The two trees stand "at a great distance from each other," yet the stem of the gaze skewers and sticks them together on an unspecified background, on any canvas. Very well, but this flattening makes the "picture,"[6] not a page covered in writing, which is a kind of table. One does not read or understand a picture. Sitting at the table one identifies and recognizes linguistic units; standing in representation one seeks out plastic events. Libidinal events.

That the world remains to be read basically means that an Other, on the other side, transcribes the given objects, and that with the appropriate point of view I could theoretically decipher it. This is still giving objects a lot of credit—a sign of Claudel's paganism, of which he was well aware: he had no choice but to disassociate poetry and prayer. His entire oeuvre arises from this drama, for a Christian, of being able to achieve a semblance of serenity through the agreement of a pine and a maple, to experience a fervent faith—both desire and pleasure—in the sensory. The road to Chuzenji is the Calvary of an absolution of the sensory. By climbing up to Chuzenji, Claudel wants to catch a glimpse of the flip side of the picture, but from Nikko he wants to take the frontside with him to the other side. Such is the imaginary: to possess both front and back. Such is sin and pride: to have both text and illustration. This ambivalence is that of Christianity itself, the same Christianity in fact that lies at the core of the issues we Westerners have: the audition of the Word, but at the same time a philosophy of creation. Through the first we ask to be delivered from the thickness of the flesh, to close our eyes, to be all ear; through the second we are forced to acknowledge that the objects' mobility, which constitutes them as world, that their shimmering, that the appearance (and the depth that informs it) be absolved in some way, insofar as they derive from what is all-powerful and all-loving. An ambivalence outlined by the history not only of Western thought but of the painting, born of the Writ and daring to illustrate it, untamed, never ceasing to submit itself to it, yet always managing to elude it.

The alternative would be to forgo Creation altogether, to assert crudely the sole radicalism of ethics, to refute the transcendence of the sensory—the transcendence in immanence that Merleau-Ponty spoke of in the wake of all the painters—to attribute depth to the false transcendence, to temptation, and to go so far as to reject the false text of the world, to want only to hear accurately, maybe even still less than that. In its radicalism, this return to Script—understood as allocution of the Other and as promise, where Jewish and demythologized Christian thought converge—renounces even what the eye listens to. May it close, be ripped out like Oedipus's. Master of illusion, slave of illustrations—we are never rid of the "evil eye." Philosophy, both first and last, is, as Emmanuel Levinas reminds us, morality, the vis-à-vis of the face since the face is the presence of the absolutely Other, the only *Gegenstand* worthy of the name, which cannot be walked around, does not belong to the sensory, announces something I cannot thematize as the back of a front facing me, as noema of a noesis. The face is the presence of the word. Between it and me who listens to it lies not the thickness of the sensory, but absolute openness, absolute imbalance, true irreversibility where are to be found not objects and my gaze (as Claudel believed), but the infinite and the finite. This suffering is said to be good if it hears the infinite in the face. On the contrary, the eye's action would be passion, corruption.

This book takes the side of the eye, of its siting; shadow is its prey. The half-light that, after Plato, the word threw like a gray pall over the sensory, that it consistently thematized as a lesser being, whose side has been very rarely really taken, taken in truth, since it was understood that its side is that of falsity, skepticism, the rhetorician, the painter, the *condottiere*, the libertine, the materialist—this half-light is precisely what interests this book. "The eye," writes André Breton, "exists in its savage state."[7] For Merleau-Ponty, the sensory is the site of the chiasm, or rather the very chiasm where the site takes place: there is no absolutely Other, but there is the element dividing itself and turning over, becoming vis-à-vis and therefore perceptible; there is a "there is" that is not originally a heard utterance, but the product of a driftwork that tears the element in two, leaving the flanks in the imbalance that the ethical life indeed speaks of but that belongs to the seer and the visible, that is unheard speech.

Such at least was Merleau-Ponty's resolve: to go as deep as this originary chiasm without crushing the imbalance through the phenomenological reduction, without overcoming exteriority through the immanence of the transcendental realm, and to that end to find a language to signify what lies at the root of signifying. However, it took nothing less than the transformation of language itself into a gesture to render it consubstantial with the space of the chiasm that it was supposed to utter. Yet we know what happens in the end when one simply combines word and gesture, when saying is dissolved in seeing. Either saying goes silent, or the seen must already be something like a said. Did Hegel not challenge sensory certainty to dare declare itself without falling into the anxiety of uncertainty? And even when, leaning over its shoulder, condescending to its silence, he endeavors to follow its finger pointing to the Here, does he not in the same movement extract from this supposed immediate faith the mediation of demarcation, the trajectory that he states is a discourse, the same negativity as that of language? In the end, then, depth seems empty, in its shadow all cows turn black, and the truth of the matter is that one must begin where one is, namely, from within words.

Let us therefore start here, take up the daunting challenge, enter the arena. Let us tackle the self-sufficiency of discourse. An easy task, that of dissipating the current prestige of the system and the closure in which the specialists of language think they can confine all that is meaning. We find ourselves right back at the text, authored by no one this time and which reads itself. Trivial gains, for the impertinence remains, which is such an oversight with regard to the sensory that it is as if humans had become two-dimensional beings, with nothing for touching, but moving along the intervals [*écarts*] in the network.[8] Will we be able to tear down the closure by claiming the existence of an absolute excess of meaning in the originary word and the necessity for the finite to interpret endlessly? This infinity and this openness, which we find in Paul Ricoeur's hermeneutics, betray a reticence toward Hegelianism, but they remain in its sphere. For Hegel, before anyone else, did not take the symbol as anything other than as lending itself to thought; before anyone else he saw it above all as a moment to be overcome. In fact, he simply did not see it, for all he wanted was to hear the voice of its silence.[9] With this accomplished, hermeneutics is content to leave open the passage of consciousness toward listening. It thereby seems to respect the symbol's transcendence to all form of commentary, and the endlessness of the task. Nonetheless, its affinity to dialectics is not in doubt, in that the symbol, the starting point, is not taken as an object but a scrambled utterance. The transcendence of the symbol is that of a discourse emanating from an Other. It is not Creation as a thick thing that leaves its mark on, and that takes in, alterity, it is by being deaf to revelation, the visible is not what manifests *itself* by holding *itself* back in its reverse, it is only a screen of appearances. It is not appearing, but noise covering up a voice.

What cannot be tamed is art as silence. The position of art is a refutation of the position of discourse. The position of art indicates a function of the figure, which is not signified—a function around and even in the figure. This position indicates that the symbol's transcendence is the figure, that is, a spatial manifestation that linguistic space cannot incorporate without being shaken, an exteriority it cannot interiorize as *signification*.[10] Art stands in alterity as plasticity and desire, a curved expanse against invariability and reason, diacritical space. Art covets the figure, and "beauty" is figural, unbound, rhythmic. The true symbol gives rise to thought, but not before lending itself to "sight." And the surprising thing is not so much that it gives rise to thought, since once language exists, every object has to be signified and inserted in a discourse, falling into the sieve [*trémis*] where thought sifts and sorts everything.[11] The mystery is that the symbol remains to be "seen," that it remains steadfastly within the sensory, that there remains a world that is a store of "sights," or an interworld that is a store of "visions," and that every form of discourse exhausts itself before exhausting it. The absolutely-other would be this beauty, or the difference.

Must one therefore keep silent in order to bring it to light? But the silence of the beautiful, of perception—a silence that precedes speech, an innermost silence—is impossible: there is simply no way to go to the other side of discourse. Only from within language can one get to and enter the figure. One can get to the figure by making clear that every discourse possesses its counterpart, the object of which it speaks, which is over there, like what it designates in a horizon: sight on the edge of discourse. And one can get in the figure without leaving language behind because the figure is embedded in it. One only has to allow oneself to slip into the well of discourse to find the eye lodged at its core, an eye of discourse in the sense that at the center of the cyclone lies an eye of calm. The figure is both without and within. This is why it holds the secret of connaturality, but at the same time reveals this connaturality to be an illusion. Language is not a homogenous environment: it is divisive because it exteriorizes the sensory into a vis-à-vis, into an object, and divided because it interiorizes the figural in the articulated. The eye is in speech since there is no articulated language without the exteriorization of a "visible," but it is there because an exteriority exists which is at least gesticulatory, "visible," deep within discourse, which is its expression. In pursuing this double exteriority one may be able to take up the challenge that language poses to the visible, and the ear to the eye, namely, to show that the gesticulatory expanse that makes depth or representation possible, far from being signifiable through words, spreads out on their margins as what enables them to designate; and to show, too, that this expanse is the source of the words' power of expression, and thus accompanies them, shadows them, in one sense terminates them and in another marks their beginning. For one needn't be immersed in language [*langage*] in order to be able to speak; the "absolute" object, the language-system [*langue*], does not speak.[12] What speaks is something that must remain outside of language as system and must continue to remain there even when it speaks. Silence is the opposite of discourse, simultaneously violence and beauty; but silence is the very condition of discourse since it is also on the side of the things of *which* one must speak, *that* one must express. There can be no discourse without this opacity in trying to undo and restore this inexhaustible thickness. Silence is the result of the ripping-apart that allows discourse and its object to stand vis-à-vis each other, and the work of signification to begin; it is the result of the tear, integral to language, where the work of expression occurs.

Such violence belongs to the depth of language. It is its starting point, since one speaks in separation and the object must first be constituted as lost for it to have to be signified. Violence therefore ratifies the birth certificate of the problem of knowledge, forces one to desire truth as the interiorization (completed signification) of (the object's) exteriority. The cognitive function contains within it this death that makes the vis-à-vis, the desire that produces the thickness of reference. But the expressive function contains it as well, but differently: it imports this death within discourse itself, since in the violence of the tearing-apart it is not a question of having a perfectly pure object on one side and, on the other, a pristine subject, this setup permitting those cherished mind-games about the possibility of truth. No, this violence transforms the object into a sign, while symmetrically transforming discourse into a thing: it adds depth, erects a stage in the articulation and limpidity of signification, at the same time carving, on the side of the object, its other face, the wings of its stage.

Power lies with the eye. To transform the unconscious into discourse is to bypass the dynamics, to become complicit with the whole of Western *ratio* that kills art at the same time as the dream. One does not break free at all from metaphysics by placing language everywhere; on the contrary, one fulfills it, one enacts the repression of the sensory and of *jouissance*. The opposition is not between form and power, in which case all one does is confuse form and structure! Power is never anything other than the energy that folds and crumples the text and makes an artwork out of it, a difference, that is, a form. The painting is not something to be read, as contemporary semiologists would have it. Rather, as Klee put it, it has to be *grazed*, it makes visible, giving itself up to the eye like the exemplary thing it is, like naturing nature (to borrow Klee's words again), since it makes visible seeing itself. What is more, it makes visible that seeing is a dance.[13] To look at a painting is to draw paths across it, or at least to collaboratively draw paths, since in executing it the painter laid down, imperiously (albeit tangentially), paths to follow, and his or her work is this trembling, trapped within four wooden slats, that an eye will remobilize, bring back to life. The "fixed-explosive" beauty lucidly required by *mad love*.

What, then, do you believe discourse to be? Cold prose hardly exists, except at the lowest rungs of communication. Discourse is always thick. It does not merely signify, but expresses. And if it expresses, it is because it too has something trembling trapped within it, enough movement and power to overthrow the table of significations with a quake that produces the meaning. Discourse too opens itself up to grazing, and not only to understanding. It too appeals to the eye; it too is energetic. Let us trace the eye's paths in the field of language, capture the fixed-trembled, espouse the hillocks of the metaphor, which is the fulfillment of desire: only then will we see how exteriority, power, and formed space can be present in interiority, in closed signification.

But does adopting this stance not mean siding with illusion? If I show that in any discourse, in its underground, lies a form in which an energy is caught and according to which the energy acts upon its surface, if I can show that this discourse is not only signification and rationality but expression and affect, do I not destroy the very possibility of truth? The door will be open to sophistry whereby it could always be argued that the apparent signification of discourse never will exhaust its meaning, and that far from being able to contain the entirety of meaning within the signified, discourse receives it unconsciously and passively, from an exterior authority that owes nothing to the language structure in which it is uttered, that it therefore has its other inside it and thus that the one who speaks knows not what she or he says. An open door for sophistry, an open door for a kind of "terrorism," because the moment one ignores the common call to signification made by all discourse, where the implicit or explicit reference that every interlocutor makes to a possible universality and understanding is broken, and where the speaker's words are taken as coming from elsewhere, there remains, in fact, only violence to determine whence they come. If I can no longer speak with you, that is, accept that you and I take seriously—respectively and reciprocally—the signification of what we say, and apply to it a consensually agreed-upon geometrics that will allow us to decide what is right and what is wrong, but instead if I begin to speak of you, rephrasing your speech in the third person as if emanating from an absent interlocutor, taking it as implicitly expressive speech and no longer explicitly meaningful, then communication collapses, and with it the possibility of truth. It will no longer even be a question of *knowing* what your words "mean," since this knowledge in turn is made up of words—mine and yours—but it will become necessary to mete out judgment upon them, and for that to have postulated that there exists a kind of rationality of expression, an order of causes of the unsignified, another discourse speaking from within your discourse that I can know, or that at least someone can. One will have to imagine that this someone possesses, or is, your discourse's other. One will even have to imagine the following "nonsense": that this other discourse that you do not speak but which speaks from within yours is nonetheless signifiable except by and for you, that I or someone can say it, that we can speak of you but not to you. Such is violence, or seduction. Philosophy, it is said, ends here.

Is this the reductive path we are looking for? I would like to show that on the contrary the alternative between, on the one hand, the discourse of communication, good intentions, and dialogue, and, on the other, war and schizophrenia, is not radical in itself. The common reference to an authority that the two interlocutors recognize in the absence of a judge, precisely of a third party possessing adequate guarantees, is not truth, but rather allows for the construction of a body of knowledge. The configuration of discourse as interlocution, as potential universality by reference to rules that will serve as index to dialogue at the same time that this dialogue will elaborate them—what, in short, Socrates bequeathed the West as its specific position of speech—implies in fact the end of truth. Nietzsche is not alone in teaching us this: research in the field of semantic history confirms it.[14] Far from being reducible to the alternative between well-meaning dialogue and Callicles, we must understand that such opposites themselves belong to a world of speech pitted against another world—that of ἀλήθεια (*aletheia*)—and that truth is not at stake in the alternative, but outside of it, that the alternative itself is erected when truth recedes, when truth is neglected, covered up by discourse and the desire to know. Then, admittedly, sophistry, deceit, the illusion of εἰκόνες (*eikones*), is made possible, but so too are philosophy, dialogue, and the illusion of knowledge—an illusion because truth is excluded from the very first. "Truth," says Braque, "has no opposite."[15]

One could counter that it is nobody's business to reinstate this presence of truth, and it cannot be denied that such reinstatements are generally clumsy when they are linguistic, the work of heavy-handed Nietzscheans who busy themselves like thesis-makers. Either we will all be "artists" together or no one will; those who believe themselves to be artists as of today, who adopted Nietzsche and truth to make fun of others, are not the least loquacious. All they do is perpetuate philosophy as a separate activity and the manipulation of discourse as a badge of knowledge. No one today can speak *in the name* of truth: all lofty speech is derision; everything that "officiates," far from freeing us from the alternative between knowledge and ignorance, plunges us right back into the clericalism that relies upon it. Yet one must allow for the possibility of truth, and it is likely that many among those who come across as ridiculous and pompous, or as living-room tricksters, take this task upon themselves. Is such an outcome inevitable?

Freud taught us the meaning of utopia in the strictest sense.[16] Utopia is the fact that truth never appears where it is expected. This means many things, of which the following two at least will show us the way forward. First, truth appears as an aberration when measured against signification and knowledge. Truth is discordant, and to be discordant in discourse is to deconstruct its order. Truth in no way passes through a discourse of signification: its impossible *topos* cannot be determined through the coordinates of the geography of knowledge. Instead it makes itself felt on the surface of discourse through effects, and this presence of meaning is called expression. However, not all expression is truth. Here again Freud gives us guidelines for discernment. Not that we could ever grab hold of truth itself as one picks a flower after disentangling it from the surrounding weeds. Deception and truth go hand in hand, not as opposites in a system but at least as the *thickness* made up of a recto and a verso together. Nonetheless one must fight to allow the effects of truth to come to the surface, to unleash its monsters of meaning in the midst of discourse, within the very rule of signification. Thus one must learn not to distinguish truth from falsity—both defined in terms of the internal consistency of a system, or of operativeness upon an object of reference—but to discern between two expressions, the one that exists to thwart the gaze (to capture it) and the one that is there to expand it, to allow it to see the invisible. The second requires the work that is the purview of the artist, the suspended attention, the negligence, enforced as a rule, toward what is instituted, while the first is produced by the dream-work. If the first aims to deceive, the second aims to make patent. But both are identical as far as their operations are concerned, except for an additional reversal in the first case, which turns its product into a work of art.

Second, if truth doesn't appear where one expects it to, and if no discourse can ever hope to expose it in completed signification (since it does not belong to the same field), then this book is not truthful insofar as it strives, quite obviously, to produce articulated significations. But neither is it knowledgeable, since it does not seek to build a unitary theory, not even as distant objective. Rather it is like a dislocated body whereupon speech impresses fragments that in principle can be rearranged in various configurations, but which the constraints imposed by typographic composition—those belonging to signification and *ratio*—force to present in an immutable order. Even if this order is determined, and determining, it is certainly not arbitrary, but instead arbitrarily privileged (by the constraints we mentioned) when compared to others. A good book, in order to give free rein to truth in its aberration, would be a book where linguistic time (the time in which signification evolves, the time of reading) would itself be deconstructed—a book the reader could dip into anywhere, in any order: a book to be grazed. A book, incidentally, that would be freed from the literary genre of the aphorism—I mention this thinking of Nietzsche, who was still too tolerant of it. The present book is not that good book, for it still stakes out a position in signification; not being an artist's book, deconstruction here does not operate directly, but is *signified.* It is thus, still, a book of philosophy. No doubt its signification is fragmentary, with omissions and, I hope, rebuses. Nevertheless, this makes it only an uncertain and intermediary object, which I would like to excuse by calling it an interworld (after Klee) or a transitional object (after Winnicott); but it does not really warrant these qualifications, since they pertain only to such figural things as games and painting. Once again, it is not a question here of letting the figure insinuate itself into words according to its own rules, but rather of insisting on the words' capacity to *utter* the preeminence of the figure. The ambition is to *signify* the other of signification. This book still wants, and wants too much; one is, after all, only the least of men, and the space of this book is no more than Baroque. Still, in its defense, this desire for more remains very little.

Having given up on the folly of unity, of offering the founding cause in a unitary discourse, on the phantasy of origins, we are bound by Freud's utopia to the rule dictated by the so-called death drive, according to which the unification of the diverse, even within the unity of discourse (and not least in that of Freudian theory), is continually deferred and always prohibited. Just as it follows that from a consideration of this rule the ego must be given up as a constituted unitary entity, so too it is high time that philosophers abandon the hope of producing a unitary theory as the last word on things. There is no *archè*,[17] nor does the Good exist as a unitary horizon. One never touches the thing itself but metaphorically. However, this laterality is not, as Merleau-Ponty believed, that of existence—much too close already to the unity of the subject, as he himself conceded toward the end.[18] This laterality is rather that of the unconscious or of expression, which in the same movement offers and holds back all content. This laterality is difference, or depth. But whereas Merleau-Ponty posited it as the possible movement to a point over there while remaining here—as ubiquitous aperture and continuous motion, whose model he saw in the chiasm of the sensory, thereby falling into the trap of unitary discourse[19]—we intend to yield to figural space, with Cézanne and Mallarmé, with Freud and Frege. Depth will continue to exceed by a long way the power of a reflection that seeks to signify it, to include it in its language, not as a thing but as a definition. Meaning is present as absence of signification. Yet signification will seize meaning (and it can, for one can say anything), exiling it to the border of a new speech act. Here is the death drive, always embroiled in Eros-Logos. Building meaning is never anything other than deconstructing signification. No model can be assigned to this evasive configuration. One could argue that at the beginning the violence is like castration, and that the silence or death our words want to unmask is the offspring of this initial terror that gave rise to desire. Very well, but as the place of this desire is a utopia, let us renounce once and for all finding a place for it.

This is of the highest importance for practice, for the practical critique of ideology. The present book is itself nothing more than a detour on the way to this critique. If I had to wait as long as I did to see my own resistance to writing it fall, it was (among other reasons) without a doubt out of fear of being seduced, distracted from this goal, mesmerized by language. How its practical function fares, what in it remains active and hot, is not something I can judge.

A word as afterthought: there is a gradual slackening along the string of sections below, and the reader will no doubt be sensitive to it. She or he might object that my thinking is equivocal. What is in decline, from the opening to the closing lines, is the importance granted perception. First I explore the order of discourse to disentangle what, strictly speaking, belongs to signification and what to designation, thereby delineating a phenomenological space, or a space of vision, whose characteristics are understood to be totally different from those of linguistic signification, though I skip their analysis, having sufficient trust in Merleau-Ponty's phenomenology of the visible. Then I move from sight to vision, from the world to the phantasy, and the responsibility of the constitution of the object, of the vis-à-vis, first assigned to the gaze of discourse is transferred and given over to the fulfillment of desire. Simultaneously, the figure finds itself displaced: no longer simply the image of presence or of representation, but form of the mise en scène, form of discourse itself, and, more profoundly still, phantasmatic matrix. At this point Freud's lesson supersedes Husserl's.

The point of transition is that of deception par excellence: the category of continuity. If we accept that gesture is meaning, it must be in opposition to linguistic signification. The latter constitutes itself only as a network of discontinuities, resulting in a static dialectics where thinking and thought are never confused, and where the elements constitutive of thought never interfere with one another. By contrast, gesture, as Merleau-Ponty understood it, is the experience of a meaning where the felt and feeling come together in a common rhythm—like the two folds of a single furrow—and where the constituents of the sensory form an organic and diachronic totality. Nonetheless the gesture refers if not to a subject, then at least to a kind of subjectivity, however anonymous or "natural," as Mikel Dufrenne would put it: it is experienced, lived, or in any case structures lived life, partaking of an unconscious that is not object of repression but subject of constitution.

At first sight, meaning according to psychoanalysis presents itself, too, as continuity. One would be justified in opposing it to linguistic signification insofar as the plastic expanse of condensations, displacements, and distortions is opposed to the finite and transparent space where signifiers emerge through measured intervals. Libidinal meaning and sensory meaning seem to overlap, to stand together against the signification of language. This is the overlap that ultimately is undone in this book: the phenomenological mask slipping not off the face of the unconscious that no one has seen or ever will see, but off the mask of desire. The decline is that of phenomenology.

The area where the shift occurs is the reflection on difference, on the organization of sensory space. That this space cannot be reduced to a geometrical organization entirely available to concepts is precisely what phenomenology itself underscored. Merleau-Ponty's *Eye and Mind* went as far as one could go in the direction suggested by the description of *passivity*, of the passivity of perceptual synthesis whose analysis Husserl had initiated. In pitting Cézanne's space against that of Descartes's *Dioptric*, Merleau-Ponty was saying that an articulated, discontinuist, active, logical conception of meaning and space would necessarily miss the given [*la donnée*], or rather the bestowal [*la donation*] of the visible; that this bestowal was exactly what remained invisible to this conception, just as it is in our experience made up of extended objects; and that it took Cézanne's enormous stillness to dismiss the rationalization of perceptual space and make us see the originary bestowal in its obliquity, in its ubiquity, in its lateral transgression of the rules of geometrical optics. Cézanne desires nothing more than to have Mount Sainte-Victoire cease to be an object of sight to become an event in the visual field: this is what the phenomenologist hopes to understand, and which I believe he cannot.

His ultimate concept, his finest concept for grasping the event-ness of the given is of course not intentionality but passivity. Yet this concept still can function only in the field prescribed by phenomenology as the opposite or correlate of intentional activity, as its basic support structure. The aim [*la visée*] as act rests on a passive synthesis that is the very bestowal of what is aimed at. This passivity is therefore still thought of as an *assumption* of the aiming subject, as presupposed immanence in its transcending relationship with the object. In this relationship the subject finds him/herself in a sense deposed (dispossessed), but also posed [*posé*]. This is how Merleau-Ponty attempts to go from the I to the undetermined One. But just think of the distance that still separates the One and the Id.

The "One" does not constitute an event in relation to the "I," on the contrary. What would this direction of anonymity lead to? At best the organization of the forms of sensibility, a space-time admittedly buried deeper than that of lived experience and less beholden to the laws of physical knowledge than the one Kant described, but notwithstanding a space and time that make up the *frame* in which the given gives itself, in which the event erupts, but which could never be the principle of an event. However preconceptual a system, like every system it is likely to testify not to the fact that something eventful has taken place (in the visual field or elsewhere), but precisely that the event (the bestowal) has been absorbed, received, perceived, integrated as world (or as history, etc.). The mystery of the event will remain intact, even if one tries to descend as far as the "One," for it is not the search for the condition, whether anonymous or not, of the given that immobilizes Cézanne in front of his mountain, it is the search for the bestowal. Phenomenology cannot possibly reach the bestowal since, faithful to the West's philosophical tradition, it remains a reflection on *knowledge,* and the purpose of such a reflection is to absorb the event, to recuperate the Other into the Same.

Now, the event in its initial alterity cannot arise from the world to which we are attuned in meaning. The discordance cannot come from a spoken word that, inasmuch as it is heard, is articulated signification and as such becomes object of knowledge. Nor can it come from a world with which the body cooperates to produce the sensoria that are its element. No doubt, the worldly body can become event in the order of discourse, since, quite obviously, meaning is deployed differently there than signification is in the system of language [*langue*]. This is why one will be able to detect the presence of figures in discourse according to the model of the insertion of gestural operations, based in a continuous space, in a field that otherwise tolerates transformation only between discrete elements. This is how Merleau-Ponty's notions of "encroachment" [*empiètement*] and "laterality" [*latéralité*] should be understood. These effects are useful to define the poetic or rhetorical order in general. But to what should they be attributed?

We must remember that this disturbance in the order of signification has always been conceived of—whether in myths, tragedies, or philosophies—as reprehensible. To lay this guilt on the body alone is impossible. This body is not a privileged place for the disturbance and the event. There is a silent underside in the life of the flesh—its ὑγίεια (*hygieia*)—and it is true that, as Merleau-Ponty believed, it is merely a chiasm in the element of the world, grasped by it, grasping it. It is on such a euphoria that the philosopher attempted to build a pagan philosophy. But his paganism remains caught in the problematic of knowledge, which leads to a philosophy of knowing flesh, a joyful flesh untroubled by dispossession. The event as disturbance is always what defies knowledge, either by challenging knowledge articulated in discourse or, just as well, by shattering the quasi-comprehension of the body itself, putting it out of tune from itself and from things, as in emotion. There is as much guilt and impropriety concentrated in a look or a sudden pallor as in a slip of the tongue. The body is not the culprit of language's dismay: something else can disturb both language and body. To accept the body as the locus of the event amounts to endorsing the defensive displacement and the vast project of rationalization carried out by the Platonic-Christian tradition aimed at covering up desire.

The event cannot be situated elsewhere than in the vacant space opened up by desire. This vacancy of space is precisely the preferred site of the bestowal. This becomes immediately apparent in the anguish that undergirds all emotions,[20] but also in the presence of words in discourse, of turns of phrase that declare zones of turbulence where the person who speaks receives. Such vacancy is not an "attitude" to be recommended, nor an ethics—such as the paradox of Kierkegaard's horseman of faith or of Levinas's an-archy.[21] Wanting to promote oneself as partisan of the event, or to predispose oneself to the event, is still an ethical delusion. It is a property of the bestowal to dispossess us—one cannot predispose oneself to dispossession. The event does not arrive where one expects it; even a state of non-expectancy will be disappointed. One cannot cross over to the side of the primary processes: this is merely a secondary illusion. Desire has its rejection embedded within itself, which is the principle of the dispossession of its effects. Desire is truly unacceptable. One cannot pretend to accept it, for accepting it is still to reject it. It will become event elsewhere.

In fact, one cannot begin to place the event if one begins by removing it from the vacant space left in the wake of repression, or at least of rejection in general. Neither discourse nor the body possesses in itself this crossed-out, distorted disposition that *authorizes* the bestowal precisely because it *prohibits* the recognition or comprehension of the given. This would be Cézanne's prayer: that the well-known mountain dispossess him, that it appear elsewhere than where the eye expects it, and that it thus seduce him; a prayer of *de-conciliation,* an anti-prayer. It ties the visible neither to the I-You of language nor to the One of perception, but to the Id of desire; not to the immediate figures of desire, but to its operations.

This, then, is the displacement, or the rotation, that will be discernible in what follows. It can be located with greater precision in a reflection on opposition and difference. One might ask: since you argue that the order of the perceptive One covers up that of the Id, why not simply discard the mask and erase the former? I would answer that this displacement is precisely what constitutes the event for me in this book. By virtue of what order, of what assumed function of the book, of what prestige of discourse, should one attempt to erase it?

SIGNIFICATION AND DESIGNATION

Dialectics, Index, Form

With negation, reflection positions itself at the juncture between two experiences: speaking and seeing. A juncture, because each of these crosses paths: on the one hand the mouth sees—just as Claudel said that the eye listens—otherwise one speaks of nothing, even if one says something, for linguistic reference points to the depth of the visible. On the other hand, how would this depth itself, constituting things in thickness, with a front and a back, be at all possible were there not in human language an arbitrary principle, the self-sufficiency of a system entirely dependent on its internal intervals, and thus capable of provoking and supporting the separation of discourse from its object? Would one see if one did not speak?

Negativity is a position that directs two heterogeneous experiences. There is a negation involved in the visible—the distance, the spacing that determines space itself—a negation experienced in variability. The experience of this mobility, which engenders expanse, thickness, and the figure, is for the phenomenologist a privileged object of description: for Husserl, it is the constitutive seeing he tries to locate under its collapse in formed vision; for Merleau-Ponty, it is the permanent genesis of objective space and body that stirs beneath them in the flesh. To speak of a *beneath* could suggest that it is unconscious, but this unconsciousness belongs to the order of the transcendental. We are dealing here with an originary *ekthesis* as Kant and Husserl understand the term: originary so that something may be seen. Its originarity ensures its unconsciousness. Now by unconsciousness I do not want to merely imply that this initial force, which distinguishes and brings into relief, is destined to lodge itself in the dead casing of a language or an academicism (though the chances are high that this is indeed the fate awaiting it, as Merleau-Ponty suspected and Francastel demonstrates). Nevertheless, *ekthesis* is involved in seeing to the point of not being seen, as that which makes visible. This power, on which the visible and the seer are deployed, generates their conjoining precisely because it generates their separation: an unconsciousness, therefore, pervading even the most revolutionary moments of plastic activity. At the moment when Cézanne and Picasso show us how there is to see, how the object comes into relief as we face it in its essential elision of what is visible, they are still showing us this object, drawing upon the same relief-giving power that separates us from the picture and makes it visible to us. No doubt painting is what brings us as near as possible to transcendental activity, insofar as this activity is indeed a disjoining rather than a synthesizing power. What the picture shows is the world in the process of becoming, how objects can emerge, with the help of the eye, from nebulae in the watercolors of the last Cézanne, a line from the adjoining edge-to-edge of a yellow and a blue in Van Gogh, a gaze on either side of the green trickle dividing Matisse's famous portrait. From this perspective, the picture is the strangest of objects when it fulfills the function assigned to it by modern painting: an object where the becoming-object is made visible—transcendental activity itself. It should be able to stand in for all of philosophy, at least for the philosophy that argues that perception is not an ideology but that it holds the entire secret of being. Indeed, it is this very secret that the painter makes visible: the secret of manifestation, in other words, of depth. However, we—the painter and we beholders—miss this secret precisely because we see it, and because this exposure of becoming, this constitution of the seeing and the seen would be pointless and fall flat if there weren't a sharp eye to register it, expose it, and constitute it in turn. The picture is such an inefficient trompe l'oeil that it requires the eye to access the truth, and it is, in a sense, nothing more than a call to the eye to be acknowledged. Even if the picture resembles nothing (and it really does resemble nothing, even when it is figurative, since its visible function is to give the given), the eye takes back from it the right it had given up in order to allow the picture to be: the right to believe itself the place from which the world—even in the process of manifesting itself—is seen manifesting itself, manifests its manifestation. It is up to the painter, therefore, to bring this unconsciousness of the negativity of seeing to light, in a kind of chthonic upheaval. But nothing doing: there is no such thing as a painting for the blind, and it is in the eye of the beholder, or at the least in its co-action with the artwork, that this seismic power seeks cover—the power Cézanne or Picasso revealed, or thought to have revealed to it.

The negation that operates in the system of language [*langage*] seems to be of a different kind, as does its unconsciousness. Here I am referring to the lessons of structural linguistics, which, in its initial "parting of the ways,"[1] takes language [*langue*], the system, as its object. No doubt, we are far from having said it all regarding the presence of the negative in our experience of language [*langage*] by identifying in the latter this force that keeps apart the elements that make up the table of phonemes and monemes. There are other modes of negativity, as well as other forms its labor can take in language. There is the distance that discourse clears in front of itself and where it objectifies for itself its reference, a distance that brings us back to the experience of vision. More immediately, indeed first in the order of phenomenality, there is negation pure and simple, as quality of judgment, and form of discourse: mystery of the word *No.* This negation is the closest and most essential for a phenomenological description, since it is, apparently, through it that the negative comes to the subject and even—since there is no subject without negativity—through it that the subject constitutes itself in her or his opposition. The No is death attracted and tamed, the entrance into language and the coming-unto-oneself, arrived at through the experience of violence—a threat that henceforth accompanies all discourse and all subjectivity, while at the same time subjectivity and discourse play off the non-being it carries. It should be possible at this point to establish an initial connection between the symbolic No and the transcendence of seeing: the visible object is, no less, an invisible, and to manifest is also to conceal; in discourse, the No is the explicit presence of the reverse of things, and to deny is to aver. To constitute a visible object is to be able to lose it. This virtuality of lack, which must remain present even in the actuality of the thing, is represented in speech by the *not.* Here a path begins to appear, bringing together the visible and the negative quality of judgment. Freud leads the way: in an ambitious text, he linked the constitution of the visible, of the imaginary, and of the utterable with the use of the couplet *fort-da.* As we know, with and since Freud, the necessary mediation is that of desire, for it is upon the lack associated with desire that all negatives hinge.

However, the non-being involved in the system of language [*langue*] seems to be an exception to this elaboration. Its axis is not in lack; on the contrary, one is tempted to say that lack and desire only make sense in this non-being. Here again Freud shows us the way. To say that the subject constitutes itself from the experience of death—as when it sees the free interplay of pleasure denied by the threatening restriction of having to respect certain intervals—to equate Oedipus's journey with that of the mind, does this not show that negation for itself, the quality of judgment, and perhaps, too, reference's transcendence, comes after a negativity in itself: a mute negativity that nonetheless structures in silence by establishing and ensuring invariable intervals between sex partners and elements of discourse alike? This negativity, founder of order and disorder, is so immanent that it seems, as language-system [*langue*], to be the unconscious of discourse and, as kinship structure, the motive for the originary repression that gives rise to the unconscious *tout court.*

Yet this unconsciousness is at the furthest reaches from that of seeing. This second unconsciousness refers to a phenomenology, whereas the first refers to an archaeology. It is the act itself that, by way of the first unconsciousness, loses both consciousness and memory of itself in the naive, natural fascination of the object it has in sight. As for the second unconsciousness, it belongs to the order of the virtual; it precedes and surrounds the act, for it is what makes the act possible, investing the act while remaining unrecognized by it, for it erases the unconsciousness by its mere presence. Actual unconsciousness is the shadow that light is for itself, the anonymity of seeing that sees the thing and does not see itself. Virtual unconsciousness, on the other hand, occupies not the core of the act but its fringes: it is the other upon which the act seizes itself and that the act obliterates by its existence. This fundamental function of misrecognition could be described as preconsciousness—as belonging to an act that, by definition, turns its back on what makes it possible. Saussure does not cease to stress this very misrecognition in the order of language [*langage*]: the system of language [*langue*] is what is "passive," unconscious, "involuntary," almost "fatal." But this passivity is not simple, nor is it a non-activity. "Deposit," "treasure," sum of everything that is "sanctioned" through usage, that is, through speech, in which one seems to thus relegate all of activity: for Saussure language [*langue*] is also a "system," even a "grammar," an order that prescribes, at the very least, discourse's form.[2] A generative passivity, then, for the negation that operates in the system, both outside and preceding the subject, encroaches on the latter's prerogative to act. The subject cannot experience this negation since it is inherent in his or her experience of language [*langage*]: it is the subject's inner lining, what she or he can only apprehend reflexively, as Husserl does in the *Fourth Meditation* when he draws out from behind constitutive acts the passive genesis that prepares them.

By hinging on negativity, reflection thus settles on one side in familiar territory while, on the other, it stretches outward toward absolute otherness. One may indeed speak of familiarity, since it is of the essence of the reflexive to nullify its object and, as such, reflection operates just as all forms of thinking do inasmuch as it remains a form of seeing—the only difference being that in reflection the seeing of thinking is redoubled and tries to come unto itself. This reflective redoubling is to the sight involved in speech what pictorial redoubling is to vision proper. Painting offers reflection both an exceptional object and an exceptional model. For when we reflect on a picture, we reflect on reflection itself—a reflection one must call elementary, after Merleau-Ponty, because it embeds its looking in the very stuff of the world, and keeps it there: a re-turning of the sensory into the aesthetic which, on the one hand, announces that of thinking into thought, and on the other repeats the originary turning of the sensory of the object into the sensory on the body. In obeying this injunction to speculate issued from painted matter, we should be able to isolate the transcendental negativity that undergirds all aim [*visée*], along with its essential property: variance. By crossing plastic space, reflection stays in its element, or rather, descends into itself, seeking out a view—within the limits defined above—of its undergirding, of the redoubling of the sensory into painted figure, and, deeper still, of the redoubling of the sensory into felt and feeling.

(Mirror, redoubling: such words in no way imply recourse to an aesthetics of imitation, a theory of faithfulness in painting, or a materialism of reflection in a theory of knowledge. The relay of sensation in perception is not repetition pure and simple; the relay of perception in the picture is creative; and to think is not the same as to reflect. This is precisely what the descent to the sensory sources of negativity teaches us. However, the metaphor of the mirror [which is much more than a metaphor] remains valid in this case because it encapsulates on the one hand the mystery of depth, of a concealing manifestation, that is, what falls under all forms of semiology, and on the other, that of variance, of commutation, which is the axiom of reflection.)

But what the painter's as well as the philosopher's reflection brings out, and what the body's reflection harbors, is the fact that negation is at the heart of seeing as distancing. There is nothing to see without distance, without the separation between seer and visible; nothing to think if I know what there is to think; nothing to paint if I cannot remove myself from the game the world plays with itself on my body. By constituting both object and subject, this scission is exactly what endows them with a hidden side, with a "background" slipped under their figure, thus instituting them as signs with the power to manifest and conceal themselves, with their depth. When reflection discovers this disjoining power, it encounters itself, or believes it is encountering itself. Here nothing seems more legitimate than to follow the lead of intentional analysis, for speaking, too, is always speaking of something: this referential dimension, which the structural method assumes to be negligible, is nothing other than the presence of the distancing of seeing in the experience of discourse. Phenomenological description is not only one possible method among others. No other approach preserves the negativity that extends what one is speaking of to the outer limits of what one is saying about it, like an object to be reached, because it is the only approach that rests on the speaker's experience, and in this experience it is not signs that are given, but rather something to be signified by what Merleau-Ponty called a linguistic gesture which, like every gesture, requires depth—precisely that of reference. By allowing itself to slide along the line of this distancing, reflection recognizes itself not only in the *Bedeutung*[3] of discourse; it finds itself further down the line in the variability inherent in the order of the picture, and, finally, in the exteriorization of the touching and the touched that unlocks the initial mirror of the sensory. These voids follow one another, so to speak, and these discontinuities continue one another: there is no difference in position from the one to the other vis-à-vis reflection, since they themselves are all reflection.

On the contrary, negation in language does not allow for reflection, even according to the loose definition just provided, which encompasses everything up to and including the chiasm of the sensory and that of art. Reflection claims its own space in reversibility, in a negativity authorizing the permutation of the terms that it nonetheless keeps apart. But this permutation is precisely what the system prohibits: the intervals must not be trespassed, nor the prohibitions flaunted, lest they lose their significance (*sinnlos*). As a result of phonological analysis, the distinctive units of a language [*langue*] can be organized in the orders and series of a grid that will show what phonetic oppositions must be respected if one wants to be understood in this language [*langue*]. We arrive here at a set of constraints so elementary that, no matter how great the freedom of combination the speaking subject may otherwise enjoy, or the manipulation of the terms deployed in her or his discourse, they affect only the units of a higher order—words, sentences—while leaving intact the basic network of phonetic oppositions upon which rests the entire hierarchy of units. Regarding these constraints, the differences and variations in the act of realization are negligible precisely so long as they do not impinge on the units' distinctive function. The variance that culminates in reversion and that grounds all reflexivity seems to have no place here.

One fails to see, therefore, how the system could be read or thought through by itself, for the structure is and remains beyond its grasp. It seems impossible that reflection could engender itself from the structure alone—the collapsing that would bring a part of the grid to fold back upon itself—since such a fold presupposes a three-dimensional space, in other words depth, while the systematic grid of orders and series takes place in a two-dimensional space without thickness and, strictly speaking, without sight. A language [*langue*] does not speak itself: one speaks it. One need not of course rush to "explain," by way of the subject's "intention to signify," how the elements of the grid settle and arrange themselves in the vertical axis of discourse; at the least, the possibility of this intention itself needs to be explained. But it remains that, without introducing in the system something other than the strictly measured negativity that informs and measures its internal intervals, it is impossible to see reflection carve out its depth within the system. One cannot even see—and this is a second consequence to be inferred from the properties of the grid of language [*langue*]—why and how the latter grid could aim, or show, or designate, or depict something *other,* outside of itself. Now there is a fact that our experience of speech renders incontrovertible, which is that every discourse is projected toward something it seeks to grasp, in other words, that it is incomplete and open, not unlike the partiality of the visual field, hemmed in and extended by a horizon. How to account for this quasi-visual quality of speaking from the point of view of this theoretically closed object, shut upon itself in a self-sufficient totality, which is the system of language [*langue*]? How can language [*langue*] combine with the obviously referential function of discourse? The only mediation available does indeed seem to be negativity's. There is the *No* of speech [*parole*], and there is the spacing of referential transcendence, but within the anonymous system itself there are the intervals that keep the terms at a constant distance from one another, so that this "absolute object" is shot through with holes, so to speak, and holds within itself a static—yet nonetheless generative—dialectics that conveys the definition and value of one term through the other terms with which it is connected. There must be communication between the *No* of language [*langue*], which is that of the object, and the *No* of discourse, which is that of seeing. Such is the hypothesis, familiar to philosophy, that we need to scrutinize.

*

* *

The *identity* that in other orders one would be tempted to assign to these negativities is out of the question, at least as far as language is concerned. It is worth pausing here, since what is at stake is the position of *dialectics.* Conceivably (even if it can be debated) *praxis* can be understood as the same constituting negativity that—sedimented in works, crystallized in institutions—finds itself reduced to maintaining the invariant intervals between terms, such as in relations of production where, admittedly, the structure does not occupy, relative to the "vertical" negativity, a position of anteriority comparable to that of language [*langue*] relative to speech. Indeed, even if the mode of penetration and establishment of the relations of production is not the object of a decree, but rather due to an involuntary, perhaps even unconscious dynamic, it cannot be ascertained that this characteristic is an essential property of this order's structures. It is conceivable that the same praxis that animates—in captivity, so to speak—these established relations works, and consciously, to establish others, and even believes this to be feasible. There is a underside to capitalism, perhaps a beyond, but in any case there is the possibility of conceiving of non-salaried relations within salaried relations themselves, and this possibility is not random but constitutive. Here the "vertical" negativity goes so far as to contest the intervals maintained in the "horizontal" system, to the point of producing a new structure in thought, and developing it as far as possible in reality. At issue here is not whether this experience of alterity, of which the labor movement was the receptacle and expression, can actually break free from the imaginary and become a truly different society—in other words, if praxis can come to master the system. Yet it must be conceded that the system is such that it allows, maybe even requires, its own contestation, that is to say, in a critical form, the coming-unto-itself of the negativity of praxis as constitutive of the very relations in which it is trapped. In this sense, and within these strictly defined limits, "dialectics" can appear to be a legitimate expression of the socioeconomic reality of capitalism.[4]

Such is not the case with language. Dialectics, in Sartre's definition, is unfeasible in language—one cannot see how the system, even as critique, could give rise to its own objectification. The existence of metalanguage should not lead one to believe, erroneously, that the possibility of speaking of language [*langue*] as system—a possibility offered with any language [*langue*]—enjoys a relation with the system in any way comparable to that of critical praxis with the relations of production. This can be grasped very easily: sociopolitical critique can only take effect by breaking away from the constraints that characterize the capitalist system, by attacking the invariant intervals that govern its terms' distribution. On the contrary, discourse on language [*langage*] is produced entirely within language [*langage*], and if it should attack the semantic, syntactic, possibly even phonological invariances, it is always within the bounds of communicability, that is to say under the laws of language [*langue*], lest it turn into nonsense. Under certain conditions one could argue that the negativity that binds the social system and that which upsets it are related. But it is impossible, without resorting to a philosophical sleight of hand, to argue that it is the same negativity that upholds the system of language [*langue*] and in which discourse's momentum flows. Language [*langue*] precedes speech since no speaker can believe to have, however modestly, founded the first language [*langue*], nor aspire to institute another, and since every attempt to reform it runs up against the circular reasoning that it is our basic toolbox, containing all the tools available to us to change it.

This is not to argue that new discourses are impossible in this language [*langue*], quite the contrary. But when Saussure posited in principle that the modifications that upset the balance of the linguistic system all find their cause in speech acts, and that diachrony thus seeps into the structure by means of this event that is a new discourse—even if this was placing too great a confidence in the system's homogeneity and inertia, and not enough in its nimble generative power—in any case the linguist did locate the problem of language's [*langue*] becoming, and of its relation to the speaking subject, unambiguously *outside* the field of dialectics, and no one has revised this view ever since. More or less continuous internal readjustments run through a system because it never reaches in itself perfect equilibrium, and also because it is never perfectly isolated from a context, linguistic or otherwise, that constitutes an event in relation to it, disturbs it, thus forcing it to constantly re-adapt. One enters a world here where structures are in a perpetual state of coming undone and being re-formed, like the interplay of colors of several kaleidoscopes whose rate of rotation would be measured in centuries. One does not step into a story at all; the opposite is true: one comes out of it to immerse oneself in a nature. Diachrony belongs to a physical time, not historicity. The amazement that the moderns experienced at the thought of language [*langue*], and the sometimes passionate attachment they felt for it, betray at once the paradox and the reassurance of discovering, so close to the mind, even within the mind, something like nature. Even if we need to correct what taxonomical eagerness there is in the structuralist view of language [*langage*], and even if taking the fact of discourse into account highlights the generative power of language [*langue*], the resulting shift in orientation—of the highest importance for the linguistic method, as well as for the philosopher paying close attention to the position of speech in relation to the system—will have no impact whatsoever on the a-dialectical character of language [*langue*]. Undoubtedly, by thinking of language [*langue*] as a generative grammar instead of an ordered set of values, discourse will more readily find its place, and the relation between "vertical" negativity and the negativity that separates and conjoins the elements of the system will allow itself to be articulated with greater certainty. Yet one can already be sure that this articulation will not be dialectical in Hegel's or Sartre's definitions, and that it will remain as impossible as it is in the strict structuralist or functionalist view to make language [*langue*] the fallout and inert sediment of a power of speech that would logically precede it.

The communication we are after between the two *No*'s cannot lie in their dialectical identity. And this is without even broaching the difficulty inherent in *all* dialectical thought from Hegel, maybe even from Heraclitus and Parmenides, up to Sartre, stemming from the possibility of the "false," the "alienated," the "inert," in other words from the mutilation, reification, and obstruction of process, i.e., from *recessus*. This is probably a difficulty too great for the project at hand. The difficulty we do wish to underscore is more specific and more decisive, namely that, from the negativity separating discourse from its object to the negativity maintaining intervals internal to language, the consequence is not good; in this case, the dismissal of dialectics is based on concrete evidence. But we will encounter the other difficulty again, lodged at the heart of our problem.

It might then appear foolhardy to want to persevere toward structure with the help of reflection alone. The preferred methodology in the field of structure passes as rigorously objectivist. The procedures required to establish a structure seem to owe nothing to reflection, to the auscultation of "experience" in the phenomenological sense, to intentional analysis. On the contrary, the linguist has chosen to banish what she or he calls the "psychic" from her or his preoccupations. As for the ethnologist, who has made it a rule to mistrust any immediate meaning, she or he is determined, if not to ignore the significations the indigenous person attaches to the rules of her or his social life and to the mythical tales upon which she or he bases, these significations, then at least to record such admissions as merely incidental behavior offering additional information, a possibly useful hint for the only task considered essential: to erect the structure of the system of these rules and myths. If there is indeed a latent meaning, reflection alone will not be able to reach it; on the contrary, reflection is imbued by it, and to extract it one must get rid of immediate significations and treat sociolinguistic facts as objects. From the reflective point of view, this objectification is akin to cutting up the field of science with a diamond-tipped implement, dividing the seer from what is seen, what I say from what I speak of. After which "truth" is cast as a reconciliation of the two halves (but such a conjoining is in fact as impossible as the flawless reassembling of pieces of a single pane of glass). Or one will have to reject categorically the subjective hypothesis, go so far as to elide the subject of science itself, and commit to positivism. Both of these directions demonstrate to what extent reflection and structure are incompatible.

Yet this exteriority is worth preserving: here the structuralist wins out over the dialectician, or at least the responsibility between the two is shared unequally, in any case as far as their intentions are concerned. For the structuralist method does not seek to pass as a philosophy—a conceptualization of totality—but instead as a procedure related to its object by a strategy. The dialectician, on the other hand, seeks to paint a general picture in which the subject and the structure would be mediated. At least structuralism can hide the partiality of its approach behind the epistemological demand, whereas dialectics is unabashedly a "phenomenological ontology." Keeping the negative of transcendence separate from that of the system is simply to recognize that something radically original begins with language, an *other* that one cannot "infer" from the sensory but that commingles with it. This can be demonstrated if, by reversing the situation, or perhaps by putting it straight again, one observes that in sensory certainty language encounters an order it cannot exhaust, but from which it itself draws, and endlessly, its dimension of depth.

Phenomenology of Spirit opens with this very admission, of an insurmountable exteriority from the sensory to the sayable. What one first comes across, in the beginning of the first chapter, is undoubtedly the exact opposite: that the *Meinen*—the signifying concrete aim [*visée*][5]—cannot be uttered without losing itself, and thus called upon to exhibit itself it must own up to its insignificance and abstraction. But *Meinen* only appears thus because it is challenged by language and from language's standpoint, and because the philosopher, betraying his promise not to become involved in the development of the object, summoned sensory certainty to utter itself (even to *write* itself), and hence to contradict itself, since its *now* will sometimes be night, sometimes day; its *here* sometimes tree or sometimes house; in any case a hollow universal, a *now* and a *here* that have no organic connection to their content. However, this abstraction does not belong to the movement itself of sensory certainty, but results from this certainty's encounter with language; it belongs, in other words, to the logophilic bias, which gives preference to the utterable conclusion over that of mute immediacy. To contradict oneself is not to *contrafeel* oneself. Hegel is sufficiently aware of this to try, in a second movement within the same chapter, to do justice to the claim of immediacy issued by the *Meinen,* by ceasing to force it to pronounce itself and be inferred in the mediation of discourse, and by attempting to seize it, or at the least to approach it through a truly pre-linguistic act of signification: "*Zeigen* müßen wir es [das Jetzt] uns lassen; denn die Wahrheit dieser unmittelbaren Beziehung ist die Warheit *dieses Ich,* der sich auf ein *Jetzt* oder ein *Hier* einschränkt."[6]

To indicate is to extend the index finger toward a place. Along its vector, this silent gesture constitutes an originary spacing at the ends of which the showing and the shown find themselves polarized. In this gesture, therefore, one must recognize the engendering of the opening itself in which the sensory and sensibility come to pass. But does indicating belong to language? Hegel tries to bring out the dialectics concealed in so-called immediacy, even up to this resumption of reflection toward sensory certainty. The act of indicating does not establish a simple reference by which a something would be manifested unequivocally; it is a movement—a movement engendering the *here* indicated as its result. For no *here* can be indicated in itself if it is not situated, placed in relation with other *heres,* and therefore included in a sort of mute, gestural "discourse" of dia-deictics pointing to "a Before and a Behind, an Above and a Below, a Right and a Left."[7] Thus the gesture becomes a dialectics of gestures, the place becomes a dialectics of places, and to situate becomes to include laconically the other in the same and mediating it.

The logos thereby appears to have won the day, once again, and this time without having had to *impose* itself extrinsically upon sensory perception, but emerging through its clinging motion—a motion in which it reflects itself, dis/uncovering itself already present as mediator. Yet one cannot be so quick to declare it the winner, to have language seep into the sensory, and thus to have the latter entirely absorbed by discourse. It is no doubt in keeping with Hegelianism to be rid of the exteriority first established by Kant, between speech or understanding and between meaning [*sens*] or sensibility, to shatter the autonomy of forms relative to the categories—the same autonomy that, in critical thought, marks the irreducibility of the given to thought. Yet the operation fails, and it is easy to identify, at the very threshold of the project of totalization through language represented by the *Phenomenology of Spirit* what will forever evade totalization, what will always act in the project like the silence contained in speech: *Aufzeigen, indication,* itself.

If one cracks the shell of immediacy, what one finds at its core is not the διαλέγεσθαι [*dialegesthai*], but something else, which is in any case not language. The specification of the *here* does indeed relate to that of *before, behind, right* and *left,* and of *above* and *below.* But these terms do not entertain the same relation to the *here* as that uniting a word to the other contiguous words of the same language [*langue*], and even less to the relation uniting a phoneme to its neighbors in a phonological grid. Nor is their correlation reducible to that of the elements of discourse—of the words of a sentence, for example—or even to that of propositions in an argument (which is what Hegel seems to have had above all in mind). The space of indication is neither the grid of the system nor the line of speech. The points through which the movement indicating "where is *here*" passes are not like middle terms, like mediators which, for meaning or sound, are confronted with the word or chosen phoneme, and finally discarded in those operations of virtual selection and concatenation that structural linguistics believes to be at work in the speech act. To the contrary, the indicated place—the *here*—is included in a *sensory field,* of which it is no doubt the focal point, but not such that its margins are eliminated, as is the case in the choices made by the speaker.

The margins remain, in the uncertain, undeniable, and curvilinear presence of what stands at the periphery of vision, as an absolutely necessary reference to the indication of place as defined by Hegel, but whose nature is completely at odds with that of a linguistic operation. The latter relates to a discontinuous inventory, while sight relates to a topological space; the first is subjected to the rule of the spoken chain that requires the unicity of the actual and the elimination of the virtual, whereas the second circumscribes a sensory field governed by the rule of the quasi-actuality of the virtual and the quasi-virtuality of the given. Hegel is undoubtedly correct in stating that there is negativity in the sensory, that being prone to doubt is natural, that animals are wiser than the sensualists when they despair enough of the reality of things to devour them. But this nullification that resides in the field of the sensory is not the invariant negativity that transforms language into the means of understanding itself.[8]

To put it another way, above and below, right and left, before and behind, are places that need to be ascribed *to* a generating volume—the living and speaking body, as well as its gestating gesture—but these places need not, however, be perceived as dimensions *of* this body. The indication of the *here* refers to a coexistence of body and space which has no equivalent in the experience of language [*langage*]. No doubt the system of language [*langue*] has at its disposal what Émile Benveniste calls "indicators," about which we will need to say more. But the interesting and mysterious aspect of such words as *I, this, here,* which expect their "content" to come from their actualization in a discursive act, is specifically that they open language to an experience language cannot take in, since this experience is one of a *hic et nunc,* of an *ego,* that is to say, precisely, of sensory certainty. Any other word is charged with its latent significations in the virtual grid of language [*langue*], though it remains unuttered: it is not my discourse that creates this content of the word; rather its position in the sentence only serves to actualize one of the meanings attached to it. Whereas, in fact, the indicator's meaning *is* not; it can only *exist,* for we cannot produce a definition of *I* or *here* while remaining at the semantic level in which they are placed, without performing from and upon them a metalinguistic operation that amounts to a change in level—as, for example, in the grammarian's definition "*I* is the first person pronoun," which consists in transferring the term to the level of its syntactical function, thus apprehending it on an altogether other level than the lexical one that I occupy when I define, say, the whale as a marine mammal.

The difficulty derives from the fact that the signification (*Sinn*) of an "indicator" is inseparable from its designation (*Bedeutung*): what it means is what it speaks of, and one cannot identify its signified independently of its designated if it is not placed back in the spatiotemporal situation in which it is uttered. It is as if language, with these "indicators," were riddled with holes through which the gaze can slip, through which the eye can see and anchor itself outside. But this "outside" itself refers back to the original intimacy between the body and its space (as well as its time)—a corporating-spatializing intimacy where the above, before, and right cited by Hegel, which could be applied to the body itself, are engendered in the gesture that situates them as it goes through them. The *here* might very well be the result of this gesture, but certainly not the conclusion; diadeictics can be a type of dialectics, but it is not a discourse. A dialectics, because it is true that the *I* and the *here* emerge together in the movement that goes through, and that creates what it goes through, just as the subject and the object of speech take shape at the two extremities of its signifying motion. However, the act of indication eludes the saying because it is presupposed in the sphere of designation. Every totalization occurs in the three-dimensional space first opened by a twin de-totalization, that which sets apart discourse and its object, signification and reference. This reference belongs to the act of showing, not to that of signifying, for it is unsignifiable.

And this is precisely what Hegel recognized: "what they mean [*visent*] is not what they say. . . . The sensuous This that is meant [*visé*] cannot be reached by language. . . . What is called unutterable is . . . what is merely meant [*visé*]," and this meaning is the "untrue," the "irrational."[9] This could be construed as a condemnation of the system if, beneath the concept of system, one keeps alive the hope for a reconciliation of seeing and saying, of form and category. But it could equally be an authentication of the no-longer-totalizing system theorized, developed, and deployed by modern structuralists (with undeniable, if irritating philosophical modesty), indifferent to the sensory, restricting their scientific ambition to what can enter the language-system [*langue*], and neglecting the "merely meant" because it "cannot be reached" by language [*langage*]. Yet, by a significant reversal of positions, it is the dialectician who speaks the structuralist's truth, and who, by conceding language's shortcoming with regard to the *Zeigen*, also speaks of the structure's inability to exhaust language. The reason for this shortcoming is indeed that the meant or aimed-for [*le visé*] is inaccessible to language [*langage*]—*too close* to it, as if wrapped up in its movement. And it is inaccurate to say that perception truly apprehends (*wahrnimmt*) the sensory insofar as it composes and dialecticizes what was given in the false immediacy of sensory certainty. If one abides by Hegel's hierarchy of moments, one should say that what upholds perception does not come from perception but from the transcendence of sensory perception, and that the *Wahrnehmung*, far from revealing the truth of this transcendence, both presupposes and silences it for lack of anything to say about it, since the upholding is the *Zeigen* itself—transcendental negativity—that originally informed sensation itself as initial difference, and that will accompany the *Geist*'s movement until the end, applying to each of its formations the *discession*, the *Entzweiung*, without which there would be no subject and no object, no depth of an intentionality, nor this moment's "inequality" with its self, and thus nothing to speak of.

*

* *

Hegel concluded the first chapter of *Phenomenology of Spirit* by declaring the uncertainty of sensory certainty. Its immediacy is the result of its forgetting. It is made up of the forgetting of the movement by which the *here* is determined; it takes the *here* as an immediate given when in fact it derives from a mediation. This is how the logos will be smuggled back in—in itself-for us [*en soi-pour nous*], in the apparently primitive for-itself [*pour-soi*]. If there is such a thing as mediation in the most basic bestowal [*donation*] of a something here-now, it is because language already inhabits the sensory, and not only as what comes from elsewhere to immobilize, preserve, and remove it from the fluctuation of the instant (§ I), but rather as what (§ II) inside it—acting from within as its unconscious as it were, its rational unconscious—determines it through repeated negations applied to the elements of its spatial and temporal environment. The way Hegel understands this negation, acting on the surface of the grid of the world, is similar to the negation that, for structuralism, acts on the surface of the table of linguistic signifiers, where it cuts out distinct elements. Place and time would thus be determined *as* signification.

We nonetheless have the right, as I have tried to argue, to come to the opposite conclusion from Hegel's reflection, namely, that language [*langage*] does not manage to take the sensory seriously. The philosopher, of course, has no trouble demonstrating in his discourse that the unique status claimed by sensory certainty is unthinkable and unsayable, and that if it needs to be established, then it has to be said, and therefore embedded in a semantic field that ushers it into universality. But what he cannot incorporate is the showing, manifestation itself. Diadeictics is not a dialectics in Hegel's sense, precisely because the latter operates on the surface of a semantic grid, while the former presupposes the empty interval, the depth that separates the showing from the showed. Even if this interval is applied to the grid of the showed, it will lend itself to a possible index, in a distance that is never completely signifiable through language.

True, to designate does not mean to point fixedly at something: the eye that did not allow itself the slightest movement would not see; the index belongs to the stone statue. But there is another kind of movement than the mind's acting in the order of signification, going through the semantic subsets where it can sample the concepts it needs and articulate them in an intelligible discourse. There is a kind of movement that cannot be reduced to the activity Roman Jakobson calls selection and combination.[10] The movement by which the sensory presents itself is always a gesticulation, a dance, a movement that, assuredly, combines with itself, since to designate and to see require the constitution of a space, an order of the coexistences. And just as assuredly, designation and seeing determine a place as their end result. Yet such a combination is not a combinatorics, and such a determination is not an implication. The result of sensory activity is a *Dasein,* not a *Sinn.* The negativity that opens its distance between the eye and the object is that of form, not of category. The sensory lies in an unbridgeable gap in relation to the sensible [*sensé*].

Hegel's theory of the sensory—his aesthetics—provides unwitting proof of the existence of this gap. The critical assessment of the sensory's communication with the sensible [*sensé*] does in fact confirm the absorption of seeing by saying, which is the Hegelian phantasy. Jean Hyppolite picks up on the two uses of meaning [*sens*] Hegel distinguishes: "Meaning is certainly a curious word, which is, in turn, used in two opposite ways. On the one hand, it indeed identifies the organs that govern immediate apprehension; on the other, we call meaning a thing's signification—its idea, its universality. Thus meaning refers on the one hand to the immediate exteriority of existence and, on the other, to its interior essence. Reflective consideration, instead of separating the two parts, ensures that the one presents itself at the same time as its opposite: when it perceives something through sensory intuition, it simultaneously apprehends this thing's meaning and concept. But since these determinations are received in a non-dissociated state, the beholder is not yet conscious of the concept that she or he only vaguely feels."[11] Which Hyppolite goes on to explain in these terms: "There are, therefore, intermediaries between the sensory and the signification that is only present in language, and the transition from one to the other appears in the dialectics of the arts as well as in that of the mind. One should not, however, be misled by the term *intermediary*, since Hegel's philosophy is a philosophy of *mediation*. Signification as it comes to the fore in language, and meaning as the concept's becoming in discourse: these come before the movement that seems to generate them. There is no meaning before language, no more than there is an ineffable Absolute, and no more than there is a dream-state for the person who never wakes up."[12]

This straightforward explanation succinctly identifies the Hegelian problematic at issue here, for on the one hand it locates the Hegelian difficulty on the opposition between exteriority and interiority—in other words, on exactly what we referred to as the two definitions of meaning: meaning in interiority, which is signification (*Sinn*); and meaning in exteriority, namely designation (*Bedeutung*). The importance of this opposition will become clear. But for now, suffice it to note that in some respects the entire Hegelian problematic is indeed to resolve the meaning from exteriority—that which is given as coming from elsewhere, *Bedeutung*—in a signification that is entirely immanent in a system. The aim is to build an enclosure that can hold openness within it.

On the other hand, Hyppolite rightly notes that art is *not yet* this integration of meaning with itself, and therefore can only be, for a system thus haunted by the obsession of signification, an *intermediary.* But as Hyppolite also observes, in a philosophy of mediation there can be no intermediary, for everything is intermediary; only a dualist thinking can accommodate the intermediary, the μεταξύ [*metaxy*], the merging of body and soul, and the schema. In a philosophy of Logos-driven mediation, there is no given before mediation, and thus no meaning before signification: "There is no meaning *before* language." One can understand why Hegel does not manage to grant art a status of sufficiency, if the *aisthèton* is for him merely a *logikon* oblivious of itself that has "not yet" acceded to the in itself-for us.

Yet it is not for lack of trying to draw a clean line between symbol and sign, to show that, and how, in the former the sensible is immanent in the sensory:

> Now the symbol is *prima facie* a sign. But in a *mere sign* the connection which meaning [*signification*] and its expression have with one another is only a purely arbitrary linkage. In that case this expression, this sensuous [*sensible*] thing or picture, so far from presenting *itself,* brings before our minds a content foreign to it, one with which it does not need to stand in any proper affinity whatever. So in languages, for example, the sounds are a sign of some idea, feeling, etc. But the predominant part of the sounds in a language is linked purely by chance with the ideas expressed thereby, so far as their content is concerned, even if it can be shown, by an historical development, that the original connection was of another character; and the difference between languages consists chiefly in the fact that the same idea is expressed by a difference in sounds. Another example of such signs is afforded by the colours which are used in cockades and flags to express the nationality to which an individual or a ship belongs. Such colours likewise have in themselves no quality in common with their meaning, i.e. with the nation which is represented by them. Therefore, when symbol is taken in *this* sense as

> a mere sign with such an *indifference* between meaning and its expression, we may not take account of it in reference to *art,* since art as such consists precisely in the kinship, relation, and concrete interpenetration of meaning and shape. Therefore it is a different thing when a sign is to be a *symbol.* The lion, for example, is taken as a symbol of magnanimity, the fox of cunning, the circle of eternity, the triangle of the Trinity. But the lion and the fox do possess in themselves the very qualities whose significance they are supposed to express. . . . ; and the triangle as a *whole* has the *number* of sides and angles as that appearing in the idea of God when the determinations which religion apprehends in God are liable to *numeration.*[13]

Lucid reasoning: in the sign, the signifier is arbitrary in relation to the idea; in the symbol, the idea is immanent in the signifier. Here we come extremely close to Saussure, particularly to the explicit opposition he makes between a motivated semantic system and an arbitrary or unmotivated system.[14] Does such a differentiation of language with regard to any other signifying set not give us the assurance that the sensory as non-sensible meaning will gain an autonomous status, that it will not be annexed by the rational? Is the Hegelian symbol not what we are after—a true immanence of meaning in the signifier?

One has reason to doubt it. Let us return, among the examples of symbols Hegel provides, to the one of the triangle which, he says, symbolizes God, and let us analyze the procedures involved in this symbolization. On one side we have, not the signified "triangle," but the figure Δ; on the other, the phonological signifier /gäd/ with its signified "God." If the figure can symbolize God, this is because it has three sides and God, in Christian mythology, comprises three persons. The mediation appears to occur via the number 3, shared by the two terms and thereby assuring the immanence of the idea in the figure. But this is going too fast. The relation between the two concepts "God" and "Trinity" is, in structuralist terms, a paradigmatic one: "Trinity" can intervene in the signifying chain at the same places where "God" does. The two terms are substitutable; placed in the same expression—"God is the Trinity," "The Trinity is God"—they constitute what Jakobson calls a metaphorical proposition, such as "A hut is a small house," that is, one characterized precisely by the appearance of two terms or phrases that can be substituted for one another at two different places of the chain: such is the model of the metalanguage of definition. With these operations, we remain entrenched within the semantic field, instigating shifts aimed at isolating the *Sinn* of a term by placing it in opposition to others. Between "God" and "Trinity," the relation is strictly one of signification, entirely internal to the field of language.

This is not the case with the relation between the figure Δ and the significative unit "has three sides." Between the two a term is missing—"triangle"—which is, strictly speaking, the *name* of the figure. If the relation between this name and the phrase "has three sides" remains, as was the case with "God" and "Trinity," entirely internal to language, it is impossible to assert that the figure itself and the name belong to the same order. The figure is not made of articulated language. The name it carries is wholly extrinsic to it. The relation Δ-/'trīạɴɢgəl/ is totally arbitrary.

One could argue that the relation between the figure and the linguistic unit "has three sides" is not arbitrary, but this is because the level of analysis has changed, and the level relevant to the problem at hand has been left behind. For the *motivation* of the three-sided property with regard to the figure implies that we have slipped under language, so to speak, and that we have acknowledged that if the figure and the signified property share a community, this community takes place in an order representing the sensory in the intelligible, as well as the intelligible in the sensory, precisely the order Kant refers to as schematism. In fact, we need to resort to the schema of the ternary, to something like the sequence —∪— (every schema being temporal), to a dance, to what is sensory-sensible, to a poly-esthetic body capable of making the triangle's visible form, the rhythm of the tracing hand, and geometrical signification overlap. It is important, however, to stress that this synthesis operates directly between the fields of the sensory and the intelligible, whereas the order of the linguistic signifier, where the syntagms /'trīạɴɢgəl/ and /gäd/ lie, is not affected by schematism and remains enclosed in its arbitrariness. So that one could very well oppose Kant to Hegel in order to allow for the communication of the sensory with the sensible, without having the former dissolve in the latter. But this would be at the cost of neglecting what Kant effectively ignored, namely language's arbitrariness, the radical power of emancipation in relation to the sensory contained in the system of language [*langue*]—in other words, what will eventually give rise to the entire formalism of logic and modern mathematics. If the act of foundation is inconceivable (for you and for Kant) as merely the inscription of a given in a system, but further requires to be placed on an "aesthetic" plinth, then you over-motivate, your symbol becomes too heavy, and science as scission, as separation, becomes impossible. This is the paradox of a dualist philosophy (form-concept): going too far in tightening the same connections it had initially loosened.

But Hegel's paradox is no less striking. However hard he comes down on mathematics for their lack of motivation, their arbitrary character, their extrinsic character in relation to the object, what does he do if not ignore precisely this lack? For Hegel's system, far from respecting referentiality by effectively allowing the object to remain exterior to itself as its other, has moreover the pretension of signifying it totally in the system. But simply having the object signified in the system does not entail that the system loses its arbitrary relation to the object. The lack of motivation is inscribed in language as its dimension of exteriority in relation to objects. Once signified, this exteriority is no doubt internalized in language; but the latter will not have lost its margin for all that, and this margin is the face that looks elsewhere.

Let us return to God and the triangle. It is clear that there is no real immanence of the signified (God as Trinity) in the signifier (the triangular figure), since the analysis of the transfer processes brings to light a void, a "solution of continuity," located between the word and the figure.[15] If Hegel nonetheless offers this case as an example of a symbol, of an exemplary immanence of meaning in the signifier, this is proof that he takes the word for the object, the name of the thing for its presence, and thus dwells and persists in the order of language, where indeed one can say that triangularity is "symbolic" of Christian divinity, on the basis that one is speaking not of the triangular figure but of the concept of "having three elements."

Of course, we will have to identify and locate carefully the metaphor within language itself. Stating that "God is three" certainly does not go without saying, since it means taking as predicate of the utterance a term that does not belong to the same sub-system as the subject. In this detour or bridge—which constitutes the metaphor—there already exists, as we will soon see, a figural power working over [*travaille*] discourse.[16] This power is discourse's first expression, the closest, the easiest to grasp, and also the easiest for discourse to capture and put back in the order of signification. Hence the fact that all metaphors eventually wear down, and every expression, once "colorful," becomes commonplace. But this metaphor in language is not the one Hegel has in mind with the symbol, for he aims to go much further, to disclose meaning in the figure. He fails, because he understands meaning as signification, or, if you prefer, because he understands the name of the figure instead of the figure. Hegel gives us yet another innocent account of this systemic failure when, immediately after the example under discussion, he accuses the symbol of being ambiguous, equivocal, for containing at the same time an excessive measure of signifier over signified—of the triangular figure over the concept of God—and of signified over signifier—of God over the triangle—as well as a primary uncertainty, namely that once a triangle is given, one cannot, on the face of it, know if it is a symbol or only a figure, since it does not carry with it the index of its function or the formula of its usage.[17]

Now this ambiguity, adds Hegel, will be resolved only in the complete exteriorization of the image and of its signification (assuming, of course, that in the symbol there is immanence of the latter in the former—precisely the assumption that we are challenging), an exteriorization requiring that the image and the idea both, and *equally*, be *named*. "Such dubiety disappears only when each of the two sides, the meaning [*signification*] and its shape, are expressly named and thereby their relation is enunciated at once. But in that case the concrete existent set out before us [*vorgestellte*] is no longer a symbol in the strict sense of the word but just an image, and the relation between image and meaning acquires the familiar form of *comparison*, i.e., simile. In the simile, that is to say, there must float before our minds both, first, the general idea and then its concrete image. Whereas if reflection has not yet advanced far enough to take good note of universal ideas independently and so to set them out by themselves, then the related sensuous shape in which a more general meaning is supposed to find its expression is not yet thought to be separate from that meaning; both are still immediately at one. . . . [T] his constitutes the difference between symbol and comparison."[18]

The comparison is the "truth" of the symbol. It is of course undeniable that the comparison makes explicit what the symbol-metaphor keeps implicit, and thus begins to bring order to the latter's polysemy. But what matters is, first, that Hegel interprets this resolution as the truth of immanence; and, second, that the exteriorization he expects from the function of articulated discourse be, at the same time, the interiorization of what was exterior to it. The comparison exteriorizes the terms implied in the metaphor: "God is triangle" becomes "God is like a triangle." This "like" (to which we will return) is the switch, the signal of the change of field, and thus what posits the exteriority of what was once fused. It dissolves the confusion, and this is why it is, argues Hegel, the truth of the symbol. Thus truth is placed in discourse as discontinuous, and the continuous (or the con-fused with what is not itself, with the figural) is symmetrically cast as falsity, if not as absolute falsity (we are dialecticians, after all!), then as momentary falsity, falsity leading to truth, which will be disimplication.

As for this disimplication, it is indeed an exteriorization of the two terms—God and triangle—intertwined in the symbol, but this exteriorization takes place in the sealed-off order of discourse. In other words it is at once the interiorization of the symbolic figure (a process in fact already begun, as we saw, in the presentation of the example itself), its uprooting from its position of object of which one speaks, that is, of designated, and its assimilation to the order of signification, its transformation into signified. In so doing, we swapped the deep exteriority bordering discourse—where the object's figure stands—for a flat exteriority, an exteriority between two concepts laid out on the surface of the linguistic order, an exteriority guiding the search for a combination that would allow them to be brought together. We can always count on Hegel to come up with absolute expressions, and in the case of this recuperation he certainly does not disappoint. Here it is: "the perfect element in which interiority is just as exterior as exteriority is interior, is language."[19]

The first chapter of *Phenomenology of Spirit* performs the operation of showing that the exteriority of the sensory is interior, a discourse, a dialectics internal to language. The task of showing that interiority and the immanence of meaning in the signifier, in the symbol, is in fact the exteriority of two semantic subsystems, falls to my reading of the *Aesthetics.* For on the one hand the fluidification of the margins of discourse and, on the other, the petrifaction and articulation of its internal field can occur in language, and thus, too, can the swapping of the two exteriorities, the shuttling between the two negations. This is why Hegel considers art, which is the order of symbols, as fundamentally unstable and doomed to disappear; why the hierarchy as well as the chronology of the arts partake of an increasing abstraction, that is, of an increasing freedom vis-à-vis the figure and an increasingly rigid closure of language upon itself; and why the fate of art is its already quasi-realized disappearance; why the beautiful figural, sensory, Greek totality is lost and can be restored only as *Wissenschaft,* only as real discursive, linguistic, modern (and obviously clerical-bureaucratic) totality.

Who will deny that we are not Greek, and that we cannot be? Who will deny that this separation from the sensory, this preeminence of speech, this obsession with totalization, this faith in redemption belong to the legacy of Christianity? But who does not feel that the time has come to do away with it? Totalization by and through language is the necessary complement of a process of detotalization. The exteriority of the object at issue here is not a matter of signification but of designation, belonging to an experience that has no place in the system, but which is the speaker's, and proceeding from a break, from a split that is the price to pay for the system of language [*langue*] to be usable. This exteriority is pried open by seeing and desiring, in a withdrawal of meaning as old as any experience and any utterance. Hegel's totality represents the (entirely imaginary, ideological) filling of this space of dispossession in whose absence, however, we would not be able to see, or even speak: this imaginary representation, which is the Hegelian system, itself presupposes this void to be filled. Every act of signification takes place in a space of designation that is at once that of intentionality and of dispossession.

Can nothing then be said about this space of designation, about the deep exteriority located on the border of discourse, given that discourse misses (interiorizes) this exteriority in the very process of signifying it? There is, however, outside of language, the possibility of a redoubling: that of re-presentation. Re-presentation can render visible what seeing is. Indeed, painting not only shares with discourse the privilege of being able to represent itself (as in a picture representing a picture), and not only the aptitude to represent itself in the act of being made (as in a picture representing the painter painting the picture); it also has the power to represent visibility itself—what we called the space of designation or bordering exteriority. Hegel knew this: "To express inner feeling, painting reduces the triad of spatial dimensions to the surface, as that to which, in exteriority, is the closest interiority.... For painting is not involved in the activity of rendering visible in general, but rather in visibility in the process of particularizing itself in itself, and in visibility that has become interior. In sculpture or architecture, forms are rendered visible through exterior light. In painting, on the other hand, matter, in itself obscure, contains in itself its interiority, the ideal character, light: it is permeated by light, and for this very reason light is permeated by obscurity."[20]

Yet this knowing was just that, a form of knowledge. Let us go one step further: this making visible is equally possible in the order of language itself, only not as signification but as expression. In front of discourse there is the figure-image, while in discourse dwells the figure-form. The redoubling of the one upon the other is what possibly allows poetry to represent presenting distance [*distance présentante*]. But one can only gain access to this structure through unstructured desire, which is precisely what Hegel excluded from his purview. This unstructured unmotivation is painting's subterranean impulse. By following this impulse we will come to realize that the possibility itself of manifestation—the space of designation, which discourse unconsciously uses to keep its object at a distance—is already there in the sensory, as far as the latter exceeds mere bestowing and holds within itself the power to reflect itself; thus, as far as the sensory constitutes itself at the same time as desire and receives from the latter its thickness, its hidden side.

The figure-form is the presence of nonlanguage in language. It is something that belongs to another order lodged in discourse, granting the latter its expressivity. We cannot hope, as Hegel did, to grasp the immanence of meaning in signification at the level of the linguistic or visual *unit*—i.e., the word, the triangle. The relevant level is always that of the sentence or the form. The word in itself has no expressive power in relation to what it designates; indeed, it became a word precisely at the cost of losing this power, of becoming arbitrary. Nor does language partake of the sensory through its "matter";[21] rather, it is through its figure that language will be able to measure up to the sensory.

There is nothing more to add on the subject of "flat" and as it were "motionless" dialectics of space passing through concepts, organizing semantic fields. All thought proceeds in this way; discourse takes shape by interiorizing in its text the significative units it needs. Thus the truth of the same can be said to lie in the other. But then the other of the concept is nothing other than another concept, and this truth lies firmly in the identity of the sayable. No doubt for the speaker the sayable remains to be said; there is a kind of discovery of the signified, which can provoke in her or him the feeling of alterity. This alterity, however, remains enclosed in the discursive element. When dialectics extends its claim to the object—to the other of the concept that is the sensory—it stretches beyond its own reach, and from knowledge turns into ideology. True, we have every right to contend that everything is sayable; but what cannot be said is that discourse's signification embraces all the meaning of the sayable. One can say that the tree is green, but saying so does not put color in the sentence. Yet color is meaning. The negativity of signification comes up against that of designation, not because there would be an insurmountable unsayability of the world and a destiny of silence, but because a symmetrical deferral of the act of designation accompanies any effort to signify. The hope of enclosing the whole object within discourse must be abandoned if this is indeed our hope—and this is what one must attack in Hegel. On the other hand, the space of designation does indeed dwell in discourse, but on this side of what it signifies, in its expression. I call it provisionally "space of designation" because its properties seem analogous to those of that space and contradict those of linguistic space. What they have in common is the figure, which I will call figural space. The latter surrounds discourse, offering it its object as image; and discourse also harbors this space within itself, which determines its form. But let there be no mistake: this "interiority" of figural space in relation to discourse is not dialectical.

Recessus and Hyper-Reflection

Reflection, which thought itself comfortable in the negative, having set up camp there as if on a peak from which to contemplate both sides of language, now finds itself—after the structuralist critique of showing, and the dialectical-phenomenological critique of the system—turned out and apparently doomed to nomadism. It realizes that it is invested from both sides, by the unconsciousness of language as system [*langue*] and of sight, and that it cannot take possession of these two kinds of elementary intervals—one constituting signification, the other, reference. Captive of language [*langue*], in the absence of which it would be no more than sight, yet chained to the distancing of seeing, without which this language [*langue*] would be merely a thing and could not be spoken, reflection must travel the border zone where the first silence—that of structure—touches the second—that of the phenomenon—to produce speech. Reflection, threatened with lapsing at any moment either into the positivism of the system, or into the intuitionism of the aim [*visée*], is barred from achieving the dialectical "solution" that offered the synthesis of the two axes of the negative; it is condemned to moving forward by preserving its imbalance as the sole witness to its intact existence.

The evacuation of dialectics leads one to take different paths. As long as the philosopher doesn't also become a painter, she or he will remain prisoner of the sphere of language [*langue*], of structuralist unconsciousness. But what speech can still accomplish is to carry out, upon its own language [*langage*], this transgression of the spacings, this mobility and this depth that characterize the reference of discourse and that structuralism neglects. It is not even a question of drawing or painting, but rather of painting and drawing with and in words, what Merleau-Ponty called hyper-reflection [*surréflexion*].[1]

What philosophy "finds in thus returning to the sources, it says," obviously,[2] but this saying, Merleau-Ponty thought, could have a texture such that it would respect in itself this source quality, this ontogenesis it seeks to signify. Discourse as it takes shape would thus try to measure itself against the "origin" it wishes to say. Discourse on the origin, originary discourse: for Merleau-Ponty, an opening discourse as opposed to "eloquent" language, which would be that of closure. The "words most charged with philosophy are not necessarily those that contain what they say, but rather those that most energetically open upon Being, because they more closely convey the life of the whole and make our habitual evidences vibrate until they disjoin."[3] The philosopher quickly adds, on the heels of this statement, in something of a retreat that is not only a sign of modesty, nor a kind of concession in the form of denial, but rather a safeguard against the contraction of this hope into a "thesis," against a renewed alienation of language—in the end not dissimilar to that one he has just denounced in Sartre's analysis of nothingness: "Hence it is a *question* whether philosophy as reconquest of brute or wild being can be accomplished by the resources of the eloquent language, or whether it would not be necessary for philosophy to use language in a way that takes from it its power of immediate or direct signification in order to equal it with what it wishes all the same to say."[4] One would have thought that the "answer" to this "question" was already known, since it reappears throughout the book. "As the world is behind my body, the operative essence is behind the operative speech also, the speech that possesses the signification less than it is possessed by it, that does not speak *of it,* but speaks *it,* or speaks *according to it,* or lets it speak and be spoken within me, breaks through my present."[5] "As the nervure bears the leaf from within, from the depths of its flesh, the ideas are the texture of experience, its style, first mute, then uttered. Like every style, they are elaborated within the thickness of being. . . ."[6] And if one had to characterize the "style" in question, this is how one would go about it: ". . . there could be a language of coincidence, a manner of making the things themselves speak. . . . It would be a language of which he {the philosopher} would not be the organizer, words he would not assemble, that would combine through him by virtue of a natural intertwining of their meaning, through the occult trading of the metaphor—where what counts is no longer the manifest meaning of each word and of each image, but the lateral relations, the kinships that are implicated in their transfers and their exchanges."[7] "There could be . . . , it would be a language . . .": expressions of reverie, composed in the mode and time of the unreal present, but also a glimpse of the style of hyper-reflection, which connects and assimilates it to that of the dream. This meditation on a language gives way to the "language" of dreams. The "natural intertwining" of meanings, the "occult trading of the metaphor," the "lateral" relations of words and images: it's all here, condensation, displacement, figurability—all the operations that combine to produce the "style" of the dream but also of poetry, all their "work," as Freud would say.

Of course Merleau-Ponty did not intend to *replace* philosophy with the dream. Rather, he thought that a model of discourse enclosed or obsessed with closure, such as that of "rational" philosophy, must be stripped of its originary imperative if it wants to let speak from within itself what otherwise, in all its "eloquence," it cannot succeed in speaking. But with what to replace it? Can one philosophize outside of discourse, and discourse without *ratio*? It might appear arrogant to declare that what is sought here, in light of what I have just quoted, is why and how poetry and the dream resemble hyper-reflection, why and how, by giving up the armature of scientific logos, language can, if not *come closer* to the "origin," then at least offer, in its very texture, an approximation of what it is not. This might appear to betray the spirit of *The Visible and the Invisible,* if indeed revealing the reason behind the secret goes hand in hand with something akin to the restoration of a philosophy of the negative—precisely what Merleau-Ponty constantly seeks to isolate and free himself from. The negative we will thus uncover, however, is not Sartre's negative, nor a Hegelian dialectics. It subdivides, I have argued, into invariant interval of the system and mobile spacing of seeing. This self-dividing is so essential that if hyper-reflection can lean toward poetry and the dream, this is because both equally imply, quite obviously, language [*langue*], but language undone; and quite obviously too, the invariant interval of the grid, but an interval worked over and subject to distortion, "vibrating until it disjoins."

To undo the code without, however, destroying the message, while instead releasing from it the meaning and the lateral semantic reserves concealed by structured speech, is to carry out a series of operations that Freud called dream-work and that, as I will try to show, consists entirely in the transgression of the measured intervals underpinning the weave of language [*langue*], and is thus, indeed, "fulfillment of desire." Such a description calls upon at least two negativities: that of the structure of language [*langue*], and that of visual experience, both implicated in our use of discourse; the first as invariant code shared by the interlocutors and all the words uttered in this language [*langue*]—in any case as condition of communication, even if it does not allow one to infer that two people may be communicating; the second as distance to be crossed, as a distance indicating the place toward which what I say goes, as horizon opening before words and pulling them toward it: a negativity that lies at the heart of our spatial existence, a mobility constitutive of depth. This mobility of gesture in which the energetics and the flash of desire are concealed is, once censorship is lifted, what seems to collapse on the *ratio* of language—which Merleau-Ponty called speaking speech [*parole parlée*][8]—where it will produce the "disorder" of dreams, poetry, and the figure, revealing, in fact, the unstable, impossible "order" of a being torn between Eros-death and Eros-reality, between variant and invariant, between figure and discourse.

With this disassociation of the two negativities, one can walk the same path as Merleau-Ponty, but in the opposite direction, our back toward him. He wanted to introduce the gesture, the mobility of the sensory, even into the invariance characteristic of the system of language, to articulate what is constitutive of saying, to restore the act that inaugurates the possibility of speech: the ultimate attempt on behalf of transcendental reflection. To no avail. The system is always already there, and the gesture of speech that supposedly creates signification can never be grasped in its constituting function, for it is always and can only be grasped as *deconstruction.* What one can show to reach this order sought by Merleau-Ponty is how the beyond-Logos dwells in language, how it invades it to transgress the invariances—the keys to signification—and arouse in it the lateral meaning that is surreality. But if this meaning is indeed surreality, this is because the energy of deconstructing is not only on this side of the Logos, but also on this side of the real, or of perception, and because this sensory, or rather this *visible* with which we will have to deal is not that which surrenders to the utilitarian or scientific eye of the busy individual, of the Westerner, not even the visible seized by the eye trained to wait, to see the invisible (which is Cézanne's, according to

Merleau-Ponty). No, it is the visible of a subject-less gaze, the object of nobody's eye. And it is not enough to try, along with the phenomenologist, to go beneath the realist view of the constituted or the given, for sooner or later one will have to give up phenomenologizing if one wants to reach this something that comes close to phenomenological constitution, this something that is not constitutable, but only graspable through an entirely different method—deconstruction—and on grounds of completely other, unexpected, effects—of recessus.

Phenomenology has always had to correct, or be relieved of, its naïveté as a philosophy of consciousness. As for perception, Merleau-Ponty strenuously placed it under the authority of the body, demonstrating that there is structure before signification, that the former supports the latter, and that the nullification through the for-itself is a phantasy. But when it comes to language, the importance granted the linguistic gesture seems to have distracted the philosopher from considering this other preconscious of structure in which, after all, this gesture is performed, without which it would not be possible, which forms the anonymity and transitivity where all speech acts are immersed, and which serves as a guideline for this gesture in roughly the same way as the natural agreement between color and movement that suffuses the body can govern its attitudes and gestures. One should give back to the *ratio* of language [*langue*] its scope, even if it should be anti-phenomenological, as Merleau-Ponty did for the body's *Gestalt* and *Aufbau*. The need for this re-adjustment is what prevents one from granting the art of writing the privilege of activating, on the philosopher's own discourse, the movements, distortions, osmoses, and associations that make up speaking speech. There is no reason to declare the latter and spoken speech exclusive to one another. To state that discourse is a gesture is in any case a metaphor, and the distance between the two terms of this metaphor—movement and utterance—depends entirely on the fact of language [*fait de la langue*].

One should stop interpreting language [*langue*] as inertia, without consequence, through a Manichaeism inherited from Henri Bergson, and take another look at this division. For at the moment when we describe the transgressions of the order of language [*langue*], we are speaking, signifying, and communicating them, thereby introducing them back into the transgressed order. Herein lies the limitless power of the system, to still be able to utter what reduces it to silence, and to allow the commentary of precisely what resists it, namely the operations of condensation, displacement, and figuration. For everything can be described, that is, signified, transmitted, even the silences that in language [*langage*] are not those of language [*langue*], even uncoded blanks, even the intervals that resist being regulated, even the torsions that lie outside of syntax. Articulated language [*langage*] carries within itself its own limitation, that is, the inability to place outside, to consider as object and to signify its actual aim [*visée*]. At the same time every aim [*visée*] can be taken as object, can fall under language's jurisdiction once placed outside. It is upon this same limitless jurisdiction that the commentary on art relies, that interpretation with Freud relied, and that we too will rely. Mute sight, the gesture of desire, condensation and displacement, the entrance of the figure in the text via the rebus, and finally the merging of spaces, can all be uttered and articulated in discourse. Such discourse of course does not grant us the possession of seeing, desiring, moving; but then no discourse possesses its object. If one wants to stay within the sphere of this concept of possession, one should say that language can, at best, allow itself to be possessed by its object—which is what Merleau-Ponty wanted—and this is the artist's discourse, not the philosopher's, which must give up possessivity one way or another, since philosophy is born at the same time as the dwelling of speech by the world or the gods comes to an end, and since it is its destiny to speak soberly, at a distance, to never completely "be part of it." We must accept this particular gap in the contact, which is the burden of philosophical speech—neither art nor science—as well as its guarantor and model, namely the order of language [*langue*]. For it is through the constraints the latter imposes, all of which result in invariants and constant intervals, that the order of language founds this speech at an arbitrary distance from the order of things, pitting against the unhampered movements underlying perceptual space the unconditional markers of linguistic "space."

The relevant opposition here is not between spoken and speaking speech—the former assimilated to language [*langue*], the latter to gesture or movement. But in every utterance there are two dimensions: one in which operate—at the different levels identified by linguists (such as of the first and second articulation in André Martinet's functionalism)—the oppositions and correlations connecting the units available to the speaker; and the other in which the speaker's intention to signify thrusts itself. On the one hand the dimension of language [*langue*]—which is not merely spoken speech, but the matrix of innumerable propositions—and on the other the dimension of intention, of linguistic gesture, which is "speaking" by its expression, but primarily because it respects the constraints of language [*langue*]. The utterance can better obey the constraints imposed by language [*langue*], its intention to signify respectfully following the latter's shape. Or it can undo the constraints so as to subject the elements of language [*langue*] to the vector of desire, in which case it can harm the code, inserting between words, and possibly in the words themselves, the same unpredictable intervals that separate and bring together imaginary things, and infuse the space of language [*langue*] with the mobility of desire, built on the polarity of the close and the distant. Yet even in this last case the utterance must meet certain conditions of signification if it wants to avoid total chaos. This is exactly the moment we want not to mime on the surface of our writing, but to capture at the tip of our gaze. This activity—that of the poet, the writer, and the dream—places the figural into abstraction, the "real" into the "arbitrary," endowing discourse with almost the same flesh as that of the sensory. This labor of regression, as Freud would say, reveals that the truly pertinent opposition is only between variant and invariant, between mobile and rigid negativity, and that the order of language is to the order of expression as that which is twice articulated is to that which is once.

What is invariance? Variance plus the negation of variance. But what then is variance? Variance is the spacing whose unbridgeability is denied—spacing transgressed. So what, again, is invariance? It is the negation of this negation that lies in mobility.

But the relation between these two negations is *not dialectical*: one is not the moment of the other. If one really wants to articulate them together—that is, by keeping them in their exteriority, in their unsurpassable inequality, in what we will call their *difference*—one must consider them in relation to the fate of desire. For it is only by considering desire that we can hold reflection *at bay* from the dialectical reconciliation of the two negations, and that the horizon may be kept free to show (through hyper-reflection) how invariance and variance—that is, secondary and primary processes—always, and simultaneously, present themselves together and can never form a unity. What guarantees signification is the respect for the oppositions between the terms of a system. Yet it is by virtue of the same respect of instituted intervals (through the prohibition of incest) that the mother will have to retreat before the subject's request—a withdrawal that opens up for the subject the space of seeing-imagining. Far from promising the reconciliation of signification and meaning, this articulation of the Father-negation and Mother-negation forces one never to be able to think of the one except as the other's transgression. To want to measure up to the imaginary interworld through pure representational and ineffable intuition is a fulfillment of desire that depends on the repression of its taboo: "There is no law." And to want to measure up to the law in a formally enclosed and wholly signifying discourse is also a fulfillment of desire—a desire hinging upon its foreclosure: "There is only the law." Merleau-Ponty's philosophy is Father-less, or has too much of it: in any case, this leaves his discourse in an insatiable longing for the Mother.[9]

We impinge here on a Freudian problematic that we cannot possibly survey in its entirety, let alone domesticate and put behind bars—which is what philosophy tends to do when it encounters something. But one need not resort to torturing, chaining up his texts to be struck by the fact that Freud's reflection, from the beginning to the end of his career, from *The Interpretation of Dreams* to *Moses and Monotheism,* centers on the relation between language and silence, signification and meaning, articulation and image, interpreting or constructing commentary and figuring desire. It is no less striking that this relation is constantly understood by Freud, if from different angles, as *Verneinung*: negation of discourse in the phantasmatic realm of dreams and negation of the phantasy in the patient's discourse; negation of the religion of the image in that of the book and negation of this negation in Moses' purported murder. By thus holding reflection in negation a while longer, we have no intention of placing it under Hegel's tutelage—totalizing negation where nothing is lost—but rather of announcing Freud—negation as suppression of the other and of myself. This negation is what constitutes the transcendence of saying in relation to the said, the dimension of reference that is the rebound of seeing in the order of discourse. It is also what sets in motion the machinery of the image even in articulated language [*langage*], producing the dream, poetry, and, lastly, the very possibility of this hyper-reflection that phenomenology, tired of mulling over intentionality, finally longs for. Freud arrives just in time to teach it how the subject is a being who dreams of the coincidence of which she or he is deprived. It would be misinterpreting Freud's lesson, I believe, to conclude simply that since all transcendence of consciousness is imaginary, we must ignore it. Yet it would not heed his lesson at all to found, just as simply, a philosophy of hyper-reflection that took from a philosophy of reflection the idea that the whole of the unconscious is in the aim [*visée*], adding to it only the principle that one can bring to light this unconscious through style alone. Freud's negation, which goes under the name of castration and generates anxiety, produces the transcendence of seeing—which is that of desire; but it also implies the entrance into the structure, into its *archè,* that is, the set of measured intervals of the law. By occupying this hinge, we should be able to articulate the two spaces one on top of the other, that of language [*langue*] and of the figure. This is still reflection, because we will continue here to produce a discourse of signification, but also hyper-reflection, because we will attempt to articulate what in speech remains silent and shows.

One can track the recessus of speech as it undoes itself, on its way toward anti-speech or the rebus. It can be followed because there is anti-speech in speech, seeing in saying, continuity in the articulated, difference even in opposition. This is regressive flexing rather than reflection, the opposite of dialectics: the truth of hyper-reflection. One can track it, and one must, because it is precisely this mobility that, when introduced in the order of invariant spacings, can detect them—the ironic contribution of Eros-death to Eros-Logos. How do the two forms of negation overlap; how can that of showing enter into that of discourse; how can text become figure: these are the questions that interest hyper-reflection and can guide it. It will come as no surprise that philosophy arrives too late here, and that it has everything to learn from poets.

A text is that which does not allow itself to be moved. The intervals that keep its elements apart and punctuate them—letters, words, sentences—are the projection on the sensory support—page, stone—of the intervals separating the distinctive and significative terms in the grid of language [*langue*]. But language [*langage*], too, is deep, and as such should be capable of undergoing fictionalizing operations. If there is evidence to confirm this hypothesis, it will be found in the work itself of establishing language [*langage*], specifically in that the linguist, at the very moment she or he assigns positions to the terms in the depthless plane of the structure, makes use of a procedure—commutation—that nonetheless requires depth. But there is further evidence that a text should be able to be read not only according to its signification—a matter of linguistic space—but actually seen according to its configuration, upheld by the sensory-imaginary space in which it is inscribed. Fiction, which is what produces figure from text, consists entirely in a play on intervals: the figure is a deformation that imposes another form on the layout of linguistic units. This form is not reducible to the constraints imposed by the structure.

When it comes to large units—for example, Claude Lévi-Strauss's *mythemes*[10] or Vladimir Propp's functions[11]—given that the intervals separating them are not controlled with any precision by the code of language [*langue*], and that they do not belong to a rigid space and are, for the most part, left up to the speaker, the game that gives rise to form at this level of discourse does not come across as violence against any rule; thus structural linguistics easily relinquishes the study of this level's combinations, handing it over to stylistics. It is here that literary activity comes into play, producing stylistic devices and narrative forms. Such an additional organization of literary discourse, this supplementary constraint brought to bear on larger units, is sometimes called structure. But this is a mistake, for such forms do not belong to the structure of (linguistic) matter from which they are made, which is precisely why they are expressive.[12] Hence the order of structure appears able to remain independent from that of form, linguistics from stylistics, and by the same token reason from passion. The methodological option chosen by Saussure, in favor of a study language [*langue*]—thus automatically at the expense of speech—runs the risk of overlooking the question of the coexistence of the two negativities, that of structure and form.

Radical poetry (which is not the same as "pure" poetry) is necessary to make this coexistence tangible and visible. In the search for what Paul Valéry calls the "figure of thought," this poetry descends to the lowest reaches in the hierarchy of linguistic units, importing the agitation and insurrection no longer only in traditional prosody—that is to say, in the supplemental constraints through which poetic discourse is connoted—but in the fundamental laws of communicable discourse itself. With *Un coup de dés jamais n'abolira le hasard,* Stéphane Mallarmé radically deprives articulated language of its prosaic function of communication, revealing in it a power that exceeds it: the power to be "seen," and not only read-heard; the power to figure, and not only to signify.

First of all it would be absurd to take Mallarmé's book as a score or a picture, to pretend that the words are not words and have no meaning. Gardner Davies is right to underscore the fact that the text is read, like any French text, from left to right and top to bottom.[13] But if such is the case we cannot avoid taking into consideration the *signification* of these inscriptions bizarrely scattered across the space of the book. The connection Davies draws with *Igitur* indicates clearly that the same problematic is at issue: to produce the ultimate work, speech standing outside of time and space just as it stands outside of the relation of author and reader—timeless, nonextended, incommunicable and uncreated, "the text speaking of itself and without authorial voice"[14] because the spirit that finds expression here is "located beyond circumstances."[15] This place-less place and this moment without time are chance abolished. Discourse placed upon this space, "vacant and superior" as it is described at the end of *Un coup de dés,* no longer owes anything to sensory, social, affective circumstance; it has cut all ties to its other, and the object is no longer present within it at all, like an unconscious parasite. Such is the requirement discourse must satisfy for it to produce what Mallarmé calls the "essential notion," the true poetic object.

This process of elimination ("My work was created only by 'elimination'" Mallarmé writes to Eugène Lefébure, adding, "Destruction was my

Beatrice"[16]) is the fulfillment of the loss of the object, without which there is no literature. This "illusion," this "hoax" that is poetic fiction, and this "divine transposition"[17] of fact into ideal, occur in a "vacant space" from which the constraints of sensibility in the Kantian sense and those of the language of interlocution are eliminated. Speech already carries out this exclusion of the object (and subject) thanks to the immaterial, "vibratory" nature of its support.[18] Mallarmé's poetics seems to bring to completion the fundamental property of language, which Saussure was developing at the same time, namely, the sign's arbitrariness in relation to the object it signifies. The "elimination" Mallarmé performs is the deepening of the spacing of reference as an unbridgeable distance separating the word and the object, and ensuring the former's ideal scope.

Now this poetics gets more complicated, however, as *Un coup de dés* testifies as much by its content as by its form. Through literature, one must indeed "ascertain that one is in fact where one should be (because, allow me to express this apprehension, there remains an uncertainty),"[19] by "assuming . . . some duty to re-create everything." But such re-creation allows its object to be *seen,* and this seeing, should it even be ideal or notional like its object, is nonetheless borrowed from the libidinal constitution of vision. If "the agony in which one resuscitates what one has lost in order to *see* it"[20] is in fact the work of death that literature exacts upon the world, it is not, however, the latter's simple abolishment, having still to *represent* it. Mallarmé indirectly flagged this importance of the visible, present even in the vacant space of withdrawal, when in his letters he insists on the sensual character of his notional approach: "I discovered the *Idea of the Universe* through sensation alone—and . . . in order to perpetuate the *indelible idea of pure Nothingness,* I had to fill my brain with the sensation of absolute Emptiness."[21] The operation of transposition passes through the register of affect: it is the "sensation" that preserves the reminiscence of the abolished object. And this sensation is not only knowledge, but pleasure: "I want myself to *enjoy* every new idea, not learn it."[22]

This is not a case of an author's idiosyncrasy, at exactly the moment when the author is in the process of disappearing. This sensuality in the use of negativity finds its counterpart on the side of the text itself. Writing distinguishes itself from speech in that it offers, through its signs, a visible trace of the idea. For Mallarmé, however, this trace cannot be arbitrary: "to go from the *sentence* to the *letter* via the word; by resorting to the Sign or to writing, which links the word to its meaning."[23] The written letter acts as a link to meaning—a "meaning" that presents no small ambiguity, impossible as it is here to know whether it is the word's signified or the object it designates. As we will see, it is neither one nor the other, but a kind of schema included in the word, its action plan, a motivated choreography, concealed within its arbitrariness. Notwithstanding, and unlike speech, writing institutes a dimension of visibility, of sensory spatiality, that will allow precisely to make visible the universe re-created from the divine transposition. The notion (or the signified) must therefore be represented sensorially, "expressed" in a space that is the object's, and without losing anything of itself, its content and its discontinuity as concept.

This very contradiction motivates *Igitur,* and generates, too, the writing of *Un coup de dés.* At stake in both texts is an act by which contingency must be halted. The act in question is the one of writing the work, of producing an absolute discourse, the "Book," represented as the Number—in *Un coup de dés,* the number possibly brought about by the Master's throw of dice before it founders. The work, because it speaks in the vacancy of all condition extrinsic to pure discourse and grants only the notion, must abolish chance, that is, language's other, its reference. But what *Un coup de dés* says is that language does not abolish its other, that the work itself belongs to the sensory, and that there is no need to choose between writing and giving it up, that, in sum, the problem is a false one and, in any case, "nothing will have taken place but the place."[24] Language and its other are inseparable: such is the lesson of *Un coup de dés, Igitur,* and Mallarmé. But we have yet to show how Mallarmé expects us to devote ourselves and yield to this inseparability: not by politely tipping one's hat from within language, by *signifying* it, but by making it *visible,* again, thereby smuggling the plane (the emblem of contingency) into the sign (the seal of the notion). Hence the attention to typography, which is far from "childish."[25]

That nothing should have taken place but place would be an inaccurate formulation in its pessimism were it to suggest that writing is nothing, that only the sensory remains, the abyss of *Un coup de dés.* This place—which will have taken place after the poem, or which will even have taken place after the poet founders without having produced anything—is not nothing. We know that at the end of *Un coup de dés,* precisely where the dice are not thrown, where the work is not written, there nonetheless appears the figure of the Big Bear: nothing has taken place but this constellation. Davies reminds us that this celestial figure, "which counts down . . . the regular jolting . . . of a total computation in progress" and thus belongs, with writing, to the Number, to anti-chance, differs from text insofar as the text takes the form of black on white, while the star is white against the black background of the sky. "You noted, one does not write, luminously on a dark field, the alphabet of the stars, alone thus appears, sketched out or interrupted; man continues black on white."[26] Is the night sky, then, the negative of the text? Not exactly, and not only, for to write white on black is to write with the ink of chance across the element of the absolute, where the absolute is the immutable trace as sign, the presence of the word [*verbe*] (the word is Mallarmé's, in his essays on language), and white is absent meaning. The constellation, then, is the "fixed infinite," the white of the indefinite intercepted in the sign. Only this sign is not a book but a form: neither shadow nor white, but both. And it is in this sense that it is a place.

Now, the volume of *Un coup de dés* represents the answer to this place, as itself a place of meaning, but the negative of the Constellation, writing black on white. The establishing of the place is achieved in the most straightforward manner possible, practically without sentences (Figure 1): through the transgression of the usual spacings between textual elements, through an arrangement of the words that takes into consideration, beneath the constraints imposed by the structure of language [*langue*], spatial values borrowed from our visual and gestural experience, whether perceptual or imaginary.[27]

To confirm that Mallarmé indeed sought, through the sensory layout of the book, to render expressive a space normally destined to be overlooked, we need only read the spiritual instrument that is The Book: "The book, which is a total expansion of the letter, must find its mobility in the letter; and in its spaciousness must establish some nameless system of relationships which will embrace and strengthen fiction. . . . The making of a book, with respect to its flowering totality, begins with the first sentence. From time immemorial the poet has knowingly placed his verse in the sonnet which he writes upon our minds or upon pure space. We, in turn, will misunderstand the true meaning of this book and the miracle inherent in its structure, if we do not knowingly imagine that a given motif has been properly placed at a certain height on the page, according to its own or to the book's distribution of light. . . . A tremendous burst of greatness, of thought, or of emotion, contained in a sentence printed in large type, with one gradually descending line to a page, should keep the reader breathless throughout the book and summon forth his powers of excitement. Around this would be smaller groups of secondary importance, commenting on the main sentence or derived from it, like a scattering of ornaments."[28] And in the letter to André Gide, quoted by Valéry, Mallarmé writes, "The poem is now being printed in the form in which I conceived it, including the pagination, which will be its true originality. Certain words in large type will need an entire blank page. . . . The constellation, obedient to the strictest laws, will move as fatefully as constellations do—at least insofar as it can in a printed book. The ship will heel over from the top of one page to the bottom of the next, and so forth. The big point (which I couldn't explain in a periodical) is that the rhythm of a word group, if it is to make sense, must imitate the action or object in question."[29]

"It seemed to me that I was looking," writes Valery, "at the form and pattern [*la figure*] of a thought, placed for the first time in finite space. . . . With my own eye I could see silences that had assumed bodily shapes."[30] So here it is, this language dreamed of by Merleau-Ponty, or at least its protocol of experience. It has brought the sensory into itself: no longer speaking only through its signification, it expresses through its blanks, its typefaces, the folds of its pages.[31] It has agreed to deconstruct itself, has abandoned some of the typographic constraints that belong to language [*langue*], accommodated certain expectations, emphases, accelerations that take shape from a sensory expanse. Radical poetry thereby testifies to the presence of a latent sensory

OVERLEAF: Figure 1. Stéphane Mallarmé, *Un coup de dés jamais n'abolira le hasard* (Paris: Gallimard, 1914). Half-size facsimile.

C'ÉTAIT
issu stellaire

CE SERAIT
pire
non
davantage ni moins
indifféremment mais autant

LE NOMBRE

EXISTÂT-IL

autrement qu'hallucination éparse d'agonie

COMMENÇÂT-IL ET CESSÂT-IL

sourdant que nié et clos quand apparu

enfin

par quelque profusion répandue en rareté

SE CHIFFRÂT-IL

évidence de la somme pour peu qu'une

ILLUMINÂT-IL

LE HASARD

Choit

la plume

rythmique suspens du sinistre

s'ensevelir

aux écumes originelles

naguères d'où sursauta son délire jusqu'à une cime

flétrie

par la neutralité identique du gouffre

in the sensible. Where does it dwell? Not directly in the "matter" of words (what would this be, exactly? their written, printed figure? their sound? the "color" of letters?), but in their disposition. One will counter that the sensible too—signification—depends entirely on the disposition of units. But our understanding of disposition—the poetic dispersal across the page—is a disturbance of the disposition that ensures signification; it upsets communication. Mallarmé already says it of verse: "Out of a number of words, poetry fashions a single new word which is total in itself and foreign to language—a kind of incantation. Thus the desired isolation of language is effected; and chance (which might still have governed these elements, despite their artful and alternating renewal through meaning and sound) is thereby instantly and thoroughly abolished."[32] He refers to verse as chance "vanquished word by word,"[33] and sees in the typographic blank the sensory presence of an initial contingency that the regular return of the paragraph break will incorporate as "silence" in words. The disruption of significations consists in forms: the elements (words) are isolated by unforeseen distances, struck by variability, occupying "variable places." This "mobility" enables the book to become "spacious," and this spacious spatiality, made up of "correspondences" (this is the form), is the way through which "fiction" is "confirmed," asserts itself, and through which the other of discourse takes shape in it.

What then is this space of *Un coup de dés*? Logical, because words are inscribed in the space; sensory, because what lies between the terms is as important as the terms themselves (this is, according to André Lhote, the figure's essential character); and imaginary, because the figure of these intervals is determined only by the fiction upheld by discourse. "Poetry—unique source."[34] When speech becomes object, it is not to reproduce something visible, but to make visible an invisible, lost "thing," taking on the form of the imaginary of which it speaks. The correspondences mentioned in the letter to Gide rely exclusively on the words' designation: thus the Page (double-page spread) "that the abyss . . ." will obey a slipping motion, of burying into the depths. This Mallarmean "naïveté"—of taking the word at face value by endowing it with the form of the object it designates, or at least, rather than its closed outline, its movement, its plastic presence, what we called earlier its schema—is very edifying. It reveals that the referential distance itself, after a right-angle rotation, places its figure in the line of discourse, distending and dispersing it into a thing "simultaneous" to itself. Designation migrating into signification; discourse, without losing its power of relay, taking on another power, namely, that of the things of desire, and, like these, soliciting the eye. This is how contact is made, the thing of which we speak introduced in what we are saying—introduced not intelligently but sensorially—thanks to the sensory's inexhaustible resource, this chance that escapes every effort to abolish it, which is its ability to accommodate both text and non-text; sensory reality transforming itself into both stage and seating area, reproducing itself as constituted, mirror-like, by the play of text and figure on it: anamorphosis.

There is no accrual in this *recessus,* no development. Davies bases his reading of *Un coup de dés* and *Igitur* on a Hegelian influence on Mallarmé's thought, but nothing is less Hegelian than this thought: *Un coup de dés* can only belong to the chance-abyss. Holding on to the question of meaning until the very last in the element of contingency is contrary to the assertion that the entire real is rational; to consider thought as a chance combination among other potentials is, according to the Preface of the *Phenomenology of Spirit,* to dwell in exteriority and in the formalism specific to mathematics, notably to combinatorics; finally, to plunge all actual combination as thought or work into the absolute neutrality of the sensory, to the point of locating its equivalent in a constellation, amounts to nothing less than blurring of the inequality between the for-itself of natural immediacy and the in-itself for-us of mediated knowledge. With Mallarmé, the crisis of knowledge deepens, for not only does it articulate itself in a discourse of signification that, in a sense, entrenches knowledge in its element and in its presumption, but reflection grasps precisely this discourse of signification as a delusion, as a trick that knowledge plays on non-knowledge, and it outwits this trick by playing the game of *recessus,* by positioning sensory and libidinal space in its very discourse, in other words, the trick of the trope. Thus the fact that the true notion is given by sensuality, and that transcendence is immanent, is *expressed.* This hyper-reflection finds its match not in Hegel, who belongs to Western tradition, but in Cézanne and in the entire plastic upheaval for which he was both the seismograph and the detonator, in Nietzsche, and, soon thereafter, in Freud.

Surreality is this book itself, *Un coup de dés jamais n'abolira le hasard*, insofar as it occupies the "vacant superior" space (of which it speaks). Without attempting to explore here the configuration of this surreality offered by representation, one can nonetheless already underscore its mirror effect. The object-book contains two objects: an "ideal" object, of signification (comprised of concatenated signifieds according to the rules of syntax) that states "there is no notion (no signified) outside of the sensory." One *comprehends* such an object. Then there is a meaningful object [*un objet de signifiance*], made of graphic *and plastic* signifiers (blanks, typographic variations, use of the double page spread, arrangement of signs across this surface), actually of writing disturbed by considerations of the sensory (of "sensuality"). The first object allows the second to become intelligible; the second allows the first to become visible. They mirror each other: signification is presented visually as meaning, and meaning is presented intelligibly as signification. This is a first mirror, coexistensive with the entire book; but this book itself, insofar as it is of signification and of meaning, is reflected in the form of a chiasm:[35] the expression "A throw of dice" [*Un coup de dés*], upon which the book opens, is answered by the line of the last page "every thought emits a throw of dice" [*toute pensée émet un coup de dés*]. Chiasm in the linguistic signifier, as well as in the signified: thought fails to abolish the unthought, but the unthought contains thought. A chiasm is a rhetorical *figure* of the *ab-ba* variety, analogous in its form to a figure of prosody—such as the alternate rhyme—and therefore introducing in the course of the text a depth that is not of pure signification, but that conceals and signals a kind of excess of meaning. The figure of the chiasm gives to this meaning—situated on this side of explicit signification, and which exceeds it—the form of the mirror, and therefore inspires a feeling of reflection, the same set of elements repeated, but reversed. This is the second mirror, this time inscribed in the book's diachrony.

From these basic remarks one can already identify three types of figures at work in *Un coup de dés*: the image, or the figure that takes place in the order of language, specifically in the plane of the signified (comparison, metaphor); the form, a kind of figure also located in language but which affects the linguistic signifier and which is not signified in discourse; and the sensory figure, a configuration that allocates the linguistic (that is, in the present case, graphic) signifiers according to requirements that are not strictly speaking those of discourse but of a rhythm (here a visible one). Thus these tiered figures, from pure signified to plastic signifier, via linguistic signifier, constitute a chain or switch between the intelligible discursive order and the sensory spatiotemporal order, confirming the presence of forms likely to cross the divisions separating the intelligible world and the sensory world—forms independent of the context they inform (just as Freud will argue that the phantasy is a sufficient configuration capable of crossing as-is the border between unconscious and preconscious). Thus this tiered succession of forms gives discourse access to what is alien to it, establishing the mirror function it has in *Un coup de dés*: the fact that the other of signification—the figural—can come to dwell in discourse endows the latter with a thickness that will make reflection possible.

But one notes that this reflection is a hyper-reflection insofar as it does not consist in reflecting the designated in signified, but that on the contrary some element of the space of reference, as it comes to lodge itself in discourse, produces anomalies there, thereby making itself visible. One can get to the bottom of this operation only after having studied the work of dreams, for it is important to separate the regression or direct expression mobilized in the latter work and the *recessus* or doubly inverted expression that alone produces the art work. At the end of *Divagations,* Mallarmé defines the form he seeks as "critical poem."[36]

Linguistic Sign?

One could start (again) by stating that language is not made of signs. It would be the same discussion as the one on the symbol in Hegel, but taken from a different vantage point. Turning around the object that interests us is far from useless; it is a task we cannot shirk as long as we remain in the order of signification. We only always perceive one side of this object at a time; it never changes, but if we have gone around properly, what we observe from the newly revealed side introduces us to a new discourse. Different repetition.

The object in question is in fact the space in which discourse operates, and the proposed thesis is that this space is not homogenous, but doubled: on the one hand, the space of discontinuity where signification takes shape (on the model of the signifier); on the other, the space of designation that surrounds discourse and opens it to its reference. Ferdinand de Saussure's importance in this regard is obvious. By subsuming his reflection on language, from the very first, under the heading of a general semiology,[1] he made it necessary (for himself) to think the linguistic element under the category of the sign. Thus he formulates the concept of the arbitrariness or unmotivation of the linguistic "sign": the latter is opposed to another sign as what is "instituted" to what is "natural," or as what is "unmotivated" to what is "motivated."[2] Let us therefore approach our object along the path cleared by Saussure: is it true that the word differs from the sign on account of its arbitrariness, or is this arbitrariness not the symptom of a far more radical condition, namely that the word does not belong to the semiological sphere, but is tangential to it?

Whatever the object of which one speaks, and no matter how the utterance relates to it, every speech act speaks of something. It is an essential characteristic of articulated language that it should always have a referential function, and this is the characteristic one should recognize in the

Saussurean notion of arbitrariness. No denial, writes Émile Benveniste, can "abolish the fundamental property of language, which is to imply that something corresponds to what is uttered, some thing and not 'nothing.'"[3] Every language presupposes a respondent outside of itself, and, as Gottlob Frege has argued,[4] an impulse toward the designated never ceases to exceed the grasp of the signified, forcing us to rush from one place of discourse to another, around what we speak of. Benveniste's remark should not fool us: this "something" that must correspond to each and every utterance is precisely ungraspable and unseizable; it is, admittedly, established by the speech act, but established over there, in a space created by an originary spacing. Speech faces its object, opens onto it, at the very least through a kind of sight, and in the absence of a point of contact or direct grip—which it lost in being constructed and which haunts it—it unceasingly puts itself to the test, measures itself, tries to align itself with objectness. There exists in language—however inhabited by what Merleau-Ponty called its "presumption of totality"—a contrary and no less radical position of insufficiency owing to the primary excision by which the silhouette of the thing, in negative, sets itself apart on the edge of the words that refer to it. In this respect every speech act is a means of adducing something that is not of language [*langue*], that cannot find its place within the utterance, but which stands, as its impregnable theme, in the opening of discourse.

Following this lead, it seems impossible to imagine the order of discourse as a closed system. Language [*langue*] is indeed such a system, but the use to which the subject puts the "signs" provided by language is referential, where the calling-up and organization of these "signs" are motivated from without through a kind of preview of the object. The order of discourse does not have all of its reason behind it, in the structure, but also in part in the speaker's intentionality, which is none other than the subjective aspect of designation. Now, as Charles Sanders Peirce noted, "replacing something for someone" applies not only to the linguistic sign, but to all signs: the opening of the sign onto the other, its nature as substitute, are what define it; and words, if they are to be counted as signs, are no exception to this rule of indicative immanence. Edmond Ortigues (on this point very close to the tradition of the *Logic* of Port-Royal) stresses this immanent character of the referential function (of transcendence) that defines the sign.[5] The latter is, he writes, "a sensory event referring to something belonging to *an order other* than itself."[6] The sign "shows something or brings something to light," understood that the absent other thing, thus presented, cannot be presented in person.[7] The sign is therefore inseparable from a rift through which being and appearing, or meaning and the sensory, are cleaved; in this way it cannot be reduced to a certain relation between two terms, but is "the generating principle of all relations, of all possible forms."[8]

From this, one can see that the above concept emerges in a metaphysics of presence, thanks to which, precisely, this other signifier—the concealed term—appears in person, the thing itself given; one can see, too, that the West's madness is to believe the trace effaceable as such, and that what traces showable.[9] Regardless of the implications to be derived from this critique, one must acknowledge that the archi-writing called upon to account for the primitive fact of meaning's withdrawal is in no way strictly speaking a form of writing—inscription of arbitrary signs on a neutralized space—but, on the contrary, the constitution of a thick space where the game of concealing/revealing can be played out. Difference is not opposition. The former constitutes the opacity that opens the order of reference; the latter upholds the system of invariances in the plane of the signifier or the signified. About the former—the crux of the matter at hand—the question is whether the linguistic "sign" (either written or spoken, the distinction is irrelevant here) is inhabited by it in the same way that it opens or distends every other sign. Does the depth of referral—to which Merleau-Ponty ascribed, as ultimate model, the figure-ground relation in form, as a means of locating the entire mystery of transcendence in the sensory—operate in the same place depending on whether we are dealing with a word or, for example, a color or a line? By depth of a color or a line I understand, as all painters do, the directed force emanating from a blue or a red, a curved or vertical line, which arouses in one's body an expectation, the rudiments of polarized motion. In this case I think one can speak of an immanence of meaning in the sign, of immediate thickness. Not arbitrariness, but immediacy: an untaught montage of the body with the sensory, so that the blue or the vertical line tugs at it in a given spatial direction. Yet this is still a case of transcendence, for one cannot argue that this meaning is *given* in the line or the color. On the contrary, it is hidden there, and from there must appear.

One might object that to present the problem with reference to the signification of the sensory is to resolve it, for no one will deny that words are not sensorial elements. However, Saussure's positioning of the problem of the linguistic sign is not as far as one could imagine from the reference to the sensory; it is, in fact, determined by a very similar reference, to the symbol. Saussure specified that by the linguistic sign's arbitrariness he did not want to suggest that the speaker has the power to shape sounds or words at will, but that it is impossible to derive the sign from the thing it designates. To support his claim he points to the fact that the same thing bears different names in different languages. Rather than arbitrary, he prefers to name this relation unmotivated.[10] Now the model guiding Saussure's reflection here is that of a relation that he himself calls symbolic,[11] such that there would be continuity from the signifier to the signified, that the "content" would be indicated on the signifier—through the sign's substance or through its form, or both—which brings us very close to the sensory signifier. Hence a signpost indicating a ridge on the road is a motivated sign: the thing is recognizable by the outline featured on the signpost. Motivation in this case consists of the schematic rendering, figured on a plane, of a corporeal rhythm connected, in actual experience, to the passage of a vehicle over a ridge. If the signpost features two bumps where most ridges have one, (one might imagine) this is because the mediation between signifier and signified is sought on the side of the body, because corporeal signification is always akin to a rhythm, and because the latter requires an interval between two pulses—those very bumps figured on the signpost. Here is one such "motivation" in Saussure's sense that, without being, properly speaking, expressive, depends nevertheless, somewhat as in painting, on this matrix of rhythm and of correspondences between rhythms (in this case kinesthetic and visual) that is the body.

Is it not possible to find something similar in the linguistic sign? This is where one comes across Benveniste's remarks as an essential prolegomenon to any discussion on the subject.[12] It is indeed impossible to think positively about the linguistic sign's arbitrariness if one has not accepted beforehand the distinction Benveniste proposes between two relations that take part, in equal measure, in the constitution of language: that of signifier to signified, and of the sign to its object—the former immanent in, the latter transcendent to the object. If the linguist declares the latter arbitrary, it is merely, Benveniste assures us, because he must refrain from broaching "the metaphysical problem of the agreement between the mind and the world."[13] But the relation internal to the sign, that which binds signifier and signified together, is hardly arbitrary: "There is such a close symbiosis between them that the concept 'beef' is like the soul of the sound pattern /'bif/. The mind does not contain empty forms, concepts without names";[14] there is "consubstantiality of the signifier and the signified."

By positing this distinction, Benveniste is obviously following the speaker's ordinary experience. It is in the speech act that the distance from words to the things they speak of is unbridgeable. No doubt this distance can be, in principle, if not bridged then at least turned around through the use of what "thingness" there is in the word, through the mediation of its flesh, and of the echo its flesh can produce in response to the resonance the thing emits in the cave of the sensory.[15] But this poetic experience, of the connatural relation between discourse and its object, far from belying the shared experience of their difference, finds in this experience its counterpoint and its mirror: it is unusual that the sensory would come to inhabit the signifier, and that discourse would transform itself into symbol—at the same time *sinnliche* [sensuous] and *sinnvolle* [meaningful], as Eugen Lerch put it in an article in which he tried, quite desperately, to salvage the symbolic value of sound against the thesis of arbitrariness (including Benveniste's corrected version).[16] This unusual character is the product of expression, but expression is not the only, indeed not the main function of language. The other function—communication—requires the almost total exhaustion of the *Wortkörper* [word's materiality], the translucency of words, and the sort of freedom enjoyed by the signified from the signifier that communication makes possible for the speaking subject. This other aspect of our common linguistic experience highlights what Merleau-Ponty called its "virtue": "to efface itself," "in the way it works, [to hide] itself from us," "to efface itself and to take us beyond the words to the author's very thoughts."[17]

One cannot argue, therefore, that motivation is excluded in principle from the order of linguistic signs, for this would be to banish the poetic and preclude describing and comprehending an experience of speech that, however exceptional (at least in our societies), is no less essential than the other. But one must specify that motivation affects the relation of the whole sign to what it designates, and not the signified-signifier relation, which is a "relation" only under the linguist's knife, and one that we do not experience. Having said this, however, this motivation, when it exists, is of the same order as the motivated signpost: the thing is not "inserted in" language [*langage*]—which is only a manner of speaking—rather the disposition of language [*langage*] induces upon words and between them rhythms that resonate with those provoked on our body by the thing discourse speaks of. This invasion of rhythmics in the invariant space of language [*langue*], of unhampered mobility in measured discontinuity, is so fundamental that the one cannot go without the other, and that, in the linguist's commutation, in the analysand's free association, as well as in the work of the dreamer or the painter, the order of language [*langage*] must be violated by this rhythmic power for it to be perceived.

But let us put aside for a moment the question of expression. What we shall say is that two directions of meaning intersect on the linguistic sign, involving three poles in all.[18] On the one hand, the sign is constituted by two facets, inseparable in practical use—the signifier and the signified—and whose adjoining determines signification proper. This is Saussure's specific term for the effect of meaning produced when the concept or signified merges with what he calls the sound pattern or signifier.[19] On the other hand, the linguistic sign, taken as a whole (as it is in fact), relates to what it designates, to a real or unreal object about which the speaker is speaking. It is the latter relation that Benveniste distinguishes from the former in order to show that it alone deserves to be qualified as arbitrary or unmotivated, while signification is so little unmotivated that we are unable to think the concept without its "formulation," and the word without "what it means." This relation of the sign to the object can be called designation.

If we want to insist on speaking of linguistic *sign,* then, it becomes necessary to state that in one or the other of these dimensions, or in both, one encounters the thickness, difference, or force of reference to something else, that constitutes the sign. Let us first turn to signification to see if the expressions "replacement" and "representation" apply to the signifier's relation to the signified as Saussure theorized it. Can we assert, for example, that the syntagm /hôrs/ *replaces,* for the speaker and the listener, the notion "horse"? If we absolutely must—indeed at the cost of making an egregious mistake—we could go so far as to concede that the sign in its totality, the *word* horse, is the "representative" of the real horse, and that its "value" in the system of signs is the same as the animal's in the system of perception. Needless to say, this thesis suffers from crude approximation, since it relies on the confusion pure and simple of designation—which is a matter of discourse alone—and representation (*Vorstellung* [idea] in Frege's terminology)—which defines the function of the symbol. We will come back to this. But this thesis becomes decidedly absurd if, when applied to signification, one contends that the signifier is the signified's sensory substitute, its expression.

When faced with the spoken chain, we hear meaning, and meaning is again what we pronounce as our mouth articulates sounds: such is our experience of words. This is because of the linguistic signifier's ability to become completely transparent in favor of the signified—except of course when the opposite intent, namely, to highlight the signifier, drives the organization of the message, as in the use to which art puts language.[20] But this use, which aims to subvert the signifier's strictly linguistic function of communication in order to intensify its expressive power, requires precisely that the words' symbolic potential be given or restituted to them, and that linguistic matter be, through particular arrangements, burdened with sensory value. This is why it is essential in poetry that the term's natural transparency be clouded for the utterance to take effect through its "see-through" linguistic semantics, while generating "affective"[21] resonances thanks to the ordering that the poet has imposed on verbal matter. Such artistic manipulation of the utterance constitutes precisely the exception: through the effects with which it is laden, the poem—in the fullest meaning of the word, as for example Michel Butor understands it[22]—eschews language's communicational vocation, dwelling in the border zone between the word and the thing, writing becoming like an object. But the condition of everyday language—whose tenets are communication and economy of means—is the erasure of phonic matter in favor of signification, that is, the signifier's transparency. In the messages we exchange, even those that depart from simple routine, sounds are not produced as "replacements" of ideas, they "take the place" of nothing: they are what they signify. Benveniste says exactly this when he underscores, in relation to the Saussurean thesis of arbitrariness, the powerful motivation that "from within" the sign, so to speak, welds signified and signifier.[23]

The limpidity that allows the signifier, in the experience of articulated language, to disappear almost completely behind meaning is not easy to grasp: I invoke a meaning, words form in my mouth, and the interlocutor hears a meaning. There is no way to separate significations from signifiers. This is not to say that to each "moneme" a corresponding "notion" attaches itself, as Saussure sometimes suggests. Rather, the meaning of the utterance emerges from the order that the signifiers receive or take on in the utterance; in return, the signification of each of them is circumscribed according to the surrounding words: a kind of lability specific to the signifier allows it to slip under meanings that are doubtless related but diverse enough to render fruitless any attempt at attaching one and only one "concept" (to borrow Saussure's terms) to it. This is not the sort of univocation—object, or dream, of an exact *mathesis*—I have in mind when stressing the solidarity between signifier and signified. The idea of the signified hardly requires that to every signifier correspond one and only one signified; in practice all that it requires (and we will say no more on the subject) is that a syntagm should be "well formed," articulated in accordance with the rules that govern the phonetic level and with those of the level of significative units, for it instantly to "mean something" clearly. It is this immediate clarity of discourse that is obscurity itself.

This clarity hardly prevents other meanings from also stepping forward. The thickness of discourse or the polysemic nature of the message is instead the norm; but it remains, in a way, secondary to the signifier's translucency, that is to say, to the immediacy of signification. When a word in a statement is difficult or generates uncertainty, the resulting delay in comprehension is not due to a structural opacity in the relation between signifier and signified. If I speak of "palindrome" and my interlocutor is not familiar with the word, any obscurity will derive from this lack of familiarity (that is, because the term is absent from her or his code, or is present but with a very low probability of occurrence), and not from the fact that there is in language [*langue*] a signifier available without its signified, or *before* it, so to speak, as is the case with the color blue announcing (revealing and concealing) the adduction in the order of the dynamics of the body itself. Now if I say about such and such a ruined royal family "here is a crumbling house," the play on words is based on the polysemy of the word *house* in English, and therefore on an excess of signified in relation to signifier; but this polysemy is regulated in the lexical order of language [*langue*], and the speaker is not entitled to overstep it, short of not being understood. Again in this case the relation of signifier to signified is not opaque in and of itself as merely multiple: it is the term's position in the sentence, or the sentence's in discourse, that will dispel the plurality of significations and determine which one to retain. In structuralist or functionalist terms, this comes down to saying that the choice or selection of the signifying unit at a point in the spoken chain is not, as it stands, entirely completed—except in an exact, scientific discourse, from which all polysemy is theoretically evacuated—but that this choice must continue to operate on the given utterance in order to identify the relevant signifieds. Nevertheless these "choices" do not have any connection to the search, the investigation set in motion by a true sign whose "signification," indicated only by the signifier and without appearing anywhere in any preestablished system, must be built. It is not up to us to build the significations of our language [*langue*] from the signifiers we hear: the signifier-signified relation is in itself infallible, and arbitrariness plays no part in it. Nothing could be less fortuitous for the English speaker than the concept "horse" as the signified of the phonic syntagm /hôrs/. This unmotivation has no equivalent in the experience the speaker has of her/his mother tongue [*langue maternelle*].

Saussure could build the concept of unmotivation only by crossing out this experience, with a stroke that amounts to the epistemological cut, and by positing a speaker *deprived of mother tongue.* For in Saussure's eyes, arbitrariness needs no other justification than the fact (which no speaking subject experiences as fact) that "horse" is signified here by /hôrs/, there by /pfɛrd/ [*Pferd*], etc.: an epistemological abstraction that will in fact soon be amended when it will become obvious that the articulation of the signified is not the same here and there, that the one-to-one translation is unreliable, and that it is necessary to go through the general articulation of experience—in other words, the general organization of semantic fields—that is the supposed structure of a language's [*langue*] signifieds. The result is an excess of abstraction that allows one to go from the term to the system, but a better abstraction too, since it keeps perfectly intact the inseparability of the signifier and the signified within a language [*langue*], and hence within the experience of the speaker using it. In sum, the signifier *stands in* for nothing; its "content" isn't one, insofar as a "content" is something that the sign holds back, the inside of what it encases. The linguistic signifier does not conceal anything *within* it (*Inhalt*) because it has no interiority, no volume, and does not occupy a thick space.

As for the relation of designation (that which, from the "sign," refers to the object it speaks of), we may indeed qualify it as arbitrary, since one is hard pressed to locate any rhythm, any corporeal schema, or any sensory assemblage ensuring the mediation between words and things, and transforming the former into a stand-in of sorts that would prefigure the latter. One can only endorse the linguist's caution in determining the origin of language [*langage*], especially with regard to the hypothesis that sees primitive language [*langue*] as a vehicle for expression, and that thus tends to divert signs from an emotive situation and to understand them as originally motivated.[24] But if words once possessed such an expressive value, weighing almost as much as the things they designated, nothing remains of it in today's experience of language [*langage*].[25] One would be more inclined to back André Leroi-Gourhan's well-argued hypothesis, according to which the oldest language performed a sacred function, and the first significative spoken units were uttered by a narrator who simultaneously gestured toward the corresponding painted figures during ceremonial processions followed by the tribe in temple-caverns.[26] The hypothesis is very appealing since the function of designation immediately comes across in all its power and specificity. The latter hinges on two decisive points: speech is not uttered in the absence of the designated thing, but *in its presence*; and the designated thing is not a thing but a symbol, which legitimately can be said from the outset to be opaque. This dual property of the situation in which the referential function is deployed allows this function to be located with precision and distinguished from the symbolic function. Far from placing itself before the thing and blocking it, the word dissolves in order to bring the thing into relief. Neither a substitute hiding the thing, nor itself a symbol re-presenting the thing through its own substance or form, the word is merely, in the speaker's experience, a perforation [*percée*] through which the thing comes into view, a line of sight that makes it visible. There is thus indeed a distance from the word to this thing, from the utterance to its object in general—but this distance, far from being a thickness to be crossed, is the one in which the gesture points to its object; it is the depth of atmospheric space that assumes light to be the medium where seeing takes effect.

Opacity is in the object, not in the word, nor in its distance to the object. Words are not signs, but the moment a word appears, the designated object becomes sign. For an object to become sign means precisely that it conceals a "content" hidden within its manifest identity, that it withholds another side of itself for a different glance upon it, a glance that might never be taken. For it to become sign requires that it be afflicted by a dimension of absence. When the finger points to the tree to designate it, it sways the tree, making it tip forward over an abyss of meaning. Or, put differently, designation implies this profound eschewal, this drainage of the back of things. Before, there is no tree; every object as such presupposes speech, the power of nullification that the latter wields over what it designates. The object derives its *thickness* from this speech. The word that designates it and that makes it *visible* is at the same time what strips it of its immediate meaning and deepens its mystery. This is why it is remarkable that the word designates a symbol, as Leroi-Gourhan believes: it has to show a presence and an absence, to make visible—but a front, a façade; it has to intimate that something remains to be made visible, an unseen, which is an invisible insofar as the operation never ceases to renew itself, and that this other side, supposedly connected to the one we see through a continuous *motivated* relation, when we see it, it is up to us to signify it, that is, to place it in the arbitrary and discontinuous order of signification, and to have it shed its immediate relation with the former side.[27] The thickness of the world and its very possibility as always incomplete synthesis, as horizon hollowed out behind its sensory presence, are in this way a function of language [*langage*]. As we will see, Freud arrives at a similar observation.

But this observation should not lead us to the absurd conclusion that there is nothing but text, for if the world is a function of language, language possesses a world-function, as it were: out of what it designates, every utterance makes a world, a thick object waiting to be synthesized, a symbol to be deciphered, but these objects and symbols offer themselves in an expanse where showing is possible. This expanse bordering discourse is not itself the linguistic space where the work of signification is carried out, but a worldly type of space, plastic and atmospheric, in which one has to move, circle around things, make their silhouettes vary, in order to utter such and such signification heretofore concealed.

Words or linguistic units are not signs through signification, nor are they signs through designation, rather they produce signs with the objects they designate (make visible) and signify (make intelligible), and from which they are separated; presence and absence together become world on their margins. Motivation is the other of discourse, its other assumed to exist outside of itself, in things-signs.

From where does this difference come that distinguishes linguistic terms from signs? How do the former set themselves apart from motivation? Through arbitrariness, clearly—but this arbitrariness must be supported by an intrinsic property that would allow the linguistic term to escape the attraction of motivation. Such a property does exist: it is that of double articulation, characteristic of articulated language; its function is easy to grasp from a discussion of the sign's *temporality*.

The sign is thick. The visible surface of a layer of cobalt blue is a chromatic value; its hidden "face" is the corporeal repercussion (in terms of tonicity) of this value.[28] The *meaning* of blue lies in its power to condition the body as if it had to seek out the area of blue slightly beyond the latter's space. This corporeal adduction has, as its correlate, the value of the blue's withdrawal;[29] this value is the hidden side, complementary to the one that presents the color to us. The grasp of meaning in this sense is slow, because the body must allow itself to be inhabited by the chromatic power or settle in this withdrawing area, for the blue's meaning to actualize itself.[30] In the absence of such a settlement, the color will be *recognized* at best, able to function as the element of a communicational code, that is, as a graphic signal. The space in which it is situated in this case is entirely different from the expanse the eye carves out and opens in the picture when the body is allowed to cohabit with the color. Temporality is related to the sign while achrony belongs to the purely recognizable linguistic term.

This achrony, which guarantees linguistic signifiers their omnitemporality, proceeds from the double articulation.[31] The first articulation to which speakers have immediate access is the one that assembles significative units, but this articulation in turn rests on a layer of secondary articulation where smaller, exclusively distinctive units are combined. This organization isolates the signifying linguistic term from its referent, guarantees its autonomy in relation to all forms of motivation, and places it in a position independent of the speaker's or the situation's temporality. If the smallest unit of language were motivated, signifying could not be distinguished from expressing, and the configuration of the signifier could not be separated from the situation in which the sign is produced: a scream, for example, or a groan, which are concrete expressions. This would match the case imagined by André Martinet, where motivation puts such pressure on the signifier that the former alters it at each occurrence.[32] It would then be impossible to attach constant signification to an expression itself deprived of stability. The double articulation allows expressions that should otherwise never be compared to achieve recognition since, however different one from the other, they appear successively in the experience of speech. The double articulation freezes the configuration of the signifier in such a way that it becomes recognizable at two different moments, despite the duration that has already swept up the first expression in its flow while the second comes into being.

In principle, it is impossible to establish the identity or the gap between two sounds produced at intervals, particularly when these are significant, if one does not have at hand a referential system allowing the sounds to coincide, thus freeing them from the position they occupy at the time of their utterance, in order to bring them back to an order of simultaneity in which they can become comparable. Here one comes up against a classic problem, that of measurement in the temporal order, except that communication requires from the linguistic sign that it be recognizable in every respect, and not only by its length. The opposition between short and long might well constitute what Paul Claudel calls the "fundamental iamb" which, in its simplicity, can pass as the paradigm for all significative opposition. Nevertheless, language [*langue*] draws upon many more distinctive features than duration, if only because the organs of phonation form a group with a much richer array of distinctive features than a mere whistle.

Writing seems to offer the possibility of constituting such a referential system, by resorting to the sign's inscription in an exterior space that is the order of simultaneities; it appears to owe nothing to spoken language, as far as solving the problem of the signifier's positioning is concerned. Indeed, it is the material support upon which writing inscribes its figures that ensures the function of omnitemporality indispensable to the recognition of signs and their communication. This solution appears to be denied speech, which, if we are to believe Saussure, has to do with a one-dimensional continuum, namely time.[33] Here the concrete nature of the signifying unit, the fact that it is impossible to decompose it in independent and stable units, would have as its inevitable corollary, as we said, its unicity, since it would be impossible to establish any relation, whether of identity or difference, between this and another unit produced at another moment. How to prevent the signifier from being valid only in the context in which it has been uttered, and its expressive potential from increasing at the expense of its communicability?

It should be noted that speech itself presupposes a form of spatializing and that the vocal signifier is no less composed of unmotivated elements than writing. No doubt a fine ear and a well-trained memory are prerequisites if one wishes to recognize, from one utterance to the next, a sound with its distinctive amplitude, frequency, and intensity—in other words, its physical identity—all the more if the interval between the different auditions is considerable. Moreover, an accurate voice and extensive practice are necessary to produce it. On the other hand, to emit and hear a sound that can be deemed identical to itself through repeated utterances is easy if there is always the possibility of situating it distinctly in a system of sounds. Such is the difference Troubetzkoy established between phonetics and phonology.[34] The principle behind the latter is that one need only distinguish a sound from the nearest surrounding sounds to convey signification in the most efficient way possible. In this respect, the voice's timbre or intensity counts for little, for what in fact is heard in speech is not the acoustic vibration itself, but the gap separating it from others nearby—gap thanks to which the signifier may be identified and signification understood. When speaking, the speaker need not concern her- or himself with executing faithfully the indications provided by a kind of (entirely imaginary) score. Suffice it for her or him to produce an /s/ that cannot be confused with /ʃ/, an /əʊ/ that cannot be mistaken for /uː/, etc., if the language in which she or he expresses her- or himself relies on these oppositions to distinguish meanings (/səʊ/ "so," and /ʃəʊ/ "show" in English). The phoneme is thus defined not by its audible identity, but by its placement in a constellation of units; it stands out in relation to each of these through the position it occupies on different "axes" corresponding to the various "distinctive features": vocal/nonvocal, consonant/inconsonant, compact/diffuse, etc.[35] The distinctive feature is the smallest unit making the distinction between two phonemes possible.[36] From one language to another, two apparently identical phonemes—say, /ʃ/ in "shoe" and /ʃ/ in *Kirsche*—must in reality be distinguished if one of the two enters in an opposition that the other does not recognize: as is here the case of the German /ʃ/, which is opposed to the /ç/ of *Kirche,* a phoneme absent in English. What allows the appreciation of the linguistic sign to be immediate and foolproof, and thus what facilitates fluid communication, is that sound recognition can always be reduced to the simplest possible operation, determined by yes or no. I have no knowledge whatsoever of the physical properties of the /h/ uttered here and now by my interlocutor, while he holds forth about a hat; at the very least, for the utterance to be recognized and the message to be unambiguous, he and I need only to be able to distinguish it from a /k/ and an /m/.

This articulation of the spoken chain into purely distinctive units is what sets language apart from all other semiological systems. The double articulation's essential function is not merely to compensate for the fleetingness of the uttered sign, by making its identification possible; it would be if spoken language represented the totality of communicative language. The latter, however, can also be written. Now what distinguishes writing is not at all that it is a trace in visible space (for drawing, too, is such a trace) but that this trace, like spoken language, makes use of strictly distinctive conventional units (letters) to form significative units (words), and that the letters are easily recognized only because they belong to an invariable system of strokes (graphemes). The space of signification is not visible space, but the space of the system. This is why, in the order of oral communication too, the anchoring of significations can be carried out only by the same kind of spatialization imposed on the signifiers. The distinctive feature is "dimension," the y-coordinate registering the gap between two neighboring phonemes. We imagine this gap as a distance on an "axis,"[37] a legitimate move if we consider that the distance between /h/ and /k/ is that which, on the frequency reading, separates the low from the high pitch, and which, as such, actually marks a discontinuity of position observable across the expanse. Further, the space described by the spectroscope is itself a derivation, for there is a basic spatialization acting as its support: the production of words implies that the volume and form of the body's interior expanse—of this kind of intimate exteriority where the fate of words is played out—be affected in a finely tuned manner. This is where the principle determining the realization of distinctive phonemes resides: in the differences in position of the organs used for phonation. The abstract configuration of the table of distinctive features has as its empirical equivalent the configuration of the phonatory cavity.[38] Speech, like writing, frees itself from its site of inscription, by registering and observing gaps that are entirely unmotivated as far as the expressive power of this locus is concerned; the visible aesthetic space is reduced to the level of mere support for signs that are intrinsically alien to it; and as for the space constituted by the phonatory cavity, the gaps will be registered and observed with such precision that the slightest variation provoked in this hollow by the interplay of the different resonators will suffice to produce easily identifiable signifiers and to communicate signification.

Here the difference we sought to establish between the linguistic term and the sign comes across vividly. The formation of phonatory habits enabling the production of words entails the elimination of numerous phonic possibilities. The fine-tuning of the organs of the phonatory cavity is obtained through the repression of the force that uses these organs to produce harshly motivated expressions: the scream, the groan, "chirping." This fine-tuning is mainly the work of the ear;[39] it signifies the interiorization of the virtual space of language [*langue*] into the real space of the body proper, as well as the latter's expropriation. Following Antonin Artaud, we can assume that a highly developed use of articulated language [*langage*] comes at the cost of a dispossession of expressive phonic space. The thickness of the groan, the pant, the laugh, and the scream makes these sounds into signs: motivated by situations, they can be extracted from the speaking body only when words fail it, when its distance to itself, conquered and embodied by the phonic space measured against the linguistic code, no longer holds and anti-language takes over and subverts the apparatus of communication. It is with respect to this subversion, to the deconstruction it performs in the production of distinctive units, that we perceive the existence of another side of the sign, a hidden—that is to say "expressed"—side. There are sounds in the aphasic's scream that are irrelevant to her or his mother tongue; in the pant there is an irresolvable equivocation that only the context can lay to rest, by determining if it refers to pain or pleasure; breath can be one's last or the one one catches; the nervous breakdown and hysterical laughter are, for a moment, indistinguishable. In all these sounds, the voice clouds over, turns its back to the order of arbitrariness, dips deep into other layers of its register for configurations that, even if not wholly natural, do not belong solely to communication; and what it brings back is not signification, but meaning. Freud stated that the dream treats words as things,[40] that is, it cuts the syntagmatic chain differently than language, combining the pieces of the chain with no regard for linguistic pertinence.[41] Likewise Artaud in the theatrical order: "It is not a question of doing away with articulated language, but rather of endowing words with more or less the same importance they have in dreams. . . . To produce the metaphysics of articulated language is to encourage language to express what it does not express usually: it is to use it in a new, exceptional, unusual way; it is to restore its capacities of physical shattering; it is to divide and scatter it in space; it is to adopt the intonations in a concrete, absolute manner, giving them back the power they had to tear and truly manifest something; it is to turn against language and its utilitarian, one could say monetary, preoccupations, against its origins as hunted beast; it is, lastly, to consider language in the form of the *Incantation*."[42] Similar concerns are to be found in Luciano Berio's studies, whose aim is to identify the trajectory from vital noise to communicable term: you hear signification conquer or lose itself as the terrible expressive violence of the scream and of silence is relegated or discovered; you apprehend by what repression the constituents of discourse take shape, and how the term is the annihilated sign.[43]

Effect of Thickness in the System

Once evacuated from the spoken and written chain through the elimination of the expressive function of sounds and lines, does opacity not retreat to a higher level, in signification? Is there not a thickness of the signified, in the very existence of words; for example, in the possibility of breaking them down into monemes?[1] And is this not what the theorist stumbles upon when discovering that the lexical system, as opposed to the syntactic system, has the property of being an "open" inventory, of taking on new terms and abandoning old ones—all of which suggests the metaphor of a semantic *field*, and therefore of a *horizon* on which significations would come into relief and disappear in turn, like *things*?

If an inventory is not limited, which indeed seems to be the case with lexical monemes,[2] it would be difficult to deny signification an evanescent and intangible character that would prevent the term that carries it from occupying a fixed place in a system of oppositions. Signification would thus find itself pushed out beyond the system of significative units, inasmuch as it could embody any one of these units, then abandon it, only to invest another, without ever seeming to be frozen in an invariant set of oppositions. It would therefore be tempting to sideline the strictly systematizing pronouncement of the Prague School—"Since in lexical consciousness words are opposed to one another and mutually coordinated, they constitute systems that are formally analogous to morphological systems and likely, as such, to be available to the linguist's inquiry"[3]—in favor of the definition of the linguistic field given by Jost Trier in 1934: "Fields are linguistic realities existing between single words and the total vocabulary; they are parts of a whole and resemble words in that they combine into some higher unit, and the vocabulary in that they resolve themselves into smaller units."[4]

Without going any further, these two formulations allow one to grasp what lies beneath the question of signification. Josef Vachek establishes the formal analogy between the system of significative units and that of distinctive units, but he does so with reference to the speaker's experience of vocabulary. No hiatus here between the speaking subject's lexical consciousness and the most unconscious system of all, the phonological system: the phoneme's transparency is positioned on a par with the thickness of the word. Hence the absence of anything like the idea of a *field.* This idea refers to a finitude in which the word's openness onto its surroundings and the system's closure are combined.[5] Notwithstanding, it is the one who introduces this concept in linguistic reflection, Trier, who carries the formalist ambition the furthest in the study of semantic fields.[6] What remains in question, for us at least, in these curious torsions is the localization of the level of language [*langage*] where the effect of thickness of signification is produced. This localization can occur in two orders, of language [*langue*] or of speech [*parole*] (to follow Saussure's terminology); and in each of these two orders, it can occur at various levels: in the order of speech, at the level of significative unit—word, sentence, and discourse; and in the order of language [*langue*], at the level of paradigmatic groupings—"fields," subsystems, and lexical system.

Here we will only pinpoint an anxiety and an uncertainty in Saussure's reflection that foreshadow his followers' hesitations. His conception of structure leads him to subsume all of signification under articulation, that is, under the system of intervals between terms or system of *values.* Yet, at the same time, he does not give up on an idea of signification that opposes the latter to value as the vertical is opposed to the horizontal or depth is to surface. What could pass as a weakness for a linguist bent on limiting his study to the structure of language [*langue*], that is, the temptation to introduce the thickness of the sign in the transparency of the system, is in fact much more than a mistake or a sign of naïveté. Rather, a fact, which one could call transcendental, thus comes to light: that every discourse constitutes its object in depth. When this discourse is the linguist's, and she or he takes signification as the object of study, she or he spontaneously thematizes it as something thick, and is led to posit signification as a sign. In fact, this depth is an effect of the object's position produced by actual discourse, the latter keeping signification at bay, establishing it as sign to the same extent as any object.

The editors of Saussure's *Cours* lay considerable stress on the duality of axes required to think signification through: "The paradoxical part of it is this. On the one hand, the concept appears to be just the counterpart of a sound pattern, as one constituent part of a linguistic sign. On the other hand, this linguistic sign itself, as the link uniting the two constituent elements, likewise has counterparts. These are the other signs in the language [*langue*]."[7] The handwritten notes are no less explicit: "We have just asserted that language [*langue*] represents a system where all the terms may be considered connected. The value of a word results only from the coexistence of the different terms; the value is the counterpart of the coexisting terms. How does this combine with what is the counterpart of the sound pattern?"[8] The counterpart of the sound pattern is what Saussure sometimes calls signification, while value is always the counterpart of the other coexisting terms. One could say that they stand at a 90-degree angle from one another. Indeed, rectangular vectors figure in the notes of students: "Value [in its general sense] is determined by a dissimilar thing that one can exchange: ↑; it is also determined by similar things that one can compare: ←→."[9] From this opposition between the two dimensions, Saussure draws a comparison borrowed from economics: "In a 20 franc coin, determination of value: 1. I can exchange it for so many pounds of bread; 2. I compare it with a one franc coin from the same system. . . . Likewise, we will not be able to determine a word's signification by only taking into account the exchangeable object. We must also relate it to the similar series of comparable words."[10] It is one thing for the signifier *mutton* to be exchangeable for the signifier *mouton* in order to determine its value's aspect of signification; but it is only when the signifier is compared, or not, to another signifier—*sheep*—that it will receive its exact, clear value.[11] In this last case, one recognizes the measured opposition, the product of the constant intervals in the plane of the linguistic grid,[12] while the exchange of "sound pattern" for the "concept" belongs to the model of oral communication that Saussure took as the starting point for his reflection, and which obviously illustrates not the system of language [*langue*] but the experience of the situation of speech. Now, it is from speech that the major theme derives, that of the linguistic sign's immanent duality in signified and signifier, a theme that evokes a kind of *thickness* of this sign, as can be seen with the comparison of the sheet of paper, which, like the sign, possesses a *back* and a *front.*[13]

But then how to understand that signification offers at once the transparency that we saw in it at the outset, and the opacity that the duality of the sign determines in it? Signification, we argued, is translucent, marked by the immediate presence of the signified and the transparency of the signifier; we opposed it to the thickness of designation, to that distance that makes what one speaks of something on which we have our sights, something on which to keep one's eye, something to be looked at, something one seeks to approach. Now that we have been encouraged by Saussure to place "signification" in another pairing where it finds itself contrasted to "value," we observe that this new opposition grants it the opposite meaning to the one it received previously. When it found itself opposed to designation—which indicates what one speaks of, and belongs to visual experience[14]—signification seemed to be only a matter for the system of *language* [*langue*], which is what permitted us to refer it to the negativity immanent in this system; we indicated as much when we placed it at the heart of the presumption of sufficiency that characterizes language [*langage*]. But placed in opposition to value—which, according to Saussure, is strictly "horizontal"—the same signification finds itself endowed instead with a kind of thickness, or vertical depth. And undeniably, we have just seen that Saussure introduces the theme in a way that places signification on the side of speech and value on the side of language [*langue*]. Overall, then, signification appears sometimes endowed with the transparency of ideality, to which the opacity of reference or designation is opposed, and sometimes with the depth of the visible—its "positivity," writes Saussure[15]—against value that belongs entirely to the grid's system of spacings.

Is this due to an uncertainty at the level of concept, a consequence of a terminology that, by borrowing the image of oppositionality from spatiality, contents itself with necessarily imprecise metaphors? Or does this slippage in the status of signification not betray, rather, the position of hinge that signification occupies between the two spaces? One should recall that on this term of signification two nomenclatures with different destinations overlap. The first belongs to Saussure's reflection on the sign's arbitrariness, later developed and amended by Benveniste; the other comes out of the reflection on the structure immanent in the linguistic system, which is already present in Saussure, and which Jakobson (after Troubetzkoy) aimed to extend to all aspects of language [*langage*]. No need to return to the first; as for the second, there is no doubt that Saussure tended to reduce signification completely to value, thereby privileging the negativity of language [*langue*] over that of speech [*parole*]. "The meaning of a term depends on the presence or absence of a neighboring term. From the system, we arrive at the idea of value, not of meaning. The system leads to the term. At that point we will recognize that signification is determined by what is around.... The word does not exist without a signified and a signifier: but the signified is only the summary of the linguistic value presupposing the interplay of terms between them.... What is in the word is never determined by anything else than the combination of what surrounds it, associatively and syntagmatically."[16]

Extending this line of reasoning, Jakobson, after having distinguished the syntactic from the semantic, will be quick to claim the "intrinsically linguistic" character of the semantic.[17] By "intrinsically linguistic," read that the dimension of signification must be, according to Jakobson, entirely conceived of according to the principle of the constant spacing that governs phonological analysis and allows for the construction of the grid of language [*langue*]. Giving back to linguists the characteristic of the semantic, or at least the concern for it, is necessarily, from a structuralist perspective, to identify signification with value, thereby refusing to understand signification as the relation between the sign and the thing. Jakobson thus adopts the distinction Benveniste had established from the other direction of thought, between signification and designation. This is precisely what allows Jakobson to deny signification the depth of visual space that we recognized in designation. The inclusion of signification in the linguistic field, conducted under Peirce's authority, is justified by the fact that, to be understood, all signs require an "interpretant" and that "the function of this interpretant is fulfilled by another sign, or group of signs that are provided concurrently with the sign in question, or that could be substituted for it."[18] Jakobson goes on to write: "Peirce gives an incisive definition of the *main structural mechanism of language,* when he demonstrates that any sign can be translated by another sign in which it is more fully developed."[19] As for our question of whether or not signification belongs to the measured interval or to movable distance, it is obvious that if the interpretant is itself conceived of as a sign, we will be forced to admit that the signified of a signifier is itself a signifier—thereby doing away completely with the rift between a plane of the signifier and a plane of the signified. Saussure seemed to concede that however unrealizable this rift was in practice, it had to be preserved as a necessary theoretical opposition. Signification thus finds itself ousted from its position of verticality, emptied of its depth, and subjected to the same treatment as the horizontal "opposition" that served as guide for the elaboration of phonological models. "All linguistic signification is differential. *Linguistic significations are differential in the same way as phonemes, which are differential phonic units.* Linguists know that, besides phonemes, the sounds of speech offer contextual as well as optional, or situational, variants (in other words, 'allophones' and 'metaphones'). Similarly, at the semantic level one finds contextual significations and situational significations. *But only the existence of invariant elements makes it possible to recognize the variations.* At the level of meaning as well as of sound, the problem of invariants is crucial for the analysis of a given state of a given language. . . . If you do not like the word 'meaning' because of its ambiguity, we can speak simply of semantic invariants—and these are no less important for linguistic analysis than phonological invariants."[20]

In this passage, in which the ambiguity of meaning[21] is challenged explicitly, I have italicized the two sentences that constitute an answer to my question on the space of signification. The answer being that this space is identical to that of value, in the Saussurean sense of the term; that the variations that can be observed there are, logically, secondary; that these presuppose invariant intervals between the signifiers; and that these fixed spacings *are,* strictly speaking, the signification—the latter requiring the identification of the terms of the segments and, at the same time, the absence of the one when the other is present in discourse. Such a reduction appears legitimate: from the structuralist perspective, which grants primacy to facts of language [*langue*] over those of speech [*parole*], it becomes necessary to abandon the Saussurean concept of signification, whose source, we noted, is rooted in the actual dialogic experience, and accept only, as epistemological category, the one that applies to the system in general—that is, the invariant interval. It follows that signification must be "laid flat," so to speak, over the grid of signs, just as oral expression had been over the grid of phonemes. Thus the scruple that held Saussure back from extending the principle of difference to relations of signification is overcome, and the positivity he glimpsed in the semantic order eradicated.

Signification can then be restored in the clarity we assumed it possessed on the basis of the speaking subject's experience, for if /hôrs/ immediately conveys "horse" for the English speaker, to the point, as we said, that it is impossible to have the "concept" without the "sound pattern" or vice versa, it is precisely, argues Jakobson, because the two planes—of the signified and the signifier—are in fact inseparable. Indeed, the whole signification of /hôrs/ is determined by the grid of adjoining monemes that can establish with /hôrs/ the paradigmatic and syntagmatic relations included in the code of the English language. Take the simplest case, that of lexical monemes (*lexemes* in Martinet's nomenclature), and open the dictionary to know the signification of "horse." The entry corresponding to the word indicates two types of operation, usually distinguished typographically: on the one hand, it offers other monemes likely to be substituted for the one under consideration; on the other, it indicates exemplary instances in which the word appears, each context circumscribing a meaning with the least ambiguity possible. In the first case, the proposed operation is what Jakobson calls substitution or selection; in the second, combination or contexture.[22] The word can be placed in a relation of similarity with other words (what Saussure called associative relation); it can also be placed in a sequential, or syntagmatic, relation. In short, the word's signification provided by the dictionary is nothing other than the virtual set of constraints governing its use by the speaker. And the latter is so aware of these that when she or he uses the signifier /hôrs/, all the constraints converge as it were toward the area of full luminosity—that is, the pure actuality of the uttered word—and that some of them will in turn be actualized to grant the utterance its substance. The lexeme's signification is therefore nothing but the system of paradigmatic and syntagmatic oppositions in which it is positioned by the code of language [*langue*]. Its depth is a consequence of the fact that the speaking subject obviously cannot say everything at the same time—providing in her or his utterance all the substitutable and combinative options surrounding the word in question—but that, on the contrary, she or he must cut through the table of syntagmatic and paradigmatic relations along a single vector which is that of the discourse she or he is uttering; and thus, never actualizing more than a small part of the semantic field in which the word is located, she or he must *cast in shadow* the rest, thereby creating opacity and depth. The latter is an empty depth, while the "fullness" of signification lies in the measured intervals of language [*langue*]; and if the speaker cannot have the signifier without the signified, she or he knows that the term, as an inseparable entity, *is* nothing but the tip of a multiplicity of segments that keep it at an invariable distance from the terms situated at the other tips.

Now if one were to ask upon what, nonetheless, depends this appearance of depth that signification takes, one might think it easy to show that its roots go back to the same "mistake" Benveniste denounced regarding the thesis of the linguistic sign's arbitrariness. The illusion of the signified—a clinging one, forged by centuries of idealist realism—originates, one will argue, in the transfer of the relation of designation onto that of signification in a kind of 90-degree rotation that aligns the designated onto the signified, leading the latter to merge with the object. A kind of lining of the world is thus founded, which Platonic myth named "thinkable," intelligible, but whose character Platonic dialectics (for example, at the beginning of *Parmenides*) easily shows precisely to be unthinkable in its relation to the signifier. It is because the signified is granted the same status as the designated, because it is placed at the end of a mutable distance separating it from the signifier; because it is turned into an essence conceived of exactly on the model of the thing's being [*étant*], and therefore because within the grid of language [*langue*] is brought to bear a "perspective" that is impossible there—according to which what is aimed at and intentionalized offers itself to the speaking subject—that signification, in the end, can appear simultaneously to manifest and conceal a signified, and can signify it according to this relation of depth, of figure on ground, that belongs to our experience of the visible. What is true is the immediate presence of the signified, which is none other than the potential of the operations that envelop the signifier when it appears in the spoken chain: there *is no* signified, except as mirage.

Still, it is difficult to be satisfied with this "clarification" argued in positivist terms, for there remains in any case to be understood where this "mistake" comes from that redoubles seeing in comprehension, that transforms the signified into a horizon for the mind's eye. In the end we will have to concede that, like all illusions, the illusion of the depth of signification is well-founded, so well-founded, in fact, that even the linguist inevitably falls for it. When an English speaker says /hôrs/, the signified is here, for her or him, immediately given with the signifier: thus is transparency "glued," in opposition to the spacing of designation, for, as far as the object is concerned, it is still over there. But if the linguist, when attempting to locate the signified, is led to set it back onto another plane, to turn it into a "substance" of sorts as we saw with Saussure, it is not only due to a kind of realist naïveté, and for lack of fluency in transcendental philosophy. The truth is that, even after Kant and Husserl, this "realism" is, in fact, natural, and one must explain how it insinuates itself even into the scholar's description of the semantic plane. I would argue that this inability to seize the negative in its pure state, as Godel put it, that this impulse to place there something that is not there, that this reifying drive is wholly attributable to the fact that the linguist *speaks* in the very act of uttering the system of values. The mutable space of the aim [*visée*], which is that of speech, infiltrates the system's phonological or semantic description not as a blunder, but rather as the linguistic method's acknowledged right. To grasp the clarity of /hôrs/ one must obscure it by varying the gaps that define its semantic environment. Such an obscuring aims to institute the invariable space of language [*langue*], but the result can be achieved only through the variations of utterances, through the game of depth—the game that will make signification go from the position of felt immediacy to the status of intellected mediation. The inclusion of thickness or depth in signification—that is, the introduction of a "visible" space precisely where the speaker is deprived of one—results from the work of "mobilization" of what was implicitly stable. The system of values, according to which the use of the word "horse" is determined in speech, is indeed detected thanks to the technique of selection, which is merely the implementation of the principle of pertinence: could I use "horse" in the same way if, for example, the oppositions "horse/mare," "horse/horses," or "horse/Norse" came to disappear from the system of language [*langue*]? This simple question is enough to inject mobility into purportedly invariant intervals and is, strictly speaking, the negation of negation: thanks to it, depth burrows itself under the signification of /hôrs/.

This does not prevent signification from remaining transparent in ordinary use, and it would be superficial to declare this transparency an illusion. For such an immediacy belongs irrevocably to our experience of speech: to try to "demystify" it would be about as logical as a psychoanalyst deciding to give up the study of consciousness on the pretense that the latter is deceived by the unconscious and is intrinsically misconception. On the contrary, this transparency of the signified in discourse is necessarily presupposed, including, foremost, by the linguist even when she or he strives to make known its "conditions" by replacing the term in an underlying and autonomous system, that is to say, by casting it in shadow. For every speaking speech [*parole parlante*], opacity comes "before" discourse, in that dimension of openness we refer to as designation. When the linguist takes this very signification, its transparency, as the horizon line of her or his discourse and attempts to thematize it, to manifest it as an effect of meaning strictly subordinated to an environment of values in a system so tightly measured that the slightest modification of one of the values can only have repercussions on this signification—as she or he speaks like this, mediatizing the immediate, obscuring transparency, relativizing the un-relative—her or his speech again combines other equally "transparent" significations, in order to measure itself against the theme it aims for, to incorporate what it designates into it as signified.

One thus sees in the linguist's very practice the clear and the opaque trade places. It is conventional wisdom to say that all thought "implies a somber share of shadow," since one imagines intentionality as that fiery paintbrush setting the noema ablaze, and since fire does not illuminate itself. This yarn is accurate insofar as it applies to our experience of meaning: the unveiling of the *quid* [what] goes hand in hand with the concealment of the *quomodo* [how].[23] But if one thinks about the plane of language [*langage*] in and through which this "clarification" takes place, and if one takes a closer look at the torsions and rotations provoked in this plane by the linguist's activity, one observes the opposite effect: this work, which like any scientific work consists first in obscuring clarity, in dispelling the obvious, in transgressing limits, can occur only in the immediate clarity of the language [*langue*] in which it operates. By clarity here I mean that though this language [*langue*] could be as scholarly and sophisticated as one would like, it will always in the end need to fall back on linguistic experience, on terms and on syntagmatic and paradigmatic relations that it will not have *established* but *found,* to draw upon a lexis and a syntax "older" than itself. It is a known fact that the strictest axiomatic requires the use of a common language [*langue*] through which to comment on its elaboration. This is the ground that remains when all scaffolding is removed and the axiomatic appears suspended at its apex.

This play of light and dark, of signification and designation, belongs to every metalanguage. Linguistics marks that moment when language takes itself as object. So long as it positions itself at the tip of the aim [*visée*], it obscures itself as designated: linguistic discourse is thus a discourse that draws the night over discourse. This night is the depth of designation. It consists precisely—like the night of dreams and of incest—in violating the *ratio,* in varying the invariants. On the one hand these variations can only be imaginary, as they presuppose, in their formulation, the invariants they subvert. On the other, these invariants themselves are "constituted," in a Husserlian sense, by the acts of unbridled freedom that are the variations, and the latter, far from being illusory, appear "archaeological." Once again we need not decide if the negative of the figural comes logically, ontologically, or epistemologically before the verbal negative. We must be wary of this temptation to decide: structuralism already fell victim to it, as we learned from Jakobson. But temptation also lurks when we are inclined to respond to the enthusiasm of the structure with that of intentionality, and to counter the preeminence of the invariant over variation with the argument that, after all, it is through the latter that the former is constituted.

There is, therefore, no such thing as a "thickness" of signification, other than through an epistemological illusion apparent in Saussure's *Course* that leads the linguist to redouble and transfer onto linguistic signification the configuration that applies to designation. My speech aims for something: this is the mobile distance from the word to the "thing"; but this depth originates in discourse. In the system of language [*langue*] taken as object, in the architecture of signification, this distance does not exist at all: here there is no "verticality," only the horizontal spaces that determine the values in the signifying order. Yet it is this depth—in reality none other than that of intentionality or of the separation of a subject from its objects—that first Saussure, followed by other linguists, reintroduce at the core of the *object-*language [*objet-langage*], *between* the signifier and the signified, something like a perpendicular dimension to that of the relations of value. But once again, there is no eye to "see" within the object-language [*objet-langue*], and signifiers could not "signify" anything of the signifieds, could not "replace" anything other than themselves, "a concept" for example, as Saussure says.

The thickness of the sign is that which opens in front of the object of discourse. It is hardly aberrant that at its beginnings structuralist linguistics would have been tempted, if not to confuse this thickness with the relation of signification, then at least to maintain it alongside this relation. The linguist is destined to suffer the same fate as any other speaker: we cannot speak without tracing this distance between our discourses and its object. This distance is what Saussure placed at the heart of the "sign," yet it is this very distance that must be evacuated from the sign by the consideration of the system of language [*langue*]. What lies behind this parapraxis [*acte manqué*] is the impossibility of settling in the absolute of totality. Our kinship with the visual and the libidinal reaches even in our logical claims to combinatorics. Reflecting on the way to reconcile the presence of the two axes in Saussure's thinking—the vertical axis that relates signifier and signified *within* the "sign," and the horizontal axis that relates the terms with one another in their *exteriority*—Godel observes that "The internal relation presupposes the external relation. However, *in the order of the account,* the latter comes after the former: the nature of the sign is the first question to come to the fore, once language [*langue*] has been distinguished from speech [*parole*]; the nature of the system and of the terms appears only at the moment when one broaches static linguistics."[24] Hence the horizontal concept of signification—the external relation of the terms between them—belongs to the order of the system, of developed science, while the order of the account, belonging to *Bildung,* to science in the making, to the mind building the mediation between the terms, requires that one start from the sign as opaque immediacy and from signification as the signified's overhang on the signifier.

But how to understand this "starting from"? Does it announce the program of a phenomenology, the story of a mind marching toward totality, dissipating the illusion of thickness? I believe nothing of the sort. No knowledge-discourse will ever get the better of the opacity in question, regardless of Hegel's claims to the contrary; difference is not a moment acting as a springboard toward identity or opposition; the fact that signification itself passes as sign only serves to indicate that there is a power of the sign, a power of the being-sign capable of investing the object with any referential relation. A compulsion of opacity exists that requires that what one speaks of be declared lost.

Thickness on the Margins of Discourse

A decade before Saussure, Gottlob Frege had understood and developed this effect of positionality, establishing that the words' opening onto reference belongs to actual discourse and not to the virtual system of language [*langue*], suggesting moreover that there is silent meaning or thickness on this side of significations, lodged this time at the heart of discourse itself, in its form. The separation of the two vectors that allowed Benveniste to locate the arbitrary nature of linguistic signs overlaps exactly with the distinction Frege posits between *Sinn* and *Bedeutung*.[1] This last remark is more than a mere anomaly, for Frege's reflection goes far beyond a formalist revision regarding propositional calculus; it follows a Kantian lineage when it starts from the separation between an $a = a$ type equation, which is analytical, and the equation of the $a = b$ variety, which implies an increase in knowledge, but needs to be justified. Above all, Frege's reflection culminates in an organization of the space of discourse and thought that will serve as reference for the Husserl of the *Logical Investigations* as much as for the Wittgenstein of the *Tractatus Logico-Philosophicus,* becoming, with its intersecting dimensions, the matrix of intentional as well as analytical philosophy. It is important to return to the point where, on the one hand, the exclusion of designation in favor of signification, and on the other, the burying of the *Sinn*'s key structure under intentional analyses, are not yet completed, where the union of the two great Kantian themes of the transcendental as subjectivity and the transcendental as structure is not undone, but on the contrary refined—especially since Frege's conclusions find, in certain results and omissions of structural linguistics, an echo that makes his reflection all the more timely.

An expression such as $a = b$ encapsulates the whole problem of the sign. If it turns out to be true, it would mean that one could take b instead of a; but a is not b, and their difference is maintained in the formulation of their identity. What constitutes this difference? If *b* differed only from *a* as an object (*als Gegenstand*), for example through its form and not in the way it designates (*bezeichnet*), the expression $a = b$ would have the same knowledge value as the expression $a = a$, and their difference would be trivial. However, their difference is so important that it contains the entire opposition between the analytic and the synthetic, the entire gain in knowledge. The difference, then, consists in the way in which the designated is given respectively by *a* and by *b*.[2] Let us assume M is the point where the three median lines *x, y, z* of a triangle intersect. One can designate M as the point of intersection of *x* and *y*, or *y* and *z*. These two designations each indicate (*deuten*) a different way of presenting the designated object: this is what grants the statement "the point of intersection of *x* and *y* is the point of intersection of *y* and *z*" a positive knowledge value. One must therefore distinguish between the sign's *Bedeutung*, its designation, involving the exteriority of the designated, and its *Sinn*, consisting in the way the object is given (*die Art des Gegebenseins*). The *Bedeutung* of the expression "point of intersection between *x* and *y*" is the same as that of the expression "point of intersection of *y* and *z*," but not its *Sinn*.

This is not to suggest that if reference is objective, signification would be subjective. To emphasize how far he stands from a psychologizing interpretation, and to locate signification precisely within objectivity, Frege provides a new coupling where signification is this time opposed to "representation" (*Vorstellung*). The latter can vary from one subject to the next, while signification is independent of the word's or the expression's formulation. The phrase "a new day is born" can elicit various representations, images, feelings, depending on the listener, but each and every listener, if knowledgeable of the English language, will understand it in the same way. Thus emerges the concept of a non-reifying objectivity, for which Frege provides as model the image of the moon in the lens of a telescope: "I compare the moon itself to the reference (*Bedeutung*); it is the object of the observation, mediated by the real image projected by the object glass in the interior of the telescope and by the retinal image of the observer. The former I compare to the sense [*signification*] (*Sinn*), the latter is like the idea [*représentation*] (*Vorstellung*) or experience [*intuition*] (*Anschauung*)."[3] Signification is thus endowed with the same objectivity as that of the physical image in the "objective": it is *einseitig* [one-sided] and depends on the position of the observation point, but is the same for all the observers standing in any one place. Hence signification has no more to do with persons than designation; what does is the world of images that signification can give rise to in each of us. The correlation between our representations and, say, the text of a poem is unverifiable, "free"; similarly, the dream separates us from the objectivity of *Sinn,* pressing us into another element that is not communicable, or at least not easily so.

If Frege chooses not to dwell on this relation between sign and *Vorstellung*—since the problem he sets out to elucidate is not that of the expression of "subjectivity," but rather that of the position of objectivity in discourse—his analysis of the two dimensions of meaning is, for its part, crucial. As Frege writes, a "proper noun"—that is, any sign or group of signs, whether words or not, to which corresponds a definite object and not a concept or a relation[4]—"expresses its sense [*signification*] (*drückt seinen Sinn aus*), stands for or designates its reference (*bedeutet oder bezeichnet seine Bedeutung*). By means of a sign we express its sense [*signification*] and designate its reference (*wir drücken mit einem Zeichen dessen Sinn aus und bezeichen mit ihm dessen Bedeutung*)."[5] This duality of the dimensions of meaning [*sens*] is inescapable: it is pointless to object that, after all, one can make do with signification [*signification*] alone, and that nothing forces us to look for the reference behind the sign. To the skeptic who wonders why we should need to have "moon" find a respondent in reality, Frege answers: "when we say 'the Moon,' we do not intend to speak of our idea [*représentation*] (*Vorstellung*) of the Moon, nor are we satisfied with the sense [*signification*] (*Sinn*) alone, but *we presuppose a reference* (*sondern wir setzen eine Bedeutung voraus*)."[6]

When what is at issue is no longer the proper noun but the declarative statement, Frege will go on to assert just as vehemently the inalienable character of the search for the designated. Understood in its totality, the declarative statement possesses an objective thought content, independent of the thinker; just as in the case of the proper noun, signification is not subjected to the whims of the speakers' imaginations. But what about reference, of the dimension of designation in such a statement, to which not *one* object can correspond? Can we simply do without it? "Is it possible that a sentence as a whole has only a sense [*signification*], but no reference?"[7] When I assert that "Odysseus was set ashore at Ithaca while sound asleep," the sentence possesses signification but seems to lack a dimension of designation since, in all probability, no object corresponds to one of the proper nouns it contains (Odysseus). Frege's answer to this question warrants our attention. When, he argues, we listen to the epic poem in an aesthetic attitude, what fascinates us through the musicality of language is signification, and the images and sentiments it arouses. "Hence it is a matter of no concern to us whether the name 'Odysseus,' for instance, has reference, so long as we accept the poem as a work of art." But "the question of truth would cause us to abandon aesthetic delight for an attitude of scientific investigation."[8] For we are inclined to want the proper noun to possess not only a signification but also a designation; on its own, the thought content of the statement leaves us unsatisfied. "It is the striving for truth that drives us always to advance from the sense [*signification*] to the reference [*designation*]."[9]

In the above answer we see the first sketch emerge of a complete table of the attitudes of speech that would force us to reflect on the language of art. When the statement is grasped for the *Vorstellung* it can generate, the grip on the axis of language occurs at the pole of images, which is individual, and this approach determines the aesthetic existence of speech, the poetic. A second grip should be possible through signification alone, stripped of its phantasmatic resonances as well as its referential power; it would then induce a formalist attitude, using language as an objective totality in that the signifieds would always be verifiable from one speaker to another—which would imply that we remain confined to the order of articulated language—and thus as a *closed* totality, since there would be no need to reveal signification by pitting it against something beyond itself. But Frege seems to suggest here that such a formalism is impossible since it is not in our power to summon words, and groups of words, in thought without referring their signification to an "object" that is not in them, but outside. This explains why this second type of grip on language finds no place in Frege's terminology, and why he considers the language of knowledge a form of speech in search of the absent object of which it is speaking. Thus all language is essentially open onto nonlanguage: the discourse of knowledge requires a transcendence directed toward things, within which it hunts down its object, while the discourse of art requires the opposite transcendence, issuing from the images that come to inhabit its words. On the one side defining speech, which tries to force the designated into invariant structure relations and to assimilate completely the designated into signified; on the other, expressive speech striving to open itself up to the space of vision and desire and to produce figurality with the signified. In both cases, language fascinated by what it is not, attempting in the latter case to *possess* it—this is the phantasy of science—on the other to *be* it—the phantasy of art.

It is with considerable insight that Frege sees as a motive in the discourse of knowledge a striving, a *Streben,* a desire, thus provoking (this logician, this professor) in the meticulously sanitized problematic of knowledge a crack through which the theme reputed as being most foreign to knowledge could creep in, whereas it is doubtless its core: the theme of desire. Frege even shows that the transcendence that refers every utterance to an object is essentially unknown to language: "If anything is asserted there is always an obvious presupposition that the simple or compound proper names used have reference. If one therefore asserts 'Kepler died in misery,' there is a presupposition that the name 'Kepler' designates something; but it does not follow that the sense (*Sinn*) of the sentence 'Kepler died in misery' contains the thought (*Gedanke*) that the name 'Kepler' designates something." This could almost be Kant's refutation of the ontological argument: existence is not a concept. Frege adds, "If this were the case, the negation would have to run not 'Kepler did not die in misery' but 'Kepler did not die in misery, or the name "Kepler" does not have a reference.'"[10] Note in passing this proof's method: by negation.

Yet an elementary Kantianism still lingers in the sketch of the table of meanings. In it the expressive and cognitive forms of discourse remain separate, just as the celestial body and its retinal image are in the comparison of the telescope. Wanting-to-know and having-lost are not articulated with one another; art is not seen as "memory" of an identity of the word and the thing of which science is the forgetting and the desperate repetition in the possessive register; knowledge as desire is not articulated with misrecognition as phantasy. No doubt Frege is absolutely right to stay clear of the totalizing dialectics of the sensory into sensible, a dialectics by which he was hardly tempted as far as we know. Frege nevertheless falls victim to the same psychologism that haunts the *Critique of Pure Reason* (but which Kant will progressively shed as he advanced in the critique of his criticism) when he places *Vorstellung*, and all the power of meaning that poetry attaches to the image, on the side of the individual subject and of a communication-less interiority opposed to an objective and universally observable exteriority supposedly belonging to science. As if this subject and this object were not fragments from a primary explosion of which language was precisely the initial spark; as if reality, far from being that about which there is never anything but unanimity, could be approached otherwise than as that which is lost and must be found again; and as if, on the other hand, poetry and art in general didn't have everything to do not with *Vorstellungen* but with tried-and-true objects. The real and the imaginary are not faculties, nor levels, nor even poles. One certainly cannot avoid falling into this spatializing of Being: it finds its justification precisely in the explosion that divides by unifying, since this exteriority and this unity are space itself. But one must continually resist the convenience, even up to the validity of this imagery, if we want to recapture what made and continues to make possible the polarization of the object and the subject, of the thing and the image, of science and art, that is our lot.

It would naturally be unfair to ask of Frege's article what it is not meant to give (despite the fact that this "mistake" awaits every text, as it is the general law of reading). But what it does give—the transcendence and the rule of commutation—deserves thorough consideration. Frege's double question is: What does it mean to say $a = b$? And under what conditions can one say it? This is the problem of synthetic judgment, here understood in terms of semiology and no longer of criticism, which is how it comes up directly against the problem of arbitrariness and the modern theme of the two meanings of meaning. The answer to the first question is that one says $a = b$ when a and b are expressions that refer to the same object. "The Stagirite philosopher" and "Alexander's tutor" are equivalent expressions because they share the same reference and aim for the same object. One thus sees what for Frege grounds the synthesis of judgment or, as one would say, governs the sentence's formation, namely, the discourse's opening onto what it speaks of. We can replace a phrase with another without betraying the truth when both have the same referent in sight. The synthesizing process at work in the production of discourse must be seen as the movement of the speaker from one observation point to another from where the object seen from the first point will still be recognizable; as the experience of a mobility whose rule is to leave the aim [*visée*] untouched. In this description of synthetic judgment two primary metaphors are seen to come into play, that of moving and of seeing. To speak is to jump from one reference point to another without letting what one is speaking of out of one's sight. The object is constituted as a horizon line toward which the expressions, like glances cast in its direction, will converge. A description remarkably close to the one we can venture, and which Husserl did, of perceptual experience and the constitution of the visual object: a unit of drafts, site where these grips take hold, where these instantaneous caresses take shape into a thickness in which the object holds itself back like an X. We recognize the kind of negativity at the heart of Frege's analysis—visual transcendence—and what matters most in this transcendence: the remote bestowal in the mobility that engenders depth. This is the ekthesis of all synthesis, the originary explosion in which the sequence of linguistic terms stretches out, the $a = b$.

This vertical negativity does not do away with internal conditions regulating the syntagmatic chain, which limit the right to commute a and b, even when they share the same reference. The close study of these prohibitions is of great interest, revealing as it does the presuppositions of a methodology from which we will barely need to stray in what follows. Frege identifies three types of such restrictions, all of which have to do with subordinate clauses. When I state "Copernicus believed that the planetary orbits are circles,"[11] my statement is true despite the fact that, taken separately, the subordinate is false, as lacking *Bedeutung*. I can replace this statement with this one: "Copernicus believed that the apparent motion of the sun is produced by the real motion of the Earth," in which this time the subordinate, taken separately, is true (since it possesses a referent), without this substitution altering the truth value (*Warheitswert*) of my statement. This particular trait also applies to all subordinate clauses completing verbs such as to say, etc., that express a conviction, an appearance, a goal, an order, a request, or a denial.[12] A first obstacle to a selection determined solely by the consideration of the reference lies therefore in *indirect* speech, where words are no longer taken for what they designate (as is the case in direct speech) but rather only for what they signify. Thus in the expression "I believe it is raining," "it is raining" counts in fact as thought content (*Gedanke*), not as reference to "actual," real rain. The rule is therefore that the *Bedeutung* of a proper noun (or of a clause) taken indirectly is its *Sinn*. We will return to this rule, which is of great importance and comes into play each time language is taken as object.

The second case in which selection finds itself restricted occurs when the subordinate, separated from the entire set of propositions, does not constitute an autonomous thought content. When I declare that "Whoever discovered the elliptic form of the planetary orbits died in misery,"[13] I am unable to think the subordinate separately. Of course I can utter the clause for its own sake ". . . whoever discovered the elliptic form of the planetary orbits," but its *Sinn* does not form an independent thought content, as one cannot transform this subordinate into a main clause. It possesses moreover no distinctive *Bedeutung*, thus preventing me from replacing such a subordinate by another with the same reference: since its signification is only a part of the signification of the whole set of propositions, by modifying this part I modify the thought content of the whole.

Finally one must isolate the case—the most common in ordinary language—where the entire thought content is not expressed in the set of propositions taken as whole (main + subordinate), and where, therefore, there is more *Gedanken* than clauses. For example, causality, reservation, or mediation can be suggested by the disposition of clauses without any one proposition, or part thereof, corresponding to it.[14] In this case, the use of the rule of selection with equal *Bedeutung* must come after an analysis of the utterance detecting the presence or not of an implicit notion. Thus in the statement "Napoleon, seeing the threat to his right flank, personally led his Guard against the enemy position," I can replace the relative subordinate clause by another of equal *Bedeutung*—for example, "suffering from liver problems"—only after making sure that no sequential relation holds between the sight of the threat and the decision to take personal command of the Guard.

One notes that the method used by Frege constitutes a kind of experimentation with propositions that is, long before it became known as such, the *commutation* test itself. When am I entitled to replace *a* with *b*? The most basic condition is that both must have the same reference, that is, converge in the depth of discourse's transcendence. An added condition is that the change in signification resulting from the selection—this time in the linear dimension of discourse—should not produce nonsense. One understands nonsense to be inevitable if, as is the case with certain indirect subordinate clauses, the expression's reference is identified with its signification; it is inevitable, too, if the subordinate clause's *Sinn* is an integral part of the *Sinn* of the whole clause or if, conversely, a non-expressed "signification" emanates from the statement's organization itself. These cases can be subsumed under two overarching instances. The speaker does not speak in her or his name but reports the object of a thought, an utterance, a wish, or an order for whose content she or he does not take responsibility. In the spatial metaphor, this translates as: from the observation point 1 with a view on object X, I express what is said, thought, wanted, or ordered from the observation point 2 with regard to this same object. Thus it is clear that the object of my statement is not object X but rather what occurs at point 2, that in this way the actual transcendence of my discourse aims for this point and not for my object, and consequently that the *Bedeutung* of the terms I use to express what occurs at point 2 is indeed these terms' *Sinn,* that is, the thought content corresponding to them. The sole condition of having to keep one's sights on object X no longer suffices to measure my movement from one observation point to another, for what is at issue in my discourse is the view of the other observation point on X—that is, the other's gaze—and to express it requires respecting its perspective, not unlike certain Gothic altarpieces organized according to "reverse" perspective, which would be to the figure what reported speech is to discourse. The method of selection brings out in subordinate clauses that are apparently similar as to their meaning, the radical difference resulting from a change of reference, such as between "the firefighters claim that a house is on fire" and "the firefighters are heading toward a burning house." It is remarkable that this method, which we know, forty years after Frege, will become instrumental for phonology and structural linguistics, and which was already the whole secret behind Leibniz's logic,[15] far from confining itself to discourse's longitudinal dimension, of bringing to the fore only structural invariants—that is, a measured and horizontal negativity, a formal law—first relies on the transcendence of vision, on the reference to the object of which one speaks, and declares as ground rule, as a rule more radical than formal laws, the safeguarding of *intuitus* [immediate cognition]. The first situation where the freedom of selection is hindered consists therefore in the fact that actual discourse can include in itself another discourse, aiming for another object.

Here we already begin to see the outlines of the critique of structural linguistics that we will need to develop. Such a critique does not apply to the strategic choice of language level [*niveau de langue*], otherwise perfectly legitimate, but to the double consequence this choice entails, which needs to be circumscribed. On the one hand, the aim [*visée*] of the discourse in question is covered up, the words are no longer taken for their "truth value" but for their *Sinn*. This blocking out of reference is what will simultaneously allow speech to be treated as a chain, the extraction of the units articulated in the latter, and their organization into a system. The closure of language [*langage*]—structuralism's fundamental hypothesis—is the correlate of this epistemological relation, in which the other's discourse is not considered according to its own aim [*visée*] but to mine (the linguist's discourse). Reference as "truth value" is driven out of the language under scrutiny, lodging itself between the scrutinized and the scrutinizing language. The relation between discourse thus objectified and its object is lost in its specificity, which is that of a sighting; at best, this relation can be restituted only as a theory of "context," which assumes that the scrutinized discourse and its object are of the same nature and can be dealt with according to the same methodology, with the result of doing away with the possibility of all "truth value." On the other hand, by objectifying the other's discourse, by making it into an object identical in nature and position to that about which it speaks, one transforms words into signs: one ceases to hear them, one strives to see them, thereby granting them a semantic thickness comparable to that of a sensory sign—which is the opposite effect of that by which the linguistic units are organized in the transparent system. One notes how these two effects are contradictory: as signs, the elements of discourse are opaque; as units deprived of reference, they are mere terms. Signification's effect of thickness brings the contradiction to a head, by implying that the system's element is opaque.

As for the other overarching instance that places a limit on the scope of the selection between *a* and *b*, one could say that it consists entirely in the laterality of meaning and in the polysemy of signs. If we sometimes find ourselves unable to replace a subordinate clause with another of equal *Bedeutung* (or truth value), this is because it partakes fully of the statement—for example as the relative clause of a hinge itself unspecified—or because it forms the necessary moment of a meaning not supported expressly by a group of words but that emanates instead from the form itself of discourse, and from the position words and phrases occupy in discourse. In one case, the terms await their signification from their articulation in the statement; in the other, on the contrary, this articulation generates lateral, secondary significations (*Nebengedanken*): in the first case, the discourse's organization evacuates polysemy by actualizing one of the word's *Sinne* and eliminating the others; in the second, it maintains or produces polysemy at the next higher level by combining the significations thus obtained. What does this mean? That mobility is the rule of ordinary language; that the point from where the object of which we are speaking is seen and uttered is not static like an observatory, but rather that the signification with which we endow the object is always produced only at the juncture of two operations, one of which consists in eliminating secondary meanings while the other consists in reconstituting them; and that, therefore, once beyond the level of elements, if one focuses no longer on the terms but on the living statement, one must be prepared to concede, after Frege, that "the clause expresses more through its connexion with another than it does in isolation."[16] And one must acknowledge that a certain movement is not what in language makes it confusing but what makes it possible, just as sight would be impossible if the eye were deprived of its capacity to move around the thing. What impedes selection in the semantic order in which Frege situates himself is, in the final analysis, that in this order one is not really in the presence of the discontinuous, that one is not dealing here—as is the case with distinctive or significative units—with fixed intervals separating and unifying terms that the trajectory of selection could reveal without ambiguity. Here this trajectory, this motion is as good as already integrated into words. It constitutes their polysemy, which could be considered its testimony, since it is the sedimentation upon them of the torsions the speakers inflicted on their initial meaning, of the ebbing and flowing through which the speakers dragged them, only to deposit them, in the lexicon, laden with the new significations acquired in the course of these wanderings.[17]

Frege's analysis thus teaches us not only that there are two axes of discourse that intersect perpendicularly on linguistic "signs"—the axis of signification and that of designation or reference. It further posits that the observance of the latter is the most elementary rule of truth; it teaches us that a discourse reported through ours finds itself deprived of its transcendence, having itself become the object of the present transcendence; lastly, it suggests that we have but one means of speaking, which is to "walk" to see and make visible, and but one means of knowing, which is to continue to move, trying out new substitutions. In his review of *Philosophy of Arithmetic,* Frege admitted to sharing Husserl's belief that the Leibnizian definition "eadem sunt quorum unum potest substitui alteri salva veritate" [Those things are the same which can be substituted for one another without loss of truth] does not deserve to be called a definition. But, he adds, "my reasons are different: since all definitions are expressions of identity (*Gleichheit*), identity itself cannot be defined. One could qualify Leibniz's formulation as an axiom, for it exposes what is the nature of the relation of identity, and this is why it is of the utmost importance."[18] Yet this "nature" of the relation consists in the movement of substitution or selection; and this movement takes place in a positional space that is not where the terms are positioned.

The No and the Position of the Object

Not by chance did Freud's reflections on negation lead Émile Benveniste to recognize "the fundamental property of language" in the presumption of reference involved in all discourse.[1] By drawing on Freud's work, one can clear a path toward an essential aspect of the constitution of transcendence: the interlocking of the impulse's silence with articulated language, which all at once erects desire, its object, and the dream or art.

Let us begin by extracting what, at the beginning and the end of Freud's *Die Verneinung* [see Appendix at the end of the present book], constitutes the essay's theme, namely, the function of grammatical negation in knowledge, or the definition of knowledge as the lifting of another and originary negation: repression.

Freud begins by wondering about a kind of logical scandal that arises in analytic interpretation. "It is *not* my mother," says the analysand. "We amend this to: it is therefore his mother," says Freud. This strange permutation from No to Yes rests on the hypothesis that the negation of the object in the analysand's discourse—here, of the mother—is at the same time the positive presentation of this object. By cancelling, for him- or herself, the negation made explicit in speech, the analyst seems to be in violation of its strict interpretation, but this is to give it a dimension that strict literalness and formalism overlook: that of its violent separation from what it is speaking of. We are in a position to state that the statement "it is not my mother" signifies, or at least *also* signifies, "it is my mother," granted we give the axis upon which we implicitly place the message a ninety-degree turn and if, rather than as a negative judgment, we take the message as the expression of surprise and anxiety through which one refuses to *see* what presents itself. The question is whether or not this turn is justified.

It can be justified only if the syntactic negation, the negation *within* discourse, expresses a negativity that transcends the latter, establishing it alternatively as language [*langue*] or sight. By considering it only as a segment sampled from a closed system—that of language [*langue*]—the statement "it is not my mother" presents negation as one of the possibilities offered by the system's syntax, as one of the ways to articulate experience: for the logician, it represents a determination of judgment according to the category of quality. The synthesis this negation brings to light consists entirely in the simultaneous positioning of two terms between which one asserts there to be no relation, "no connection." Here we find ourselves in the order of signification where No means No. If, notwithstanding, the analyst believes her- or himself entitled to interpret No also as Yes, this is because she or he leaves behind the order of formal signification, of the closed system, in order to open under this No the transversal, vertical dimension of designation. "Negation," Freud stated, "is a way of taking cognizance of what is repressed."[2] "Is it not apparent here," writes Benveniste in his commentary, "that the linguistic factor is decisive in this complex process, and that negation is in some way constitutive of the negated content? . . . His discourse {the subject's} can produce denials [*dénégations*[3]] in abundance, but it cannot abolish the fundamental property of language, which is to imply that something corresponds to what is uttered, some thing and not 'nothing.'"[4] The No, then, should not be understood merely as *the position of exclusion within the system of language* [*langue*]; one can and should take it as the position of exclusion *within which all discourse is actualized.* Negation is not only the quality of judgment, it is the condition of its possibility; not only a category of discourse, but its locus: the speaker has torn her- or himself from what she or he is speaking of, or it tore itself from her or him, and by speaking the speaker continually holds it from afar, as the object of her or his discourse, in a "vision." The No that the analyst hears is thus not only one embodied by a particular quality of judgment: it signals this other negation, which every discourse requires as its permanent origin, by which the object and its speech, speech and its object, are excluded from one another. In the first sense, the No is the formal property of a segment of a closed system; in the second, it stands as the transcendental mark of reference, which is openness.

Now the passage from one dimension to another—as it is spontaneously performed by the analyst—seems to be authorized by a characteristic of the negative in discourse that one could clarify by comparing it to the property Benveniste discerns in "indicators" and, more specifically, in the first-person pronoun.[5] *I* cannot be treated as just any other signifying unit. *Tree* is endowed with a signification that, however multiple and ambiguous, is nonetheless fixed within the grid of language [*langue*], independently of the discourse in which the moneme is actualized. On the contrary, *I* does not have any signification, being only an "indicator" that will obtain its meaning from its insertion in actual discourse, where it designates the speaking subject. It *designates* the subject rather than *signifies* her or him, as I argued; or, to put it differently, its signification is its designation. For the noun, one can provide standard phrases that will allow its usage to be circumscribed, and each of these phrases authorizes the word, or at least the moneme, to be replaced by one or more other monemes, which can be said to define it if they "clarify" its signification. Let us put aside the problems raised by this notion of "clarification." It remains that similar operations cannot be performed on *I.* This last word will hardly be defined by being placed in statements such as: *I*'ve slept, *I* love you, *I* would add. In truth, *I* has no "content," as philosophers would say, no "concept" in Benveniste's terminology, that is, no signification that can be assigned to the grid of language [*langue*]. We cannot possibly substitute other words for it that would make it more understandable, as when we say that *to dread* is *to fear intensely.* Its only value is of designation, referring unequivocally to the actual speaker. *I,* therefore, finds its counterpart not in words but in perceptions. One cannot understand it without recourse to the experience that is not of language [*langue*], but essentially of speech [*parole*], which requires one to hear and see without metaphor, to be able to locate the instance of discourse [*instance du discours*], to situate it in the spatiotemporal order.[6]

Admittedly, negation does not offer the same originality. To begin with, it is not lexical but syntactic, identifying not an object but a relation. Language [*la langue*] being the system par excellence, that is, a sum of relations, negation easily finds its place and function within it, alongside other relations equally marked by syntax. However, this formal negation, inscribed in grammar, and realized in the course of a denying discourse (as in the "it is not my mother" of Freud's analysand) should not make us lose sight of the negative's universal reach. Before being a relation within the system, negativity informs every relation, be it of resemblance, even of identity, as long as the position of a relation in general presupposes the composition of terms, in other words their distinction "before" their combination. Thus the Sophist places negation on the border of Logos, Hegel difference at the heart of dialectics, while modern linguistics after Saussure makes the discontinuous its most basic working hypothesis. So long as language [*langue*] is *the* system and a system is a sum of relations, it is no longer enough to say that negation finds a place in it: language is held, indeed *maintained* by negation. The negative, which we may not perceive *in language* [*langage*] though it is its silent support, is not what grants a negative claim its quality; rather, it consists in the fact that the terms of the system have no other being than their value, and that they receive the latter entirely through the measured intervals they maintain together: negative in the sense that, as the editors of *Course* have Saussure say, "in a language [*langue*], everything is negative."[7]

This negativity remains horizontal, so to speak, circumscribing spacings between distinctive or signifying units that belong to the system, and are intelligible without resorting to anything outside of it. But here we must recall Benveniste's remark, as well as Frege's analyses: discourse always speaks *of something*. Designation or reference is that negativity that is not immanent in the fact of language [*langue*] itself but rather in the fact of discourse; nor is it a quality of this discourse in the sense of category that we mentioned earlier: if not explicitly present in discourse, it is implied in the latter, as its intentionality. The negation upholding the relation of designation is the split that, as it opens between discourse and its object, allows us to speak, since we can only say and have nothing else to say than what we are not, and since it is certain that, conversely, what we cannot say, we are. This is why the confrontation between negation and the personal pronoun is warranted: by actualizing an empty form given over to the grid of language [*langue*], the use of *I* designates a fact that is not strictly speaking of language [*langue*] but that is taken up in every speech act and, it follows, that governs each and every actualization of language [*langue*]: the Ego is that which speaks. As suggested above, the personal pronoun thus opens a breach in discourse, initiates a descent in an underside of language [*langage*] toward an experience that is not verbal but perceptual, as it requires the here-now of sensibility. Likewise, the negation that distinguishes itself formally in the utterance affords a glimpse of the supporting structure of discourse, suggesting a hole punched in its floor through which we fleetingly catch sight of the persistent distancing that protects the order of language [*langage*] from that of the objects of which it speaks, and that allows it to cut them up, in total freedom, according to its own logic—just as a window on the underbelly of a plane flying over water offers a view of the liquid surface's mobility, above which the order of technical reason supports itself and moves forward.

Thus we find ourselves in the presence of three instances of the *No*: the negation of the grammarian and the logician, which comes across in negative statements; the discontinuity of the structuralist and the linguist, hidden in language [*langue*], which holds the system's terms apart from one another and, by respecting the invariances, integrates them into a whole; and, lastly, hidden in speech, the lack acknowledged by the logician and the analyst that runs through discourse and grants it its referential power. Syntactic negation, structural negativeness [*négatité*], intentional negativity: is it possible, of course not to reduce them, but to articulate them? In what follows I will limit myself to Freud's indications that touch more specifically upon desire's relation to the negative.

In the *Verneinung* essay, as the competent phenomenologist that he is, Freud observes that it is necessarily through the first of these negations that the others can become manifest in discourse. Without the quality of judgment, signification and designation would remain inexpressible. Indeed, we would be incapable of identifying the content of a significative unit if we were deprived of the grammatical means to say also what it is not, to distinguish it from its immediate context. One need only look at any text on semantics to measure how essential the use of exclusion really is in these cases. The semanticist's "one should not confuse" and more generally the linguist's "relevant opposition" are the expression, in discourse, of the measured intervals they detect between the analyzed term and its neighbor: this is how signification signifies itself. As for designation, its expression in discourse may at first seem less dependent on syntactic negation, insofar as it seems to re-pair, to reunite, rather than separate. Does one not grasp the referential function as a position of the object about which the speaker speaks rather than as its negation? Nonetheless, one is forced to recognize that this position is a remote one, that it is only ever metaphorically that one can qualify a discourse as exhaustive and a signification as "full." In any case, to "re-pair," to "reunite" imply, as signaled in the prefix of reiteration, the presence in them of a negative magnitude in the Kantian sense, which discourse's positivity would consist precisely in re-covering, in covering in the opposite direction. I specify "would consist" because such a conception is not devoid of naïveté, as much as that of *adaequatio intellectus et rei* [adequation of intellect and thing] with which it is closely connected. But assuming for just a moment that this conception is valid, the very challenges facing the philosophy (whether basic or sophisticated) of adequacy could not be voiced—indeed, one would not even be able to know that one is in a relation of adequacy—if the latter could not be distinguished from what it is not, if it did not stand in contrast to inadequacy, not only as to what it is not, but as to what allows it to be. Adequacy, or its phantasy, embeds itself in a space opened by a prior inadequacy, by a lack of contact that gives the desire to know some leeway, just as Kant's boat needs, as it sets sail to America, the ocean's vast interval between continents—the expanse of mobility and risk that is the mind's element, as Hegel would put it—for its route to be mapped out, including the "negative" moments of this route when the winds push it back.[8] Yet this negativity of lack—the expanse to be covered separating Columbus from the object of his desire, but also the buffer zone preserving the "object" from ever being attained (to the point that Columbus, upon reaching land, believes he is setting foot in Asia)—also requires the use of negation in language [*langage*]. As Freud points out, in the absence of the positive force of the symbol of negation, the withdrawal of the object would not be graspable, we would remain trapped in a blind "sensory certainty" for which desire would not exist but only the alternative between want and pleasure, and where, therefore, there would be no vis-à-vis (nor subject) but the fluctuation of two not even identifiable states.

When the analysand asserts "It is not my mother," through the grammatical use of negation she or he establishes a relation of exclusion between two terms, the person of her/his dreams and her/his mother. The relation of exclusion, however, is much more than a quality of judgment: it possesses, not once but twice, universal value. First, it is essential for the order of language [*langage*] to be able to distinguish an "object" from all the others it is not—in this case, another person's mother who is not the mother—since there can be no language [*langue*] if the fixed intervals between units—here at the level of first articulation—are not strictly observed. So much for the system's negativeness [*négatité*]. Second, and particularly in the case at hand, the analysand's denial has universal value in another sense, this time referring us to the negativity of designation. If the analysand has to deny that the object of her or his dream is her/his mother, this is because this dream is indeed a negation of her/his mother insofar as desire harbors the transgression of fixed spacings and the dream is the fulfillment of desire. The mother is the woman placed theoretically outside of desire; to dream of her is to overturn the prohibition and cancel her in her quality of tabooed partner. In *denying* having dreamed of her or his mother, the analysand effectively carries out the constitution or reconstitution of her or his mother as "lost object," and from what she or he says as discourse the analysand exits the plane of the dream and desire to settle in that of knowledge,[9] instituting once again the order of language [*langage*] and of objectivity to which language [*langage*] refers through the distancing of what is assumed to come before all discourse and all objectivity, that is, the mother—through the severing of originary identification. The analysand's negation *repeats* the negation that makes discourse possible, just as it expresses that which is the condition of the system of language [*langue*]. And this is what authorizes the analyst to go from the formal negation present in the analysand's discourse to the negation as fundamental distancing. So that it would not even be true to say that the interpreter replaces No with Yes. Rather, she or he goes from the No of syntax to the No of transcendence, the latter being a position "outside": *ekthesis*.

Now this idea of a "repetition," of a primary negation in the analysand's denial, encourages us to look a little further than the function of negative language in the lifting of repression. Freud himself is led to take this extra step since, from a reflection on the acknowledgment of the repressed and on the role that spoken negation plays in it, he very naturally segues into a meditation on the possible correlation between the Yes-No of articulated language and the introjecting-rejecting of the drive, and from there on the constitution itself of exteriority. This transition is remarkable in that in it a complete reversal occurs in the relation of the negation's symbol to the drive.[10] When he considers the analysand's denial, Freud sees in the *Nein* what allows for an intellectual acceptance of the repressed, a first lifting of repression. But when, in the course of this reflection, he comes to examine how the intellectual function of judgment can rely on the polarity of the drives between Eros and death, then the *Nein* of speech no longer fulfills the sole function of intellectual acknowledgment of the repressed. It is the "substitute for repression; its 'no' is the hall-mark of repression, a certificate of origin—like, let us say, 'Made in Germany'";[11] it is the "successor of expulsion" and as such falls under the destructive drive.[12] Thus syntactic negation—negation in discourse—maintains with this destructive drive—the impulse to reject, to place outside, to repress, or rather to foreclose—a fundamentally ambiguous relation, since it is at once the emblem of its presence and the means of its disappearance.

Added to this first difficulty is the enigmatic passage, located at the center of the *Verneinung* essay, bearing upon exteriority and interiority. Freud begins by asking what it means to judge. Following philosophical precedent, he accepts two kinds of judgment, of attribution and reality: the first acknowledges in or denies an object a given property; the second acknowledges or denies an object's existence. Now the initial form of this "property" is value (good/bad), and the initial polarity of valorization is that of the drives. The unifier Eros orders the object's introjection in the subject; the destructive drive orders their separation, the object's expulsion. Thus, judgments of attribution appear to be reducible to expressions of the drive, the polarity of judgment entirely covered up with that of value, and the latter with that of the drives. This "materialist" hypothesis may seem shocking, but it is not exactly what Freud has in mind. What he does have in mind becomes apparent when he turns to the judgment of reality. Here again, he writes, it is "a question of *external* and *internal.* What is unreal, merely a presentation and subjective, is only internal; what is real is also there *outside.*"[13] However, what is at stake here is no longer to valorize, but to understand if the object itself is outside or only inside, and therefore if it has been rejected (and lost) or on the contrary incorporated, if it has been object of destruction or subject of pleasure. Reality is what has been rejected, it is what one encounters without at first recognizing. Does this amount to arguing that the rift—in which exteriority (and interiority) originate—is indeed that of the archaic polarization of the drives? Is the negation of language nothing more than a stamp of the rejection motivated by the drives?

But a stamp would already be something, and it would still be necessary (a customary, if impossible, task for the materialist), once this reduction is performed, to go on to explain why and how there exist two levels, or states, or moments, or places—here, the death drive and its emblem—and not just one. Freud's essay, however, does not even go that far; rather it states: "The antithesis (*Gegensatz*) between subjective and objective does not exist from the first. It only comes into being from the fact that thinking possesses the capacity to bring before the mind once more something that has been perceived, by reproducing it as a presentation without the external object having still to be there."[14] Exterior and interior do not simply coincide with spat and swallowed that are "from the first." The reality-ego [*Real-Ich*] is not just another figure of the pleasure-ego [*Lust-Ich*]. And, once again, from where would the latter obtain such a power of distortion? The pleasure-ego, as it spits out what is bad, does not constitute reality. What is spat out is what is spat out, and no longer exists for the body of pleasure: it is obliterated. For what has been rejected to *be something* nonetheless, the drive to destroy must be supplemented by the opposite power to appresent [*apprésenter*] absence. Then loss may count as loss, the presence of a lack, and the object may count as reality, something that *is* even when it is not there. But what exactly is this power to render present, to "reproduce as representation" an absent object? It is, says Freud, the power of linguistic negation.

Reality and desire are born together at the threshold of language. Benveniste's remark, that the analysand's denial is "in some way constitutive of the denied content," finds more than assent in Freud's reflection. Already in the last of the *Three Essays on the Theory of Sexuality* it is stated that the object constitutes itself as something lost in search of which the libido wanders, but it is still only the "sexual" object that is at issue, while the theme of loss is not explicitly linked to that of language.[15] Starting with the great texts from the 1920s—*Group Psychology and the Analysis of the Ego* and *Beyond the Pleasure Principle* (to which belongs the *Verneinung* essay)—the emphasis shifts to the simultaneous constitution of reality, subjectivity, and desire as the result of the breakup of an originary situation, which is that of identification,[16] and to the function of language in this breakup. Through the game of *fort-da*,[17] the child constitutes the object as something that can be both there (*da*) and not there (*fort*), since one can make it disappear when it is present and call it back to "presence" when it is absent. This ability to slip away while never ceasing to be is what makes the spool at the end of a string that the child throws over the edge of its bed the model of all objects, and this string, the model of all referential distance. Freud specifically connects the constitution of objectivity to the retraction of the mother who has gone missing. Yet the loss of the mother is not sufficient in itself for her to be objectified. The "mother" is ambiguous (good-bad) well before objectification is possible. But this ambiguity is, precisely, pre-object and pre-objective. The pulsing between eaten-introjected and spat-expelled does not determine a *relation* with the breast. Instead it marks the pleasure-ego's rhythm—non-cumulative and non-referred—oscillating between release and tension and governed by the pleasure principle: "we never discover a 'no' in the unconscious," writes Freud.[18] The *difference* between the two poles of the oscillation is not the *reference* separating and connecting interior and exterior. This reference can establish itself as possible reality only if the expelled-missing is retained (through objectification) and supported (through accumulation) outside of the pleasure-displeasure pulse. This is why the first retraction, that of the breast, far from tracing the fault line between Ego and reality, only establishes autoerotism, the coiling of the corporeal surface upon itself, and the reconstitution of the pleasure-ego's self-sufficiency, and only grounds childhood's polymorphic perversion, which relies on such a denial of reality. This narcissistic wandering comes before objectification: what the former is to the latter, an art form is to a science. With the child's entry into language the + and – of *jouissance* can be collapsed onto the axis of reference opened by designation, and the mother can be placed at a distance as a visible object. This distance is strictly speaking depth, for what the child experiences with the spool is the object's two-sidedness, like the moon in Frege's telescope: one through which it surrenders itself, the other in which it holds itself back forever. And this depth built upon the spool is the model of objectivity to which the mother, too, conforms: "reality" is what eludes. Now this elision that makes up the flipside of things can be established only because there is the *fort* and the *da*, the No and the Yes, because, that is, the initial opposition between absence and presence allows every speaking subject to posit in and through her/his discourse what is not. Language establishes the third dimension insofar as it is understood not as dimension number three but as the first dimension with respect to representation—the dimension according to which the imaginary scene is set, and at the extremity of which, so to speak, "reality" will be circumscribed by the test of words and actions.

Desire thus begins, as long as it is preceded, heralded, and marked by its procession of representatives, because the negativity of the object-sign begins and because the distance and tension—which forever separate the "interior" and the object—spread out. The representation of the drive, which is what constitutes desire, requires the possibility of the negative being established: such is the referential function of language. There is much in Freud's work to reassure those who fear that the *Verneinung* defends a straightforward and reductive thesis. Benveniste believes that Freud "reduced the polarity of linguistic affirmation and negation to the biopsychical mechanism of acceptance within oneself or rejection outside oneself, connected with the appreciation of good and evil."[19] A vulgar materialism with which the linguist cannot be satisfied: "But animals are also capable of this evaluation which leads to acceptance in the self or rejection outside the self." A truly linguistic negation is not merely expulsion, adds Benveniste, for in the order of language "negation is first acceptance." Why? "It has to set up for the express purpose of suppressing"; "a judgment of nonexistence has necessarily the formal status of a judgment of existence."[20] Indeed, Benveniste makes the analyst's right to interpret the No as a Yes dependent on the thetic power of discourse, a power whose inverted symptom is the speaking subject's powerlessness to make what she or he is speaking about disappear, even by denying it. Linguistic negation implies an affirmation, and, according to Benveniste, the latter consists in the necessary uttering of what is denied, in the "formal" position of what is denied in discourse. The positivity of the linguistic negative would therefore consist in the proposition, even a negative one, being positional. But when Freud writes, at the end of the *Verneinung*, that the "creation of the symbol of negation has endowed thinking with a first measure of freedom from the consequences of repression and, with it, from the compulsion of the pleasure principle,"[21] he invokes precisely the *symbol of negation* and, thus, the form of negative judgment to indicate what speech adds to (or takes away from) the pleasure principle and the pulsating of the drives. Far from the materialist reduction Benveniste feared, what is necessarily presupposed in negation is the transmutation of the drive into desire as it passes into language, and the fact, essential for the analyst, that the negative judgment—the grammarian's No, the analysand's denial—is like a repetition of the negation constitutive of judgment, a repetition of the pulsating of the drives, perhaps, but rerouted through the negativity of transcendence, through the play of language.[22]

For Freud, to deny is not and cannot be synonymous with expelling outside of the self as when the animal rejects what it dislikes. The act of judging is, argues Freud, the "continuation, along the lines of expendiency (*die zweckmässige Fortentwicklung*), of the original process by which the ego took things into itself or expelled them from itself, according to the pleasure principle."[23] This is at the furthest reaches of simply reducing the intellect to the drive: we are faced with an operation by which the pleasure-ego, wrapped in the pulsating of the drives, finds itself involved and repressed in a teleology, which is that of knowledge. No doubt, when Freud writes that "with the help of the symbol of negation, thinking frees itself from the restrictions of repression and enriches itself with material that is indispensable for its proper functioning,"[24] one may be struck by the dynamism he ascribes to this end. One could then argue that if thought needs to attain fulfillment, if it cannot do without repressed content, this is because it draws its energy from the same reservoir as the drives. This takes place, however, after the transmutation whereby the energy of the drives is bound in groups of invariant relations, forming systems. The *fort/da* relation is the simple and absolute model for this systematic binding, under the two criteria in play in reality-testing. On the one hand it signals the horizontal interval that makes possible, in the linguistic system, the anchoring of the terms by placing them in pairs of opposites, thus circumscribing the space where the object's "word-presentations" will take place. Yet on the other hand, as we pointed out, the child associates the *da* and the *fort* with an activity of presentation and concealment of the object, which this time sets the stage for the object's "thing-presentations" to appear. We recognize in these two axes—respectively, of signification (opposition) and of designation (thickness)—those of articulated language. It is in the referential determined by their intersection that the energy of the drives will find itself caught. This referentiality is integral to the reality principle; it is out of the question, therefore, to infer it from the "order" issued by the drives, which it represses while reality institutes itself. For Freud there are *two* principles of psychic "becoming," between which not the slightest continuity can be established, were it dialectical.[25] Any reconciliation (spiritualist or materialist) is illusory.

With Freud, *Bedeutung* is no longer taken as a merely theoretical distance: it is an *Entzweiung,* the splitting in two of what was "originarily one," *infans* [infancy] to the breast. All objectiveness [*objectité*] will come inscribe itself in the distance opened up by a loss. Perception presupposes this pulling apart, which will serve as model for the theory of knowledge: both the back and the front—that is, the deep negativity of the thing, of the object as something to-be-known—have their point of departure in this distance. Here the space of the *Bedeutung* is invigorated: a space where the eye moves, no doubt, but this eye is the symbol of desire; its perpetual mobility is the movement of desire. One must set forth the equivalence of knowing and desiring, which Socrates inaugurated and embodied. Wanting to know is implied in discourse: turning *around* its object, in deep space, the object always managing to escape by one of its facets. Being the object—the fifth mode of knowledge in the seventh Platonic Epistle[26]—is what makes possible and prohibits this *Entzweiung.* The latter places an unbridgeable interval *along the edge* of discourse. A voided edge. This void is the reason why when we speak, we are not what we are speaking of, and why our speech awaits its respondent (its reference), on the other side, just like our desire.

Does language [*langage*], then, hold this power of severing ties with the breast, with the pre-world? No, as we said, and as Freud conclusively showed, the ambiguity of the breast, of the "mother," goes back much further than the acquisition of language [*langue*]. Yet it is this acquisition that allows the ambiguity to appear as such; it is because the child has at its disposal the No (*fort*) of language [*langue*] that the mother's evasion—its hidden face, its thing-like thickness—can be posited. The quality of negative judgment will be able to provide, in the layout of language [*langue*], an "equivalent" of the thing's thickness. Language [*Le langage*] does not make up this thickness, which is, indeed, first a matter of the alternation of pleasing-displeasing, but it brings it to the fore; it is its phenomenological, not ontological, reason.

In borrowing these themes from Freud, we have begun to tackle only a small part of the problem. For the hypothetical splitting of the pre-world not only opens up the distance in which the eye settles on the edge of discourse. This tearing-away produces effects of distortion *in* discourse. A figure is lodged in the depth of our speech, operating like the matrix of these effects, attacking our words to make forms and images out of them. The space of desire paves the way for thoughts and takes them in. Through *Entzweiung* the object is lost; through phantasy, it is re-presented. We will need to return to this eye that no longer is peripheral, but buried deep in discourse.

Opposition and Difference

Beyond the Alternative

Signification does not exhaust meaning, but neither does signification combined with designation. We cannot be satisfied with this choice of two spaces, between which discourse—the system's as well as the subject's—insinuates itself. There exists another, figural space. One must assume it buried, for it shuns sight and thought; it indicates itself laterally, fleetingly, within discourses and perceptions, as what disturbs them. It is desire's own space, what is at stake in the struggle that painters and poets tirelessly wage against the return of the Ego and text.

In trying to characterize this space, or at least its effects in the facts of discourse or sight, one is not only attempting to separate it from the order of signification or from the depth of designation; rather, one positions oneself to approach the site where truth is at work. Truth is not to be found in the order of knowledge: one encounters it in its unruliness, as an event. Knowledge assumes the space of signification where all the syntactic limitations regulating the consistency of its discourse dwell; and inasmuch as it is referential discourse, it requires, too, the space of designation within which the knowledgeable speaker gauges the reference of her or his discourse.

Yet truth arises (*e-venit*) as that which is not in its place, essentially displaced, and as such destined to be elided: deprived of a place, neither foreseen nor pre-heard. Indeed the stage is set, in the two spaces of signification and of designation, for its effects to pass as mere mistakes, blunders due to inattention, to an ill-considered fitting of discursive elements, to the eye's improper adjustment. Everything is ready for the rubbing out of the event, for good form, for clear and precise thinking to be restored. Truth presents itself like a fall, like a slippage and an error, exactly the meaning of *lapsus* in Latin. The event clears a vertiginous space and time; untethered from its context or perceptual environment, this discontinuity or hovering goes hand in hand with anxiety: "*Quantum of anxiety in a freely floating state* . . . [which] is always ready to link itself with any suitable ideational content."[1] The unexpected is not anguishing because it is unexpected, as the enforcers of good order would claim; it is unexpected because it is anguishing, unexpected insofar as anxiety commingles with "presentations" (significations, designations) in which it appeared entirely out of place, affecting them in a mad way. For the expectancy not to be such that this madness is foreclosed or repressed, unwelcomed, or if it is welcomed, is disguised, that it lends itself to the event, this also requires on the part of the ear or the eye (the ear for discursive signification, the eye for representational designation) something free-floating, the deployment of a zone of eventness and, deep down, a disordering.

The attentive reader will have already understood on the basis of *Un coup de dés* that the deep space of chance where the encounter can take place with this madness—madness that no significative arrangement (throw of dice) will be able to abolish—is precisely that which Mallarmé unfolds in the well-measured, discrete expanse of typography. But he may have misjudged, as I did, the reach of this spatial transfer. What is called for now is to dispel the perceptual representation under which what is specifically the event was able to be covered up in our understanding of the Mallarmean situation, to show that we have not given full account of this situation by attributing the responsibility for it to the properties of the plastic expanse. Performing this disillusion will thus amount in particular to showing that the latter expanse is itself at stake in a battle between good and bad form, between the recognizable and the ordered on the one hand, and the unknown, the strange, and the anguishing, on the other.

It would be false to contend that we are always immersed in the world as though in a bath of perceptions and meanings. Nor have we said the last word on the subject of our spatiotemporal experience by characterizing it as an enwrapped depth, an immanent transcendence, a chiasm. The world, too, is open to events: it is prey to slips, to surges of non-immersive zones, to crises of "transcendence" without counterpart; worldly space and time can fail us, just as language can. This world of presentation, however much we thought we could anchor it in the body assumed to be one's own [*supposé propre*], thereby preserving it from the nullification of discourse and returning it to an undeniable presence, an originary faith, this world is not exempt from the risks of "meaninglessness" [*insignificance*]: it might be less exempt, but it is, above all, exempt differently. This time the meaninglessness will obviously not be the lack of linguistic signification (through non-lexicality or a-grammaticality). It will be the erasure of top and bottom, or of stereognosis, or night, or silence—all the losses of position of the relations between world and body, thetic losses: "Concerning the factors of silence, solitude and darkness, we can only say that they are actually elements in the production of the infantile anxiety from which the majority of human beings have never become quite free."[2] Claiming to consider perception outside of emotion is a misguided abstraction, for emotion would be impossible if our corporeal hold on the world were not, at its core, uncertain, if the possibility of a non-world were not given at the same time as its "certainty."[3] This possibility is not only a theoretical power to suspend the thesis of worldliness, but this power of *epoché*, insofar as it is not reducible only to a discursive denial [*dénégation*]—which, as we know, can always easily be turned around as an involuntary symptom of an assertion—itself derives from a specifically corporeal power of annihilation, of undoing the ties linking body and world. We normally experience (so to speak, for it is really the interruption of experience) this "inexperience" in the occurrences of orgasm and sleep. One could say that this inexperience depends on experience, that some of its edges abut, as it were, on what constitutes presentation, that even if there is no retention of presence in climax or deep sleep, these can only ever be not only thought but "lived" through difference, in opposition to the states of grasping of the world and of Dasein [*d'être-là*].

One cannot possibly refute this. But one should distinguish between this difference and the opposition that we said is the key to signification in the order of language, and one should especially dissociate this difference from the depth of the negation involved in the subject's experience of the sign. As we will see, difference is neither the flat negation that maintains the elements of a (linguistic) system apart, nor that deep-seated denial that opens the referential or representational field in front of discourse. In attempting to define the field of difference it is hardly coincidental that it should be the event, the slip of the tongue, or the orgasm that come to mind as examples. For in each of these "cases," in contrast to what occurs in signification or designation, *the gap is not what stands between two terms* located at the same level, inscribed on the same support, and possibly reversible, pending certain operative conditions, but on the contrary *the "relation" of two "states," heterogeneous yet adjoining in an irreversible anachrony.* Hegel was right to argue that the mind quickly heals its wounds: this is because there is no such thing as a wound, as far as language is concerned. Nor was Merleau-Ponty wrong to subsume all relations of the body to the world under originary faith, since both the one and the other need to be there together, bound by this faith, or else neither are there. Nevertheless, we will be able to detect effects of difference as far as in the discursive order, and as far as in the perceptive order, without even having to invoke silence and obscurity, that is, the void of one and the other order. All there needs to be within these orders are nullifications irreducible to the intervals of opposition or to the depth of designation, mad events, that is, operations or effects of operations calling for an "order" that cannot come under the negativities we have identified *precisely because this order only registers itself negatively there,* an order we may thus be tempted to assume is positive. However, the Yes of this order, upsetting the No of discourse and the No of perception, is that of desire as death drive.

Nonhuman Sex

Let us begin with discourse once more. If difference is not opposition, this is because the terms do not belong to the same being or the same order. In the case of language, this means that one term belongs to language and the other does not. A critique of opposition leads therefore again to that of Hegelian dialectics. Yet this time it is not a question of identifying, in the latter's position, the elision of the sensory and the distance of designation, in other words of waging a critique from a philosophy of perception that can only be thought of as a philosophy of the subject (however corporeal). One must go beyond the principle of subjectivity as well as of non-subjectivity, past the system/subject alternative, challenge not only dialectics but also dia-deictics inasmuch as the latter, like the former, is inclined to erode sensory difference and to swathe the body in the *order* of a world. Let us follow, for a moment, a radical critical observation made by Marx, taken from a passage in which he reflects on a particularly provocative claim of Hegel's *Philosophy of Right.* Here is this claim: "It is one of the fundamental principles of logic, that a definite element, which, when standing in opposition, has the bearing of an extreme, ceases to be in opposition and becomes an *organic* element, when it is observed to be at the same time a *mean.*"[4] Marx says of the interplay of these moments: "They are like Janus with two-faced heads (*Janusköpfe*), which now show themselves from the front and now from the back, with a diverse character at either side. What was first intended to be the mean between two extremes now itself occurs as an extreme; and the other of the two extremes, which had just been mediated by it, now intervenes as an extreme (because of the distinction from the other extreme) between its extreme and its mean. This is a kind of mutual reconciliation society (*Es ist eine wechselseitige Bekomplimentierung*)."[5] This is, adds Marx, the story of the man who attempts to break up a fistfight and who ends up having to be separated himself; or of the lion in *A Midsummer Night's Dream* who states "I am the lion, and I am not the lion, but Snug": "So here each extreme is sometimes the lion of opposition and sometimes the Snug of mediation."[6]

However—and here we note that a separation from religious dialectics is under way—"Actual extremes cannot be mediated with each other precisely because they are actual extremes. But neither are they in need of mediation, because they are opposed in essence (*Wesen*). They have nothing in common with one another; they neither need nor complement one another. The one does not carry in its womb the yearning, the need, the anticipation of the other."[7] One could argue that "Les extrêmes se touchent,"[8] that "the North and South poles attract each other" just as "the female and the male sexes also attract each other," and that through the union of their differences they constitute what is human. Now, indeed, the poles and the sexes are not different beings (*Wesen* [*êtres*]): they are only differentiations within a single being, whereas "*Truly real* extremes would be Pole and *non*-Pole, human and *non*-human gender,"[9] they would be two beings [*êtres*] and not only two existences in the same being [*être*]. Hegelian logic confuses "the difference (*Differenz*) within the existence of one essence [*être*]" with "the *actual* opposition of mutually exclusive essence [*êtres*]."[10] Yet "no matter how firmly both extremes appear, in their existence, to be actual and to be extremes, it still lies only in the *essence* [*être*] of the one to be an extreme, and it does not have for the other the *meaning of true actuality*. The one infringes upon the other, but they do not occupy a common position."[11]

The subject of the above discussion matters little here.[12] What does is what is sought, namely, the possibility to think a relation through without including it in a system of oppositions; in other words, insofar as thinking and placing the object in such a system are one and the same operation, the possibility to think a relation through without thinking it. If Marx arrives, at the end of this passage, at the notion of *Stellung*, this is because positioning appears to him as what in thinking remains unthought. This *Stellung* would no doubt need to be compared with the *Position* Kant discusses in the refutation of the ontological argument to press the point that precisely the difference between the thought [*le pensé*] and the given [*le donné*] depends solely on the latter's position, that thought [*la pensée*] cannot give itself the given, but only the possible, and that if it takes possession of the possible through an analytic judgment, it can think the given only through the enigma of a synthetic judgment. And we know that this Kantian synthesis, in contrast to Hegel's, is not in turn reducible to analysis.

Marx argues that it is not a matter of positional difference between the male and the female sexes: the *no* at stake here is merely that of the systematic interval. This means that from one of the sexes the other can be thought, engendered, through a simple eidetic variation consisting in a nullification that reveals the resulting term's complementary nature with the initial term. It is this complementary nature that is granted from the outset with attraction. Marx starts with the example of polarity because the metaphor of the pole in itself betrays the essence of opposition: the mind bent on analyzing a pole can grasp its essence only as a complementary function and must therefore devise—literally, deduce—the possibility of an anti-pole. Here, in the organization of natural things, we find a kind of mimetism of the order of concepts whereby the earth's polarity reproduces in the gravitational field what conceptual dialectics produces in that of thoughts. When this complementarity is applied to the order of the sexes, it inscribes them in a possible, thinkable totality, in which each one is but a moment for the other, an altogether transitory moment of detotalization, a negligible remnant quickly sutured in the comforting conclusion that this negative moment presented itself as opposite only through abstraction, and that it was merely a development in the constitution of the initial moment into truth. This is basically a religious operation, one that does not apply to all religions—the religion of the infinite does not fall into the unifying movement of totality—but that does apply to the redemptive function of archaic religion, which consists in the confession and atonement of sin, in its position, within a (mythical) "system," as negative dialectics, that is, as simple opposition.

As far as "sexual difference" is concerned, it would hardly be inconsistent to argue, closely following Freud, that the function of religion in general, and of Hegelian dialectics in particular, is precisely the transcription and inscription of this difference as simple opposition on the level of thinkable dialectics. For the question of this difference is that of castration, and every religion, as cultural phenomenon, aims to absorb the event of castration into the advent of the condition of the son, that is, the recuperation of meaning and violence in signification. Thus, by imagining real difference as that between human and nonhuman sex, Marx comes close to what will constitute Freud's object of study, since he refuses to suture the difference between the sexes into the male/female opposition; since he entertains, if only for a second, the possibility that there is in the fact of human sex (male as well as female) an unredeemable violence, the reference to an exteriority (nonhuman gender) that can find no place in the conscious order of what constitutes legitimacy; and since, lastly, he concedes that the issue of the sexes is not at all that of the polarization between them, but on the contrary that of their non-attraction and unthinkable distinction.[13]

It is untrue that the female sex holds for the male "the meaning of true actuality," nor the male for the female. They hold this meaning for one another only in the order of the appearance of desire, in the order of the conscious, already instituted text where the interplay between man and woman can be read on the surface of what one calls human relations. This surface is that of reality and of the imaginary. On the other stage, the sexes are not complementary. The truth of sex does not lie in the remark, often made by Freud, that there is basically one sexuality, which is male. Even if it is true that the girl discovers her own sex only later and comparatively, and boys and girls perceive the female sex as absence, such a *position* still remains that of sexuality, in other words, of a system in which one goes from male to female through negation, and not the position in the order specific to desire. This order distinguishes itself in that the acknowledgment of this absence exceeds, by far, the acknowledgment of an absence, but that it gives rise to the strangest, most rambling presentations and at the same time to the most unexpected affects. When, in possession of the North Pole, one discovers the South, one is not gripped by the violence of an irremediable event requiring all the power of the imaginary to quell through presentations, and all the disorienting power of the affect to displace onto other representatives. Quite the opposite: such a discovery is that of a complement, a form of recognition. But the subject's entry into desire by way of castration is always something like its death. The No of nonhuman, inhuman (*unmenschlich*) sex indicates difference, another position (stage) that unseats that of consciousness—that of discourse and reality.

Opposition Is the Significative Difference

The discourse: "Language [*langue*] requires only difference. . . . In stating this, one should go much further and consider every value of language [*langue*] as oppositive, and not as positive, absolute."[14] "In language [*langue*] there is nothing but differences, and no positive quantity."[15] Can one distinguish opposition from difference in Saussure? To disentangle the two terms, Godel refers to a passage of the *Course* from 1910–1911: "In a state of language [*langue*], there are only differences. . . . When we arrive at the terms themselves, resulting from the relation between signified and signifier, then we can speak of opposition. . . . Because these differences mutually condition each other, we will have something that can look like positive terms, through the vis-à-vis, the correspondence between such and such a difference of the idea and such and such a difference of the sign. We will then be in a position to speak of opposition, on the basis of this positive element of the combination."[16] For Saussure, therefore, opposition involves both difference and relation. Difference, writes Godel, "in itself is indeed a negative character: if *a* is different from *b*, this only means that *a* is not *b*, regardless of their degree of non-coincidence; but the moment a relation otherwise exists between *a* and *b,* they become members of the same system, and difference turns into opposition." And, he adds, "it then appears that, in a system of signs, difference must always coincide with an opposition and the negative character can never be observed in the system in its pure state."[17]

The question left unanswered in Saussure's text is whether what conceals difference in the system is indeed the "thickness" of the linguistic sign, that is to say, the effect of signification. In accepting this explanation, does one not cross again the line separating a philosophy of the system and a reflection centered on the speaking subject? If opposition is made to depend on signification—accepting that the latter, in its opacity, is given only in the experience of speech—must one conclude that it is the speaker who organizes in a totality terms that are different in themselves, and who, through her or his positional activity, transforms them into opposites? An untenable claim, insofar as it would place the position of linguistic relations under the responsibility of the speaking subject. The criterion used by Godel (even though it later falls by the wayside somewhat) seems more apposite: it is the system itself that conceals the differences, for it includes the terms into relations, thereby limiting and measuring pure non-coincidence into invariable intervals. The "positivity" of the opposition consists in the measurement of the interval. If, then, "one can define opposition as a significative difference,"[18] this is not due to the signifier's relation to the signified, but because of the regulation of the spacings in the signifying order.

This is the principle that Jakobson strictly applies at the level of distinctive features: "All differences of phonemes in any language [*langue*] can be resolved into simple and undecomposable binary oppositions of distinctive features. Hence all phonemes of any language [*langue*] can be fully dissociated into further indivisible distinctive features."[19] The hypothesis of the "primary triangle" developed in 1956, even if it betrays a rather debatable geneticism, rests entirely on the polarizing power of units by opposition: articulation of the *p* / *a* couple on the vertical "vocalic" axis, followed by that of the *p* / *t* couple on the horizontal "consonantal" axis, etc.[20] I am not qualified to judge the linguistic value of this hypothesis, but what is certain is that it offers a kind of epistemological model on two counts. First, being a figure closed upon itself, the triangle, like the circle, thereby illustrates the system's closed nature. But where, in the circle, all that is needed to generate all the points is a segment of a straight line (the radius) and an operation (rotation of the segment around one of its extremities), to build Jakobson's triangle one needs to determine two intervals (the segment constituting the height and that which forms the base) and an angle (formed by the two segments).

It would be easy to show that the same rule of the invariance of intervals determines and makes signify the lexical units (*teaching / education*) or the grammatical morphemes (*they captured the city / he captured the city, we will sing / we are singing*). The commutation test is convincing only because the intervals are measured. Sheer noncoincidence—in other words, pure difference—cannot lend itself to any recognition. It is worth remembering that in the phonologists' view, it is by means of signification that the relevant character of a phoneme in a given language [*langue*] can be tested. This passage through signification, performed by the speaker, refers us back to the invariant organization of the intervals in the system. One even finds this characteristic in generative linguistics, albeit no longer in the guise of an opposition as in phonology, nor is it evaluated by a commutation test. Nonetheless, if one takes a simple rewrite rule such as N P → Det + N, which reads as "the nominal group can be rewritten as: determiner + noun," it becomes apparent that we are dealing with a transformation rule prescribing the operations authorized on the symbols to the left of the arrow. It is noteworthy that by adding generativism to structuralism, linguistics has reinforced the *positive* aspect of the interval to the point that simple difference, understood as noncoincidence, appears entirely concealed under rules that no longer have merely a diacritical function but positively a genetic one. Still, this difference persists at the most basic level, which Chomsky calls grammaticality. For here again the linguist will seek confirmation that a particular organization is grammatical or not by resorting to linguistic feeling [*sentiment linguistique*]. It is easy to grasp that the gap between the given sentence and the model of grammaticality provided by the rewrite rules, if the gap is such that the former passes for a-grammatical without, however, being nonsensical, will determine a modality of meaning that is no longer that of lexical or syntactic signification based on the system of oppositions, but that, precisely, derives from a difference. This is the case in poetic language. One could say that the latter is to ordinary language what difference is to opposition. Difference does not *enter* the system of oppositions, it *exits* the system. Like Artaud's scream: "I do not know / but / I do know that / space, / time, / dimension, / becoming, / future, / destiny, / being, / non-being, / self, / non-self, / are nothing to me; / but there is a thing / which is something / only one thing / which is something, / and which I feel / because it wants / TO GET OUT: / the presence of my bodily suffering. . . ."[21]

And if one had to provide an example to show how "the presence of my bodily suffering" *gets out* in words, here is one: "—a its the hole question / if God goes or if God stays / now the question is posed / They dance the dance of the vile friction / of the whoran with the wôman and / and of the coupling of ron and saun."[22] The case is extreme, and one will eventually manage to find the signifiers and the signifieds suggested by the deviant units (*woman* → *wôman*; *Rhône* and *Saône* → *ron* and *saun*). Yet the shift in spelling (which marks a corresponding shift in Artaud's declamation) is such that it *gets* discourse *out* of the system of oppositions and invests it with potential affects and presentations.

Trace of a Working-over

Let us try to clarify this by taking a more accessible example where the "exit" is less fraught with risk:

I print you / I swim you / I music you,[23]

and where the deviance (the difference) looms progressively larger, so to speak: *to print* is a verb that ordinarily does not accept for its object to be animate; *to swim* is an intransitive taken here as transitive; *music* is a noun displaced and used as verb. But let us put aside for now these variations of interval and simply compare—to render palpable what is at stake with difference and not with opposition—the phrase *I music you* with a "correct" utterance such as *I know you.* There is an effect of meaning, which I call here signification, that is conveyed immediately with the last statement. If *I know you* is endowed with signification, this is because it enters into virtual opposition to *I know him, you know yourself, I don't know you. . . .* The terms, or the relations that are in opposition to the stated term or relation, are virtually present, virtually co-present (or co-absent). That is to say that their absence is that of an element belonging to what Freud calls the preconscious. These elements (terms, relations) were put aside when the speaker (or whatever held this function) uttered this sentence; they were not selected to appear in the statement. But this does not mean that they suffered any disruption; on the contrary, it is because they are there, virtually, in their assigned place in the interlocutors' preconscious—that is to say, because there is a code, and this code is shared by the speaking subjects—that the utterance possesses its signification and that this signification can be transmitted. The system is *absent,* and will always be, since it is in the nature of the order of structure never to present itself as does the utterance: the (vocal or graphic) signifier is a sensory datum whereas the system of signifiers is not.

However, this absence of the system—and therefore of the terms or relations that the utterance leaves aside, and in opposition to which it signifies—is in no way the result of a rejection, of operations associated with the process of repression such as displacement or condensation. It results instead from a concealment that is itself measured. Proof of this can be found in this essential fact: the statement *I know you,* taken in itself as a simple signifier (i.e., without reference to the situation in which it is uttered) contains no charge value, no difference of tension. The situation in which it takes place may grant it such a value, but the statement is denied the latter in the signifying order proper. In this order it does not act as event: it is possible.

The same cannot be said for *I music you. Music* is not in opposition to the terms that one would expect to find here (*I cradle you, I charm you*). These terms are not kept virtually co-present (or co-absent) in their place; they are displaced, or more exactly, *music* is a displaced term. The interval separating *music* from its neighbors is not a measured, coded interval. This interval does not belong to the system. The system is not kept in its place, intact in its virtuality. The concealment that accompanies the statement *I music you* is no longer the erasure of the system in the dusk (or preconscious) thanks to which *I know you* stands in broad daylight. The withdrawal of the absent elements does not create virtuality, but violence. *Music* is a term actualized through transgression; its presence bears witness to the fact that there lies underground not a system but forces, an energetics that disrupts the ordering of the system. When you produce a verb with a noun, an event happens: the system of the rules of language [*langue*] not only is unable to account for this novel use, but opposes it, resists it; the relation that arises between it and the statement is one of conflict.

I music you is like a symptom: a compromise between an order (of language) and its other (the pleasure principle?). The symptom carries the truth: something appears where one does not expect it. If I choose to call the statement *I music you* a figure, I should add that this figure (and I would postulate: every figure) is linguistically charged—that is, acts as linguistic event—because it is an effect of *discharge* issued from another order. By taking another point of reference, every figure is destined to be neutralized in a form of script [*écriture*] (what is, for example, commonly referred to as the erosion of metaphors; however, it is not a question of erosion, but of the neutralization of discourse's other by discourse, of the signification of the nonsensical). Before this neutralization, the figure offers itself as a straying *trace* that defies reading, that is not a letter, and that can be grasped only in energetic terms. This figure is supported by displacements, condensations, and distortions. This means that *before* its incorporation in the order of language (for example in a rhetoric), the figure is the mark, on the units and rules of language, of a power that treats these units and rules like things. It is the trace of a *working-over* [*travail*] and not of knowledge by signification. Through this working-over, what is fulfilled is desire.

Notes: One should make this distinction between the two areas (of the system and the force) not merely into an opposition within a system, but into a difference such that language cannot lay claim to what lies beyond the system and signify it positively in itself. Where the *Id* dwells, *I* will never come to pass.

When Benveniste corrects Lacan in concluding that dream-work is closer to rhetoric than to linguistics, at issue is not a change of level within language, for rhetoric, while it is indeed the reconstitution of an order comparable to that which holds among elementary articulations, is still just that, its *re*-constitution. Any form of rhetoric is a deferred language, and what defers language *in this way* is not in language but outside of it, like an untamed silence or a cry exterior to the system. With this remark, Benveniste acknowledges that there is a mode of bestowal-concealment [*donation-occultation*] that is *meaningful* in a way that is irreducible to the modality of signification.

This view corresponds to the irreducibility Freud recognized between secondary process and primary process (in the first topography) or between reality principle + Eros on the one hand and death drive on the other (in the second topography).

In light of these two modes of signifying, the methodological unity accepted by structuralism, in particular when it applies to complex orders (sentence, tale [*récit*], genre), requires the difference we detect to be *crushed.* With this postulated unity, and with the displacements and condensations to which its search gives rise in the field of metalanguage, a desire is fulfilled. (The reader will notice that certain tools are or will be assembled here that are necessary for the critique of ideologies—among them structuralist.)

Sex and Dispositio

Let us now turn to a much more complex order of discourse than *I music you,* and at the same time a much less explicit discursive genre with respect to what interests us: a mythological tale, for example the one Lévi-Strauss borrows from an account by Lloyd Warner:

> These North Australians [the Murngin of Arnhem Land] explain the origin of things by a myth which is also the basis of an important part of their ritual. At the beginning of time, the Wawilak sisters set off on foot towards the sea, naming places, animals and plants as they went. One of them was pregnant and the other carried her child. Before their departure they had both indeed had incestuous relations with men of their moiety.

> After the birth of the younger sister's child, they continued their journey and one day stopped near a water hole where the great snake Yurlunggur lived who was the totem of the Dua moiety to which the sisters belonged. The older sister polluted the water with menstrual blood. The outraged python came out, caused a deluge of rain and a general flood and then swallowed the women and their children. When the snake raised himself the waters covered the earth and its vegetation. When he lay down again the flood receded.[24]

The structural analysis of this tale yields the following system of semantic opposition:

sacred, pure	male	superior	Rain
profane, impure	female	inferior	Earth

The natural and social context is as follows: the Murngin live in an area where there are two highly differentiated seasons: one of great drought, the other of great rainfall, associated with southeasterly winds and northwesterly winds, respectively. During the rainy season, large tides flood the coastal plain over several kilometers inland. The Murngin then disperse and take refuge in the hills. At this point they are without resources. With the return of the dry season, the sea withdraws and vegetation grows in abundance; the population then gathers in the plain. From this context we can draw a second table of oppositions:

rainy season	NW winds	distress	dispersal
dry season	SE winds	abundance	Reuniting

Lévi-Strauss believes it would be contradictory to consider the second table as an extension of the first—what is sacred would then at the same time be distress, what is abundance would at the same time be impurity—and that mediations must therefore be found. This is how he interprets the function of an initiation ritual concerning the young men. Through this ritual, a third term is instituted (the non-initiate), allowing the units of the two lines to communicate with one another, that is, the male and the female:

Man	man	initiate	Pure
woman	youth	non-initiate	Impure

Initiation clearly fulfills the function of a third term, third not because it ranks as such, but because it condenses in it the first and second, and thus enables the mind to restore circulation between seemingly contradictory elements. The Hegelian *Aufhebung* (and indeed Christian redemption through the mediation of Jesus) belongs to this same model, which is that of every religious discourse.[25] Note that in fact the introduction of the third term is the product of an operation of *condensation.* The non-initiate is at once man and woman, good and bad, pure and impure. This condensation transgresses the system of oppositions, since it conjoins what is separate in the system. If, therefore, the resulting term (the non-initiate) is granted some meaning, this meaning cannot be of the same kind as the signification of the opposed terms in the semantic tables. It would be only for the sake of convenience to confine ourselves to the table above, for then we would pretend to count the initiate/non-initiate couple as belonging to the same system of oppositions as pure/impure and man/woman, when in fact its function is to rid the system of the separating bar. Nonetheless, one has to admit that the difference embodied in the condensed term (non-initiate) remains concealed in the institution, precisely because the latter aims to absorb the discrepancies between myth and socionatural "reality." The institution of the non-initiate functions as a symptom because it testifies to the process of a desire (desire to bring together sacredness and fecundity, that is, to reconcile meaning and life, or, just as well, to overcome castration) working over the mythical "text" as well as the social and natural "context," at the same time that it falsifies desire under the guise of a relevant element of the system governing both text and context.

One may find the same disguised-disguising [*masquée-masquante*] operation of condensation in the very organization of mythical discourse, where one will discover the trace of desire engaged in the act of forming an element equivalent to the *non-initiate,* but within the order of discourse and taking only into consideration this discourse's *form.* This form is cast aside in the construction of the table of the semantic structure (though admittedly it is in principle irrelevant to this table).[26] What I call *form* of mythical discourse corresponds to a large extent to what in Latin rhetoric was referred to as the *dispositio* of the harangue or the tale [*récit*]. If one determines large semantic units corresponding to the "functions" that Vladimir Propp identifies in his selection of folktales, then the *dispositio* would be defined by the order of presentation of these functions. Inasmuch as we are dealing with a tale, this order is subject to the consideration of verisimilitude. One cannot return before having left, prevail before having fought, die without being born, be redeemed before having sinned: such are the minimum requirements of the reality principle. In truth, even these basic requirements are not always met.[27] Notwithstanding, let us assume that the grouping of functions is always consistent with the reality principle; the latter's requirements in any case would not account for the overall disposition offered by the tale. The reality principle does not require that the "schema covering the entire development of the tale"[28] open with a committed wrongdoing, transition to an endured punishment that repairs the damage, and end with a reward. To argue (in the words of Claude Bremond) that the model Propp proposes for the Russian folktale represents "the most economical arrangement toward which the combination of 'motifs' available to storytellers gravitates, as if towards its state of perfect equilibrium" and to assert that "the sequence of functions is the 'good form' of Russian folktales"[29] is to resolve the question of the form or *dispositio* in strictly Gestaltist terms. This stands to reason, since this form must indeed be "better" than others, having imposed and maintained itself, but it fails to question the principle of goodness and badness of forms. Here the analysis of the condensed third can show us the way, allowing us to see that the good form is a form of compromise between death drive and pleasure principle, between destruction and preservation of a complex set.

I am not in a position to demonstrate this on Russian folktales. But let us go back to the Murngin myth and lay out the functions successively presented in the tale, marking them as + or — depending on whether they belong to the upper or lower row in the semantic tables. We arrive at the following disposition:

— + — ± +

which corresponds to the sequence:

incest, naming of beings and things, pollution of the water hole, punishment, fertile lands.

It is apparent that the initial couple — + is recurrent (the pollution of the water hole repeating the incest). The simplified version would thus read:

— ± +,

where ± symbolizes the punishment inflicted by the totem snake: positive through the agent's sacred nature and the purification that follows the act; negative through the barrenness and desolation it sows over the earth-woman. This punishment is the exact equivalent, in the institutional system, of the term *non-initiate.* But the formation of this condensed term, as an element in the tale, cannot be considered apart from the tale's form itself. This is how: if one wanted to transcribe the "contradiction" that emerges from the semantic tables, one would obtain the following set:

(1) *The impure season is good, the pure season is bad.*

Now, in its disposition, the tale articulates these two clauses as follows:

(2) *If the impure season is good, this is thanks to the punishment (that is, to the bad) inflicted by the pure.*

Several operations are necessary to go from (1) to (2):

(a) The formation of the condensed term *punishment.*

(b) The subsuming of the second clause in (1), in the form: if X, then Y.

(c) The inversion (or reversal) of *the pure is bad* into *the bad through the pure.*

These operations do not appear in the semantic tables, nor can they be deduced from the latter, as they constitute the support of mythical discourse's *form.* If this support remains a blind spot in structuralist discourse on mythical discourse, this is because it is transgressive in relation to the semantic tables and their corresponding syntax, that is, either it is irrelevant as to the chosen methodological strategy, or this method is irrelevant as to the support. It may very well be that the operations (b) and (c) are not independent, and (b) no doubt merely a rationalization (secondary revision) of (c). One would then have a condensation and a two-term maximum displacement (or reversal) as the fundamental operations upholding the *dispositio.* These operations do not belong to the secondary (logical) process, but to the primary process: they lead into the discourse of the event, that is, of difference. Certainly once a so-called opening situation is created, an action may or may not be set in motion, and this act may or may not be successful; if a choice is called for, it is indeed due to the "unidimensionality of the temporal segments whose bundle makes up the story."[30] Yet this constraint (that of discourse's linearity) in no way explains why there would be an "opening," that is, a wrongdoing at the outset in the order of the signified, nor why the tale would be devoted to erasing it through "illogical" devices in the order of the signifier. "Good form" owes its very existence to the prior occurrence of a bad event (which is a pleonasm). What is important to understand is that the work of form is signifying in itself, but signifying in another way than linguistic signifiers that draw their signifying power from the system of oppositions to which they belong. The *dispositio* of the myth is both a trace of the primary process and its suturing. The ambivalence is double. In the signified, incest and its lethal impact on the social group are traces of desire, while punishment represents desire's repression and the cultural transmutation of values. In the signifier, desire presents itself negatively as the story's beginning, as *difference,* such that there is something to tell because there is something to restore; but operations (a) and (c) take on the role of censorship to suture difference and transform it into opposition. It should be quite obvious that by considering only the opposition *man : woman :: pure : impure,* one falls victim to the myth's function of deceit, blocking out the work of truth that is next to it. Here again sex is foremost nonhuman, non-opposite, transgressive with regard to oppositions. And it is the tale's *dispositio* that, in the signifier, hints at this brutality of the primary process by covering it up.

Time Represses

The temporal configuration comprised in *dispositio* is not only that of the myth, but of history. Of course, from the former to the latter there is a considerable shift. The time of myth is held to be nonhomogenous to that of the speaking subject, whereas that of history seems to be an extension of this subject's historicity. Moreover, this shift itself corresponds to a very deep rift in the position of the social with respect to meaning. In the archaic position, the signified is absent (*in illo tempore* [at that time]) but the signifier is active; from the organization of men in the *polis* and the appearance of the political, the signifier seems lost, sacredness finds itself in crisis, while the signified increasingly aligns itself with the human subject in its presence to itself. Put differently, in the myth reconciliation is achieved (in uchronia); in history, we are in the process of achieving it. Nevertheless, setting this shift aside for a moment, it is legitimate to recognize the same configuration in the organization of time according to the Murngin, Condorcet, Hegel, or certain Marxists (like Plekhanov): for all of these this organization has the function of absorbing a primary event through the institution of a third term and a *dispositio* of the discourse signifying history as redemption of this event. One could object that this figure concerns the *content* of the discourse, not the *form* of temporality itself, and that the latter frees itself completely from history in the work of Augustine, Kierkegaard, or Husserl. Thus opposed to history conceived of in objectivity is a temporality described entirely as flux of the lived experiences of consciousness, which would constitute the noetic pole of the thinking of history. And this form of interior time has little to do, one could argue further, with the *dispositio* observed in the myth and assumed applicable to history.

I am not so certain. Does the *dispositio* change when one goes from a reflection on history as general organization of the states of humanity to the analysis of temporality as organization of the lived experiences of consciousness? Actually, the entire question may be made to pivot on the difference/opposition couple. In myth, and still to a large extent in so-called rational history (Enlightenment history), *dispositio* is an oppositive organization intended to make initial difference enter into the signifying system. For Condorcet, this event is the obscurantism of priests and despots. This is a true event, coming from elsewhere, impossible for an Enlightenment thinker to account for, a given that the philosophy of history nonetheless transforms into a moment. The stated problem appears altogether different in an analysis of the internal consciousness of time, becoming that of the unity of the temporally diverse in consciousness. The question here is: how is the non-present (the future, the past) present? We know that Husserl's search for an answer led him in the direction of a hyper-presence capable of containing in its form not only the lived present but also its horizons of retention and protention, and which in his last manuscripts he called Living Present.[31]

If one remains wedded to the problems of origin and subject, one will become aware of the fact that this Living Present is not a present at all, that it is instead only an absence, and that one must come to terms with an absolutely archaic interval, with an archi-interval that cannot be overcome in any presence, that is, in the un-intervalled [*du non-écarté*]. One could argue that what produces the synthesis is not itself unitary, thus re-engaging with what was most subtle in the Kantian problematic of time and the I. This might, however, come at the cost of the other critical approach.

Freud wrote in 1920:

> At this point I shall venture to touch for a moment upon a subject which would merit the most exhaustive treatment. As a result of certain psycho-analytic discoveries, we are today in a position to embark on a discussion of the Kantian theorem (*Satz*) that time and space are "necessary forms of thought". We have learnt that unconscious mental processes are in themselves "timeless". This means in the first place that they are not ordered temporally, that time does not change them in any way (*die Zeit nichts an ihnen verändert*) and that the idea of time (*die Zeitvorstellung*) cannot be applied to them. These are negative characteristics which can only be clearly understood (*deutlich*) if a comparison is made with conscious mental processes. On the other hand, our abstract idea of time seems to be wholly derived from the method of working (*Arbeitsweise*) of the system *Pcpt.-Cs.* and to correspond to a perception on its own part of that method of working (*einer Selbstwahrnehmung derselben*). This mode of functioning may perhaps constitute another way of providing a shield against stimuli (*ein anderer Weg des Reizschutzes*). I know that these remarks must sound very obscure, but I must limit myself to these hints.[32]

In going from mythical belief or the philosophy of history to the phenomenological analysis of the time of consciousness, I do not believe one *leaves behind* the preconscious system. Admittedly, it would be difficult to argue that Husserl theorizes the "not yet" as a redemption of the "now" or the "already past." However, one can assert—and this is what characterizes the continued presence in the preconscious—that the construction of the notion of Living Present obeys the same requirement as that of a third term, that is, the requirement of a systematic placing in opposition.[33] In this case what the third term mediates is no longer the – and + of myth or history, but the – and the + *of consciousness*. The function of the Living Present is to unify what offers itself with what does not. Despite the emphasis critique places on the fact that this unification itself does not offer itself, it remains in the shadow of the preconscious, in the order of the opposition, for it is clear that within this order there is absence: the absence of the terms initially paired with a term selected by the speaker, which she or he then eliminates in the course of speaking. The absence and non-presentability of the Living Present is no more than the absence—as it appears to the speaking subject—involved in every oppositional system and that literally makes it signify. From this observation regarding the absence of the Living Present one could develop a philosophy of the system and/or the subject. In so doing we would be again overlooking this fundamental fact: that the system and the Ego play the part of defense against the "stimuli," as Freud puts it, and that the archi-present (i.e., absent) *dispositio* that holds together the "already past," the "now," and the "not yet" constitutes itself over another "order" to contain it.

How does this other order appear? If it cannot appear as order, this is not because, by definition, an order is never wholly present, but because it is not an order. By this I mean, because it is not a *chronic dispositio* governing what seems to be the basic condition of any form of temporality, namely the distribution of elements in "before" and "after," in "already past" and "not yet." In reality this *dispositio* is an effect of language [*langage*]. It would no doubt be easy to show that the articulation of the temporal continuum varies considerably from one language [*langue*] to another, as well as the modalities of expression of this articulation (through adverbs, verb tenses, and nouns). Yet all languages contain the *I*, and therefore the postulate of the presence of a present and of the present of a presence, as a focal point in relation to which the periphery of the temporal field is organized along the main past/future axis. What Husserl describes in terms of vision could be rephrased in terms of diction. Thus phenomenological reflection remains in the order of discourse, that is, in the order of what distributes data in a set of positions that constitutes them as meaningful. Difference can be grasped in the order of the temporal as the non-temporality this order aims to quell. Difference is the indifference to this order. This is what Freud meant by the timelessness of the "primary psychical process."[34] And let us not fear being radical, let us follow in the footsteps of Freud, who had the courage to write: "In themselves [the unconscious processes] cannot be cognized, indeed are even incapable of carrying on their existence; for the system *Ucs.* is at a very early moment overlaid by the *Pcs.* which has taken over access to consciousness and to motility."[35] Out of the question, after such a statement, to confuse what *exits* the temporal system—what can only enter it by exiting it, what can only be in it by being absent from it—with what is in it as condition of possibility. Opposition is the condition for the preconscious system, including for temporality, to exist; difference is the threat of its impossibility.

What is outside time "acts" within temporality simultaneously as past and future. This action accounts for the fact that what is familiar, *das Heimliche,* which is also what is hidden, is *at the same time* what is strange, unsettling, *das Unheimliche.*[36] This means that what is about to happen, or what is happening, *has happened.* Freud stresses that anxiety does not follow from frightening *content,* but only from the frightening element being "something repressed which returns."[37] The *Unheimliche* is repressed *Heimliche,* the *Un-* being the mark of repression. The relation between what is assumed "past" and what comes, the present or imminent event, is not really that of temporal diachrony, but of repression.[38] And it is one of the characteristics of repression to make what in fact is still active (and still hidden) pass as something past, to deploy in visible temporality what is not and never was a future moving toward the past by coming to the present. Here the protective function of the temporal system comes into relief. When we say what occurs *has occurred,* the temporal system entitles us to understand that there is a cause, an initial trauma, which is an effect of recurrence of a past event: nothing more is needed to repress the event, since a past event is a nonevent. Clearly, it is the temporal system itself that functions here as mediator. Mediation is no longer given in a third term, in a signified, as was the case in the form of the myth; rather mediation is given, in a strictly formal way, in *dispositio* itself, while repression has shifted from the content, where it was relatively easy to uncover, to the form itself in which one plans to uncover it.

Note: In moving from Hegelian to Feuerbachian discourse, one does not leave behind ideology (read: the secondary process as rejection). Instead one goes from an ideology in which mediation is signified to an ideology in which it is eliminated in the signified and transferred into the signifier itself: existential discourse, by its very *position,* takes on the role of mediator. The same goes for temporality. But the real temporal disarray is that the event does not appear where it should, where everything is ready to receive it, that is to say, in the future.

Laterality

Let us try to locate the modality of difference in perceptual space. The visual field undergoes a "correction," a constant leveling, which aims to eliminate difference and homogenize space into a system of oppositions. For the speaking animal, the most spontaneous treatment of perceptual space is inscription [*écriture*], that is to say, abstraction.[39] Spontaneity leads to constructing the field as a system's fragment that "speaks" through colors, lines, and values.[40] The goal of attention is to recognize; and recognizing does not go without comparing. The eye darts here and there, weaving its familiar web: with this movement, consisting at once in sweeping across the field and accommodating the optic system, each part in turn becomes a focal point, identified in central vision, and arranged in relation to others in an entirely intelligible, Euclidian composition. Attention scripts [*écrit*] space, inscribing it with lines and triangles; for attention, colors are like phonemes: units that operate through opposition, not motivation.

But has the ambition of a phenomenology of one's own body [*corps propre*] not been precisely to carry out a critique of this equalization of the visible world, to reinstate the genuine specificity of the field that is non-referential depth, that is, precisely, difference as origin and not distance to an origin? For the living eye, the "here" and the "elsewhere" are not equalized; their dissymmetry is radical, and this dissymmetry's master configuration is, as we know, the Gestalt. In the latter, the elsewhere, the thing's reverse, its absence, is given in its obverse, in presence. The *figure/ground* organization constitutes the a priori of the experience of any spatiality, the visible's constitution into a field comprising its invisibility, the key to the mystery of depth that remains staunchly resistant to any elucidating effort, either intellectual or empirical. It makes sense that a philosophy of consciousness, such as Merleau-Ponty's, which aimed for an underside of consciousness, would come up against this configuration as its last word, as the impassable organization of the most elementary contact between body and object. Yet the Gestaltist organization of visual perception is itself the outcome of secondary rationalization. Before the ordering of the thing according to "good form," the given offers itself in a halo, in superimpositions and deflections that the eye's movement will end up precisely eliminating.[41]

At this point, what is called for is nothing less than a reversal in methodological procedure, by which one will be able to measure the change of level required of reflection and which tests the transition to hyper-reflection. Phenomenological reflection sees the eye's movement as producing (passively, it is true) the synthesis of the here and the elsewhere, and thus as going against the concept of pure exteriority one finds at the level of categories. Hyper-reflection, however, sees this same synthesizing motion as the main procedure, thanks to which "reality" constitutes itself as a set of elements articulated according to constants. For hyper-reflection, apprehending difference—the fundamental imbalance of the visual field—requires suspending the operation that triggers this constitution of a world. Such an operation is the *movement* of the eye traveling the field, constructing the latter in order to *recognize* it, and thus rejecting on the way everything that is not instantly identifiable. Here the bias is mobility—the mobility that "makes" the world and represses difference. Critical painting—and the hyper-reflection that maps itself on it—replaces the mobility and active ease that belong to our body immersed in its milieu with the discipline of immobilization.[42] It is only by suspending mobility that not only the diachronization of spaces, their linear arrangement in a succession, and their juxtaposition in a legible order, but also the Gestaltist organization through well-measured depth, are rendered inoperative, and that the fundamental heterogeneity of the visual field can be approached. The deconstruction of the field that brings its true unevenness to light requires the trussing up of the eye. Learning how to see is unlearning how to recognize. The eye's movement must be made to stop without altering the very wide aperture of the ocular system, so that the field constituted by the juxtaposition of theoretically equally distinct points can give way to the preeminently figural space, to the field of vision which focalized attention represses, and which presents around the tiny area of clear vision (the foveal zone) a vast peripheral fringe of curved space.[43]

Spatial difference is even more paradoxical than the gap that in Gestaltist articulation "gives" the invisibility of the object's other side; more rudimentary, too, it is the ungraspable distance between the visual field's periphery and its focal point. This gap gives much more than the here and the elsewhere, the front and the back. It gives the qualitative discontinuity of the two spaces in their simultaneity: the curved, twilight, fleeting, lateral space of the first peripheral contact with something, and the stabilized, constant, central rectangular space of the grasp in the foveal zone. This grasp is a seizing, a prehension, an impounding akin to a preying, laborious, linguistic grip. The first contact, the entrance of something at the edge of the field—this is visual otherness, an invisible of the visible; yet this is not merely the back of what is grasped frontally at the center. This fragile, oblique tactility gives the visual event that is before even the sketch.

The sketch is conceived of retroactively on the basis of the form or the thing viewed a little later in clear sight; in other words, the sketch (but this can be said only after the fact) is the thing approaching, before it is constituted by its position at the center of the field and the synthesizing activity of sight. With the sketch, one imagines oneself to be in possession of a more radical moment in the constitution of what is perceived, a pre-subjective and pre-objective moment, when in fact all one is doing is taking from the constituted object fragments one assumes were perceived before it gave itself as a totality (however open), and projecting the object in the "past" of perceiving activity. But in so doing one is erasing difference, imagining the sketch as an incomplete object and the object as the completion and totalization of sketches; one is blotting out the heterogeneity of the field according to which what appears in the field is not first "seen" in the sense of foveal vision, and what is seen there ceases to appear as event. In the thing's entrance into the field, the sketch is merely what will remain as element of the seen object; on the contrary, the event is what is excluded from the field.

What is deviant in the sketch will be eliminated to allow for the constitution of the "thingist" [*"chosiste"*] and Gestaltist constant.[44] To have the visual event one must therefore fix one's eye on a point for a long time and let come from the side, without turning toward it, what precisely is eliminated by prehensile, secondary, and articulated vision. The event is an anomaly good form will rub out, the same anomaly Cézanne sought through his monstrous immobility in front of Mount Sainte-Victoire. What will then move and deconstruct will no longer only be the objects as constants of value and color (for Impressionism, and perhaps the Baroque, had already understood this) but space in its homogeneity. The relation between *focus* and *fringe,* center of field and periphery, will not be that of the no/yes or *fort/da*—which is no longer difference and already opposition between two spaces potentially equalized through focalization—but that of diffuse/clear vision.

You might counter that this is not a case of qualitative difference but only of quantitative difference between center and periphery; that diffuse vision is merely confused sight, an effect of overlaps in need of disentanglement. Besides, one could obtain an equivalent of the sketch's peripheral presence in the field by overlaying several motifs on the same sensitive plate in photography. This is a comforting misconception. For on the photograph, even the blurring is contrived: it can be studied and analyzed by the attentive eye, which will reconstitute at length the many superimposed images and the varied adjustments these will have required. The space of the camera is an orthogonal space that obeys the laws of traditional optics, whereas visual space is a curved space. What I call diffuse perception is the curvature of the space evaluated and identified on the basis of the Euclidian bias. In so-called diffuse vision, the peripheral is not only blurred, it is other, and any attempt at *grasping* it loses it. This is where difference lies within the visible. In the front/back pair, there is reversal and possible equalization of the terms; we are on our way to language by way of stereometry and geometry. In the diffuse/punctual pair, there is qualitative change and irreversible loss at the same time as retention of the lateral in the focal: no equalization possible. We are not talking about the opposition between two terms, but about a difference in *qualia* that involves their irreversible inequality as well as their juxtaposition. It is striking that to reveal this difference, one has to interrupt not only the movement of speech between terms, but also that of the eye between objects or their facets. Hence there is something false even in the eye's movement, lending itself as it does to the construction of the knowable, repressing truthfulness. Truthfulness is the unbalanced configuration of space before any construction. It requires the deconstruction of the eye's movement into an immobility that is not a state of mobility. Such immobility bears no comparison with that of the system's dialectics. Between the two stands the difference between seeing and reading. As for the eye's movement, it makes only recognition possible, treating things as letters.

Braque pits "the profile against the silhouette":

"It is the accidental that reveals existence to us."

"Let us not conclude: the present, the accidental will set us free."

"I am not looking for definition. I stretch toward the infinite."

"The present, the circumstance."

Of course, the last thing Braque wants to do is philosophize—we owe him our apologies; with words, he paints the space of a painting where the power of "metamorphosis" would be in play, instead of the order of the "metaphor."[45]

VEDUTA ON A FRAGMENT OF THE "HISTORY" OF DESIRE

Veduta on a Fragment of the "History" of Desire

1. Neutral space and position of discourse
2.1. Figure and text in illuminated Romanesque manuscripts
2.2. Text and figure in Romanesque writings
3.2. The space of the new philosophy
3.1. Rotation of pictorial space
4. Inverse rotation

The reader will have noted, or will note, that the references upon which the present reflection is based belong for the most part to a European corpus from the period between 1880 and 1930: Saussure, Frege, Freud, Mallarmé, Cézanne, Lhote, Klee . . .

This corpus rests on a fractured topography that possesses, as Pierre Francastel has demonstrated in relation to pictorial space, a seismic scope and sensibility comparable to that of the Quattrocento, which is what authorizes a study of the latter. Admittedly, the relation between the two is not one of mere comparison. We are products of the Cézannian and Freudian revolution, thanks to which we may come to understand the revolution of the Renaissance. The former therefore plays, in relation to the latter, the role of an operative concept or group of concepts. This is how, in the following fragment, the categories derived from the critique of the Hegelian confusion—based on the work of Frege, Saussure, Freud, and Cézanne—will help us determine the transformation of the pictorial space of the Renaissance. The relation between the two areas is thus, foremost, that of a theory with a single field of reference. To illustrate the consistency of the group of concepts we subsume under it a fragment of "reality." As far as this relation is concerned, the fact that reality and the concepts belong to the same history—the West's—does not appear immediately relevant. Applying the same group of concepts to Balinese theater or Dogon masks would be no more or less convincing; it would most likely allow us to set the limits of validity in the use of the categories, and from there, most importantly, to circumscribe negatively *these expressions, in function of the specific twists they inflict on the sign's configuration in cultural contexts alien to the area under consideration.*

Yet the relation between the late-nineteenth-century revolution and the Quattrocento cannot be reduced to that of simple epistemological exteriority. Renaissance space functions, in relation to us, like the mirror in which Cézannian space finds reflection. For it is with respect to the rules of the geometric inscription of representational space—laid down at the end of the first quarter of the fifteenth century—that Cézannian space fulfills its deconstructive function. Had the viewer of Madame Cézanne in a Yellow Chair *or of* The Large Bathers *in Philadelphia not had in sight the virtual organization of the field of vision imposed by Alberti and his followers, the reversal contained in Cézanne's oeuvre would have remained imperceptible. The critical function of the figural, its work of truth, comes to fruition in relation to a "script"* [écriture] *and consists above all in the deconstruction of this script.*[1] *Impressionism had merely overturned the "outlines"* [tracés révélateurs], *the contours, by drowning them in light; Cézanne pushes deconstruction much further, dealing a blow to the "regulating lines"* [tracés régulateurs],[2] *to the organizing forms of Renaissance space.*[3] *This last space belongs, therefore, to the seismic upheaval that concerns us; but it does so, first of all, negatively: it is what undergoes the shock.*

Still more needs to be said on the subject. A third relation becomes apparent between the late-nineteenth/early-twentieth-century movement and that of the fifteenth century. The Cézannian crisis is reflected in Albertian space; retroactively, however, it suggests that there is no such thing as a natural organization of visual space at the scale of cultures, and that Renaissance perspective was no less shocking to those used to reading the images of the international Gothic style than Cézanne's perspective was to those who appreciated Pre-Raphaelitism. Thus one does not understand Cézanne through Masaccio or Leonardo, but rather the latter two with Cézanne. What do "through" and "with" mean in this context? Are these epistemologically valid categories? Leonardo allows Cézanne to be understood because the former is the script the latter encounters and strives to overcome. Here the relation is that of censorship with desire: Renaissance order burdens the free interplay of plasticity with constraints that this plasticity will transgress. But when

Cézanne allows us to enter Masaccio's oeuvre, he is like the psychoanalyst's unconscious listening to the analysand's: by opening our eyes to the power of meaning contained in the deconstruction of a plastic script, Cézanne enables us to perceive this force in Quattrocento painting.

1. The space of the text and the space of the figure are not beholden to a single neutral expanse where traces—sometimes graphic, sometimes plastic—would be inscribed. One should be critical of the notion that the expanse is neutral, for the latter is hardly an immediate given, but instead presupposes a container-space, neither textual nor figural (ne-uter) *in its own organization, equally likely to receive either text or figure—in short, geometric space. Now, this space is constructed, and its construction, while it may allow the difference that we want to reveal between the two spaces to be revealed, that is, while its construction is this difference's* ratio cognoscendi *[reason for knowing], it is not this difference's* ratio essendi *[reason for being]. The reason for this difference appears in a profound transformation of the relation between the script and the figural. The hidden organization of the visual field is the difference, the irreversible heterogeneity between focal area and periphery. This difference is normally repressed, to the point that a philosopher like Bergson, otherwise capable of recovering and bringing out difference from temporality, completely abandons spatiality in favor of the realism of adaptive action and of the geometrization of technical thought that extends from it.*[4] *For his part, Freud understands the constitution of reality as a process of* Gestaltung: *elimination of topological organization, of the infant's relation with the breast and transitional objects.*[5] *Yet both thinkers recognize, for different reasons, the role language plays in the organization of "adult" space. Modern anthropological research suggests that this last function is the only real constant: the function of active adaptation implies that the problem of defining a norm of reality has been resolved. Even for the animal, this norm is conditioned to a much greater degree by the genetic code that determines, for example, its instincts, and thus selects the situations in which the animal will have to act, than by a hypothetical unprocessed reality given objectively. All the more when it comes to the human child, for whom the reality it must engage with is always mediated by a cultural system acting as a grid or language* [langue]. *This is precisely a very important function of culture, to allow the members of the group to decipher the event, to recognize the unknown, to signify disorder. This function may well be operative and adaptive, but it does not apply directly at the level of the individual's relation with "reality." It concerns instead a collective order that functions as mediator for the individual, and this order partakes of language* [langage]. *One could say that this order's purpose is to transcribe difference (the event, irreversible atemporality, dissymmetrical spatiality) into opposition, by incorporating disequilibrium into a structural system. Clearly, this transcription goes hand in hand with the repression, and more generally with the rejection, of figurality.*

This rejection can take very different forms, depending on the kind of "discourse" held by the culture under scrutiny. By kind *of discourse, I do not mean to suggest variations within a single genre, but rather a break between different genres. Take for example the organization of space in Asdiwal's gesture,*[6] *a discourse held by the society of Tsimshian Indians, and that of the founding myth as told by the Australian Murngin society.*[7] *One could oppose them as elements in a system comprising all the spatial organizations that account for a topography* through a narrative: *by this measure, both organizations are isomorphic. But if you want to pursue this operation by amalgamating these discourses with Giordano Bruno's in* Camoeracensis Acrotismus *or, better still, with Galileo's discourse in* De Motu[8]*—both of which* signify *a spatial organization—you will be forced to acknowledge that the operation is impossible, for the* genre *of discourse has changed, or more specifically its* position. *I would define the latter by the transformation or set of transformations that allow one to go from the discourse to its object.*

As discourse, the mythical tale belongs to the narrative genre. Galileo's discourse, on the other hand, tells of processes of variations that are for the most part intellectual, conducted intentionally, and that allow definitions to be established: it is thus the constitutive discourse of an axiomatics. As such, this discourse's aim is, as much as possible, to eliminate all that qualifies as figure from its vocabulary and syntax, by the definition taking the place of the metaphor (figure of words) and the rule governing the combination of units that of rhetoric (figure of style). On the contrary, the mythical tale belongs to the category of figural *discourse. Every tale depends on the observation of a difference, of a dissymmetry between an initial and a concluding situation. By telling a story, one introduces a dissymmetry, a disparity in the order of the signifieds, and one organizes this disparity in temporal succession: narrative diachrony will come to signify, by redoubling it, the diachrony of the signified story, since for the linguistic order it is the very form of irreversibility. Narrative discourse thus finds itself positioned parallel to its object, and its configuration is analogous to that of* the res gestae *[things done]. Furthermore, the mythical tale is eminently figural in that its form impacts not only religious discourse itself, but all the activities that are identified in the culture in question: it is the spoken trappings of a matricial figure, open to numerous other trappings (danced, woven, erected, painted). However, as discursive signification, the function of the mythical tale is to allay the difference it narrates, to establish this difference in a system, that is, to transform difference into opposition. By relying on this last function—strictly speaking that of signification, and no longer of expression—structural anthropology can build matrices of culture that are no longer matricial forms at all, but mathematical structures. Indeed, in these structures difference can be specified according to a few simple transformations, such as reversal, inversion, and negative transformation. But such a method will always have a remainder to account for, which is narrative form, the destabilized and restabilizing figure that the virtual matrix dons when embodied in mythical discourse.*

The gap between the respective positions *of the mythical tale and the discourse of knowledge is not hard to define: in the first, the sensory lends itself to being scripted and the script is figural; in the second, the script is strictly textual, while the sensory shifts to the referential pole of scholarly discourse. One can see why the two kinds of discourse on space cannot share the same taxonomy: the first entails the transfusion of the two spaces into one another, figural and textual; the second, their separation. A mythological culture* represses *difference in the sense that it covers up the sensory figure with a function of language, but also in that the repressed figural order reemerges within mythological language itself as its unconscious ordering, its narrative form. A scientific culture* forecloses *difference because it evacuates the latter from its discourse and can only* encounter *difference as returning from without.*[9]

This separation of the two spaces is at the root of our problematic. Before, difference as such, that is to say, difference as different from opposition, cannot appear. Sensory data [le donné sensible] *at least has to stop being "scripted," to shed the clarity of a text and acquire the opacity of a sign located outside of discourse as its reference, for it to be conceived of as discourse's other. What is a gain in problematic is a loss in signification.*

The effects of the fission we are discussing come, and come repeatedly, to the surface of the historical panorama presented by the West. It is out of the question to identify, describe, and signify each of these traces. What is certain, however, is that they form a series of events, each truly contemporary to one another regardless of the position they occupy in chronology, so that these events come to form "another (his)story" than the reality that is the object of historical knowledge. An apposite image of this synchrony of traces could be provided by the inscriptions the unconscious leaves behind in the subject's "waking" life: contemporary to one another in the achrony of the primary process, and the result of a labor of truth rather than of a discourse of knowledge. If this image seems apposite, this is because the articulation of discourse with the figural is in every way attached to the fate of desire, even in artworks.

Suffice it to examine one such surface manifestation here, among the easiest to grasp. Through it, the unity of the figure and the text, so meticulously crafted by the Middle Ages, becomes fractured in the Renaissance, and in this fracture we can grasp the shift in the distribution of the terms defined above.

2.1. Architecture is the art in which the Middle Ages brought the "scripting" of the sensory to its acme.[10] *Nevertheless, it is in the field of illuminated manuscripts that I will select two examples, because the manuscript allows for an immediate, nonmetaphorical confrontation of textual and figural spaces, and because it was less exposed than public artistic expressions (capitals of columns, stained-glass windows, frescoes) to the monks' censorship over images: the literate, as the only ones with access to manuscripts, were believed better equipped than the lay people at resisting the images' power of illusion.*[11] *Needless to say, these examples are not meant to "test a hypothesis." Such a test would require the strict identification of relevant features for the two spaces, and the statistical processing of the large body of miniatures at our disposal. My more modest ambition is to make this hypothesis* visible, *so to speak. I have deliberately selected my two examples among works of the same period, the late eleventh century, as it is particularly noteworthy on two counts. For manuscript illumination, this period is one of intense activity, so intense and inventive—especially in Cluny and in the Burgundy tradition—that several decades later (in 1137) Bernard of Clairvaux will bar monks from practicing manuscript illumination.*[12] *As for the status of discourse, these final years of the eleventh century are decisive, witnessing the emergence of a generation that, on the one hand, with Abelard and the Sententiaries, will counter the monastic tradition of* auctoritas *with the first arguments of the scholastic method*—disputatio *and* conclusio—*and, on the other, with the Victorine school of thought, will extend Neoplatonic optimism so far as to justify sensory delectation. At stake in both cases is the traditional articulation of the textual and the figural: in the first, a will to free discourse from those figures embedded by Christian mythology that had escaped scrutiny; in the second, an effort to conceptualize the visible as a Divine trace different from writing. It is at the very moment when the balance between word and image instituted by the Augustinian tradition finds itself most at risk that it will best reveal its inner forces: under fire from Abelardian dialectics, Hugh of Saint Victor is a kind of catalyst that turns incandescent.*

Let us take the beginning of the Book of Numbers in the Saint-Martial Bible from Limoges (Plate 1).[13] *Here space is organized as follows (Figure 2): let A be the folio's (white) plane where the letters are inscribed; B, the plane (crimson, L-shaped, cut out on the first) in which the initial and the small figure are placed; C, the (white L-shaped) plane bounded by the body of the initial; and D, the (blue, vertical and rectangular) plane serving as the image's background. A is a graphic space, but one where the letters are nonetheless arranged according to specifically figural criteria (symmetry, ornamentation); B stands out against A as a function of its value as a plastic form, and as a letter as a function of its outline. C instead is neutralized chromatically, but its contour is highly ornamental, while D's contour is neutral, but with an intense plastic and chromatic internal relief. If one were to posit that the sign x (y) represents the relation "x contains y," the planes of this leaf interlock as follows: A (B [CD]). By factoring in each plane's indexes of figurality and textuality, one observes that a figurally wrought textual plane contains a figural plane endowed with sculptural value, which itself includes two planes where text and figure are combined. In itself, this page's construction* en abyme *already implies the homogeneity of the two spaces.*

More clearly, the text Locutus est Dominus ad Moysen in deserto Sinai *and the image of the Lord giving his orders to Moses are in a face-to-face relation.*

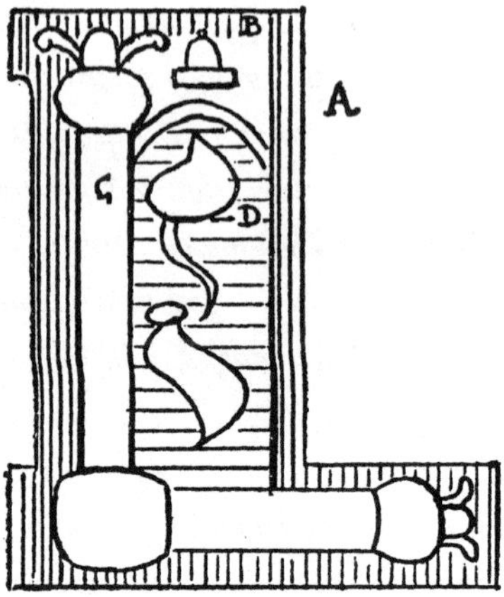

Figure 2. Schematic rendering of the initial of the Book of Numbers, *Bible of Saint-Martial* (Paris: Bibliothèque nationale, ms. lat. 8 [1]), second half of the eleventh century, Limoges.

On one side, the letters (capitals and uncials) occupy the page plastically, and not merely so as to be read. For example, the initial and the text are not at the same scale; one reads a text, one notices that a letter is missing, and one sets out to find it: a space that slows down the gaze, forcing it to spend time within its borders. The meaning of the letters, too, is figural, as a passage from the holy story through which difference is signified (creation-fall-redemption). On the other side, the figure is the text's designatum, *its* Bedeutung; *it must therefore be inscribed in a space theoretically heterogeneous to the graphic plane, and the miniaturist's use, in this space, of curves and verticality for purely expressive purposes is heavily emphasized. Yet the eye can move unceasingly from the textual plane to that of the image, thanks to the mediations offered by the inclusions noted above. Moreover, the image's plastic organization hardly excludes recourse to the traditional signs that punctuate Romanesque representation and that make it a kind of pictographic script: the nimbus with the T-shaped cross, or the vaporous cloud as celestial signal of the Almighty; the symbol of the Holy Spirit, flying under Moses's feet; the ritual positioning of hands, the teaching hands of God and those of Moses in worship; the dome and the canopy overlooking the scene, a traditional indication that the world is a temple and that the very exteriority of the desert is embraced by the gaze of God as the expression of His ubiquity. All these constituent elements of the image are coded, easily recognizable for the reader trained to decipher its vocabulary. Not to mention the scroll, ultimate plane embedded in that of the image, once again bearing text, but here laid out according to the iconic plane's verticality and curvature—making, in other words, a significant concession to figural expression.*

This is no doubt an ideal case, given the care with which the imbrication of difference and opposition is crafted. The analysis of the manuscript's other miniatures only goes to confirm this impression (Plate 2, and the commentary in "Notes on Figures and Plates"). Here is, at first glance, a less convincing example (Plate 3): the leaf with the beginning of the Book of Generations according to Matthew, in the Gospel believed to be from the Moissac monastery.[14] In this case the text and the figure are placed in a position of mutual exteriority: the words are clustered in the lower right corner like a caption, in a separate plane from that of the figure upon which the words comment. Unlike what we saw before, the figure of the Evangelist is not confined to the plane of the dropped initial, but is isolated in its entirely plastic space; the initial itself loses some of its legibility, invaded and devoured by the chimerical figures attaching themselves to the letter's lines, whereas in the Limoges Bible, the ornamentation from Albi, made of abstract arabesques, did not hinder the L's identification. In short, this page does seem to show the signs of a break under way between the two spaces.

Still, let us examine the image that is the most independent from the text, the representation of Saint Matthew. One can easily see how "scripted" it is, how in it persists the overlapping of the two spaces. This overlapping first occurs through the mediation of the narrative figure of Christian discourse: each of the figure's components acts as a signal referring to a significative feature in the Holy Story's cast of characters: the halo indicates the saint, the raised finger the Apostle, the book the Evangelist, and if there is no emblematic animal, this is because the image will be "read" by someone learned who can identify the character from the inscription of the titulus. It becomes apparent that the function of this image is to allow itself to be recognized rather than to be looked at—a "figurative letter," so to speak. Indeed, the image obeys a kind of language-system [langue] made up of invariable markers—with or without halo, finger raised or not, etc.—to signify terms. The artist could not afford to take liberties vis-à-vis the system of features, short of provoking the worst confusion, since he or she would thereby be subverting indirectly the Holy Story's canonical form. We are thus unquestionably in the presence of a system of oppositions,[15] the same in terms of figures as that which governs the semantic field of Christian history. What is more, certain relevant features of this quasi-script are as arbitrary as they are in written form strictly defined, or in phonation. For example, the phonetic opposition open/closed, which is relevant for French vowels (jarre/jour), is completely independent from the objects it allows to designate. The *chromatic system used in the Moissac miniature (red, purple, blue, green) could no more be derived from the object represented than the vowel /eɪ/ can be from daylight. It cannot even be derived from what Kandinsky will call the "language of colors,"*[16] *that is, from the system of opposite and complementary colors that make up the color wheel. The four colors employed here follow one another in the spectrum; their value is the result of conventional oppositions and does not derive from sensorial differences.*[17]

Thus, if it is true that the dropped initial in the Moissac manuscript is much more representational than the one from Limoges, and if it is true that the overlapping of the spaces is much more developed in the Saint-Martial Bible than in the Moissac Bible (which is indeed the manuscript's overall characteristic—see Plate 4, and the commentary in "Notes on Figures and Plates"), on the other hand the space in which Matthew is represented, detached from the plane of the text, is even more distinctly scripted *than the space depicting Moses receiving God's command. Overall, then, text and figure balance each other out in both spaces. But in the Moissac Bible this balance is achieved through a kind of direct overlapping (compare with how the encounter between the two spaces is rendered on any capital from the same cloister {of the same period; see Plate 5 and the commentary in "Notes on Figures and Plates"}): script takes over plastic expression and contracts it, while the figurative invades the letter and begins to deconstruct it. In the Limoges Bible, the balance is achieved through a process of hierarchically ordered immanence: the two planes are sharply differentiated thanks to the simplicity of the initial on the one side, and on the other to the relative plasticity of the image's curved space; yet both skillfully interlock to form a series leading from text (of the leaf) to text (of the scroll), via the letter and the figure. In this last example, the result is more satisfactory for the* intuitus, *just as it was for the* significatio *in the other example.*[18]

2.2. *Subordinating* intuitus *to* significatio, *visible meaning to articulated signification, is the basic rule imposed by the Fathers of the Church on the use of imagery. In the* Caroline Books,[19] *which constitute the doctrinal corpus of the Carolingian Renaissance, Alcuin had vigorously laid down the function of the image in the doctrine and teachings of the Christian West, by contrasting it with* the alternating crises of veneration and destruction of idols that were convulsing Byzantium: "imagines quas prior synodus nec etiam cernere permiserat, alter adorare compellit. . . . Nos nec destruimus, nec adoramus" [the images that the first council had not even allowed us to see, the second compelled us to revere. . . . But neither did we destroy, nor did we revere].[20] But the image is accepted only on the condition that it serve a specific purpose, which is to make accessible to the illiterate what the literate know through the Scriptures: "Illiterati quod per scripturam non possunt intueri, hoc per quaedam picturae lineamenta contemplantur" [By means of a picture's several brushstrokes, the illiterate contemplate that which they are unable to observe in writing].[21] This is a pedagogy indebted to the antique doctrine of Horace's "Ut pictura poesis" [as in painting, so in poetry], a doctrine whose original formulation Plutarch ascribes to Simonides of Ceos.[22] Thus if painting is to be tolerated, it will be on the condition of clear "speaking." This clarity should be understood literally, as the transparency of signification in the linguistic term. Just as the latter's agency does not depend on the nature of its signifier, but on what it signifies, so must the image be produced in such a way as not to have the gaze stop at its opacity of plastic signifier, but rather to induce directly the recognition of what it represents. "Artistic consciousness is a movement 'per intuitum ad memoriam': from the perception of the image qua image, one comes to the recollection of reality in imagination. The image is present to sensory intuition; represented reality is present only to intellectual memory."[23] With the figure so strictly subjected to script, it cannot possibly deceive; for the same reason its opacity will not be able to divert and lead astray the motion of worship. The function of the visible is to signify the invisible.

In the evangelistary of Hitda of Meschede, at the back of a Majestas, one reads: "Hoc visibile imaginatum figurat illud invisibile verum cujus splendor penetrat mondum cum bis binis candelabris ipsius novi sermoni" [This visible conception represents that invisible truth whose splendor pierces with four (twice two each) candelabra the world of someone who is new to speech].[24] This "figuration" could not be less figural; the way for the radiance of truth to illuminate the world is through the sermo: "images, just as letters and writing, are visible signs, some of them concrete, imitative, sensory, others conventional, more abstract, intelligible, whose mission it is to signify an absent reality."[25] It is not coincidental that the illuminator from Cologne thought to provide, on the back of the Majestas, *guidelines for its proper use: not only does the illuminator signify it through the* hoc visibile imaginatum . . . , *but he expresses it, placing signification on the back of the visible, in its own order—that of the invisible, or presence of absence, which is precisely that of text.*

The constricted figure performs essentially the same function as the letter, to afford its "reader" the instant recognition of the "signified." When Alcuin declares the "memoria rerum gestarum" [recording of actions] to be the aim of figurative representation,[26] *he demands that it operate as a graphic signal, whose whole function consists in reminding the reader of the signified associated with the symbol. It follows that the painter, the illuminator, the maker of images must construct the figure as a message, that is, as a set of signifying elements whose nature (the lexicon) and rules of construction (the syntax) are defined in a code with which "the image reader" is already familiar. To see will be to hear, like reading—the "reading" of those who cannot read.*[27]

Notwithstanding, this suppression of difference in an oppositional system is not unequivocal, and above all not definitive, even in the aesthetics of the High Middle Ages. As early as the eighth century, Alcuin adds to the function of recording past actions, which he assigns to painting, the function of "embellishing walls";[28] *to its pedagogical usefulness he adds the eye's enjoyment, which seems almost unabashedly aesthetic. The door is thus left ajar for the figural to be set free, for a space of difference to become autonomous. In the* Caroline Books, *this becoming autonomous is far from within sight, as the criteria for such enjoyment remain stringently subordinated to those of pedagogy, that is, of the* subject *of representation, and hence of its* scripting. *Pictorial technique itself must surrender its materials and their uses to scriptural code. There is no such thing as beautiful monsters. It is only one hundred years later, with the arrival and circulation in the West of the* Corpus aeropagiticum, *that the dissimilar is granted the status of beauty in figurative representation and the right to feature in aesthetics.*[29] *A watershed moment: when Pythagoras-inspired Platonism gives way to a Neoplatonism heavily reworked in light of the position of discourse particular to Judeo-Christian legacy, namely, narrative discourse. By emphasizing the unfolding of primordial (hi)story—the diversity of successive moments leading from God to God through the creature—the new schema fulfills a double function. On the one hand it introduces the figural into the very order of the discursive, since it stamps the latter with the* figure-form *of the Fall and of Redemption, the purportedly primary difference. On the other, it thereby allows the discursive to better signify what had previously appeared to it out of bounds, even antagonistic: the order of the sensory where the figure stands. This double legitimization of the order of discourse will reach its culmination in the writings of Hugh of Saint Victor.*[30]

Thus the creatures' own beauty—their "formal" beauty—joins their expressive beauty, that is, their function as signifier referring to the signified of the Scriptures, to the signified of the absent Father's speech. This "formal" beauty no longer derives from the "beauty" of their subject; no longer will the compliance with the code in which the primordial (hi)story is written determine the work's emotional power. Rather, the latter is due to an immediately obtained agreement between the harmony of the object's components and that of the soul's.[31] *Contrary to what Bernard of Clairvaux desires, it is impossible to reach the contemplation of* invisibilia *directly: "non potest noster animus (ascendere) nisi per visibilium considerationem eruditus ita videlicet ut arbitretur visibiles formas esse imagines invisibilis pulchritudinis" [Our understanding is unable to increase (grasp the truth) unless it has been so clearly instructed through the consideration of the visible that it believes the visible shapes to be images of an invisible beauty].*[32] *And this is why "constat quod plus simulacrum evidens (Dei) est decor creaturarum":*[33] *the most obvious trace of the Divine is the beauty of creatures. The visible ceases to be merely a site of transit, mere lit signal to be crossed on the way to hidden signification, mere script: on account of its recognized formal beauty, it gains its own consistency, thickness, even mystical fertility. It becomes* symbolum, *"collatio formarum visibilium ad invisibilium demonstrationem" [the collation of visible shapes for the representation of the invisible],*[34] *what we called* sign. *Now, if this sign clearly continues to refer to something other than itself, it no longer refers to it based on the world of the linguistic pseudo-sign. Not only does it possess its own criteria of beauty,*[35] *bringing into play a specifically aesthetic order, an order of the meaning immanent in the signifier, but the autonomy of this order is discernible even in its dissimilarity, through its difference from the order of the signified, that is, of the Story told by the Scriptures: "The figures may appear worthy of admiration for their size, large or small, or because they are rare or beautiful, or, equally,* by a certain agreement in absurdity, *so to speak (aliquando ut interim ita loquar, quia quodammodo convenienter ineptae)."*[36] *Signs are signs through the similar or the dissimilar.*[37] *In reality, they are signs through both: were they similar on all counts, they would not be signs, but the signified itself; dissimilar on all counts, they would be arbitrary and lose their symbolic quality. Their specific status is that of* dissimilar similarity, *for it is thanks to its element of dissimilarity that the similar has the ability not to fulfill a function of decoy, by preventing the eye from mistaking it for what it represents: "Omnis ergo figura tanto evidentius veritatem demonstrat quanto apertius per dissimilem similitudinen figuram se esse et non veritatem probat. Atque in hoc nostrum animum dissimiles similitudines magis ad veritatem reducunt quod ipsum in sola similitudine manere non permittunt."*[38] *This difference is what prevents the mind from remaining at the level of the signifier, of the visible side of the symbol: apparent disorder induces latent order; the ugly, that is, what is deconstructed of divine text, appeals to absolute beauty. "Signum veritas esse non potest etiam cum veritatis est signum" [A sign cannot be the truth even when it is a sign of the truth].*[39] *Here, the transparency of the textual as unique presentation of meaning is abandoned; the textual is called upon as unseen signification, while the visible is recognized as a presence of the word irreducible to its discursive manifestation. Irreversible thickness stands in the way of the mind's rush toward signification; but this obstacle, conversely, is what allows one to accurately locate the verb, beyond the eye's grasp. If things "speak," it is not in words but in figures. No doubt the person who "in visibilibus istis creaturis foris videt speciem, sed intus non intelligit rationem" [sees appearance in those visible creations on the outside but who fails to comprehend the inner meaning] is just as mad as the illiterate who, seeing an open book, "figuras aspicit, sed litteras non cognoscit" [sees shapes without understanding the letters].*[40] *Yet, after Hugh of Saint Victor, one will be able to qualify as equally mad any attempt to dispense with the figures' truth function.*

This function lies precisely in the figures' dissimilarity in relation to the signified: by deconstructing similarity, truth appears in the order of the figure. And the Victorines are well aware that this order of dissimilar similarity is not confined to the visible strictly defined, but that it encompasses the whole of the imaginary, in particular that which the metaphor can generate from discourse itself. We never have the signified in immediacy; nor do we have access, in the Scriptures, to the divine word stripped of allegory, for the Bible, too, requires figural beauty. It should come as no surprise that Hugh in turn makes use of a comparison to convey this function of figurative expression in the sacred text: "In an admirable way, and this throughout the divine text (in the same way as in citharas and other related instruments), God's wisdom coordinated and arranged the various parts with such skill that everything involved either produces the melodious sound of spiritual intelligence (spiritualis intelligentiae suavitatem) *as would the strings or, by containing and connecting the tales of the mysteries in the sequence of history and in the consistency of the letter* (per historiae seriem et litterae soliditatem mysteriorum dicta continens et connectens), *combines with the taut strings the power of the wooden box to emit a sweeter sound for the ears to enjoy."*[41] *This solidity and this series in which the scattered traces of the mysteries achieve consistency and diachrony—such then are the elements through which the signified figures itself. The Victorines stress the need to buttress any allegorical interpretation, any attempt at grasping the spiritual meaning of the Scriptures by a meticulous study of literal, historical meaning. "The third type of speculation," writes Richard of Saint Victor, "consists indeed* in ratione," *but it can only come about* "secundum imaginationem, *for it is from the image of visible things that similarity is conveyed to speculation."*[42] *Likewise, the Bible's "immediate" meaning is, so to speak, the imaged figure of the hidden meaning. The literal is the allegorical of the spiritual. Thus the Bible, which is the compendium of all doctrines and the manual of all pedagogy, is still the model for all works of art and of every reality insofar as it aims to satisfy not only the reader's power of understanding, but equally her or his power of image.*

The figural is therefore present in texts, including holy ones, and its presence is felt on two levels: historiae series *and* litterae soliditas. *The "sequence of a story," of the primordial story of past actions, constitutes a figure, one that organizes the form of Christian myth: a narrative figure, occupying a subterranean realm, set back from the surface of immediate discourse, yet which produces the latter's relief. The "consistency of the letter" refers to its immediate opacity; it is to the reader's eye what color is to the eye of the beholder of a painting or a landscape: what stops the eye, so that this literality, far from suggesting transparency in this case, indicates instead, in Hugh's comparison, the obscurity that can cloud a text from the presence within it of stylistic* figures. *This time we find ourselves at the level of the spoken or written chain itself, since these figures are the result of intervals ("dissimilarities," differences) exercised in the organization of semantic or syntactic fields.*

To summarize: on the one hand the "sensory world is like a book written in God's hand, and the individual creatures are like its figures, not invented by man for his own pleasure, but instituted by divine will to bring God's invisible wisdom to light," in other words, reduction of the sensory to the textual. On the other hand, however, "in one and the same script, one person will note the form and the color of the figures, while the other will praise its meaning and signification"; that is, the textual itself splits into signification and figures. Yet "It is recommended to contemplate and admire the works of God assiduously." To study the figure is legitimate, even in the apprehension of a text, "on the condition, however, that one knows how to turn the beauty of bodily things to the benefit of the spiritual."[43] *Such allegorical use of signs does not entail the elimination of their opacity, since only God can read the world, having scripted it. The mind can attempt to figure a metaphysical narrative on the basis of creatures and the script. But for this it must learn the figuring function that will allow it to develop allegorical signification; and it is by opening itself up to the sensory* insofar as it is illegible, *by yielding to unmediated figurality, that it will be able to construct the figurative meaning of script.*

This hierarchy of orders that, in the realm of the sensory, distinguishes similarity (through which it is scripted*) and dissimilarity (constituting its* difference*) and, in the textual, literal meaning identified as historical (announcing the other meaning) and allegorical meaning (the figure or difference concealed in the latter), represents in the doctrinal order a configuration that corresponds exactly to the one offered, in the order of the sensory, by the painted initials several decades before Hugh of Saint Victor, in Moissac and particularly in Limoges. Whether the combination of letter and image occurs through an osmotic relationship between the two spaces (as in the evangelistary from the South of France) or through the interlocking of figurative and textual planes (as in the Limousin Bible), we notice a projection,* at the level of the signifier, *of the arrangement of the signifieds (or rather, the meanings) that conforms to the teachings of Victorine mysticism. The only noticeable discrepancy concerns the autonomy granted difference, or dissimilarity, and therefore the sensory as unscripted, which is not as great in the miniatures as in Hugh of Saint Victor's texts. Western painting will be nothing but a struggle for the manifestation of difference; or, as Hugh would put it: "Ubi amor, ibi oculus" [Where love is, there is insight].*

3.2. With the Renaissance comes an entirely different relation between the figural and the textual. Romanesque as well as (to put it hastily) medieval organization assimilates the textual to the figural through the coding of visual representation, and the textual to the figural through the narrative (mythical) configuration of canonical discourse. Starting in the fourteenth century, an effort to disentangle the two spaces, as much at the level of visual representation as of discourse, aims to produce a thoroughly new redistribution of difference and opposition. The medieval unification of the fundamental forms of alterity consisted in pushing difference out of the sensory into the discursive, which is oppositional: uttering difference, but only making script visible. The "moderns" activate a double shift: at the discursive level, building the formal rules of all possible discourse instead of the concrete narrative provided exclusively by sacred discourse; at the plastic level, producing the visible as such instead of using the visible to symbolize the invisible, that is, instead of scripting it. Difference thus finds itself excluded from discursive space and placed, theoretically, in the sensory. Script and painting would then appear to be opposed, in the same way that what is inscribed in the flat and homogenous space of oppositionality is opposed to what resorts to perceptual difference. Nonetheless, this new articulation of strictly textual discourse and purely figural reference is misleading: the visible is not freed from script, nor the intelligible from difference.

Let us start with this last point. The discourse of knowledge, as a formal system defined by a lexicon (definitions) and a syntax (transformations), is indeed what takes shape in the work of Galileo. Axiomatics—a set of propositions independent of a content, discourse under which any field of reference may indifferently be subsumed depending on whether it meets the formal system's requirements—is prefigured in Galileo's oeuvre as the inescapable position which the scientific text will later achieve.[44] *This elimination of "content" is exactly synonymous with the elimination of difference. Difference is present in discourse as "form" (as configuration, montage) and as (rhetorical) figure: it is a matter of stylistics, at least insofar as it, in turn, can yield to systematic organization (recategorization).*[45] *The Christian tale, which, on the one hand, obeys a fundamental narrative form describing an ontological trajectory and, on the other, cannot dispense with allegory, metaphor, synecdoche, and all the tropes to convey the Other or Elsewhere of which it speaks—this tale is a preeminent example of a discourse of difference. The evacuation of content from the new discourse implies the neutralization of textual space with respect to all forms of difference. The new discourse finds its place at a level beneath that of stylistics, namely, of lexicon and syntax.*[46] *Speaking will no longer stand for retelling the founding story, but for establishing a priori the properties of a set of rules in which various possible "(hi)stories" can be told. By the mere fact of being subsumed under the formal set, these (hi)stories must in principle give up their figural quality, this irreversible ordering that has Adam and Eve expelled from Paradise lost, Jesus die on the cross and, by its very configuration, reconciliation as hoped-for outcome.*[47]

Alexandre Koyré left us a remarkably detailed case study of this neutralizing effect of discursive space, notably that of the formation of the discourse of new physics.[48] *For Koyré, the destruction of the notion of Cosmos, and its replacement by that of Universe, sums up the essence of the transformation.*[49] *Instead of the hierarchy of "spaces" that had defined the Cosmos, the new physics gives rise to the concept of a space without center or limit, where movement loses all "natural" or "violent" quality, to become merely a spatiotemporal shift relative to an observation point arbitrarily assumed to be at rest. The geometrization of space and infinitization of the universe are already completed in Giordano Bruno's metaphysics.*[50] *To Galileo we owe the emptying of all "content" from movement: the pure (Archimedean) cinematics he introduces pits itself against the physics of the* impetus, *according to which the setting in motion of the object corresponds to the insertion in the latter of an "impressed" force that departs it when it comes to a halt.*[51] *Finally, we owe to Descartes the explicit formulation of the law of inertia that reduces both movement and immobility to "state-relations" equally endowed with the same inertia.*[52]

Sensory reality is no longer "spoken" according to the narrative discourse that recounts the creature's adventure; it does, however, continue to hold a discourse. It is only much later that its intelligibility will become unintelligible, that one will only speak of it, *that it will, therefore, side entirely with reference. For this to happen, the order of the system will have had to divorce itself completely from that of the field it is speaking about, and the latter will have had to appear as only one of the fields the system can establish. Geometry is the language* [langage] *in which the new universe finds expression. For all of his contemporaries, Galileo was a Platonic mathematician or an Archimedean physicist.*[53] *His innovation is to have introduced movement itself into the language* [langue] *of arithmetic and geometry, movement whose mathematicization the Peripatetics, in the wake of*

Aristotle, believed impossible, and which they saw as the insurmountable hurdle to a complete mathematical theory of physis. *Galileo seeks to lay down the "alphabet" as well as the syntax of the language "spoken by the nature God created."*[54] *The unmooring in relation to this major position of sensory discourse, which understands the latter as a text or document emanating from an absconded divine word, is therefore not consummated. The Other is still very much the one speaking in physical geometry. And as far as it speaks and we can understand it, it speaks clearly; for the few terms and propositions of its discourse within the scope of our understanding, we possess a comprehension of the objects denoted by these terms and propositions equal in intensity* ("intensive" *in Latin*[55]) *to that which God possesses of them. But where our mind is "separated by an infinite gap from divine intellect," it is "with regard to the mode and multiplicity of the things understood":*[56] *not only does God comprehend "an infinite number of propositions more (than man), since he knows them all," but while we are forced to* hear *those propositions to which we have access, he* sees *them all at a glance.*[57] *"Where we, for example, in order to acquire the understanding of some of the circle's properties (which has an infinity of them), start with one of the simplest and, establishing it through a definition, move on discursively to another, and from this one to a third and then a fourth, etc., divine intellect, by the simple grasp of its essence, understands without temporal discourse the entire infinity of these properties. . . . These passages that our intellect performs over time and step by step, divine intellect, like light, spans in an instant, which is the same as saying that it is always present to all of them."*[58] *The language is the same, but Galileo understands the difference between the two ways of articulating it according to the pairs of opposites diachronic/synchronic, finitude/infinite, or darkness/light. God is in transparency, encompasses the entire system at once without any reverse, embraces it; we are* in *the system, which enshrouds us, restricts our field, imposes on it a horizon line, subjecting us to discursivity. Despite the immediate meaning of these formulations, which could lead us to believe that the divine order is that of the visible and the human order that of discourse, the truth is that God* is *the pure language: in him elements have no thickness; they are only terms in the system of properties "that while being infinite are perhaps, in their essence and in divine understanding, only one"; whereas our understanding—"as if clouded by a thick and deep darkness"*[59]*—is stationed in this language as in a world of which it never glimpses more than a part, which it* *must travel, and where truths arise like events. God is the pure ubiquitous gaze that pierces the system of oppositions, instituting the textual without shadow and three-dimensional form, while we are plunged in difference.*

Unsurprisingly, we find this same break in the writings of Descartes, except that it is brought into such stark relief that its observation is made easier still.[60] *In Descartes, one notes a particular vividness granted the motif of sight, a passion for seeing, for a seeing that is passivity, of such power that it underpins even the theme of the system's constitution. Merleau-Ponty tried to show that the* Dioptric *essentially depends on the elimination of the living eye, its space-generating mobility, and the "power of icons" that corresponds to it: an optics of the blind whose function is indeed to rid the realm of the visible of its intrinsic heterogeneity in order to turn it into a space of reasoning, a "a space to be heard."*[61]

As Merleau-Ponty observes, however, this project of total geometrism is kept in check by many resistances. The "thought of seeing" does not manage to mask sight in action completely, for in this active sight there is a passivity that one can only attribute to a complicity between body and things that precedes the mind's inquiry and from which the latter will have to wrest clear and distinct understanding. Experienced space cannot enter thought space without remainder, and the union of body and soul hinders their separation.

Nonetheless, these remarks still rely on the hypothesis put forward by the phenomenologist of perception, in that the privileged, exclusive reference he makes is to the experience *of the visible, as opposed to its intellection. Things are not so simple, however. The essence of the visible is not object of experience, and good form is not its rule. The defining characteristic of the visible—namely, difference—reappears even in the theory of intellection itself. Admittedly, the theory of vision requires that seeing reduce itself into touch.*[62] *No doubt, too, the critique of the piece of wax depends on a symmetrical transformation of the mind into a geometric eye. And, just as undeniably, Descartes's method at its core is no more than a means of "proper sight." But in Descartes there is also a contrary impulse, the acknowledgment of the a priori of the field's thickness, of its radical heterogeneity to all geometrism. "Accurate" sight is never unmediated, but reclaimed from blurred vision. The mind's inquiry has a childhood, which is the murky and the phantasmagorical. It is essential for the Cartesian problematic that the mind find its origins in multiplicity and chaos, and that its initial state not be geometric "optics," but that it must reclaim itself from opacity and curvature.*

Such a fate, which allows for the ratio *to be born in its other, finds its model in the world of culture. This world is like a city*[63] *that holds, within the visible layout of its streets and neighborhoods, another layout, which it possessed a century ago, and yet another layout, each one connected to the others through urbanistic developments—some visible, some hidden—so that by wandering across this city, which is the world of the mind, the latter experiences a fundamental mobility: not only its own movement in relation to a map of the city assumed to be immutable and self-same, but the simultaneous movement of this map's various parts, such that by going from one neighborhood to another, or even by looking at a single monument or seemingly unified building, the mind goes from one city to another, from one moment of itself to another, and each one of these moments organizes all the other moments around itself, becoming like a focal point around which the other moments (the other areas of the city, each, in turn, having previously been focal points) appear deformed, twisted, unrecognizable. Each time the mind believes itself to be capturing an* intuitus *of the whole city, a sight free of prejudice, the act of seeing produces the anamorphosis of what is not located at the point of proper sight. This anamorphosis is not an anomaly: even though he sometimes hopes to get the better of it by rebuilding the entire city at one go, Descartes is well aware that the anamorphosis is an inherent in the field, and that the rationality of a "proper" point of view can only be built at the cost of neglecting on principle this peripheral curvature, this childhood, this event.*[64] *The crisis in the world of the mind, the crisis of culture, refers—by way of the metaphor of the city—to the crisis provoked, in reasoning, by the world of vision, which is that of passion. Never will Descartes forget the figural, even though he* neglects *it by methodological convention. The gap between the sign and the word will never be crossed out.*

In the end, this theme is similar to the one Galileo formulated in the Dialogo, *but here it finds itself transposed entirely in the analogy of the visible. This analogy runs through Descartes's whole oeuvre; even the demonstration of the method resorts to it. One could argue that the method's basic function is to constrict the object's anamorphosis. It seems to me that it is in this ambivalent relation to the visible, considered at once as ultimate context of reference and as site of the deformations, that the key to the arbitrary character that Descartes sometimes acknowledges in the method is to be found. Certainly, true knowledge is given by what meets the eye, by pure seeing, itself underwritten by divine veracity—and as such it is "natural light." But what is there to see at the outset of the search? The given must be put in order, an "order of reasons" different from that of "materials," and whose sole raison d'être, in the first place, is its utility: "by supposing an order even among those which do not naturally precede one another."*[65] *The only possible convention is to prefer the straight to the oblique, the simple to the complex, the identical to the dissimilar, the one to the multiple. Descartes knows this, and even when he does not rely on this artificiality of the method with regard to the given, his metaphors evoke it.*[66] *For us, these metaphors bring to mind the technique by which the Florentines, a century and a half earlier, had gained mastery over the field of deep vision at the very moment when they allowed it to "perforate the wall."*[67] *We know that Brunelleschi*[68] *had built a box-like device whose burnished metal back panel caught the light of day, and another side of which, representing the façade of the Duomo in Florence, was reflected in the mirror on the box's opposite side. The drawn panel had a hole in it, at the level of the cathedral's main entrance, offering a view of the façade's reflected image only to a single eye. This bridling of the gaze is the condition of the geometrization of the field of vision. The edge of the hole had the effect of blocking out the peripheral field, thus of "de-curving" perceptual space and rendering it as consistent as possible with the central focal area where the curvature (the anamorphosis) is negligible. It would henceforth be possible to enforce precise guidelines for the production of any object whatsoever on the picture plane: the golden rule of these guidelines is that this object be represented as it would appear to the eye observing it through the hole of Brunelleschi's box.* Costruzione legittima *depends on this convention, whose essential function is clear: to repress figural difference in favor of a unified Euclidian field.*

What does Descartes do when he wants to be rid of the phantasmatic and the sensory? He sets out to build a kind of mental box. *The mind, by placing its eye to it, will lay claim to an object freed, as much as possible, from all obscurity and confusion. If* intuitus*—the pure and attentive mind*[69]*—is "proper" sight, this is because it is cleared of the anamorphosis provoked by the overlapping of surfaces or outlines (confusion) and that of values (obscurity) one on top of the other. The Cartesian answer to the question "what does it mean to understand" consists in the fixing of the gaze* *on the object. This fixing is not merely that of the distance between the mind's eye and what it sees—a distance that must be optimal, just as the focal distance is in the field of optics.*[70] *It also affects the field's delineation, its "distinctness."*[71] *As with Alberti, legitimate vision is defined by the exclusion of everything that does not appear to the observer in "an obvious way," by the repression of the lateral.*

In contrast to Alberti's legitimacy, however, Descartes's knows itself to be arbitrary with respect to the object. The establishing of a proper depth of field and of a frame eliminating all confusion assumes that the physical properties of the optical system (thanks to which visual perception occurs) are known. These properties are fully independent from the object under scrutiny. For intellectual intuition, Descartes believes that we have no choice between systems: there is but one clarity and one distinction possible, which geometry, arithmetic, and analysis offer human understanding; their privilege derives from this mathematical discourse being the same as that in which God utters the world. Therein lies the metaphysical limit to the arbitrary's expansion. And it is this limit that subsequent mathematics will force open. But in the field of comparison—that of the visible—we experience different optical systems that betray the arbitrary nature of "proper" distance and "proper" aperture. The system's optical properties are entirely divorced from the object: no derivation *possible from the latter to the former. Consequently one must forgo all ambition to grasp any resemblance between the object and the image one has of it. This is not to say that Descartes performed this leap: it is all too obvious that the whole conception of ideas as set forth in the third Meditation and in the Replies to the second Objections* (more geometrico, *definitions III and IV) continues to rest on an implicit problematic, namely, that of* representation. *Take, for example, a picture representing a dog. This picture is "in" the mind. As far as it is composed of matter (in the case of a real painting, what plays the part of the canvas and color), its material reality is that of thinking substance. Yet it represents a dog. There are thus two dogs: the first is the visible dog painted on the canvas (the signifier or representative), which is the idea's objective reality, that is, "the entity or the being of the object represented by the idea, insofar as this entity is in the idea." A second, absent dog—the represented dog—is the idea's formal reality. When one no longer seeks to represent a* dog, *but* God, *the reality of the represented is no longer formal in relation to the painting-idea, but eminent: there is no longer conformity between the idea of*

God and God; rather, God infinitely exceeds the idea.[72] *Still I "conceive" of him, I see a recognizable representation of him.*[73]

Nevertheless, on the basis of this problematic, and even assuming a benevolent God who does not lie, who grants his unconditional guarantee to the principle of derivation, errors remain, and there is a need to invent rules of legitimate construction for the paintings in the mind. To avoid mistakes, one will need to, if not abandon the derivation of the representative from the represented, then at least not be satisfied with it, cut the cord that directly connects the object and the eye, and establish an autonomous order of the signifier that would contain, in itself and in its own plane, the principles of its effects of signification. There is another opportunity to consider this passivity that gives us the image; its model is provided by the arbitrariness of the elements of language: "We ought, however, to bear in mind that there are several things besides images which can excite our thought, as for instance, signs and words, which have no manner of resemblance to the things they signify."[74] *Now this reference to the arbitrariness of linguistic designation is what allows the arbitrariness to be revealed—to a lesser degree for us, but in itself identical—that differentiates the real object from its representation projected onto a plane. Taking the model of the word as starting point, the critique of representation can challenge the axiom of continuity between the image and its reference: "We must at least recognize that none of them [the images sent to the brain] can resemble in all respects the object it represents; for there would then be no distinction between the object and its image. It is sufficient that images resemble their objects in some few respects; and often, indeed, their perfection depends on their not resembling them as much as they might have done." This is where the comparison with graven figures comes into play:*

> *Thus, in the case of engravings, made up of a little ink disposed here and there on the paper, we see how they represent forests, towns, men and even battles and tempests, while yet of the infinity of diverse qualities which they make us conceive in these objects, the only one of these qualities to which they bear any proper resemblance is the quality of shape* [figure]; *and even this is a very imperfect resemblance, since it is on a completely flat surface that they represent bodies diverse in height and distance, and further that in accordance with the rules of perspective they often represent circles better by ovals than*

> *by other circles, and squares by four-sided figures which are not squares, and similarly in the case of all other shapes* [figures]. *And thus it comes about that often, precisely in order to be more perfect in their quality as images, i.e., the better to represent an object, they ought not to resemble it. Now it is in this way that we must think of the images which take form in the brain, and must recognize that the only question we need raise is that of knowing how the images can supply to the mind the means of sensing all the diverse qualities of the objects to which they stand related, and not how in themselves they bear resemblance to them.*[75]

Dissimilis similitudo? *As we saw with Hugh, the two sides of the sign tend to come apart, and the one is all the truer when its production obeys the rules of its own order. But this relation has shifted entirely. In the Middle Ages, the signifier is the sensory, and the signified is divine discourse: their dissimilarity or* diformitas *is negative proof of the existence of truth. Here, however, the "signified" is no longer what is signified, but represented, and what is tasked with its representation is a fiction inscribed on a plane. Yet what is inscribed on a plane and is fictional is likely to take the form of writing. In principle, like any other linguistic system, writing signifies in itself, without analogy the designated. The representative has its own rules, and projective geometry constitutes the set of these rules.*[76] *Before, the figures of the sensory "uttered" the Creator's discourse, which was itself figural (narrative): they were its plastic signifiers. Now they have become the possible objects of designation of an abstract discourse. The dissimilarity between the latter and the things of which it speaks derives from discourse's internal* conformitas *to itself. This discourse* is *truth. Admittedly, it is still thought to be that held by God. However, first of all, this God combines elements chosen arbitrarily: his function is no longer to test and absolve a creature thrust in an ontological tragedy; rather, he is only the hypostatized anticipation of the nineteenth-century mathematician. Second, and more important, we now have access to an equivalent of another order than what the creature is for him, namely the object "seen" ("conceived" would be more apt) in the box, that is, reduced to the two dimensions of the projective screen, scripted, perfectly legible, made obvious, seen to exhaustion. The obvious being the (impossible) sublimation of the figural in the textual.*

3.1. This shift in the conception of space began to take hold of pictorial theory and practice long before speculation drew philosophical implications from it. It is there, in the spontaneous formation of the new plastic order, that we can properly see, and therefore fully signify, what we glimpsed in the theory, namely, the separation of the signifier from the signified and its anchoring in the designated—in short, the constitution of representation. One can hope to catch sight of this process in progress by placing side by side the last great painting that remains as faithful as possible to the textual tradition, and the first great painting that presents itself as representation: Duccio's Maestà,[77] *and the frescoes Masaccio painted in the Brancacci Chapel of Santa Maria del Carmine.*[78] *The choice of these works warrants a few words of explanation.*

Duccio has been cast as one of the precursors of the deep space that will come to prominence a century later. By following the evolution of certain motifs (notably that of the Putto, *the little naked boy ubiquitous in Hellenistic and Roman traditions, who will take the place of the Christian "virtues" in a* Last Supper *attributed to the studio of Pietro Lorenzetti, c. 1320–1330), Erwin Panofsky*[79] *demonstrates that these conventional objects derived from Classical art, especially sculpture, find their way into Trecento painting, where they determine entirely different iconographic properties than those associated with the pictorial space of the Sienese tradition.*[80] *This particular late Gothic space had for the most part retained what Panofsky calls the "surface consolidation," the "cartographic" tendency typical of Romanesque miniature painting, which treats the background as "a solid, planar working surface" and the figure as "a system of two-dimensional area defined by one-dimensional lines."*[81] *Panofsky's argument is that the problem Duccio tried to solve was already that of the constitution of a "picture space," of an "apparently three-dimensional expanse, composed of bodies . . . and interstices, that seem to extend indefinitely, though not necessarily infinitely, behind the objectively two-dimensional painting surface."*[82] *It is still, however, saying too little to assert that Duccio attempts to find a solution to this problem by different means than Giotto,*[83] *that the former is much more beholden to the Byzantine tradition than the latter.*[84] *The truth is that the means employed by the Sienese painter imply the exact opposite of what will be the basic requirement of perspective, which is the illusionistic opening of the background into the support's dissolution. Duccio's means imply precisely the support's presence, and it is up to script to ensure that the support on which it is inscribed does not dissolve. One would be hard pressed to see in the* Maestà *a modern space—that is, a "Greco-Roman space* 'vu à travers le tempérament gothique.'"[85]

Panofsky provides four illustrations of this work that he believes substantiate his thesis, namely the panels depicting the Last Supper, the Crucifixion, the Descent from the Cross, and the Annunciation of the Death of the Virgin. One can accept that the painter offers us "perfectly consistent, boxlike interiors, their ceilings, pavements and side walls 'fitly framed together.'"[86] *However, this coherence is not that of sight. Panofsky astutely remarks that these interiors are not seen from within, but from without: "the painter, far from introducing us into the structure, only removes its front wall so as to transform it into a kind of oversized dollhouse."*[87] *But Panofsky omits to mention that the perspective ordering these dollhouses is in most cases inverted; that the Crucifixion takes place "out-of-doors," against a gold background handed down directly by Gothic tradition; and that most of the outdoor scenes confront the eye with this same background plane, which is none other than the clearly displayed surface of the plastic screen. With this in mind, one cannot conclude that "the works of Duccio and Giotto confront us with a space no longer discontinuous and finite, but (potentially at least) continuous and infinite."*[88] *As Francastel has argued, the whole problem of the new space cannot be reduced to that of perspective,*[89] *and if Giotto is so important it is not for having depicted, on the wall of the Scrovegni Chapel, auxiliary chapels seen at an angle rather than frontally.*[90] *Likewise, the reappearance in Trecento art of types of codified objects inherited from Antiquity is undoubtedly significant, but it involves only a strictly iconographic level, that is, the language* [langue] *of conventional objects. What matters to us is not so much to determine what the figurative units are as to know in which space they organize themselves. In this sense, the opposition between Duccio and Masaccio is indisputable: from the one to the other a tremendous shift has taken place, which clearly concerns the figure's relation to its support. And this relation is strictly subordinated to that of the figure to meaning, for the relation to the support defines the nature of the sign, thereby implying a particular kind of relation between its three poles.*

The choice of Masaccio seems less debatable than that of Duccio. It would be difficult to deny the former the feat of having accomplished what Vasari had already acknowledged: to have "perforated the wall," something for which every painter who has come to study in the Brancacci Chapel has paid tribute to him. Francastel, who demonstrated that when it comes to perspective, Masaccio's master was still Masolino,[91] *admits to having overemphasized linear perspective to the detriment of other aspects of the figurative space of the Carmine frescoes.*[92] *Because these are precisely the reasons that lead me to prefer the latter over other, no less celebrated works such as the* Trinity *in Santa Maria Novella, I quote them here in full: "Masaccio is a painter like Poussin, Manet or Cézanne: it is through color that he directly models form. A good example . . . would be the figure of the soldier accepting the tribute money in the well-known composition in the Brancacci Chapel. Firmly planted on his feet at the edge of the space and of the fresco, his back to the viewer, this impressive swordsman, with his taut calves, insolently leaning backwards, no longer harks back to the figures of Gothic cathedrals, but to the visual experience of each and everyone. He no longer owes his poise to the weight and volume of his cloak: his tunic molds his body. He exists in and of himself, isolated from the background, suspended in space according to laws that are equally unrelated to the methods of measured perspective; oscillating under our eyes through the illusions only painting can produce. As for Adam and Eve, they too are placed at the edge of the frame, detached from the wall, hovering in the viewer's space. . . .* Henceforth the human figure will be defined not by the acts and tales [récits] that situate it in a story [histoire], but by an immediate physical and sensorial grasp that creates presence. The goal of figuration will be appearances, and no longer meaning."[93]

Through the use of color and, I would add, of value, Masaccio produces on the chapel wall a space of oscillation, distinct from that of the wall as well as of the beholder, which occupies a radically new position: that of representation. The Trinity *(Plate 6) is undoubtedly more significant when it comes to linear perspective, but it is less so from the point of view of representation, for while its aim is to create the illusion of an altar located under a loggia, this illusion is undermined by at least two features: the kneeling figures in prayer at the foot of the purported loggia strike the altogether "scripted" pose of donors in Gothic altarpieces; and the group standing within the space of the loggia makes it impossible to ascribe to this space an illusionistic function. The appearance of the three divine figures refers directly to Christian symbolism, and the space in which they appear cannot communicate plastically with the beholder's own space: through its signified, the space in which the Trinity stands is a symbolic one, whose model is to be found in the depictions* of Christ in glory in the mandorlas of Romanesque tympana. This piece, therefore, suffers from a kind of strain between the use of perspectival means and the subject,[94] between plastic signifier and sacred signified.[95] Here the signifier's rotation is much less bold than in the Carmine frescoes, already caught in the grips of linear perspective's architectural script. To understand fully the implications of this rotation, it is helpful to contrast these frescoes with Duccio's *Maestà*.

I would like to suggest that it is thanks to this rotation that the repressed of medieval civilization—that is, difference as attribute of the figural—briefly emerges, and that it will immediately find itself rejected once more through the geometric organization of the field of vision. We need to pinpoint the moment when the Christian balance between the figural and the discursive is destabilized; to indicate the nature of this destabilization; and to identify by what (fundamentally different) means it is neutralized. The area through which runs the fault line comes across as a privileged moment, when the primary space in Freudian terms—the space of desire—erupts in the secondary field instituted by script. The Carmine frescoes are at the epicenter of the upheaval, while the *Trinity* is on the sidelines where the shaken strata once again find their equilibrium and geometric order regains the upper hand. I will argue that Masaccio's frescoes are opposed to Duccio's altarpiece as the representational is to the textual. What follows is an inventory of the characteristics that stand in relevant opposition to one another in this regard.

1. The value of Duccio's line is essentially graphic, whereas with Masaccio the contour is plastic. Compare the faces and limbs in the *Descent from the Cross* and those of *The Expulsion from the Garden of Eden* (Plates 7 and 8). In the former, a continuous outline delineates the bodies' silhouette; in the latter, not only has the line disappeared—making it possible for tones and values to enter into direct contact—but passages interrupt the contour, allowing the body, the face or an element thereof (Eve's mouth) to communicate with its immediate surroundings.

2. Nowhere does the *Maestà* stray from the chromatic code inherited from Byzantine tradition: the Virgin and Christ wear a blue cloak over a red garment, the Magdalene is in red, etc. The chromatic unity of the whole belongs to a system independent of its visual effect in actual perception. The chromatic unity of *The Tribute Money* is plastic, built on the green-orange-purple triad (the three intermediate primary colors), which bathes the scene in an atmosphere of half-tint, endowing it with an immediate visual unity (Plate 10).

3. In Duccio's work, relief itself is scripted: the shadows cast by the arch of the eyebrows and the curve of the mouth are rendered independently of the face's position. A striking example can be found in the Descent from the Cross, *where even though Mary and Jesus face each other, their faces are lit symmetrically. With Masaccio, light and shadow deconstruct the faces, bodies, clothing, and backgrounds in such a way as to sculpt them into volumes whose values are independent of the represented entities.*

4. The figures' arrangement in Duccio's panel is essentially informational. This becomes apparent when one compares the number of feet and heads in the Christ before Pilate *(Plate 9). It will also be noted that the group of Pharisees standing outside of the small chapel is not articulated plastically with the group of soldiers inside it. In* The Tribute Money, *the apostles are arranged around Jesus in a kind of semicircle; more telling, however, is the fact that the unit they form as a group is communicated by the distribution of values defining a light swath of faces, and by the composition that grants the gestures and cloaks of the six figures in the foreground a garland-like rhythm. Taking a step back, one sees that on the whole the* Tribute *sums up three consecutive episodes—a "narrative" logic that seems to recall the Gothic scripting of the Holy story.*[96] *Yet it should be noted that the three episodes cannot be read according to textual diachrony, since their order—from left to right—follows the sequence 2, 1, 3. This sequence forces the eye to scan and scrutinize the space, preventing it from carrying out a straightforward act of recognition, and thereby, once more, placing the work in a profoundly unscripted space. By contrast, the back of the* Maestà *that describes the Passion "reads" from left to right and from bottom to top.*[97]

5. Duccio is not concerned with perspective, nor even with realistic verisimilitude. In the panel depicting the Funeral of the Virgin *(Plate 11a), the city wall's angle of curvature contradicts that of the hexagonal structure: the wall is represented as if seen from below, while the chapel is from above. The plastic effect is otherwise impressive, allowing us to see the city from a number of points of view simultaneously, so that it "dances" as if in a dissolve or a Cubist painting.*[98] *What is more, the Virgin's bed is depicted in reverse perspective, with the vanishing point positioned out in front of the painting. Likewise, in the* Christ before Pilate, *one notices that the Christ figure interrupts the middle column:*[99] *as many indications that the figure's function is to signify a text, and not to represent visible action.*

With Masaccio, not only do we have the use of linear perspective (whose vanishing point coincides with Jesus's head) but something like an aerial perspective (Plate 11b) of the kind Leonardo would later develop, which slowly leads the eye toward the backdrops through storied planes of contrasting value.[100]

6. All of the scenes in the Brancacci Chapel attributed to Masaccio are located "out-of-doors." The eye does not enter into the houses. The trick afforded by the illusionistic chapel, allowing the outside viewer to see what goes on inside, is abandoned.[101] *Not only is the perspective in the two back frescoes consistent,*[102] *but in all of those painted by Masaccio the lighting is distributed as if its source were positioned above the chapel's altar,*[103] *that is, at the right for the frescoes to the left of the altar (which is the case of* The Tribute Money*), and at the left for those placed to its right. In the* Maestà, *interior and exterior are not differentiated plastically but rather by a convention (noted by Panofsky*[104]*) that consists in including a proscenium when the viewer is assumed to be outside of the structure in which the scene takes place, and removing it when the viewer is assumed to be inside it. We are thus able to tell that Herod is seated outdoors and that Pilate sits inside a loggia, yet the lighting is the same in both cases (Plate 12). If one may be tempted to speak of interior lighting, this is because the modeling of the clothing and the faces—fully coded and unrelated to the lighting in which the field of perception is normally immersed—gives the impression that each figure possesses its own source of lighting and its immutable angle of illumination. Hence these panels' hidden power of ubiquity: the story they tell does not unfold either in the space or the time of perception; instead their meaning is like their plastic value—true everywhere and localized nowhere—and, as such, identical to the position of writing that, as linguistic phenomenon, is subject to a system (not a substance), and as inscription implies the absence of a scriptor. Scripted meaning, therefore, "unexists" doubly.*

7. This is why the relationship with the support is crucial, for all the oppositions enumerated above find embodiment in it. The Maestà*'s scenes occur* on a background *rather than* against a background. *They are deprived of depth, and the figures are inscribed on the wood as if they were graphemes.*[105] *The altarpiece is painted on both sides: the faithful would come up to it, "read" the cycle of Mary, then go behind to "read" that of the Passion. This mode of inscription is the same as that of letters on the leaves of a book. The size of the panels further encouraged a "reading," the minute recognition of events signified in a story with which all* *viewers would have been otherwise intimately familiar. The Brancacci Chapel may well be much smaller than the main altar of the Siena Cathedral; nevertheless Masaccio's frescoes in the former are meant to be seen, not read.*[106] *The faithful would of course have recognized fragments of the same holy story as in Siena. But this recognition—akin to reading, that is, to the immediate grasp of the signified on the signifier—finds itself vehemently contested by an entirely different operation, to which Duccio paid no heed: the reverie. A window open on a bleak chiaroscuro where a debt-related transaction is unfolding silently between very somber individuals: such a scene lends itself to phantasies. In Siena, we are of course free to fantasize on the basis of, and according to, the text, but in the Carmine chapel there is no longer any folio, there is a* mise en scène. *And Masaccio takes a huge step forward at once, for he even does away with the backdrop that in Late Gothic illuminated manuscripts was commonly stretched behind the figures,*[107] *and that he himself knew perfectly well how to render as the background of a piazza in Masolino's* Tabitha.[108] *A scene devoid of backdrop is an open space for desire and anxiety to represent their progeny endlessly and lawlessly. The discovery of infinite and continuous space*[109] *is not primarily that of a neutral substance where an axiomatics will put all of its possible propositions into play. Nor is it the discovery of a world given over to human activity. For Masaccio, it is rather the discovery of the absence of a world, of a space where the phantasmatic, hitherto harnessed and sublimated in the Christian tale of Redemption, asserts itself in it, promising to shatter it: the discovery, in other words, of a space no longer sacred (textual) and not yet geometrical (textual), but imaginary.*

Before specifying how this mobile expanse will become frozen in neutral space, we need to locate as precisely as possible the rotation at work in Masaccio's oeuvre. It is here that the previously analyzed separation between linguistic term and sign will prove valuable.

In the visual arts of the Middle Ages (a cavalier way of putting it, though legitimate if used simply in opposition to the phase Masaccio inaugurates), the iconic signifier *is built "like" a text. This is not to say that it is a text, for however big the scope for the arbitrariness of lines and colors may be, it does not eliminate all resemblance with the facial or scenic models given in perception. Nevertheless, the treatment of the figures obeys a code, an oppositional system that is never transgressed and an adherence to which guarantees the subject's quick recognition. In their relation to the signified, these figures tend to enjoy a status similar to that of letters of a text, authorizing the combinations of the two spaces discussed above. The* signified *to which the images and texts refer is the biblical tale; this signified is constituted by a narrative and metaphorical discourse. On account of these two points, we are justified in claiming that in the art of the Middle Ages, the figure is in the signified. Lastly,* the reference *or* designated *is reduced to a degree zero, for the same reason that the figure turns into a quasi-graphic signifier: what one "speaks" of is perceptually absent, present only* in illo tempore *[at that time], and its figurative reality amounts only to the possibility of recognizing it easily.*[110] *No doubt, we should not overlook the power of* dissimilitudo *in opening the painter's eyes toward the designated taken as such. But this power will never clear a free dimension of representation in the order marked by the signifier-signified relation. As a whole, therefore, the medieval system can be defined as follows: difference is in the signified (discourse of the ontological [hi]story); opposition is in the plastic signifier (quasi-script); and reference is crossed out (no representation).*

In the art of Masaccio, the signifier *is no longer scripted as a text would be, nor is it yet fully reconstituted according to the rules of geometric optics. This means, first, that the signifier has lost the close, theoretically inseparable relation that in a linguistic system weds the signifying side of each term to its signified side. Indeed, secular "subjects" (or signifieds) will be able to take place in the new space on the same footing as biblical subjects, followed, ultimately, by "non-subjects" such as the still life. Second, this means that the signifier's subordination to the strict type of designated of geometric optics—which is the basis for Alberti's* costruzione legittima, *and which will impose itself as the new script—is not yet achieved for the figures of the Carmine. The latter draw their signifying power by obeying a whole other set of rules—those, precisely, of the phantasy.*[111] *As for the* signified, *it too now finds itself crossed out, particularly in its narrative function (it will be possible to have still lifes and portraits that signify nothing, in the sense that they do not tell any story), while all of the figural power that once resided in the Christian narrative is transferred onto the* designated, *what is* "shown." *Thus what we have, in sum, is a system in which the lost meaning in the order of discourse crosses over to reference, and where the signifier organizes itself as the*

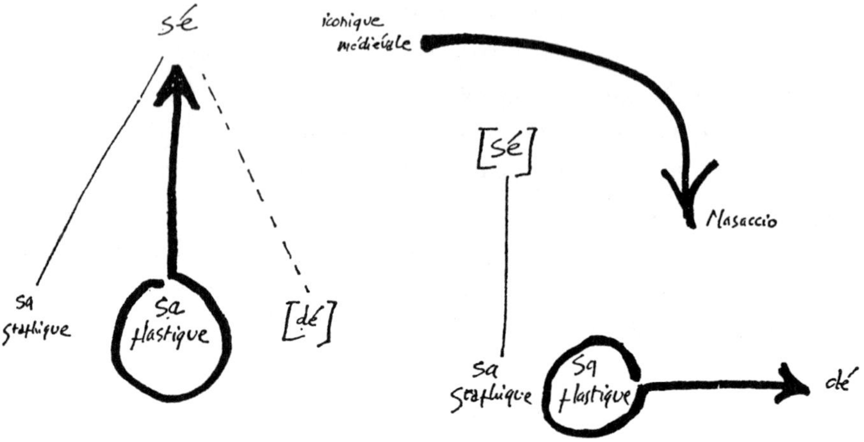

Figure 3. Diagram depicting the rotation of the plastic signifier when the pictorial space of the Quattrocento replaces medieval "graphics" with the illusion of depth.

re-presentation, behind a pane of glass, of an object for which various types of "mise en scène," *that is, various pictorial schools, may be deployed. Painting ceases to signify; it makes visible. This rotation can be seen in the diagram above (Figure 3, and the commentary in "Notes on Figures and Plates").*

In the Middle Ages, thickness, or difference, was to be found in the discourse narrating sacred History (signified); then it switched sides, to that of the designated. This shift of thickness corresponds to the constitution of representation. To say that from now on the function of the signifier is to make something visible (the designated) is to say that it acts as a stage director, and no longer as the material face of a particular discourse. The position of the image changes completely: no longer discourse's lining, it becomes a theater or mirror, carving out behind its glass pane a deep stage where the phantasmatic becomes hallucinatory [où la fantasmatique s'hallucine]. For one stages what one cannot signify, and one makes visible what is unsayable. *Representation depends on the disjuncture of the discourse-figure couple.*[112] *Even when this mirror-image once again begins to "become scripted"—that is to say, almost immediately (the* Trinity *in Santa Maria Novella postdates the frescoes of the Brancacci Chapel by two years; and it is for the former that Vasari has the greatest praise)—this new "script" will fulfill an entirely different function than that of Romanesque manuscripts or the* Maestà. *I will return to this.*

But first, one more point: the constitution of representation as neither real nor mythical space on a chapel wall is obviously connected with the constitution of a new discourse of knowledge. The intersection of the two movements occurs, as we know, with Manetti and Brunelleschi, and again with Leonardo. But even if this intersection were undocumented, the articulation would remain indisputable. The discourse of knowledge has a tendency to constitute itself as a text that claims to rid itself of all figural trace: hence its potential break—slow at first, but effective in the end—with Christian discourse. Hence, too, the figural's foreclosure and its constitution as exteriority. Christian myth had a symbolics at its disposal to express difference; the new physics has none.[113] *Difference moves to the outside, as what is unsaid, like something residual. Representation is the position of meaning that enables this residual to be shown, if not signified. I see in the return of antiquity during the Renaissance precisely the return of the repressed of Christian civilization. It is not surprising that this return should happen by way of forms borrowed from classical statuary. Sculpture in the round was not the glorification of the human body; rather, it is the total unmooring* [dérive] *of the plastic signifier. Before, when it was engraved in low or high relief on the wall of a sacred monument, this signifier was to be read: it recounted the sacred legend; it was the temple's speech. Now we can move around the god. The statue's complete three-dimensionality will be a measure of how far the god has retreated. This retreat is not of the same nature as the absence of a speaker who would have left behind a written document, a testament, before disappearing. Zeus's (or Poseidon's) absence from Cape Artemision is that of the object of perception, of an autonomous object that exists for itself. This god speaks no more; it offers itself up to be seen. How not to relate the bringing into representation of the divine in statuary with the development of the city? When the political sphere opens up, the dimension of the sacred shifts: the political and philosophical word is uttered by human beings and no longer received by them as emanating from an Other; and both the linguistic and plastic signifier desert the temple and move to "the middle,"* ἐς μέσον [es meson]. *The opacity now belongs to the naked man, standing on his pedestal in the middle of the Agora.*[114]

One must be clear about what the appearance of depth in the pictorial order means in this context. The rotation described above separates discourse from its object, and this schism is science (skizein, scire). *The object is placed at the edge of discourse, in the position of the designated, and science is the language that will take care of signifying it. But the break will remain, irreversible, consubstantial with the object's position. A discourse that banishes the presence of the figural from itself cannot bridge the gap separating it from its object, denying itself the possibility of becoming expressive. The function of pictorial representation is precisely to show the figural as unsignified. The window Masaccio traces on the wall does not open onto the discovery of the world, but onto its loss, or, rather, its discovery as lost.*[115] *The window is not open, there is the pane of representation that separates by making visible, that makes that space* over there *oscillate, neither here (like that of a trompe l'oeil), nor elsewhere (like Duccio's). If, at the beginning of the Quattrocento, the West elevates painting—which until then had been a minor craft, a "mechanical art"—to the dignity of art par excellence, this is because the West must now re-present: represent what is absent to it (reality),* but was once present to it, *and what is not signifiable in discourse. The world, from the Renaissance onward, withdraws into the silence of the foreclosed. Yet great artworks still manage to* show *this silence, which is that of the figural itself, through the same reversal the Greek tragic authors taught us: the payment of the debt depicted on the walls of the Brancacci Chapel is steeped in a somber light, demonstrating*—negatively—*that this settlement is nothing more than a fulfillment of desire, just as Sophocles makes visible, through the ruthless unfolding of events, that the Oedipal quest for constituted knowledge is an illusion.*

4. Science quickly smothered Masaccio's wisdom. The painter died in 1428 at the age of twenty-seven. The Latin manuscript of Alberti's De pictura *is dated 1435; its Italian translation, 1436. It is unnecessary to go over what Francastel has so persuasively argued: not only that Renaissance vision is not "natural," that legitimate construction bears no relation whatsoever to the immediate perception of a reality, and that the modern way is no less conventional than its predecessor, but, moreover, that one must be careful to dissociate two strands in the early Quattrocento movement, and distinguish their contrasting effects: "The conception of closed space, and that of open space combining on an equal footing both close and distant objects, but exclusive of any exact reproduction through the reduction of scale or the elimination of the background."*[116] *One should not confuse this spatial openness with the "linear projection of space on a flat surface based on the system of geometrical coordinates reduced to a single point of view."*[117] *In fact, the gridding of the plastic screen through "legitimate construction" is compatible with the upholding of the principle of the plastic cube that we saw systematically applied in Duccio's work. According to Francastel, compositions based exclusively on the principle of the open space are exceedingly rare.*[118] *Most often, compromises are reached between the principle of the cube and the requirement of openness that appeared with Masaccio. The* veduta *is one such compromise. In a cube, it allows another scene* [scène] *to be made visible through a window.*[119] *"Another" scene, since it cannot be integrated—through either its atmospheric perspective, linear construction, or chromatic spectrum—with the cube's interior space. It is a case of compromise-formation: compromise between the cube's closure and the openness of a boundless space, but above all between script and figure.*

For the important thing, it seems to me, is not the fact of the veduta *so much as the principle of compromise that establishes the representational position in its universality. The expanse glimpsed through the* vedute *of a cubic space constitutes an arrangement in which the open and the exterior are presented as the* elsewhere *of the interior and the enclosed, while the latter is presented as a scene staged in a world wholly different from what goes on "outside." In most cases the interior is what remains scripted, coded in accordance with Christian narrative; on the contrary, the exterior (landscape, city, second scene, still life, and even another interior*[120]*) allows for a different plastic handling, due to its secular nature. The effect of representation is achieved through the combination of a textual space and a figural one: in the former, the plastic screen is treated like a graphic support; in the latter, like a windowpane overlooking a deep space.*

Now, the veduta's *compromise between cube and open space is but an initial episode of representation. Even when, in subsequent generations, the cube will be abandoned, even when Leonardo will attempt to introduce the total unification of pictorial space through the interplay of the three perspectives, representational effect will not be abolished. In fact, the combination between the support's graphic and plastic treatments (i.e., the compromise specific to representation) is maintained. Figurative representation requires that the object be designated as unsignified. Insofar as painting designates the object and makes it visible, it treats the medium as a translucent window; but for the object to be understood as something situated elsewhere, its trace on the window must still be registered in such a way as to render this elsewhere identifiable. If the perspectival code were not observed, the trace could not function as trace, that is, refer to something beyond the support. The power to designate the elsewhere, the flip side, is subordinated to the existence of a system that inscribes its own combinations on the front side. The referential function presupposes a combinatorics of signs that is like a discourse inscribed on the plastic screen. Descartes, as we saw, will say that an oval refers to a circle, an oblique to an orthogonal line, an elevation to a receding into depth, etc. The painters of the Quattrocento will therefore establish a syntax and a lexicon of the correspondences between the object theoretically visible "on the other side" of the screen and its trace on the screen. Projective geometry emerges in order to fulfill this function; it tells us how to combine and inscribe on paper geometrical figures endowed with referential power. Inasmuch as the painter wants to designate something beyond the support, she or he has no choice but to signify it* on *this support as if it were a blueprint.*

Representational painting regards the support at once as a transparency that makes visible and an opacity that makes legible. Such is the compromise in its purest form; it reveals the truth of the compromise Francastel discovered between the cube and the open space: the cube is still beholden to the scripted signifying order of Gothic painting, while the veduta *opens the dimension of designation. As early as the second generation, in part with Mantegna, the initial solution of cube plus* veduta *subsides, and the system of segregated planes takes hold of plastic space altogether.*[121] *Now the beholder finds her- or himself in the cube, and the picture itself is the window. The latter is no longer represented; it is the painting-window that represents. The signification of loss, of the presence of absence, which is specific to representation, is entirely invested on the transparent yet impenetrable screen, where the traces of something happening over there are registered.*

I want to argue that it is this compulsion to represent that provides the true reason for the victory of closure over openness in Quattrocento painting.[122] *The force of habit and the still vibrant legacy of the International Gothic style*[123] *are not enough to explain why the school of thought represented by the narrow geometrism of Alberti's* Treatise *prevailed over the floating and quasi-anamorphic position indicated in the background of* The Tribute Money. *In any case, the script is no longer the same in both cases. There is a different reason, I believe. By following the direction suggested by Masaccio, one moves toward the space of the late Cézanne. This space is not at all representational any more. Instead, it embodies the deconstruction of the focal zone by the curved area in the periphery of the field of vision. It no longer makes an "over there" visible according to geometric optics, but manifests Mount Sainte-Victoire in the process, as it were, of making itself visible, that is, manifests the landscape with its distortions, overlappings, ambiguities, and discrepancies, such as one can* see it before looking at it, *before the orthogonal coordination of its sites take effect. It is as if the painter no longer placed us in the spatial cube, but at the threshold of the eye, to allow us to see what is supposed to occur on a retina looking at Mount Sainte-Victoire—as if, in other words, the painter made us see what seeing is. And since the beholder, in this hypothesis, stands at the same spot as the object, it is exactly as if it were the mountain looking at the retinal image of itself through the aperture of a pupil.*

Brunelleschi's box, Manetti's geometry, Alberti's treatise, and all the subsequent treatises on perspective perform a specific function: to learn how to script the traces of the designated on the windowpane.[124] *"Perspective," says Leonardo, "is nothing else than seeing a place behind a plane of glass, quite transparent, on the surface of which the objects behind that glass are to be drawn. These can be traced in pyramids to the point in the eye, and these pyramids are intersected on the glass plane."*[125] *The proper projective method is the subject of endless debate. As usual, however, what is overlooked is what matters; as Leonardo succinctly put it: "Perspective is the bridle and rudder of painting."*[126] *What is overlooked in all the treatises lies indeed in the regulating function of perspective, and this function consists entirely in the right-angle rotation by which the distance from the "eye-point" to the screen is transferred onto the latter so as to establish the oblique from which the objects' foreshortening will be determined (Figures 4, 5*[127]*). From this rotation, we come to understand exactly the operation of script: the transcription of depth into length and width, and the corresponding transformation of the clear sheet of glass into opaque surface. This rotation of meaning is directly opposed to that which I described to convey the importance of the Masaccian revolution: rather than the exteriorization of what was scripted, it is the scripting of exteriority. This simple operation is enough to make clear what is at stake in the new form of closure involved in, or applied to, the representational function. This closure is no longer that of medieval script, but of geometrical optics, acting not through the*

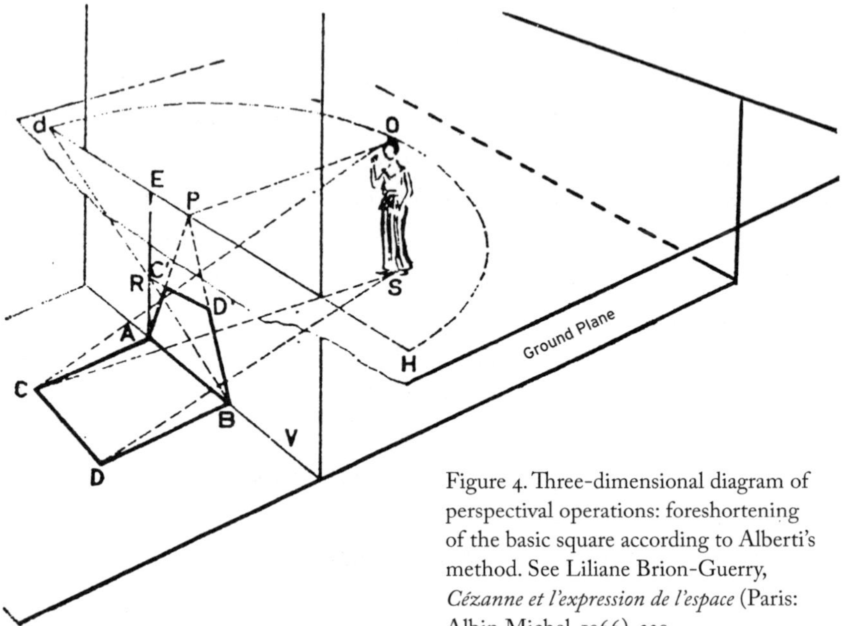

Figure 4. Three-dimensional diagram of perspectival operations: foreshortening of the basic square according to Alberti's method. See Liliane Brion-Guerry, *Cézanne et l'expression de l'espace* (Paris: Albin Michel, 1966), 229.

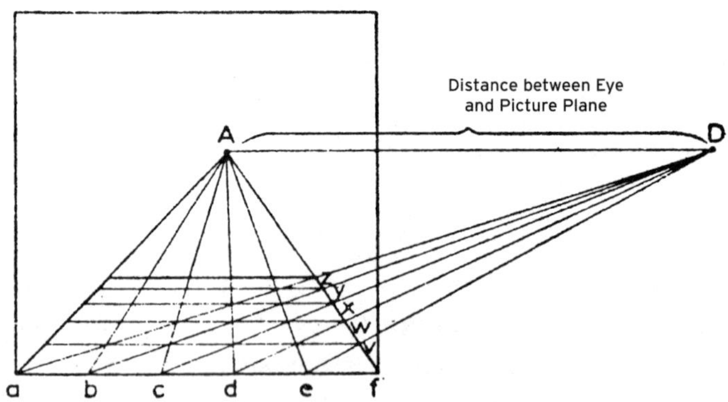

Figure 5. Two-dimensional rendering of perspectival operations: perspectival construction of a checkered floor by means of the *Distanzpunktverfahren,* or method of the distance point, first described by Giacomo Barozzi da Vignola in his treatise *Due regole della prospettiva pratica,* published in 1583. See Erwin Panofsky, *Renaissance and Renascences in Western Art* (Uppsala: Almqvist and Wiksells, 1960), 125.

symbolic—that is, through the channeling of the figural in a sacred text whose signified is unalterable and essentially unintelligible—but through the measured combination of geometrical elements into figures entirely independent of what they "say," that is, of their signified.

This is how the neutralization of space comes to be specified. The two rotations constitute the two moments and the two directions that run through the Quattrocento, at the same time as the two operations of this neutralization.[128] *The process of exteriorization is the expression of the phantasy; the process of scripting is its rationalization. In the end, this double rotation altered the site of inscription: the Quattrocento figure no longer belongs on the leaf of a Bible,*[129] *because it no longer is a plastic sign (close relative of the written "sign") enjoying a similar relation to the signified of the Scriptures as the holy text does to what it means to say. So where does the figure's inscription now take place? Alberti offers the following observation at the beginning of the second book of his* Treatise: *"Painting contains a divine force which not only makes absent men present, as friendship is said to do, but moreover makes the dead seem almost alive. Even after many centuries they are recognized with great pleasure and with great admiration for the painter."*[130] *For his part Leonardo will state that "the first painting was merely an outline of a man's shadow that the sun projected onto a wall."*[131] *The figure has become* representational sign *because it refers to something set back, beyond its immediate plane, in a space opened behind the support where it stands. It is therefore essential for the figure that this support be transparent.*[132] *Leonardo perfectly identified and explored this new function of the support: "Have a piece of glass as large as a half sheet of royal folio paper and set thus firmly in front of your eyes that is, between your eye and the thing you want to draw; then place yourself at a distance of two-thirds of a braccia from the glass, fixing your head with a machine in such a way that you cannot move it at all. Then shut or entirely cover one eye and with a brush or red chalk draw upon the glass that which you see beyond it; then trace it on paper from the glass, afterward transfer it onto good paper, and paint it if you like, carefully attending to the aerial perspective."*[133] *Leonardo moreover understood no less perfectly the essential relation connecting in pictorial reality the windowpane's function with the mirror's. For if "the mirror is the master of painters,"*[134] *and if the picture representing the object is to be compared to the object's image reflected on the mirror's surface (and not to the object itself), this is because*

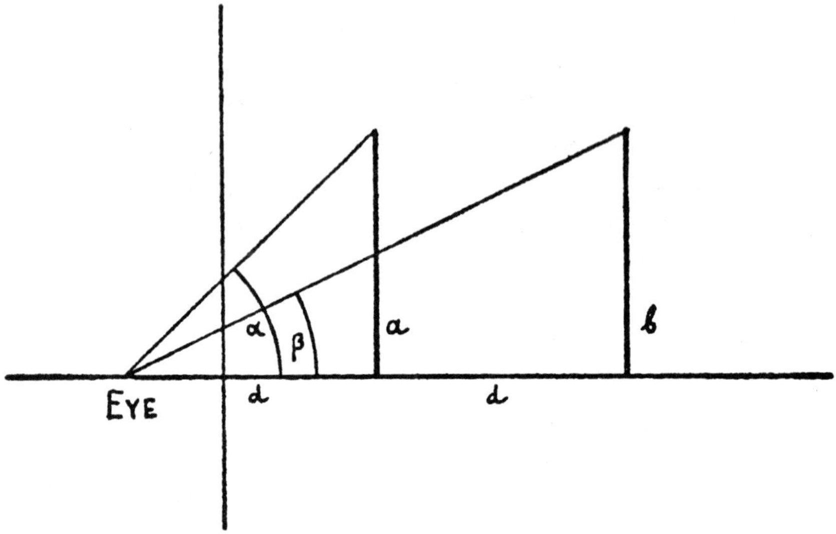

Figure 6. Difference in perspectival reduction depending on whether it is obtained by the "distance axiom" or "angle axiom." See Panofsky, *Renaissance and Renascences,* 129.

the mirror represents in itself the "physical" solution to the problem of inscribing on a plane objects placed outside of this plane. The painter will adopt the precepts of geometrical optics in order for the plastic surface to play a representational role identical to that of the mirror.

The following fact, reported by Panofsky,[135] *is particularly symptomatic of the real compulsion motivating this attitude: the translators of Euclid's* Optics *leave out or amend the eighth Theorem, which stated explicitly that "the apparent difference between equal magnitudes seen from unequal distances is not inversely proportional to these distances" but rather directly proportional to the respective width of the angles (Figure 6). The significance of this rejection is clear. Taking* α *and* β *as apparent magnitudes would be to admit that a spherical space* surrounds *the eye from all sides, and would suggest that both spectator and spectated are immanent in the same world. The calculation of apparent magnitudes based on the distances betrays the primacy granted by Renaissance architects and painters to the imaginary or real—imaginary and real—transparent plane* separating *the object from the eye. (See "Notes on Figures and Plates.")*

The representational plane has, therefore, a double function: as "transparency" it opens the gaze onto a scene placed beyond reach, showing the lost object; as surface awaiting plastic treatment, it subjects the staging of this scene to a strict geometry. This geometry is the scene's script, traced on *the support. The scene appears* behind *the support, sometimes far behind it. The same oblique line possesses two incompatible values: as element of regulatory operations, it is a surveyor's line inscribed on a blueprint; as contour of an object in the represented scene, it leads the eye toward the fulfillment of desire. Representation will come under fire when the two positions of the line come into conflict on the same support.*[136]

THE OTHER SPACE

The Line and the Letter

Between opposition and difference lies the difference of the space of the text to that of the figure. This difference is not of degree; it constitutes an ontological rift. The two spaces are two orders of meaning that communicate but which, by the same token, are divided. Rather than space of the text one should speak of *textual* space; instead of space of the figure, *figural* space. This terminological distinction is meant to underscore the fact that the text and the figure each engender, respectively, an organization specific to the space they inhabit. This space is not the container of an extrinsic content; even when it presents itself as such, as in the case of textual space, it is not a universal feature, but one specified by a property characterizing it. I define textual space, then, as the space in which the *graphic* signifier inscribes itself. As for the space of figure, "figural" qualifies it better than "figurative." Indeed the last term, in the vocabulary of painting and contemporary criticism, opposes the space of the figure to "non-figurative" or "abstract." The relevant feature of this opposition resides in the analogy of the representative and the represented, and in the spectator's ability to recognize the latter in the former. This feature is secondary to the problem at hand. The figurative is merely a particular instance of the figural, as we saw in the window that Renaissance painting opened for us. The term "figurative" implies the possibility of deriving the pictorial object from its "real" model through an uninterrupted translative process. The trace on the figurative painting is non-arbitrary. Figurativity is thus a property that applies to the plastic object's relation to what it *represents*; it becomes irrelevant if the picture no longer fulfills a representational function, i.e., if it is the object itself. The object in this case is determined by the signifier's organization alone, which oscillates between two poles.

It can be either letter or line. The letter is the support of a conventional, immaterial signification, identical in every respect to the presence of the phoneme. Moreover, the support disappears behind what it upholds, since the letter occasions only instantaneous recognition, in the service of signification. The graphic (as well as phonic) signifier owes this evanescent quality to its arbitrary nature. However, the sense in which I employ arbitrary here no longer applies to the relationship between the purported linguistic sign and the thing it is meant to indicate; rather, it applies to the relationship between scriptural space and the reader's own body. This relationship is arbitrary, for no connection could possibly be established between the distinctive graphic value of the lines or clusters of lines that form a T or an O, and the plastic value of the figures formed by these letters—the crossing of a vertical and a horizontal line, a circumference. The body is led to adopt certain dispositions depending on whether it encounters an angle or a circle, a vertical or an oblique. When a trace owes its value to this ability to induce bodily resonance, it inscribes itself in a plastic space. But when the trace's function consists exclusively in distinguishing, and hence in rendering recognizable, units that obtain their signification from their relationships in a system entirely independent from bodily synergy, I would claim that the space in which this trace inscribes itself is graphic.

Disentangling the two expanses is not an easy matter. We are constantly *tempted* to have the one encroach upon the other.

Take the letter N, a figure formed by the articulation of three straight-line segments, or take A—same definition. The two letters can be distinguished only by their particular composition of segments, since the nature and number of their basic elements are identical. Yet does this mode of composition not call for relationships of textual displacement in the reader's optical field, and therefore for figural properties? The horizontality of the bar in the letter A and the obliquity of the bar in the letter N exist relative to a point of view. Now oppose N to Z. The discrepancy no longer proceeds from the composition of segments between them, since it is the same in both cases, but from the composite's position relative to a biaxial system, vertical and horizontal. From N one obtains Z by a 90-degree planar rotation around the N's lower vertex. Now, this axial system could not be called arbitrary, for it possesses its reference-point in the reader's body, which determines verticality and horizontality. Lastly, N can follow or precede A, as in NA or AN. The order of these two groups differs, and the distinctive value of each will obviously depend on the chosen convention of reading, from right to left or left to right. But does this convention not rely on a general organization of spatial coordinates based on the reader's own? Left and right make sense only when related to a body's own actual verticality—a body that is not only locality, but also localization.

An effect of this confusion between textual and figural space can be found at the outset of Western scientific thought, in the earliest atomist tradition. Seeking to imagine the world as a text, it naturally found in the structure of oppositions between letters the model for the system of atoms. Leucippus and Democritus[1] argue that just as A and N contrast by their ῥυθμός [*rhythmos*], their rhythmic figure, likewise atoms contrast by their σχῆμα [*schema*]; that just as θέσις [*thesis*] distinguishes N and Z, the τροπή [*trope*] or direction allows one to place the atoms in opposition; and that if words differ according to their τάξις [*taxis*], the order of the letters that constitute them, complex bodies are made of atoms whose points of contact, the διαθίγη [*diathige*], varies. The relevant features identified by Leucippus and Democritus seem to suggest a space of reference that, as it stands, is not that of the text but that of the world. The moment one endeavors to transform the world into a text, one is tempted to smuggle a little of the world back into the text.

However, although it is true that the letters' "rhythm," "position," and "sequence" refer to a position occupied by the reader, which serves as reference-point, this calibration owes nothing to the body's aesthetic power. The text is inscribed *vis-à-vis the reader*; its letters are formed so as to permit the recognition of significations, in the same way that words are spoken by the addresser for the addressee to hear them. The text in-visages [*fait visage*]. It stands like a face in front of the person reading it. Between two faces there is a relationship, symmetrical to a point—the point where the exchange of speech takes place. It is this symmetry that determines the axis of actual speech. With regard to the written message, the same symmetry determines the reciprocal positions of the reader's face and the text. Notwithstanding, this reversion marks the relationship with the other as speaker, and not with the object of my senses. It is not the sensory body that finds itself implicated in this relationship; on the contrary, the body suffers a complete cancellation in the latter: interlocutory symmetry is achieved at the cost of the transitive nature of spontaneous aesthetics. The same occurs in the relationship to text: the letter's form, energy, thickness, size, "weight" do not have to make themselves felt by the reader's body. In the interlocutory situation, this body only needs to hear what the other is saying. Space is not involved as sensory expression of the body proper [*corps propre*], but merely in the function of reversibility that language-based communication grants it.

With the text firmly in place, *facing* the reader, it will be obvious that these oppositions between letters are true oppositions, that the graphic trace is formed strictly diacritically, and that the line does not allude in any way to the body's resonating capacity. It is necessary and sufficient that A, N, and Z, as well as AN and NA, be distinguishable from one another in the plane of text for them to exist as elements of a linguistic system. Clearly, they do not "represent" anything, even if they derive from pictograms or ideograms.[2] When the graphic ceases to present itself as something to be seen and begins to operate only negatively, as a term to be recognized by its place in a system, there occurs a radical mutation not only of its function but of the *space* of inscriptions. Where figural difference once reigned, now only *informational* space operates.

The extent of the mutation can be judged from the typographical gaps that will define and maintain the oppositions between intervals, depending on whether they separate the letters of a single word, the words of a single sentence, the sentences of a single paragraph, and so on. Such intervals have no plastic value: they are only particular cases of punctuation. The latter is composed of signals that in a text read aloud do not appear in the spoken chain as phonetic elements, but which simply control intonation. Thus intonation can be defined as expression, not signification, and as continuity, not discontinuity. But things are not so simple, for linguists, consistent with their own principles, make a clear distinction between significative and expressive intonation.[3] The intonation marked in the text by the sign /?/ after "still raining" has the exact same function as the syntagm /ɪz ɪt/ (is it). Although this intonation may well stand outside the chain of discrete components, it nevertheless belongs to the system of language [*langue*] and, as such, is absolutely independent of the speaking subject's production. Conversely, expressive intonation overlays significative, obligatory intonation; it partakes of rhetorics so long as it can itself be codified as a kind of second-degree connoted "script"; and it can be subsumed under "style"[4] if its nature violates not only the habits of language, but also those of rhetorics. Whether connoted or not, intonation fails to translate into punctuation. This explains why text allows for interpretation in the sense of a comedian or an orator: through intonation, interpretation will bring out a text's expressive quality. On the contrary, punctuation always indicates significative intonation,[5] and, in particular, the intervals. And it is often through the absence or displacement of precisely this punctuation that expression will erupt in the order of signification and communication. Aristotle confesses that he dares not punctuate (διαστίξαι [*diastixai*]) Heraclitus's texts out of fear of making them say what they do not mean—proof that polysemy arises from the absence of indications regarding pauses.[6] Mallarmé prohibits the punctuating of verse, since its rhythmics suffice, and he strives to distort the punctuation of prose through shifts that delineate no longer signification but the drawing of a figure.[7]

The blanks in the text transcribe, at the level of writing, the gaps separating and constituting the terms laid out on the grid of language [*langue*]. They have no more individual consistency than these terms themselves: the blanks are segments, while the terms are their extremities. Louis Hjelmslev is quite right in wanting to call the linguistic signifier a "ceneme":[8] the continuum from which the segments are cut does not contribute to the production of signification. The letter is not the exact counterpart of the phoneme, yet the substance constituting it is as neutral for the reader as can be sound matter for the receiver of speech.

Here begins our reflection on the line. Intonation, as I just argued, is poised on the blade of a knife. On one side it lends itself to the production of sounds and rhythms, and tends to adapt to their melodic or metric force in order to engender meaning and expression. On the other, intonation is entirely subordinated to the demands of signification and confined to its flat surface. What Denis Diderot acknowledges and applauds in Italian opera is the victory of expressive intonation over discourse, the latter's deconstruction carried out for the benefit of musical requirements, that vast area where form enjoys free rein through and in text. Diderot understands that what seeps in here is desire, through the song freed from the constraints of script. He establishes strict parallels between the cause defended by *Rameau's Nephew* for a space of passion in music that upsets eloquence, the position of its advocate in society—that of a "madman," a site-less person liable to take on all superimpositions and disguises—and the campaign for "sexual freedom" carried out in *A Supplement to Bougainville's Voyage.*

Now, the line presents a level of ambiguity comparable to that of intonation. On the one hand it touches upon an energetics; on the other upon writing. The means by which the line enables writing are well known: precisely by the fact that the verticals, curves, downstrokes, horizontals, and angles can be stripped of their plastic meaning and count only as constituting distinctive features of the scripted signifiers. Assuredly one can expend great care in achieving the "good form" of the letters and their layout on the page—a task on which the best printers have never given up[9]—but it has to be conceded that this good form is always caught between two contradictory demands: of articulated signification, and of plastic meaning. The former requires the highest degree of legibility, while the latter aims to give adequate space to the potential energy accumulated and expressed in graphic form as such. It goes without saying that if one wins in the latter case, one loses in the former.

It would be worth understanding how this loss and gain occur. One could begin by measuring them in temporal terms: one qualifies as "legible" what does not impede the eye's racing, that is, what lends itself immediately to recognition—think of the experiments monitoring the eye's movements while reading. Whereas in order to enter into communication with the energetics of the plastic line one must stop at the figure. The more the drawing makes way for this particular energetics, the more attention, waiting, and immobility it will require. Why is this?

The word "recognition" puts us on the right track, at least provisionally. The line-letter is an acquired skill: as a known quantity, it needs only to be recognized within a new combination, either word or sentence. The distinctive element is invariant. What is more, the physiognomy of the signifying groups—words, even sentences—further lends itself to a punctual grasp in ordinary reading. I say punctual rather than general because the eye needs only to touch a part of the physiognomy for the mind to take note of its signification. A general grasp would imply the opposite: the understanding of the graphic form in and of itself, and thus the patient probing of the plastic meaning it carries. This truly general and organic grasp can only be slow. In the end, what separates legibility from plasticity is the fact that in the former the eye needs to register only signals. These are associated with significations, and despite their small number, the combination of distinctive elements generates a wealth of significations. The saving of time in ordinary reading reflects the larger economic principle that regulates the usage of linguistic communication, finding its most exemplary model in the fact of language [*langue*], according to Saussure.

It is thus legitimate to challenge the visibility of the legible. Reading is hearing, not seeing. The eye merely scans the written signals. The reader does not even capture the distinctive graphic units: she or he does not *see* the misprints. Rather, the reader selects the significative units. It is only when she or he combines these units to construct the meaning of discourse that her or his activity begins—*beyond* inscription. The reader does not see what she or he reads, striving instead to hear the meaning of what the absent speaker—the author of the text—"meant to say." In this respect writing puts up no more resistance to the comprehension of discourse than can speech. The difference between the two forms of the presence of articulated meaning begins elsewhere, namely with the position and interlocution in the spatio-temporal context. Indeed, speech implies the co-presence of speaker and receiver. Eliminate the presence of the speaker, you end up with writing—the relevant feature here is the relationship between subject and discourse. The figural, on the other hand, opposes the discursive through the trace's relationship to plastic space; in this sense, recordings on wax cylinders or magnetic bands are already forms of writing. This observation allows one to pinpoint the relevant oppositions between phonic signifier, written line, and plastic line. The second falls squarely on the side of speech, both opposed to the figural line in the same way as the audible is opposed to the visible.[10]

One can posit in principle that the less "recognizable" a line, the more it becomes visible, and thus the better it is at eschewing writing and the closer it sides with the figural. However, this rule remains negative; its only value is to clarify the relationship between the figural and the act of waiting, by pitting it against the graphic's complicity with the eye's racing. What is a barely recognizable line? Is it simply a line that differs from those one is used to seeing? And what about the patience or even the passivity that the figural space calls for: is it nothing more than that time supplement necessary for the "never seen" to become visible? One should not simply discard this last hypothesis, for it goes beyond the obvious. Every plastic line submits to linguistic usage, which grants it straightforward informational value; the moment the artist's hand frees plastic vision by offering it a properly figural drawing, a script emerges from this drawing. Thus faced with the graphic, with a drawing laden with connotations—that is, with the "touch" that generations of painters once strove to acquire by endlessly repeating the master's signature style—the figural power of the line can only break out, like a scandal. Once again it will slow down the eye, and judgment, forcing the mind to take position in front of the sensory.

This slowness required by the figural comes from its impelling thought to abandon its element, which is the discourse of signification. No more than sound in speech, the trace as such is unwelcome in this discourse since it is only a distinctive or significative element in the grid of significations. The trace must leave behind communicable transparency; the mind used to language can only perceive as opacity the way in which meaning invests the line (or any part of the figure). An almost infinite effort is required for the eye to give in to form, to become receptive to the energy stored therein. Here one must keep at arm's length the assumptions, interpretations, and habits of *reading* that we contract with the predominant use of discourse. It is precisely of this skill that discursive education and teaching deprive us: to remain permeable to the floating presence of the line (of value, of color). From the very beginning our culture rooted out sensitivity to plastic space. If there is such a thing as a history of painting in the West, it is for the same reason that there is a tragedy of the figural in a civilization of the text. This situation informs the very manner in which the problem of their relationship is posed: if the line is to be continually wrested from writing that frames the figural as signal, it is because drawing evolves in the atmosphere of a culture where rationalist discourse prevails. This prevailing presupposes the desire to enclose every object in the field of signification. Such a desire—the desire for knowledge—will never reach *satisfaction*; it only *takes effect,* and this taking effect, far from fulfilling it, only feeds new requirements. Desire's rebound in the order of structured discourse (scientific progress) literally drags with it the desire we see in the pictorial order. Here too there is a *search,* which is why writing is continually spurned—because it signifies the blocking of plastic experimentation. Yet since at the same time it is scientific discursive inquiry that provides the model and motivation for plastic experiments, a space of a textual nature risks putting an end to these experiments, and script risks becoming the culmination of painting. In its very success, the effort to make visible the visible is threatened by the illusion of making it understandable plastically, as it were, that is, of making it legible. By allowing itself to be connoted, the figure becomes language, an underperforming language at that.

The line is an unrecognizable trace, so long as it does not refer the eye to a system of connotation where this trace would receive fixed, invariant meaning. It is unrecognizable when it does not fit in an order of relations that would inevitably determine its value. The line is therefore figural when, by her or his artifice, the painter or drawer places it in a configuration in which its value cannot yield to an activity of recognition—for to recognize is to know well. From here on we must proceed with caution.

We will let the painters speak for themselves, or rather two painters, contemporaries of each other and of the Cézannian upheaval, both of whom are draftsmen, yet who stand in stark contrast: Paul Klee and André Lhote.[11] We have no intention of resolving their conflict with all the elegance of the philosopher. For this conflict emerges from the ambiguity of the line; it transcribes the latter in significations and lends the line its scope, locating it in either textual or figural space. In this conflict we will stake a claim.

To repeat, we must move forward cautiously because no sooner is the negative principle stated—that the line is truly a figural element when it eludes the system—than we come up against the opposite thesis, or at least apparently opposite, put forward by Lhote. The thesis is well known: there are, he believes, "plastic invariants" in painting. The first three, which in 1939 he called "pictorial elements," are drawing, color, and value, to which in 1940 he added rhythm, decorative character, reversal on the plane, and monumentality.[12] The very first invariant, to which we confine ourselves here, is introduced as "drawing, or expressive sign, or ornament that pre-exists all color or model."[13] Pure drawing, unhampered by all effects of light and shadow: it is thus unquestionably a question of line. It *preexists* value and color, the two other invariants, that is, it can exist without them, not they without it. Here Lhote appears to agree with Klee, who argued that "Color is primarily quality (as color). Second, it is weight for not only is it color, but value as well. Third, it is also measure since it is constrained by its limits, dimensions, breadth—in short, its measurable characteristics. Chiaroscuro is primarily weight, and secondly measure, by virtue of its span or limits. The line however is only measure."[14] As we will see, the consensus is only skin-deep.

In Lhote's definition one must pay attention to the phrase that contains his thesis: "expressive sign or ornament." This expression lays down the function the line must fulfill—a function of signification as opposed to value (chiaroscuro) which is imitative. Why of signification? One can hope to understand Lhote's position only by analyzing his methodology, which, proceeding by oppositions, is fundamentally linguistic. Tracing enters in opposition to modeling: "the objects can be expressed either by imitation of the effect of lighting appropriately reduced to bare essentials, or by the simple sign. The operation of modeling dispenses the painter from the trace, and the trace . . . obviates the need for modeling. . . . Note that things can be *modeled* or *signified* and that the *sign* does away with the need for *imitation*."[15] Modeling produces the illusion of relief: herein lies its imitative function, which Lhote deplores. Instead the trace fails to suggest depth, running across the surface and separating not volumetric planes, but intervals cut into the two-dimensional support. The example for this form of tracing that pays no heed to optical illusion or to imitation in visual space is provided, Lhote contends, by the most archaic forms of plastic expression—by the "primitives," in both a pictorial and an ethnological sense.[16] The entire practice of drawing—from that of the animals silhouetted in Paleolithic caves, Neolithic earthenware, that of the scenes painted on Egyptian and Mycenaean walls and those fired on the sides of Greek vases, that of the sacred passages depicted in Byzantine and Italian-Byzantine art and by the Irish miniaturists, up to Sienese, and even Florentine (Giotto, Angelico, Baldovinetti) painting—for Lhote bespeaks the "expressive sign" or the "ornament," or at least a space governed by it.[17] From the origins up to the Renaissance—here portrayed as an inexplicable "decline"—the drawer will have used the line not to produce the illusion of plastic thickness, of a breakup of planes in depth, but to inscribe signs on a two-dimensional surface that he or she never thought to "perforate."[18]

From such a perspective, this ornamental space closely resembles a textual space, and the "primitive" tracing seems to be nothing other than a script. Lhote does speak of an "*expressive* sign," which would appear to bring us away from signification in the strict sense of the term, and to refer to the purely plastic values related to the line's sensory configuration: to its direction, thickness, curvature or straightness, and its position on the support. Nevertheless, one will look in vain for an analysis of these sensory characteristics of the linear constituent. Instead what one encounters everywhere is a reflection on the *relations between* the elements of the tracing. It is as if there were no plastic value specific to the curve, the vertical, the oblique, or intervals that they could determine; as if the value of the element rested exclusively on the group of oppositions in which the drawer placed it. "If one traces a line on any sheet of paper, either straight or curved, one immediately defines on either side of this line, and as far as the edge of the page, uneven areas that will enter into a relationship which instinct (or knowledge of the laws of rhythm) will declare agreeable or monotonous."[19] Here the figure's value is set by the opposition between the two areas adjoining the line. This opposition allows for precise knowledge: Lhote's parenthetical remark—his Platonism in a nutshell—means that instinct is merely a vulgar form of noetic knowledge. "Careful to organize his or her representational signs on the paper or panel, and out of consideration for the harmonious exchanges between all the lines, the drawer will be led to pay as much attention to what lies *between the objects* as to the objects themselves. For the drawer there are neither voids nor solids, only surfaces that require, in order to ensure the beholder's enjoyment, to be in a particular relation—where analogies and differences will be measured according to immutable laws."[20]

There are therefore laws of knowledge and of the production of the expressive sign, and these are of two kinds: laws pertaining to the rhythmic organization of the surface that govern a different invariant (rhythm) than drawing proper; and laws specific to the latter intended to sustain plastic interest by providing the eye with "a series of clean and well-articulated signs mutually enhanced by virtue of their reactions to one another: a right angle flatters the width of an obtuse angle or the shapeliness of a taut curve."[21] Here again we observe that the tracing finds itself endowed with "plastic" value through the opposition of its elements. Indeed Lhote goes so far in this direction that he brushes against the economic principle of linguists when he adds: "If the pure signs I call, for lack of a better term (may the mathematicians forgive me), geometricized, are few in number, their combinations are infinite."[22] One could argue that Lhote speaks of geometry rather than language [*langue*]. Nonetheless, for this Neoplatonist, geometry remains the language [*langue*] of space par excellence.[23] When he attempts to explain what constitutes the *abstraction*[24] through which drawing frees itself from the imitation of the model and produces not a representational but a "summarizing" or "revealing" outline,[25] Lhote proposes the image (the metaphor) of a "plastic metaphor," that is, a set of operations with which the painter (as well as the poet, he believes) rather than "describing the object, rendering its outline precisely," seeks and arrives at its relation with the geometric form(s) of which it is but an approximate image. "To express an object comes down to affirming the relation it entertains at any moment in its worldly evolution with a given transcendental figure, such as a sphere, cone, or cylinder, or with a complex figure resulting from their combinations."[26] The lyrical verve that overcomes Lhote when he imagines the field of geometry—in his own words, "space of the gods where the painter, servant of the earth, is forbidden to tread, but to which he is forced to allude"[27]—is that of a man whose eye, tormented by *difference*, has discovered the means to restore order in the area of sensibility, namely, invariants, immutable laws, and constant intervals capable of reducing the opacities, superimpositions, rhythmic irregularities, and variances, and of filtering the madness of ποικίλον [*poikilon* (variegated)] in the grid specified by these rules. Now the role of the painter comes into full view: to hold up the formidable disorder of the figural to the luminous organization of the scriptural.

In other words: to repress difference, and sublimate it into opposition. Lhote himself introduces and locates the vocabulary of desire: "A very special sensuality characterizes every lover of painting, something like greediness but more profound, which provokes a very particular frenzy when the painting's matter caters to this *penchant for edibility*, if I dare say of something primarily addressed to the mind. Some enthusiasts and painters prone to the disorder caused by this passion go so far as to make pictorial matter the essence of their painting."[28] It is noteworthy that this (contradictory) allusion to the innermost motive of every painting-enthusiast is made only to describe the passion that drives the adversary and to dismiss the latter's "inadmissible thesis." The love of pictorial matter, which distracts the eye from pure geometrical ornament and forbids sublimation, is what—with other devices—mobilizes the work of Lhote's sworn enemies: Leonardo, the Baroque, and realism. "Intervals, inconceivable at first sight, which led the goddess Painting to flee paradise, illuminated by the seven colors of the spectrum, assembled geometrically and embellished with the ornament's embroidery, and enter the baroque purgatory of chiaroscuro where geometry is torn asunder and the incorruptible thread of the ornament is forever broken."[29] Of course Paolo Uccello and Piero della Francesca, although two "angels of painting," had ever so slightly begun to introduce depth, but in drawing only, not in color, which they continued to apply uniformly in keeping with traditional rules of opposition governing the chromatic rhythm of the surface to be painted. Before, there were only "malicious allusions" to depth, "as one can speak of the *devil* without extolling his *splendors*." "Perspective was created out of pure *desire for change*, as a *conceit of the mind*." For Lhote, it is Leonardo who carries this desire's conceit to its climax. Before him there was nothing more than a "*temptation* a tad *perverse,* an almost *childish need* to give more *depth* and a little more *sensual* warmth to objects." But Leonardo's passion is fueled by the "gyrating forms," "space" (read three-dimensional space) and "light" that will become his utmost pictorial goal, will provide painters with the excuse to practice and "outperform" (whereas painting calls above all for "sacrifice"), will, in short—let us not be afraid to call it by its name—offer the painter the opportunity to boast his or her "spiritual pride" and satisfy the "urge to measure him/herself up against God."[30]

The entire passage would deserve to be quoted. But these few remarks suffice to make clear the role the line plays in Lhote's understanding of painting: to reduce the diverse, the singular, and the deformed to the universality of geometric form. Drawing's function consists in making sensory space *speak* in geometric figures. At issue is the need to rid the eye of the shimmer that beguiles it, and to return it to the clarity of the intelligible. The relation between the given and the drawn is that of a catharsis snatching the eye from the phantasm of thick presence and of the interrupted line, and reestablishing it in the two-dimensional plane, its place of choice. Significantly, color for Lhote plays the same role as drawing in relation to modeling.

Klee titled *Auserwählte Stätte, Chosen Site* (Plate 13), a 1927 watercolor and pen sketch on colored paper.[31] The piece's dimensions are almost those of the golden section: 30.5 × 46 cm. The rectangle stands vertically, suggesting a view from a window. However, what leads me to choose this particular work as an example among thousands is the way in which its line and color intermingle. With Klee, the line and the chromatic element are in conflict—a conflict that overlaps with that of interior and exterior, masculine and feminine. Here the function of drawing, mastered at the cost of grueling effort, no longer consists in geometricizing "matter" by taking refuge in the closed outline, but rather in taking part, with color as a companion whose shifts it embraces, in the origins of a creation *free from any model.* Where once the challenge was to constitute and make recognizable an intelligible world, it now centers on an "interworld," another possible nature,[32] extending creation, making visible what is not—without, however, falling prey to subjective imagination.

Drawing for Klee is the plastic medium through which the phantasmatic expresses itself spontaneously.[33] Its "initial position" is "the line in itself."[34] So powerful is this initial position that at the very moment when he first attempts (in 1910) to found and enact compositional techniques of drawing with color, "before even the 'pure genera' have had time to develop," suddenly, he writes, "the devil of combination" appears—which he tries to scare off with this caveat: the line "at most in certain situations, and never so as to produce a massive effect."[35] The line is the element the artist will never cease to have to tame, for in it floats and contracts his desire. "My mother once inadvertently fell upon some pornographic drawings of mine. One showed a woman, her belly full of children; another, a woman with a very revealing neckline. My mother unfairly reproached me of moral wrongdoing, since the décolleté was part of an illustration of a theatrical ballet performance. In the drawing a rather plump sprite leaned over a strawberry, offering a view of a deep recess between protruding hillocks. I was mortified" (Klee, age eleven to twelve).[36] Here is an almost direct transcription of the phantasy: "I imagined the face and genitals as if they were corresponding poles of the female sex, and in my mind I pictured weeping girls, their sex in tears."[37] But also delirium of the primary process, capable of violating any representational writing: "My uncle—Switzerland's fattest man—owned a restaurant furnished with polished marble-top tables, their surface a tangled web of veins. In this labyrinth of lines one could discern and pencil in grotesque physiognomies. I was transfixed, indulging my taste for the bizarre" (Klee, age nine).[38] His first drawings will inherit this ambivalence of the line: on the one hand, a direct, intimate, obsessive submission to a phantasmatics grafted on the enigma of the opposite sex, and on the other the discovery and development of the critical (ironic) power of distortion[39] (Figure 7). The drawing of desire enables the recognition of the lost object,[40] outlining it, hollowing it out, and shaping it. It fantasizes the restitution of what it lacks with mirthless brutality (*Maiden in a Tree*, 1902/3) or with vile wantonness (*Woman and Beast*, 1903/4)[41] (Plates 14a and b); it tends to become *script*, so exacting is the burden of a primordial, profound figure in which desire is trapped, and that guides the hand without consideration for the artwork. Thus even when the drawing is clearly meant to be ironic and denounce, it maintains its critique in the same space of modeling and representation where the phantasmatic flaunts its figures.[42] Thus the distance from the fantasized is secured first through the play alone of signification proper: the critique "says" the opposite of what desire says, but with the same plastic means and the same technique, so that desire takes revenge on critique by harboring it on its own stage. Soon, the line begins to seek out a different space of inscription; or, at least, spontaneous script (that of phantasmatic modeling) vanishes, leaving behind a coarse, hesitant trace outlining elongated silhouettes that are all members, dotting the space through a frozen gesticulation. Only the shadows cast on an indistinct terrain reveal that the reference to the representational scene is not entirely abandoned. Klee had the opportunity to subjugate drawing with the illustration of Voltaire's *Candide* (1911). The drawer knows full well that "towards the middle of 1911 . . . the first bout of inspiration comes to a halt"[43] and that the merits of the compromise between the impulse "to stray graphically" and the acquisition of "modeling from nature" have run dry.[44] What destabilizes Klee in *Candide* is the economy of literary means, the sobriety, the interiority. As early as the end of 1903 he writes, "Strain to purify and isolate my virile ego. Although ripe for marriage, retract inwards and prepare myself for the most absolute solitude. Disgust at the thought of procreation (ethical hyper-sensibility)."[45] Purified virility is a euphemism; but this virility, which he attributes to drawing as its most essential property, is still far from genuine "purity." The Ego can still be virile without this virility necessarily being pure. Where, then, will the catharsis of this interiority—which for now is haunted by the ghosts of the opposite sex, the progeny of the fear of castration—find an outlet?[46] Is it toward a more arbitrary, more geometric graphism, as Lhote would like, that is, toward writing per se, toward the scripting of the intelligible (after having been through that of the phantasy)?

In 1924 Klee asserted that "measure is the defining attribute of this element of form" (the line); that "any hesitation on this subject betrays an imperfectly pure use of the line"; and that "the symbol for the essence of the pure line is the graduated ruler with its many sections."[47] And when later in the same lecture he segues from the definition of pictorial elements to the examination of what he calls content, it might seem at first as if he is resorting to Lhote's opposition-based system in the hope of highlighting the line's expressive potential: "For each angular zigzag motion opposed to the steadier course of a horizontal, one finds a given expressive contrast," or "A similar discrepancy occurs when one linear formation displays a uniform

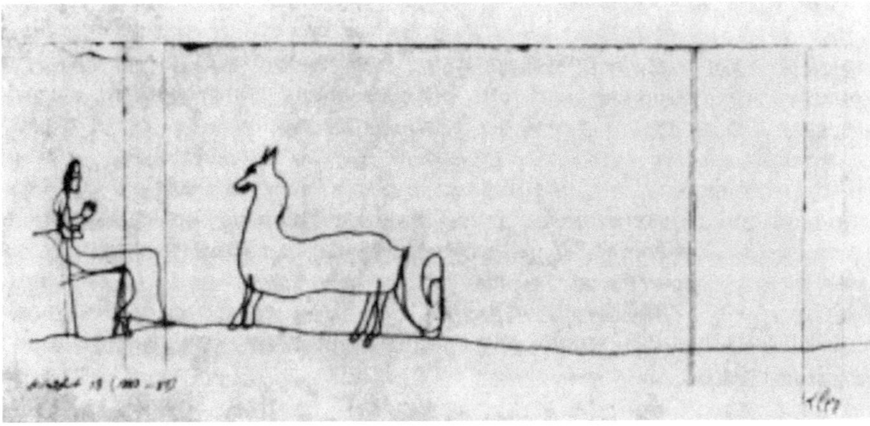

Figure 7. Paul Klee, *Azor Takes Orders from Ms. Frog*, 1883–1885/13. Child's drawing, pencil, 8 × 18.6 cm. Klee Foundation. Reproduced in Félix Klee, *Paul Klee par lui-même et par son fils Félix Klee* (Paris: Les Libraires associés, 1963), third flyleaf.

mass and another a loose scattering."[48] Is it, then, a question of establishing and developing, through a combinatorics, the system of oppositions from which every particular line would gain signification, in the same way that in matters of language a significative unit does from the sub-group in which it is sampled?

In 1914 Klee wrote in his *Diaries*: "To see with one eye; to feel with the other."[49] How to make sense of such a riddle? By looking on the one hand, and groping on the other? Rather, the distinction should be between the visible and the invisible. To feel will mean to draw the interior, the unpenetrated of the visible silhouette, in which case to see is simply to identify. The visible, recognizable silhouette covers the object and the person, familiar in their immediate exteriority, as if transformed into letters. The eye that sees in this way does no more than read or recognize; sooner or later it will cease *to see* altogether. Sensory power is that of the eye deployed not in the field of legibility, but in that of form that escapes from legibility, not in the field of immediate exteriority, but concurrently in the fields of exteriority and interiority.[50] Klee was in the habit of telling his students: "Practice your hand. Better yet, practice both, for the left hand writes differently than the right: *precisely because it is less adroit, it sometimes is more manageable.* The right hand runs with greater agility; the left hand instead designs hieroglyphs. Writing is not clarity but expression—think of Chinese script—and this exercise renders it more sensitive, intuitive, spiritual."[51] One hand operates in the register of the legible; its trace is neat, lively, and easy to recognize: it is the hand that traces for the "seeing" eye. The left hand labors clumsily and pays no heed to my desire: it can lure us to the never-before-seen form and to expression, as interiority turned inside out. Such are the two types of figures that hands can produce; using the left hand, while feeling with the eye, is to *free* the linear constituent from its spontaneity, from its poor innate scriptural ability.

Here then is the indigent spontaneity of the line: "I wanted to describe only controllable things, limiting myself to my interior life. As time passed and my inner life grew in complexity, the compositions themselves became increasingly strange. Sexual confusion arouses the monsters of perversity. Hordes of Amazons and other terrifying creatures. A three-part cycle: Carmen—Gretchen—Isolde. A *Nana* cycle, *Théâtre des Femmes*. Disgust: a woman spread out, her breasts pressed flat against a table, pouring refuse from a vase." Elsewhere: "To this period belong a few motifs approaching plasticity: chained female nudes.—*The Day Breaks* (after a lustful night the youth sleeps while the woman is hidden).—*Farewell to the Woman. The Maiden Defends Herself.*"[52] A year later Klee adds: "There was also a drawing portraying a woman as the prize of an unfolding game of dice. The depiction of such banalities could be attempted only if the one appropriate form were found."[53] Klee is well on his way to discovering "a small, unclaimed property,"[54] that is, to guiding his hand toward the other register—that of the invisible to be made visible—and no longer that of the phantasm awaiting recognition. In Rome he saw Carolina Otero dance: "Apart from the orgiastic character of this dance, an artist has much to learn from such a performance. He would no doubt have to spend more time surrounded by a dancer's movements to have not merely a feeling for the laws of movement, but also to know them. In the end it might be a question only of the difficulty in capturing the linear relationships of the body at rest."[55] In the lecture from 1924, Klee invokes mobility and liberty as attributes of *natura naturans* [nature naturing]. Dancing thus dispenses with the woman, allows the good eye to open and the left hand to trace its autonomous web of lines. "Dancing consists in softly modulating the body's lines."[56]

I believe it is here that Klee's fundamental claims on the origin of the work of art should be located: "Genesis as formal movement is the work's most essential part. / In the beginning, insertion of energy, sperm. / Works as form-engendering in the material sense: *ur*-feminine. / Works as form-determining sperm: *ur*-masculine. / My drawing belongs to the masculine sphere. / The engendering of form is energetically mitigated in relation to the determination of form. / The ultimate consequence of the two kinds of forming is form itself. Pathways toward a destination. From action to perfection. From the genuinely alive to the conditioned. / In the beginning the male specialty of energetic thrust. Followed by the carnal growth of the egg. Put differently: first the blinding bolt of lightning, then the clouds of rain. / Where is the spirit at its purest? At the beginning. / Here, creation that (subdivides). Over there, creation which is."[57]

These are essential claims on two counts: they affirm, first, the primacy of the point of view of movement, genesis, and creation over the artwork itself; and second, the allotment of creative tasks according to a system of gendered oppositions:

MALE	FEMALE
more energetic	less energetic
determining	conceiving
discontinuous	continuous
(thrust, lightning bolt)	(growth, rain)
spiritual	carnal
drawing	?

The status of drawing will be clarified in Klee's theoretical writings. The line must be thought of in relation to an energetics: "An example of a two-dimensional element that does not break down into smaller units: energy, either uniform or modulated, released from a large point. An example of an indivisible spatial element: the diffuse stain, applied unevenly, with the brush soaked through."[58] In the *Skizzenbuch* Klee explains that this energetics is the outcome of a universal energetics, strictly bracketed by two limits: on one side by "the active, gamboling line," whose vector is "a mobile point,"[59] and on the other by the passive line dissolving in the field of activity (surface) that it engenders through displacement. The lateral displacement of a line segment generates a square or a rectangle; transposition by rotation around a point in the middle of the segment generates a circle. The trace of the movement (of the point) is no longer the line; rather, the line is the motive that leaves the two-dimensional figure behind as trace. In this case the line is passive.

This energetic grasp of the line gives it access to a number of applications from which it had traditionally been barred. For example light, as energy, can be rendered by tracings. The object and the drawing no longer communicate through the outline (as classroom exercises from life teach us) and through the vectors of plastic space. By placing energy at the center of his concept of creation, Klee instigates a radically different space of communication between object and line, which is neither the recognizable text of visible appearance nor the geometric script of the plastic screen, but a site (or non-site) achieved through procedures such as a systematic deviation from laws of perception and conception (see Plate 15a, and the commentary in "Notes on Figures and Plates"); the displacement of objects outside of their space of origin; the simultaneity of successiveness; the co-affirmation of the contrary; the condensation of distinct constituents; the making of what appears alien correspond: in effect, signaling the presence of light with a large black arrow: "To represent light with brightness is old hat. . . . Now I attempt simply to render light as deployment of energy. And should I opt to treat energy in black on a white ground, I should arrive at the same result. / I need only refer to the unquestionably rational black light on photographic negatives."[60]

In the artwork's genesis, the line's "spermatic" function is to determine form by and through its own impact. As Klee noted, "The spirit is at its purest at the beginning"[61] (Figure 8). The following unusual characteristic substantiates the claim that the line is a mental construct: "The sort of graphics I pursue—which bear witness to the hand's movement by means of the registering implement—differs so completely from the customary use of tone and color that one could just as easily practice this art in total obscurity, in the darkest of night."[62] Drawing is interiority, what "drives the soul": the line

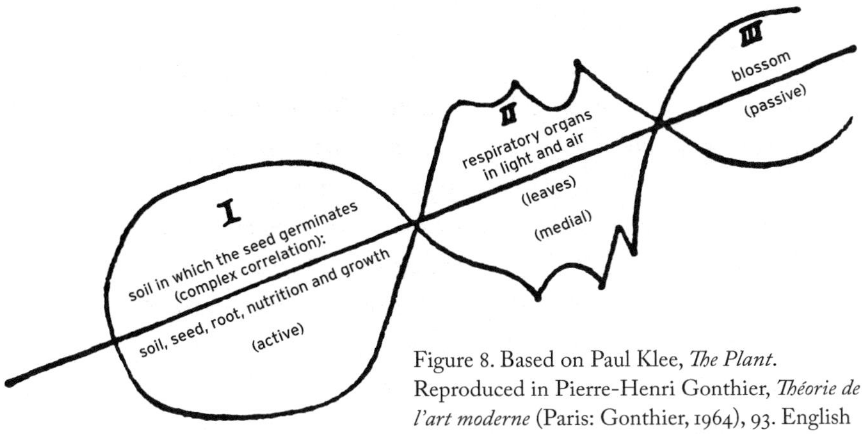

Figure 8. Based on Paul Klee, *The Plant*. Reproduced in Pierre-Henri Gonthier, *Théorie de l'art moderne* (Paris: Gonthier, 1964), 93. English translation from Paul Klee, *Pedagogical Sketchbook*, trans. and intro. Sibyl Moholy-Nagy (London: Faber and Faber, 1968), 32.

traces "experiences that can, in the depths of night, convert independently into tracing."[63] Are these phantasies once more? Will their children turn out to be the Amazons, the women raped or gambled at the throw of dice, the spontaneous figures of castration?

Here again things are more complex than they seem. In 1908 Klee writes that "my lines from 1906–1907 were my most prized possession. But I had to relinquish them, for their lapsing into some kind of convulsion, into what was perhaps even the ornamental, was imminent. In short, I interrupted them out of fright, however much I felt them imbedded in me. I simply could not uproot them. So difficult was it to harmonize interiority and exteriority that I failed to discern them in my midst."[64] This is evidence that the phantasmatic has been here and that virility incised such obsessive lines that they could not possibly endure reality-testing. But for virility to become thought it must first prove itself ready to encounter that which it is not, and to seize it as well as to succumb to it as if through the passive fertility of matter. This is where Klee's method takes a sharp turn away from Lhote's. Drawing does not accrue truth-value by observing a pure geometry that it imposes on all data. For Klee this kind of drawing *remains phantasmatic*, presenting a *regressive* virility and determination that cannot withstand reality-testing and the challenge posed by sexual difference. This is the trace of unitary phantasy, premised on apparently objective and transcendent—yet truly imaginary—unity. For the sperm-drawing to assert itself as it is, it must first accept being met and passively acted upon by the ovum. At the plastic level, what is required is an operation, which Klee elucidates in the same passage of his *Diaries*, and whose simplicity strikes me as attracting attention to (rather than giving away) the secret to the transformation from phantasmatic representation to critical creation: "Genesis of an artwork. / 1. Draw meticulously from nature, if necessary with the aid of a telescope. / 2. Turn drawing no. 1 upside down, emphasizing the main lines according to feeling. / 3. Turn the page back to its initial position and harmonize no. 1 (nature) and no. 2 (picture)."[65] Put differently: upend nature according to feeling, but also upend feeling to achieve the co-construction of picture and object. If one stops at no. 2 there is only the imaginary, not painting, and the line is servile. No. 1 gives access to the visible and no. 2 to the invisible of phantasmatic interiority, but the combination constructs *another invisible,* which is the phantasy overturned through artifice rather than exposed. "Art goes through *things,* beyond both the real and the imaginary."[66] This passage is a double reversal.

The entire theory of modern art, understood as *natura naturans* producing a "Zwischenwelt," or interworld, stems from this double reversal.[67] By obediently deferring to *plastic* requirements, that is, to the innumerable (but not indifferent) combinations made possible by the plastic levels, one can possibly "encounter" an object and recognize it. In any case this encounter is secondary, since the object is the composition itself—a composition whose purpose is not to represent something else, for it is something else: something that neither the visible of nature nor the invisible of the unconscious gave us, but which art constructs. If the artwork must somehow manifest its strangeness, the fact that "on this side" (*diesseitig*) it eludes our grasp (*greifbar*), then the object that it is cannot allow itself to stabilize in completed form. In the artwork's actual constitution, its genesis—and thus the movement that brought it to its present configuration (yet that overshoots it to generate other configurations)—must remain palpable. As *possible* world, the artwork does not shed its *otherworldly* appearance, despite its reality. Creativity exceeds the creature.

This transcendence can be intimated only if all possible combinations of plastic levels are accounted for and utilized. The relation between drawing and color takes place within this matrix; its position is of the utmost significance given drawing's rabid deployment in Klee's work.[68] Only in Hammamet, in 1914, does the interior line truly accept to be subordinated to the conditions imposed by its relationship with color. The eye's unsettling, or its re-settling, was necessary to trigger the unstoppable infringement of chroma in interiority. Klee remembers this adventure as his personal *defeat* by color: "I now give up work. I can feel it pervade me so utterly and surreptitiously that it builds up my confidence without the slightest effort. Color possesses me. No need for me to pursue it. It has me in its grip, this much I know. Herein lies the meaning of this joyous moment: color and I are one. I am a painter."[69] "The evening is indescribable. To top it all, the full moon rises. Louis eggs me on: I have to paint it now. I reply: it will be at best an exercise. Naturally, I am no match for nature such as this. Still, I know a little more than I did before. I can appreciate the ground I still need to cover, between my inadequacy and nature. This is the inner task that awaits me over the coming years. / This does not depress me at all. One should not hurry when one expects so much of oneself. The evening is forever etched deep in me. Many a future northern blond moonrise, like a muted reflection, will incite me softly, will never cease inciting me. This image will be my bride, my alter ego. A stimulus to find myself. I, meanwhile, am the southern moonrise."[70]

Thirteen years later Klee paints *Chosen Site.* Here, for all to see, his silver moon (and therefore the painter himself); solved "the synthesis urban architecture = pictorial architecture," which the painter had fought so hard to achieve on site;[71] put to good use the "small, unclaimed property" discovered in 1902, a "particular kind of three-dimensional surface representation."[72] Indeed, even a quick overview reveals that the composition's essential features all seem to answer the problems encountered by Klee's drawings. The graphic system is a non-representational rectangular network where the line determines areas of different colors—ranging from grayish-white to faded pink through yellowish-gray, yellow, salmon, and orange—yet whose value is uniformly washed-out, pale gray. The moon, too, is gridded, but only two complementary colors differentiate the enclosed areas, yellow and purple, their values equally faint. In the graphic element only the "town's"

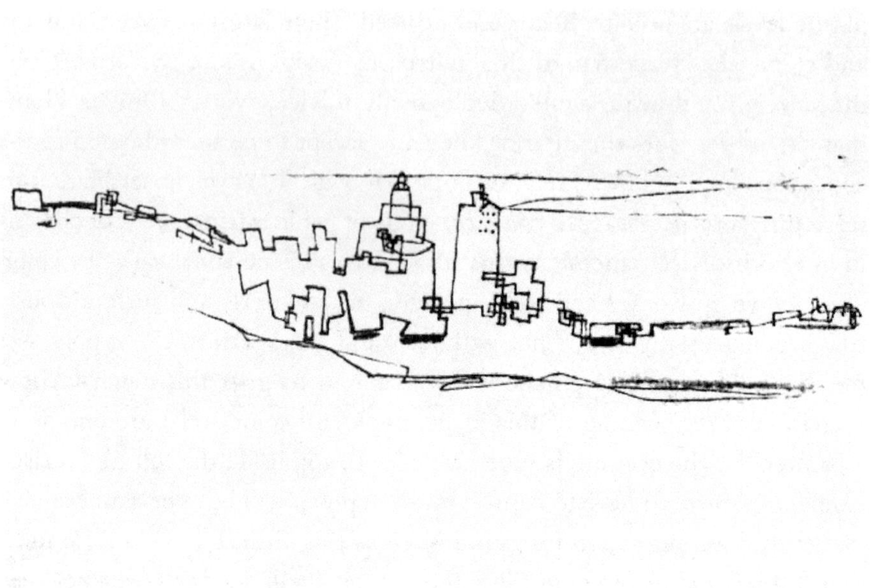

Figure 9. Paul Klee, *Calvi (Phantasmatic)*, 1927/U7. Pen and color pencil, 30.6 × 46.6 cm. Klee Foundation. Reproduced in *Paul Klee par lui-même et par son fils Félix Klee,* 48.

surface—out-of-kilter, tilting downward from left to right—gives an indication of movement. The dynamic effect appears to have transferred to the "backdrop's" color-value system, with warm hues throughout and entire areas devoid of all linearity (in this case, the linear system as surface "draws the line" between the green and the brown). The quantitative element has not disappeared for all that: four bands alternate from top to bottom (not counting the gray band formed by the edifice), namely, red, green, brown, and blue. From the point of view of pure or postural chromatic effect, where the reds and browns are abductors, and the greens and blues adductors, we arrive at the series + — + —; this series is checked by another, — + — +, which on the scale of values twice changes from a dark to a light hue, from top to bottom. Most important, the first series merges with an intrinsically quantitative series, 2 8 4 1, formed by the respective widths of the bands starting from the top, and which gradually compresses the picture toward the bottom. A set of acute tensions therefore strains the "background" plane, and it is along these tensions that the graphic trace inscribes its diligent ant-like shuttling.

In fact, the line deployed here corresponds to what Klee called "linear-medial" (Plate 15b, Figures 9 and 10). No better commentary on this line exists than his explanation given at the Bauhaus: "Neither line nor surface, but a sort of hybrid (*Medium*) between the two. It begins in linear fashion—as the movement of a point—and ends as appearance of surface. An intermediary (*mediale*) line: building up surface through linear circumscription. The line articulated at specific points, with its cramped, temporally finite character (*mit knappen, befristetem Charakter*). In these new examples, the finite line defines surface figures, such as triangles and squares. The forces mobilizing a line issue from the combination of other forces in different directions. Tension means connection (*Spannung ist Bindung*)."[73] The hybrid line leads to the endless circle without beginning or end; the surface then eliminates the line, as well as the impression of movement: "No one is inclined, looking at the lunar disc, to install a merry-go-round on its edge."[74] In terms of energetics, the moon's circumference in *Chosen Site* brings full circle the hybrid line's confined trajectory that reticulates its surface and comes from the "city."

Neither of these tensions *speaks*; rather they *act*, as the energy's specifications. Drawing yields this energy as inhibited, sealed off, differentiated, microscopic, while the colored areas convey the other infinite, mapped out in taut differences across the flesh-like cosmic dome. The line produces man, the city, the discontinuous, shock; color produces nature, quality, consuming growth: "She did not count among the endearing young girls; she was

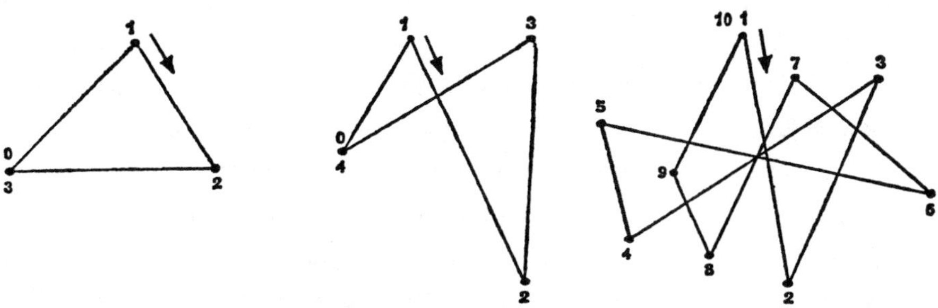

Figure 10. Paul Klee, *Linear-Medial.* Pencil. Based on the sketch reproduced in *Das bildnerische Denken* (Basel-Stuttgart: Benno Schwabe, 1956), 109.

a woman, almost as strong as I. As I seized her, I felt the pulse of her fiery blood, her breath seared my face. With this breath my entire being was consumed in longing for the redemption only the woman can offer."[75] Klee writes these lines in March 1902, in Rome, as he is about to leave for Naples. He is describing the composition of the work in progress entitled *The Three Boys*: the boy who finds redemption in the woman is the third. A few days later, in Naples, the redemption is repeated: "Lastly, Naples again, like a hushed pollination of lights at my feet. Oh, the overwhelming confusion, the shifting of planes, the bloodied sun, the deep sea covered with small tilted sailboats. Matter upon matter, to the point of drowning in it. To be human, to be ancient, naive and nothing, yet happy. Just once, exceptionally, as a special occasion. . . . May the day come when proof is revealed. To be able to reconcile opposites! To express the manifold in a single word!"[76]

I see no reason to elaborate further. In sum,

1) Lhote confines the drawer to the alternative between having to reveal the contour of the figure of desire and organizing the plastic screen geometrically—either modeling or the intelligible. He unequivocally opts for the latter. Klee allows us to see what Lhote fears in the former, something he himself dreads but with which he wrestled openly, namely, addressing the question of desire. When the dynamic point leaves behind its trace, in which space does this trace inscribe itself? What it spontaneously inscribes is the phantasmatic figure, the figure staged by desire. This figure is representational; its role is to present absence, reproducing the spontaneous phantasm directly, without reversal. The line becomes "revealing" [*révélateur*] because it indicates a presence where there is nothing, because it "gives shape" to a body, a face, an action, where there is only a bare surface.[77] It deceives, turning the sheet of paper into a window: the surface as opaque support is denied, treated in such a way as to hint at the presence of another scene evolving beyond it, on the other side, and to make this scene recognizable. The desire to figure is spontaneously that of figuring the figures of desire. When figurality takes on the trappings of representation, it remains in the immediate space of what Freud calls the dream-"content," which is representational.

For Klee, however, as for Lhote, after Cézanne, representation is divested of all truth; it has become simply symptomatic.[78] Drawing, painting, perform a cathartic function. Whatever holds them back in representational space holds them back in the figure-image of the phantasy of desire. Klee knows this, tragically; Lhote steadfastly refuses to. In this respect, the former displays a perverse constitution that will translate in the polymorphism of the "freed" work, while the latter holds fast in a monolithic rejection. Lhote's line will always have something of a crossing out about it.

2) This difference in catharsis is not merely picturesque. It means that Lhote's alternative is not relevant. For the regulating line [*tracé régulateur*] is not the only possible opposite of the outline [*tracé révélateur*]. The choice is not between an imaginary that represents and a geometry that scripts. Klee never was a cubist. What he learned from Cézanne[79] was not to script with geometric volumes, but rather to deconstruct representation and invent a space of the invisible, of the possible. Klee is closest to Cézanne when he sets out to locate the painting's polyphony, the simultaneity of different perspectives, in a word, the interworld. What Cézanne teaches him is Delaunay: Klee goes straight from one to the other—a path which alone succeeds in casting Lhote's cubism aside. Klee's task is not to testify that the intelligible regulates the sensory; it is to make an object out of the picture. Nature did not produce this object. Indeed, far from conforming to its plane, the object is denatured or transnatural, attesting to the fact that creation exceeds created nature, and that the artist is a site where nature continues to bear fruit. Creation holds sway over both nature and art. The latter, however, owes nothing to the former. To Lhote's Neoplatonism—which aspires to produce a "good nature" through geometric reason, a nature closer to the intelligible than visible nature—Klee might have replied with Aristotle's two apparently contradictory statements, analyzed by Martin Heidegger and Jean Beaufret: "Technē brings to completion what phusis failed to craft"; "the way it is crafted determines the way it grows, and the way it grows determines the way it is crafted: each and every thing."[80] Klee states that the artist is no more than a tree trunk in which sap rises—but no one had seen the fruit borne by this tree before, making recognition, even reminiscence, impossible.

3) A strange plane, then, Klee's plastic screen: no longer window or showcase through which to contemplate a distant scene, any more than page from a geometry treatise or mathematician's chart in which the eye would read the forms. Since the line (but also value and color) behaves on the screen not according to the laws of good form but to the power it exerts on the beholder's eye and body, it positions this plane in the field of sensibility, even sensuality. Yet insofar as drawing polyphonically offers lateral and facial views, elevation and plan, outside and inside, trace that orders and one that makes visible—for all this, it thwarts desire's impulse to fantasize on the plastic plane and carve on it the beyond of the imaginary. Through these combinations and deconstructions, desire faces nothing but itself; rather than find fulfillment in the represented object, it is stopped in its tracks by this object—the picture—that bears all the traces of desire's own processes: displacements, deviations, reversals, unity of opposites, and disregard for time and reality. Klee's interworld is not an imaginary world: it is the displayed workshop of the primary process[81] (Plates 16a and 16b). Here one does not speak or "see," one works. In this space, the line records neither the signifiers of a discourse nor the outlines of a silhouette; it is the trace of a condensing, displacing, figuring, elaborating energy, with no regard for the recognizable. "The essential question begs to be settled, namely, what is the ultimate goal of making visible (*das Sichtbarmachen*). Should one preserve in one's mind what one has seen or, further, bring forth that which is invisible?"[82] Here the invisible is not the verso of the visible, its flip side. It is the unconscious capsized: the potential of plasticity.

"The Dream-Work Does Not Think"

Translated by Mary Lydon

It should come as no surprise that the problematics of work versus discourse is the nub of chapter 6 of *The Interpretation of Dreams.* In the course of this chapter Freud examines the dream-work and enumerates the essential operations by which it proceeds. It is easy to show that each of these operations is conducted according to rules that are in direct opposition to those governing discourse. The dream is not the language of desire, but its work. Freud, however, makes the opposition even more dramatic (and in doing so lets us in on a figural presence in discourse), by claiming that the work of desire is the result of manhandling a text. Desire does not speak; it does violence to the order of utterance. This violence is primordial: the imaginary fulfillment of desire consists in this transgression, which repeats, in the dream workshop, what occurred and continues to occur in the manufacture of the so-called primal phantasm.

The figure is hand in glove with desire on at least two counts. At the margin of discourse it is the density within which what I am talking about retires from view; at the heart of discourse it is its "form." Freud himself says as much when he introduces the term *Phantasie,* which is at once the "façade" of the dream and a form forged in its depths.[1] It is a matter of a "seeing" which has taken refuge among words, cast out on their boundaries, irreducible to "saying." We will dwell a little on secondary revision because the *Fliegende Blätter* inscriptions, in spite of their dismaying aesthetic impoverishment, provide an excellent opportunity for formulating the relationship between image and text. Considerations of beauty aside, art begins here.

I

At the end of chapter 6 of *The Interpretation of Dreams,* which deals with the dream-work, Freud recalls the question with which he began: "whether the mind employs the whole of its faculties without reserve in constructing dreams, or only a functionally restricted fragment of them."[2] His response is that the question must be rejected: it is badly put, "inadequate to the circumstances." On the basis of the terms in which it is stated, the answer would have to be in the affirmative in both cases: the mind contributes *both* totally and partially to the production of the dream. What Freud calls the *Traumgedanke,* the dream-thoughts, what the dream thinks, *what it says clearly,* its latent pronouncement [*énoncé*], must be attributed *in toto* to waking thought. It is "perfectly proper thought" (*vollig korrekt*) which belongs to the same genus as conscious thought. Even if it retains some puzzling aspects, these have no "special relation to dreams and do not call for treatment among the problems of dreams."[3]

What the dream says *at bottom* is fully intelligible. Its motivating discourse is an intelligent one, subject to the same rules as waking discourse. No doubt that is why Freud believes that an interpretation (something quite different from pure invention on the interpreter's part) is possible, because such an interpretation does not have to recover a meaning [*sens*], but a *signification* just as explicit as that which pertains to "normal" discourse. It is for this very reason, however, that the essence of the dream is not to be found in the dream-thoughts. Freud makes this clear in a note added in 1925:

> Many analysts have become guilty of falling into another confusion which they cling to with equal obstinacy. They seek to find the essence of dreams in their latent content and in so doing they overlook the distinction between the latent dream-thoughts and the dream-work. At bottom, dreams are nothing more than a particular *form* of thinking, made possible by the conditions of the state of sleep. It is the *dream-work* which creates that form, and it alone is the essence of dreaming (*das Wesentliche am Traum*)—the explanation of its peculiar nature.[4]

This work, however, does not belong to the category of waking thought: "it diverges further from our picture of waking thought than has been supposed even by the most determined depreciator of psychical functioning during the formation of dreams."[5] It is a transformation. The dream-work is "completely different . . . qualitatively" from waking thought, so that it is "not immediately comparable with it." The dream-work "does not think, calculate or judge in any way at all; it restricts itself to giving things a new form."[6]

It is advisable, if one wants truly to grasp Freud's intention, to take seriously the opposition he establishes between dream-thoughts and dream-work [*Gedanke* and *Arbeit*], and the transforming action (*umformen*) of the dream. The discourse that resides at the heart of the dream is the object of this work, its raw material. The dream-work does not relate to this primary discourse as another discourse, such as that of interpretation, might do; the gap between latent content (*Traumgedanke*) and manifest content is not the empty distance, the transcendence separating a "normal" discourse from its object (even if that object is itself a discourse), nor yet that which separates a text from its translation into another language. That difference is "intrinsic" according to Freud. The problem of the dream-work is therefore to discover how, from the raw material of a statement, a qualitatively different though still meaningful object can be produced. The work is not an interpretation of the dream-thought, a discourse on a discourse. Neither is it a transcription, a discourse based on a discourse. It is its transformation.

This statement of the problem sets the tone for all the descriptions of oneiric elaboration in chapter 6. From beginning to end of the study, Freud assimilates the dream-thoughts to a text and the dream-work to a sum of operations carried out on the ("correct") meaning of the text, but by means of procedures which are non-linguistic, and which hence must operate on the text as if it were material. How must a *text* be *worked over* in order for its stated meaning to be modified?

To begin with, a word about chapter 4, which deals with the notion of *Entstellung* [distortion]. The help it offers might appear to be slight, given that we might justifiably expect it to contain the heart of the matter, if it is indeed the case that in the notion of *Entstellung* an entire way of working on the initial text is summed up. In everyday speech, the word indicates the use of force: *sich entstellen,* to disfigure oneself; *die Sprache entstellen,* to do violence to language. According to Sachs and Villate, the semantic field of the particle *ent-* is constructed along three axes: that of privation, of deduction (de-position); of distancing (ex-position); of progress from a given point of departure (trans-position). But Freud's thought in this chapter is focused elsewhere. He wonders why, if the dream is the fulfillment of a wish, it frequently contains failures, disappointed wishes, and frustrated desires. It is at this point that he shows that the motive of distortion is censorship: a power exerted by an authority forcing desire to disguise itself. At the end of chapter 4, the canonical formula for the dream posited in its third section has to be modified as follows: *"a dream is a (disguised) fulfillment of a (suppressed or repressed) wish."*[7] This is a statement whose parentheses at once record the chapter's acquisition and echo its tone: that of repression. It is therefore the first trace of the theory of repression, rather than an analysis of the concept of *Entstellung,* which is to be found in chapter 4. This is not to diminish the importance of the theory of repression. It teaches us the fundamental truth that repression and desire are born simultaneously.

There is, however, a short meditation on *Entstellung* in *Moses and Monotheism,*[8] Freud's last piece of writing. In it Freud advanced the hypothesis that the Jews, who had rebelled several times against the over-austere, over-paternal religion which Moses, allegedly an Egyptian, had imposed on them, killed him; and that after the subsequent reconciliation of the people with itself and with religion, under another Moses, oral and then written tradition indefatigably worked and reworked the story of Moses, the Pentateuch, in order to conceal the murder. The dream-thought in this instance is therefore parricide, and the work of disguise is called *Entstellung.* I am deliberately ignoring the other secondary operation whose objective is the pious conservation of the text, thus interfering, so Freud presumes, with *Entstellung.* He writes as follows:

> In its implications the distortion [*Entstellung*] of a text resembles a murder {in this instance a murder, that of Moses; but the latter was already an *Entstellung*: a distortion of the father's Word}: the difficulty is not in perpetrating the deed, but in getting rid of its traces. We might well lend the word *Entstellung* the double meaning to which it has a claim

> but of which today it makes no use. It should mean not only "to change the appearance of something" but also "to put something in another place, to displace." Accordingly, in many instances of textual distortion, we may nevertheless count upon finding what has been suppressed and disavowed hidden away somewhere else, though changed and torn away from its context. Only it will not always be easy to recognize it.[9]

At first glance, Freud's remark appears to take *Entstellung* in the weak sense. The displacement of its fragments does not demand that the body of the text undergo the pressures, slippages, and thrust faultings which arise in *The Interpretation of Dreams.* A bit of text may be displaced without interfering with the space of writing, of language. Consequently *transposition* would be an adequate translation of *Entstellung*: a piece is taken out here and replaced somewhere else. But that is to forget the act itself. On reflection, it seems that such an operation cannot fail to have recourse to a spatial dimension that is precisely excluded from the linguistic system. To erase a fragment from one place on the page (remove it from a particular point in the chain) and put it elsewhere (where space will have to be made for it) demands that the extract move *above* the text. This movement takes place, therefore, in depth, the same depth required by Kant for the superimposition, by rotation, of two triangles symmetrical with respect to a perpendicular, and which cannot be made to coincide by a simple planar movement. In what does the murder that is the *Entstellung* of the Pentateuch consist? In precisely this: text is inscribed on plane surface, the two-dimensional spatial limitations of which reproduce the linguistic restraints governing the units that constitute the text, while it symbolizes, for Freud, the strictures of the Law itself; and this text is still subjected to processes inscribed in a three-dimensional space. Writing belongs to a space of reading (letters without depth), the process of displacement has a gesticulatory, visual scope, and the result of displacement, which encompasses both the readable and the visible, is illegible.[10] It is this that constitutes a kind of murder: desire, with its dimension of depth, disfigures the *table* of the Law. And simultaneously, by the same token, it is illegible, hence hidden. Its concealment demands the depth that discourse excludes. Here, in the violence of the Law *vis-à-vis* desire, and the violence of desire's disrupting the space of the Law, we have the two demands of the dream-work: the wish and censorship, both violent, the former undecidable.

With this understanding of *Entstellung*, let us return to an inventory of the processes instituted by the dream-work. We know that Freud enumerates four of these: condensation (*Verdichtung*), displacement (*Verschiebung*), considerations of figurability (*Rücksicht auf Darstellbarkeit*) and secondary revision (*sekundäre Bearbeitung*).[11] It would be an easy matter to show precisely how each of these operations is based on a spatiality that, far from being the locus of the discourse's meaning (*Traumgedanke*), can only be the sensitive, plastic surface where the text is supposed to be inscribed.

I will limit myself to the following remarks:

1. *Condensation* must be understood as a physical process by means of which one or more objects occupying a given space are reduced to a smaller volume, as is the case when a gas becomes a liquid. Consequently, when condensation is applied to a text, it has the effect of telescoping either the signifiers (the *Norekdal* dream, etc.),[12] or the signifieds (dream of the botanical monograph),[13] or both, into "objects" that, in any case, are no longer specifically linguistic, and are even specifically non-linguistic. As far as the signifiers at least are concerned, Freud is categorical: condensation is a *Spielerei* (the dream of the *Autodidasker*)[14] that treats words as if they were things, like the *Sprachkünste* of childhood and of neurosis.[15] Condensation comes under an energetics that plays "freely" with the units of the initial text, freely, that is, relative to the constraints peculiar to the message, to any linguistic message. Hence condensation is a transgression of the rules of discourse. In what does this transgression consist? In condensation itself! To squeeze signifiers and signifieds together, mixing them up, is to neglect the stable distance separating the letters and words of a text, to scorn the distinctive, invariable graphemes of which they are composed, not to recognize, in a word, the space of discourse. This space, neutral and empty, plane of pure oppositions, does not appear by itself. It is invisible, but all the elements of language (or of writing) attain specificity in it, and it is thanks to it that we are able to "hear" (or "read").

Condensation is a change of "state" (a difference in "nature"). The geometric space of language, where the differential lines that lend order to the line of discourse (of the written text) meet, is invaded, as a result of this process, by a movement that violates its taboos, and constructs word-things, words that are "comical and strange,"[16] from the units it finds there. Their "thingness" lies in their depth. Normally, in the linguistic order, a word is transparent: its meaning is immediate, and it is that meaning that is received, the phonic or graphic vehicle passing, so to speak, unperceived; the product of condensation, as its name implies, is, on the contrary, opaque, dense, hiding its other side(s).

Now this mobility that manufactures things out of words, is it not desire itself, pursuing its usual course, producing the imaginary? If this is the case, then we should not say that condensation is an exercise by means of which desire disguises itself, but rather that it *is desire working over* the text of the dream-thoughts. In the first of these interpretations, the force is located *behind* the manifest content, itself assumed to be a disguised text; in the second, and apparently correct one, the force, on the contrary, compresses the primary text, crumpling it up, folding it, squabbling the signs it bears on its surface, fabricating new units that are not linguistic signs or graphic entities. The manifest content is the old text "forced" in this manner; it is not a text. Force occupies the very scenario of the dream as Van Gogh's brushstroke remains recorded in his suns.

This hypothesis would appear to run counter to Freud's own explanation: that the force that crushes the text, pulverizing and combining its elements, is censorship. It would follow from that explanation that desire would be the initial discourse of the *Traumgedanke,* and the work of condensation (and all the revision) would be the product of censorship. But this imputation raises great difficulties: the censor understands what he reads before he cuts, and *in order* to cut. As far as preconscious censorship is concerned, "meaning" belongs to articulated language; it is in the realm of the "readable." Cutting a text after having understood it is a parapraxis if it was a matter of not knowing it. This would be a regression to the Sartrian hypothesis of bad faith. The dream, however, is truly initially opaque: between the text from which it comes and the "reader" (the interpreters), there is no third knowing authority that embellishes the first for the benefit of the second. It must not therefore be the agency to deceive that assumes the responsibility to disguise (transitive verb), but desire itself that disguises itself (reflexive verb). Only that reflexiveness is unreflecting, pre-reflexive, and one can understand how. Desire is a scrambled text from the outset. The disguise does not result from the alleged deceiving intent of desire; the work itself *is* disguise because it is violence perpetrated on linguistic space. There is no need to imagine that the Id has an idea at the back of its head. "The dream-work does not think." The mobility of the primary process is deceptive in itself; it *is* what deceives, what sends the "faculties" using articulated language into a spin: the figural versus the mind.

So much for the principle. It raises several difficulties, however, and Freud's thought on the subject is by no means unequivocal.[17] How do desire, dream-thoughts, and censorship interact? The hypothesis could be advanced that there is a decentering of their relationship in the course of Freud's work, a decentering which does not in any way prevent the terms from occupying different positions at a given period.

In the first kind of relationship, the dream-thoughts are the intelligible text which an exogenous censorship renders undecipherable, thus inviting the analogy with political censorship.[18] In this case it is censorship that represents force, which is exerted on an unconscious desire that speaks. In the second kind of relationship, the dream-thoughts [*Traumgedanken*] are always opposed to the dream-content [*Trauminhalt*], just as the latent is to the manifest content. But this latent content no longer possesses the limpidity of a text; the *Traumgedanken* are composites of text and figure. There are ready-made symbols in the depths of the dream,[19] material designed to lead censorship astray, because it already contains elements of the unreadable and the figural. There is, therefore, a precensorship, which is in fact the originary repression. Freud subsequently emphasizes the ambivalence of censorship,[20] which thus also serves the interests of desire. If we apply the capitalist/entrepreneur metaphor to this relationship, desire is the capitalist, furnishing the energy; the entrepreneur provides the ideas (the thoughts).[21] But, says Freud, it is only a question of two *functions*. They may both be embodied in the same man: there are capitalists with ideas (= the textual may be present in desire), and entrepreneurs with capital (= desire profits by the perceptions and traces that make up the *Traumgedanke*).

In other words, desire is forbidden long "before" the censorship of the dream comes into play; it is intrinsically forbidden. And it is necessary to dissociate, not a pure force from a discourse, but the "discourse" of desire (which, figural and figurative, constitutes the matrix of the primal phantasm) from the preconscious material, diurnal perceptions and traces, which this matrix attracts and works over to the point of making it unrecognizable, the objective being both to fulfill desire—repeating the matrix form by imprinting it on a material—and to disguise and to clothe that form with elements deriving from reality. The censorship that Freud speaks of in *The Interpretation of Dreams* is therefore the operation by which the silt of daily experience (the day's residues) comes to cover over archaic desire. But this desire already carries within itself its primary repression.[22] This means that it is a travesty from the "outset," that it *has never spoken,* in any real sense of the word, that is, of emitting communicable utterances. This would even mean that "to disguise" is a bad metaphor, since the word implies the identity of the thing under different clothing. This means that the correct metaphor would be "to transgress," in the sense I have indicated.

On the other hand, the finality of the dream, wish-fulfillment (*Wunscherfüllung*) would be more satisfactorily explained. The principle of *Is fecit qui profuit,* formulated à propos of censorship in the case of displacement, ought to read: "it is desire (and not censorship) that did it," since it is desire that the dream fulfills. It would be understood that the fulfillment of desire, an important function of the dream, consists not in the representation of a satisfaction (which, on the contrary, when it occurs, wakes one up), but entirely in the imaginary activity itself. It is not the dream-content that fulfills desire, but the act of dreaming, of fantasizing, because the Phantasy is a transgression.

2. *Displacement.* Freud calls it "the essential portion (*das wesentliche Stück*) of the dream-work," "one of the principal methods by which that distortion [*Entstellung*] is achieved." There is no need to dwell on it any more than Freud does,[23] for displacement is treated in these pages as a preparatory step to condensation. The latter has been shown to be closely connected to overdetermination, but to overdetermine supposes certain changes of emphasis in the initial text of the dream-thoughts. In condensing themselves,

the dream-thoughts crush certain parts of the discourse, leaving others visible. Take a text written on a sheet of paper and crumple it. The elements of the discourse take on *relief,* in the strict sense. Imagine that before the grip of condensation compresses the dream-thoughts, displacement has reinforced certain zones of the text, so that they resist contraction and remain legible. The result is the "textual difference" between dream-content [*Trauminhalt*] and dream-thoughts [*Traumgedanke*].[24]

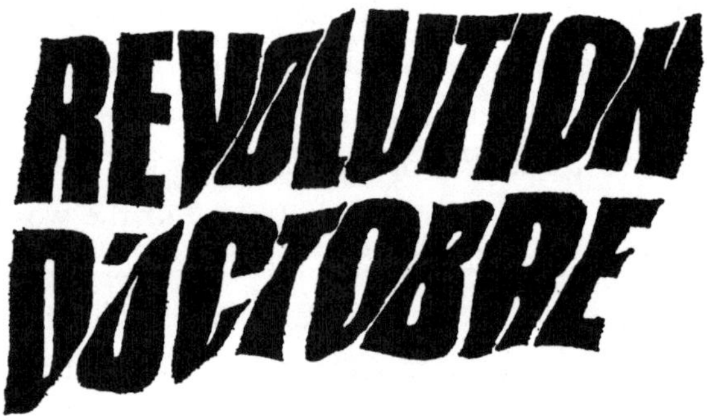

Figure 11. *Révolution d'octobre,* advertisement panel for Frédéric Rossif's film *Révolution d'octobre* (1967), a Télé-Hachette/Procinex production, distributed by Paramount. Based on the original reproduced in *Revue d'esthétique* (Paris: Klincksieck, 1968), vol. 1, 35.

We have a simple example of this in the poster for Frédéric Rossif's film *Révolution d'Octobre* (Figure 11). The letters of the title are deformed in such a way as to give the impression that a wind is blowing the flat surface on which they are written. This is enough to make this plane movable, to turn it into a piece of cloth, the cloth of a flag carried by someone who is walking fast toward the left (which, as well as being politically symbolic, also carries a plastic value: the eye moves from the left when reading; hence the letters move ahead of the glance, complementing its movement). But this is only the beginning of condensation. If the wind were to blow harder, if the horse of the standard-bearer were to gallop flat out, if one were able to "freeze" the inscription, certain letters would disappear altogether into the folds and others would undergo radical changes. B, whose base was masked by a fold, might be read as an R, D as an O, etc. Certain differential or graphically relevant features would be transgressed. It could happen that *Révolution d'Octobre* might read *Révon d'Ore* and be heard as *Rêvons d'or* [let's dream of gold]. So much for condensation, which clearly requires the third dimension, that in which the flag forms its folds. But such a distortion would have required a preliminary choice; in our example, it is the beginning (*REV, D'O*) and the end (*ON, RE*) that must remain visible, must stand fast to windward. It is the work of displacement that effects this choice by reinforcing certain parts of the cloth, stiffening them, enabling them to preserve certain sites of the—primary—text in position. "Textual difference" might be imagined in these terms. It remains, however, to conceive of it. If desire is the mobile element (here the wind, elsewhere water) that crumples the text, can it also be the fixative that keeps certain parts of it readable? I know of only one notion which can satisfy these conflicting demands: the notion of Form, of Phantasy.

3. Look out for the figure: *Rücksicht auf Darstellbarkeit* [considerations of figurability]. We must proceed cautiously here, because here desire seizes the text in a quite different manner. By condensation and displacement it acts on the *supposed site* of its inscription. One might say that by figuration, desire, in addition, takes words literally [*au pied de la lettre:* at the foot of the letter], the foot of the letter being the figure. Surrealist art might shed some light on this. I am thinking particularly of the paintings of Magritte, many of which are not plays on words but games played by the figure on the words that form its legend. For example, the painting called *Reconnaissance Infinie* (Plate 17)[25] shows an enormous bare planet floating above desert mountains, bathed in a dull cosmic light, and on it a man in a double-breasted suit scanning the void, doing a reconnaissance of it. The examples that Freud borrowed from Silberer and which support his entire theory of figuration show that exactly the same procedure takes place in the dream. "'Example 1. I thought of having to revise an uneven passage in an essay. Symbol: I saw myself planing a piece of wood.'"[26] The literal in the figure, at least if one accepts the hypothesis that all discourse aims at an object exterior to language, which may be presented (*darstellen*) as its referent. We rely, therefore, on the function of designation, rather than signification, in which the relation between the sign and the thing gels, where, as a result, magic [*magie*] can take place, the possibility of conjuring up the thing by the word, of making an image. *Image-magie,* the luck of the anagram, but objective luck, and Freud in any case was a firm believer in the relationship between the two.

To become convinced of this one has only to read *Moses and Monotheism,* a meditation built exclusively on the opposition between the Jewish religion, sober and image-less, and the Egyptian one, full of magic and images. Beware of the figure because it is the thing supplanting the word, because it is desire fulfilled, not only childhood, but paranoia, hysteria, obsession.[27] Do not crumple the pages of the book! Do not illustrate it!

The *Rücksicht auf Darstellbarkeit* is that arrangement of an initial text that, according to Freud, has two objectives: to illustrate it, but also to replace certain portions of it by figures. In the illustration the figure is outside the text, and text and image are, as a rule, presented together (which gives rise to other problems). In the rebus, corresponding figures will be substituted for at least some fragments of the primary text. The *Rücksicht* is that operation on the text that consists in replacing "colorless, abstract" expressions "such as might be used in a political leading article in a newspaper" by expressions for which it would be permissible to use a figurative equivalent *or* substitute.[28] The text must become an "imaged" text, by virtue of the fact that the "imaged" (the imageable, *das Bildliche*) is, for the dream, "particularly capable of being figured (*darstellungsfähig*)."

An imaged text is a discourse that is very close to the figure. It will be necessary, then, to analyze the different ways in which such a proximity may be established: the figurative power of a word, or course, but also the rhythmic power of syntax, and at an even deeper level, the matrix of narrative rhythm, what Propp called form. We will see revealed what I consider to be an essential paradox. At the lexical level, the figure is given as *outside the word* (Silberer's "roughness," Magritte's "reconnaissance"); at the (still rhetorical) level of syntax, the figure is the rhythmical schema (the rhythm of a given writer's sentence, Flaubert's as Proust studies it, for example). We are no longer in the domain of the visual. Here language communicates with dance by diffusing its range and frequency throughout the body of the reader: recitation, declamation, song are intermediaries between reading and dance. At the stylistic level, the figure is submerged in the words but only in order to support and control the articulation of the large units of the narrative. There is no longer anything visible, only the visual haunting narration. We are approaching the matrix. It is clear that the notion of the figure leads to image, configuration, form, and therefore a lexical and/or syntactical, but also stylistic, proximity, because there are figures that correspond to words, figures of style, of discourse, in each case, the figural surrounding the substance of language and permeating it. Pursuing this tack, we inevitably stumble, once again, on the question of the phantasm, which is pivotal. The great linguistic figures, of discourse, of style, are the expression, right in the heart of language, of a general disposition of experience, and the phantasm is the matrix of that ordering, that rhythm, which will henceforth be imposed on everything that happens on the levels of "reality" and expression. Thus these figures figure a primary figure. It is through their agency that a discourse may enter into communication with the images that are reputed to be external to it, but which in fact depend for their organization on the same signifying matrix.

It is not fortuitous that Freud, in the passage under discussion, ends up spontaneously citing poetry as an example of the work of figuration, not on account of its powerful external images, but as an immanent rhythmic force (both rhythmed and rhythming): "If a poem is to be written in rhymes, the second line of a couplet is limited by two conditions: it must express an appropriate meaning, and the expression of that meaning must rhyme with the first line."[29] We will see that it is precisely this rhythm that Jakobson calls metaphor. The constraints of rhyme impose a scansion [*découpage*] on the signifier, and if the poem is a good one, on the signified, simultaneously. Similarly, there is a "distribution and selection" of signs (signifier and signified) in the dream, which allows one particular sign to exercise and influence over the others by remote control, as it were, comparable to that which forces the poet to choose *retour* over *rentrée* because it must rhyme with *alentour* three lines earlier. This remote action, which takes place in the body of the work, is the very principle of form: all along the linear body of a text, an utterance or a piece of music, flat on the plane surface of a picture, in the volume of a sculpted object or a building, it is form that establishes communication between the parts, in keeping with certain constraints, and in order for it to be form, these constraints must not be inscribed in any *language*. Why? Because whatever is language is dedicated to communication between interlocutors, while the figure, as described above, has to jam that communication. By virtue of the fact that it sets up a closed circuit intercom system of the work with itself, the figure surprises the eye and the ear and the mind by a perfectly improbable arrangement of the parts. Thus there is no more restraint in the figure of discourse than in any other image. And it is futile to attempt to bring everything back to articulated language as the model for all semiology, when it is patently clear that language, at least in its poetic usage, is possessed, haunted by the figure.

II

Before dealing with the fourth operation of the dream-work (secondary revision), which I should particularly like to illustrate more fully, the most important implication of what I have just said must be examined, i.e., that the dream is not a discourse, because the dream-work is intrinsically different from the operations of speech. I have already indicated as much in the preceding remarks, but since this statement runs directly counter to what I believe to be Jacques Lacan's interpretation, as well as counter to the current tendency to stuff all of semiology into linguistics,[30] it is worthwhile confronting these positions.

The operations that have guided Lacan's interpretation of the dream-work are those elucidated by Roman Jakobson with regard to the speech act, in his article "Two Functions of Language and Two Forms of Aphasia."[31] The origin of the separation he makes in that article between metaphor and metonymy is to be found in the Saussurean thesis according to which meaning is ultimately reducible to a value, that is that the signified of the linguistic sign "is only the resumé of the linguistic value, given the interplay of the terms."[32] Saussure says, even more explicitly, that "what the word contains is never determined by anything but the convergence of what exists around it, associatively and syntagmatically."[33] In the table of language, what surrounds a given term organizes itself according to two kinds of relationships. The first, which are syntagmatic, determine the position and function of the term in every possible statement; the second, which Saussure called "associative" or paradigmatic, link the term with others that may be substituted for it. I consider it very important to establish a link between the syntagm-paradigm opposition and the theory of meaning as a value because this theory, in turn, has meaning only insofar as a language refers back to a closed system (*la langue*) that is independent of its object, and precisely because of this exteriority can speak of that object. The closure of the system is pivotal to both these properties of language at once, the double internal function (paradigmatic and syntagmatic) and the external (referential) function.

Corresponding to the double setting of the term in language is the double operation in the speech act which Jakobson visualizes summarily as follows: the speaker chooses each term he utters from among all those that are linked to it by paradigmatic, substitutive relationships; and he combines the chosen terms according to the constraints of concatenation (syntagmatic relationships) which regulate the linking of each term used to its context in the line of speech. Thus for the speaker an act of selection corresponds to the paradigm, and an act of combination to the syntagm. Jakobson shows that given this disentanglement [*désintrication*], two forms of aphasia may be distinguished, according to whether the illness attacks the selective activity (disruption of similarity), leading to the loss of the capacity to define and of metalanguage in general, or whether, on the other hand, it affects the combinatory activity, leading to the disappearance of double articulation (agrammatism) by scrambling the relations of contiguity.

Jakobson's analyses are perhaps arguable for the linguist; they are extremely fertile for the philosopher. But in any case they make a strong assertion: that speech supposes twin, indissociable activities;[34] that it is illness which separates them in fact and the linguist who separates them in theory; and that it is the equilibrium of both functions in the speech act which guarantees, as a rule, the "normality of the discourse,"[35] that is to say, its communicability. Doubtless one function could gain precedence over the other without causing the discourse to become immediately aphasic. Jakobson attempts to apply his criterion of similarity/contiguity to literary discourse, an essential characteristic of which, in the eyes of linguists, is to "unbalance" "normal" discourse. He comes up with a classification of three difference levels of discourse—rhetoric, genres, schools—which the following table summarizes:

Levels	*Paradigmatic Relationships*	*Syntagmatic Relationships*
Language	similarity	contiguity
Speech Act	selection	combination
Trope	metaphor	metonymy
Genre	poetry	prose
School	Romanticism, Symbolism	Realism

It has been noted that the extension of the criterion does not so far exceed the field of articulated language, properly so-called. But at the end of the article, Jakobson permits himself to take the plunge: "The respective prevalence of one or the other of the two procedures is not in any way exclusive to literature. The same oscillation appears in sign systems other than language.... The competition between the two procedures, metonymic and metaphoric, is evident in every symbolic process, whether intra-subjective or social."[36] It is at this point that he considers dreams: "Thus in a study on the structure of dreams, the decisive question is to know if the symbols and temporal sequences used are based on contiguity (the Freudian metonymic 'displacement' and synecdochic 'condensation') or on similarity (Freudian 'identification' and 'symbolism.')."[37] The result of this formula is that displacement and condensation belong in the same column of our table, that of the syntagm, while identification and symbolism are consigned to the paradigmatic column.

Nicholas Ruwet, the translator of Jakobson's article, notes that this classification does not coincide with Lacan's: "The latter identifies, respectively, condensation with metaphor, displacement with metonymy."[38] In the table, therefore, condensation would go under paradigm, and displacement under syntagm. Jakobson and Lacan agree, therefore, in situating displacement in the syntagmatic order. The disagreement arises over condensation: syntagmatic for Jakobson, paradigmatic for Lacan. Ruwet adds: "Roman Jakobson, to whom we have pointed this out, believes that the divergence is explained by the imprecision of the concept of condensation, which, in Freud, seems to encompass cases of both metaphor and synecdoche."

This is to put the blame on Freud a little precipitously. Another hypothesis must be advanced, i.e., that the imprecision results from applying to one field of expression categories borrowed from another, an undertaking that is motivated by the desire to find in the dream-work the operations of speech. It is, I believe, that desire which is really "imprecise," if it is to "spell out" Freud's text that is involved without "deducting anything from it."[39] Failing recognition in the dream of a true discourse, true precisely because it conforms to the only two operations defined by the linguist—which the analysis of the dream as well as that of *The Interpretation of Dreams* preclude—the desire of which I spoke runs the risk of backfiring on the two operations of selection and combination in order to bend them to the project. The dream cannot be made to speak? Then we will try to make discourse dream. That is more accurate, closer to what really happens, and I am convinced that the figure dwells in discourse like a phantasm, while discourse dwells in the figure like a dream. The only thing is that it must be agreed that the "language" of the unconscious is not modeled on articulated discourse, which, as we know, finds utterance according to a language. Rather, the dream is the acme of the inarticulate, deconstructed discourse from which no language, even normal, is entirely free. Metaphor and metonymy must, therefore, be understood, not in the strict sense attributed to them by the structural linguist in his theory of the speech act, but in a sense which is itself metaphoric. From this it would follow that it is not Freud who is imprecise but Jakobson himself in his use of concepts that he had begun to construct, in all rigor, on the basis of a structural analysis of the language activity.

Let us limit ourselves to an examination of condensation, which seems to be the nub of the disagreement between Jakobson and Lacan. Here is what the latter has written about it:

> *Verdichtung,* or "condensation," is the structure of the superimposition of the signifiers, which metaphor takes as its field, and whose name, condensing in itself the word *Dichtung,* shows how the mechanism is connatural with poetry to the point that it envelops the traditional function proper to poetry.[40]

First of all, what is metaphor? Its formula, as Lacan has already explained, is "one word for another." Its "creative spark . . . ignites between two signifiers, one of which is substituted for the other while taking its place in the signifying chain, the eclipsed signifier remaining present in its (metonymic) connection with the rest of the chain." The example given is the line from *Booz endormi*: "Sa gerbe n'était point avare ni haineuse" (His sheaf was neither miserly nor spiteful).[41] A perfectly appropriate definition. And it includes the notion of substitution, the very one that according to Jakobson characterizes the paradigmatic, hence metaphoric, relationship between two terms. Nonetheless two observations must be made.

The first is that the essential feature of metaphor, for the poet a least, is not covered by this definition. In the poetic metaphor, substitution *is precisely not authorized by usage,* is not inscribed in the paradigmatic network surrounding the supplanted term (it is not, for example, common usage to substitute "his sheaf" for Booz, if this line is accepted as metaphorical). When the substitution is authorized, we no longer have anything like metaphor in Lacan's sense of a *figure* of style. We have simply an instance of a choice between terms that stand in a paradigmatic relation to each other, any one of which would serve equally well at that particular point in the chain. Hence the choice of one of them at the expense of the others results in no overloading, no "overdetermination" of the statement. The substitution will, however, *determine* the amount of information which the message conveys to its recipient. Thus: "I — dread —, or — hope for —, or — await — his arrival." Here we are "ante" style, in the realm of language [*langue*]. The true metaphor, the trope, begins with the too-wide gap, the transgression of the range of acceptable substitutes sanctioned by usage. Jakobson starts off from a notion of substitution based on a strictly structuralist concept of language, and proceeds (unjustifiably, as we will see) to a rhetorical meaning of metaphor that is applied to discourse. Substitution is indeed based on usage, but the true metaphor defies usage. André Breton is right in this instance: "For me the strongest (surrealist image) is the most highly arbitrary one. I don't deny it."[42]

And he is doubly right. Lacan accuses the surrealist notion of the image, as it is implied in automatic writing, of confusion, because, he says, "the doctrine behind it is false. The creative spark of the metaphor does not spring from the presentation of two images, that is of two signifiers equally actualized,"[43] but rather, as we have seen, from the eclipse of one term for which another is substituted. Hence the sheaf of Booz. This is to appeal to the current meaning of the word, which must be called into question here, and in the name of the very Jakobson who is invoked on the same page in a footnote. In his essay on aphasia Jakobson distinguishes the metaphoric from the metonymic process, in keeping with psychological notions of substitutive and predicative reactions.[44] For example, in a word-association test, "hut" is proposed as a leading word to the child. If the response is on the order of "has burned down" or "is a wretched little house," the reaction is said to be predicative. If it is on the order of "hut, cabin, palace" the reaction is said to be substitutive. Let us examine the predicative response more closely. Its nature is to constitute a sentence, hence to open the possibility of a narrative. But two kinds of opening must be distinguished. "Hut—has burned down" is a purely narrative statement. "Hut—is a wretched little house" is doubtless a syntagmatic organization (Jakobson calls it syntactic) by virtue of the positioning of the terms within it. But semantically, the statement is paradigmatic: as far as meaning goes, "wretched little house" could be substituted for hut; "has burned down" could not. Jakobson, therefore, distinguishes a positional aspect (within the statement—*l'énoncé*) from a semantic aspect (within the table of meanings accepted by language). A metaphor may be a predicative reaction positionally, but it must in any case be semantically substitutive.

A statement such as "his sheaf was neither miserly nor spiteful" would be entirely unacceptable as a metaphor for Jakobson. Not only do the terms constitute a clearly predicative statement, but on the semantic level they are not amenable to substitution, unless it were claimed that the signifieds "generosity" and "benevolence" are implicit in the signifier "sheaf"—which is not, in any case, the thrust of Lacan's argument. The fact remains that for Jakobson metaphor is characterized precisely by what Lacan judges to be a surrealist error: the coexistence in the discourse, hence in a syntagmatic position, of two or more terms whose semantic relation is one of substitutability. The spark of meaning ignites, not perpendicularly to the axis of the discourse, in its encircling depth, but all along that axis, like a short circuit between two poles of the same sign. It seems to me that "his sheaf" is a good instance of metonymy, the sheaf being understood as an emblem of Booz, while the use of the imperfect confers, in addition, a typically narrative connotation on the statement.

Now, given Lacan's interpretation of metaphor, how can one say that condensation is one? Lacan formulates the metaphoric structure as follows:[45]

$$f\left(\frac{S'}{S}\right) S \cong S\ (+)\ s$$

which reads: the metaphoric function of the signifier is congruent with the emergence of signification. The metaphoric function is transcribed $f\left(\frac{S'}{S}\right)$, the emergence of signification S (+) *s*. The plus sign placed in parentheses indicates the crossing of the bar —— and the role that crossing consistently plays in the emergence of signification. The bar (——) is, in Lacan's algorithm, what separates the signifier and the signified, it is the mark of "nonsense." Crossed (+) by the metaphor, it reestablishes contact between signifier and signified and thus establishes meaning. As for the notation of the metaphor itself $\left(\frac{S'}{S}\right)$, it conforms to Lacan's own definition: S' is the stated term that eclipses the signifier S, just as his sheaf is supposed to eclipse Booz. If I am not mistaken, finally, about the "crossing of the bar," metaphor for Lacan is the trope by means of which the signified is adduced. It "takes up its position at the precise point at which sense is produced in non-sense."[46]

Can the same be said for condensation in the dream-work? Here we will be obliged to return to Freud himself, since his interpreter is not very forthcoming. At this point Lacan's real preoccupation and the root of the displacement of the term "metaphor" in his account becomes clear. Obliged to explain how condensation is metaphoric, he explains how the subject is never present in discourse except metaphorically, and that it is in losing himself in it that he can be present. The signifier is *never given,* so he believes, and the "unique key" to metaphor and metonymy is that "the S and the *s* of the Saussurian algorithm are not on the same level, and man only deludes himself when he believes his true place is on their axis, which is nowhere."[47] When he says "signified," Lacan thinks "subject." The entire theory of the metaphor is the theory of the metaphor of the *subject,* which only apprehends itself through the ruse of the metaphor, that is, in missing itself, because it is signified by a signifier. And the signifier is the Other. It is this expressive repression which the bar between S and *s* conveys.

We have seen how the use of the word metaphor diverges from Jakobson's definition. We are now obliged to register the strongest reservations about such a reading of the Saussurean algorithm. To begin with, Saussure placed the signified *above* the signifier, and the line which separates them in the schemas, far from representing repression or censorship, has so little consistency that it will tend to disappear as the notion of value will supersede that of signification in the later lectures, the signified of a term being nothing more than a summary of its *value,* that is, of its syntagmatic and paradigmatic entourage. And that entourage is not hidden, but transparent. Lacan, preoccupied for his part with that deafness—the Greeks called it *Atè*—which constitutes the unconscious, omits to say that Saussure's reflection on the linguistic sign takes its departure from the transparency necessary to interlocutory experience. To such an extent that in the end one might wonder if the sign is indeed a sign, since it has no depth. In other words, it seems to me that here in Lacan's thought there is a confusion between *signification* in the strict sense Saussure accorded the term by shifting it back to linguistic value, a sense which, precisely because it reduces signification entirely to the ensemble of syntagmatic and paradigmatic relations surrounding a term, controlling its functioning in the statement and its place in the semantic field, robs that signification of all the depth of hiding/revealing and explains the enigmatic limpidity of words in use, a confusion, then, between signification thus isolated, and *meaning* [*sens*]. When a French speaker says *La nuit tombe* [night is falling], the statement does not preclude signification, which is completely transparent to the French ear. The indissociability of the signifier and the signified that Saussure never ceases to underline, and Lacan to suppress, is complementary to that transparence. On the other hand, the statement may yield depth by virtue of its *meaning* [*sens*], but it will be necessary, most of the time, to refer to the context (whether, for example, the sentence has to do with the advent of Hitler to power) in order to interpret this meaning.

The manner in which Lacan understands metaphor has to do with meaning, not signification. That is why, incidentally, his metaphor is that of Hegel or

Alain and could not be Jakobson's strictly speaking. The depth produced by the movement of a term shouldering aside another and eliding it, a depth in which I understand that the subject must lose himself at the brink of constituting himself (as a speaking subject), is absent from "metaphor" if it is accepted that, for the linguist, metaphor is equivalent in the order of tropes to the paradigm in the order of the structures of language, and to selection in the order of the operations of speech. Or, if Jakobson's metaphor is already itself "profound," the responsibility for the confusion ought to lie with the imprudent transition the linguist permits himself to make from language [*langue*] to rhetoric. According to his strict structuralism, there is no figure of language, only rules, no figure of speech, only controlled operations, and the figure enters language only at the stylistic level, when the units are sufficiently large so that the order to be followed is no longer constrained and the phantasm can "freely" (that is to say, under constraints that are not linguistic) situate itself, not *behind* words, but *among* them, invisibly. And such is indeed the doctrine professed elsewhere by Jakobson with regard to the hierarchy of units: the freedom of the speaker growing in proportion to the size of the units.[48]

It seems to me that it is his overweening preoccupation with the theory of the subject, under the guise of the theory of signification, that causes Lacan to take metonymy for metaphor, as in "Sa gerbe n'était point avare . . . ," and metaphor itself as constituting a depth, a beyond, resulting from eclipse [of one term by another]. A structural theory of language could not agree with him on this point. Can the Freudian theory of dreams do so? The *Verdichtung* [condensation] for Freud is a genuine compression. It must be conceived of spatially. The given account of a dream takes up a few lines; its interpretation, that is, the exposition of the dream-thought, "may occupy six, eight or a dozen times as much space."[49] One must abstain, it is true, from measuring the coefficient of compression (*Verdichtungsquote*) failing direct knowledge of the "real" scope of the thoughts. Nonetheless, we are dealing with a topography, having two superimposed levels, thought underneath "content," the dream-work operating between the two, in depth, producing the latent/manifest opposition. Thus the need to reduce the second space relative to the first allows us to understand the two properties which Freud singles out in the *Verdichtung:* it is an "omission" (*Auslassung*) and "a multiple determination" (*mehrfache Determinierung*).[50] An omission of thought that cannot pass to a higher level, an over-determination of dream-elements that subsume several strands of thought. The topographical inspiration is so powerful here that it would seem that condensation is no longer motivated by censorship, but by limitations of space, in the strict sense, the locus of our dreams being narrower than the locus of our thoughts.

And by dwelling at length on the fate of words in the course of this compression, Freud assures us that it is a fundamentally nonlinguistic operation. Where can we best grasp ("*am greifbarsten*") the work of condensation? When it seizes on words and names. The dream frequently treats words as if they were things (*Dinge*), subjecting them to the same combinations as representations of things (*Dingvorstellungen*).[51] And this is not a rare occurrence, it is "extremely frequent," which is why the analysis of "nonsensical verbal forms" (*unsinnige Wortbildungen*) is "particularly well-calculated" to provide a grasp of the operation of condensation.[52] Here is formal proof that for Freud this work affects articulated speech (which gives at first silent, and ultimately, at the end of the interpretation, explicit expression to the dream-thoughts) in a deconstructive fashion. Substitution, for Jakobson, was constitutive of discourse; condensation, for Freud, is a transformation *dismissive* of discourse. Here we are at the opposite pole from Lacan, who writes: "What distinguishes these two mechanisms [metaphor and metonymy] which play such a privileged role in the dream-work (*Traumarbeit*), from their homologous function in discourse? Nothing, except a condition imposed upon the signifying material, called *Rücksicht auf Darstellbarkeit* which must be translated by: 'consideration of the means of representation.' (The translation by 'role of the possibility of figurative expression' being too approximative here.) But this condition constitutes a limitation operating *within* the system of writing; this is a long way from dissolving the system into a figurative semiology on a level with phenomena of natural expression."[53]

It seems unnecessary to pursue the discussion with regard to metonymy; it leads to the same conclusion. It doesn't matter that Jakobson and Lacan agree, this time, to ascribe displacement [*Verschiebung*] to metonymy; it takes a real play on words to do it. Metonymy is already hard-pressed to play in rhetoric the role that Jakobson attributes to combination in the speech act and to the syntagmatic relation in the table of language. The difficulty is aggravated, if, leaving discourse behind, metonymy is required to function as a mainspring for oneiric displacement.

Neither is it possible to agree with Lacan about the dream-work's considerations of figurability. Not only does he relegate these considerations to the background, unjustifiably, in the light of Freud's text, but above all he refuses to concede to figurability its two functions: the one operative *inside* the writing system, creating figures with letters, heading not only in the direction of the hieroglyph, but in the direction of the rebus; the other, however, about which Lacan says not a word, trading on the designatory power of language, and simply replacing (as in the Silberer and Magritte examples) the signified by one of its designates, the concept by one of its objects. It is the prejudice in favor of the closure of the system that prevents justice being done to Freud's text.

It can perhaps be said that the dream is articulated like a language. It must then be accepted that the word "language" loses the precision conferred on it by post-Saussurean linguistics. It refers to a study not of language, but of enunciation. It is particularly the theory of signification as a value, and of value as a syntagmatic and paradigmatic framework that must be, if not abandoned, at least completed by a theory of meaning [*sens*]. It is, at the same time, the doctrine of the indissociability of signified and signifier, that is of the transparence of the sign, which must be balanced by justifying the depth of discourse. The language to which one appeals must be "weighty," laboring, concealing, revealing, in a metaphorical sense, no doubt, but metaphor must be understood here as in the case of an artistic work. So that, at first glance, the "language" of the dream seems to be nothing more nor less than the language of art.[54] It is its primary cause, perhaps its model. The same distance separates Jakobson's substitution and Lacan's metaphor as exists between discourse and figure. On the one hand, the space of invariances, on the other the terrain where the plasticity of things "seen" is deployed. Legible or audible space, open space of the visible (and invisible).

III

The fourth operation, *secondary revision,* remains to be explored. It seems to bear a paradoxical relationship to our thesis. Freud says of it that its function is to make a day-dream [*Tagtraum*] of the dream, to make it conform to the laws of intelligibility. He even goes so far as to maintain that it derives from normal thought,[55] the result being that this revision might indeed appear to be secondary, relative to the primary process, imposing articulated language on material to which, as Freud insisted in the section on figurability, nearly all the categories of rational thought were foreign. We have here, in a word, "this work which does not think" resorting to the discourse of conscious or preconscious thought. How, then, can one continue to maintain that the operations that transform the dream-thoughts into the dream-content are real work? Must we not make an exception, at least, of the fourth operation, which seems to derive exclusively from language? But how can we understand this exception? The order of discourse that it is the function of the dream-work to render unintelligible, according to Freud, which in any case it violates, does this order participate in it own eclipse?

Freud is not as formal on the subject of this revision as the foregoing remarks may have indicated. It is true that he ascribes it to normal thought, that he entrusts to it the task of building the dream's façade.[56] But first of all he resists making it *posterior* to the three other operations,

> We must assume . . . that from the very first (*von allem Anfang*) the demands of this second factor constitute one of the conditions which the dream must satisfy and that this condition, like (*ebenso wie*) those laid down by condensation, the censorship imposed by resistance, and representability, operates simultaneously (*gleichzeitig*) in a conducive and selective sense upon the mass of material present in the dream-thoughts.[57]

And this is not all. The "façade" that this revision must construct, the order it must impose on the chaos resulting from the upheaval of the three prior operations, may present itself quite unexpectedly. It happens, says Freud, that secondary revision may find that "a formation of that kind (*ein solches Gebilde*) already exists, available for use in the material of the dream-thoughts."[58] Thus the dream may wear its heart on its sleeve. "I am in the habit," Freud continues, "of describing the element in the dream-thoughts {he does indeed say "thoughts"} that I have in mind as a 'phantasy.' I shall perhaps avoid misunderstanding if I mention the 'day-dream' as something analogous to it in waking life." A footnote to this sentence reads "'Rêve,' '*petit roman,*'—'day-dream,' [continuous] 'story.'" Some of these novels are conscious, others unconscious. It is around such phantasms constructed from memories, and not on the memories themselves, that hysterical symptoms are constructed. The essential characteristics of these novels are precisely those of the night-dreams. Freud writes: "their investigation might, in fact, have served as the shortest and best approach to an understanding of night-dreams."[59] I indicated above that phantasms, rather than a discourse, should perhaps be classified as dream-thoughts. This passage invites such a conclusion. The dream's wrapping is also sometimes its core. The "novel" is never an ulterior arrangement, and it is sometimes an archaic one, in which the memories themselves (of primal scenes) are involved, articulated. The phantasm is not only both diurnal *and* nocturnal, but belongs to the façade *and* to the foundations.

Clearly the recurrent "sometimes" and "it happens that," juxtaposed with the attribution of secondary revision to normal thought, scarcely constitute a coherent doctrine. But the hesitancy itself merits attention. We must be guided by Freud. Immediately after these reflections on phantasy, he states that secondary revision stands in the same relation to the dream-content as waking (preconscious) thought does to the material of perception: a quasi-pulsional ordering that obliterates the difference between the given and the anticipated and jams proper *reception.* Secondary revision is commensurate to that *pseudein* (to deceive, to cheat) which calls to mind what Plato said about painters and sophists, but which appears to be attributed by Freud in this instance to discourse itself.

And it is in order to illustrate this deceptive function that he cites the "enigmatic inscriptions" that he takes as an example from the newspaper that had regaled Bavarian and Austrian households for a century, and of which, according to Lacan, he was "an avid reader."

> If I look around for something with which to compare the final form assumed by a dream as it appears after normal thought has made its contribution, I can think of nothing better than the enigmatic inscriptions with which the *Fliegende Blätter* has for so long entertained its readers. They are intended to make the reader believe that a certain sentence—for the sake of contrast, a sentence in dialect and as scurrilous as possible—is a Latin inscription. For this purpose the letters contained in the words are torn out of their combination into syllables and arranged in a new order. Here and there a genuine Latin word appears; at other points we seem to see abbreviations of Latin words before us; and at still other points in the inscription we may allow ourselves to be deceived into overlooking the senselessness of isolated letters by parts of the inscription seeming to be defaced or showing lacunae. If we are to avoid being taken in by the joke, we must disregard everything that makes it seem like an inscription, look firmly at the letters, pay no attention to their ostensible arrangement, and so combine them into words belonging to our own mother tongue.[60]

It is worthwhile to analyze the kind of hoax employed in these inscriptions: it presumes an interesting interplay of reading and seeing. Leafing through the issues from 1884 to 1898, years during which Freud was collecting material for *The Interpretation of Dreams,* I found thirteen of these inscriptions. They are all entitled *Rätselhafte Inschrift* [enigmatic inscription]. Some have no figure; the reader passes from the manifest text (which usually looks like Latin), to the latent text (in the dialect of the South), by a simple displacement of the divisions in the phonic continuum. For example: Integram addi coenam gymnasium ista nix vomia galata in trina (= In de Grammatiken am Gymnasium ist a' (auch) nix vom Jaga-Latein drinna!).[61] Freud is primarily concerned with figure-bearing inscriptions. Nonetheless, this first category teaches us something: that the passage from manifest to latent text takes place through displacement of the *phonic* reality of the original statement. We will see the importance of this remark. In order to classify the illustrated inscriptions, three elements, not two, must be taken into consideration: the latent "text" (*Traumgedanke*), which is the solution of the enigma; the manifest text (*Trauminhalt* after secondary revision), which is the text of the inscription; and the scene illustrated (*Darstellung*).

Let us proceed from the manifest text to the scene. They can be joined in three ways: unity of place, when the linguistic signifier and the figure are inscribed in the same representational space; unity of culture, when both refer to the same civilization; unity of meaning, when the *signified* of the manifest text can be related to the *scene.* Hence, in theory, there are eight possible categories:

Categories	*Unity of Place*	*Unity of Culture*	*Unity of Meaning*
1	+	+	+
2	+	+	–
3	+	–	–
4	+	–	+
5	–	+	+
Etc.			

The categories preceded by the minus sign are excluded here. They would not be inscriptions, but legends, texts belonging to a space other than that of the figure. The categories 1 through 4 remain. The collected inscriptions fall into groups 2, 3, and 4. Group 1 would be typified by an inscription lodged in the same space as the scene, referring to the same culture, endowed with a signification that is related to the scene. The inscription of Plate 18a[62] comes close to being this type. Nonetheless, because the character is Austro-German rather than Latin, it would be better placed in group 4. The inscription of Figure 12[63] belongs to group 2; it lacks unity of meaning, since the pseudo-Latin text is absurd. Finally, we will put the inscription of Figure 13[64] in group 3.

If we now proceed from the scene to the latent text, two possibilities present themselves. Either the text is pronounced by one of the characters in the scene, or not, in which case the text becomes a commentary attributable to a third party (the author, the reader) who is outside the situation. Figures 12 and 13 are in the first category; Plate 18a is in the second. This second criterion is independent of the first one. Figure 14 corroborates this.[65]

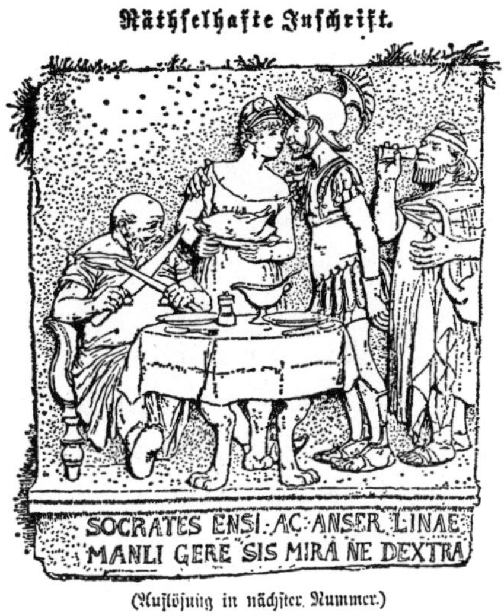

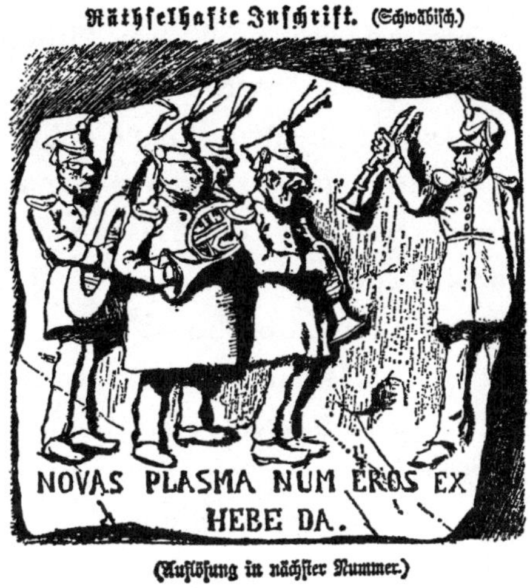

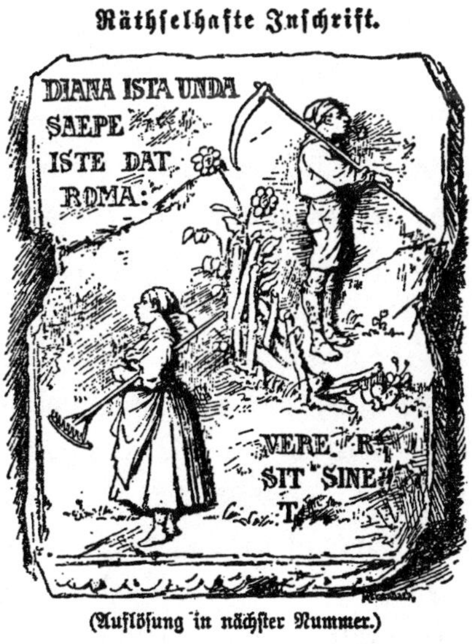

Above left: Figure 12. "Rätselhafte Inschrift," *Fliegende Blätter* 2034 (1884): 20. Based on original reproduced in *Revue d'esthétique,* vol. 1, 49.

Above right: Figure 13. "Rätselhafte Inschrift," *Fliegende Blätter* 2241 (1888): 15.

Left: Figure 14. "Rätselhafte Inschrift," *Fliegende Blätter* 2078 (1885): 168.

Like Figure 13 it belongs to group 3 by virtue of the relationship between the manifest text and the scene represented; but as regards the relationship of the scene to the latent text, it belongs in the same group as the enigma of Plate 18a: the hidden text is a commentary on the scene, not a statement issuing from it.

Clearly the link between latent and manifest texts and the figure is established in a great variety of ways. But we cannot really understand the function of the image until we have seized the nature of the relationship between the latent and manifest texts, a relationship which I touched on with regard to the unillustrated inscriptions. This passage consists in a double transformation: from one tongue to another, from phonics to graphics. First of all, the latent tongue is the mother tongue, a living tongue taken in its most common (phonic) manifestation. The manifest figure of the inscription is foreign, dead. Above all, it is a pseudo-language: the inscription does not conform to the syntactical and/or lexical restrictions of Latin. This first transformation should suffice to show the illusory finality of secondary revision. It puts forward a triply incomprehensible text: the majority of the *Fliegende Blätter* readers do not read Latin; it is a dead language whose statements remain unheard; it only *looks* like the language. We are thus discouraged from too hastily attributing secondary revision to a rational agency inasmuch as what results from its intervention is precisely not rational! Finally, this first transformation is in no way a translation. Every translation passes through the signified; here it is simply an equivalence in the order of the signifiers that is given.

This leads us to examine the second transformation, that from phonics to graphics, which is even more interesting. It is impossible to pass from the latent text to that of the inscription, or vice versa, without recourse to homophony. If you, an Austrian peasant, do not *pronounce* the text, *novas plasma,* you will never hear *No, was blas'ma?* This is half the secret (the other half is that the intervals must be displaced). The manifest text is the graphic notation, imitating another language, of a statement pronounced in dialect. The (oneiric) revision thus carries out a phonic analysis of the words and the redistribution of the letters (which are taken to be the written equivalent of the phonemes of the initial language) in words of another tongue. This operation is similar to that of the spoonerism [*contrepèterie*], with these two differences: one switches languages, and the resulting arrangement does not necessarily make sense (in fact it rarely does: see Plate 18a for one example.)

A comparison with the operation leading to what Saussure called a *hypogram*[66] might be more fruitful. For example in this line from the *Iliad*:

῎Ασεν ἀργαλέων ἀνέμων ἀμέγαρτος ἀϋτμή,

[Aasen argaleon anemon amegartos aütme: "The dreadful breath of winds infatuated (him) . . .]

the syllables of the name *Agamemnon* are disseminated throughout other words, so that the name is, so to speak, a subscript, hypographed, in that line. Nonetheless what distinguishes our inscriptions from hypograms is yet again the switching of languages (although this is not essential); it is above all the fact that in the hypogram the manifest text contains repetitions, inversions, conversions of the syllables of the hidden name, whereas in secondary revision the space occupied by the manifest and latent texts coincides. As in a true anagram, the completed operation, in both directions, leaves no remainder. The repetitions, chiasmus, etc. of the anagram make it similar to a musical (the Ricercare of *The Musical Offering*) or literary (Raymond Roussel's *Impressions d'Afrique*) combinatory system, as Bally in a letter to Saussure, and Starobinski in his commentary, suggest. The thing is that in these cases the manifest "text" (in the broad sense of the word) must be "readable," that is intelligible, audible by itself. It harbors the name, the canonical formula, but by allowing its scattered elements to reverberate within its own form, which must therefore be *similar in nature* to theirs. Hypogrammatic depth is of the order of resonance (assonance, consonance), and of harmonics: the line of the *Iliad* underlines the name of Agamemnon, and Saussure accepts for his hypogram this meaning of ὑπογράφειν [*hypographein*] which is "to emphasize the features of the face with make-up."[67] But the depth of our inscription is opaque. It is not a graph, but a pseudo-graph, homophonic with the originating text, like Saussure's hypogram, but at the expense of a double heterosemia. Transcribed from the phoneme to the letter so as to produce a presumptive other meaning, it supposes the transformation of the nature of the sign and of the alleged signification.

Provided with this scholarly definition—a homophonic, heterosemic pseudo-graph—we can return to the function of the scene. The single constant which appears in the classification of these pseudo-graphs is, as we have seen, the unity of place joining scene and inscription. This unity constitutes the very stuff of the inscription. It is written in the same space as something else, in this case an image. Now the topical unity of writing and scene indicate that the text, having taken up a position on the same plane as the image, will submit to the strictures of that plane and betray the strictures of writing. By this simple placing of the inscription, we pass from linguistic space, that of *reading,* where one *hears,* to visual space, that of painting, where one *looks.* The eye no longer listens, it desires. Now the manifest text does not deceive, does not allow itself to be taken for another, except in the exact measure that one looks at it without hearing it. What is inscribed is a kind of non-writing; the space in which it moves is that of an object, not a text. An object's space is to be seen, not read. And this seeing is desiring.

The function of the image is to consolidate the pseudo-graph. Written, but written above all as an inscription, inscribed, a text lends itself to pseudology because by its letters it belongs to the object in which it is traced. It presents itself to view at the same time as that object, and it will remain graphic as long as the celebrant does not intervene to make it *heard,* as André Leroi-Gourhan suggests in the case of rock-paintings.[68] The support of the image casts a spell on the text; the image fulfills its antique function of deception [*pseudein*]. But there must be an element of *pseudein* in writing. The text deceives not by the ear, but by the eye. An essential deception: the dream, says Freud, makes use particularly of visual images. Seeing interferes with hearing and speaking, as desire interferes with understanding. Such, at least, is the Freudian algebra.

These observations ought to be expanded. The ambiguity of writing, object of reading and of sight, is present in the initial ambiguity of drawing. An open line, a line closed on itself. The letter is an unvarying closed line; the line is the open moment of a letter that perhaps closes again elsewhere, on the other side. Open the letter, you have the image, the scene, and magic. Close the image, you have the emblem, the symbol, and the letter. These remarks find their commentary in the admirable treatment of capital letters in Romanic manuscripts, of which the R taken from the *Moralia in Job* done at Citeaux in the twelfth century gives us a glimpse (Plate 18b). The letter is threatened, invaded by the line, the spirit by the eye, the Church by the Barbarians, the very Book by the plastic ornament which comes from the Irish, while the repressive vertical of the Saint sets its face against the good-natured baroque of the dragon: the letter is opening itself up, we are heading toward the miniature and painting in depth. The birth and re-birth of painting from writing. That supposes the ambiguity of the line that André Lhote talks about: it can delineate a contour, enclose a space, confer formal identity. That is called writing; it may be the trace of a gesture that creates a space, the wake of a movement that situates, organizes, and painting returns endlessly to that enigmatic gestation, endlessly offering it to the eye that desires it, so that it may err, and erring, may recover its spatializing truth. In Breton's words, "We who have always preferred the shadow to the prey . . ."

The read-heard text is without depth, even without perceptible space; the seen text dwells over there, beside the image. That "over there" is its mystery, renders it enigmatic. By virtue of its opposition within the range of vision it appeals to a distanciation of the eye from itself, which is the distance of representation, whereas read, it matters little from what angle, it is read from nowhere. From the read to the seen, we pass from a "horizontal," flat, atopic negativity, to a "vertical," deep, place-making negativity; the read belongs to the system of gaps that constitutes the language code; the seen requires openness, transcendence, showing and hiding. The enigma gives a sign to the eye, hence the dream's preference for visual images.

Let us return, finally, to secondary revision and try to understand it on the basis of this status of inscription. Where does its specific work come in? We have said above that Freud hesitated to place secondary revision within the topology of the dream-work: it acts from *as great a distance,* from as great a depth, as the three other operations; nonetheless it derives from normal thought. Is not this ambiguity the same as the ambiguity of the read, half-seen, half-heard inscription?

Freud says that the function of secondary revision is to expunge from the dream the absurd incoherent fashion in which it was produced by the three prior operations left to themselves. Desire, acting "freely" within the constraints of the initial text, would leave in its wake the tortured, illegible relief of the "content." Secondary revision interferes with this operation by fabricating a manifest text like the "Latin" inscription. This work consists in ostensibly *flattening out* the relief by using the humps and hollows, the peaks and valleys, to produce writing. Suppose that an upheaval of the earth's crust had distributed the figures of the relief so that, viewed from an aeroplane, they could be taken for letters, for words. Secondary revision would be the selective power directing these upheavals to deposit their products in a readable manner. At this point we pass from the energistic to the linguistic, which is readable. And this is how secondary revision belongs to normal thought, supposes intelligibility and intelligence.

But this readability is a pseudo-readability. The readable signification of the dream, its immediate content, cannot be read; and even when it is, it *ought* not to be: Freud reiterates that we must not treat the content as text, but as an object. The reason is that even when the inscription means something (in Latin, but this is an exception, as we have seen: Plate 18a), its meaning is suspect, and can only delude the interpreter. It is necessary to disbelieve "rêvons d'or" in order to grasp "Révolution d'octobre." We must reconstruct a primitive text, hidden under the gilded text, which the work has deconstructed, or if you prefer, we must deconstruct the edifice, the figure that the operations have constructed. Thus what is intelligible in the text is pseudo-intelligible: that part of the text which is preserved in every case is precisely the distinctive unit (phoneme, grapheme) that is non-signifying; and it is the signifying unity (the moneme) that in many cases is destroyed. What is most often lacking is the unity of discourse, because the Latin syntax is not respected; and, finally, in those very rare cases (*Naevia*) where the entire architecture of the linguistic units is respected, the very meaning that emanates from the ostensible discourse leads the mind astray. The closer we get to true language, the more vulnerable we become to the true lie. The figure cannot lie, since it has no pretensions to univocality. Intelligibility is therefore rather simulated, aped, than truly satisfied. That is why Freud speaks of "misunderstanding."[69]

If he also says that secondary revision is like a pre-interpretation,[70] it is only because the content borrows its tool, articulated language, from interpretation, but only to divert it from its linguistic position and put it to criminal use, the text being taken as a thing, a phonic, visible thing, and not a conglomerate of empty signs, of cenemes. Secondary revision interferes with two functions: it introduces the textual into the plane of the figure (*Inschrift*), and it protects the figural implanted in the text. The text of the inscription is therefore false and deceptive, but it also bears witness: the oddness of its divisions, not counting the image itself, whose commentary it is supposed to be (we rediscover here the *two* modes of figuration: in the letter and in the designation), testifies that something must inform this double figure: it is *a figure to be read.*

Now this double function, this double position, constitutes the very *foundation* of the dream. At bottom there is the *Gedanke* [thought], and for Freud it is a text which is lodged in the *Inhalt* [content] as in a figure. Only, and it is time to say so, no one has ever heard or read this text. The *Gedanke* is never rendered other than figuratively, in an *Inhalt.* The figure inhabits the allegedly initial text.

This remark allows us to understand Freud's hesitation about secondary revision: façade or "foundation," *Inhalt* or *Gedanke*? The revision duplicates a deep-seated constitution. That is why it operates at once on the surface and at the heart of the dream, by a kind of analogy. If this is the case, it is because at bottom this movement of exchange, this whirlwind, has already occurred, continues to occur: the figural is immediately present in the context; the figural is always already there. The textual is already there in the core-figure. We are deaf at first. We do not begin by hearing in order subsequently to repel the awful utterance. Desire does not manipulate an intelligible text in order to disguise it; it does not let the text get in, forestalls it, inhabits it, and we never have anything but a worked-over text, a mixture of the readable and the visible, a no man's land in which nature is exchanged for words and culture for things. We must presume a primordial situation where repression and the return of the repressed are born together. Here, precisely, for Laplanche and Pontalis, is the phantasm.[71]

Reverie, dream, phantasm are mixtures containing both viewing and reading matter. The dream-work is not a language; it is the effect on language of the force exerted by the figural (as image or as form). This force breaks the law. It hinders hearing but makes us see: that is the ambivalence of censorship. But this composite is primordial. It is found not only in the order of the dream, but in the order of the "primal" phantasm itself: at once discourse and figure, a tongue lost in a hallucinatory scenography, the first violence.

Desire's Complicity with the Figural

The figure enjoys a radical complicity with desire.[1] This complicity is the hypothesis that guides Freud in his exploration of the operations of the dream. It allows for a strong articulation between the order of desire and that of the figural through the category of transgression: the "text" of the preconscious (day's residues, memories) undergoes shocks that render it unrecognizable and illegible. In this illegibility, the deep matrix in which desire is caught finds satisfaction, expressing itself in disorganized forms and hallucinatory images.

Let us take a closer look at how this machinery works. For this, it is useful to isolate three types of parts. The *figure-image*, that which I see in the hallucination or the dream, and which the painting and film offer me, is an object placed at a distance, a theme. It belongs to the order of the visible, as outline [*tracé révélateur*]. The *figure-form* is present in the visible, and may even be visible, but in general remains unseen. This is Lhote's regulating line [*tracé régulateur*], the Gestalt of a configuration, the architecture of a picture, the scenography of a performance, the framing of a photograph—in short, the schema. By definition, the *figure-matrix* is invisible, the object of originary repression, instantly laced with discourse: "originary" phantasy. Nonetheless the figure-matrix is figure, not structure, because it is, from the outset, violation of the discursive order—violence against the transformations authorized by this order. By replacing it with a schema of intelligibility, one would render unintelligible its immersion in the unconscious. This immersion is proof, however, that what is at stake is indeed the other of discourse and intelligibility. To establish this matrix in textual space, all the more so if the latter is systematic, would be to imagine it as an ἀρχή [*archè*], to entertain a double phantasy in relation to it: first, that of an origin; second, that of an utterable origin. Yet the phantasmatic matrix, far from being an origin, testifies to the contrary that our origin is an absence of origin, and that everything that presents itself as object of an originary discourse is a hallucinatory *figure-image*, placed precisely in this initial non-site.

Image, form, and matrix are figures insofar as each of them belongs to figural space according to a particular, though strict, articulation. Freud helped us to understand this articulation by invoking the energetic model of the reflex arc. The economic hypothesis he draws from this analogy is that any form of displeasure is a charge, and any form of pleasure, a discharge. Pleasure follows the principle whereby the energetic discharge is always pursued by the most expeditious means: the goal is to return the psychical apparatus to a state of least stimulation.[2] In accordance with this principle, energy flows freely within the psychic system, ready to invest indiscriminately any zone, so long as it offers a possibility of discharge. This property, shared by those processes subjected to the pleasure principle, reveals the *unbound* character of the energy at work. When the use of energy is subjected instead to the reality principle, the function it obeys is no longer to eliminate all tension, but rather to maintain the energy at a constant level. Above all, in this case discharge cannot come at the cost of any zone in the psychical apparatus, since some of these zones communicate through facilitation while others are protected by contact-barriers, and since all the bindings through association and exclusion fall under the Ego's control. The principle of this reality subordinates the possibility of discharge to the transformation of the relation between system and external world, either through the use of language or through motility, or both. The path followed by energy thus begins with perceptions and memories of perceptions, through word-presentations, moving toward the centers and motor organs—what Freud calls progredient movement.[3]

Although the above description may well owe much to Fechner's psychophysics, it already contains metaphorically a theme that will never be recanted and is essential to the position of the figural. The space in which energy flows is qualitatively different depending on whether this energy is bound or unbound. The space of pleasure and that of reality are alien to one another: this comes across already in Freud's analysis of the situation of the infant, which is and remains that of the human being. Faced with an "internal" source of excitation—while the secondary process is not yet established and does not allow the external world to be organized in order to effect the discharge—the subject finds itself in a state of *motorische Hilflosigkeit*, of motor helplessness.[4] In the absence of the *spezifische Aktion* [specific action] whose realization would relieve the pressure of need, the satisfaction of this need is entirely in the hands of an external person.[5] This is how three factors will come to be distinguished: the motor factor of reflex movement that accompanies discharge (suction, for example); the affective factor of satisfaction; and the sensory factor of the object whose mediation eliminated anxiety and made the discharge possible. When need reappears (as endogenous excitation), the object image and the motor image will be reinvested so as to achieve discharge. "The first wishing seems to have been an hallucinatory cathecting of the memory of satisfaction."[6] Desire is therefore born through "anaclisis":[7] as search for pleasure, the sexual leans on and is supported by the instincts of self-preservation. The latter attains satisfaction only through the specific operation of a defined organ, whereas the former takes hold of the instinctual aim (satisfaction) and its object (the organ of the specific operation) as means of pleasure. Desire constitutes itself as power of pleasure without gratification of need.

The fulfillment of desire, or wish-fulfillment (*Wunscherfüllung*), holds in itself the absence of the object. This absence is essential to desire and constitutive of its relationship to any object that has the pretension of passing as *its* object. Similarly, one could say that the "absence" of the organ characterizes desire's use of the body: body parts are not taken by desire as means to satisfy a need, but as erogenous zones whose excitation leads to the phantasmatic mise-en-scène. The body thus finds itself subverted [*détourné*]. Moreover, it finds itself in pieces. In self-preservation, the specific function is subordinated theoretically to the survival of the organism as a whole. For desire, as each organ is a potential erogenous zone, the charge's cathexis of this organ is its own end, as long as it ensures the production of the phantasies fulfilling the desire. Here one observes the extent of the upheaval of realist and biological space that accompanies anaclisis.

Freud gives us an idea of this upheaval when he stresses the importance of regression.[8] Hallucinatory fulfillment is regressive in three ways. First because it is premised on the regredient movement of the psychical apparatus, as opposed to what happens in specific action. This action begins with excitation, passes through memories, verbal traces, and zones of motility, produces a transformation of reality, and finally achieves satisfaction as external discharge. In wish-fulfillment, excitation crosses the layers of the apparatus in the other direction, cathecting memories of perception with such intensity that it provokes hallucination. Regression is therefore the shift of energy to the perceptual pole instead of the verbal-motor pole. This regression is the result of the principle of immediate discharge at minimal cost, also known as the Nirvana principle. But regression is also to be understood historically, for there is reactivation of the memory of the first satisfaction, the return to infantile experience. Above all, regression is marked by the use of "primitive methods of expression and representation [*figuration*]" that "take the place of the usual ones."[9] "We call it 'regression' when in a dream an idea is turned back into the sensory image from which it was originally derived."[10] There is a "selective attraction exercised by the visually recollected scenes touched upon by the dream-thoughts."[11] Regression occurs as much through this attraction as through the complementary operation of censorship. In the elaboration of disfigured figures instead of recognizable figures, of rebuses instead of texts, what is at work is as much desire's own power, in its space and particular relationship with representation, as prohibition. Here, the figural is conceived of as the polar opposite of the verbal and of motility, that is, of the reality principle with its two functions, language and action. Desire turns its back on these functions.

This same alterity is still the focus of the analysis formulated later to characterize the unconscious.[12] Indeed, Freud strives to make unconscious space understandable by continually placing it in opposition to the space in which occur the processes under preconscious control. The four features he identifies are, first, the fact that there is "no negation, no doubt, no degrees of certainty," in other words "exemption from mutual contradiction": unconscious "judgments" have neither modality nor quality, being always assertive and positive.[13] Second, "The cathectic intensities {in the unconscious} are much more mobile."[14] Primary process is what Freud will call this energetic unbinding, and the "free" movements of this energy, Freud writes, are displacement and condensation. These operations are defined explicitly here as checking the secondary process, that is, perception, motility, and *articulated language*. The third feature characterizing unconscious processes is that they are "*timeless*; i.e. they are not ordered temporally, are not altered by the passage of time; they have no reference to time at all."[15] Lastly, unconscious processes "pay just as little regard to reality," as they are subjected to the pleasure principle, to the "replacement of external reality by psychical reality."[16] So not only do these processes fail to fall under the categories of judgment (modality, quality), they do not even abide by the basic constraints of discourse: condensation violates lexical constraints, just as the displacement and disregard for temporality violates those of syntax. As for the indifference to reality, it demonstrates explicitly a refusal to take reference into consideration and a contempt for the dimension of designation. The two spaces of discourse—of the system and reference—are transgressed in unconscious processes. The space where these processes are inscribed and which they generate is therefore another space, different from that of the system in that it is incessant mobility, and from that of reference in that it takes words for things. Mobility in the systematic field of language [*langue*] and of the order of discourse brings about short-circuits of meaning and "non-sense"; the transgression of referential distance brings us back to magic, to the "omnipotence of thought." Violation of the two negations, therefore: of the negativity that keeps the terms of the system at a distance from one another, and of the negativity that keeps the object of discourse at a variable distance.

It should be clear that it is not enough to assert that the unconscious is the insertion of the second negation (as variability) into the first. Such a reasoning runs the risk of opposing the philosophy of the system with a philosophy of the phenomenological "gesture," the chiasm, and depth. At its core, however, unconscious space is no more that of gesture than that of invariants. It is a topological space. If one may be misled by its effects, this is because, from the point of view of language, the transgression of systematic space by displacements and condensations can just as well be attributed to the characteristic mobility of the space of reference (sensory space) as to that of the primary process. This overlap of the two functions itself is perhaps not entirely innocent. The force that moves at full speed in the wild space of non-binding can, thanks to the latter, pass as the elegant and spacious mobility of the gestatory gesture postulated by philosophies of body consciousness. What adds to the confusion (and what at the same time forces us to be suspicious of it) is that among the operations of the dream, there is something other than the distortion condensing and displacing the dream units: there is the taking into account of figurability. Is this not proof that we are dealing with the dimension of designation, and that this dimension—folded into the flow of discourse and in the well-measured, well-tempered space which is that of communication—is what sows havoc and generates effects of meaning deriving neither from signification nor from syntax, but from sight?

Were one to stop here, a philosophy of the subject could possibly be developed, but one would disqualify oneself from understanding the dream, and more generally the symptom. In the dream, aesthetic space does not simply apply itself onto linguistic space; rather the bodily expanse itself is stretched, so to speak, beyond the mundane dimensions it hews to while awake. One cannot afford to ignore the fact that we *sleep* while we dream, and thus that the connaturality between body and world is suspended by an immobility whose function is not only to eliminate the world, but whose effect is to take the body as world.[17] Above all one must consider that the figures appearing in this world—a world that hollows itself out and offers itself within the expanding bodily scene—are not in the least subject to the laws of connaturality, by the stage directions of perceptual space, and by the constitution in depth that produces "real" things from signs presenting us one of their sides while concealing the others. In the dream and the neurotic symptom, these properties of the worldly figure disappear. So when Freud tells us that one of the basic operations of the dream is representation [*figuration*], we must be vigilant: it behooves us to infer that we are no longer in the order of language, but equally to assume that we are no longer in referential or worldly distance either, since this figure is no more *bound* to the constraints of designation (among which are both the variability of the viewpoint and the unilaterality of the visible) than to those of language [*langue*]. We are indeed faced with a performance [*représentation*], but the rules of scenic space are no longer those of sensory space. It is not merely the author's text that is censored, overlaid, blurred; the figure of the actors, the

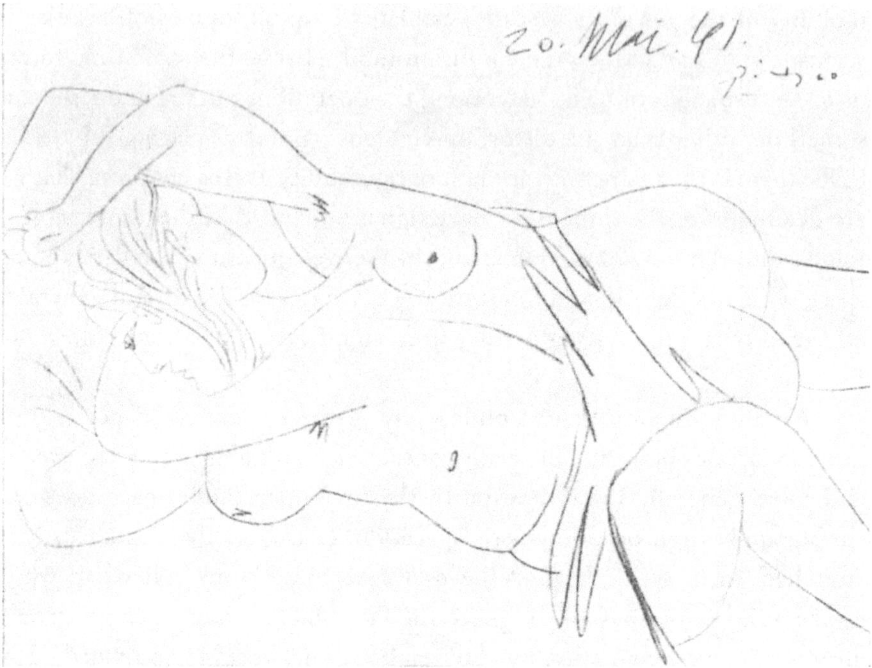

Figure 15. Pablo Picasso, *Étude de nu,* 1941. Lead pencil drawing. Louise Leiris Gallery. Reproduced in Pierre Francastel, *Peinture et société* (Paris: Gallimard, 1965), 225.

place where they stand, their clothing, and their identity are too. As for the stage sets, they change in midscene, without notice. The scene's action itself is deprived of unity.

We can now return to our rows of figures and specify their respective articulations with unconscious space. The *figure-image* is that which comes into view on the oneiric or quasi-oneiric stage. What suffers abuse here are the rules regulating the formation of the perceived object. The figure-image deconstructs the percept, taking effect in a space of difference. We can articulate it precisely: what it deconstructs is the silhouette's outline; it is the *transgression of the contour* [*tracé révélateur*]. Picasso's drawing is an exact illustration of this transgression, where the object of deconstruction is the edge, the line that indicates that there is a single and reifying point of view; the coexistence of several silhouettes results in the simultaneity of more than one point of view (Figure 15). The scene in which this woman sleeps does not belong to "real" space; it allows a single body to display several positions in a single place and time: erotic indifference to time and reality, except for the postures. Other similar examples would need to be found for the deconstruction of values and colors (see the corresponding commentary below in "Notes on Figures and Plates").

The *figure-form* is the figure that upholds the visible without being seen: the visible's nervure. It can, however, be made visible itself. Its relation to unconscious space is given by the transgression of *good form* (Gestalt). "Good form" is the Pythagorean and Neoplatonic form, heir to a Euclidian geometric tradition. Upon it rests a philosophy, even a mystique, of the number and its luminous cosmic value.[18] This form is Apollonian. The unconscious figure-form—form as figural form—would instead be an anti-good form, a "bad form." As an energetics indifferent to the unity of the whole, one could qualify it as Dionysian.[19]

It is undoubtedly difficult to find examples of figure-form in art, since the latter requires that Apollo cooperate with Dionysus. Jackson Pollock's action painting—at least in its versions from the period 1946 to 1953, where the dripping process (or what could be called *passion painting*) is brought ruthlessly to its limits—might give us an idea of what bad form could be: plastic screen entirely covered by chromatic runs; absence of all line construction, of all tracing even; disappearance of echo or rhythm effects produced by repetitions or recurrences of forms, values or colors on the painting's surface; indeed, elimination of all recognizable figure (Plate 19). It does seem as if we have sided with Bacchic delirium, sunk underground where the plastic "invariants" (at least the linear invariant) start to boil, where energy speeds from one point of pictorial space to another, thereby preventing the eye from finding a place to rest, from cathecting, even for an instant, its phantasmagorical charge either here or there.[20]

And finally, the *figure-matrix*. Not only does it remain unseen, but it is no more visible than it is legible. It belongs to neither plastic nor textual space. It is difference itself, and as such does not suffer that minimum of *oppositionality* that its spoken expression requires, of image- or form-conditioning that its plastic expression entails. Discourse, image, and form: all equally pass over the figure-matrix, for it resides in all three of the spaces. The artist's works are only ever the offshoot of this matrix. One may be able to catch a glimpse of it through their superimposition, in thickness.[21] But the spatial confusion that prevails "originally" is such—words being treated as things and forms, things as forms or words, and forms as words or things— that deconstruction no longer applies only to the textual trace [*tracé textuel*] as in the literary figure, to the contour [*tracé révélateur*] as in the figural image, or to the regulating line [*tracé régulateur*] as in figural form. Rather, deconstruction now applies to the site where the matrix stands: a site belonging at once to the space of text, of mise en scène, and of the stage. Script, geometry, representation: each deconstructed as a result of the interference of the two others. We must pay this matter further attention, with Freud.[22]

Such are the fundamental modes of complicity that desire entertains with figurality: transgression of the object, transgression of form, and transgression of space.

Desire in Discourse

Knowledge and Truth

Now I would like to turn to the presence of the figural in discourse. The field of inquiry is restricted to the work of poetry. The latter can be defined, hastily, as constituted by a text worked over by the figure. Here, then, is a paradox: how can a figural discourse—invested by the forms of desire, offering the illusion of fulfillment—perform the function of truth? The properties of a text taken as such have, as it were, their destiny mapped out and their model imposed by the very properties of the linguistic signifier. Just as these properties inform a system of oppositions that free discourse completely from both the subject of the utterance and the object it designates, discourse's signified similarly tends to constitute itself into a system of terms bound by specific transformations. The properties of this system are internal: consistency vis-à-vis negation and independence of the axioms, as well as saturation and decidability of the system. The property of completeness or incompleteness that defines the relation of the system to the area of interpretation subjected to it adds nothing to the "syntactic" properties.[1] Knowledge constitutes itself by building its "object"—building here means the establishing of a system of relations between terms, and this establishing occurs through variations enacted upon terms. Instead of the field in which the object first appeared, a system of concepts will now take over. Clearly, what is considered ideal for any system of knowledge, at least in its relation to the two other spaces that interest us, is the system of language [*langue*]. With the designated—that is, the object first presented in its field—we witness the same break taking shape as referential (arbitrary) distance in language and as epistemological split in knowledge. As for the figural, for the presence of a form within discourse, we encounter the same ambition to specify all internal relations as a system and thus to impose discontinuity as rule of intelligibility: in the use of relevance at the lowest degree of communication (phonology), and in the use of the independence of axioms at the highest level of knowledge (formalization).

The text's mission as such is to free itself from the figure, be it designation or expression, and to sever the adhesions and continuities by which the movement of the mind that performs the variations runs the risk of being hindered, and the significations that it simultaneously produces of being unilateral. Knowledge's vocation is to hold true at all times and in all places, without consideration for the meanings that might remain active and silent in discourse. It would seem, therefore, that the poetic text has no right to any claim to truth, because it is riddled with figures. The figural is to the textual what illusion is to knowledge.

Still, here is my hypothesis: that this alternative—between deceptive figural space and a textual space where knowledge is produced—can be avoided. On this side of this alternative one can discern another function, absent from the alternative itself, that would, *as a matter of principle*, turn on figural space: a truth function.

Against what is implied in revelation, I would argue that this truth is not the sign of the Word uttered by the Other, which would be scrambled merely by effects of reverberation, omissions, and condensations that would make it into a symbol given to us as food for thought. Figural opacity is not that which belongs to a second discourse in discourse. A discourse occupies a position in front of us so that we may understand and read it. One can read a discourse on lips; short of lips, the paper or support of scripted discourse is turned toward us like a face, showing its front to us. A second discourse is merely a second front in the first. God would be only this kind of transcendence, of an invisible, possibly inaudible vis-à-vis, but gripping us by the presence of its absence. I have no intention of leaving the ideology of knowledge behind only to return to that of revelation. What Freud appreciated in art is that it does not allow something to pass as what it is not, nor the unconscious to be mistaken for the sky. The truth that signals to us in artworks comes from below, fathered by desire. This truth teaches us nothing, is not edifying, does not look at or face us. Instead it erupts beside the point where we expected it to. The unexpected and the reverse are its points of emergence. Desire has no lips upon which what it is saying can be read.

It does not present itself to us, but elides us, dragging our eye over there: it represents. Desire and we are about to lose ourselves on the other side of the sheet of glass. Unless, by some artifice, the windowpane is treated in such a way that we could not misrecognize it and fulfill what desire demands, that we be thrown back on the very motion of this thrust that first projected us toward the scene, and that we have the strength to hold up, open-eyed, before it. The truth function would be this treatment of the phantasy-generating window. Not exactly a mirror.

How the Figural Is Present in Discourse

Before attempting to bring this window to light, we must elucidate precisely the way or ways in which the figural inhabits discourse. It is essential that we refine our analyses with regard to both the axes of discourse and the rows of figures. We identified two sets, each composed of three terms: on discourse, the signifier/signified/designated triad, and on the figure, the image/form/matrix triad.

The first group simply adopts the articulation Frege discerned on the linguistic "sign." It indicates, first, that a discourse always occupies a formal space of measured intervals, subdivided in a space of diacritical units and that of signifying units; and, second, that a discourse always stands in relation to its object in a space of designation where mobility and laterality are the rule. The two axes of signification and designation, upon which the three terms signifier, signified, and designated are positioned, are involved simultaneously in actual discourse. The second group of terms concerns the rows of figures. The criterion used for classification is that of visibility: seen, visible; unseen, invisible. The first term applies to the image of an object with its outline; the second, to the form (*Gestalt*) of the visible, which can be brought into relief through analysis even if it was not seen at the outset; the third, to a still deeper configuration to which analysis could possibly come near, but that can never become object either of vision or signification.

By taking the visible as the criterion for the classification of figures, we are immediately suggesting that an articulation is possible between the orders of figures and the axes of discourse. Is not the visible the axis upon which the object is given to discourse through designation? In Frege's example, reference (*Bedeutung*) is the moon itself; it is, therefore, a contour [*contour révélateur*], a recognizable object. The point of articulation between the two tables (of the figure and of discourse) would therefore be the figure-image or designated. This would be due to the fact that since all discourse points to a reference, the latter is given to the speaker in a field of vision—such as a silhouette or an image. The characteristics of this bordering space are altogether different from the internal space of the system where discourse is lodged. Yet discourse is precisely what articulates the one with the other, for mobility and the "perspective" on the object are what guides the speaker in the elaboration of her or his discourse, what makes her or him prefer one term over another at a given point in the signifying chain, and in the end why she or he says one thing rather than another. There can be no analysis of speech without resorting to the distance of sight.

From this first articulation of the figure with discourse we were able to derive a further proposition, namely, that the existence of the space of signification—with its properties of autonomous, non-derived, and invariable system—is also what enables us to constitute the visible as *lost*; to touch the object remotely without *possessing* it; to uphold absence; to posit or assume the other face of the given, the face that it does not turn toward me; and to constitute the given as thick sign. The articulation of the designated or image with discourse is thereby redoubled. Moreover, this articulation finds itself placed in the field of desire: the position of the lost object touches directly on the latter's constitution.

Parenthetical Remark on the Lack of Reality

By this point, however, the reader is well aware that a clarification is needed, one that has not been made heretofore: the real and the imaginary need to be distinguished! Discourse is positioned differently depending on whether its designated is one or the other. Frege stresses that the truly aesthetic position is precisely that of the discourse that becomes disinterested in its object's existence, or, as Freud put it, that does not call its reality into question, that avoids reality-testing. What does this test consist of? Of words and actions. How to know whether the object of which we are speaking exists? Answer: if we can give it a name that will allow it to be recognized (persistence of perceptions), and perform on it operations that will allow it to be transformed (satisfaction of needs). The criteria thus introduced confront us with issues that do not relate to our primary concern, however easily they map onto it: the issue of praxis, that is, communication with others, and transformation of the external world; and the issue of knowledge, that is, constitution of reality and of a coherent discourse. I need only note that reality is constituted from the imaginary. What is given at first is the phantasmatic object. The forming of a "real" object is a test corresponding in the subject to the constitution of the reality-ego. Reality is never more than a part of the imaginary field that we have agreed to relinquish and from which we have agreed to decathect our phantasies of desire. This section is surrounded along all of its borders by the imaginary field where wish-fulfillment by phantasy is perpetuated.

The relinquished part itself shows scars of the struggle over its occupancy between the pleasure principle and that of reality. "Reality" is not the fullness of being as opposed to the void of the imaginary, since it preserves some lack within itself, and this lack is of such importance that in it—in the rift of inexistence at the heart of existence—the work of art takes place. The artwork is real, it can lend itself to being named and manipulated before witnesses, assuring them there is indeed, here and now, a painting or a statue. But it is not real, the expanse of Claude Monet's *Water Lilies* does not share the same space as the room in the Orangerie Museum, and Auguste Rodin's *Balzac* at the Raspail-Montparnasse intersection in Paris is not erected on the same soil as the trees lining the boulevard.[2] In front of the image's powerful consistency, reality is so fragile that in the contest between the two expanses, of the artwork and of the world in which it is placed, it is the first that seduces and attracts the second to it: the basement of the Orangerie allows itself to be sucked through its walls into the light-filled mist floating over the painted pools, while the statue's backward tilt endows the boulevard with its particular slope leading down toward Saint-Germain. Not only does the presence of artworks attest to the object's absence and to the world's scant reality, but the absence that is "realized" in them pulls toward itself the given's purported existence and reveals its lack. The world throws itself into artworks because there is emptiness within it and because the artist's critical expression provides a shape to our object-seeking desires. What is crucial here is that there is, at the tip of the axis of designation, an image, which we have assumed is ungraspable. As such, it may be no different from the "real" object: the "grasping" does nothing more itself than provide images; it is probably no more phantasmatic than sight, impregnated as it is by vision. There is but the slightest difference between having one's head in the clouds and being in them.

The dividing line that is relevant to our problem does not run through the imaginary and the real, but through the recognizable and the unrecognizable. This is where the third space enters into consideration, a space different from both that of language and the world. The difference is strictly speaking the unconscious; by entering the space of the signifier or the signified, it transgresses the system of measured oppositions, concealing the message, blocking communication, treating phonemes, letters, and words like things, preventing the eye or the ear from recognizing text or speech, from "hearing" it. When difference lays claim to the space of designation, of sight, it undermines the outline that revealed the object and allowed us to recognize it, the good form that allowed the multiplicity of given plastic elements to stand together in the field of the visible. This difference pulls us into another world, devoid of recognizable face and form. Such misrecognition of the respective orders of discourse and world—rendering unrecognizable the former's units and the latter's objects—is the sign that desire pursues its fulfillment by appropriating givens [*données*] organized according to rules alien to it, in order to impose its own law on them. The essential characteristic of the figures to which desire gives rise, in language as well as in the field of vision, is that they disconcert recognition. At best, as we will see, they allow themselves to be recognized as unrecognizable.

The Metaphor and the Gesture

In light of this property of figural space, the hierarchy of figures—image, form, matrix—takes on a meaning that could have gone unnoticed before. Previously, it seemed like a convenient attempt at classifying the various types of figures. In fact, what this hierarchy does is restore the complexity of the figural's relation with the visible. There is a profound affinity between the visible and the figural, but this affinity must be critiqued, for it conceals a discordance that is even further removed—the discordance by which the figures of the visible can, in turn, be upheaved, fragmented, compressed, and disfigured by desire.

It is worth pausing here to counter an objection we have already encountered. When it comes to the presence of the figure in discourse, phenomenology adopts a stance it deems strong: let structure (or generative grammar) take care of signification, phenomenology tells us, but ordinary and poetic language [*langage*] defies description of both language [*langue*] and discourse thanks to one feature: they are full of figures. These figures, according to the linguists themselves, are violations of the system's order, whether the system be taken as structure of language [*langue*] or deep grammar engendering utterances.[3] What do such violations mean? That another space than linguistic space makes its way into discourse, and that in the latter it produces meaning-effects that cannot be the result of the normal interplay of semantic and/or syntactic givens, but rather proceed from their transgression. This transgression implies that there is a force at work in linguistic space, bringing together poles that were once isolated. Such an action, say these philosophers, can be thought of in terms of a *gesture*.

This action places the elements of discourse in perspective, ordering them in a deep expanse where they play the role no longer of carriers of signification, but of things-signs that show us one face while withholding the others, and that we will need to circumvent in order to understand. This suggests that the poet (the everyday speaker when she or he invents expressions, turns of phrases, metaphors) introduces into discourse properties that derive from the sensory. To which this new suggestion must be added: not only does this discourse become opaque, difficult to fathom, perilous like a world, but it acts upon our bodies! The key property of arbitrariness, which radically distinguishes language from all sign-systems, is precisely what the figure subverts in discourse. Through the figure words begin to induce in our bodies (as would colors) such and such a hint of attitude, posture, or rhythm: yet further proof that discursive space is dealt with as a plastic space, and words as sensory things.

Phenomenology claims to have more than enough evidence to warrant its confidence.[4] In what follows, I give only one illustration of this confidence, but an illustration so essential that it applies almost universally.

A Few Metaphors: Where Is Their Gesture?

"The metaphor," writes Du Marsais, "is a figure by which one carries, so to speak, the particular signification of a noun over to another signification with which it agrees only by virtue of a comparison in the mind.... When one simply declares 'he is a lion', then the comparison is only in the mind, not in the terms; such is a metaphor."[5] The metaphor is therefore a non-signified comparison. This in-signification is already in itself a breach of the law of communication without equivocation, but it could also be put down to the principle of economy, when usage imposes it. But the metaphor in a nascent state is precisely condemned by usage.[6] Recall what surrealism professed: "For me, their greatest value {of surrealist images}, I must confess, is the one that is arbitrary to the highest degree, the one that takes the longest time to translate into practical language, either because it contains an immense amount of seeming contradiction...."[7] "The ruby of champagne" (Lautréamont) is an illustration of this first form of image. The metaphor transfers the stone's properties—hard, red, heavy, odorless—onto the blond, sparkling, and luscious liquid. The terms stand at opposite extremes with regard to physical state (solid/liquid-gaseous), direction in space (the stone's fall/the cork's explosion), odor and taste (0/+), and separated moreover with regard to color and value (bright red/ashen blond). Notwithstanding, one must be aware that one speaks of a red wine's "rubies" to indicate its transparency, its boldness, its brilliance. The association of the two contradictory terms is achieved through this common area. The mind is, as André Breton puts it, "disconcerted," "put in the wrong."[8] Indeed, the form of the fixed syntagm "the rubies of Burgundy wine" is tapped to bring together terms whose objects they respectively designate clash in sensibility: thanks to the inertia of a habit of speech, an object is brought into a relation with another despite their dissimilarities. Discourse thus finds itself endowed with an enigmatic thickness. The signifiers come forward and seem to be hiding something, something that is not their "signified" (for the latter, on the contrary, is grasped), but rather a meaning held back beyond their screen.[9]

Here is another kind of striking image: "In Rose Sélavy's sleep, there is a dwarf emerging from a well who comes to eat her bread at night." [*Dans le sommeil de Rose Sélavy, il y a un nain sorti d'un puits qui vient manger son pain la nuit.*] "It derives from itself a ridiculous formal justification," as Breton says of this image.[10] The latter depends on the spoonerism *nain-puits/pain-nuit*, which is one of the dream's weapons. In this case, the sensory that riffs on the sensible belongs to the words' acoustic substance itself: yet the permutation of consonants—an operation that occurs in a nonlinguistic space—nonetheless gives rise to meaning. A signifying sequence, which is in a relation of chiasm, a relation of mirror and reflection vis-à-vis the first sequence, far from producing a doubling of the first signified, a reverse copy, emits a new meaning. It is as if, by placing a child's face in front of a mirror, and turning the mirror upside down, one saw appear in it a head of a dog. This is a game familiar to children and lovers: to lie in wait for the other mask to emerge from the face turned upside down. The double is neither the same nor the contrary, but the other. What is linguistic in this operation are the constraints that determine the signifier: however extra-linguistic the inversion of consonants may be in principle, it must nonetheless generate significative units (words or monemes). For a play on words to occur, rigor is mandatory, a "mathematical rigor (displacement of letters within a word, swapping of syllables between two words, etc.)," as Breton writes in *Littérature* about Marcel Duchamp's puns.[11] Achieving a heterosemy by reverse homophony depends on this faithful observation of the laws of language [*langue*], for there are intra-linguistic "correspondences." But from a Merleau-Pontian perspective, the permutation of elements (here of consonants) is a matter of the sensorial and comes directly from perceptual experience. Not only does permutation rely on assonances which language [*langue*] considers fortuitous, and which it enjoins every reasonable interlocutor to neglect in favor of signification—thereby introducing into language [*langage*] the appreciation of its sensorial charge—but permutation repeats, in its very own *chiasma*, the constitutive figure of the sensory, the constitutive figure of the figures. It is indeed, as the author of *The Visible and the Invisible* will argue, in the power of reversal, of permutation, that the depth of field resides.

This brings us to another surrealist image, whose power, Breton warns, lies in the fact that "it belongs to a hallucinatory order": "On the bridge, the dew with the head of a tabby cat lulls itself to sleep" [*Sur le pont, la rosée à tête de chat se berçait*].[12] We reach here the limits of a phenomenological interpretation: with hallucination, we move beyond the sensory. The chiasm does not explain the phantasy. No use in coming up with endless associations based on this image, the figure is unmistakable: the Sphinx, feline devourer of those attempting to cross which river? transgress which injunction? as young as dawn and as patient as a soft swaying to and fro. First, we note a (typically surrealist) observance of syntactic invariants, but also a lexical conflict between words depending on their context, owing to nonlinguistic disruptions whose principle is to be found (as the phenomenologist would say) in sensory mobility [*mobilité sensible*]. Thus there is combination of linguistic space with that of perceptual experience: the insertion, at the spot reserved for the attribute, of a noun, the morphology of which still shows signs of its adjectival origin, transforms "the cat lulls itself to sleep" into "the dew . . . cat lulls itself to sleep." However, this last image still does not differ from the previous ones since, like them, it results from the inclusion of an illegal mobility in the linguistic order.

But of what infraction are we speaking? Breton's warning gives us a clue. The daydreamer thought she or he had recognized an initial configuration in the imaginary representation, which may very well be essential to the logic of her or his unconscious: the configuration of a young female gaze fascinating that of an onlooker determined to allow himself to be devoured in exchange for his glance. The phantasy of seeing-being-seen, with its aspect of taboo—represented by the monster's threat issued against the bridge's trespassing—does indeed seem to be the matrix in which the elements of this metaphor come to be pulverized, unrealized, and reorganized. Moreover, the power of this metaphor is certainly due to the fact that it exceeds the personal phantasies of the poet who overturns it and presents it as metaphor of metaphors. The bridge to which it alludes is the one the metaphor builds between words; the youthfulness that fascinates and awaits he who crosses the bridge is the dawn promised to the language that has been violated; the commingling of the gazes represents the coitus of words; and the possible death stands for the risk taken by verbal transgression. Leaving this train of thought aside for now, suffice it to say that the infraction is the product of the primary process: it owes nothing to the gestatory gesture of sensory spaces and everything to the mobility of desire.[13] The image's secret does not lie in the experience of space; rather, it is engendered by an unconscious matrix that is this side of any experience (at the same time as the representation of the expressive process itself). This is not a case of a subject establishing a new distribution of elements in the invariant space of linguistic terms, carving out unknown meaning. Rather, these images have been received as a gift, their "author" experienced "an absence."[14] They are not born out of a kind of connaturality with words comparable to that of the body with things. This last connaturality is at one remove, covering up and taming a strangeness that is admittedly no more explicable than the "natural" but that, in contrast to the latter, does not place us in agreement with words and things, but in check.

Phenomenology and Connaturality

This theme of agreement doubtless lies at the core of philosophies of expression. To argue that words treated poetically recover the power to bring us in agreement with things would mean that language is essentially like a world or a body. Like a body, because through significations language ushers us into an ante-reflexive relation analogous to that through which the body unites us with rhythms, colors, and lines. Like a world, since language is not only the active agent actualizing significative data [*données*], but also the field of these data, which poetic activity, as opposed to the speech act described by structural linguistics, does not apprehend as a system of possibles among which the speaker chooses, but as a horizon from which emerge and take over words and sequences of words through whose event-ness something is said that does not belong to the poet's intention, but to an affinity between signifiers and meanings. As Mikel Dufrenne writes, "the word is expressive when it brings us into harmony with what it designates; when, as it reverberates, it makes us resonate as we would to the object at the very moment that it presents itself to us in the still ambiguous fullness of the first encounter, before we even come to know it exactly through a specific aspect."[15]

Expression may thus be defined as the immanence of the designated in discourse, and it is this immanence that reveals in language a voluminosity by diverting it from its informational function.[16] Expression "is also the power the signifier has to stretch the signified to the dimensions of a world—as if what is evoked was a form carrying its ground with it."[17] Language has a nature. It provokes effects of depth, like a visible figure that stands out against its ground. One can appreciate how the metaphor is the model of language, as it were, since it deploys the signifier as a façade or a scene, relegating meaning to the background. To what are these effects of depth due? To the repercussions triggered on the body by a discourse that awakens several sensorial fields at once: synesthesia and correspondences revive in language the body's own volume.[18] But above all, says Dufrenne, the word itself possesses a voluminosity that can be rediscovered when one rids it of its syntactic binder, allowing its polysemy to ring in the space connecting us to the world.[19] Expression is nature in language, and "the conception of language as nature . . . leads . . . to the idea of a language of Nature." In expression, it is "Nature that expresses itself."[20] The chiasm from language-Nature to Nature-language is a perilous one, but one that was already announced by the decision to grant the evocative force and imaging power to the words themselves, so long as they are not placed in the position of sentence. If the words "day" or "sea" (or "nature") have by themselves the function of summoning, of inviting me (recurrent terms in Dufrenne's terminology) to certain fundamental relationships with being, it stands to reason that what is addressing me in them is being. (For my part, I would attribute the word's force in this case to its de-syntaxisation.) One must therefore assume a kind of continuity and at the same time of chiasm between the language of nature and linguistic nature. Nature already "speaks"; it is the "mother of images," and it imagines in man.[21] There is already openness and therefore potential expression in Nature: Dufrenne calls this spacing, which is something like the a priori condition of all language, temporal transcendence. The latter is not constituted by the subject. Instead, the subject encounters it; it is given to her or him before any concept, as the possibility of concept or language. This time of the ground, which is not the temporalization of a For-itself, is what makes appearing possible.[22] "Temporality . . . in the temporal being is this distance to the self, this remove, this clearing where the light of a glance, of an *Augenblick*, can play."[23] Nature speaks through images in the sense that there is, set in the order of the sensory, the space of a seeing. Poetry acts as relay to this primordial seeing by bringing out in language the power of visual appresentation, which the use of pure communication smothers and makes languish. Poetry extends the expressivity present before the speaking subject. It fulfills this expressivity, because poetry grants it space within language itself, in the labyrinth of significations.[24]

Expression as Reconciliation

The main flaw in this metaphysics of continuity, explicitly inspired by Schelling, is glaring: the language of nature it cites as ground of the nature of language is not a language. The chiasm renders visible, not speakable. Temporal transcendence produces a world, not a semantic field. It is only for Hegel that time is a concept and the sensory discursive. In Kant, time is a form of sensibility; and if it is indeed the a priori of all a priori, what cuts across and occludes even the *Ich denke*, this is precisely because it is not language or reasoning, but a universal condition common to seeing and speaking, sensibility and understanding. However, this universal condition hardly stops there from being an always unbridged gap between the forms of one and the categories of the other: even if the two had "a common root," this root, as Kant says, remains unknown to us. Language begins with the loss of nature. Between understanding and sensibility, the connections are not direct, unless one reintroduces teleology. Art is assuredly one such connection: it engenders speech and presupposes, for it to be produced, a speaking subject—although art itself, strictly defined, does not speak.[25] Yet the connection it attempts to establish is always under threat, critical, mediate, constructed. Nothing is less natural.

This is a crucial point: the thesis of connaturality of poetry and the world inevitably rests on a certain poetic idea that privileges its power of reconciliation while ignoring its critical power of reversal. What the philosophy of expression acknowledges most readily in the work of poetry is the enactment of procedures capable of inducing a "state."[26] As the many comparisons with melody and dance suggest, this state is understood as something soft, moreover is understood softly: "Here one should think of a gentle and discreet flow of the imagination. . . . Imagination at once docile and discreet, wanting to be merely an attentive commentary of what is perceived, refraining from undue agitation."[27] To follow Bachelard's distinction, this is a state of daydreaming, not dreaming. Behind this softness it is easy to recognize the tempering brought by the reality principle's regulating function to the acts of violence of the primary process—a tempering that is the condition of reconciliation. The only recommended "subject" for the work of poetry is the world. The acts of violence of the interworld are banned from such poetry. Banned for the same reason are the techniques modeled on the primary process, techniques that would hurt the melody and the rhythm and that, by attacking recognizable music, would block the soft reverie, upset lawful phantasmatics, and put off reconciliation. True, poetry always appeals to the body, but to which one? Exclusively to the cradled, caressed, seduced body, possessing or thinking itself in possession of the "good object," convinced of its "good form"? Or also to the body capable of letting the "bad object" be, of surrendering to "bad" forms that are no less true than the good ones; to the body capable of having an ear for disharmonies, glissandos, and clashes, and of hearing meaning in these; of having an eye for dischromatisms, "abstractions" of value, and errant traces, and of seeing meaning in these? A body, in other words, able to face non-conciliation without softness.

This is not a question of taste, but a decisive issue. It is not even a question of "art." Instead it is the question of the critical function of artworks. Let us tackle the problem from the other end, in order to convey what repercussion the position taken from the subject of "connaturality" can have. This other end is political. It encompasses, on the one hand, Louis Aragon justifying the return to rhyme at the height of an imperialist war because "it is the link connecting things to song, what makes them sing," and because "never before perhaps making things sing was a more urgent and noble task required of man, than in this hour when he is most profoundly humiliated, more fully dishonored than ever. . . . In this hour when the unreasonable rhyme once again becomes the sole reason."[28] And, on the other, Benjamin Péret who, in *Le déshonneur des poètes*—on the subject of the underground poems published in Paris during the Nazi occupation and collected under the title *L'honneur des poètes* (poems among which featured several from Aragon's *Le crève-cœur*)—harshly denounces the Aragonian "song" in these terms: "Accustomed to the Stalinist censer and amens, Aragon nonetheless does not succeed as the preceding 'poets' {Loys Masson, Pierre Emmanuel} in alloying God and country. He meets the first, if I may say so, only at a tangent and obtains a text that would make the author of the French radio jingle 'Levitan's furniture is guaranteed for life' turn pale with envy." Péret observes "in passing that the form of the litany comes to the fore in the majority of these 'poems,' no doubt because of the idea of poetry and lamentation the form implies, and of the perverse taste for misery which Christian litany tends to exalt in the hope of earning celestial rewards."[29] Rather than by such naive anticlericalism, this critique would have been better served by an analysis of the system which, in Aragon, connects at a deep-seated level the regression toward rhyme and melody (a regression easily perceptible under the flimsy guise of a total renewal of the rhyme through its exclusive subordination to phonation) with, on the other hand, what his ideological affiliation could have advised him to discern and do in the imperialist war. But Péret's critique is sincere, pointing vividly to what must be held against a poetics of propriety, namely that by rewarding lawful soft fantasy, it opens the door to the maneuvering of the powers that be. Reverie, too, is the guardian of a certain sleep.

It was necessary to insist on this point, for it allows us to detect the existence of an essential illusion in the figure's position. Even when it is obvious that something is deconstructing the order of signification to elicit meaning in it, this something is not easy to identify, since it persists in appearing in disguise. What the phenomenologist sees in poetic disorder is nature's intrusion into language, at most the constitution of language into visible/invisible. The phenomenologist fails to see that the visible conceals another type of invisible than that of the other side of things; that such figures are not the fruit of the "generosity and benevolence of the sensory";[30] and that the god who prepared for us the feast of figures is not Apollo. But the philosopher is only partly to blame, for nocturnal and repressed Dionysus wears the mask of light to appear.

Rebus (Loquitur)

The articulation of the figure with discourse cannot, therefore, hinge only on the figure-image (or the designated), even if one argued that the figure of language is the result of the collapsing of the designated onto the signified.

Satisfying oneself with this argument would amount to opting unwittingly for a methodology, even an ontology. To gain a clearer view of the complexity of the articulation in question, I propose to analyze the ways in which the rebus operates. Close to the dream, the rebus imposes powerful forms of subversion on textual space. At the same time, it offers the double advantage of submitting its work to *designation* (whereas dream figures are only restored as *signified* in the dreamer's account) and of bringing its operations to bear on a text, which is its solution. The table of figure-text relations which I developed in relation to secondary revision and the *Inschriften* finds a match in the material of the rebus because the latter contains many more of these relations, since they are not limited by the constraint of spatial continuity of text and image as in the *Inschriften*, that is, by the constraint of a revision that complies with the secondary process. In this respect, the following analysis is certainly incomplete. Its aim here is first to test the three sets of categories I have identified: of language (signifier, signified, designated), of the figure (image, form, matrix), and of the subversion of these two spaces by the primary process. The analysis below further endeavors to draw a line from the dream to poetry.[31] The articulation of these sets of concepts will constitute the basic network of hyper-reflection.

Freud has taught us that instituting discourse as separated from its object, or the object as designated, and resigned, by a discourse, requires the *Verneinung*, the sidelining of the speaker and that of which she or he is speaking. By contrast, the unconscious is assumed to be able to express itself only in a language of positivity, through an incessant *Bejahung* that tends to confuse object and subject and the things between them. The deconstruction of the articulations of language, which entails the subversion of the most deep-seated categories, is the task of the *Bejahung*, if one understands the latter not as a brute affirmation situated *before* language, but as a secondary affirmation, a re-affirmation that covers up what language had uncovered, reassembles what it had separated, and confuses what it had distinguished. This task requires that the *Verneinung* be no more destroyed than *aufgehoben*, preserved while at the same time eliminated through dialectical recuperation. A task one can well call regressive, on the condition that due attention be paid to the specific rebound effect triggered by the prefix re-, which clearly indicates that to return somewhere is not the same as to go somewhere, for between the two one had to come back—which is precisely the *Verneinung*. As Freud writes: "The way in which dreams treat the category of contraries and contradictories is highly remarkable. It is simply disregarded. 'No' seems not to exist so far as dreams are concerned. They show a particular preference for combining contraries into a unity or for representing them as one and the same thing."[32] "{Dreams} reproduce logical connection by simultaneity in time. Here they are acting like the painter who, in a picture of the School of Athens or of Parnassus, represents in one group all the philosophers or all the poets. It is true that they were never in fact assembled in a single hall or on a single mountain-top; but they certainly form a group in the conceptual sense."[33] "In interpreting any dream-element it is in general doubtful

(a) whether it is to be taken in a positive or negative sense (as an antithetic relation),
(b) whether it is to be interpreted historically (as a recollection),
(c) whether it is to be interpreted symbolically, or
(d) whether its interpretation is to depend on its wording."[34]

"One and only one of these logical relations is very highly favored by the mechanism of dream-formation; namely, the relation of similarity, consonance or approximation—the relation of 'just as'. This relation, unlike any other, is capable of being represented in dreams in a variety of ways."[35]

The dream's "story" [*récit*] is not, therefore, strictly speaking a story told in an articulated language that one may be unable to translate but that would, at least in principle, be translatable into our own. If Freud ventures to say of the productions of the dream-work that they "present no greater difficulties to their translators {*dem Übersetzer*} than do the ancient hieroglyphic scripts to those who seek to read them,"[36] it would be showing a lack of appreciation for his sense of humor to argue, on the basis of the term *Übersetzer*, that interpretation and translation are interchangeable. Freud himself warns against this conflation by inserting in the same sentence this relative clause, which he underlines: "Productions of the dream-work, which, it must be remembered, are not made with the intention of being understood {*die ja nicht beabsichtigt verstanden zu werden*}"[37]—if it weren't for the fact that they could not be understood anyway. This is to say: a hieroglyphic script already laden enough with its own difficulties, to which however more are added by a scribe who, in her or his use of it, has no intention to make her- or himself understood, and who, therefore, can be expected to divert its signs from their destination and combine them according to ends entirely foreign to those of communication.

The comparison with hieroglyphic script already features at the beginning of chapter 6 of *The Interpretation of Dreams*—"the dream-work"—where it once again intersects with the theme of translation. Through terminological ambiguity, Freud manages to identify precisely what he has in mind, namely that the hieroglyph eventually gives way to the rebus as does, simultaneously, translation to transposition:

> The dream-thoughts and the dream-content are presented to us like two versions of the same subject-matter in two different languages. Or, more properly, the dream-content seems like a transcript {*Übertragung*} of the dream-thoughts into another mode of expression, whose characters and syntactic laws it is our business to discover by comparing the original and the translation {*Übersetzung*}. The dream-thoughts are immediately comprehensible, as soon as we have learnt them. The dream-content, on the other hand, is expressed as it were in a pictographic script {*Bilderschrift*} [*écriture figurative*], the characters of which have to be transposed {*übertragen*} individually into the language of the dream-thoughts. If we attempted to read these characters according to their pictorial value {*Bilderwert*} instead of according to their symbolic relation {*Zeichenbeziehung*}, we should clearly be led into error. Suppose I have a picture-puzzle {*Bilderrätsel*}, a rebus, in front of me. It depicts a house with a boat on its roof, a single letter of the alphabet, the figure of a running man whose head has been conjured away, and so on. Now I might be misled into raising objections and declaring that the picture as a whole and its component parts are nonsensical. A boat has no business to be on the roof of a house, and a headless man cannot run. Moreover, the

> man is bigger than the house; and if the whole picture is intended to represent a landscape, letters of the alphabet are out of place in it since such objects do not occur in nature. But obviously we can only form a proper judgment of the rebus if we put aside criticisms such as these of the whole composition and its parts and if, instead, we try to replace each separate element by a syllable or word that can be represented by that element in some way or other. The words which are put together in this way are no longer nonsensical but may form a poetical phrase of the greatest beauty and significance. A dream is a picture-puzzle of this sort and our predecessors in the field of dream-interpretation have made the mistake of treating the rebus as a pictorial composition: and as such it has seemed to them nonsensical and worthless.[38]

Thus interpretation is not a translation since it goes back from the image to the signifiers, and even to the distinctive units (which, for Freud, are the syllables) replaced by the image. The sentence that holds the key to Freud's understanding is this one: "whatever the nature of the relation may be {*nach irgendsolche Beziehung*}." The relation between the dream-content and thought is not a *constant* one as is, in theory at least, or ideally, that between a statement or a text formulated in a language and its translation in another. The reciprocal is equally true, since interpretation and elaboration are always symmetrical. The latter could not have been a case of "translating" a thought into content, for such an operation would take place entirely in the plane of language, but of "transposing" one or the other through the use of means of expression that are not based in this plane. In this sense, Freud's reflection first shifts from the model of translation pure and simple to that of a passage to another "mode of expression" that leads him to the comparison with hieroglyphs. Then, unsatisfied with the fact that this comparison still remains confined too narrowly to the sphere of articulated language, Freud's reflection drifts once more from this comparison to the example of the rebus, whose property in this respect is obviously that articulation remains assumed, but that it is also "performed" [*jouée*] in it. Thus the theory of oneiric elaboration starts from the *Übersetzung* of the dream-thought into a foreign *Schrift*, goes through the *Übertragung* that produces a *Bilderschrift*, and finally points to an *Ersetzung* [substitution] without defined rules, whose result is the *Bilderrätsel*—at each stage distancing itself a bit more from the field of script and granting a bit more room to figural space.

What is this "picture-puzzle," what is a rebus? The *Littré* dictionary offers the following illustration:

pir	vent	venir
un	vient	d'un

which, it says, "represents '*un sous pir, vient sous vent, d'un sous venir,*' which can be transcribed as '*un soupir vient souvent d'un souvenir*'" [A sigh often comes from a recollection].[39] This definition may seem surprising, as it includes no figure whatsoever, in contrast to the rebus to which Freud alludes, where the image enjoys by far the upper hand on speech, and the latter is present in the figure of the "puzzle" only through debris—syllables, letters, and punctuation marks. Nonetheless, the text chosen as an example by the *Littré* does constitute a rebus, insofar as signification, in the strict sense of the word, cannot be returned to it without us having deciphered and transposed in language something that does not belong to language, namely, the position that the six words occupy in relation to one another on the plane of the page. By means of wordplay, the inventor of the rebus—that is, the person who carried out its "work"—had to perform on the syllable *sou-*, previously selected from the syntagmatic chain, a topographical transposition figured in the space of the page. The inventor took *sou-*, as one would say, literally, meaning that she or he took the thing for the word, replacing the syllable for what it in fact designates in French: a subordinate position on a vertical axis. For the reader, the result is a spacing between *pir* and *un* that is fundamentally ambiguous, since its position in space replaces its signification in discourse. If we want to reconstitute this signification, we will first have to treat the syllables *pir* and *un* as objects situated in space, *observe* that the latter is under the former, and then *say* what one has observed: not only that *un* is under [*sous*] *pir*, which is not enough to constitute a signifying statement, but rather that there is "*un*" *sous* "*pir*," ["*un*" *sous* "*pir*"→ *soupir* → a sigh], which instantly includes the figure into a meaningful spoken chain, and thus solves the puzzle. The surprise the *Littré*'s example can afford is due to the fact that the space used in its rebus is not the one Freud has in mind. The latter is the space laid out immediately on the plane of the page by the image itself, that is, a representational expanse. The *Littré*'s space does not harbor any figured representation. It merely organizes a text according to an implicit system of axes that determine relations directed between unspecified objects (in this case, syllables). What stands out in both cases with the same vividness is that one is speaking "through things"—rebus—and that the articulation of the signifier merges with the spacing of the sensory. "Writing *in rebus*," according to the *Littré*, is "a script in which one expresses the things one wants to say through figures. Certain primitive peoples use a script *in rebus*."[40] A statement, needless to point out, that can only leave us pensive, since this primitiveness—pure fantasy of a contemporary of Lewis H. Morgan and Friedrich Engels—is indeed what today and always gives shape to the dream and art, freeing them from "civilized" discourse. Besides, what would *saying* be without resorting to any "thing"? But in Freud's rebus, the "things" are mainly figure-images; in the *Littré*'s, the text itself takes on figure-form, its typographical spacings partially transformed into topographical spacings.

The Rebus Works over Discourse . . .

Let us widen the scope of our analysis. The rebus is discourse disguised as visible object. Hence it offers the perfect material for reflection on the different "transpositions" necessary for this disguise. It should be straightforward to uncover the presence of operations that replace an element located in one of the sites of discourse with another originating elsewhere, since the result is always a challenge to linguistic usage. The processes that determine how this challenge is made can be divided into two broad kinds of operation, depending on whether they are brought to bear on the spoken chain or the plastic screen.[41] Within each of these groups, different operations can further be identified. This is where our categories become useful.

Acting upon oral discourse, one first encounters operations that are linguistically correct. In rebus Figure 16,[42] whose solution is "there can be no effect without a cause" [*Il n'y a pas d'effet sans cause*], one notes that the first operation enabling the passage from text to image consists in the transformation of the doubly negative sentence into a positive: "all effects have a

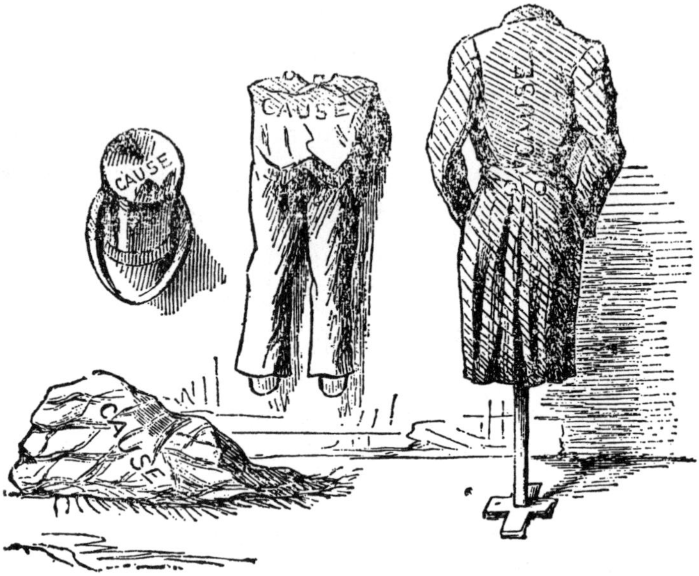

Figure 16. Rebus: "Il n'y a pas d'effet sans cause" [There can be no effect without a cause]. Reproduced in Roland Topor, *Rébus* (Paris: Pierre Horay, 1964), 60. Reprinted by kind permission of the publisher.

cause." Such a transformation appears to be linguistically correct.[43] In this case, the transformation is one of the necessary operations to go from the rebus's "thought" (its solution) to its manifest "content." The elimination of negation in favor of affirmation obviously brings to mind what Freud says of the unconscious process: it ignores the negative. But here this ignorance obeys operations deemed acceptable by the linguist.

In the same rebus, the use of homonymy that will allow effects (the results of causes) to be represented as items of clothing can also seem relatively respectful of the linguistic order. Both terms exist in French vocabulary, have the same pronunciation and the same spelling. What deviation there is concerns only the signifieds. This is not to say that this deviation is trivial, but that it acts on only one level of discourse, while the phonic and graphic signifiers remain intact.[44]

However, the most frequent deviation in the making of the rebus consists in the redistribution of the acoustic chain in order to obtain fragments from which the play of homophony or homonymy can occur. Thus in the next rebus (Figure 17), whose solution is "qui casse les verres les paie" [Who breaks the glasses must pay for them], the segmentation has shifted so as to cut *verres* in two: *qui casse les V/erres les paie*, which—at the cost of the false homophony *les V = l'ève*—allows the fragment *erres* to become a proper name R.[45] Here the work of the rebus runs counter to the diacritical function performed by the distinctive units, that is, by neglecting phonetic oppositions and by not hesitating, in order to arrive at a very rough homophony, to upset completely the measured distribution in words. In so doing, the

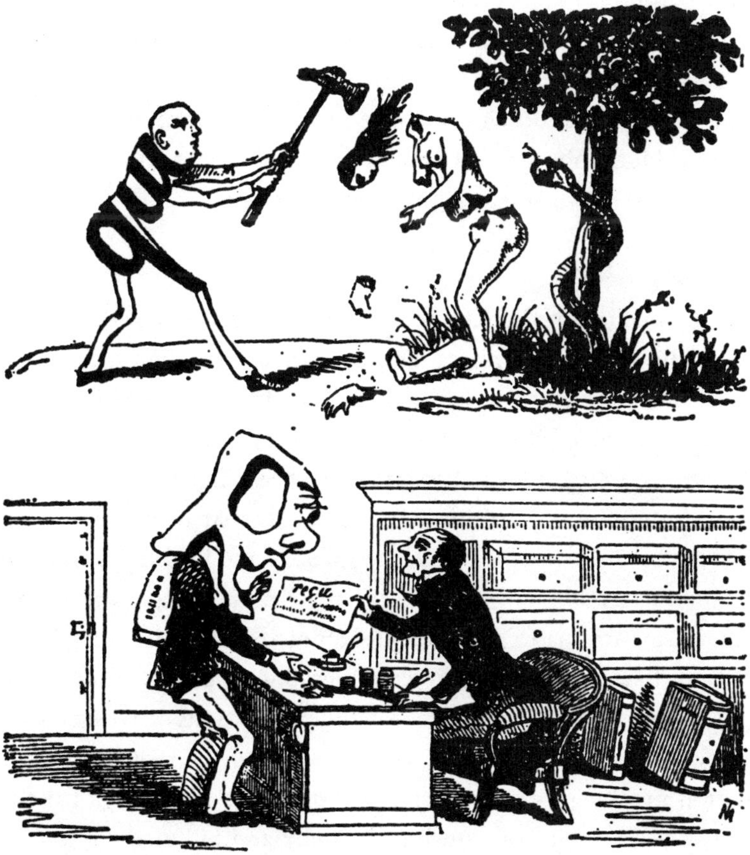

Figure 17. Rebus: "Qui casse les verres les paie" [Who breaks the glasses must pay for them]. Reproduced in Topor, *Rébus*, 53.

work that produces the rebus strips language of the property of guaranteeing the rapid communication of significations—i.e., the listener's immediate recognition of what the speaker is saying, thanks to the identification of the distinctive units and their disposition in the spoken chain.[46] As a result, the sentence becomes opaque, and another meaning than its recognizable signification takes shape behind this signification. It is this other meaning that the rebus-decoder first encounters (once she or he has traveled the path from image to apparent text) and that she or he will have to transcribe into communicable signification. It need not be stressed how different this transcription is from a translation; it is more like breaking a code, where perceptive vision [*voyance*] consists in seeing where the normal spacing has been displaced and putting it back in its rightful place. But there is no law governing this displacement. Its overriding goal is to produce "wild" homophones. Moreover, homonyms are often sufficient for the rebus, as they are for the joke. Homophony is the result of a displacement on the phonic signifier; homonymy of a displacement on the signified.

. . . and Works over Plastic Space

Next in the making of the rebus comes the transformation of the units obtained on the spoken chain into figures inscribed on the page of the book. At this point I identify three operations. The phonic unit can be represented by its *graphic equivalent*—letter, syllable, or word. In the last rebus (Figure 17), *qui* and *R* are figures of this kind. Are these figures? One could argue that these are letters, or groups of letters, and that it would be absurd to speak of figures since the perfectly recognizable and legible graphic signifiers are hardly inscribed in a figural space. Furthermore, the graphic equivalence that allows for the passage from phonemes to letters is itself a linguistic convention. True, these elements remain graphic and, as such, are to be read. But it is no less true that they are not laid out as signs of writing on a page should be. On the contrary, they are subjected to the requirements of representation in which they are integrated: *qui* forms the body of the convict breaking Eve. The line constituting the body and tail of the q is registered on the page in such a way as not only to trigger the recognition of the signifier (and from there, of the signified) on the part of the French reader, but

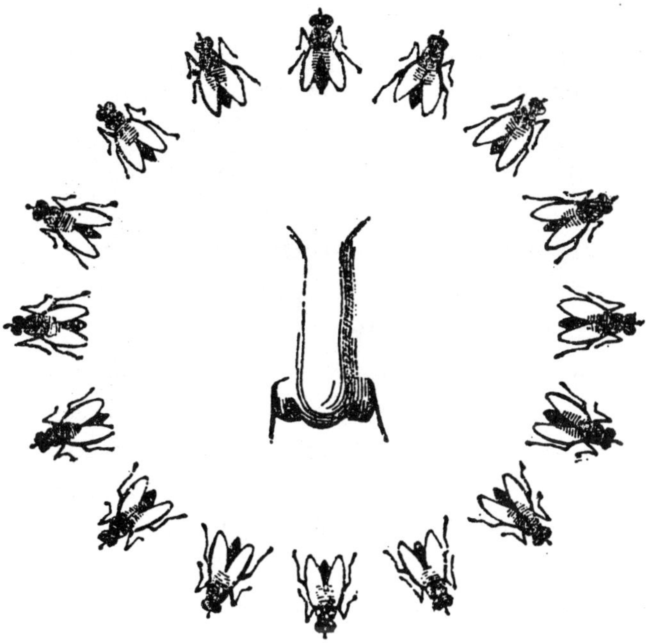

Figure 18. Rebus: "Un essaim d'abeilles" [A swarm of bees]. Reproduced in Topor, *Rébus,* 1.

also—and contradictorily—to outline the silhouette of the stone-breaker. In which space, then, is this line inscribed? At once in a graphic and plastic space. Far from dispelling the confusion between the textual and the figural, the presence of letters or words in the rebus brings it to a head. After being treated as things through the phonic displacement, words can once again be treated as things in graphic figuration.

A second operation consists in representing the unit, arrived at by redistributing the spoken chain, by its *designated.* Such is the case of the image of the nose in the next rebus (Figure 18), whose solution is "un essaim d'abeilles" [a swarm of bees]. The substitution of the axis of signification for that of designation is not an operation that qualifies as linguistic. No need to return, I believe, to the discussion of this issue in Hegel and in our critique thereof: between the word and the thing, the distance is unbridgeable; the word is a universal that denotes a class of objects, whereas the thing is a sensorial given. The representation of the word by the thing requires a "choice" among all the denoted objects. There is no linguistic reason to represent the word *nez* [nose] with the image offered by the rebus in Figure 18. On the other hand, there are nonlinguistic—or at least plastic—reasons for representing frontally a nose that will need to be encircled by a ring. Thus we witness here the displacement of the lexical space, where the term *nez* [nose] can be substituted legitimately for other terms that make up its definition, toward a plastic space where the outline reveals the presence of a nose. This plastic space prompts two comments: first, the nose is recognizable; the line determines a *contour*, a three-dimensional rendering; we are dealing, therefore, with an outline [*tracé révélateur*], a plastic "script" that represses figurality. Second, however, the nose is separated from the environment that the eye would expect to see. The face, in the middle of which sits the nose, is missing; the latter has been displaced, this time through a wholly figural operation.

On this same rebus, we may observe a third kind of presentation of the units redistributed in the acoustic chain. This presentation results no longer in a figure-image, but in a *figure-form*: in a "nez ceint d'abeilles" [a nose girded by bees], the phrase *ceint d'* is not strictly speaking represented, yet it is present as the image's form: the bees encircle the nose. Here, one no longer goes from the phonic unit to the image of the designated, but instead to the formation (*Gestaltung*) of its signified. For this to occur, the work on the phonic level must have produced significative units. On the plastic level, the *Gestaltung* generates a *Gestalt*, a regulating line [*tracé régulateur*] that normally remains unseen but that allows us to see, and that here must be detected and seen, that is, transformed into an outline [*tracé révélateur*] if we want to be able to decipher the form of the image and articulate the word *ceint*. To compare this operation to the last, this one is meant to conceal more thoroughly the signification waiting to be uncovered, since what represents it can no longer be seen, even though it is visible. We saw the same process at work in the example given by the *Littré*: the preposition *sous*, homophone of the syllable *sou-* (detached from *soupir*, *souvent*, and *souvenir*) is concealed as the form of the text's layout. It should be noted that the *Gestaltung*'s limits are here imposed by language. Just imagine the case where the

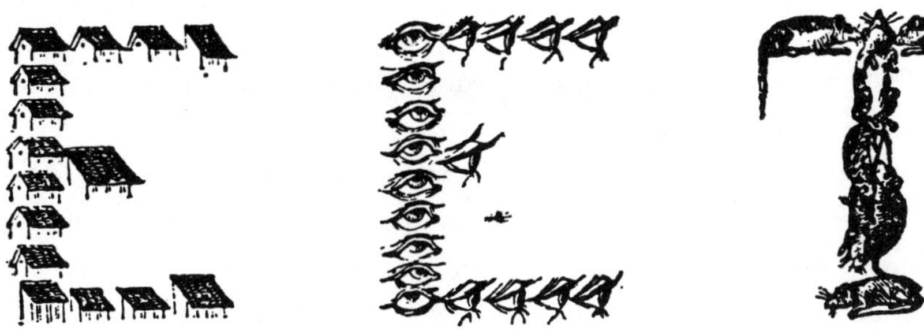

Figure 19. Rebus: "Aide-toi et Dieu t'aidera" [Help yourself and God will help you]. Reproduced in Topor, *Rébus,* 53.

spatial relation between visible elements could not be articulated: it would simply go undetected. Now the register of ordinary language only has to signify practical geometric relations, which are Euclidean; it fails to account for relations that fall under a curved or topological space. The rebus's *Gestalt* must therefore be "good," and this example provides an eloquent definition of good form: recognizable and signifiable form.

Lastly, certain fragments are purely and simply eliminated: neither seen nor visible. This is frequently the case of the link-word. In the rebus in Figure 17, the *les* of *R les paie* appears neither as image nor form. This is all the more pronounced in the last rebus (Figure 19), which reads: "Aide-toi et Dieu t'aidera," where *de* remains invisible [Help yourself and God will help you; visually in French "É de toits É d'yeux T de rats"; and literally in English: E of roofs, E of eyes, T of rats]. Here we have in a nutshell the incompatibility Freud observed between the primary process and the articulation and connection specific to the secondary process. Condensation covers up syntax.

The Rebus and the Rules

On the basis of these modalities of the figure's construction, and of the previously discussed operations bearing upon text, one discovers that a considerable number of combinations are possible.[47] But regardless of the operations used to produce the rebus, what matters is that the decipherer does not know with which operation she or he is dealing, since the exact nature of the confusions of location within linguistic space, and of the substitutions of a linguistic term for a plastic element, is in no way made clear. One finds oneself faced with something truly opaque. Constructions must be applied to it in order to signify it.

One could counter that I have just outlined a grammar of the different ways of generating a rebus from a text, and that the very possibility of such a grammar suffices to undermine the claim of the result's opacity. This counterclaim does not withstand scrutiny: all one can concede to the rebus with regard to regularity, and thus to a semantic "reading" of rebuses, is that the operations are contained within relatively narrow boundaries. I am not referring to those operations working over the solution-sentence, where one can observe a rather extended range of displacements (although condensation is infrequent). But I am certainly referring to those operations that generate the figure: the modeling line [*le tracé plastique*] is always reifying and gestaltist, proposing a silhouette or identifiable forms. As I mentioned, this limitation is imposed by the existence of the "solution." If there is no chance of finding the solution, the rebus is no longer a game. Yet the solution is a text. The image's reifying and gestaltist properties are the result of the compromise that the (preconscious) constraints of language manage to extract from figural space. While the dream, unconcerned with making itself understood, goes very far in displacement and condensation, the rebus is kept in check to a greater extent by the secondary process, notably at the level of figurability.[48]

This is the opposition between the rebus and the dream that emerges if we take the preconscious as reference-point. If we take the unconscious, the opposition is reversed: the dream relies to a much greater extent than the rebus on the phantasmatic matrix. This reliance is evident in the production itself of figure-images, in which desire finds fulfillment—that is to say, is momentarily extinguished. With its playful aspect, the rebus brings to the surface (of the sheet of paper and the psychic apparatus), along with traces of the matrix (indecipherable except in analytical treatment), operations of the unconscious process. In the rebus desire does not achieve immediate fulfillment as it does in the dream, and these operations come to light only partially: the search for the object of the drive is abandoned, while the search for the drive itself has begun. Desire desires itself. One senses the reversal to come.

I would like to return to this question of the generative grammar performed on the rebus. This grammar brings us to the heart of the problem of the poem as it should be formulated. Desire can target every level of language in order to generate the figural; and, at the very least, the poetic is the presence of the figural in discourse. Does this mean that in poetry one is still speaking *with things*? Yes, but these things are no longer confined to the sheet of paper. Where are they then? In the mind, as images? This is going too fast,[49] for poetry has much to do with the signifier: the figures of discourse are registered on paper or in the voice, or both—these are hardly "spiritual" materials. The relevant distinction between rebus and poem lies elsewhere, namely in the fact that the poet refrains from drawing images on the page, working instead exclusively with the linguistic signifier. Even when the text is read on a calligramme, the outline of the "stabbed dove" is traced with the letters forming words and sentences.[50] The legible is never renounced. Such is the paradox of the figural finding refuge in a text without destroying it. As I argued, the figural deconstructs the text—but how do such deconstructions work?

Intra- and Extratextualism

This is where it becomes imperative to step back and discuss methodology. Putting the question as I just have ("How do the deconstructions in the poetic text work?") is immediately to take sides. Indeed, thus formulated, the question amounts to adopting a negative approach toward the problem of the specificity of poetic language (since the frame of reference is the language of communication). In principle, the linguist starts from the opposite hypothesis: poetic language [*langage*], whatever its distance from ordinary language [*langue*], remains a language [*langage*], and it is far more interesting to establish the internal rules governing it (intratextual relations) than to try to measure its differences with the language [*langue*] of reference (extratextual relations).[51] James Peter Thorne offers a particularly forceful view of this approach in an article in which he argues that an (English) poetic text is an example of another language [*langage*] than Standard English, and that its linguistic analysis does not require the application of other rules in addition to those offered by the generative and transformational grammar of ordinary English.[52] Instead, the analysis of a poetic text requires the elaboration of new rules that allow not only the sentences of the poem to be generated, but also many other possible utterances. The poetic work would thus be neither speech articulated in ordinary language [*langue*] nor language [*langage*] onto itself, but discourse uttered in a different language [*langue*].[53]

Here Thorne is taking aim at a method of analysis that remains at the text's surface and does no more than enumerate the relevant stylistic features on the corpus that this text constitutes in and of itself.[54] Such a method would not allow for any useful comparison to be drawn between the text and English grammar, since the observations would take only surface manifestations into account. For it to be enlightening the comparison must apply to the same level on either side. This is why it should not mediate between a text (speech) and a language [*langue*], but between two languages [*langues*], namely, English and another language [*langue*] of which the poem is one possible discourse among others.[55] If such is not the case, the comparatist method will remain of little use and banal: "it would amount to saying nothing more than that [two texts] are different because they are different." The solution? "To take the text as a sample of a different language and to construct a grammar for it of the same kind as we would construct for English."[56]

Here is the rub. On the basis of his demonstration, Thorne believes that such a working hypothesis would allow for certain intuitive insights to be taken into account:

> It has been suggested by psychologists that "If we spoke a different language, we would perceive a different world".... For example, it has been suggested that Russians and Arabs have a different concept of color from ours because they speak languages in which there are verbs of color as well as adjectives of color: "Perceiving a different world" seems a pretty good description of the experience I receive reading a poem such as *Anyone lived*.[57] To account for this one would have to provide an explication for some such statement as "The meaning of this sentence is not expressible in Standard English." It is by no means clear how one should go about this in the case of a natural language. But the fact that in the cases we are

> considering we can link difficulty in understanding a sentence with difficulty in incorporating rules which would account for its structure into a grammar of Standard English, might provide a clue. Such an explanation would also have to account for the fact that Standard English is obviously an inadequate metalanguage in which to discuss these sentences.[58]

Let us study this passage. To read a poem is to perceive a different world. We can only concur when the difference in meaning is thematized (by a linguist no less!) as a difference in sensory data [*données*]. But this concession is invalidated as soon as it is proffered: the difference in perception, we are told, is the result of a difference in language [*langue*], and the latter stems from the heterogeneity of the grammars of each of these two languages. Granted, the poem's opacity, its resistance to translation into ordinary language, would be due to the fact that it relies on a different "distribution of experience" than that which upholds this language. Except that this difference in distribution is itself considered analogous to that which distinguishes two "natural" languages (English and Arabic, say, in relation to color). The former difference even has the privilege over the latter of making intelligible to us the reason for opacity, which is the incompatibility between the poem's rules of generation and those of language [*langue*]. If, then, ordinary language cannot be an adequate metalanguage to discuss the poem, this is because of the heterogeneity of the respective grammatical rules of the language of the poem and that of the commentary.

As one can see, this heterogeneity is radical only for linguistics, since it distinguishes two languages. It goes without saying that one is not the metalanguage of the other. However, each has its own metalanguage, which is that of the linguist, whether structuralist or generativist. The two languages (Arabic and English, the language of the poem and the poet's mother tongue) belong to the same "reign," the same space, where they occupy positions more or less apart from one another, but where they occur merely *in opposition* to one another. They come under the same universals of language.

It should be clear that this hypothesis leads one to favor what Henry Widdowson calls "intratextual relations" over "extratextual relations." The latter can furnish only a negative proof, that is, the knowledge that one is not dealing with the poet's mother tongue [*langue*]. Positive proof is given by the construction of the grammar that would enable the generation of, among others, the sentences of the poem under consideration. This is precisely what Thorne does in his remarkable analysis.

Site of Meaning

This requirement may seem technical, yet it is much more. It covers a real option on the very essence of meaning, and this option consists in rejecting all meaning that is not signification (at least syntactic signification in Thorne's generativist hypothesis). In particular, what is excluded is, first, sensory meaning [*sens sensible*], the model of which is provided by color's particular mode of action on the body; and, second, unconscious meaning, which functions through such operations as condensation and displacement. Again, the first meaning of meaning is a deviation from the arbitrariness of reference, while the second is of the rules internal to the system which uphold all signification. The intratextual method applied to the poem overlooks these meanings that depend on an energetics or an economy (in the Freudian sense). This method positions itself between two choices: either the metalanguage is that of the natural mother tongue, and it produces the banalities of literary analysis; or it is that of generative grammar. In both cases the metalanguage is a language [*langue*] that makes use, whether immediately or mediately, of rules of generation. That the metalanguage could draw upon a set of nonlinguistic categories; that it could consist not in placing poem and prose in the same reign, but in signifying the fact that the poem is discursive matter permeated with figurality; that the latter could refuse to obey all generative grammars (as well as the structuralist's supposed metonymy and metaphor), and instead obey another order of meaning production (the phantasmatic matrix) where the fundamental rules of language are rejected (such as those that distinguish in every discourse the object of one's speech and what one is saying about it): this is what the linguist is loath to consider, and this is precisely our hypothesis.

This option on meaning entails a decision as to the treatment to be applied to the text. If one takes the poem as a discourse realized in a different language than the natural language, it will be up to the linguist to decide what in the poem is a feature of language and what is a feature of speech. Only on this condition can the linguist hope to arrive at its deep grammar. The linguist is led, therefore, to privilege certain features over others. If, on the other hand, one posits the text as a corpus coterminous with language in its entirety, "any syntactical feature in the text has to be regarded as being as important as any other syntactical feature."[59] Now this is exactly the treatment required by the figural, as Freud demonstrated with the dream and the work of art, but for this one difference: that the object is treated precisely not as a language but as a compromise between preconscious and unconscious. Far from having to evaluate the degree of generality of a given feature, we must be attentive to all of them, and it is legitimate to begin the analysis by studying the most apparently trivial detail.[60] When it comes to the by-products of the unconscious process, there can be no trust in the rules of language (or of realist perception) that allow levels or forms to be distinguished, since condensation can cover up an essential element of meaning, and displacement renders it unrecognizable. The decipherer's attention must let itself be "evenly suspended" over all parts of the material, allowing her or his own unconscious to detect the figures of the unconscious present in the artwork.[61] In the end what opposes the intratextualist method to ours is the opposition between the discontinuous and hierarchical space of discourse, and the undisciplined continuity of the games played by the primary process in the latter space. Our approach could only be called extratextualist if we modify Widdowson's definition of the term: any comparison between the text of the poem and ordinary language would have to be carried out not only with linguistic categories, but *also* with those corresponding to the operations of the primary process.

A Reasonable Chart of Poetic Folies

Nonetheless, this last difference is only superficial. Indeed it seems to me that Widdowson's meticulous description of stylistic operations, even though it may refer explicitly only to those levels of language recognized by generativism, makes implicit use of categories generally ignored by linguistics. Before showing this to be the case, I summarize Widdowson's analysis in the following table.[62]

I. Extratextual relations

1. *Deviations with regard to language* [langue]

1.1. Phonological level: rhythm—deviation from the rhythmics of language.

1.2. Syntactic level:

1.21. Level of surface structures: poetic licenses (nonenforcement of transformational rules, such as, for example, omission of *do* in interrogatives and negatives in English, of *ne* in French interro-negatives).

1.22. Level of deep structures.

1.221. Level of the rules of selection: personification (the attribution of an animate subject to a verb requiring an inanimate subject).

1.222. Level of the rules of category: recategorization (noun taken as verb, or noun taken as adjective: "I shall see / Some squeaking Cleopatra *boy* my greatness / In the posture of a whore . . ." [William Shakespeare]).

1.223. Level of the rules of subcategory (transitive verb taken as intransitive verb, or vice versa: "J'ai besoin de me sentir *voyagée* comme une femme" [I need to feel *traveled* like a woman] [Henri Pichette]).

N.B. 1.222 and 1.223 are incompatible.

1.3. Semantic level:

1.31. Level of the system of meaning relations: paradox ("Cette *obscure clarté*" [the *dark light*] [Pierre Corneille]).

1.32. Level of the relations between lexical units: homophony, play on words.

1.33. Level of the lexical units themselves: invention of new words ("eggtentical" [James Joyce], "Urchs" [Paul Klee], "merdre" [Alfred Jarry]).

N.B. In the invention of these words, one should distinguish between deviations from the order of language [*langue*] and those that concern the order of speech, such as "Cette furtive ardeur des serpents qui *s'entraiment*" [This furtive ardor of snakes *in love*] (Guillaume Apollinaire).

2. *Deviations with regard to speech*

2.1. Phonological level: alliteration, assonance, consonance (anomalous concentration of certain phonemes or phonetic features ("Du lundi au / Dimanche l'idiot speaker te dédie O / Silence l'insultant pot-pourri qu'il rabâche" [From Monday to / Sunday the idiot *speaker* dedicates to you O / Silence the offensive mish-mash of his ramblings] [Aragon]).

2.2. Syntactic level: anomalous elaboration of the elements of the sentence.

2.21. Level of coordination: multiple branching construction (Chomsky).

2.211. Level concerning the nominal syntagm ("Only you can hear and see, behind the eyes of the sleepers, /the movements and countries and mazes and colours and dismays /and rainbows and tunes and wishes and flight and fall and /despairs and big seas of their dreams" [Dylan Thomas]).

2.212. Level concerning the adjective.

2.213. Level concerning the verbal syntagm ("Je t'imprime / je te savoure / je te rame / je te précède / je te vertige /et tu me recommences / je t'innerve te musique / te gamme te greffe /. . ." [I print you / I savor you / I swim you / I precede you / I dizzy you / and you begin me again / I innervate you music you /scale you graft you /. . .] [Pichette]).[63]

2.214. Level concerning the relative clause ("Ils sont / Ceux qui punissent, ceux qui jugent, ceux qui vont" [They are / Those who punish, those who judge, those who move on] [Victor Hugo]).

2.22. Level of subordination: right-branching construction (Noam Chomsky).

2.3. Semantic level:

2.31. Lexical level: images, metaphors, comparisons, highly unlikely groupings of terms ("Quelquefois je vois au ciel des plages sans fin couvertes de blanches nations en joie" [Sometimes I see in the sky endless beaches covered with white nations full of joy] [Arthur Rimbaud]).

N.B. Frequent use of such a grouping eventually cancels out its character of deviation.

N.B. Deviations of the 1.221 type engender those of type 2.31. The opposite is not necessarily true.

2.32. Contextual level:

2.321. Level of the "types" of language: juxtaposition of several types of the same language in a single text ("Notre Père qui êtes aux cieux / Restez-y" [Our Father who art in heaven / Stay there] [Jacques Prévert]).

2.322. Level of situational context: always redoubled ("*Mon* enfant, *ma* sœur . . . / *Vois* sur *ces* canaux" [*My* child, *my* sister . . . / *See* upon *these* canals] [Charles Baudelaire]).

II. Intratextual relations

1. Equivalence: projection of equivalence from the axis of selection onto that of combination (Roman Jakobson) (phonological: "Lune melli-fluente aux lèvres des déments" [Mellifluent moon on the lips of the mad] [Apollinaire]; semantic: "Stable trésor, temple simple à Minerve, / Masse de calme, et visible réserve, / Eau sourcilleuse, Œil qui gardes en toi / tant de sommeil sous un voile de flamme, / O mon silence! . . ." [Sure treasure, simple shrine to intelligence, / Palpable calm, visible reticence, / Proud-lidded water, Eye wherein there wells / Under a film of fire such depth of sleep / O silence! . . .] [Paul Valéry]).[64]
2. Coupling: convergence of equivalences of different levels ("Quel repli de désirs, sa traîne! . . . Quel désordre / De trésors s'arrachant à mon avidité, / Et quelle sombre soif de la limpidité!" [What a coil of lusts, his trail! . . . What a riot / of riches wrenched away from my longing, / And ah, that obscure thirst for limpidity!] [Valéry]).[65]
3. Variation of level: displacement of the equivalence from one level to another: phonological, syntactic, semantic ("Till I am indifferent and cannot enjoy it; till I am solitary and cannot impart it; till I am known and do not want it" [Samuel Johnson]).

We now have at our disposal one of the more detailed tables of the "figures" of style, a table that can easily withstand comparison with the classificatory system Tzvetan Todorov proposes.[66] The latter does not mention the distinction between level of language [*langue*] and level of speech; instead he distinguishes between a weak requirement for the classification of figures (namely, that they can be described) and a strong requirement, which is that they contain a "deviation from a certain rule of language [*langage*], either explicit or implicit."[67] Now the strong requirement should correspond approximately to the deviations Widdowson situates at the level of language [*langue*]. And when Todorov asserts that there is no such thing as deviations in the figures themselves, which in his classification satisfy only one condition, that of describability (weak requirement), he confirms Widdowson's observation regarding the syntactic or semantic deviations that affect speech alone, namely, that they belong merely to the order of improbability and violate what in computer science is termed constraints of usage, but not those of the code (of language [*langue*]).

Yet Todorov's characterization of the four levels where the anomaly or figure can appear lacks precision when compared with the subtlety of Widdowson's generativist analyses. These levels are: the sound-meaning relation, syntax, semantics, and the sign-referent relation. To begin with the sound-meaning relation: it is not a level of language [*langage*], but a relation between levels (if that). By stopping at this relation, one misses the formal analysis of the operations that bear upon the distinctive units themselves, concentrating instead all of one's attention on the effect of these operations on meaning. This is not to say that this approach is invalid, but only that it relies on a different reference point than the approach concerned with syntax or semantics. For there can be operations affecting phonetic features, phonemes, or prosody, whose effects on meaning one would be incapable of describing, and which would thus not even come under Todorov's weak requirement, although they constitute profound modifications of language's phonic system. Such is clearly the case of rhythm, which, as formal unit of movement, forces one to accent normally unaccented syllables and transforms verse into a compromise between two different demands.[68]

One could therefore conclude that Widdowson's classification fulfills all linguistic requirements as far as stylistics is concerned. Still, the question of the extratextual method's shortcomings remains: figures are described according to their effects on the level they deconstruct, but the nature of what it is that is deconstructing and the processes at work remain elusive.

Who Is Working, and How?

One might think that this question is addressed in section II of the above table, under the heading *Intratextual relations*. Indeed it is, but only very indirectly. "These relations are established in reference to the various ways in which the deviations relate to one another within the literary text."[69] The equivalences, couplings, and variations of level concern the relations between deviations or figures; they do not tell us what these deviations or figures consist of, since they are at one remove from the latter. Or at least they seem not to tell us—they do, but indirectly.

Let us come back to extratextual relations, specifically the deviations regarding speech (I.2), which all operate in the same way regardless of the level of language they disturb. Alliterations, assonances, etc., concentrate in a weak segment of the spoken chain an excessive number of phonemes or features that would normally be distributed less densely. "Multiple-branching or right-branching constructions" act similarly upon the constituents of a sentence: through coordination or subordination, they concentrate nominal or verbal syntagms, or adjectives, to an uncommon degree. Likewise, the work affecting the lexical level consists in juxtaposing (collocation) terms belonging to different semantic fields. And on the contextual level, the effect is the result of the same process, whether it involves combining within the same discourse normally different units of language, or mixing incompatible situational contexts, notably through the interplay of pronouns. In all of these cases we are dealing with *condensations* and *displacements*, but *tempered*. The process of concentrating the worked-over units does not go so far as to disfigure them and render them unrecognizable: it ceases when groups are produced whose units are identifiable but whose relations are unexpected.

By turning to the deviations of language [*langue*], one will recognize the same operations, but this time affecting even more essential rules. The condensations listed under section I.2 in Widdowson's table obviously involve displacements, yet the gap between the displaced terms must not be so great if in the end one wants to arrive at what one in fact observes, that is, concentrations of recognizable units. To the contrary, I.1.33 presents an altogether different situation: the creation of new words is achieved in most cases through the condensation of syllables coming from different words, and the power of this condensation is such that it crushes fragments of old units one against the other. Hence the cover-up effects one also finds under I.1.21.

Yet there is more, namely, displacement without condensation. We already made a note of it when we compared the dream, the rebus, and the joke: pure displacement produces in the worked-over material a denser opacity than when it is coupled with condensation. To treat a noun like a verb or an adjective (1.222) is to alter the placement of a term in deep syntactic space without having it undergo any compensatory transformation. Similarly, paradox (1.31) deserves its name because of the semantic distance it has the terms that it linked cover. It is as if unadulterated displacement brought us in direct contact with the unbound nature of the energy at work in the primary process. Condensation reconstitutes units; displacement does not.[70]

In the end it seems to me that a correlation exists between, on the one hand, Widdowson's distinction between deviations of language [*langue*] and deviations of speech, and, on the other, the difference in the intensity of the force (or forces) that displaces and compresses the units of various levels of language [*langage*]. The discontinuity that the linguist introduces is relevant, but it masks the existence of processes doubly subject to continuousness: processes that act in linguistic space as if it were not made of unalterable intervals, and that can vary continuously in intensity.[71]

The Acknowledgment of the Interval and Its Recuperation

As Jean Cohen says, poetry is the anti-prose.[72] Its specific function is to assail the normal intervals acknowledged by language [*langue*]. (Cohen himself admits that his method is in this respect fundamentally extratextualist, "negative.") The deviation creates an interval, an "impertinence": at the phonic level, Cohen identifies the dislocation of the system of pauses, the disjuncture of the phono-semantic pairing, and the dedifferentiation of phonemes and prosody; at the semantic level, he lists the redundancy of the attribute in relation to the noun, the non-determinative use of the pronoun, and the inconsistency of coordination; lastly, at the syntactic level, he notes the reversal in the order of words. Clearly, these linguistic categories differ from Widdowson's, covering fewer levels; nonetheless, they easily find a place in the latter's classification.

But this is not the issue. As opposed to a linguist who would be content with description, Cohen ventures an explanation of the poetic function, modeled after the analysis of the metaphor. "Why the change of meaning? Why does the decoder not abide by the code of language [*langue*] dictating that a signifier be assigned a given signified? Why does this decoder resort to a secondary decoding, which brings a new signified into play?"[73] The significance of this question is immediately apparent: why poetry, or, to put it differently, why the figure in discourse? For Cohen, "the answer to this question could not be simpler: because in its primary meaning, the term is not pertinent, whereas the secondary meaning restores its pertinence."[74] For example: "le vent crispé du matin" [the shriveled-up morning wind] (Paul Verlaine). Primary meaning of shriveling: the crumpling and contraction of an object's surface when exposed to fire, cold, wind, etc. In this case, the secondary meaning would be: the wind is as if crumpled and recoiled upon itself by the freshness of dawn. According to Cohen, one moves therefore from a primary to a secondary signified.

What then is the difference between these two signifieds? Meaning "has undergone a metamorphosis along the way."[75] From the denotative function of language, which grants a cognitive signification to the designated (the wind), we shifted to a connotative function.[76] By connotative function one must understand here that the metaphor draws from a layer of meaning different from that of the primary signifieds, and where can be found networks of equivalence and systems of evaluation.[77] The term of connotation is justified if one understands by it that *shriveled* for example acts not only as signifier of a signified (which would be the primary signified), but as a total sign (signifier + signified) referring to another signified (signified 2).[78] Such an understanding, however, obviously presupposes that that connoted level—that of signified 2—is of the same nature as the connoting level (signifier + signified 1), that is, organized like an articulated language [*langage*]. This is exactly what is already suggested by the use of the term *signified* to identify this second meaning, and what Cohen states explicitly when he writes that "the poetic metaphor is the shift from denotative to *connotative language* [*langue*], a shift obtained by way of a word [*parole*] that loses its meaning at the level of the first language, only to regain it at the level of *second*."[79] The essential similarity between the two languages is so crucial to Cohen's demonstration that it becomes his final word on the matter: "Why the metaphor, why the change of meaning? Why not call things by their name? Why say 'this golden sickle' and not simply 'the moon'? The answer lies in the antinomy of the two codes. Notional meaning and emotional meaning cannot coexist within the same consciousness. The signifier cannot give rise simultaneously to two mutually exclusive signifieds. For this reason poetry must resort to taking a detour."[80]

But then what difference is there with Thorne's (and I would add, Hegel's) position? The other language is a language [*langue*], assumed to obey rules that, though undoubtedly different in their specificity, are identical when it comes to their principle, which is universal. This means, among other things, and without looking beyond structuralism, that the signifieds 2 that the metaphor draws from language 2 belong to an oppositional system and function only when replaced in the network of discontinuities that Jakobson proposes. In other words, the position of meaning is no different in the connoted and the denoted. Now, connotation is a category introduced in semiology precisely to show how a nonlinguistic element (a color)—whose value is not in itself arbitrary, but instead motivated (at the perceptual level and/or that of the libido)—can, moreover, acquire an arbitrary signification by virtue of its position in a system.[81] Connotation is strictly speaking the script of figural space, that which allows the latter's polysemy to be reduced, its opacity leveled, and the object of sight to be converted into legible object. Not surprisingly, connotation is plentiful in all the forms of production of figures that reduce the latter to a function of communication—advertisement, propaganda, audiovisual instruction—and use images as a vehicle capable of transmitting significations and orders without incurring the receiver's scrutiny. One can see why, on the one hand, they rely on a code, and multiply connotations accordingly: the desired effect (the understanding of a sentence in a foreign language, consumer habits, political affiliation) must conform to the aims set by the emitter, and thus the vehicle must be as devoid of ambiguity as possible. If, however, the emitter chose the image instead of discourse (which after all would be the most monovalent of all "languages" [*langages*]), this is because, on the other hand, the emitter wishes her or his message to escape the receiver's censorship. Connotation represents a compromise-formation between these two requirements.

The poetic metaphor is the opposite of a compromise. It achieves poetic status not when it refers to an already scripted language [*langue*], or in any case to a code generally accepted by the speakers, but when it transgresses it. Such a transgression does not consist in the shift from ordinary language (of signified 1) to the supposedly affective language (of signified 2), but instead in the use of *operations* that have *no part* in language 1. Cohen's anti-prose is merely another prose. As for myself, I believe poetry to be prose's other.

A Kind of "Affective Language"

Besides, what could an "affective language" [*langue affective*] be? If it were true that we needed to go through this language first in order to decipher at level 2, one of these two implications would necessarily follow: either this language would be, strictly defined, a connoted language [*langage*], that is, a language "of culture" determining the sensibility of a community at a given time and place; or, short of being a proper language of communication, this "language" [*langue*] would be that which is "spoken" by the poet's unconscious, and its message could be heard only if one were in possession of the same code as the emitter.

In the first hypothesis (where "connotation" is understood literally), poetry and "writing" become one. The function assigned to the former—which could not have been more tangible in all essentially noncritical societies—is that which is fulfilled by every cultural formation of these societies: the subsuming, so to speak, under the metaphoric (or, for Claude Lévi-Strauss, symbolic) level of the contradictions that inform these societies. It would be easy to show that this integrating function of poetry, and of art in general, prevailed in most societies for millennia. The West begins to lose sight of it, and irreversibly, only from around 1860, when, as Roland Barthes puts it, "writing" becomes impossible.[82] Yet we cannot simply exclude Rimbaud or E.E. Cummings from poetry because they cease to be "writers," that is, stop expressing themselves in a socially accepted metaphoric language [*langue*] capable of mobilizing large units of meaning such as mythemes.[83] It is up to us to build a concept of the specificity of poetic language [*langage*] that can account both for its function of integration in societies invested by mythology and for its critical function in ours.

Deconstruction (or recessus) is such a concept, in that it introduces into language extra-linguistic operations that slow down communication. The classic alexandrine evinces such a deconstruction in relation to ordinary language, and the principle of this deconstruction is no different from the "excesses" committed by Dada, except that it affects fewer linguistic levels and is boxed into connoted writing by strict rules that limit its usage.[84] Take Cummings, for example:

> there is a here and
> that here was a
> town (and the town is
> so aged the ocean
> wanders the streets are so
> ancient the houses enter the
>
> people are so feeble the feeble go to
> sleep if the people sit down)...[85]

and Corneille:

> Die without obtaining satisfaction!
> Seek a death so fatal to my honor!
> Allow Spain to ascribe to my memory
> the refusal to defend the honor of my house!
> Respect a love whose collapse
> my dazed mind knows is certain!
> I must stop thinking of that enticing image
> which only increases my suffering.
> Come! At least I will save my honor,
> since in either outcome I will lose Chimene.[86]

Cummings breaks several rules: of the sentence's construction, by turning the last word of a line into the first word of the next (transgression of the order of language); of subordination, by stringing together consecutives (order of speech, right-branching construction); of the arbitrariness of terms, through the use of alliterations (people, feeble, sleep). For his part, Corneille runs afoul of coordination (multiple-branching construction), but also of the signifier's arbitrariness through the use of rhyme and meter (and, furthermore, of the meter's variation). In Corneille's poem, the transgression of syntax does not go beyond the constraints of usage (speech), but contrary to Cummings, the transgression targeting the phonetic level does indeed have the seriousness of a deviation of language. As far as the extratextual method is concerned, what is at stake is the same for the classical and modern author: both texts are poetic because they are laden with deconstructions.

Poetic language [*langage*] is not, therefore, a social or socially connoted language [*langue*]. The heart of the matter is that the poetic function is not a matter of communication. Today, this function is a matter of critique; it was once of integration, but even then this integration of the community to itself occurred in another register than that of the secular language [*langage*] of communication. It is individuals who communicate with one another, and the very category of communication can come to dominate only in a society where the crisis of institutions produces isolated groups or individuals seeking to establish social ties on "horizontal" contractual grounds. The integrative function of a poetic type of discourse presupposes instead a coherent system of institutions culminating in a founding myth, to which the poem—just as dance, the plastic arts, or warfare—continuously refers as they would to a shared meaning. The question is whether this myth is an "affective language." I doubt that it is, strictly speaking, a language, for it is itself a figure-form.

The Other "Affective Language"

The other hypothesis that remains to be considered to justify connotation is that of an "affective language" that would no longer be that of a community, but rather of a poet who would be understood only by a reader endowed with the same sensibility. Union, insight, *Einfühlung*, fusion, wedding of one phantasmatic to another—these must be involved, otherwise the preference for a given poet or style could not be explained. Yet two things would remain to be shown. First, that this fusion is a fundamental poetic function, and second, that the phantasmatic is a language [*langue*]. For now I leave aside an in-depth discussion of the second point. But even if one can speak of communication from one unconscious to another (which Freud invokes with regard to the analytic relationship), we will see that this communication does not take the same forms as oral communication, but instead takes position against them.[87] As for fusion, if one were to see in it the essence of poetic pleasure, the latter's form would not differ in any way from the pleasure afforded by the amorous relationship, which provides the model for the merging of affects. But the amorous relationship remains closely dependent on each partner's phantasmatic: in this respect at least, and with all due respect, this relation has the same value as the symptom.[88] The loved one is the image (albeit worked over) of the lost object. The matrix produces these images on either side, and love is the "discovery" of their complementariness. If poetic pleasure were the product of this same revelation, it could be experienced only on the basis of a single type of object, a single style of poem, a single set of images, a single genre of "writing," that is, on the basis of a single form.[89]

Poetry itself would then need to be seen as symptomatic expression. This is precisely the critique one could level, for example, against Charles Mauron's method, in that it takes the artwork as a symptom, striving to find in its thickness the traces of an originary phantasy, a "personal myth," with the "obsessive metaphor" assumed to be the direct descendent of the unconscious matrix. I am convinced that such a phantasy operates within the artwork, just as it does in the course of life, forming its always-active core. Yet even more so than the dream, poetry is interesting not for its content, but for its work. This work does not consist in *externalizing* in images forms in which the poet's or our desire finds fulfillment once and for all. Instead, it consists in *reversing* desire's relation to the figure, in offering desire not so much images in which to fulfill itself as it loses itself, but (in this case poetic) forms through which it will be reflected as game, as unbound energy, as process of condensation and displacement, as primary process. Discourse is not poetic because it seduces us, but because it also makes us see the *operations* of seduction and of the unconscious—illusion and truth together, ends and means of desire. Our poetic pleasure can thus exceed by a lot the limits set by our phantasies, allowing us to accomplish this strange thing: to learn how to love. The pleasure of the game reverses the game of pleasure. Thus fusion becomes nonessential. The poem may indeed elicit images for the reader, but it does so only by making the latter let go of her or his phantasmatic images, and by giving her or him access to the laboratory of images, that is, the forms.[90]

Illusion Does Not Depend on the Image

Therefore the image is not the figural's preferred mode of presence in poetic discourse. To make this claim is to grant this discourse the sole function of the phantasy, the oneiric function. At its core, poetry is not constitutive of a stage on which desire finds fulfillment. The artwork is not the dream.

This opposition is to be treated here with caution; it must be placed at the right spot for its relevance to be uncovered. Desire can find fulfillment in the imagery of dreams only because the subject is asleep. If one were to present the conscious subject with the same scenes she or he encounters in dreams, her or his desire would clearly fail to find anything worthy of fulfillment.[91] The space in which the sleeper's desire is staged and fulfilled suffers the worst transgressions, whether in relation to the rules of language or of perception (reality). If these deviations are deemed acceptable in sleep, despite the fact that they bear the unmistakable mark of the primary process, this is because the preconscious's requirement level could not be set lower. The effort to uphold a division between exterior and interior is abandoned. Similarly, the pressure demanded of us in our waking lives to constitute others as total objects slackens.[92] Inversions between outside and inside, what comes before and what comes after, myself and the other, speech and silence, occur in abundance. The drama thus staged would appear incoherent, irritating to the non-sleeping subject. This irritation indicates that the very operations that allow desire to be fulfilled, and thus allow it to escape preconscious oversight during sleep, would function on the contrary to alert us to it when we are awake. For then the subject will have gone over to the side of the preconscious (or the ego), to the other side of her or his desire. The reversal in the function of deconstruction corresponds to this reversal in the subject's position. Condensations, displacements, and distortions in general now work over a material that one expects to obey the preconscious rules of discourse and action. How could they not be felt? They are reflected on preconscious material as would be, simultaneously, figures in a mirror and waves against a breakwater. A wholly other energy emerges, but one which obviously remains *unrecognizable*, since recognition belongs to the order of the preconscious, the order of discourse and of reality. This energy manifests itself negatively, in a threatening and anguishing way—in a word: disorder. But it also denounces order, announcing another "order," of another kind, by unmasking good form, the good object, and clear discourse. Hence any oneiric representation seen in a waking state could only be a "bad" representation, a representation in which our desire could not find fulfillment, which would return desire back to us as a reflection. Thus the same image that was illusionistic in the dream would become—once transcribed in reality (in the artwork)—a disillusionistic image. A critical image.

Critical images therefore exist. The opposition between the dream and the artwork does not hinge on the presence or absence of images. This is not a relevant criterion. There are poems brimming with "images" that are critical, and others that are not; "imageless" artworks that are not critical, or on the contrary that are. What is relevant is the presence of the function Mallarmé called critical, a function that depends on the *interval* identified by linguists between poetic language [*langage*] and ordinary language [*langue*]. This interval is much more than an interval: in it the order of discourse remains open to its other, namely, the order of the unconscious process, which appears in the first order as figure. The presence of figures (from all the levels) in discourse is not only deconstruction of discourse; it is also the critique of discourse as censorship, as repression of desire. But it must also be the *unfulfillment* of the phantasmatics from which these figures originate, at the risk of being no more than trivial alienated-alienating expression. This was only a preliminary sketch of this reversal, to which I will return.

Poetics Depends on Deconstruction

To take a detour, consider visual space, and put condensation to work there. Condensation can operate by gathering together fragments sampled on various objects. This leads to the constitution of the chimera, with each of these fragments remaining recognizable in its own right: head of a lion, serpent's tail, etc. The figure-image it engenders will make it impossible to find a counterpart for it in reality—it deconstructs the "good object." Yet it can fail to undermine good form, and the space in which the chimera is represented can still be a classical theatrical space. Condensation can attack the other rows of the figure: if it deconstructs the figure-form, the good order expected in the arrangement of the staged objects is what is disconcerted—such is the case, I believe, for double exposures in photography and cinema.[93] Even representational (Euclidian) space itself can suffer harm, through curvatures and anamorphoses. In any case, the presence of the figural distinguishes itself negatively, through disorder. However, no single type of disorder ranks higher than the others. One cannot claim that the deconstruction of a space of figurative representation is any less provocative than that of abstract "good forms." The artwork's critical power depends much more on the nature of the interval upon which it draws than on the levels (here of figures) upon which it impresses the effects of this interval.

The same goes for figural discourse, where the image does not enjoy any privileged position. Indeed, in the table based on Widdowson's essay, the image appears only once. The operations of the primary process in the order of language [*langage*] produce many other figures, most of which are forms that have no name either in rhetoric or stylistics. Just as in visual space, desire can attack all levels of language. What matters for poetry is deconstruction: the presence of a power other than the rule of language [*langue*] and communication in discourse. There is no figure, image, or even form that holds in itself the poetic power to make the other scene—the unconscious—present. When one group, one network of figures (metaphors, etc.) holds the monopoly over representation to the exclusion of others, then the poetic gives way to the clinical. This formal system is a symptomatic expression of the phantasmatic matrix. From a formal point of view, the outcome is comparable to that which awaits all production of literary figures, that is, its degradation into script, its recuperation by the secondary process, its event-ness suppressed, the healing of the wound it inflicted upon words, its connotation, its repression. This is why I believe it formally accurate to speak of script not only when a "style," or a scream, becomes connoted language, but also in the opposite case when the phantasmatic's initial rigidity and indigence afford the writer only a few, and always the same, deconstructions. Just as we saw with Klee, where the phantasy that was first grafted on sexual difference held back drawing in its monotonous grip, until the reversal of the ends of desire onto its means was achieved.

It is to deconstruction, the interval, and critique that the figure owes its poetic dimension. Surrealism had understood this, although it hesitated to spread transgression beyond row 2.31 in the above table, ensuring that no harm is done to language [*langue*], only deviations of speech, and, at least for Breton, exclusively semantic deviations. This is the limit imposed by the rule of the metaphor's arbitrariness. Nevertheless, in Paul Éluard's early work one finds:

> Comment ma vie disait-elle
> Une autre ai-je été moi-même
> Qui dans la vie qui en moi-même
> Et moi les autres.
>
> [How my life, she said
> An other was I myself
> Who in life who within me
> And me the others.][94]

where deviations abound. The rhythm strays from that of French prose (the first two verses have the same meter) (1.1); there is an accumulation of similar phonic elements (particularly bilabials) (2.1); and, above all, there occurs a deviation that does not even appear in the chart (so deep it is! 1.224?) and that affects the very constitution of the core sentence "une autre ai-je été moi-même" [An other (feminine) was I myself]. The latter combines two sentences in one:

subject	*predicate*
je [I]	*ai été une autre* [was an other (feminine)]
je [I]	*ai été moi-même* [was myself]

One of the two sentences (at the reader's discretion) must forgo the subject nominal group and the predicate's verbal nominal group. English-language poetry will take this very far.[95]

And where to place the stanza below, the sixth in Antonio Porta's *Ouvrir*?

> De là, serre la poignée, vers,
> il n'y a pas, certitude, ni issue, sur la paroi,
> l'oreille, puis ouvrir, une réponse, ne s'ouvre pas,
> incertaine, les clefs entre les doigts, le ventre ouvert, . . .
>
> [Away, squeezes the handle, towards,
> there isn't, either certainty, or escape, on the wall,
> the ear, then to open, an uncertainty, it doesn't open,
> reply, keys in hand, stomach open, . . .][96]

This stanza overflows with acts of syntactic violence. But once again, there is no guarantee that their disillusionistic effect is greater than that of a surrealist comparison just because it is the result of a working-over that touches deeper strata of the generation of discourse.

"We found ourselves at the center of a dazzling precariousness, at the edge of schizophrenia, in an unstable balance between the rational and the irrational, and we made to languish the vocabulary, syntax, verse, and structure of those poems we had considered 'modern' just the day before. . . . For us, poetry was a match for the deterioration of significations and the physiognomic instability of the verbal world in which we were immersed."[97]

"The writer understands reality and transforms it by challenging it through linguistic means that shake it in its very communicative roots, or at the level of its superstructural manifestation."[98]

By now, my patient reader will no doubt have caught a glimpse of where we are headed. This last word, by Umberto Eco, will provide a further hint: "Do we really believe that the global communication system, in an advanced industrial society, still qualifies as a superstructure?"[99] The present text will not, however, reach this region itself—that of ideological critique.

Fiscourse Digure: The Utopia behind the Scenes of the Phantasy

Translated by Mary Lydon

1.

And that figure I named matrix, is it coherent? Can we say it is *one:* unified and unifying? What kind of unit does it have? The unity of a language? If so, is its unity that of a language-system [*langue*] or that of a discourse? What I want to show is this: that the matrix is not a language, not a linguistic structure [*une structure de langue*], not a tree of discourses. Of all the figural orders it is the most remote from communicability, the most withdrawn. It harbors the incommunicable. It breeds forms and images and it is *about* those forms and images that discourse eventually starts to speak. Discourse itself is not always able to recognize them. Is the matrix *even* a figure then? It is not a figure that is recognizable in itself. Neither can we establish a regulative order that would give it a stable form. The phantasy, as a figure, inscribes itself neither as an ordinary pattern, an identifiable shadow cast on the imaginary screen, nor as an explicit stage direction to be followed on the imaginary scene.

When the various components of the phantasy are disentangled, we find that:

1. Even the "word-presentations" (the signifiers of the language, the "verbalizations") it can give rise to run counter to the rules of syntax, as for example in "une autre ai-je été moi-même" ("an other [feminine] was I myself {Paul Éluard}) and of semantics, as in "plus jamais la barre d'appui ne sera un indicateur de chemin de fer" ("never more will the hand-rail be a railroad direction-board" {Benjamin Péret}).

2. The "thing-presentations" (phantasmatic images) it nurtures hardly represent "things" in the sense of objects recognizably pertaining to the external world. The images the matrix generates are both sharply defined and blurred at the same time. The effect is as if multiple scenes, having certain segments or areas, some plastic element only, in common, were superimposed on the same film, but at the right exposure.[1]

3. The figure-form itself is not unified. The phantasy contains several forms that are simultaneously active.

4. The affects too are a prey to polysemia. The relation between the drives involved in the phantasy and the pleasure principle is not univocal.

5. Indeed the libido itself, insofar as we can speak of it apart from its representatives and the affects to which it lends support, proceeds, within the same phantasy, from several different sources (genital and anal, for example) at once. The phantasy has multiple drives.[2]

As we pursue the analysis we come up against a density, an opacity: the locus, I will assume, of the figural that deconstructs not only discourse but the figure, inasmuch as the figure is a recognizable image or a regular form. And underneath the figural: difference. Not just the trace, not just presence-absence, period, indifferently discourse or figure, but the primary process, the principle of disorder, the incitement to *jouissance*.[3] Not some kind of interval separating two terms that belong to the same order, but an utter disruption of the equilibrium between order and non-order. As we sound these depths of the *pseudarchè* we may perhaps get a handle on the truth of difference, whose presence was already felt in the tangible order, the order of the visual field, but where it is simply a metaphor. Its proper field, the environment it requires in order to try to establish itself, is the pseudarchaic.

2. Tabulating the Phantasy

Freud studies the phantasy "A Child Is Being Beaten" on the basis of an "exhaustive" study of six cases—four women and two men.[4] Three of the cases come under obsessional neurosis, either severe or mild, one comes under hysteria, the fifth under psychasthenia, and nothing is said about the sixth.[5] Up to the last part of the sixth and final part of his study, Freud confines himself to female cases. We will do the same. The phantasy "A Child Is Being Beaten" is reported by patients with astonishing frequency. "At the climax of the imaginary situation there is almost invariably an onanistic gratification, that is to say a gratification in the genitals."[6] A powerful sense of shame inhibits the avowal of the phantasy, which is self-induced to begin with and subsequently undergone in a compulsive fashion. It occurs for the first time when the child starts going to school. Freud writes:

> Who was the child that was being beaten? The one who was himself producing the phantasy or another? Was it always the same child or as often as not a different one? Who was it who was beating the child? A grown-up person? And if so, who? Or did the child imagine that he himself was beating another one? Nothing could be ascertained that threw any light upon all these questions—only the one timid reply: "I know nothing more about it: a child is being beaten."[7]

The analysis will reveal that this vapid formula emerges out of three strata of meanings which it condenses and conceals. Freud puts forward a verbalization for each phase (*Phase*). The earliest phase (I) is rendered as "The father is beating the child." The formula for the second phase (II) is "I am being beaten by my father." The statement the patient herself makes: "A child is being beaten," constitutes the last stage (III) of the phantasy. Let us go back over our questions:

Who is doing the beating? In I, an unidentified adult in whom it is easy to recognize the patient's father. In II, her father. In III, an adult substitute for the father (teacher, etc.). There is, therefore, a feature that remains constant: the sex of the agent in the scene.

Who is being beaten? In I, the patient's brothers and sisters, indiscriminately. In II, the patient herself, and in III, an indeterminate number of children, almost always male. Sex and number both vary.

What is the place of the author of the phantasy? In II, evidently on the scene where the patient is receiving the blows. In I, the place is not specified. Freud suggests it is that of the onlooker. In III, the patient states: "Ich schaue wahrscheinlich zu" [I am probably looking on], thus introducing a variation in regard to the imaginary screen.[8]

Let us add the following questions, the answers to which already suppose a *construction:*

What kind of affect (Bedeutung) *is associated with the phantasy?*[9] In Phase I, the satisfaction of jealousy: the father loves me alone. It is the ego's drives (the child's "egoistic interests") therefore, says Freud, rather than sexuality that is at issue. There is probably no sexual excitement. II and III, by contrast, are accompanied by acute sexual arousal.

What is the clinical content of the phantasy? Freud temporizes as far as Phase I is concerned: "As is well known, all the signs (*alle die Kennzeichen*) upon which we are accustomed to base our distinctions tend to melt (*pflegen zu verschwimmen*) as we come nearer to the source. So perhaps we may say in words like those of the promise given by the three Witches to Banquo: 'Not clearly sexual, not in itself sadistic, but yet the stuff from which both will later come.'"[10]

This diagnosis, for all its prudence, will not be retained. In the same text, at the beginning of part VI, Freud unhesitatingly combines Phases I and III, both of which he claims are sadistic, as opposed to the masochistic second phase.[11] But most importantly, six years later, in 1925, Freud harks back to that phase of the beating phantasy in the light of the concept of penis-envy which he had just established. He writes:

> Even after penis-envy has abandoned its true object, it continues to exist: by an easy displacement it persists in the character-trait of *jealousy*. . . . While I was still unaware of this source of jealousy and was considering the phantasy "A Child Is Being Beaten" (1919), which occurs so commonly in girls, I constructed a first phase for it in which its meaning (*die Bedeutung*) was that another child, a rival of whom the subject was jealous, was to be beaten. This phantasy seems to be a relic (*Relikt*) of the phallic period in girls. The peculiar rigidity which struck me so much in the monotonous formula "a child is being beaten" can probably be interpreted in a special way. The child which is being beaten (or caressed) (*geschlagen-geliebkost*) may at bottom be nothing more nor less than the clitoris itself, so that at its very lowest level the statement will contain a confession of masturbation, which has remained attached to the content of the formula from its beginning in the phallic phase up to the present time.[12]

Thus we are obliged to revise the meaning as well as the content of Phase I. Instead of being a mere matter of "egoistic interests," its meaning was already libidinal: bound up with intense, phallic, sexual excitement. Its clinical content is neither neutral nor originary, like some as yet undifferentiated material or a witch's conundrum. Its origin goes deeper. Phase I is itself a product built on top of other strata, a residue (*ein Niederschlag*), a scar (*eine Narbe*) left by something else.[13] By what other wound? In 1919, Freud is inclined to think that it is a matter of incestuous desire for the father, which Phantasy I stages and disguises: the scar left by the Oedipus complex. But in 1925, at the moment when he is developing the notion of the difference between the sexes, the feminine Oedipus complex appears to him to be, in its turn, "a secondary formation."[14] The function of castration in the genesis of the complex in girls is the inverse of its function in boys: "Whereas in boys the Oedipus complex succumbs (*zugrunde geht*) to the castration complex, in girls it is made possible and led up to by the castration complex."[15] The wound results, not from the impossibility of being loved by the father, but from the absence of a penis. The narcissistic scarring consists in substituting the desire for a child for penis-envy and it is at this point that the father is taken as love-object. Far from being originary, Phantasy I is grafted onto a deeply buried drama. Its motivating jealousy does not even result from the father's "disavowal" (required by the Oedipal organization) but rather from the established fact of castration. Phantasy I bears the mark of a lack that is not the lack of an object, but of a signifier. It is therefore understandable that it imposes the role of the beating's victim not on the mother, as might be expected if one were to hold to the hypothesis that the Oedipal drama is the determining cause, but rather on children of the same age and of both sexes, whom jealousy alone, inspired by castration, has reason to expose to the father's blows. As to the clitoral masturbation that accompanies or precedes the phantasy, it is possible to see in it the symptom of denial of castration through identification with the male sex, a symptom that will reappear in Phase III, as we will see, if it is true that the boys being beaten are substitutes for the phantasizing girl, as Freud believes them to be.

Now we can put the two-fold question ("What is [a] the meaning, and [b] the drive-content of the phantasy") once again. The meaning, for all three phases, is *jouissance*. As to the drives that impel the phantasy, for Phase I, they are sadistic and for Phase II masochistic. For Phase III, "only the form (*die Form*) of this phantasy is sadistic; the satisfaction that is derived from it is masochistic."[16] Hence *jouissance* remains constant while there is variation in the drives that produce it. If one were to draw up a table of the three phases, pinpointing their distinctive features, here is what one would get (see opposite page).

This table has no epistemological value, but it allows us to identify certain constants that appear to dictate the fate of the drives and their representatives bound up in the phantasm.[17] The agent on the scene is always an adult male; the phantasy is always accompanied by *jouissance*; it always represents a beating. These constants occupy different positions and perform different functions. *Jouissance* determines the function of the phantasy as far as the pleasure principle is concerned, but its recurrence throughout all the phases does not exclude the possibility of its being accompanied by different affects. When, in the course of the transition from I to II, the scene acquires a masochistic "content," one can justifiably assume that a "reversal of content" joins forces with the turning round upon the subject and the reversal into its opposite that are characteristic of the drive.[18] The love that was felt for the father becomes glazed over with hate, while some of the repressed affect is discharged in the form of anxiety. Consequently the affect-content of phantasies II and III is probably much more ambivalent than that of phantasy I.[19]

As far as the adult male who does the beating all through the "story" of the phantasy is concerned, the apparent invariability of the figure he cuts should not obscure the fact that he is Protean enough to represent other familiar figures besides the patient's father. The fixation is not based on an individual, the real father, but on a kind of imaginary archetype who can be readily identified by the rod [*verge*] he has and the one with which he beats the child. This doubling of the phantasized penis is adequate proof that the imaginary roles are anchored, not in the father's *person,* but in the symbolic function of the phallus.[20]

Only "beating" seems to be irrefutably invariable. Nonetheless, what it is in "beating" that does not vary remains to be determined. If indeed there are invariables in the recurrence of the beating phantasy we must be suspicious

TRAITS					
	Kind of agent	Kind of victim	Place of subject	Drive "content"	"Meaning" in terms of pleasure
PHASES					
I	adult, father	child, masculine or feminine	onlooker	sadistic	genital arousal
II	father	subject	victim	masochistic	genital arousal
III	adult	male children	onlooker	masochistic with overlay of sadism	genital arousal

of their absence from the order of representations and affects (where one would expect to find them) and concentrate, therefore, on ferreting them out, beyond these lures, in a configuration.

3. The Fate of the Drive

Let us briefly outline the fate of the drives involved in this phantasy (without pretending to discuss them exhaustively).[21]

Freud's first diagnosis is as follows: in Phase I there is a movement of love toward the father, accompanied by a strong component of sadism. Phase II introduces a masochistic reversal and in III the subject vanishes from the scene without a trace. After 1925 this diagnosis is revised so that Phase I becomes secondarily, rather than primarily, incestuous. In the beginning is penis-envy, and the incestuous impulse is merely the scar-tissue with which the wound is eventually covered over.

What we have to determine is the nature of the drive-operations that the phantasmatic unit contains within its boundaries. These operations are two-fold. The first transforms I into II, the second II into III. The first is a regression, the second a repression. Freud insists on the violence of the first operation, associating it with the intensity of Phantasy I and its accompanying guilt. "The phantasy of the period of incestuous love had said: 'He (my father) loves only me, and not the other child, for he is beating it,'" Freud writes. "The sense of guilt can discover no punishment more severe than the reversal of this triumph: 'No, he does not love you, for he is beating you.'" Why does this reversal take place? So that the daughter can be punished for having her desire fulfilled? And why should she be punished? Because the dissolution of the Oedipus complex is at stake, says Freud: "These love-affairs are bound to come to grief sooner or later, though we cannot say on what particular stumbling block."[22]

But does a real dissolution take place here? Remember that we are dealing with obsessional personalities; that we are considering the genesis of a perversion. Perverts, no less than neurotics or so-called normal subjects, have passed through the Oedipus complex.[23] But what part does the passage play in this instance? The violence of the regression from I to II proceeds from the violence of the libidinal formation in I. But what is the intensity of the incestuous impulse a sign of, in this first phase? Of the repercussions of castration for the subject. Let us look then at the first formation: It is not simple, as far as the object of the drives is concerned. Certainly there is acceptance of castration in the feminine love-impulse, but there is also a phallic protest which leads to an identification with the father. (I hate the other child—the father hates the other child.) This same complexity is to be found in the sources of the phantasy, which are genital (clitoral masturbation) but also anal-sadistic. It is this latter element that provides the phantasy with its constant: beating.

Thus the masochistic regression (from I to II) indeed fulfills a repressive function with regard to incest, but it also acts to preserve the partial drive, at once castigating the demand for love and turning it into its opposite: a procedure that allows the eroticization of the anal-sadistic zone to be maintained.[24] Clearly the "reversal (*Umkehrung*) of [the] triumph [of incest]" is at the same time a reversal into the opposite (*Verkehrung ins Gegenteil*) of the very element that had eluded the love-impulse—sadism—into its opposite. The overdetermination of this inversion is obvious, as is the fact that from the first phase on, two issues are at stake: the sadistic component and the Oedipus complex. The former is either a given or (as Freud thinks by 1925) the residue of an initial rejection of the trauma of castration. In any case it has its part to play in the action of the complex. And if the latter is destined not to be "overcome" in obsessional neurosis or perversion, it is because the normal outcome has been barred from the start by the rejection of castration. To repeat: Phase I not only bears witness to a demand addressed to the father (to have the phallus), it also attests to an identification with him (to be the phallus). The regression would thus derive its significance not from the strength of the complex, but from its weakness.

There is not much to be said about the repression at work between II and III. It "covers up" the "being beaten by the father" of the second phase. It changes the girl into a boy, the singular into the plural, the first person into the third, and it blocks out the agent of the beating. These are operations that have to do with the linguistic or imaginary representatives of the drive, but the drive itself no longer shifts, as in the regression from I to II, either by changing zones (according to the 1919 hypothesis), or by reversal, turning back on the same zone (the hypothesis of 1925).[25] The fate of the drive is fixed. Repression will no doubt keep the ideational representatives at a distance from the preconscious, but "The vanished affect is transformed without any diminution, into dread (*in der Verwandlung zur*) of the community, pangs of conscience, or self-reproaches. . . ."[26] It will become the non-ideational (i.e., non-representing) representative of Phase II in obsessional neurosis.[27]

One final remark on the fate of the drives: the three states of the libido do not succeed each other in linear fashion. Jacques Nassif, discussing the temporality of the phantasmatic configuration, pertinently cites the passage from "Instincts and Their Vicissitudes" (1915) where Freud tries to settle the question of libidinal development in a few words.[28] Here is the text:

> With regard to both these instincts just examined as examples, it must be said that transformation of them by a reversal from active to passive and by a turning round upon the subject never in fact concerns the whole amount of impelling force pertaining to the instinct. To some extent its earlier active direction always persists side by side with the later passive direction, even when the transformation is very extensive. The only correct description of the scopophilic instinct would be that all phases of its development, the auto-erotic, preliminary phase as well as its final active or passive form, co-exist alongside one another; and the truth of this statement becomes manifest if we base our opinion, not upon the actions which are prompted by the instinct, but upon the mechanism of its satisfaction. Perhaps yet another way of conceiving and representing the matter may be justified. We may split up the life of each instinct into a series of "thrusts," distinct from one another in the time of their occurrence but each homogeneous within its own period, whose relation to one another is comparable to that of successive eruptions of lava. We can then perhaps picture to ourselves that the earliest and most primitive instinct-eruption persists in an unchanged form and undergoes no development at all. The next "thrust" would then from the outset have

> undergone a change of form, being turned, for instance, from active to passive, and it would then, with this new characteristic, be superimposed upon the earlier layer, and so on. So that, if we take a survey of the instinctual tendency from its beginning up to any given stopping-point, the succession of "thrusts" which we have described would present the picture of a definite development of the instinct.
>
> The fact that, at that later period of development, the instinct in its primary form may be observed side by side with its (passive) opposite deserves to be distinguished by the highly appropriate name introduced by Bleuler: *ambivalence.*[29]

If indeed there is any "development" it occurs by virtue of an effect that is properly speaking kinetic, since it induces the "eye" to combine the changes it observes in a single continuous sweeping movement. In fact the drive proceeds by discontinuous bursts or "thrusts" but each succeeding thrust does not wipe out its predecessor. This text of Freud's should be compared with *Civilisation and Its Discontents,* where Freud imagines the three Romes (ancient, Christian, and modern) all separately and simultaneously occupying the seven hills.[30] The space occupied by the formations of desire is not merely topological. What makes it impossible to represent is that it stands for the *atemporality* or *omnitemporality* of the primary process, in space. The primary process knows no such thing as negation. Whatever the drives produce lasts forever; an investment made by the unconscious is never liquidated. The formation may be submerged by a new libidinal surge, the investment overcompensated for by a counter-investment, but there is no going back to the blank page. Erasure is out of the question. Localizations accumulate, one on top of another.[31]

That is what Freud says yet again when he maintains that the unconscious knows only one tense and one mood: the assertorial present. All the formations of the unconscious are contemporaneous, posited simultaneously with the same intensity, invested with the same charge. The result is that in the space of the unconscious locations are not *partes extra partes.* If an area is invested, it is not necessary for it to be cleared in order to be reinvested. The interval that the order of perception requires so that the things in the external world can be distinguished from one another, to keep them from blending into one another, in a word, depth of field, negation as phenomenological transcendence, is abandoned here. In that sense, the erotic body (which is not the same as the body experienced erotically, but rather the surface where the localizations of desire are inscribed) is the opposite of a world, at least as far as the child, the hysteric, or the pervert is concerned. It is a jigsaw puzzle of areas where the charge-discharge of *jouissance* discovers its favorite sites, but a puzzle that no one or nothing holds in his/its gaze so as to give it the unity of a picture: a puzzle in which each zone can signify a multiplicity of pleasures simultaneously. By the same token, regression is not the abandonment of a genital investment in favor of a zone that had been previously invested and abandoned in the interim, but the eroticization of a non-genital region, which as such, represents an obstacle to the unification of the drives under the dominion of sexuality that has never been surmounted.

Neither this *atemporality* of the phantasmatic matrix nor the *discontinuity* of the drive's impulsions should warrant taking the matrix for a *structure.* What the matrix and the structure have in common is that both are invisible and synchronic. But these two characteristics derive in their turn from qualities that are diametrically opposed to each other. A structure's invisibility is that of a system, which is a virtual but intelligible entity. Its intelligibility manifests itself precisely in the observing of formal rules, the rules of logic that define the properties of a system in general, internal rules governing transformation. One might say that these rules always serve to establish an operational function: to fix products of intervals [*produits d'écarts*] and intervals of production [*écarts de production*] once and for all, by consensus.[32] Negativeness has an essential function here. The unconscious, on the other hand, does not recognize negation; it does not know what contradiction is. The matrix does not consist in a series of fixed oppositions, and whatever "propositions" might be attributed to it that would combine the aim (to beat), the source (the anal zone) and the object (the father) of the drive in one sentence, are themselves condensed into a formula-product—"A child is being beaten"—whose apparent coherence conceals the fact that the life of the psyche contains a multitude of "sentences" that are mutually exclusive, that cannot possibly coexist. Of course it is only word-presentations that are in question here, and we will study them more closely later on, but the same holds true for the impulsions of the drive they represent. The latter do not form a system but a block. By block I mean that in contradistinction to the propositions of a system, the impulsions occupy an identical position in (libidinal) space simultaneously. The intervals of production are never observed in the case "A Child Is Being Beaten." The drive to "be the father" and the drive to "have the father" are presented together. The investment is at once phallo-genital and anal-sadistic. The products of intervals, the terms, display the same characteristic. By a series of displacements that are highly irregular, the singular becomes plural, the feminine masculine, the subject becomes object, the determinate indeterminate and here becomes elsewhere.

If therefore the matrix is invisible, it is not because it belongs to the realm of the intelligible. It is because it occupies a space that remains on the far side of the intelligible, that is diametrically opposed to the rule of *opposition* and completely under the control of *difference.* We will discuss just how this is the case in part 6. But we can already grasp that this property of unconscious space (a property it shares with the libidinal body)—its capacity to contain several places in one place, to form a block out of what cannot possibly coexist—is the secret of the figural, which transgresses the intervals that constitute discourse and the distances that constitute representation. The word-presentations and the thing-presentations spring from the matrix and inherit their deviancy from it.

4. The Fate of Word-Presentations

The phantasy "A Child Is Being Beaten" is a matrix figure. It produces forms and images as well as words. This material constitutes the *drive-presentations* bound up in the phantasy. (Freud makes a distinction between ideational-representatives and affects, which also point to the repressed drive.)[33] The representative is called ideational in contrast to the affect when, in order to fulfill its proper function of representing absence (the drive "itself") it has recourse to the representation of objects. The affect also represents the drive within the psyche, but without representation. The ideational representative

(*Vorstellungsrepräsentanz*) is therefore stretched between two poles—that of the drive invested in it and that of the object by means of which the drive represents its fulfillment. The first is a relation of "expression," the second of "designation." Speaking metaphorically, the drive is the "author" of the text and of the stage-production, the representative is the actor and the object is the play's referent (what it is about). As in the theatre, the relation of representative to object is not simply verbal, it is also visual. What the actors (the representatives) talk about is represented both in figures (makeup, costumes, décor, lighting, sound, scenography) and in words (text). Freud remains true, then, to the theatrical metaphor when he makes the distinction elsewhere between word-presentations and thing-presentations of the object.[34]

It is as well to respect this distinction in the analysis of the phantasy, since it appears that the fate (or working-over) that each of these two categories of representatives (those that are properly speaking imaginary and those that are verbalizations) undergoes is not analogous. It is interesting to compare them so as to establish their relationship to each other in addition to their mutual relationship to the fate of the drives themselves. Beginning with the study of the propositions of the phantasy, we seek to pinpoint the construction of an *ideological speech* [*parole*] by establishing the operations that its *discursive position* implies, and which divert it from the desire which is its origin.

Freud gives, as we have said, a verbal formula for each phase:

I. The father is beating the child (whom I hate).
II. I am being beaten by my father.
III. A child is being beaten.[35]

We must begin by recalling that these three verbalizations do not all have the same status. The third is pronounced and even spontaneously repeated by the subject. The first is Freud's summary of the meaning of the phantasy of Phase I according to the subject's own account. The second is an analytic construction. It is not provided by the patient, either directly or indirectly. The three positions correspond to three variations with respect to the preconscious. Passage into the preconscious is linked to verbalization. In form III the phantasy has crossed the unconscious/preconscious barrier. In form II the phantasy is out of reach of any verbalization: there is no word-presentation available. The analyst will have to "construct" this phase in its entirety.[36] Form I is less distant from the preconscious. It can dispatch word-presentations to it to some extent. Freud breaks this "delegation" down into several statements, only the last of which is uttered.[37]

0.1 The father loves only me (fem.)
0.2 I hate the other child (fem. or masc.)
0.3 The father hates the other child (fem. or masc.)
0.4 The father beats the other child (fem. or masc.)
I.1 *The father is beating the child*

There are three observations to be made concerning this verbal formula I:

1. Phantasy I harbors a weighty heritage. Its point of departure is a destination, as we have already indicated.

2. In Freud's perspective at that time (1919) the legacy descends directly from the Oedipus complex. We know that another series of formulae running from 0.1 to 0.n (representing verbally the operations related to castration and penis-envy) need to be added. The heritage is even weightier than it appears to be here. Nonetheless, it bears the mark of castration. For example, the transformation that the nominal syntagm undergoes between 0.2 and 0.3 supposes an identification: "I (the girl) = the father," an identification that is itself the residual trace of the denial of castration. In contrast, the formation 0.1 supposes castration (femininity) to be acknowledged and scarred over in the demand for love addressed to the father. The existence side by side of two relationships to the signifier (to be and to have) is certainly characteristic of the cases being considered. More generally, it is this coexistence of mutually exclusive situations that will allow the subject to "enter into" the phantasy, both as "father" (being the phallus) and as "the child being beaten" (having the phallus).[38]

3. The transformation of 0.4 into I is an extension, to use the linguistic term. Its importance is not inconsiderable. By hiding the identity of that *other* child (the subject's brother or sister), it definitively cuts off the relationship between the subject of the utterance [*énonciation*] and the terms of the proposition or statement [*énoncé*]. The subject remains negatively represented in *the other child*, since it is only from *me* that the latter can be

different. The suppression of the term *other* (in form I.1) hides the presence of the subject.

In phase II, verbalized by the analyst alone, let us note that Freud is again induced to dissociate two intertwined formulations:

2.1 The father is beating me (fem.)
2.2 I am being beaten by the father[39]

But since this phase remains completely unconscious, the transformations that occur in it have nothing to do with word-presentations. What the modification of 1 into 2.1 and 2.1 into 2.2 alters profoundly is the imaginary stage-setting [*mise en scène*] itself. I will speak about this in regard to thing-presentations.

Phase III is verbalized as "A child is being beaten." But (a) the indefinite article here is an indeterminate signifying "any given number," (b) the victims are boys, and (c) the agents are adult males in the paternal position (teachers). It is therefore legitimate to introduce an intermediary formulation which will make it easier to distinguish between several types of operation:

3.1 Children (masc.) are being beaten by an adult (masc.)
3.2 A child is being beaten

The complete table (excluding the statements supposedly corresponding to castration 0.1 etc.) of the verbalized stages of the phantasy is therefore as follows:

	0.1	The father	loves	me alone (fem.)
	0.2	I	hate	the other child (fem./masc.)
	0.3	The father	hates	the other child (fem./masc.)
	0.4	The father	is beating	the other child (fem./masc.)
I	1	*The father*	*is beating*	*the child* (fem./masc.)
II	2.1	The father	is beating	me (fem.)
	2.2	I (fem.)	am being beaten	by the father
III	3.1	Children (masc.)	are being beaten	by an adult (masc.)
	3.2	*A child* (masc.)	*is being beaten.*	

If we stick to the actual verbalizations (i.e., to what passes into the preconscious) that are italicized in the table, the trajectory from 1 to 3.2 implies (a) a transformation from the active to the passive voice; (b) a modification in the gender of *child* (neuter = masculine); (c) a modification in the determinative of *child* (the = a); (d) the disappearance of the extension of the predicate (whose presence would normally be anticipated after a final transformation) from the last sentence.

The first of these operations, (a), appears to be linguistically correct. So is the fourth, (d), which adds ellipsis to the transformation into the passive voice.[40] The two others, (b) and (c), are not transformations but equations that have to do with syntagmatic grammar (the rules governing rewriting). In Freudian terms,[41] these equations signify the substitution for one representational element, *that child,* boy or girl, whom the father is beating, of another element that on the one hand is not too different, so that the substitution is tolerable, but which is on the other hand sufficiently different to provide a cover for the subject of the utterance [*énonciation*] within the statement [*énoncé*]. Hence girl → boy. The father's disappearance (first in 3.1, where he is disguised, by extension, as a teacher, etc.) serves the same purpose, but is a more drastic operation. The absence of an extension of the predicate in 3.2 cannot fail to attract attention. What are we to make of this void? But caution is recommended. This apparently wide-open gap is perhaps more of a decoy designed to trap us than a lowering of the censor's guard.

I rather admire the fact that Freud, probing operation (a)—the only one that is linguistically beyond reproach—discerns in it the most devastating operation. Transformation into the passive voice is correct if it makes no alteration in the meaning, says the linguist: "X is beating a child → a child is being beaten by X." But why the switch to the passive? the analyst wonders. Might it not represent, syntactically, masochistic regression? In fact, it is on the basis of the passive form (and its accompanying ambivalent affect) that Freud must have been led to construct a masochistic second phase, at the time the case-studies took place. Here we have the exact analogue of an instance raised by the rebus. In that instance a part of the text passed into the figure-form (*un nez ceint d'abeilles* [= *un essaim d'abeilles*]) and ceased forthwith to be immediately obvious to the gaze, having been transformed into an outline [*tracé révélateur*]. In the present instance it is a part of the libidinal configuration that passes into the syntactic figure-form of the statement (the passive voice) and thus passes *out* of the field of designation. Desire is working to perfection here. It does not attract attention; it follows the rules. Nonetheless, within this law-abiding transformation that is completely contained by the system of *oppositions*, the urge toward an anal-sadistic regression with the objective of masochistic *jouissance* is "represented," that is to say a movement in the direction of the greatest possible *difference* is "represented." But this representation is inaudible; this undertone remains unheard. The phase in which masochism appears (II) achieves no direct verbal expression. This is characteristic of *regression*, which, according to Freud, is the specific operation that heralds masochism (between 1 and 2.1). There are no identifiable traces left on the word-presentations. *They* are talking about something else. At a pinch, the slide into the passive at the formal level of the discourse indicates the reversal into the opposite[42] which is also the "reversal of [the] triumph" that the love-impulse had won in Phase I.[43]

But the passive form makes no impression on the discursive order. It performs no perceptible displacement or condensation on it. It has no figural value. Only the affect might arouse suspicion in this instance. It is in fact the acute genital arousal of Phase III, as well as the anxiety that accompanies it, that leads Freud to suspect the paradox: to discover in the beaten boys the substitutes for the phantasizing girl and to "construct" a masochistic phase. The silence of regression consists in the fact that the work of displacement no longer figures in the word-presentations. Figurality operates within the space proper to itself here, without pushing any recognizable offshoots into the space of discourse. Its own space is the surface of the erotic body insofar as it is a field of *jouissance.* Regression marks out a figure on it, displacing the difference between maximum charge and discharge (i.e., *jouissance*) from the genital to the anal zone. This displacement has no metaphor with which to express itself in words. It remains *this side* of rhetoric itself. Nonetheless, the reversal that occurs in the libidinal order is not totally silent. It has a very weak and uncertain representative on the surface of the discourse in the grammatical vacillation by which *the father beating the child* is transformed into *a child is being beaten.* In the "time" it takes for the negligible oscillation to occur, the phantasizing subject will have switched places on the scene and *jouissance* will have changed its preferred site on the body.

5. The Fate of Thing-Presentations

The fate of thing-presentations (images) is quite different. Some of them are unconscious figures: figure-forms without a doubt, image-figures perhaps. Consequently presentations that are expressed in images are active on the near side as well as on the far side of the barrier formed by censorship between the unconscious and the preconscious, and a fortiori, of the barrier between conscious and unconscious. In other words, even when meaning (conveyed by words) becomes impossible, representation by things (designation) remains. But then how do the displacements the libido undergoes make themselves felt in the imaginary order, and how do they tie in with the effects of language?

Desire fulfills itself imaginally (that is to say phantasmatically). The desire to be the phallus (the denial of castration) and the desire to have it (the incestuous desire of the father's desire) are the producers (in the theatrical sense) of phantasy I. The first allows the subject to come on the scene in the role of the father, the second leads up to the subject's entrance in the role of the child being beaten (II). Both are fixated on the action of *beating.* But what counts is that the phantasizing subject is not himself represented. He is not on stage and he loses himself among the spectators. He is therefore at once behind the scenes, prompting his father, and in the audience clapping. When the female patient succeeds in verbalizing this phase, she casts herself in the role of spectator.

Phantasy II brooks no verbalization. But as far as representation goes, it implies a major revision of the stage setting [*mise en scène*]. The subject is on stage, where he is receiving blows. The third party has disappeared. The identification with the father is masked by the ambivalent desire to *have* the phallus and to be punished for it. We know what is meant by an *unconscious* imaginal presentation: *the subject does not see himself seeing*; whereas in I and III he sees himself looking on at the scene. Now as far as representation is concerned, if one doesn't see oneself seeing, one doesn't see. There one is, on who knows what scene. In II, where the subject is effectively the victim, one may wonder where the scene takes place, since there is no longer anyone to see it. Nonetheless, the subject "knows his way around" in it, albeit in such a way as to get lost. The representation is an oneiric one. It is only on the analyst's couch that the subject will be able to recognize, post-construction as it were, that he occupied a place in the action. In I and III he sees himself outside the drama.[44] That is because at this point a process of specular doubling is taking place. The subject (on the couch) sees the subject (the child) seeing a child (a brother or sister in I, a boy and the ego in III) being beaten. This doubling corresponds to the phases that can be verbalized. The distance adopted vis-à-vis the scene allows meaning to function. But when I am on stage I can't speak *about* what is happening on it.[45]

The subject's presence in the dramatic action goes hand in hand with his loss of the power to produce meaning verbally. Thus the hypothesis regarding the function of representation is confirmed: what presents itself without a double is that which cannot signify itself. The implication of this is also confirmed: where meaning [*signification*] occurs, representation at least doubles itself until it fades. Here we have the precise point where the drive switches representatives, where meaning begins to slide—not onto *another* chain of signifiers, but onto another signifying position. This work that switches over from the verbal to the iconic signifier gets its energy from a displacement (that is a new impulsion, or thrust) of the drive.

This relation of exclusion explains how the phantasizing subject is not present on stage at the moment when he can verbalize his experience: that is, when the phantasy crosses the border into the preconscious, and that he only returns to the scene when the image is protected from the splintering power of words. This is an old and deep-seated insight of Freud's:

> When memories return in the form of pictures our task is in general easier than when they return as thoughts. Hysterical patients, who are as a rule of a "visual" type, do not make such difficulties for the analyst as those with obsessions.
>
> Once a picture has emerged from the patient's memory, we may

> hear him say that it becomes fragmentary and obscure {*zerbröckele und undeutlich werde*} in proportion as he proceeds with his description of it. *The patient is, as it were getting rid of it* {*trägt es ab*} *by turning it* {*umsetzt*} *into words.* We go on to examine the memory picture itself in order to discover the direction in which our work is to proceed. "Look at the picture once more. Has it disappeared?" "Most of it, yes, but I still see this detail." "Then this residue must still mean [*bedeutet*] something. Either you will see something new in addition to it, or something will occur to you in connection with it." When this work has been accomplished, the patient's field of vision [*Gesichtsfeld*] is once more free and we can conjure up [*hervorlocken*] another picture. On other occasions, however, a picture of this kind will remain obstinately before the patient's inward eye, in spite of his having described it; and this is an indication to me that he still has something important to tell me about the topic of the picture. As soon as this has been done the picture vanishes, like a ghost that has been laid [*wie ein erlöster Geist zur Ruhe eingeht*].[46]

The phantasy (the figure-image in this instance) is a ghost, a lost soul that discourse is called upon to redeem, because it is a meaning [*sens*] that is waiting to be signified [*signifié*], and that presents itself as a representation because it cannot find expression in words. Where Freud's youthful conviction will waver is on the belief that ghosts can be laid. Some soul-fragments remain lost to (at a loss for) words.

It is regression then, as the drive's fate, that modifies the fate of the drive's representatives. Regression must be contrasted with repression here. Scene I is a product of repression: the image of the action is feasible, the subject is excluded from the scene, his presence is that of a witness. Verbalization is possible as well. Scene III, which is once again a product of repression, possesses the same characteristics as far as word and thing-presentation go. But the regression from I to II destroys the verbal-iconic setting of the originary repression. The new anal-sadistic impulsion brutally thrusts the subject on stage in the position we all know. Within the order of representatives regression indeed consists in abandoning verbal traces and in the predominance of the visual, as Freud observed in 1899.[47]

But vision is not "seeing." Seeing is vision seen, witnessed. The third party sees seeing. Vision itself is not seen by any eye. Regression pushes the deconstruction of meaning to a point that is not only pre-verbal, but pre-outline. There is no eye to recognize, to survey the drama. The "representative" position of the latter in Phase II is thus quite different from phantasies I and III. *They* take place on a kind of perspective stage [*scène à l'italienne*]; they inscribe themselves on a screen. Stage and screen, that is the representational frame, come with the drama. Image II, on the other hand, envelops the subject, who cannot get it within his sights. This envelopment must not be conceived of as a spatial inherency within a montage in a three-dimensional space. It is rather a matter of the coexistence of mutually exclusive points of view. Such a coexistence finds plastic expression in the aerial views of "interworld" cities and rooms drawn by Paul Klee. Such aerial views imply an exploded subject, incapable of locating himself, and a non-place, where something may take place: I am being beaten by my father. This shattering of the subject and of the scene is the equivalent, in the representative order, of regression in the order of the drives. If it is true that the latter does not involve a withdrawal of investment from one bodily zone (genital) to another (anal), but a new investment that adds itself to its predecessors, the thing-presentation (in II) should simultaneously fulfill the incestuous desire, its interdiction, the sadistic drive and the superimposition of the conglomeration [*Zusammentreffen*] of this cluster of impulsions in the masochistic setting. The subject must be able to recognize himself in the father and in the child; in the beating position and in the position of being beaten.[48] He explodes, and with him the contours, the outlines, the plastic writing. It is the unseen visible.

Freud will see it and make it visible. He will let himself be guided by the verbal equivalent in the final formulation (III) of that non-representative scenario: the change-over into the passive voice. But in order to bring the mise-en-scène the words conceal under that unimpeachable artifice to light, he will have to *construct*; because regression has pushed the *deconstruction* of the verbal and iconic representatives so far that the signs produced by desire no longer satisfy the conditions for recognition by the preconscious, and there is almost nothing left to *interpret*.[49]

6. "Beating"

The affective meaning of the beating phantasy is, furthermore, a challenge to the secondary process to discourse and to "reality." Here is a possible outline of it, from which I have excluded, as before, any consideration of the denial of castration.

incestuous love:	X	loves	me
sadistic component:	X (I [*moi*])	beats (hates)	Y
reversal:	X	beats (loves)	me
turning around:	I	am beaten (loved)	by X
masochistic repression:	Z (I [*moi*])	am beaten (loved, hated)	by X

To beat is to love (in the genital sense) and to hate (in the anal-sadistic sense), but to hate in this sense is also to love. The term "to beat" is loaded with contradictory affects. It is its substratum of drives that determines its affective meaning. Nonetheless, its meaning alone is not just its affective meaning. Every transitive verb demands a subject and an object. "To beat" is therefore different from "to run" for example. From the syntactic perspective[50] the phantasy here is based on a "transitive" action, a fact that draws attention to the elision of the extension of the predicate (*by the father*) in version 3.2. But this coefficient of transitivity is too lax. One should not be able to substitute just any verb for "to beat." Recourse to strictly semantic meaning would appear to satisfy this demand, by opposing "to beat" and "to caress" for example.

And yet this is still not enough. As we saw, it is Freud himself who writes in the text of 1925: "The child which is being beaten (or caressed) (*geschlagen-geliebkost*) may at bottom be nothing more nor less than the clitoris itself. . . ."[51] What kind of consistency does the phantasmatic block have, if even the so-called meaning of the action the phantasy stages is susceptible to such variations? So far we have seen the extent to which the phantasy is figurality, difference, challenging every set system of oppositions. We have seen the extent to which it is, consequently, the Waterloo of discourse, and even of recognizable representation. But we also know that in some sense it is a "writing": a repetitive configuration, a sieve in which to catch and "clarify" all the material, rendered by chance encounters, the day's residues and the episodes of daily life, that bombards the subject. If its consistency is neither of the order of the drives (an order that is already composite before version I and therefore doubly so in version III), nor of the order of representatives (on the contrary, the three layers of the phantasy provide the scenarios for many day and night dreams), nor of the discursive order, which is the most secondary, the most reworked, of all, whose unity is the most overestimated; nor finally of the affective order, in which beating oscillates from love to hate, then it is clear that we must refrain from attributing any truth to it on the basis of its *content.* Its identity is a formal one. But how is this formalism to be understood?

I would like to show that even at the level we have now reached, underneath the layers we have explored so far, it is necessary to dissociate, if only in principle, the figural from the discursive order. The phantasmatic matrix is clearly a "form." I have no intention of studying its origin here.[52] In any case, we know that it is itself already, always already, a trace. But is it not possible to determine, on the basis of its formal properties themselves, hence formally, what makes this form the principle of the transgressions we noted in the different orders of meaning? How, in general, can a form be a transgression at the same time? In fact we have encountered the problem coming from the other direction. How can deviation, departure from the norm, deconstruction, be form at the same time? Even if the phantasy is not articulated on two levels, like discursive language, is it not necessary, all the same, that the relations between its various parts or elements remain consistent in order for this totality (about which, in the light of Gestalt psychology, it would be banal to say that it cannot be reduced to the sum of its elements) to retain its identity amid a changing content and a succession of different moments? And if such consistent relationships, such intervals exist, is not the form like a (silent) language? It's easy, it's not new, to grasp the rationale of such relationships in terms of the law of proportions, e.g., musical intervals, chromatic oppositions, the spacing of time values, diachronic rhythms or synchronic "rhythm" (of a monumental facade, for example). A mathematical language, but a language nonetheless. Lhote and all the Pythagorean Platonists will applaud at this point, if we are constrained to admit that the order of the phantasy, the mold within which the subject's unconscious "jells" so to speak, the formal matrix of his dreams and symptoms, conforms to a proportion that is thinkable.

We have to go back over the analysis and push it to the limit. With the word or the image of "beating" we have the theme (the "signified") of a rhythmics. With the sentence or the scene: "X is beating Y," we have the schema (the syntax) of a rhythmics. But with the beat of the sentences themselves, we have the disruption of a rhythmics. In other words, the "form" we are dealing with in the phantasy is not a proper one. It is certainly a form in which desire remains engaged—*form in the grip of transgression*—but it is also, potentially at least, *the transgression of form.*

Take "to beat." The verb signifies a contact that is established, interrupted, and re-established between two surfaces: the one receiving the blows, and the surface of the object that is dealing them. Thus a rhythm of + — + — (in which + stands for the moment of contact) is induced. This scansion demarcates a zone of simple opposition on the surface of the beaten body of the "absence/presence" type. In the phantasy "A Child Is Being Beaten" this contact, which is that of the father's hand, or the rod, with the child's bottom, is hypothetically erogenous.[53] The scansion + — + — has a meaning in terms of pleasure. This meaning, as Serge Leclaire appropriately recalls, consists, according to Freud, in the difference between a charge and a discharge.[54] "The time of pleasure or *jouissance* is this time of difference (in this instance between a + and a —), in tension: a difference that is imperceptible in itself, the quick of pleasure, a difference that is not itself musical time, but its condition of possibility."[55]

Let us note carefully that this difference is not the musical beat, the meter of the scansion, but that it merely opens up a spacing. And let us suggest that if it is the case that *jouissance* results from the greatest possible disparity between the charge and discharge of tension, that opening-up is not a matter of separating terms that belong on the same plane, forming part of a single area, of which they would merely delineate the lines of cleavage. It is rather a fracture, marking the subsidence, the caving-in of a surface, a fracture that leaves two ridges of widely differing altitudes suspended on either side of the chasm it has opened up.

To "forget" to note and keep in mind that there are two possible kinds of interval is to wipe out the function of scansion. If the latter is no more than the set alternation of the coming and going of a mere nothing (time —), we can discern in it the condition of all meaning, and identify the chains that desire forges out of this elementary rhythmics with those of a signifier that is at least formal, if not linguistic: Claudel's "iambe fondamental." Even if, like Leclaire, we have reservations about a linguistic interpretation of the unconscious,[56] it is possible to make the (in my view) major concession of giving the name "letter" to that imprint of desire on the body, that wound and its lips, and to aspire to read the erotic body like a book, there where those imprints are inscribed; — although we know that this letter, this articulation (literal in its graphic or vocal formality),[57] has the precise function of confining the difference of tension within a purely oppositional space, of arresting *jouissance* on the very brink of absolute difference (the difference between life and death) and thus of giving it the opportunity to repeat itself in the scansion of desire.

Jouissance is not death, but like death, at the same time that it discharges tension, it brings obscurity: the annihilation of representation, and the annihilation of words: silence. And absolute difference would be death, insofar as it is irreversible: the (+ —) that the resurgence of desire in its (— +) form, or "letter," if you like, cannot annul. That is how (+ — +) the dialectic thinks it can put death into language, "pocketing" it and mastering it. But the truth is that there is no process but rather a cycle (+ — + — + —) without end. Absolute difference would be (+ 0).

As far back as 1895, Freud distinguished between two principles. The principle of constancy aims to keep the system at a minimum of tension; the inertia principle tends to discharge all excitation completely.[58] The former cannot maintain the energy level constant except by binding it. This is the liaison of meanings and representations in language-systems and perception-systems. It obstructs the free flow of energy and the free displacement of meaning.[59] The pleasure principle, on the other hand, seems to be in collusion with "the original trend towards inertia [of the neuronic system] (that is, towards a reduction of its level of tension to zero."[60] We know that with *Beyond the Pleasure Principle* (1920), this last principle appears to have been displaced. It joins forces with Eros, with the tendency to form more complex unities, hence to bind energy into more improbable systems whose deviation potential from their milieu is increased.[61] The place occupied by the pleasure principle in the foregoing problematic now seems to be occupied by the "Nirvana" principle, which "expresses the trend of the death instinct."[62] By means of the latter, the "bound" structures of Eros are abandoned in favor of a return of the system to zero energy.

Nonetheless, this displacement of the pleasure principle is not a matter of course. In the 1920 text alone, hesitation about its localization is palpable. A few lines after saying that "The binding of an instinctual impulse would be the preliminary function designed to prepare the excitation for its final elimination (*Erledigung*) in the pleasure of discharge," from which we might conclude that Eros is on the side of the liaison, Freud writes: "The pleasure principle seems actually to serve the death instincts."[63]

This "hesitation" is, I think, the same one that we encounter in a writer like Leclaire, when he tries to make explicit the difference contained in the "letter" of desire. It is well-founded so long as it is not allowed to come down more heavily on one side than the other, as long as it is kept in the balance, and everything we have tried to establish as figurality rests on this razor's edge.[64] If it is taken in the absolute sense, difference is what the death drive seeks: zero excitation. But difference "must" come to terms with life, with the survival of the system. *Jouissance* stops short of death; it is a compromise between Nirvana and the constancy principle. If the "letter" of desire were merely a letter, death would be excluded from it and for that very reason desire would be *readable* because it would be totally contained within the stable networks of meaning and representation. That "letter" would at least be a proper form, a configuration capable of remaining constant amid the flow of events. But the order of desire is not the order of the secondary process. It is that order overthrown by a disorderly force. Beyond the pleasure principle, what Freud is surely trying to conceptualize is "the eternal return of the same," as it manifests itself in the child's game, in the symptom, in the transference, but what he is trying to get at is not the *same,* but the *return.*[65] What strikes him is not the *law* of repetition, but recurrence.

The principle of this recurrence cannot be a structural principle, analogous to the principle that makes the terms of a phonological or semantic system hang together, permitting the system to manifest itself diachronically or discursively, precisely because the appearance of these terms does not have the repetitious character that Freud recognizes in symptoms. What does not come under language, strictly speaking, in the child's *fort/da* game, is that it is not in any sense a predication: a basic sentence structure on the lines of a nominal syntagm plus a predicative syntagm. Quite to the contrary, it is the reiteration of two alternating predications that are mutually exclusive:

Nominal Syntagm	+	Predicative Syntagm
spool *(mother)*		*fort*
spool *(mother)*		*da*

It is not the same that returns, neither is it a discourse that unfurls. It is a configuration that does not succeed in liberating itself sufficiently to form a predicative identity in a sentence or in an assertive statement. The death drive sustains this oscillation. Under the guise of a simple linguistic opposition (*fort/da*), difference, like a void separating the two moments of presence, obtains. The child certainly plays difference, trying to match up the terribly unequal edges of the wound left by the mother's disappearance. But that is the subjective *function* of the game. The question that Freud puts to himself is the question of the existence of a tendency to play, to repeat. That *compulsion* is more readily observable in the child than in the adult, he says, because the language that forms in the gap created by the death drive with a view to mastering it is unable to overcome the compulsion to repeat.[66] The principle of this compulsion does not reside in a structure nor in a grammar, nor even in a form, which would still be too bound. It is Eros that is the liaison in the phantasy, and it is the reality principle (action, discourse) that brings Eros to the phantasy. Form, even if it is the form of transgression, is not transgression, but the recuperation of transgression within a consistent whole. It is a function of identity and unity.

The death drive is not in this league. It is not in league with anything, but rather a free agent. In the return or repetition the death drive is not what makes the thing return, but what makes it go away. It is what interferes with the constancy of the formation, whether it be figure-form, figure-image, or proposition. It is the "re-" of return or of re-petition, but in the sense of re-jection, not of returning. It is not the play, but the baffle, the impediment, dis-placement—the digression that is present in regression.

To take the drive for a binding force would be worse than to take the unconscious for a language and make the Id [*Ça*] talk. Because after all, there is some liaison in the unconscious—a phantasmatic and formal liaison, Eros. But the unconscious is not what it is (i.e., unknowable), except insofar as the liaison separates, comes undone, and it is here that the death drive reveals itself.

The phantasy "A Child Is Being Beaten" is indeed one of the forms of transgression. There is a "horizontal" scansion of the represented of the beating, of the *signified*: "X is beating Y." But to the extent that it is composed of superimposed layers, that it is a layered figure, this phantasy is the transgression of that form. The "vertical" scansion that transforms the figure "the father is beating the child" into the figure "a child is being beaten," via "I am being beaten by my father," obeys the compulsion of enjambement [*rejet*], of the run-on line, namely the compulsion of regression, and the function of this enjambement is to overload the apparatus with stimulus so that the consummation of *jouissance* results, but this also brings death closer. The figures in each phase are disfigured one by one as a result of the superimposition of a new figure engendered by the enjambement.[67] The order that emerges, in which desire lets itself be caught (the order "X is beating Y"), is continually deconstructed. Now we understand that the principle of figurality that is also the principle of unbinding (the baffle) is the death drive: "the absolute of anti-synthesis": Utopia.[68]

Return, Auto-Illustration, Double Reversal

Here, then, is the question: if the phantasy is what produces figural effects in the text—transgressions to the norms of signification—can one be satisfied with the argument that the text is a *phantasmatic expression* by opposing it to the theoretical or scientific text? And if the text is indeed such an expression, should one allow oneself to posit and treat it as a clinical sign available to the analyst? A discourse with a high figural index does seem at once to be the result of the misrecognition of which the phantasy is the mark, and to result, in turn, in the reader's misrecognition: what matters most is to please. Adopting the terminology proposed earlier, it would be easy to show that:

1) the figure-image makes a direct appeal to the reader's phantasmatics, by offering a stage upon which it can be fulfilled;

2) the figure-form exerts over the reader the suggestive power of its latent structure;

3) as for the figure-matrix ("A child is being beaten"), the author her/himself is its first victim, insofar as her or his entire oeuvre is an expression, or, at best, a commentary of it.

Such is in fact, roughly speaking, the approach of psychoanalysis when applied to art, and particularly to written works: the artwork is a symptom, and literature is the externalization in words of deep-seated phantasies.[1] Freud himself was not always immune from this simplistic interpretation, especially in his writings on artworks. But when he sought to locate the artistic function,[2] he never ceased to conceive of it as *labor of truth*, most notably in opposition to the religious function, which is, for Freud, one of consolation.[3] The artwork is true so long as it presents itself effectively as the work of *Phantasie*, and the artist, even when fulfilling her or his phantasy, does not present the latter as knowledge and salvation. Religious discourse or ritual is no less tied to the fulfillment of desire than the epic or the novel, theater or dance. The first two, however, actually fulfill desire, that is, dissolve it in the representations they summon. They make, in other words, believe. Of course, plastic, literary, and choreographic expressions also appeal to the art lover's impulses to identify with the content made manifest by means of forms. Nonetheless, these forms stop desire from reaching fulfillment, hallucinatory gratification, and discharge in the illusion of the contents' actualization, *for the simple reason that these forms refuse to be ignored*, that their patent presence blocks the compulsion to cross the picture plane, the screen, the perspective stage [*scène italienne*], or the page of the book, and thus that they maintain desire in a state of unfulfillment. I would argue that the "playful" aspect that Freud ascribed to art hinges precisely on this particular status of the form in artworks.[4]

It would be utterly superficial to assign this formal principle to a function of the ego.[5] What distinguishes the artwork from the symptom is not that for the artist the ego enjoys easier "access to id material"[6] than for the patient, no more than the artist, in contrast to the patient, has the benefit of being able to resort to an "orphic ego" effecting, under the guise of poetry, the "synthesis" between the conscious on the one hand, and, on the other, "two foreign universes: the outside and the unconscious"[7]—this ego thereby constituting an additional agency beyond the id and consciousness. Any reasoning along these lines must be cast aside, for its main argument is the reconciliation between primary and secondary process, between id and ego. In this vein, Charles Mauron goes so far as to formulate the hypothesis of a "reversible regression" that would allow Orpheus not only to descend to hell (regression), but also to return from it (reversion). Yet this is to forget that Orpheus fails to bring back Eurydice, precisely because, unable to dominate his desire to look at her, he turns around to face her. In this about-face, his gaze (his desire to see) resumes its direction toward the underworld (that is, toward the phantasmatic figure), all the while the ego seeks to walk toward daylight and reality.[8] In fact what the Orphic legend shows is that regression is not reversible, that the Orphic body, the artwork, is destined to be reduced to pieces, and that there is no such thing as a synthesis of the Dionysian (of the Freudian demonic) and the Apollonian. The ego's hold is that of reality on the unconscious; it is the domination of repression, which does not produce artworks but diverts energy toward verbalization (knowledge) and toward the transformation of the world (operativeness). There is no ego whose function would be to lift or reverse repression.

The same critique applies, albeit indirectly, to the position the Kleinian school grants the phantasy and the artwork. Admittedly, it is no longer a question here of psychoanalyzing the artist and of reconstructing agency theory in order to justify the notion of a reconciliatory art. The problem of expression is formulated entirely in terms of object relations.[9] The artwork is thought of not as a clinical reality endowed with an expressive function, but rather as a "transitional object,"[10] whose status in relation to the rift between exteriority and interiority is neither actually imaginary like that of the phantasy (internal object), nor real like that of the whole object. Instead, the object's status is similar to the breast's: simultaneously out- and inside, eschewing reality testing, yet nonetheless resistant to the dissolution of any imaginary scene. Just like the soldier of *The Tribute Money* in the Brancacci Chapel, this object *oscillates* between representational and perceptual space. It occupies the same position as the toy, and Donald Winnicott rightly points out that no one questions the child speaking to a doll or playing warfare on his or her level of attachment to the reality of the situations experienced in play. This transitional status is self-evident; the problem lies with us adults, who drive ourselves mad trying to reestablish contact with childhood. By positioning the artwork in this transitional space, one avoids the risk of subjecting it to the rule of the reality principle. On the contrary, one underscores the fact that the artwork takes shape in an empty space, or even—at least in the case of major artworks that innovate by breaking with tradition, that is, with a "script"—that its sole function is to deploy and preserve this space as one of dispossession.[11] It is this very function that I attempt to convey below.

But one should not underestimate the reconciliatory (recuperative) use to which the Winnicottian, and more generally Kleinian, thesis can be put. The mere term "transitionality" can immediately set in motion the mechanics of a dialectics of reconciliation. Such a transition between interior and exterior may be construed as a mediation: one could already be inclined to find traces of this work—by which the subject renounces the interior object, mourns it, and turns toward the constitution of reality taken as the site of complete and independent objecticities [*objectités*]—on the phantasy itself (which presents an interiority as exteriority), and subsequently, after having gone through the transitional object, on the work of art. One might then be inclined to understand this work as a continuous process of energy deferral and discharge toward exterior reality. It is but a small step from this understanding of the phantasy to the one put forward by Susan Isaacs, which consists in constituting retroactively the phantasy as a mediating work capable of synthesizing interior and exterior.[12]

All of this smacks of Hegelianism, and rests too comfortably on the omission of the radical heterogeneity of the unconscious process in relation to all secondary formations, be they discursive or of "reality." Adopting a tone of the utmost "seriousness," it all remains shielded by the authority of dialectical discourse, which attributes the motive of every formation (including the motive of its own production) not to the distortion (*Entstellung*) that desire creates when it comes across words and things, but simply to the end goal of knowledge, reinforced by the claim that anything real appears as good form. But phantasy does not bring us any closer to the real, or to knowledge, and neither does the artwork. Moreover—and this is what remains to be shown—the "form's" relation to "content" finds itself reversed when one goes from phantasy to artwork.

This well-worn terminology of "form" and "content" is not unhelpful on the condition that one defines it. In the phantasy, the set of drives generates mise-en-scènes with the sole purpose of fulfilling desire. This fulfillment is both "content" and "signification" of phantasmatic activity, its meaning as to instinctual organization and to the system of affects, respectively.[13] In the phantasy, form is never taken into consideration independently. Form undoubtedly plays a crucial role, since the repetition of contents, as Freud has amply shown, never goes without upheavals in presentations (and sometimes in instinctual organization itself, as is the case in the regressive phase of the "A Child Is Being Beaten" phantasy). These transformations, however, remain subject to the pleasure principle. Even difference within repetition, even alteration within identity—both products of the death drive—still aim, as became clear in our analysis of "A Child Is Being Beaten," to recharge the psychic apparatus to the full in order to attain the most complete possible *jouissance* at the moment of discharge. The forms are thus "free," in the sense that they are not caught up in bound processes and in constants, as is the case with the energy tapped by the networks of the secondary process. Still, this "freedom" betrayed by the forms' mobility and inconsistency, as well as by their rejection, does not prevent them from being subordinated to the principle of *jouissance*, or perhaps more specifically, to what in the pleasure principle belongs to the fulfillment of desire.

If art were expression or symptom, the work would have to reiterate these "free" and servile forms without any further modification than that which analysis observes in the sedimentation of phantasmatic phases. This would then legitimate the search (that Mauron performed) in the artwork's thickness for those regulating lines [*tracés régulateurs*] through which desire organizes the mise-en-scène. One would not be faced with the artwork, but with the scream. The grip of the phantasy would never loosen; the return would never be a reversal. True, the return involves this power of displacement, this *back turned* to simple repetition, the demonic compulsion seeking death. But so long as the pleasure principle has a stake in this compulsion, the latter has no choice but to negotiate with the reality principle. The compulsion does not lead the psychic apparatus to its destruction; instead it acknowledges, if not the gratification of the drives, then at least the vicarious formation of this gratification, which is precisely the phantasmatic fulfillment of desire. Hence the order of the drives, its fate hamstrung, oversees phantasmatic activity by negotiating, as it were, its mise-en-scène with the death drive, each new formation being the outcome of a compromise between fulfillment and unfulfillment (or overfulfillment, absolute fulfillment, that is, the zero of death), between the fullness of the hallucinatory substitute and the void of the scene where it performs, between the measured discharge that will make recharge possible and the absolute discharge that will bring it all to a close. If this is true, then the "utopian" or transgressive power is not what prevails in the phantasmatic system, since this power is kept in check by Eros, by the need to maintain the apparatus at a certain level of tension that testifies to its differential character. This function of the phantasy is to fill the void left behind by the object's withdrawal and negative hallucination—in a word, defense against anxiety.[14]

The function of "poetic" work (generally speaking, whether cinematographic, pictorial, etc.) is to reverse the nature of the relationship between Eros-logos and the death drive. What is reversed is not the relationship between two *objects* in a given space; such a straightforward reversal is ably, and often, carried out by the fate of the drives, when for example it replaces *X is beating Y* with *Y is beating X*. Far from cutting the (verbal or figurative) representatives loose from their attachment to the order of the drives, this reversal testifies to this attachment. Poetic reversal bears of course on "form" and "content," but we are now better qualified to replace these vague terms with the relevant concepts: whereas the phantasy fills the space of dispossession, the artwork dispossesses the space of fulfillment. The phantasy produces opposition with difference; the poetic remakes difference with *this* opposition.

In 1962, *Réalités* magazine published a "commentary" by Michel Butor, entitled *L'appel des Rocheuses* [*The Call of the Rockies*], of four photographs by Ansel Adams and Edward Weston.[15] Calling it a "commentary" hardly captures the text's relationship to the images, and this is precisely what I want to do here: arrive at a more accurate description. Two years after the *Réalités* piece, the first book of *Illustrations* comes out.[16] In it, under number V, one finds a "text" entitled "Les Montagnes Rocheuses" [The Rocky Mountains].[17] Actually, "text" is still inadequate; "fabric" or "arrangement of words" would be better. By looking at the distance between the two layouts, one can put one's finger on the "poetic" reversal that we are trying to grasp, or at least identify an instance of this reversal. But first, may the person reading these lines take the time to look (Plates 20 and 21, Figures 20 and 21; see also the commentary in "Notes on Figures and Plates").

Plates 20 and 21 are from *Réalités*, while the two double-page spreads are from *Illustrations*. For convenience, I refer to them by the numbered letters R1 and R2, and I1 and I2, respectively.

The composition in *Réalités* has, at its core, a double-page spread in color, based on the R2 model, but with a margin on the left of the image. Bracketing this core are two double pages printed in black and white: R2 and the last of the four double pages, identical to R2; this group itself comes after a double-page spread with a slightly different layout, namely, R1. Color notwithstanding, the units R2, R3, and R4 form a homogenous group: they are at the same time units of *sight* and of *reading*. As one may observe from R2 [Plate 21], the photographic image takes up ⅚ of the unit. Each unit, moreover, comprises two texts: a text I will call A ("Le Parc National de Yosemite" [Yosemite National Park] etc.), connoting a tourist document, printed in small roman type, laid out according to standard conventions of reading and placed toward the bottom of the margin; and a text I will call B ("le bruit, le grondement . . ." [the noise, the rumbling . . .]) with lyrical connotations, printed in italics, laid out vertically on the side of the image, with a margin of its own on the opposite side of the image. The image in question plays the role of reference (*Bedeutung*) for text A, and of representation (*Vorstellung*, reinforcing a figure that is already in the text) for text B. Thus the A/B opposition in R2 involves not only the signified, but also the signifier (type, space occupied on the page, layout) of the two texts.

The first double-page spread R1 offers a different appearance [Plate 20]. The image takes up only ⅔ of the unit of sight. The title and subtitle constitute a zone of gray at the upper edge of the margin instead of the white found in the following units. And, above all, alongside the tourist-like text A, meeting the criteria defined above, we encounter a text I refer to as C ("Quand les pionniers allaient vers l'Ouest" [When the pioneers set off toward the West]), whose signifier and signified depart equally from both A and B. At the level of graphic signifier, we note a subdivision in three paragraphs acting as "stanzas," the third covering seven full lines, while the first covers six lines and a half and the second six lines and three quarters, so that a kind of diagonal generator cutting across this text drags the eye toward the lower right; and a printing in heavier roman type than text A. At the level of the signified, we observe the use of figures heavily connoted by two features: the signifier's repetitive scansion ("Quand . . ." [When . . .]) and the "diegetic" connotation alluding to a narrative unfolding in the temporality of the national legend. All of this contributes to make this text C a kind of epic tale, whose relation to the image is no longer that of representation nor reference, but under which the images of the Rockies play the part of

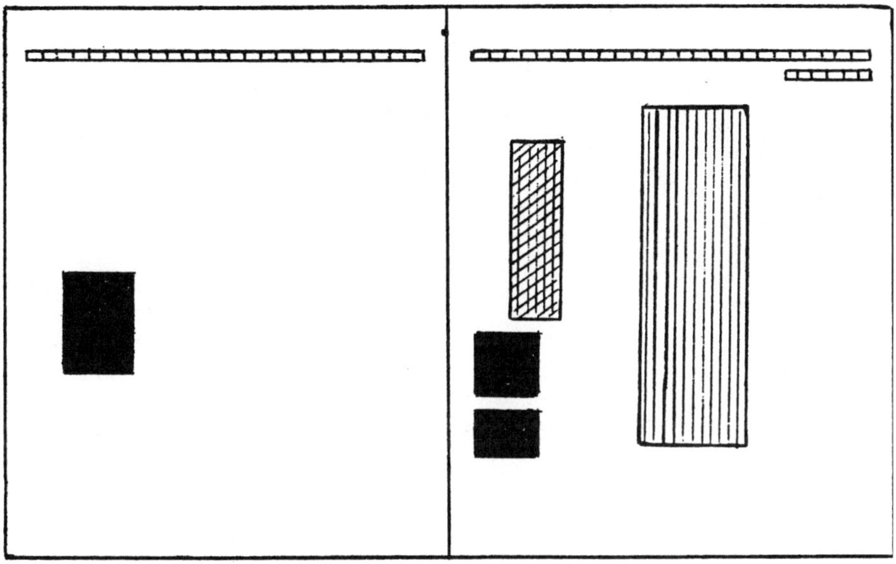

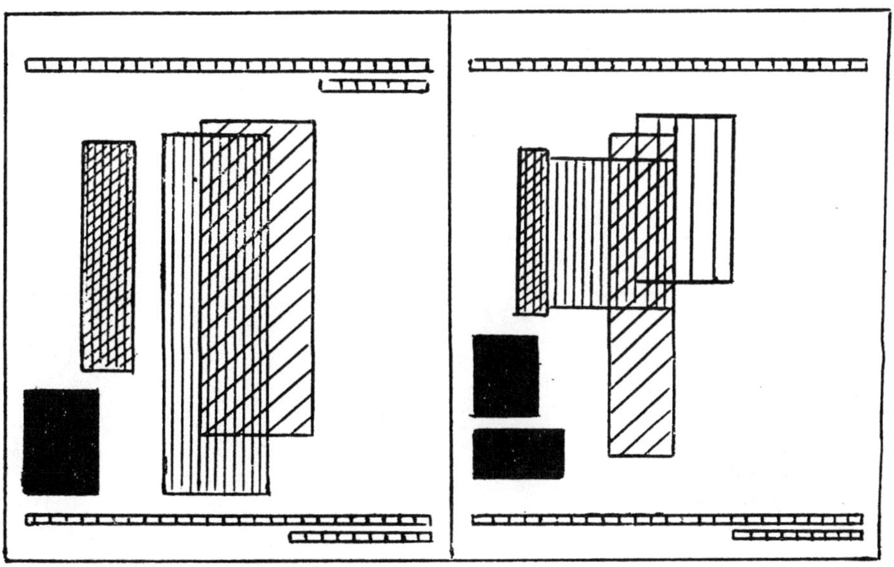

Figure 20. Diagram of the graphic signifier's layout across two double-page spreads in Michel Butor's *Illustrations* (Paris: Gallimard, 1964).

Following pages: Figure 21. Michel Butor, *Illustrations,* 94–97. Facsimile.

QUAND LES PIONNIERS ALLANT VERS L'OUEST ET L'OR,

le bruit,
le grondement
répercuté
par les parois
taillées
comme à coups
d'énormes
couteaux,

APRÈS DES SEMAINES ET DES SEMAINES DANS LES PLAINES
ET LA PRAIRIE,

LE BRUIT,

LE GRONDEMENT

RÉPERCUTÉ

PAR LES PAROIS

TAILLÉES

COMME A COUPS

D'ÉNORMES

COUTEAUX,

le souffle,

la forge

du vent,

l'énorme

râle

de la gueule

blanche

et bleue,

toutes
les paillettes
de la neige
tombant
d'aiguille
en aiguille,

le froissement
de ces rameaux,
mains
gantées de fer,

APERCEVAIENT LA GRANDE MURAILLE DE ROCS, DE PICS ET DE FORÊTS,

LE BRUIT,

LE SOUFFLE,

toutes

les paillettes

LA FORGE

de la neige

LE GRONDEMENT

tombant

DU VENT,

d'aiguille

en aiguille,

L'ÉNORME

le froissement

RÉPERCUTÉ

de ces rameaux,

RALE

mains

gantées de fer

DE LA GUEULE

le grincement
des branches
qui se tordent,
se déchirent
et tombent,
déclenchant
un geyser
de plumes,

PAR LES PAROIS...

BLANCHE

ET BLEUE

QUAND L'AUTOMOBILISTE AUJOURD'HUI APRÈS DES HEURES, DES HEURES,

ILS SAVAIENT QU'AU-DELA COMMENÇAIENT LES DÉSERTS,

LE BRUIT,

LE SOUFFLE,

le grincement
LE FROISSEMENT
des branches

qui se tordent,
DE CES RAMEAUX,
se déchirent
LA FORGE
et tombent,
MAINS
déclenchant
LE GRONDEMENT...
un geyser
GANTÉES DE FER,
de plumes,
DU VENT,
les jets
des chutes
déployant
leurs draperies
de giclures,

et le bruit du vent
qui reprend *L'ÉNORME...*
comme un hurlement.

DES JOURS DE ROUTE DROITE DANS L'INTERMINABLE
FERME DU MIDDLE-WEST,

scenery, of a stage on which three generations of Americans have continuously passed, each with its own receptivity, affects, and goals. This scene is set as an introduction to the group of four double pages; it does not recur in the following three, but persists in them in latent state.

This overall composition invites two kinds of remarks. First, the plurality of relations between text and figure-image: the latter counts as reality for A, as phantasy for B, and for C, as mythical backdrop (scenery of a "collective phantasy," and therefore half-real). Second, thanks to the configurations I have just described concerning the organization of the text,[18] one may speak of a beginning of plastic or figural treatment of graphic space. No more than a beginning, for if one can speak of a certain innovation in the treatment of text A—which one must not only read, but also see, in order to appreciate fully—in texts B and C this treatment remains within the limits of typographic tradition.

Now look at I1 and I2: the image is eliminated, as is text A, while B and C undergo extensive alterations. Text B (from R2) is divided into five segments, transcribed in five different types—each corresponding to five kinds of intervals—spread across several units of sight according to a rhythmics that a system in which types and intervals are replaced by values will reveal as similar to Mondrian's organization of plastic space. Text C suffers the opposite fate, unfurling in horizontal bands that cut cross the entire *Illustration* and that, page after page, form unusual combinations of meaning with the B texts scattered between and around them.

Here is what this transposition looks like in black and white (Figure 20). To each element I have assigned an intensity of black corresponding to the "density" in which it is printed, depending on the types and intervals involved. Had we established a correlation between the segmentation of text B from R2 and the variation of another plastic quality—say, color—Mondrian would have appeared.

Plastic requirements clearly govern the spatial organization of *Illustrations*. How does this work of the sensory plant its effects in the intelligible order of discourse? What happens on the side of the text? Now let us imagine that falling upon the fourth part of *Illustrations*—"Montagnes

Rocheuses"—and with no knowledge of "L'appel des Rocheuses," you attempted to read its pages as if they presented a consecutive piece of writing composed in accordance with the rules governing our script, beginning at top left and ending at bottom right. You would run into the strangest grammatical aberrations, faulty agreements, absences of subject, and subordinate clauses without main clause, not to speak of your complete confusion in semantic matters. To be sure, the typographic disordering could already be felt in certain texts of *Réalités*. But it was not difficult to organize the statements, to link them to one another, to "realize" them perhaps (by reading them aloud, for instance), thanks to the presence of photography, or rather to what it represented—the Rocky Mountains themselves—acting as reference to each and every one of the statements and guiding you in the comprehension of the text, while the diversity of discourses relating to the same image helped you bring out certain meanings imbedded in the image. This is exactly what has disappeared from the *Illustration*: the juxtaposition of the "window" of the image with the texts etched like graffiti on its frames, like "legends." Yet this disappearance notwithstanding, the text has not been endowed with a "normal" order, that of the linearity of writing (and speech).

Take for example a page from this *Illustration*, here transcribed linearly, while respecting the punctuation and typography of Butor's text: "ET DESCENDRE ENFIN VERS LE PACIFIQUE. Seul le crissement de votre semelle POUR FRANCHIR DANS L'ÉTAT DE COLORADO LES MONTS OUTREMER SOMMES DE NACRE, ET BAIGNER DANS LA SURPRENANTE COULEUR DU SOL qui écrase le cristal du sol. UN VENT VENU DU FOND DES ÂGES, LUI, AMÉRICAIN" [AND DESCENDING TOWARD THE PACIFIC AT LAST. Only the squeaking of your shoes TO REACH IN THE STATE OF COLORADO THE ULTRAMARINE MOUNTAINS ACCUMULATIONS OF MOTHER-OF-PEARL, AND TO BATHE IN THE GROUND'S SURPRISING COLOR that crushes the crystal of the ground. A WIND COMING FROM THE DEPTHS OF THE AGES, IT, AMERICAN].[19] This is a cryptic text seemingly blocked out, like a text chiseled on an ancient tablet reduced to pieces by time, like an "exquisite corpse" or a discourse riddled with silences or noises that we would need to complete, to fill in through a process of reconstruction. And one is all the more inclined to go down this epigraphic path and resurrect the original from which these lines are thought to have come, since the latter are far from being incoherent despite their lack of grammatical order: they unmistakably evoke a westbound trip across the Rockies. It should suffice to insert the parts of statements needed to constitute a chain whose vocabulary and syntax comply with the French language, in order to obtain finally the fully articulated message that one imagines to be at the root of this document.

This would be going down the wrong path, however. The construction of a unit of reading from a unit of sight would take us away from the latent text that this last unit (the visible document) conceals. For the latent text is made up of several statements belonging to groups C and B, whose unity therefore lies not in discourse itself, in its signified or connotation, but in an image acting as mythical frame to the epic character of some of the texts (C) and as echo and plastic harmonics to the lyricism of others (B). The hidden, lost unity is not, strictly speaking, textual, but figural. In keeping with our theme of reconstitution, the investigator who comes the closest to the truth will be the one who dares to discover (or invent) in the form—that is, in the figure-form of the units of sight of *Illustrations*—an equivalent to the figure-image of *Réalités*. A rough equivalent, a lawless analogue, like the one that allows the rebus-maker to transpose and disguise a given word or syllabus of the original text into a form of the manifest image; but here an analogue working in the opposite direction, from the figure-image to the text, since the principle guiding *Illustrations* is the anti-rebus, as it were. All differences aside, the result of this equivalence seems to have to be the impenetrability of the manifest content—in our case, of the *Illustration*.

Not least because Butor is careful not to be satisfied with rather superficial equivalences, such as the one illustrated in Guillaume Apollinaire's *Calligrammes*, where for example the sentences that make up the text "La colombe poignardée et le jet d'eau" [The Bleeding-Heart Dove and the Fountain] are arranged in such a way as to evoke the silhouette of a bird—wings outstretched, head hanging—overlooking the downward flow of water spouting from a pool.[20] In Butor's work, the text never plays the role of an illustration, that is, of a contour [*tracé révélateur*] or recognizable line: the words are not strewn like the gravel bed of Death Valley, nor do they scale the page in a mountainous outline. About *Calligrammes*, Butor writes that "they suffer from the major drawback of being, for the most part, merely texts following the lines of a drawing that comes across as very awkward once realized typographically."[21] From the point of view of craft, this argument translates as: what prohibits the transposition of drawing in the realm of the book are the constraints specific to the components and composition used in typography, that is, to the technique of the art of book-making. In fact, this argument translates much more radically as: do not confuse line and letter.

But neither should one confuse text and musical notation. No doubt, the simultaneity of phrases, their typographic marking, the *concertante* character of the overall composition of *Illustrations* indeed suggests an orchestral score. "It will become increasingly necessary for writers to learn how to handle the different kinds of letters as musicians do their string, woodwind, or percussion instruments."[22] Works built, at least in part, on the same model as our *Illustration*—such as *Réseau aérien* and *6 810 000 litres d'eau par seconde*—are deliberately intended to be performed acoustically.[23] Yet there again consideration of the letter must prohibit its assimilation to musical notation. Certainly, unlike the line, musical notation is not an immediate aesthetic value, for it represents something other than itself, namely a sound. But this sound does not allow the identification of a signified, a value in a system of significations: it is an aesthetic value, a value for a sensibility, whereas script can never be reduced to the status of the purely sensory. Butor deems Mallarmé's wish—to equate the page with a stave—impracticable.[24]

The truth of the matter is that the operations enabling one to go from the composition of *Réalités* to that of *Illustrations* comply neither quite obviously with the rules governing legitimate transformations of statements (including translations), nor with the rules regulating the transposition of a signified into plastic (or acoustic) representation. The statement is cut up in fragments that are scattered across several pages, making us lose sight of the previous fragment's signification by the time we read the fragment that would have followed in a normally configured statement. (Signification may be lost from sight, but not destroyed, since it pursues its subterranean course, producing an effect of vague recognition, a suspicion of déjà vu grounded in the experience of the book's sensory space-time.) A fragment is linked to fragments from other statements in a spatial, not syntactic, composition. The latter unleashes something like short circuits of signification corresponding to flashes of meaning, as the sequence of words is abruptly connected to an unexpected context, revealing potential, unforeseen meanings in the sequence. These are statements that discourse would identify and that the illustrated version kept apart, such as, for example, the three statements corresponding to the three "stanzas" of text C in R1. In the *Illustration* version, these statements follow one another from one page to the next, each at the same spot: the statement at the top locating the signification of the Rocky Mountains for the ancient pioneers, the one at the bottom for the motorist, and the one in the middle for the airline passenger [Figure 21]. These statements—referring as they do to three periods of America, and whose different verb forms explicitly articulate them with one another in time—nevertheless find themselves in synchrony by virtue of their parallel tracings across a single page, as well as out of sync, because they do not begin together on the same page, but instead one "after" the other as if in canon. This allows each statement to occupy, in relation to the space of the book-volume, a position comparable to that of the three historical periods in relation to the mythical time of the American nation. What gives the written text a plastic power that its "ordinary" signification does not allow to convey is precisely this textual fragmentation, this recombination of fragments in new configurations, this collapsing of times, this juxtaposition of incompatible contents. Still other operations, that one could detect with greater ease in some of Butor's more important texts, would include: the condensation of characters, or more exactly of people, determining the entire architecture of *Degrés*; the condensation of cities and situations (as in Paris-wife and Rome-mistress) in *La modification*; the shift in emphasis that, by highlighting such and such secondary observation, pushes what is important in the background and allows it to make its way into the reader's mind without her or his knowledge, as in *L'emploi du temps*.

All these operations are easy to recognize: censorship (suppression of texts A), displacement (segmentation and redistribution of texts B, which shifts the *accent* of the whole), condensation (combination of texts B with each other and with texts C), secondary revision (reconstitution of all the fragments into a "good form"), and all of these operations are the work of the dream. We thus find ourselves back to our initial question, barely modified, insofar as dream and symptom are closely related: are the units I to the units R *like* the manifest content of a dream to its latent thoughts, and *like* the clinical symptom to its meaning?

Illustrations is dedicated to the typesetter, the book worker, not to the painter or musician. The refusal to use techniques of transcription (drawing, score), deemed foreign to the book-object, has a double effect. On the one hand the text will always remain visible, since the shape of the letters and the composition's geometry remain untouched; there will remain, in other words, something to be understood. On the other hand there will be, if not something to be seen, if not something for the eye, then at least something to be danced to, matter for the body. This combined and contradictory effect is due to the fact that the work mostly targets the blanks, and always interrupts the disarticulation before it attacks the natural unit of language, that is, the word. What runs through the letters, the words, the sentences is indeed the same blankness, the same nothing that separates the units of a linguistic system. But the organization of the graphic signs is such that this nothing also counts as plastic interval, as figural area, as weak ground coursing under the strong beats serving as figure. Air or water starts to circulate between words; language lets a space other than its own seep through it. We enter the discourse of *Illustrations* as the mime or the diver would "enter" a volume to be activated through gesture, where the blanks are no longer diacritical signals but interstices in which signification recedes to give free rein to meaning. The blanks no longer simply *oppose* (or give contrast to) what they keep apart, they *differ* it [*ils le* diffèrent].

On the back cover of *Illustrations*, one reads the following inscription:

ILLUSTRATIONS
of missing images, which in turn would be
ILLUSTRATIONS
of missing texts, which in turn would be their
ILLUSTRATIONS

In the context of our text, this translates as:

this book (*Illustrations*) illustrates
the missing Adams and Weston photographs
that illustrated
Butor's (apparently missing) texts in *Réalités*
of which one could then claim that they illustrate

themselves in this book, since this book is made up exclusively of these missing texts. Thus the text of *Illustrations* is the text of *Réalités* auto-illustrating itself. It reflects itself, mirroring itself to itself; but it also illuminates, and clarifies itself, revealing something of itself that did not appear in the first form. Far from masking, concealing, or disguising, the work of transposition has fulfilled the function of acknowledging [*avérer*]. The operations are indeed those of the dream, *but they proceed in reverse order*. What is this reversal?

This reversal is double. In the movement from the R to the I configuration, one notes a first and immediately obvious reversal: the image's suppression in I is such that the text now seems to take up the entire space, whereas in R it surrounded, commented upon, and echoed an image that occupied $5/6$ of the visible surface. Limiting ourselves to this observation, one could describe the change introduced by *Illustrations* as the shift in the respective importance of two terms within a given relation: if t is the text and f the figure-image, then in R the formula is $f > t$, while in I it is $t > f$ (where f is equal to zero). But this description skips over the essential. The reversal we are dealing with is not the inversion of two objects in a homogenous space, but rather the transformation of a mutually exclusive relation between two heterogeneous spaces into a relation where they commingle to form an unstable volume, hesitating between the two original spaces. In *Réalités*, text and image are exterior to one another (despite an initial hint of combination suggested by the texts' disposition). In *Illustrations*, the printed characters act both as terms occupying a specific place in a graphic code—that is, as elements standing in measured opposition to each other, making reading possible—and as plastic units endowed, through their particular configuration (italics, for example, projecting the eye toward the right, or the capital letter deploying a more formal space around itself), with sensory power. The same goes for the intervals, operating at the same time as empty spaces that make opposition possible and as irreversible "filled" blanks, carriers of differences. What becomes clear is that the encounter between the space of the figure-image and that of the text passes through the figure-*form*.

It is not my intention here to list all the conceivable relations between figural and textual space, nor even those—much fewer in number, since they occupy only a part of the general matrix—combining text with the figure-form alone. But it is worth pointing out that there are many more relations than the one Butor makes use of in *Illustrations*.[25] Butor himself explores a certain number of them in *Les mots dans la peinture*,[26] where the author's hypothesis is premised on the opposite operations from the ones we are considering, since they consist in incorporating elements of the space of reading into that of sight. However, to limit ourselves to the subset to which *Illustrations* belongs, which brings together only those operations involving the graphic signifier (to the exclusion of the signified and the phonic signifier) by means of the figure-form (to the exclusion of the figure-image, as in *Calligrammes*), one would at least have to cite and show the work on the letter produced by Constructivists such as El Lissitzky[27] or by what I will call "Deconstructivists" like Bruno Lemenuel.[28] One illustration of each of these two "solutions" will have to suffice here (Plates 22 and 23, and the commentary below in "Notes on Figures and Plates").[29]

Without further comment, let us return to *Illustrations*. Butor's solution to the problem of the figure-form's and the text's interpenetration gives rise to a set that could only be qualified as *floating*, at once stiff and flexible, forcing the eye to interact with the page in a new way. Floating, like those convoys of logs hauled to the sea on the lakes of Scandinavia: groups whose length and width are invariable, but that hug the undulations of the water's surface and therefore fluctuate in height or depth. What remains fixed in *Illustrations* are the groups of letters, fastened together by syntactic ties that prevent them from dispersing and coming apart. This binding is the sign of the secondary process. The mobility lies in the blanks, which are of unrestricted proportions, and in the unusual use of the different printing types. Here an expanse of dispossession prevails, where meaning is event because it does not appear where we expect it. Just as the water's undulations can be perceived with much greater accuracy thanks to the distortions they provoke on the surface of the *bound* set of logs, so the linguistic consistency maintained in the text allows the reader to feel the undercurrents that sway the unwritten layers upholding the logs of language. The latter operate as amplifiers, and this is what their rigidity is for, serving as echo chamber for processes such as displacement, substitution, and condensation that otherwise would go unnoticed. These processes were already at work in the figure-images provided by the Adams and Weston photographs: the condensation on a single image of perfectly focused close-ups and extreme long-distance shots; the lowering of the point of view to ground level, distorting the object's silhouettes (*Entstellung*); the use of filters, as well as the film's over- or underexposure (displacement of values or colors). But in these photographs, such processes occurred as if in a phantasmatic scene, overlooked in favor of what they make visible, of the "subject." They themselves were not staged; rather they helped stage and represent the Rockies. They belonged to the scene's underground, occupying the forbidden space between the latent and the manifest. Their role was to be forgotten. In short, they were nothing more than evidence of fulfillment work.

This is because the operations in question bore upon an environment where they could easily disband, because of this environment's—the image's—particular complicity with dream-work. But taken back from the space of the imaginary and transposed in that of the book, which is linguistic, these operations can no longer go unnoticed, shaking the textual expanse that in turn begins to vibrate and creak. The expanse testifies. Butor's book does not *signify* these operations (as does the *Traumdeutung* [*The Interpretation of Dreams*]); rather it allows one to sense the traces they leave on the position of the constituents of discourse and on the intervals between them. It is, therefore, no longer a case of desire finding fulfillment in a phantasmatics played out on the photographic stage, as in *Réalités*. In *Illustrations*, desire can only unfulfill itself, having been deprived of its aims of reverie: in the end, all it has at its disposal are the means by which it dreams, the operations. This is what accounts for the book's strictness. The eye seeking temptation, enamored only with its own rapture, must here give up, or become strong and cold enough to desire seeing desire at work, or at least traces of its work. Polar opposites of the photographic window, the aquatic expanses—upholding written passages here and there—can only refer desire back to itself. For not only can desire no longer lose itself in plastic images, but the effects of the mobility of the lettering and the blanks on the signifier further prevent it from phantasizing from the signified, as was at least particularly the case in the *Réalités* layout.

There is, I am arguing, a "mirror" in Mallarmé's *Un Coup de dés*, where signified and signifier reflect one another.[30] But this reflection is not a true reflection; one must call it hyper-reflection. This term allows one to feel that, contrary to what happens with the mirror—which reverses the image of the reflected object while maintaining it in a (specular) space consistent with "real" space—"poetic" reversal is little concerned with the image and greatly so with the environment [*milieu*] internal to the work. This environment is floating in the sense defined above; in it one finds not reality and its specular double, but fixed and invariant elements bound together by a secondary process (what Barthes would call "written" for example), floating on moving surfaces that belong, as it were, to another element. All artwork as "critical poem" re-creates, through this combination of two heterogeneous spaces, the difference that the phantasy blocks and flattens into opposition and repetition, that is, into symptom, and incorporates this difference into itself, in its internal space. This is why the artwork is critical: it deconstructs a given "good form"; and it is placed in two heterogeneous expanses.[31]

Shakespearean Episode

For sorrow's eye, glazed with blinding tears,
Divides one thing entire to many objects;
Like perspectives, which rightly gaz'd upon
Show nothing but confusion; ey'd awry,
Distinguish form . . .[32]

In 1649, Charles I is decapitated in London. His supporters multiply his illegal portraits, among which I have selected two: one is a flat anamorphic figure, the other a catoptric anamorphosis (Plates 24a, 24b). The first follows the same principle as the one Holbein uses in *The Ambassadors*,[33] namely, the representation of an object constructed on an axis that is not perpendicular to the plastic screen (as is the "legitimate" rule), but in principle tangent to this screen in all of its points (thus forming a very small angle with it). Facing Holbein's painting, you see the two ambassadors, poised and affluent, surrounded by the symbols of knowledge. By placing your right cheek against the painting's right edge, you lose sight of these represented representatives that are the painted ambassadors; but this new angle reveals the nature of the object floating at their feet (the skull), alerting you to the vanity of success embodied by the two men.

The simple 90-degree rotation on the axis of vision is enough to dissolve representation. The truth of the latter is death. To perform this rotation is therefore an ontological act that inverts the relation between visible and invisible, signifier and represented scene. Now this inversion corresponds to the reversal of our relation to the screen.[34] When we look at the painting head-on, our desire to invest the scene leads us to ignore the screen, since we move past it as if it were a porous window through which this scene invites us to join it, through which to access this calm, this strength. If on the contrary we look at the work laterally, we give back to the support its material consistency. As a result, the scene disperses and the emblem undetected at first sight (which was a vision) begins to speak. The painted canvas no longer recedes into representation; now it is representation that explodes, resulting in enigmatic and crazed tracings streaking the canvas. Indeed, it is barely a metaphor to say that the skull *speaks*: its position vis-à-vis the support transforms it, for the frontal viewer, into the sign of an unknown script rather than a representation; its facial value seems arbitrary, making it as difficult to infer a signification from it as it would be from a set of undeciphered markings. Lateral vision gives us this "signification," which went unseen in direct vision.[35] But this signification is, in turn, nothing other than absence itself—death—and not a "content": the anamorphosis instructs us that reading requires that one die to representation, to the phantasy of presence. The strange flying saucer, at once blazing forward and stationary, uncertain whether to land on the stone floor, and casting its shadow with complete disregard for the coherence of the scene's lighting, is God's script: other space, other temporality, other light. Our rotation converts the support; through it the world becomes book, and our seeing turns into the listening of the Word.

The portrait of Charles I is similarly scripted on the sheet of paper: one must alter the angle of vision and flatten it onto the support in order to be able to identify the sitter. Here again one must therefore begin by rejecting appearance and aim for the support's nonappearance. The figure of the dead king stands in for the figure of death and of script; however it is not concealed by an immediately visible scene that would divert the eye from its quest, as was the case with Holbein.

As for the mirror anamorphosis of Charles I, it scrupulously applies the system of *The Ambassadors*, confirming that it is indeed the rotary shift of the eye's relation to the screen that alone fulfills the ontological function of these "secret portraits." You move closer to the cylindrical form so as to identify the figure of the king reflected on its surface; you discover the strange circular object that surrounds the cylinder's base; you lean forward to identify this object in turn; you remove the cylinder that is in your way; and the figure of death appears. As in Holbein's painting, representation offers itself as a scene positioned vertically (here, the reflected portrait) and truth as an indecipherable trace if one remains within the scene's axis, yet a legible one, presented moreover as absence, when the eye renounces the phantasy or the ghost and agrees to confine itself to the two-dimensional support of script.

The interplay of two overlapping spaces informs the principle of the anamorphic painting: what is recognizable in one is not in the other, and the good form of representation is deconstructed by "bad" forms (the skull in Holbein's painting, the portrait of Charles I). The critical function of the anamorphosis in relation to representation is indisputable; witness the research carried out on these distortions in Cartesian and Jansenist circles in France, inspired elsewhere by Calvinist or Lutheran puritanism, that is, by any school of thought accusing the world of being illusion. We already find an anamorphosis in Leonardo's *Notebooks*, which must be the earliest extant. From the very beginning, representation and critique have been inseparable.

Still, the latter's emergence was by no means easy, achieved at the cost of a complete rotation of the plastic signifier's position—at the cost, that is, of the Cézannian revolution. What is remarkable in the anamorphosis is that it is a critique through the representative, not the represented. Vanities will proliferate in religious painting of the sixteenth and second half of the seventeenth centuries, but these accounts of the frailness of representation are themselves representations. The laws laid down by the "perspectivalists" [*perspecteurs*] are scrupulously observed, producing their sure-fire illusionistic effects. The morality in the painting does not hinder the viewing of the painting: the two orders are kept apart, and the mediation of the discourse of commentary is necessary in order to articulate what the painting "is saying" (or "means": *veut dire*). This relation of exteriority provides a rather useful definition of an *edifying* art (just as "socialist" realism will shelter representation from the revolution it claims to represent). In the case of the anamorphosis, the signifier itself is under siege, overturned under our own eyes. The threatening objects depicted in the representational artwork belong to a space one could call graphic, as opposed to that of representation. These objects are inscribed on the "sheet of glass," making it visible instead of crossing it on their way to the virtual scene. The eye thus ceases to be taken and is given over to the hesitation of the trajectory and site, while the artwork is given over to the difference of spaces, which is the dualism of the processes. Through the injection of another space, illustration shows itself as illustration, as auto-illustration.

This intrinsic constitution of the artwork relates it to the constitution of analytic discourse, by being placed in a situation of interpretation (*Deutung*). The subject speaks; like Oedipus's discourse, the subject's, and regardless of what she or he may say, aims for a certain coherence, for not only does the subject string together the linguistic signifier according to the deep grammar of her or his language, selecting lexical elements given in the accepted vocabulary, but the subject's very effort to be "sincere" forces her or him to produce, while speaking, one or more attempts at interpretation, to build hypotheses on the meaning of the material she or he puts forward, to incorporate this material into a basic reasonable system that will later allow such and such dream element, slip of the tongue, or symptom to become recognizable, and that consequently will allow the analyst as well as the subject her- or himself, the analysand, to expect a certain kind of meaning through the recounted events. This spontaneous position of the analysand's discourse makes it a compromise-formation. In the latter one finds evidence of typically secondary work done on traces of the primary process. The aim [*visée*] of the internal coherence, of the conformity with social, psychological, and ethical plausibility, requires the erasure of what is truly difference, event, unsettling strangeness, principle of *jouissance*. This rubbing out is the operation that corresponds in the dream to what Freud calls secondary revision. But just as in the dream (albeit differently), this work of censorship in the analysand's discourse—work that subjects the material to the constraints of language and perception—although it obliterates the meaning of desire, does not erase all of its traces. One can even argue in principle that the search for a strong "binding" by the conscious is already in itself the result of a defense against the deconstructing pressure that the unconscious exerts on the bound system.[36] The challenge of course will be to disentangle what, in this revision, is secondary and what is primary, what is knowledge-illusion and what is truth, the two being always necessarily given together.

This is where what Freud calls *Deutung*, or interpretation, comes into play, which is the exact opposite of the ordinary or even hermeneutic meaning of the word as interpretative commentary, but instead consists in reversing the relation of two processes, of two spaces. One could say that within the analysand's discourse, as well as within the symptom, the traces of the primary process are concealed by their inclusion in a space of secondary signification. The marks of desire—its figure-images and figure-forms—are reallocated according to the requirements of articulated language (and of active perception). Secondary revision consists precisely in stretching over these marks the web of recognized and recognizable bindings of reasonable thought. The stamp of desire, covered up in an alien space, will then be able to go practically unnoticed. The coherent discourse addressed to the listener's ear will appeal to interlocution, and above all to a form of rational attention focused on the examination of significations and articulations.

By recommending that the analyst maintain an "evenly suspended attention," Freud intends to protect her or his listening from this illusion of rationality, articulated communication, and interpreting comprehension: "For as soon as anyone deliberately concentrates his attention to a certain degree, he begins to select from the material before him; one point will be fixed in his mind with particular clearness and some other will be correspondingly disregarded, and in making this selection he will be following his expectations or inclinations. This, however, is precisely what must not be done. In making the selection, if he follows his expectations he is in danger of never finding anything but what he already knows."[37] That this is indeed a matter of deconstructing the discourse of knowledge, that is, a discourse of communication brought to its strictest form, is undeniable: "It is not a good thing to work on a case scientifically while treatment is still proceeding—to piece together its structure, to try to foretell its further progress, and to get a picture from time to time of the current state of affairs, as scientific interest would demand. Cases which are devoted from the first to scientific purposes and are treated accordingly suffer in their outcome; while the most successful cases are those in which one proceeds, as it were, without any purpose in view, allows oneself to be taken by surprise by any new turn (*von jeder Wendung*) in them, and always meets them with an open mind, free from any presuppositions."[38] On the contrary, the purpose of the evenly suspended attention is to immerse the analysand's entire discourse in a kind of liquid element where the analyst's ear—the third ear—will let it float, so as to detect the crackling, rustling, and echoes of the distortions that the primary process impresses upon it. This rule, writes Freud, is "intended to create for the doctor a counterpart to the 'fundamental rule of psycho-analysis' which is laid down for the patient."[39] In the same way that the patient must strive, through free association, to thwart secondary revision and all the other censorship operations acting upon her or his discourse, the analyst's listening must free itself as much as possible from secondary constraints, for this is the only way for her or him to "reconstruct" the patient's unconscious, thanks to "the derivatives of the unconscious which are communicated" to him or her.[40]

Whereas the discourse-symptom is a secondary surface haunted by traces of primary operations, suspended listening and the fundamental rule reverse this relation and place this surface in a primary space where these traces will reverberate and be able to come to the fore. Thus interpretation is work in the same way as the dream: neither commentary nor metalanguage, it is before all else an operative practice that does violence to the manifest organization of language, to its syntax and articulated signification. This is precisely how—equipped with this strange method of the recessus, which grants equal importance to the individual parts as to the whole, to the detail as to entire composition—Freud will bring to light what he believed was the meaning of Michelangelo's *Moses*. Here, too, in the plastic artwork, it is when all reasonable expectation has been abandoned that the detection and capture of the phantasmatic matrix can happen. Meaning reveals itself only in opposition to significations.

Now this same reversal, or at least a comparable reversal, occurs in the production of the artwork. If the latter is not a symptom, this is because in the artwork too the space of dispossession—the space where energy flows freely in the primary process—refuses to be boxed back in, to be repressed by secondary-level bindings (linguistic and realistic) or by the complicity of Eros with Logos, but on the contrary because the artwork offers the symptom its own space of dispossession in which to resonate. When we claim that the artwork occupies an oscillating space, that it is a kind of transitional object, that it belongs to a *Zwischenwelt*, what we are thus underscoring is exactly its transgressive power vis-à-vis reality. Frege argued that the first precondition for the aesthetic apprehension of discourse is to give up the search for reference; Widdowson observes that all poetic discourse offers an ambiguous relation to context;[41] Freud stressed the gap between the realistic use of language and its use in fiction;[42] and Klee turned the realist drawing upside down to grant it plastic treatment.[43] This distinctive position of the artwork (and regardless of the sensory system to which it belongs) means that the strict organization of plastic, acoustic, or linguistic elements that it contains always presents itself in a suspended space. If the artwork seems to "oscillate," this is because there is *in itself* a to and fro between what is realistic and what is imaginary, or, to be more precise, between what is "discourse" (recognizable script in general) and what is figure. Its *playful* dimension [*dimension de* jeu] hinges on this inclusion of (linguistic, gestaltist) "seriousness," that is, of what is bound—in the element of difference—of unhampered mobility.

Based on the phantasy "A Child Is Being Beaten," one comes to understand what the symptom—and first of all, its very matrix—consists of: what encloses the free play of difference is the existence of the binding, which ensures the organism's survival. Eros and Logos then conspire to block the death drive; regression is interrupted and placed in a repetitive framework. The symptom is due to the emergence of a form, of a rigid framework as a compromise between the twin requirements of living and dying, reality and Nirvana. Thus, from the very formation of its deep figure, desire compromises itself by becoming involved with what prohibits it; its surface expressions will betray in the symptom this same configuration: bound order, dotted with displacements and condensations, marks of the death drive. What constitutes the art is the submerging of this order in the element of death: zones of displacement and condensations, peppered with islets of bound order, themselves dotted with condensations and displacements.

All art is re-presentational in a way that goes far beyond the function of perspective theater [*théâtre "italien"*], to the extent that it is overwhelming [*renversant*], that it overturns the relationship between unconscious and preconscious, that it sets out to imbed the latter in the context of the former. This reversal re-creates difference, eventfulness, and goes hand in hand with a certain unsightliness.[44] This unsightliness is the affect corresponding to the presentation of the primary operations; it is the anxiety in the aesthetic order. Such a reversal does not at all presuppose the domination of the unconscious by consciousness; it presupposes instead the rejection of this domination: what it wants is not-wanting, to keep open the space in which the order of discourse and of acts enclose themselves. The strain to keep this void voided requires strength. I imagine Orpheus *struggling to turn back* toward Eurydice, mustering the strength to desire, against all odds, a glimpse of the invisible and opt, at the cost of dismemberment, for this Dionysian vision instead of the pleasing and luminous, that is, secondary, artwork, which is the poet's share. This is the strength Hölderlin speaks of, the strength to face the thunderbolt [*foudroiement*]. The depth of the inner experience is the same for everyone. What is uncommon is the strength to want to stare at the deep figure of desire, to accommodate its space of play, to embrace the anguish of keeping open the void where it can bounce back its figures. The artist is not someone who reconciles, but one who can bear the fact that unity is absent. The artwork's "unsightliness" is a product of this absence. It shows that art is not religion.

By now it will have become clear that this reversal is double, for not only is the figure's inclusion in discourse reversed, with discourse appearing in a figural space, but the function of this second-level figurality is not to repeat around discourse the figure that was already within it. This simple reversal is simply phantasmatic, repetitive, specular, emblematized by the figure of the cow laughing on the cover of the box of cheese that bears this figure's name.[45] The earrings worn by the cow represented on the lid are boxes of the same cheese, on whose cover is the identical laughing cow wearing earrings, and so on. This sequence inspired one of my friends to conclude that the world must be a laughing cow. The simple reversal of the figure-text relation, far from bringing desire face to face with itself, fulfills and drowns it in its infinite recurrence. One suspects that this marketing campaign indeed fulfills the cheese company's (paranoiac) desire, that the laughing cow become the world, and that this world be made of soft cheese. The critical reversal on the other hand does not reinstate, around the bound elements (in this case, the printed name of the cheese), the *figure* that they harbored; instead what it repeats are the *operations* that make this figure possible among others.

The figure, by itself, is already tensed in its order, already "scripted": Eros paves the way for Logos. The primary process, understood as the mobility of cathexes, is already held in check in the phantasy. Reiterating the figure by simply shifting it in relation to the text does not amount to deconstructing this relation, does not make it critical. There is obviously a condensation in the cow, since it is laughing. But the critical function and the work of truth cannot consist in making a cow laugh again around the first (which in turn becomes the earrings of the second). Such a simple reversal is repetitive, uncritical. Rather, critical work consists in exhibiting *condensation itself* as process. The space in which the ordered elements are to appear must therefore be more than just a space of illusion (with its condensation fulfilling desire); it must *also* be one of truth, where the primary operations show themselves for what they are, instead of serving to uphold the phantasy. These operations are thereby isolated from their libidinal aim and made visible in themselves. No longer do they lead solely to desire's hallucinatory fulfillment, by which Eros carries out its mission, even into situations of distress. These operations reveal themselves as traces of pure difference, as zones of distress, in which the death drive—the movement of and toward difference—asserts itself, coiling around pleasure-, reality-, and discourse-formations.

Such is the power that strains the artwork. The latter is at its breaking-point, which is how it can afford to be more than ideological-symptomatic. Admittedly, the production of the artwork is not identical to the analytic situation: "art" is not a "therapeutics." In analytic work, reversal must extend into a turnaround that will make possible a theoretical discourse shielded in principle from primary operations, one that takes these as its object (its reference[46]). In this discourse—after the fact, at a remove, and strictly speaking secondary—all the symptomatic "givens" [*données*] put forward by the patient are literally turned around, that is, first reversed by being linked to a system of illusion and censorship, and, second, critiqued for the fact that both their immediate appearance and their reversed meaning are inferred from a phantasmatic matrix, from a script of desire. In the work of the artwork, one remains within the sensory, aesthetic element. There can be no turnaround, strictly defined, because one is not seeking to *articulate* the deep matrix and articulate it in a rigorous metalanguage with its intrinsic consistency and wholeness in relation to interpreted material. But neither is it a simple reversal, which is the work itself of desire. It is a double reversal: the work of illusion is made manifest, as such, to the senses. On the one hand, no theoretical discourse; nor, on the other, only operations subjected to the hallucinatory function, but these operations given over to the senses, and the free flow of energy acknowledged [*avérée*].

This is not a matter of sublimation, but of the strength to descend toward the death drive. And what Freud called "incentive bonus" must also be reversed, for it is, in fact, the signified, the represented, the content, and phantasmatic script that grant this incentive. The artwork's "subject," "motif," or "theme" entices us. But the artwork does not fulfill desire; it unfulfills it. Pleasure and death are cleaved in the artwork: its formalism is not the sign of the mind, but of the death drive. By reversing the relationship Freud established between aesthetic incentive bonus and libidinal pleasure, and by replacing it with the relationship between the death drive's fascination and a libidinal incentive bonus, all one is doing is bringing aesthetic doctrine up to date with the last topography.

In so doing, one is updating this doctrine in yet another way. In the elaboration of his discourse of knowledge, Freud was acted upon not by direct figurality—that is, by simple reversals of expressions of his own phantasmatics—but by doubly reversed figurality. Jean Starobinski has shown how the theatrical works *Oedipus Rex* and *Hamlet* functioned as operators in Freud's epistemological unconscious.[47] Starobinski thus assigns the proper place not only to these particular plays, but to the artwork in general in its overwhelmingness [*en tant que renversante*]. These tragedies were able to play such a role in the development of psychoanalysis because they were more than mere symptoms or reversed expressions of desire: they were entities in which the reversal was itself reversed, in which the operations of desire could already be glimpsed (though not yet heard or articulated). These tragedies were not fulfillments of desire, clogging primary space with the object's illusion, but unfulfillments preserving its voidness. This double reversal put Freud on the path of the critical turnaround.

Shakespearean Episode

Hamlet has the actors who came to the castle of Elsinore perform a sample of their repertoire, suggesting they recite Priam's murder by Pyrrhus. Following an interruption caused by Polonius complaining that it is too long, Hamlet urges them to go on:

"Hamlet: Say on, come to Hecuba." This is when is committed the slip of the tongue at the heart of the tragedy, over which Hamlet stumbles, in shock: "First player: but who, O! who had seen the mobled queen . . . —Hamlet: 'The mobled queen'? . . . —Polonius: That's good; 'mobled queen' is good" (lines 531–534). This is not a play on words that defies translation, but a verbal creation.[48] André Gide offers the excellent translation "la reine encamouflée." Through free association, one finds in the vicinity of *mobled*: *the mob*, or rabble; *motley*, or an *incongruous mixture*, and more specifically, the jester's outfit: *to wear motley* is *to play the fool*.[49] Not much further afield, phonetically, one encounters *mother*, queen and widow like Hecuba, Andromache, or Gertrude. No wonder Hamlet is shocked at such a condensation . . . Polonius is a little too quick to assent: his reckless complicity with the primary process will cost him his life, causing him to die when it should have been Claudius, displaced. The key to *mobled* is *mobilized*, the loss of invariance of the intervals that determine kinship: "my uncle-father and aunt-mother are deceived" (line 402).[50] A mobile mother is a mother misplaced, appearing where she is not expected and not appearing where she is, *camouflée*[51] because she slips away and *encanaillée*,[52] prostituted, because she gave herself in violation of the intervals imposed by the rules of exchange; and moreover "insane," since she ignores reason, the well-ordered allotment of the social fabric, the yes or no of kinship. The mobile mother is Jocasta.

Coming from the actor's mouth, *mobled* is a slip of the tongue; in the ear of Polonius, the slip of the tongue is repressed: "that's good," he says, let's move on (but there is nowhere to move on to, everything is here); and in Hamlet's ear, the slip of the tongue penetrates like a poison, like his oedipal truth. Hamlet stops short at the word—an unheard-of word that upon itself, in its form, repeats the very operations carried out by the object it designates, by the displaced and condensed mother. The function of theatrical reversal is here in full swing. Contrary to Polonius, Hamlet is out to enjoy the scene, wanting the artwork's critical function to take effect on his uncle; he turns out to be this function's first beneficiary, and its first victim. *Mobled* is a fragment of the space of the primary unconscious, which came to leave its trace in the space of discourse. But this trace is staged as a play in the fictional space of Gonzago's tragedy. The "subject," Hecuba, fades away; what remains is the operation impressed in the word. Like the "fools" clad in a patchwork of bits and pieces, this mismatched word performs a work of truth; it does not *articulate* it.

What makes this work possible is the representational relationship between Hamlet the spectator and the play staged for him. But this relationship is doubled again: Freud the spectator sees the prince immobilized for one second before this word of transgression, which is at the same time transgression within words. Freud wonders: what is this fascination for linguistic distortions on the part of this son out to avenge his father? What is this spectacle compulsion, this ear open to displacement in words rather than things? The slip of the tongue in the Gonzago tragedy gives way to a symptom on the Shakespearean stage: in the flash of an instant, the Danish king's anxiety is that of Oedipus. But this trace of the unconscious is perceived only because it is staged, because between it and Freud lies a space of play, the uncertain space of theater. In the same way that it is Hamlet's spectatorial position that makes it possible for him to pay to the actor's words an attention evenly suspended over every detail, allowing him to grasp the insignificant, so Freud can hear the question Hamlet addresses to meaninglessness—"the mobled queen?"—only because of the oscillating, mobile nature of the area in which the spectacular relationship takes place. First we have a primary reversal that produces the symptomatic condensation "mobled queen"; then a second reversal through which Hamlet falls upon and echoes, as it were, the first—this is the moment of the Shakespearean artwork; and a third reversal, in which Freud seizes the slip of the tongue in Gonzago's scene as a trace in discourse of a foreign meaning, thanks to the amplification that Hamlet's question grants the slip of the tongue in Shakespeare's tragedy. All Freud will need to do for the analytic attitude to take hold is to *turn his back* on the scene: suspended attention, but substitution of the eye with the one ear that prepares the ground for understanding and theoretical discourse. This is how the analytic turnaround will have been induced by the "poetic" double reversal.

In the technique of psycho-analysis, there is no need for any special synthetic work of synthesis; the individual does that for himself better than we can.[1]

—SIGMUND FREUD TO OSKAR PFISTER
(letter dated 9 October 1918)

APPENDIX

Jean-François Lyotard's Translation of "Die Verneinung" by Sigmund Freud

In *Discours, figure,* Lyotard wrote that he included his own translation of Freud's "Die Verneinung" (1925) "if only to give the French reader access to a text otherwise impossible to find." This must have been true in 1971, when the only available French translation of Freud's essay was Henry Hoesli's, published in 1934 in the specialist journal *Revue française de psychanalyse.* After Lyotard's version, another fourteen years would pass until Jean Laplanche's translation of "Die Verneinung," now considered authoritative, came out. (Laplanche's text, titled "Négation," first appeared in *S. Freud: Résultats, idées, problèmes,* vol. 2 [Paris: Presses Universitaires de France, 1985], 135–139, and now forms part of *Sigmund Freud, Oeuvres Complètes,* vol. 17 [Paris: Presses Universitaires de France, 1992], 11–16.)

But Lyotard is being modest when he defends the inclusion of his own translation of "Die Verneinung" in *Discours, figure* as merely a means of facilitating access to a hard-to-find essay, for his is clearly a more precise translation than Hoesli's. For example, Hoesli consistently translates *Wiederholung* as "reproduction" instead of "repetition," thus erasing Freud's key distinction in "Die Verneinung" between *Reproduktion* and *Wiederholung.* Perhaps most egregious is Hoesli's omission—corrected by Lyotard—of a crucial sentence in Freud's text: "In this stage of development [from pleasure-ego to reality-ego] regard for the pleasure principle has been set aside" (*The Standard Edition of the Complete Psychological Works of Sigmund Freud,* trans. and ed. James Strachey et al., vol. 19 [London: The Hogarth Press, 1953–], 237).

By suggesting that the sole purpose of his translation was to give wider circulation to "Die Verneinung," Lyotard was also being slightly disingenuous, because his translation represented a fairly explicit attempt at leaving his mark on an important and ongoing French debate surrounding Freud's text that involved a number of leading intellectuals from varying ideological quarters—Émile Benveniste, Jean Hyppolite, Jacques Lacan, and Paul Ricoeur among them. As John Mowitt indicates in his Introduction to the present book, Lyotard's translation of a text that had stirred such heated debate since the mid-1950s could only have been perceived, and intended, as a bold move on the part of a philosopher aspiring to the rank of *Maître de conférences*.

Knowledge of this historical background sheds light on some of the particularities of Lyotard's translation. Lyotard, for example, emphasizes (by placing the word in brackets) Freud's choice of *Aufhebung* to describe the process repression undergoes through negation (denial). In contrast to both Hoesli and Laplanche, who translate *Aufhebung* as "suppression," Lyotard, in a nod to Hegel, opts for "levée" ("lifting" in the *Standard Edition*). Lyotard makes another telling passing gesture, to Marx this time, by adding *Entfremdung* and its translation *aliénation* in brackets, even though Marx's *Entfremdung* stands at a considerable distance from Freud's in this context—something Lyotard seems ready to acknowledge by using *éloignement* ("differentiation" in the *Standard Edition*) in the text itself.

The original essay by Freud is published in *Gesammelte Werke*, vol. 14 (London: Imago Publishing, 1925), 11–15.

*

* *

La manière dont nos patients présentent ce qui leur vient à l'idée (leurs associations) pendant le travail analytique nous donne l'occasion de faire certaines remarques intéressantes. « Vous allez sans doute penser que je veux vous dire quelque chose d'offensant, mais en réalité je n'ai pas cette intention. » Nous comprenons qu'il s'agit là du refus (Abweisung) d'une idée qui vient justement d'émerger par projection. Ou encore : « Vous vous demandez qui peut bien être cette personne dans mon rêve. Ce n'est *pas* ma mère. » Nous corrigeons : c'est donc sa mère. Nous prenons la liberté, avec l'interprétation, de détourner les yeux (absehen) de la négation et de ne retenir que le contenu de l'idée. C'est comme si le patient avait dit : « C'est vrai, ma mère est ce qui m'est venu à l'idée à propos de cette personne, mais je n'ai aucun plaisir à admettre cette association. »

A l'occasion, on peut obtenir d'une manière très commode l'éclaircissement qu'on recherche sur le refoulé inconscient. On demande : Qu'est-ce qui vous paraît le plus totalement invraisemblable dans cette situation ? Qu'est-ce qui, selon vous, est placé, à ce moment-là aussi loin que possible de vous-même ? Si le patient tombe dans le piège, s'il nomme ce à quoi il veut le moins accorder créance, alors presque toujours, par là-même il aura confessé précisément l'essentiel (das Richtige). On trouve un assez joli pendant à cette expérience chez le névrosé obsessionnel qui a déjà été introduit à la compréhension de ses propres symptômes. « J'ai eu une nouvelle représentation obsessionnelle. Il m'est tout de suite venu à l'idée qu'elle pourrait vouloir dire telle chose déterminée. Mai non, ça ne peut pas être vrai ; autrement l'idée n'aurait pas pu m'en venir. » Ce qu'il retranche (verwirft) grâce à cette argumentation (Begründung), qu'il a apprise de la cure, c'est naturellement le véritable sens de la nouvelle représentation obsessionnelle.

Un contenu de représentation ou de pensée refoulé peut donc se frayer passage (durchdringen) jusqu'à la conscience, à condition qu'il se laisse nier. La négation est une manière de prendre connaissance du refoulé, à proprement parler, elle est déjà une levée (Aufhebung) du refoulement, mais certainement pas une acceptation (Annahme) du refoulé. On voit comment ici la fonction intellectuelle se dissocie du processus affectif. Avec l'aide de la négation, on ne fait faire marche arrière qu'à l'une des suites du processus de refoulement à savoir que son contenu de représentation ne s'étend pas jusqu'à la conscience. Il en résulte une sorte d'acceptation (Annahme) intellectuelle du refoulé cependant que l'essentiel reste soumis au refoulement.[1] Au cours du travail analytique, nous créons souvent une autre altération de la même situation, qui est très importante et passablement surprenante. Nous réussissons à vaincre la négation même et à obtenir la pleine acceptation (Annahme) intellectuelle du refoulé, — le processus de refoulement lui-même n'est pas levé (aufgehoben) de ce fait.

La tâche de la fonction intellectuelle du jugement étant d'affirmer (bejahen) ou de nier (verneinen) des contenus de pensée, nous sommes conduits par les précédentes remarques à l'origine psychologique de cette fonction. Nier quelque chose dans le jugement, cela veut dire au fond : voilà une chose que je préférerais bien refouler. La condamnation (Verurteilung, méjugement) est le substitut (Ersatz) du refoulement, son Non est une estampille de ce dernier, un certificat d'origine, quelque chose comme « made in Germany ». Au moyen du symbole de la négation, l'activité de la pensée s'affranchit des limitations du refoulement et s'enrichit de contenus dont elle ne peut se priver pour s'accomplir.

La fonction du jugement a pour l'essentiel deux décisions à prendre. Elle doit d'une chose dire ou dédire (zu- oder absprechen) une propriété, et elle doit d'une représentation accorder ou contester l'existence dans la réalité. La propriété de laquelle il doit être décidé, pourrait avoir été originellement bonne ou mauvaise, utile ou nuisible. Traduit dans la langue des motions pulsionnelles (Triebregungen) orales les plus anciennes : je veux manger ça, ou je veux le cracher ; et dans une transposition ultérieure : je veux introduire ça en moi et exclure ça de moi. Donc : ça doit être en moi ou hors de moi. Le Moi-plaisir (Lust-Ich) originel veut, comme je l'ai montré ailleurs, introjeter en soi tout ce qui est bon, rejeter de soi tout ce qui est mauvais. Le mauvais, ce qui est étranger au Moi, ce qui se trouve au dehors, lui est tout d'abord identique.[2]

L'autre décision que prend la fonction de jugement, celle qui porte sur l'existence réelle d'une chose représentée, intéresse (ist ein Interesse des) le Moi-réalité (Real-Ich) définitif, qui s'est développé à partir du Moi-plaisir initial (épreuve de réalité, Realitätsprüfung). Maintenant, il ne s'agit plus de savoir si quelque chose de perçu (une chose) doit être accepté ou non dans le Moi, mais si quelque chose qui existe dans le Moi comme représentation peut être retrouvé aussi dans la perception (réalité). C'est, comme on voit, de nouveau une question *d'extérieur et d'intérieur*. Le non-réel, ce qui est seulement représenté, le subjectif, n'est qu'à l'intérieur ; l'autre, le réel, existe aussi à *l'extérieur*. Dans ce développement, la considération pour le principe de plaisir a été laissée de côté. L'expérience a enseigné que l'important n'est pas seulement qu'une chose (objet de satisfaction) possède la « bonne » propriété, qu'elle mérite donc d'être accueillie dans le Moi, mais aussi qu'elle soit là dans le monde extérieur, de sorte qu'on puisse s'emparer d'elle selon qu'il en est besoin. Pour comprendre ce progrès, il faut se rappeler que toutes les représentations proviennent (stammen) de perceptions, dont elles sont des répétitions (Wiederholungen). A l'origine donc, l'existence de la représentation est déjà une caution de la réalité du représenté. L'opposition (der Gegensatz) entre subjectif et objectif ne s'institue pas dès le début. Elle s'établit premièrement grâce à ceci : que l'activité de pensée possède la faculté de rendre à nouveau présente, grâce à la reproduction dans la représentation, une chose une fois qu'elle a été perçue, tandis que l'objet à l'extérieur n'a plus besoin d'être existant (vorhanden). Le but premier et tout proche de l'épreuve de réalité, ce n'est donc pas de trouver dans la perception réelle un objet qui corresponde au représenté, mais de le *retrouver*, de s'assurer qu'il est encore existant. Une contribution ultérieure à l'éloignement (Entfremdung, aliénation) entre le sujet et l'objet procède d'une autre faculté de la capacité de penser. La reproduction de la perception dans la représentation n'en est pas toujours la fidèle répétition ; elle peut être modifiée par des élisions (Weglassungen), altérée par des fusions d'éléments divers. L'épreuve de réalité doit alors contrôler jusqu'à quel point s'étendent ces déformations (Entstellungen). Mais on reconnaît pour condition à l'institution (die Einsetzung) de l'épreuve de réalité que se soient perdus (verloren) des objets qui, un jour, avaient procuré une satisfaction réelle.

L'acte de juger (das Urteilen) est l'action intellectuelle qui décide du choix de l'action motrice, qui met un terme à la suspension (Aufschub) de la pensée et qui fait passer du penser à l'agir. J'ai déjà traité ailleurs de la suspension de la pensée. Il faut la considérer comme une mise à l'essai, comme un tâtonnement moteur effectué aux moindres frais de décharge (Abfuhr). Réfléchissons : où donc le Moi a-t-il précédemment employé un tel tâtonnement, en quelle place a-t-il fait l'apprentissage de la technique qu'il applique à présent aux processus de pensée ? Cela échoit à la terminaison sensorielle de l'appareil psychique du côté des perceptions sensibles. Selon notre hypothèse, la perception, en effet, n'est pas un processus purement passif, mais le Moi lance périodiquement de petites quantités d'investissement dans le système de perception, au moyen desquelles il tâte (verkostet) les excitations extérieures pour se retirer à nouveau après chacune de ces sorties de palpation (nach jedem solchen tastenden Vorstoss).

Pour la première fois, l'étude du jugement nous ouvre peut-être la vue sur la façon dont s'institue une fonction intellectuelle en se dégageant du jeu des pulsions primaires. L'acte de juger est le développement finalisé de ces opérations qui obéissent originellement au principe de plaisir : l'installation

(Einbeziehung) dans le Moi ou l'expulsion (Ausstossung) hors du Moi. Sa polarité paraît répondre au caractère opposé des deux groupes de pulsions que nous admettons. L'affirmation (Bejahung) — en tant que substitut de l'unification (als Ersatz der Vereinigung) — relève de l'Éros, la négation — qui fait suite à l'expulsion (Nachfolge der Ausstossung) — de la pulsion de destruction. Le plaisir de nier en général, le négativisme de nombreux psychotiques doit vraisemblablement être compris comme un indice de la désintrication (Entmischung) des pulsions grâce au retrait (Abzug) des composantes libidinales. Mais l'accomplissement de la fonction du jugement est rendu possible en premier lieu parce que la constitution du symbole de la négation a permis à la pensée un premier degré d'indépendance par rapport aux conséquences du refoulement et du même coup à la coercition du principe de plaisir.

Avec cette façon de comprendre la négation, s'accorde très bien ceci : que l'on ne découvre dans l'analyse aucun « Non » en provenance de l'inconscient, et que la reconnaissance de l'inconscient de la part du Moi s'exprime en une formule négative. Aucune preuve plus forte qu'on est arrivé à découvrir l'inconscient que lorsque l'analysé réagit avec une phrase comme : *Ça, je ne l'ai pas pensé, ou : Ça, je n'y ai pas (jamais) pensé.*

(Fischer Verlag pour l'édition allemande. Traduction J.F.L. sous réserve des ayant-droits de l'édition française : Gallimard, Payot, Presses Universitaires de France.)

NOTES TO CHAPTERS

Introduction

1. This observation is reported by Geoffrey Bennington in his introduction to *Lyotard: Writing the Event* (New York: Columbia University Press, 1988), 2.
2. Jean-François Lyotard, *Peregrinations: Law, Form, Event* (New York: Columbia University Press, 1988), 45–75.
3. Jean-François Lyotard, *Dérive à partir de Marx et Freud* (Paris: UGE, 1973), 18. My translation.
4. Precisely during this period Louis Althusser was finishing his *Diplôme d'études supérieures*, "On Content in the Thought of G.W.F. Hegel," and a few months earlier, in late 1947, he published a short review of Kojève's study, "Man, That Night" in the *Cahiers du Sud*. Although both he and Thao accuse Kojève of being a dualist, Thao's piece—both in terms of its venue and its substance—is the far more trenchant statement.
5. See Bennington, *Lyotard: Writing the Event*; Bill Readings, *Introducing Lyotard: Art and Politics* (New York: Routledge, 1991); Federico Jiménez Losantos, "Prologo" to *Discurso, Figura* (Barcelona: EGG, 1979); and Mary Lydon, "Veduta on *Discours, Figure,*" *Yale French Studies* 99 (2001): 10–26.
6. One might say that as many figures hover over *Discourse, Figure* as commentators. However, the relation between Lacan and Lyotard, as it operates in this book, has received perhaps its most sustained treatment in Peter Dews, "On the Letter and the Line: Discourse and Its Other in Lyotard," from *diacritics* 14, no. 3 (Fall 1984): 40–49.
7. The well-known quarrel between Lacan and Derrida over Poe's "The Purloined Letter" did not come from nowhere. Consider in this regard Lacan's formulation from "The Instance of the Letter in the Unconscious," that one is to grasp the letter *à la lettre,* that is, literally, and Derrida's counter in the title to section one of his *Of Grammatology,* "Writing Before the Letter," in French, *avant la lettre,* that is, before the fact, before, that is, the literal. Never to shirk a provocation, Lacan responded in the Points edition of the *Écrits* by insisting that his insight into the "instance/agency of the letter preceded any grammatology." This in turn appears to have prompted *The Title of the Letter: A Reading of Lacan* by Derrida partisans Jean-Luc Nancy and Philippe Lacoue-Labarthe. The titular phrase, *le titre de la lettre,* might also be rendered as the "deed to, or rank of the letter." Here is not the place to elaborate the stakes of this face-off, but suffice it to say that at issue is the nontrivial problem of whether philosophy can think the general economy of signs that conditions the possibility of language, whether spoken or written.

8. Jean-François Lyotard, *Libidinal Economy*, trans. Ian Hamilton Grant (Bloomington: Indiana University Press, 1993), 45.
9. Deleuze, who served as a member of the academic jury selected to evaluate Lyotard's thesis, also published a short review of *Discourse, Figure* in *La Quinzaine littéraire* where, among other things, he flags its "anti-dialectical" spirit. See Gilles Deleuze, "Appréciation," in *L'Île déserte et autres textes* (Paris: Minuit, 2002): 299–300.
10. See Gilles Deleuze, "Désir et plaisir," *Magazine littéraire* 325 (October 1994): 59–65.
11. See Gopal Balakrishnan, ed., *Debating Empire* (London: Verso, 2003) and Samir Amin, "*Empire* and *Multitude*," *The Monthly Review* 57, no. 6 (November 2005).
12. Sorting through what might be at stake in a non-dialectical Marxism would require a monograph of its own. Suffice it to say that in the context of these remarks what is at issue might be rendered in the repudiation of finitude, that is, in the repudiation of the intimate, structural articulation of death, negation, and eschatology, or, to summon their anti-Oedipal avatar, "lack."

The Bias of the Figural

[Lyotard no doubt intended the title of the opening chapter of *Discours, figure*—"Le parti pris du figural"—to cut through to the book's core, namely the role of the figural in the libidinal economy of the visible, while at the same time maintaining the figural's fundamental ambiguity between subject and object, signifier and signified, word and image. For if "le parti pris du figural" suggests taking the side of the figural, it also evokes the figural's own one-sidedness or prejudice, in blatant disregard for discourse's aspirations to structure and communication. As Mary Lydon has remarked, behind this title may lie a reference to Francis Ponge's book *Le parti pris des choses*, first published in 1942, variously translated as *The Voice of Things* or *The Nature of Things* (Lydon, "Veduta on *Discours, figure*," in *Jean-Francois Lyotard: Time and Judgment*, edited by Robert Harvey and Lawrence R. Schehr, 10–26, *Yale French Studies* 99 [New Haven, Conn.: Yale University Press, 2001], 12). Yet while "things" indeed play an important role in the figural's irruption in the visible, "voice" and "nature" run counter to Lyotard's efforts to preserve the figural's elusiveness. Hence my preference for "bias"—related to the French *biais*, meaning slanted, oblique, askew—to signify, in the context of *Discourse, Figure*, the force that unseats any perspective claiming to be "legitimate," whether in philosophy or painting. —*Trans.*]

1. Paul Claudel, *Art poétique* (Paris: Mercure de France, 1941), 50–51; *Poetic Art*, trans. Renee Spodheim (Port Washington, London: Kennikat Press, 1969), 32. [In the present translation, square brackets [ ] indicate interventions by the translator, whereas curly brackets { } signal brackets used by Lyotard in the original. —*Trans.*]
2. Claudel, *Art poétique*, 74–75; *Poetic Art*, trans. Spodheim, 48 [emphasis J.-F.L.].
3. Claudel, *Art poétique*, 50; *Poetic Art*, trans. Spodheim, 31. [Translation modified. —*Trans.*]
4. Claudel, *Art poétique*, 74; *Poetic Art*, trans. Spodheim, 47.
5. [As Lydon concedes, "the word '*sensible*' poses a thorny problem (one of many) for the translator of *Discours, figure*" ("Veduta on *Discours, figure*," note 4, 13). Although Lydon

goes on to list "'sensory,' 'physical,' tangible,' or 'material'" as possible translations of *sensible* (she will also resort to "sensitive," while Alphonso Lingis, preeminent translator of Maurice Merleau-Ponty's writings, favors "sensible"), I choose, for the sake of consistency and clarity, to translate it by "sensory." —*Trans.*]

6. Claudel, *Art poétique*, 74; *Poetic Art*, trans. Spodheim, 47.
7. André Breton, *Le surréalisme et la peinture* (Paris: Gallimard, 1965), 1; *Surrealism and Painting*, trans. Simon Watson Taylor (London: Macdonald, 1972), 1.
8. [In *Discourse, figure*, Lyotard understands *écart* differently than Merleau-Ponty. Alphonso Lingis, translating Maurice Merleau-Ponty's *Le visible et l'invisible* (Paris: Gallimard, 1964), proposes "divergence," "spread," "deviation," or "separation" (Merleau-Ponty, *The Visible and the Invisible*, ed. Claude Lefort, trans. Alphonso Lingis [Evanston, Ill.: Northwestern University Press, 1968], 7). In *Discours, figure*, *écart* is predominantly a linguistic category, referring to the measured space between signifying units. I therefore translate *écart* by "gap" or "interval" (and more rarely by "spacing"), since Lyotard seems to consider *écart*, *écartement*, *intervalle* and *espacement* as close enough to be in most instances interchangeable. —*Trans.*]
9. Compare the definition of the "hermeneutic circle" bringing together believing and understanding, religion and philosophy in *Finitude et culpabilité* (Paris: Aubier, 1960, vol. 2, 325 ff), particularly this passage: "The symbol is already in the element of speech. We have insisted enough on the fact that it snatches feeling and even language from silence and confusion, granting a language to avowal, to confession. Through it man remains language through and through. This is not the most crucial: nowhere does symbolic language exist without hermeneutics; wherever a man dreams and raves, another steps up to interpret. What was already discourse, however incoherent, enters coherent discourse through hermeneutics" (325–326 [translation A.H.]) to these passages of Hegel's introduction to his *Lectures on the History of Philosophy* (Berlin, 1823–1824): "Now philosophy has the same subject-matter, namely the absolute substance, universal reason, implicit and explicit; in philosophy likewise, the spirit wishes to make this object its own. But while religion accomplishes this reconciliation in devotion (*Andacht*) and cult, i.e. by way of feeling, philosophy wishes to reach this result in thought, in a knowledge achieved through thinking. Devotion is a *feeling* of a unity of God and man, but it is a *thoughtful* feeling. Thinking (*denken*) is implied in the word 'devotion' (*Andacht*); devotion is a drive towards thought, a thinking reaching out to the unity, a frame of mind adapting itself to the unity (*ein Daranhindenken, Sicherandenken*). But the form of philosophy is pure thinking, is knowledge and discernment, and it is at this point that philosophy's difference from religion begins. . . . It is said that what has been revealed is something to which human reason could not attain by its own effort. This calls for the remark that truth, the knowledge of the nature of God, does of course come to men at first from outside; that consciousness of the truth as of an object outside us and sensuously perceived, is the first mode of our consciousness of anything—e.g. Moses glimpsed God in the burning bush, the Greeks presented their gods to themselves in marble statues or in other imaginings contained in the poets. It is in this external fashion that any consciousness of ours begins, and to that extent the content, what we are conscious of, appears as given, coming to our minds from without, through

our seeing, hearing, etc. But the next thing is that there is not, and ought not to be, any remaining in this external mode, either in religion or in philosophy. These imaginative shapes or historical matters ought not to remain thus externally related to us; on the contrary they should become something spiritual for our spirit, cease to remain external, that is, in precisely a non-spiritual guise. . . . The universality of spirit, to which both philosophy and religion are related, is absolute universality, not external universality, i.e. it is a universality which pervades everything and is present in everything. Spirit we have to present to ourselves as free; freedom of spirit means that spirit is by itself and comprehends itself. Its nature is to overlap its other and therein to find itself, to unite itself with itself, and to have and enjoy itself" (*Introduction to the Lectures on the History of Philosophy*, trans. T. M. Knox and A. V. Miller [Oxford: Clarendon Press, 1985], 124, 130, 131 [emphasis J.F-L.]). Few are the texts where the function of *erasure of difference* assigned to dialectics, the "tautegorical" (as Schelling and Ricoeur would say) or recuperative (as I would put it) nature of interpreting discourse, and the Odyssean narcissism of knowledge (in Levinas's words) simultaneously come to the fore more explicitly. My thanks to Serge Boucheron for bringing them to my attention.

10. [Both *signification* and *sens* can translate as "meaning." Because Lyotard differentiates the former from designation as what is transparent linguistic comprehension from the gesture of reference, I translate *signification* as "signification" and reserve "meaning" (*sens*) for the "thick," "opaque" sign. —*Trans.*]
11. [Lyotard probably commits an oversight by writing that every object "tombe dans le trémis où la pensée remue et trie tout." *Trémis* does not exist. *Trémie* (hopper in English) and *tamis* (French for sieve) do. By substituting "s" for "e," Lyotard (unwittingly perhaps, but tellingly) hints at the presence of *trémeur*—terror, fright—in thought's process of sifting (*passer au tamis*) or categorizing. —*Trans.*]
12. [After Mary Lydon, I frequently translate the Saussurean category of *langue* by "language-system." As for *langage*—for Ferdinand de Saussure, the more general category, of which *langue* is a subset—I use "language," often providing the French in brackets in order to distinguish it both from *langue* and the generic non-linguistic meaning of the word. In most cases I render the third term in Saussure's terminology—*parole*—as "speech" or "utterance." —*Trans.*]
13. Georg Muche recalls the following scene: "In 1921, when Klee joined the Bauhaus, he moved into a studio adjacent to mine. One day I heard a strange noise, as if someone were stomping his foot rhythmically. Meeting Klee in the corridor I asked him if he had noticed something. 'Ah! Did you hear? Forgive me,' he said, 'I was painting away when all of a sudden—it was stronger than I—I began to dance. You must have heard me. I am terribly sorry. I otherwise never dance'" ("Paul Klee," *Frankfurter Allgemeine Zeitung*, 30 June 1956).
14. See Marcel Détienne, *Les maîtres de vérité dans la Grèce archaïque* (Paris: Maspero, 1966).
15. Georges Braque, *Le jour et la nuit* (Paris: Gallimard, 1952), 38.
16. Jean-Bertrand Pontalis, "L'utopie freudienne," *L'Arc* 34 (special issue on Freud, 1965).
17. Emmanuel Levinas, "Humanisme et anarchie," *Revue internationale de philosophie* (1968): 85–86.

18. Merleau-Ponty, *Le visible et l'invisible*, 229, 253; *The Visible and the Invisible*, trans. Lingis, 177, 202.
19. By even making preparations—as he was going to renounce what there was of a philosophy of the Cogito in *Phenomenology of Perception*—to ensure the continuation of unitary philosophy, by having Being replace the I.
20. Admirably demonstrated by Pierre Kaufmann at the end of the first chapter of *L'expérience émotionnelle de l'espace* (Paris: Vrin, 1967).
21. See in particular Levinas, "Humanisme et anarchie," 85–86.

Dialectics, Index, Form

1. Ferdinand de Saussure, *Cours de linguistique générale* (Paris: Payot, 1962), 38; *Course in General Linguistics*, trans. Roy Harris (London: Duckworth, 1971), 20.
2. Cf. Robert Godel, *Les sources manuscrites du Cours de linguistique générale de Ferdinand de Saussure* (Geneva, Paris: Droz and Minard, 1957), 145–157.
3. [*Bedeutung*, or reference, belongs to Gottlob Frege's terminology, to which Lyotard returns below in "Thickness on the Margins of Discourse" —*Trans.*]
4. I have attempted to define this sense and these limitations in "La place de l'aliénation dans le retournement marxiste," *Les temps modernes* 279 (August–September 1969).
5. [Lyotard translates Hegel's *Meinen* by *visée*—"aim" in English—whereas *Meinen* could also be translated by "design," "intention," or "meaning." In *Phenomenology of Spirit*, A. V. Miller translates *Meinen* by "meaning." However, to avoid confusion with *sens* (here consistently translated by "meaning"), and to follow the movement of Lyotard's argument—which attempts to show the proximity between *Meinen* and *Zeigen* (to indicate, to point) as well as their essential heterogeneity—I translate *visée* by "aim," except when quoting Miller. —*Trans.*]
6. Georg Wilhelm Friedrich Hegel, *Phänomenologie des Geistes,* ed. Johannes Hoffmeister (Hamburg: Felix Meiner, 1952), 85. "We must let ourselves *point to it* [the Now]; for the truth of this immediate relation is the truth of *this* 'I' which confines itself to one 'Now' or one 'Here'" (Hegel, *Phenomenology of Spirit,* trans. A. V. Miller [Oxford: Clarendon Press, 1977], 63).
7. Hegel, *Phänomenologie des Geistes,* 86; *Phenomenology of Spirit,* trans. Miller, 64.
8. Refer to Brice Parain's discussion of "sensory certainty" in *Recherches sur la nature et les fonctions du langage* (Paris: Gallimard, 1942), chaps. 10 and 11: "Hegel's beginning is . . . uncertain. He locates the drama of sensory certainty in the sentence of the now. This sentence, however, presenting itself as the expression of the moment's sensory certainty, is not of the moment itself, for it merely responds to another sentence which itself does not proceed directly from sensory certainty, but rather is a question about sensory certainty. . . . What we discover in the relations between sensory certainty and language is not . . . a dialectics, but an antagonism that only the notion of order expresses perfectly" (157–159).
9. Hegel, *Phenomenology of Spirit*, trans. Miller, 66. "Das sinnliche Diese, das gemeint wird, der Sprache, die dem Bewusstsein, dem an sich Allgemein angehört, *unerreichbar* ist . . . Sie meinen *dieses* Stück Papier, vorauf ich *dies* schreibe oder vielmehr geschrieben habe; aber was sie meinen, sagen sie nicht . . . Was das Unaussprechliche genannt wird, nichts

anderes ist als das Unwahre, Unvernünftige, bloss Gemeinte" (Hegel, *Phänomenologie des Geistes*, 88).

10. Roman Jakobson, "Two Aspects of Language and Two Types of Aphasic Disturbances," *Fundamentals of Language* (The Hague: Mouton, 1956), 58.
11. Hegel, *Aesthetics*, quoted by Hyppolite without reference.
12. Jean Hyppolite, *Logique et existence* (Paris: P.U.F., 1953), 28 [translation A.H.].
13. Hegel, *Aesthetics*, trans. T. M. Knox (Oxford: Clarendon Press, 1988 [1975]), vol. 1, 304–305. "Das Symbol is nun zunächst ein Zeichen. Bei der blossen Bezeichnung aber ist Zusammenhang, den die Bedeutung und deren Ausdruck mit einander haben, nur eine ganz willkürliche Verknüpfung. Dieser Ausdruck, die sinnliche Ding oder Bild stellt dann so wenig sich selber vor, da es vielmehr einen ihm fremden Inhalt, mit dem es in gar keiner eigenthümlichen Gemeinschaft zu stehn braucht, vor die Vorstellung bringt. So sind in den Sprechen z. B. die Töne Zeichen von irgend einer Vorstellung u. s. w. Der überwiegende Theil der Töne einer Sprache ist aber mit den Vorstellungen, die dadurch ausgedrückt werden, auf eine dem Gehalte nach zufällige Weise verknupft, wenn sich auch durch eine geschichtliche Entwicklung Zusammenhang von andrer Beschaffenheit war, und die Verschiedenheit der Sprachen besteht vornehmlich darin, dass dieselbe Vorstellung durch ein verschiedenes Tönen ausgedrückt ist. Ein anderes Beispiel solcher Zeichen sind die Farben {the colors}, welche in den Kokarden, Flagen u. s. w. gebraucht werden, um auszudrücken, zu welcher Nation ein Individuum, Schiff u. s. w. gehört. Eine solche Farbe enthält gleichfalls in ihr selber keine Qualität, welche ihre gemeintschaftlich wäre mit ihrer Bedeutung, der Nation nämlich, welche durch sich vorgestellt wird. In dem Sinne einer solchen *Gleichgültigkeit* von Bedeutung und Bezeichnung derselben dürfen wir deshalb in Betreff auf die *Kunst* überhaupt gerade in der Beziehung, Verwandtschaft und dem konkreten Ineinander von Bedeutung und Gestalt besteht. Anders ist es daher bei einem Zeichen, welches ein *Symbol* sein soll. Der Löwe z. B. wird als ein Symbol der Grossmuth, der Fuchs als Symbol der List, der Kreis als Symbol der Ewigkeit, das Dreieck als Symbol der Dreieinigkeit genommen. Der Löwe nun aber, der Fuchs, besitzen für sich die Eigenschaften selbst deren Bedeutung sie ausdrücken sollen . . . ; und das Dreieck hat als *ein Ganzes* dieselbe *Anzahl* von Seiten und Winkeln, als sich an der Idee Gottes ergeben, wenn die Bestimmungen, welche die Religion in Gott auffasst, dem *Zählen* unterworfen werden." (*Aesthetik, Sämtliche Werke*, ed. H. Glockner [Stuttgart: Frommann, 1939], vol. 12, 408–409). See also *Encyclopedia* (§ 458): "In this unity (initiated by intelligence) of an *independent representation* with an *intuition*, the matter of the latter is, in the first instance, something accepted, somewhat immediate or given (for example, the colour of the cockade, etc.). But in the fusion of the two elements, the *intuition* does not count positively or as representing itself, but as representative of *something else*. It is an image, which has received as its soul and *meaning* an *independent* mental representation. This intuition is the *Sign*.

"The sign is some immediate intuition, representing a totally different import from what naturally belongs to it; it is the *pyramid* into which a foreign soul has been conveyed, and where it is conserved. The *sign* is different from the *symbol*: for in the symbol the original characters (in essence and conception) of the visible objects are more or less identical with the import which it bears as symbol; whereas in the sign, strictly so-called, the natural attributes of the intuition, and the connotation of which it is a sign, have nothing to do with each other. Intelligence therefore gives proof of wider choice and ampler authority in the use of intuitions when it treats them as *designatory* (significative) {*als bezeichnend*} rather than as symbolical {*als symbolisierend*}.

"In logic and psychology, *signs* and *language* are usually foisted in somewhere as an *appendix,* without any trouble being taken to display their necessity and systematic place in the economy of intelligence. The right place for the sign is that just given: where intelligence—which as intuiting generates the form of time and space, but appears as recipient of sensible matter, out of which it forms ideas—now gives its own original ideas a definite existence from itself, *treating* the intuition (or time and space as filled full) *as its own property,* deleting the connotation which properly and naturally belongs to it, and conferring on it an other connotation as its soul and import. The sign-creating activity may be distinctively named *'productive' Memory*" (Hegel, *System der Philosophie*, III, ibid., vol. 10, 344–345; *Hegel's Philosophy of Mind*, trans. by William Wallace [Oxford: Clarendon Press, 1971], 212–213) [emphasis J.F-L.].

14. Saussure, *Cours*, 100 ff; *Course*, 66 ff. See also the correlations Roland Barthes draws between the semiotic nomenclatures of Hegel, Peirce, Jung, and Wallon in "Éléments de sémiologie," *Communications* 4 (1964): 103–107.

15. Here is a grid displaying the articulations implied in purported immanence:

	I	II	III	IV	
Signified	"God"	"Trinity"	"Three"	"Triangle"	1
phonic signifier	/gäd/		/THrē/	/ˈtrīaNGgəl/	2
arithmetic graphic signifier			3		3
geometric figural signifier				Δ	4

The (horizontal) orders operate on an articulated semantic field (1), a phonological field (2), a graphic field (arithmetic sign) (3), and a figural field (4). The (vertical) series define the signifiers of different orders of the same signified, according to Hegel's hypothesis. One immediately notices that the relation between square I, 1 and IV, 4 cannot qualify as immanence. Not only is there a vertical break between I and II (corresponding to Christian theology, for which God is Trinity), but there is an interruption—which is, this time, universal—separating the figure of the triangle from its name, and from the entire order of names.

16. [I adopt "to work over," Mary Lydon's translation of *travailler*. *Travailler* in its ordinary sense means "to work." In *Discourse, Figure*, however, the verb takes on a stronger character—something like "to labor" or "knead"—which Lydon's expression captures felicitously. —*Trans.*]

17. "So, for example, the lion is not only strong, the fox not only cunning, but God especially has quite different properties from those which can be comprised in number, a mathematical figure, or an animal shape. Therefore the content remains also *indifferent* to the shape which portrays it, and the abstract determinacy which it constitutes can equally well be present in infinitely many other existents and configurations. . . . So, for example, the obviously best symbol for strength is of course the lion, but nevertheless the bull or a horn can serve too, and, conversely, the bull . . . has a mass of other symbolical meanings. But altogether endless is the mass of figures and pictures used as symbols to represent God.

"Now it follows from all this that the symbol by its very nature remains essentially ambiguous.

"(*a*) In the first place, the look of a symbol as such raises at once the doubt whether a shape is to be taken as a symbol or not. . . ." (Hegel, *Aesthetics*, trans. Knox, vol. 1, 305–306) [emphasis J.-F.L.].

18. Hegel, *Aesthetics*, trans. Knox, vol. 1, 306–307. "Eine solche Zweifelhaftigkeit hört deshalb nur dadurch auf, dass jede der beiden Seiten, die Bedeutung und deren Gestalt ausdrücklich genannt und dabei zugleich ihre Beziehung ausgesprochen ist. Dann ist aber auch die vorgestellte konkrete Existenz nicht mehr ein Symbol im eigentlichen Sinn des Worts, sondern ein blosses Bild und die Beziehung von Bild und Bedeutung erhält die bekannte Form der *Vergleichung*, des Gleichnisses" (*Aesthetik*, vol. 12, 412). Again one cannot help but notice here the affinity between Hegel's thought and Ricoeur's. Notwithstanding the fact that the statement "the symbol gives rise to thought," which acts as hermeneutics's theoretical starting point, appears in the *Critique of Judgment*, it remains that the dialectics of interpretation in which Ricoeur includes the statement, as its innermost nerve and drive, is extremely close to a phenomenology of spirit, at least in that the object of knowledge (in this case the symbol) and its content (the concept) are *placed in the same space*. (See Paul Ricoeur, *Finitude et culpabilité* [Paris: Aubier, 1960], vol. 2, 323–332.) That is where the idea of a Hegelian reading of Freud originates—see Ricoeur, *De l'interprétation. Essai sur Freud* (Paris: Seuil, 1965), especially 45–53 and 444–529. In *Temps et langage* (Paris: Colin, 1967), 267, André Jacob rightly underscores the proximity between Ricoeur's thought and dialectics. To borrow the following lines from *Finitude et culpabilité* (vol. 1, 45) quoted by Jacob: "The transgression of the point of view is nothing but speech as the possibility of saying, and of saying the point of view itself" [translation A.H.]. This shift from eye to discourse, from reference to signified, coincides for Ricoeur with the shift from the demand emanating from desire to the listening to the law. There is, he writes, "another power of language, a power that is no longer the demand of desire, demand for protection, demand for providence, but a call in which I leave off all demands and listen" (Ricoeur, *De l'interprétation*, 529; *Freud and Philosophy: An Essay on Interpretation*, trans. Denis Savage [New Haven, London: Yale

University Press, 1970], 551). One clearly sees how Levinas's ethics are deployed here: as break from Hegelian discursivity, as overcoming of the state of listening to arrive at a "passivity" of doing older than all logos and all *archè*. See Emmanuel Levinas, *Totalité et infini* (The Hague: Nijhoff, 1961) and *Quatre lectures talmudiques* (Paris: Minuit, 1968). I find that the connection Jacques Derrida makes between Levinas and Hegel—on the subject of this relation of the eye to the ear—lacks rigor (Jacques Derrida, *L'écriture et la différence* [Paris: Seuil, 1967], 146–150).

19. "Das vollkommen Element worin die Innerlichkeit ebenso äusserlich als die Ausserlichkeit innerlich ist, ist wieder die Sprache" (*Phänomenologie des Geistes*, 505 [translation A.H.]). The place where this statement appears is hardly fortuitous: it is where, in the Greek world, the "living work of art"—that is, the greatest integration of the concept (the interior) into the sensory (the exterior) *in the element of the sensory*—finds itself superseded, and where *language* (the element of interiority)—through the forms of the epic, the tragedy, and the comedy—takes over in the spirit's self-becoming.
20. "Die Malerei zieht deshalb für den Ausdruck des innern Gemüths die Dreiheit der Raumdimensionen in die Fläche als die nächste Innerlichkeit des Aeusserens zusammen. . . . Denn die Malerei hat es nicht mit dem Sichtbarmachen überhaupt, sondern mit der sich ebensosehr in sich partikularisierenden, als auch innerlich gemachten Sichtbarkeit zu tun. In der Skulptur und Baukunst werden die Gestalten durch das äusserliche Licht sichtbar. In der Malerei dagegen hat die in sich selbst dunkele Materie in sich selbst ihr Inneres, Ideelles, das Licht; sie ist in sich selbst durchleuchtet, und das Licht ebendeswegen in sich selbst verdunkelt" (*Aesthetik*, vol. 13, 259) [translation A.H.].
21. I examine this question of the expressive power in discourse below. Here I am thinking of Mikel Dufrenne's argument, as developed in *Le poétique* (Paris: P.U.F., 1963), for example 27–33, 47.

Recessus and Hyper-Reflection

1. Maurice Merleau-Ponty, *Le visible et l'invisible* (Paris: Gallimard, 1964), 59–60; *The Visible and the Invisible*, ed. Claude Lefort, trans. Alphonso Lingis (Evanston, Ill.: Northwestern University Press, 1968), 38: ". . . we are catching sight of the necessity of another operation besides the conversion to reflection, more fundamental than it, of a sort of *hyper-reflection* [*surréflexion*] that would also take itself and the changes it introduces in the spectacle into account. It accordingly would not lose sight of the brute thing and the brute perception and would not finally efface them, would not cut the organic bonds between the perception and the thing perceived with a hypothesis of inexistence. On the contrary, it would set itself the task of thinking about them, of reflecting on the transcendence of the world as transcendence, speaking of it not according to the law of the word-meanings inherent in the given language, but with a perhaps difficult effort that uses the significations of words to express, beyond themselves, our mute contact with the things, when they are not yet things said." In regard to certain beings "that do not in principle elude this fixation" in eidetic invariants, starting with time, hyper-reflection would become "not a superior degree at the ultimate level of philosophy, but philosophy itself" (Merleau-Ponty, *Le visible et l'invisible,* 69; *The Visible and the Invisible,* ed. Lefort, trans. Lingis, 46).

2. Merleau-Ponty, *Le visible et l'invisible,* 136; *The Visible and the Invisible,* ed. Lefort, trans. Lingis, 102.
3. Merleau-Ponty, *Le visible et l'invisible,* 137; *The Visible and the Invisible,* ed. Lefort, trans. Lingis, 102. The pages of "Introduction à la prose du monde," published by Claude Lefort in *Revue de métaphysique et de morale* 2 (1967): 139 ff, provide a description of the experience of language based entirely on the opposition of the closed and the open. [Merleau-Ponty, *The Prose of the World,* ed. Claude Lefort, trans. John O'Neill (Evanston, Ill.: Northwestern University Press, 1973), 9 ff.]
4. Merleau-Ponty, *Le visible et l'invisible,* 137; *The Visible and the Invisible,* ed. Lefort, trans. Lingis, 102–103 [emphasis J.-F.L.].
5. Merleau-Ponty, *Le visible et l'invisible,* 156; *The Visible and the Invisible,* ed. Lefort, trans. Lingis, 118 [emphasis in the original].
6. Merleau-Ponty, *Le visible et l'invisible,* 156; *The Visible and the Invisible,* ed. Lefort, trans. Lingis, 118.
7. Merleau-Ponty, *Le visible et l'invisible,* 164; *The Visible and the Invisible,* ed. Lefort, trans. Lingis, 125.
8. See, for example, Maurice Merleau-Ponty, "Le langage indirect et les voix du silence," *Signes* (Paris: Gallimard, 1960), 94; *Signs,* trans. Richard C. McCleary (Evanston, Ill.: Northwestern University Press, 1964), 74; and below, "Effect of Thickness in the System," note 5.
9. Including his discourse on discourse: "Linguistics is nothing but a rigorous and conceptual way of clarifying, in terms of all the other facts of language, *the speech which declares itself in us* and to which, even in the midst of our scientific work, we are still attached *as if by an umbilical cord.*

   "Some would like to break this tie and get away from the confused and annoying situation *of a being who is what he is talking about*" (Merleau-Ponty, "Introduction à la prose du monde," 148; *The Prose of the World,* ed. Lefort, trans. O'Neill, 15 [emphasis J.-F. L.]. But this is, thankfully, impossible, adds the phenomenologist.
10. Claude Lévi-Strauss, "La structure des mythes," in *Anthropologie structurale* (Paris: Plon, 1958), chap. 9.
11. Vladimir Propp, *Morphology of the Folktale,* Indiana University Research Center in Anthropology, Folklore and Linguistics, Publication 10 (October 1958). Claude Lévi-Strauss, "La structure et la forme: réflexions sur un ouvrage de Vladimir Propp," *Cahiers de l'institut de science économique appliquée* 99, M series, no. 7 (March 1960).
12. In the essay quoted above, Lévi-Strauss challenges Propp's formalist interpretation, demonstrating that it relies on the hypothesis that the form and the content of the tale can be dissociated: form is the disposition of "functions" in a story to which the characters' actions, however diverse, can be reduced (for example, the two narrative fragments "An old man gives Sutchenko a horse that carries him to another kingdom" and "A sorcerer gives Ivan a ring that brings him to another kingdom" fulfill the same function). The content (old man or sorcerer, horse or ring, etc.) is the vocabulary with which form is clad. Lévi-Strauss's critique consists, first, in showing that the vocabulary is not arbitrary, that it is possible to imagine the name itself (sorcerer or old man) according

to relevant oppositions (just as the terms owl and eagle stand in opposition to each other as night does to day) and that it is the natural and cultural context that provides the relevant features; second, in taking issue with Propp for looking for form "too close" (Lévi-Strauss, "La structure et la forme," 27) to the level of empirical observation, and in formulating the hypothesis that the functions, once reduced to a very small number of elements, can all take part in a set of transformations (such as inversion, conversion, negative transformation, etc.) that would constitute the tale's matrix. The first observation is unimpeachable, while the second brings us to the question I believe structural linguistics overlooks, namely that from a given matrix several "discourses," that is, several "forms" of tales or myths can be derived. Why is it that the general form Propp observes (a form shared by the myths to which Lévi-Strauss himself ventures to give the canonical expression in *Anthropologie structurale*, 252) always obeys a double sequence in which the second "cancels out" (in the sense of *aufheben*) the first? The expression characterizing this hinged configuration (which is also that of Hegel's dialectics) prompts Lévi-Strauss to refer to Freud, for whom, argues the anthropologist, "Two traumas (and not one, as is so commonly said) are necessary in order to generate the individual myth in which a neurosis consists" (*Anthropologie structurale*, 253; Claude Lévi-Strauss, *Structural Anthropology*, trans. Claire Jacobson and Brooke Grundfest Schoepf [Harmondsworth: Penguin, 1972], 228). This is an indication, however tentative, of the direction to follow: the prevalence of this configuration, which is strictly speaking *the form*, resides in the constitution of desire—transgression of prohibition which the neurosis or the myth "cancels out" (and recuperates) into prohibition of transgression. Thus begins to appear a field that is neither of vocabulary nor of structure, but of form as presence in discourse of its other. Such is the direction I follow below, in the chapter "Opposition and Difference."

13. Gardner Davies, *Vers une explication rationnelle du Coup de dés: Essai d'exégèse mallarméenne* (Paris: Corti, 1953).
14. Letter to Verlaine, in Stéphane Mallarmé, *Œuvres complètes* (Paris: Gallimard, 1945), 663 [translation A.H.].
15. "So that Banville's mind, taking refuge within these several pages, defies civilization, which neglected to construct the miraculous Theater and Stage which the mind envisions, to which the mind alone can give true existence" (Mallarmé, "Solennité," *Œuvres complètes*, 334; *Mallarmé: Selected Prose Poems, Essays & Letters*, trans. Bradford Cook [Baltimore: The Johns Hopkins Press, 1956], 70). The book is "impersonified"; it does "not call for the reader's approach"; it "occurs alone: fact, being" (Mallarmé, "L'action restreinte," *Œuvres complètes*, 372).
16. Letter dated 17 May 1867. See Henri Mondor, *Eugène Lefébure: Sa vie, ses lettres à Mallarmé* (Paris: Gallimard, 1951), 341; and *Mallarmé: Selected Prose Poems, Essays & Letters*, trans. Cook, 95.
17. Mallarmé, *Œuvres complètes*, 647, 522.
18. "Why should we perform the miracle by which a natural object is almost made to disappear beneath the magic waving wand of the written word . . ." (Mallarmé, "Crise de vers," *Œuvres complètes*, 368; *Mallarmé: Selected Prose Poems, Essays & Letters*, trans. Cook, 42).

19. Mallarmé, Conference on Villiers de L'Isle-Adam, *Œuvres complètes*, 481 [translation A.H.].
20. Emphasis in the original.
21. Letter to Villiers de L'Isle-Adam, dated 24 September 1866, *La table ronde* (August 1952), 11; *Mallarmé: Selected Prose Poems, Essays & Letters*, trans. Cook, 91.
22. Letter dated 23 August 1866, *La table ronde* (August 1952): 71 [translation A.H.].
23. Mallarmé, *Œuvres complètes*, 852 [translation A.H.].
24. Mallarmé, *Un coup de dés* (Paris: Gallimard, 1914), *in fine*; *Stéphane Mallarmé: Collected Poems*, trans. Henry Weinfield (Berkeley, Los Angeles, London: University of California Press, 1994), 142.
25. As Davies states in *Vers une explication*, 80. Later in the book Davies returns to the same subject: "Mallarmé failed to repress a desire, in fact shared by a number of his contemporaries, to reproduce visually on the printed page the image of the object evoked in the text" (197 [translation A.H.]). The same critic who otherwise makes the signified of *Un coup de dés* readily understandable completely misses its expressive presence. The latter takes its revenge by working its way right into the words of the commentator—for this much is at stake in this unusual typography: to lift the *repression* of *desire* which in writing affects figural space.
26. Mallarmé, "L'action restreinte," *Œuvres complètes*, 370 [translation A.H.].
27. See the formulations in the preface of *Un coup de dés*: "The whole without novelty except for the way the reading process is *spread out*. . . . I don't transgress against this order of things {the use of paragraph breaks and blanks in traditional prosody}, I merely disperse its elements." "*The Paper intervenes*" writes Mallarmé at each "prismatic subdivision of the Idea." These subdivisions are characterized as "*variable*." Thus is summoned "a *simultaneous* vision of the Page." Mallarmé finally describes the latter presentation, in one bold stroke, as "*this stripped-down mode of thought*" (Mallarmé, *Un coup de dés*, "Préface"; *Stéphane Mallarmé: Collected Poems*, trans. Weinfield, 122; emphasis J.-F.L.). [Reproducing, let alone translating *Un coup de dés* is arduous, since Mallarmé set extremely precise guidelines for the poem's layout: the slightest alteration in a word's placement or length would, in principle, affect the entire composition. Even the half-size facsimile reproduced in *Discours, figure*—based on the 1914 Gallimard edition—fails in one instance (the spacing between "*CE SERAIT*" and "*pire*" on the left-hand page) to follow Mallarmé's instructions. For a comparative analysis of the original proofs of *Un coup de dés*, see Robert G. Cohn, *Mallarmé's Masterwork: New Findings* (The Hague, Paris: Mouton & Co., 1966), 106–107. Among the many English translations of *Un coup de dés*, Henry Weinfield's stands out for its sensitivity and accuracy, relying as it does on the original annotated proofs; see *Stéphane Mallarmé: Collected Poems*, trans. Weinfield, 140–141. —*Trans.*]
28. Mallarmé, "Le livre instrument spirituel," *Œuvres complètes*, 380–381; "The Book: A Spiritual Instrument," *Mallarmé: Selected Prose Poems, Essays & Letters*, trans. Cook, 27–28. This theme is already present in *Planches et feuillets* (1893): "A set of verses encourages an ideal representation: motifs of elation or of dreams interweave and separate, according to an order and their individuality. One part lends itself in a rhythm to the movement of thought, with which another drawing will clash: one and the other, to come

to completion and cease, where would intervene . . . the figure, so that the idea remain" (Mallarmé, *Œuvres complètes*, 328 [translation A.H.]). This theme comes into sharper relief in 1895, in "Crise de vers": "From each theme, itself predestined, a given harmony will be born somewhere in the parts of the total poem and take its proper place within the volume; because for every sound, there is an echo. Motifs of like pattern will move in balance from point to point. There will be none of the sublime incoherence found in the page-settings of the Romantics, none of the artificial unity that used to be based on the square measurements of the book. Everything will be hesitation, disposition of parts, their alternations and relationships—all this contributing to the rhythmic totality, which will be the very silence of the poem, in its blank spaces . . ." (Mallarmé, *Œuvres complètes*, 366–367; *Mallarmé: Selected Prose Poems, Essays & Letters*, trans. Cook, 41).

29. Quoted by Paul Valéry, "Le Coup de dés," *Variété II* (Paris: Gallimard, 1930), 200–201; *Mallarmé: Selected Prose Poems, Essays & Letters*, trans. Cook, 105. See also the following, quoted by Camille Mauclair: "I believe that every sentence or thought, if it has a rhythm, must base it on the object it aims for and reproduce, in a naked state, immediately, as if burst forth in the mind, some of this object's attitude with regard to the whole. Literature constitutes therefore the proof—no other reason to put pen to paper" (*Mallarmé chez lui* [Paris: Grasset, 1935], 116 [translation A.H.]).

30. Valéry, "Le Coup de dés," 194; "Concerning *A Throw of the Dice*: A Letter to the Editor of *Les Manges*," in Paul Valéry, *Leonardo Poe Mallarmé*, trans. Malcolm Cowley and James R. Lawler (Princeton: Princeton University Press, 1972), 309.

31. Mallarmé insists on the three-dimensionality embodied in the fold: "And since even the book's format is useless, of what avail is that extraordinary addition of foldings (like wings in repose, ready to fly forth again) which constitute its rhythm and the chief reason for the secret contained in its pages? Of what avail the priceless silence living there, and evocative symbols following in its wake? To delight the mind which literature has totally delivered? Yes, were it not for the folding of the paper and the depths thereby established . . ." (Mallarmé, "Le livre instrument spirituel," *Œuvres complètes*, 379; "The Book: A Spiritual Instrument," *Mallarmé: Selected Prose Poems, Essays & Letters*, trans. Cook, 26). Michel Butor echoes this insistence in "Le livre comme objet," *Répertoire II* (Paris: Minuit, 1964), and, generally, in all of his writings.

32. Mallarmé, "Crise de vers," *Œuvres complètes*, 368; *Mallarmé: Selected Prose Poems, Essays & Letters*, trans. Cook, 43.

33. Mallarmé, "Le mystère dans les lettres," *Œuvres complètes*, 386; "Mystery in Literature," *Mallarmé: Selected Prose Poems, Essays & Letters*, trans. Cook, 34.

34. Mallarmé, *Un coup de dés*, Preface, *in fine*; *Stéphane Mallarmé: Collected Poems*, trans. Weinfield, 123. Mallarmé assigns the layout of *Un coup de dés* to the rendering of "subjects of pure and complex imagination or intellect," leaving "the empire of passion and of dreams" up to "the ancient technique of verse" (*Stéphane Mallarmé: Collected Poems*, trans. Weinfield, 123). Does he fall victim to a musical analogy, whereby *Un coup de dés* would be to verse what the symphony is to the personal, lyrical song? Or is he on the contrary aware of the epistemological value of the process deployed in the former (displacement)? One must in any case refute Ernst Fraenkel's hypothesis in *Les dessins*

trans-conscients de Stéphane Mallarmé (Paris: Nizet, 1960) that the *forms* resulting from the text's layout conceal an "affective and dramatic content" (36) that coincides with that of the textual signified. Indeed, it is obvious that plastic form has no *content* (in the sense of signified); moreover, the method used to bring out the plastic forms is arbitrary.

35. As Davies persuasively argues (*Vers une explication*, 79).
36. "We can rest assured, the breaks in the text observe meaningfully a strict concordance, and mark virgin space only up to their points of illumination: an actual form might emerge, allowing what was until then a prose poem as well as our research to result, by better joining the words, in a critical poem. . . . No doubt there is here, for the poet who ordinarily does not work with free verse, the means to show, eventually and through experience, in the form of comprehensive and brief pieces, such and such immediate rhythms of thought ordering a prosody" (Mallarmé, *Œuvres complètes*, 1576 [translation A.H.]). I italicize the words in support of my claim: the *critical* nature of the poem is due to the fact that is *shown*, in *experience*, through *breaks* in the text, the *immediate rhythms* of thought (which I would call schemas) that govern the *prosody* and therefore do not belong to the order of simple communication.

Linguistic Sign?

1. Ferdinand de Saussure, *Cours de linguistique générale* (Paris: Payot, 1962), 32–35; *Course in General Linguistics*, trans. Roy Harris (London: Duckworth, 1971), 14–17; Robert Godel, *Les sources manuscrites du Cours de linguistique générale de Ferdinand de Saussure* (Geneva, Paris: Droz and Minard, 1957), 183.
2. Saussure, *Cours*, 100–103; *Course*, 67–70.
3. Émile Benveniste, "Remarques sur la fonction du langage dans la découverte freudienne," *La psychanalyse* 1 (1956) (collected in *Problèmes de linguistique générale* [Paris: Gallimard, 1966], 85); "Remarks on the Function of Language in Freudian Theory," *Problems in General Linguistics*, trans. Mary Elizabeth Meek (Coral Gables: University of Miami Press, 1971), 73.
4. See below, "Thickness on the Margins of Discourse."
5. Edmond Ortigues, *Le discours et le symbole* (Paris: Aubier, 1964). See *La logique ou l'art de penser*, by Antoine Arnauld and Pierre Nicole (first published Paris, 1662), 1st Part, chap. 4: "It is quite possible for the same thing both to conceal and to reveal another thing at the same time. So those who say 'nothing appears by means of that which conceals' have asserted a highly questionable maxim. For since the same thing can be both a thing and a sign at the same time, it can as a thing conceal what it reveals as a sign. Thus the hot cinder, as a thing, hides the fire and, as a sign, reveals it. . . . As things, the Eucharistic symbols conceal the body of Jesus Christ and reveal it as symbols" (Antoine Arnauld and Pierre Nicole, *Logic, or The Art of Thinking*, ed. and trans. Jill Vance Buroker [Cambridge: Cambridge University Press, 1996], 35). See Louis Marin, "Signe et représentation: Philippe de Champaigne et Port-Royal," *Annales Économies, Sociétés, Civilisations* (July 1969).
6. Ortigues, *Le discours et le symbole*, 43.
7. Ibid, 52.

8. Ibid.
9. See Jacques Derrida, *L'écriture et la différence* (Paris: Seuil, 1967), and *De la grammatologie* (Paris: Minuit, 1967).
10. Saussure, *Cours*, 101; *Course*, 68.
11. Ibid.
12. Émile Benveniste, "Nature du signe linguistique," *Acta linguistica* 1, no. 1 (1939) (reprinted in *Problèmes de linguistique générale*, section 4); "The Nature of the Linguistic Sign," in *Problems in General Linguistics*, section 4.
13. Benveniste, "Nature du signe linguistique," *Acta linguistica* 1, no. 1, 26 (*Problèmes de linguistique générale*, 52); "The Nature of the Linguistic Sign," in *Problems in General Linguistics*, 46.
14. Benveniste, "Nature du signe linguistique," *Acta linguistica* 1, no. 1, 25 (*Problèmes de linguistique générale*, 51); "The Nature of the Linguistic Sign," in *Problems in General Linguistics*, 45. [Translation modified. —*Trans.*]
15. See Mikel Dufrenne, *Le poétique* (Paris: P.U.F., 1963), and "A priori et philosophie de la nature," *Filosofia* 4, supplement (November 1967).
16. Eugen Lerch, "Vom Wesen des sprachlichen Zeichens: Zeichen oder Symbol?" *Acta Linguistica* 1, no. 3 (1939): 145–161.
17. Merleau-Ponty, "Introduction à la prose du monde," *Revue de métaphysique et de morale* 2 (1967): 143, 144; *The Prose of the World*, ed. Claude Lefort, trans. John O'Neill (Evanston, Ill.: Northwestern University Press, 1973), 10.
18. By building the linguistic sign on its two axes, Benveniste returns to the tradition of Stoicism. See the classic text by Charles Kay Ogden and Ivor Armstrong Richards, *The Meaning of Meaning: A Study of the Influence of Language upon Thought and of the Science of Symbolism* (London: Kegan Paul, 1936 [1923]), particularly 10–12, where the "linguistic triangle" is presented; see, too, Stephen Ullmann's discussion of this triangle from a functionalist perspective in *Principles of Semantics* (Oxford: Blackwell, 1959), chap. 2, section 2. The following definition of the sign by Peirce betrays a debt to the same tradition of a triangular organization of linguistic signification: "Anything which determines something else (its *interpretant*) to refer to an object to which itself refers (its *object*) in the same way, the interpretant becoming in turn a sign, and so on *ad infinitum*" (*Elements of Logic*, in *Collected Papers*, ed. Charles Hartshorne and Paul Weiss [Cambridge, Mass.: Harvard University Press, 1931–1935], vol. 2, 303).
19. Saussure, *Cours*, 99; *Course*, 67.
20. See Roman Jakobson, "Closing Statements: Linguistics and Poetics," in Thomas Albert Sebeok, *Style and Language* (New York, London: John Wiley & Sons; Cambridge, Mass.: Technology Press of Massachusetts Institute of Technology, 1960); and Tzvetan Todorov, *Littérature et signification* (Paris: Larousse, 1967).
21. Mikel Dufrenne, *Phénoménologie de l'expérience esthétique* (Paris: P.U.F., 1953), vol. 2, 543–569.
22. Michel Butor, "Le roman comme recherche" (1955) and "Intervention à Royaumont" (1959), in *Répertoire I* (Paris: Minuit, 1960).
23. Saussure, *Cours*, 144–146, 155–158; *Course*, 100–103, 110–112.

24. This is how Dufrenne can assert that expression precedes signification (*Le poétique*, 33, 184; "L'art est-il langage," *Revue d'esthétique* 19, no. 1 [1966], reprinted in *Esthétique et philosophie* [Paris: Klincksieck, 1967], 129–143), a thesis I questioned in part in "A la place de l'homme, l'expression," *Esprit* (July–August 1969), particularly 170–177.
25. This is Lévi-Strauss's claim in "Langage et Société" (1951) and in "La notion de structure en ethnologie" (1952), in *Anthropologie structurale* (Paris: Plon, 1958), 70, 326–327.
26. André Leroi-Gourhan, *Le geste et la parole* (Paris: Albin Michel, 1965), vol. 1, chap. 6 and vol. 2, chap. 14, particularly 221 and 236.
27. In his analysis of the evolution of figures through the four styles he identifies in Paleolithic art, Leroi-Gourhan stresses the fact that "the esoteric in figurative representation is practically contemporary with the birth of art itself" and that "far from being a late phenomenon, it is directly connected to the fact that figures are symbols, not copies" (*Le geste*, vol. 2, 234; *Gesture and Speech*, trans. Anna Bostock Berger [Cambridge, Mass.: Massachusetts Institute of Technology, 1993], 384). These wall figures are organized in "symbolic assemblies of juxtaposed elements" (*Le geste*, vol. 2, 248; *Gesture*, trans. Berger, 393). For example, in style II, the outline of the belly and hindquarters is rendered in roughly the same way for the horse as for the bison, and it is by adding only a few strokes, which allows one to distinguish the muzzle from the muffle, the ears from the horns, that an opposition is set up between them. Here the use of these strokes plays the same role as the graphemes distinguishing written signs from one another. Yet it is impossible to assimilate these figures fully with graphic signs, since the former will evolve, through styles III and IV, toward a greater "realism." Such an evolution suggests that the figures' initial relay function, allowing the sensory image to be integrated into the order of myth that is discourse's, loses its balance, and that the axis of representation tends to gain the upper hand over that of signification. Thus the entire problem of the sign's double attachment finds itself posed through this "evolution" (but why should there be "evolution"?): the sign oscillates between the function of signal endowed with linguistic value, inscribed on a neutralized plane (see *Le geste*, vol. 2, 241; *Gesture*, trans. Berger, 390), and that of stand-in for an absent thing located in the sensory, a representation made possible by the mediation of the support's sensory properties. The secret of this instability, and of the division of Paleolithic art into four periods—reminiscent of Henri Focillon's parsing of the life of forms into four successive stages (*La vie des formes* [Paris: P.U.F., 1964], 17–22)—might lie in the power of the sensory to attract the sign toward itself along the axis of designation. But this power is itself only that of the phantasmatic aiming to fulfill desire through images. Leroi-Gourhan makes this relation clear by linking progressive geometricization with "the disguise" of sexual symbols "in almost undecipherable geometrical forms" (*Le geste*, vol. 2, 234; *Gesture*, trans. Berger, 384); indeed his entire interpretation of wall figures revolves around the masculine/feminine opposition, that is, around sexual difference, which constitutes one of the founding enigmas of the phantasy.
28. See Noël Mouloud's analyses of pictorial space, particularly the notation of the invariancy of the intervals between chromatic contents, in *La peinture et l'espace: Recherche sur les conditions formelles de l'expérience esthétique* (Paris: P.U.F., 1964), 72. See also the studies conducted by Kurt Goldstein ("Über Farbennamenamnesie," *Psychologische Forschung*

[1925]) and by Goldstein and Olly Rosenthal-Veit ("Zur Problem der Wirkung der Farben auf dem Organismus," *Schweizer Archiv für Neurologie und Psychiatrie* [1930]).

29. See the studies on the correspondences between colors and values (and lines) in "Séminaire sur la couleur de Kandinsky au Bauhaus (1922–1933)," in *Bauhaus 1919–1969* (Paris: Musée national d'art moderne / Musée d'art moderne de la Ville de Paris), exhibition catalogue, 2 April–22 June 1969, 52 ff.
30. Mouloud observes that the preservation of the intervals between chromatic contents when the conditions of presentations vary depends on the subject's *point of attachment* in the painting (*La peinture et l'espace*, 72).
31. See André Martinet, "La double articulation du langage," *La linguistique synchronique* (Paris: P.U.F., 1965), 1–35.
32. Martinet, "La double articulation du langage," 8.
33. Saussure, *Cours*, 103; *Course*, 69–70.
34. Nikolai Sergeyevich Troubetzkoy, *Principes de phonologie* (Paris: Klincksieck, 1964), "Introduction," 1st part, and 41–53.
35. Morris Halle and Roman Jakobson, "Phonology and Phonetics" (1956), in *Roman Jakobson: Selected Writings*, vol. 1 (2nd expanded ed.) (The Hague, Paris: Mouton, 1971), 477–486.
36. André Martinet, *Éléments de linguistique générale* (Paris: Colin, 1966), 52–55, 62–66.
37. Halle and Jakobson, "Phonology and Phonetics," 497.
38. Jacqueline M. C. Thomas, *Phonétique articulatoire* (Paris: Ecole pratique des hautes études, mimeographed notebooks, 1966–1967 Seminar). Jakobson and Halle always describe features from two perspectives, genetically and acoustically ("Phonology and Phonetics," 489 ff).
39. See Alfred Tomatis, *L'oreille et le langage* (Paris: Seuil, 1963).
40. Sigmund Freud, *Die Traumdeutung* (1900), in *Gesammelte Werke*, vols. 2/3, (London / Frankfurt am Main: Imago Publishing / S. Fischer Verlag, 1952–) [hereafter cited as GW, followed by volume and page number]; *The Interpretation of Dreams* (1900), *The Standard Edition of the Complete Psychological Works of Sigmund Freud*, trans. and ed. James Strachey, with Anna Freud, Alix Strachey, and Alan Tyson, vols. 4/5 (London: The Hogarth Press, 1953–), 411, 418 [hereafter cited as SE, followed by volume and page number]. See also "Metapsychologische Ergänzung zur Traumlehre," GW, vol. 10, 412–426; "A Metapsychological Supplement to the Theory of Dreams," SE, vol. 14, 228–235.
41. See Guy Rosolato's diagram in "Le sens des oublis: une découverte de Freud," *L'Arc* 34 (1968): 36.
42. Quoted without reference by Paul Arnold, "L'univers théâtral d'Antonin Artaud," in *Lettres d'Antonin Artaud à Jean-Louis Barrault* (Paris: Bordas, 1952), 31. See also Antonin Artaud, "Le théâtre et son double," *Œuvres complètes,* vol. 4 (Paris: Gallimard, 1964), 56 [translation A.H.].
43. In particular *Omaggio a Joyce* (1959), *Visage* (1961)—a piece analyzed by Dominique Avron in the seminar *Travail et langage chez Freud* (Nanterre, 1968–1969)—and *Sequenza III* (1965). See Avron and Jean-François Lyotard, "'A few words to sing': Sequenza III," *Musique en jeu* 2 (February 1971).

Effect of Thickness in the System

1. See Paul Ricoeur, "La structure, le mot, l'événement," *Esprit* (May 1967): 801–821. Ricoeur believes that the word mediates between the language structure [*langue*] (where it keeps the units of meaning in store) and the event of discourse (where it gains new meanings from its position in the sentence); he further believes that etymology is the diachronic form of the layering of events, which appears in the synchronic system as polysemy. The latter is, however, a "measured polysemy" ("La structure, le mot, l'événement," 818). Compare with the strictly functionalist view developed by André Martinet in "Le mot" (*Diogène* 51 [1965]: 39–53), where the author demonstrates, through commutation, the impossibility of recognizing the word as a specifically linguistic unit, and arrives at the "replacement" in linguistics of the "word" by the much more flexible and more precise concept of "syntagm" (51), "for it is behind the screen of words that the truly fundamental features of human language very often appear" ("Le mot," 53 [translation A.H.]).
2. See Martinet, *Éléments de linguistique générale* (Paris: A. Colin, 1966), 4.19 and 4.38, 117 and 136–137.
3. Josef Vachek, *Dictionnaire de linguistique de l'école de Prague* (1929), 45, quoted in Jean Dubois, *Le vocabulaire politique en France de 1868 à 1872* (Paris: Hachette, 1962) [translation A.H.].
4. "Felder sind die zwischen den Einzelworten und dem Wortganzen lebendigen sprachlichen Wirklichkeiten, die als Teilganze mit dem Wort das Merkmal gemeinsam haben, dass sie sich ergliedern, mit dem Wortschatz hingegen, dass sie sich ausgliedern" (Jost Trier, "Dass sprachliche Feld: Eine Auseinandersetzung," *Neue Jahrbücher für Wissenschaft und Jugendbildung* 10 [1934]: 430; Stephen Ullmann, *The Principles of Semantics* [London: Blackwell, 1959], 157). On the school of the linguistic field, see Ullmann, *The Principles of Semantics*, 152–170. Ullmann stresses the dual influence of Saussure (with the concept of synchronic system, leading to the synchrony of the field) and of Husserl (with the concept of objective ideality that allows the linguist to eschew psychologism). One wonders if it would not be more exact to credit Husserl's influence with the concept of field, inasmuch as it is inseparable from that of horizon, the latter being already fully developed in *Ideen zu einer reinen Phänomenologie und phänomenologischen Philosophie*, vol. 1, § 27 ff, a book published in 1913 as an offprint of the *Jahrbuch für Philosophie und phänomenologische Forschung*. As for the concept of objective ideality, it seems to me that Frege's work, and the *Tractatus Logico-Philosophicus* published in Vienna in 1918 (to speak only of German-language sources) are much more influential than the *Formale und transzendentale Logik* from 1929.
5. For a more developed view of this idea see Maurice Merleau-Ponty, *Phénoménologie de la perception* (Paris: Gallimard, 1945), 240–280; *Phenomenology of Perception*, trans. Colin Smith (London, Henley: Routledge & Kegan Paul, 1962), 207–242. Merleau-Ponty starts with a (Sartrean) problematic built on the pair of opposites in-itself/for-itself, and demonstrates that the problematic cannot apply to a description of sensory experience [*le sentir*]. Blue is not the effect of a bestowal of meaning [*donation de sens*] from a nullifying for-itself, nor "an invasion of the sentient by the sensible [*sensible*]" (*Phénoménologie*, 238; *Phenomenology*, trans. Smith, 214). The sensory [*sensible*] is a "vague

beckoning" (*Phénoménologie*, 248; *Phenomenology*, trans. Smith, 214), a "hint" (*Phénoménologie*, 247; *Phenomenology*, trans. Smith, 213), and what is proposed is a "certain rhythm of existence" (either abductive or adductive) (*Phénoménologie*, 247; *Phenomenology*, trans. Smith, 213), the "suggestion of a form of existence" (*Phénoménologie*, 247; *Phenomenology*, trans. Smith, 213), a "certain living pulsation" (*Phénoménologie*, 248; *Phenomenology*, trans. Smith, 214–215). If I take up the hint, slip into the suggested form of existence, "abandon myself to it," "synchronize" with the color (*Phénoménologie*, 248; *Phenomenology*, trans. Smith, 214), only then is there sensation [*sensation*]. The latter is "communion" (*Phénoménologie*, 246, 248; *Phenomenology*, trans. Smith, 212, 213); in its constitution there is no distinct agent and patient, but coexistence (*Phénoménologie*, 247; *Phenomenology*, trans. Smith, 213) and connaturality (*Phénoménologie*, 251; *Phenomenology*, trans. Smith, 217): "The sensible [*sensible*] gives back to me what I lent to it {I lent it movement, probing, the act, the gesture}, but this is only what I took from it in the first place {the adductive impulse triggered by the blue}" (*Phénoménologie*, 248; *Phenomenology*, trans. Smith, 214). The *field* can then be understood as the site where this coitus takes place, a place both anonymous and confined: "Vision is a thought *subordinated to a certain field*, and this is what is called a *sense*" (*Phénoménologie*, 251; *Phenomenology*, trans. Smith, 217; emphasis J.-F.L.). Anonymity of perceiving: "I cannot say that I see the sky's blue in the sense in which I can say that I understand a book" (*Phénoménologie*, 249; *Phenomenology*, trans. Smith, 215). All sensations affect not the I of understanding "but another self which has already sided with the world, which is already open to certain of its aspects and synchronized with them" (*Phénoménologie*, 250; *Phenomenology*, trans. Smith, 216). The "origin [of sensation] is *anterior* [*en-deçà*] to myself" (*Phénoménologie*, 250; *Phenomenology*, trans. Smith, 216; emphasis J.-F.L.). Vision is a kind of dance, of synrhythmics, which seizes with color a nonsubjective body. Finiteness of perception. Anonymity offers a dimension of the *already*, and finiteness that of the *still* [*encore*]: the sensory withholds hidden aspects; never do I possess it in full. Definition of the field: "To say that I have a visual field is to say that by reason of my position I have access to and an opening upon a system of beings, visible beings, that these are at the disposal of my gaze in virtue of a kind of primordial contract and through a gift of nature, with no effort made on my part; from which it follows that vision is prepersonal. And it follows at the same time that it is always limited, that around what I am looking at at a given moment is spread a horizon of things which are not seen, or which are even invisible" (*Phénoménologie*, 250–251; *Phenomenology*, trans. Smith, 216–217). Merleau-Ponty's description of speech is based entirely on the model of the field. Language "presents or rather it is the subject's taking up of a position in the world of his meanings. The term 'world' here is not a manner of speaking: it means that the 'mental' or cultural life borrows its structures from natural life and that the thinking subject must have its basis in the subject incarnate" (*Phénoménologie*, 225; *Phenomenology*, trans. Smith, 193). Speech will therefore be a phonetic "gesture" borrowed, like the gesture, from the "open and indefinite power of giving significance . . . by which man transcends himself towards a new form of behavior, or towards other people, or towards his own thought, through his body and his speech" (*Phénoménologie*, 226; *Phenomenology*, trans. Smith, 194). One observes here, first, the phenomenologist's thought trying to dig, beneath the philosophy of the subject, a passage leading to a much more archaic store of meaning, and struggling to do so, as can be seen in the definition of the field, and as Merleau-Ponty will later admit with regard to *Phenomenology of Perception*; second, the attempt to deal with the problem of language in a similar way by introducing this same concept of field, that is, of an encounter between a configuration of meaning both anonymous and finite and an intention to signify. It is this concept that in Merleau-Ponty's reflection inhibits the comprehension of the system's autonomy, bringing the latter to the fore in principle (as the notion of field is opposed to that of a for-itself that bestows meaning [*donateur de sens*]) but hiding it (the organization of subsystems, lexical for instance, is inconsistent, and there is no true unconscious of language: it is always the gesture of speech that generates its order): "Here the meaning [*sens*] of words must be finally induced by the words themselves, or more exactly, their conceptual meaning [*signification*] must be formed by a kind of deduction from a *gestural meaning* [*signification gestuelle*], which is immanent in speech" (*Phénoménologie*, 208–209; *Phenomenology*, trans. Smith, 179. Merleau-Ponty can contemplate language as expression (*Phénoménologie*, 213; *Phenomenology*, trans. Smith, 183), that is, the presence of the figural in the order of the discursive, but he is unable to contemplate the order of the discursive.

6. See Ullmann, *The Principles of Semantics*, 159–160: "Another important aspect of Trier's theory is its *structuralist* orientation. In this respect it has done in semantics what the 'Gestalt' school had done in psychology, and the Prague phonologists in the study of sounds." One notes that the terms of comparison do not go without a certain confusion. An intuition close to that of the school of Münster may otherwise be found in Dubois, *Le vocabulaire politique*; see in particular the definition of the pair communism/socialism (196). The method is that of structuralist semantics, but the way in which the event intervenes in the semantic fields, how it destabilizes and enriches or instead impoverishes them, is not itself taken as reflexive or methodological theme.
7. Ferdinand de Saussure, *Cours de linguistique générale* (Paris: Payot, 1962), 159; *Course in General Linguistics*, trans. Roy Harris (London: Duckworth, 1971), 113.
8. Robert Godel, *Les sources manuscrites du Cours de linguistique générale de Ferdinand de Saussure* (Geneva, Paris: Droz and Minard, 1957), 238 [translation A.H.].
9. Godel, *Les sources manuscrites*, 239–240 [translation A.H.].
10. Ibid., 240 [translation A.H.].
11. Saussure, *Cours*, 159–160; *Course*, trans. Harris, 114; Godel, *Les sources manuscrites*, 91.
12. "The unity lies in meaning: the verb's various formations are brought together by the unity [identity?] of the meaning's *distance*; same distance between ἤνεγκον (*enegkon*) and φέρω (*phero*) as between ἔδειξα (*edeixa*) and δείκνυμι (*deiknumi*). 'Mosaic' verbs are most apt at clarifying what kind of unity is at issue. It is a methodological mistake to pay too much attention to absolute differences in meaning; what is true is that the alteration in meaning is absolutely equal in the two examples; *the reference points are equidistant, from verb to verb*. We thus obtain a *strict trigonometry* to determine the differences in meaning" (quoted in Godel, *Les sources manuscrites*, 140–141; emphasis J.-F.L. [translation A.H.]).

13. Godel, *Les sources manuscrites*, 213–214.
14. One could object that in the case of a blind person who speaks, who is deprived of this experience: how could she or he possibly come to know the dimension of designation? I would respond with Diderot's *Letter on the Blind* (1749), the same letter with which one would in most likelihood challenge me, and which is all too often read as the demonstration of an empiricist or materialist thesis, but which contains much else besides, in particular, a meditation on referential distance that, while adopting Descartes's *Dioptric* and its definition of sight as remote touching, turns it on its head. For not only is it noteworthy that in the *Letter* the blind person's touch is conceived of as sight at close range—in the sense that, like sight, touch is constitutive of the object as distant—but the fact is that Diderot subsumes both sight and touch under the category of remote position. This is precisely why the mirror lies at this problematic's core: "I asked him {the man born blind from Puiseaux} what he meant by a mirror: 'An instrument,' answered he, 'which sets things in relief at a distance from themselves, when properly placed with regard to it. It is like my hand, which, to feel an object, I must not reach to one side of it'" (151) (*Écrits philosophiques* [Paris: Pauvert, 1964], 26; "Letter on the Blind," in *Denis Diderot: Thoughts on the Interpretation of Nature and Other Philosophical Works,* trans. Margaret Jourdain [1916], [Manchester: Clinamen Press, 1999], 151). Diderot adds, not without mischievousness: "Had Descartes been born blind, he might, I think, have hugged himself for such a definition" (*Écrits philosophiques,* 27; *Denis Diderot: Thoughts,* trans. Jourdain, 151). In the *Addition* to this *Letter,* written some thirty years later (in 1782), it appears even more blatantly that what is at stake in the experience of sensory perception [*sentir*] is indeed specular distancing, of which the mirror offers only a material model. "'If the skin of my hand was as sensitive as your eye {says Miss de Salignac, blind from birth}, I should see with my hand as you see with your eyes; and I sometimes imagine there are animals who have no eyes, but can nevertheless see.'—'And the mirror?' {asks Diderot}.—'If any bodies are not mirrors, it is by some defect in their composition which destroys the reflection of the air'" (*Écrits philosophiques*, 101; *Denis Diderot: Thoughts,* trans. Jourdain, 199). When I speak of "seeing," "to have an eye for," "to look at," one should understand it in Diderot's sense, whereby the blind have eyes in their hands, in their ears: "She measured the space by the sound of her footsteps or the echo of voices" (*Écrits philosophiques*, 95–96; *Diderot's Early Philosophical Works*, trans. and ed. Margaret Jourdain [Chicago, London: Open Court Publishing Company, 1916], 150).
15. At least according to the editors of the *Course*: "But to say that in a language [*langue*] everything is negative holds only for signification [signified] and signal [signifier] considered separately. The moment we consider the sign as a whole, we encounter something that is positive in its own domain. . . . Although signification [signified] and signal [signifier] are each, in isolation, purely differential and negative, their combination is a fact of a positive nature." (Saussure, *Cours*, 166; *Course*, 118–119). For Godel, the distinction between difference and opposition actually comes from Saussure himself: difference is purely negative, while opposition is difference endowed with signification. "If *a* is different from *b,* this amounts to saying no more than *a* is not *b,* regardless of the degree of non-

coincidence," writes Godel. "But as soon as a relationship otherwise exists between *a* and *b*, they become parts of the same system, and difference becomes opposition. It seems, therefore, that in a sign system difference must always coincide with an opposition and *that the negative character will never allow itself to be observed in its pure state.* Indeed it can only be observed if, by abstraction, one considers a single side of the sign; two signifiers or signifieds are different, two signs are opposed" (Godel, *Les sources manuscrites*, 197; emphasis J.-F.L. [translation A.H.]). One can understand why Saussure's editors would have been tempted simply to credit Saussure with the claim that opposition is *positive*, but the course notes bear no mention of the term. Above all, however, were one to accept the idea of a positivity in the relation, care would have to be taken *not* to apply it to that of the signified and the signifier, that is, to signification, for Saussure only ever invokes the presence of this positivity between signifiers. If there should be a "positive," it should not be situated on the verticality of signification, but on the horizontality of "difference," insofar as the latter determines signification (Godel, *Les sources manuscrites*, 196–200). In fact, what is at stake here is what is called in linguistics the principle of relevance. / ʃ / and / ç / are *different* in both French and German, but they are *opposed* in German, since their difference determines a difference in signification (*Kirsche* / *Kirche*). Saussure's caution on the subject of the positivity of signification should be related to his tendency to reduce signification to value, as we will see.

16. Quoted in Godel, *Les sources manuscrites*, 237, 240 [translation A.H.].
17. Roman Jakobson, "Le langage commun des linguistes et des anthropologues" (1952), in *Essais de linguistique générale* (Paris: Minuit, 1963), 38–42.
18. Jakobson, "Le langage commun des linguistes et des anthropologues," 40.
19. Ibid., 41; emphasis J.-F.L.
20. Ibid., 39; emphasis J.-F.L.
21. ["Meaning" is in English in the original. —*Trans.*]
22. Roman Jakobson, "Two Aspects of Language and Two Types of Aphasic Disturbances," *Fundamentals of Language* (The Hague: Mouton, 1956), 60. It is the study of these two kinds of operations that allows structuralist lexicology to carry out the construction of the field of signification. See, for example, Jean Dubois, "Recherches lexicographiques: esquisse d'un dictionnaire structural," *Études de linguistique appliquée* 1 (1962).
23. Cf. Eugen Fink, "Concepts thématiques et concepts opératoires" (1957), in *Husserl*, Cahiers de Royaumont, Philosophie, no. 3 (Paris: Minuit, 1959).
24. Godel, *Les sources manuscrites*, 247; emphasis J.-F.L [translation A.H.].

Thickness on the Margins of Discourse

1. Gottlob Frege, "Über Sinn und Bedeutung," *Zeitschrift für Philosophie und philosophische Kritik* 100 (1892): 25–50. I am indebted to Paul Ricoeur for bringing this text to my attention; cf. his *Cours sur le langage*, Nanterre, mimeographed transcript (1966–1967), folios 24 ff. There exists an English translation of Frege's article: "On Sense and Reference," in *Philosophical Writings*, eds. Peter Geach and Max Black (Oxford: Basil Blackwell, 1952), 56–78.
2. Frege, "Über Sinn und Bedeutung," 26; "On Sense and Reference," 57.

3. Frege, "Über Sinn und Bedeutung," 30; "On Sense and Reference," 60.
4. Frege, "Über Sinn und Bedeutung," 27; "On Sense and Reference," 57.
5. Frege, "Über Sinn und Bedeutung," 31; "On Sense and Reference," 61; emphasis J.-F.L.
6. Frege, "Über Sinn und Bedeutung," 31; "On Sense and Reference," 61.
7. Frege, "Über Sinn und Bedeutung," 32; "On Sense and Reference," 62.
8. Frege, "Über Sinn und Bedeutung," 32; "On Sense and Reference," 63.
9. Frege, "Über Sinn und Bedeutung," 33: "Das Streben nach Warheit also ist es, was uns überall vom Sinn zu Bedeutung vorzudringen treibt"; "On Sense and Reference," 63.
10. Frege, "Über Sinn und Bedeutung," 40; "On Sense and Reference," 69.
11. Frege, "Über Sinn und Bedeutung," 37; "On Sense and Reference," 66.
12. Frege, "Über Sinn und Bedeutung," 38–39; "On Sense and Reference," 67–68.
13. Frege, "Über Sinn und Bedeutung," 39; "On Sense and Reference," 68.
14. Frege, "Über Sinn und Bedeutung," 46–48; "On Sense and Reference," 75–77.
15. "Eadem sunt quae sibi mutuo substitui possunt, salva veritate." [Those things are identical of which one can be substituted for the other without loss of truth.] Quoted by Frege, "Über Sinn und Bedeutung," 35; "On Sense and Reference," 64.
16. Frege, "Über Sinn und Bedeutung," 47; "On Sense and Reference," 76.
17. See Ricoeur, *Cours sur le langage*.
18. Frege, review of Husserl's *Philosophie der Arithmetik*, in *Zeitschrift für Philosophie und philosophische Kritik* 108 (1894): 320.

Husserl will ignore the distinctions put forth by Frege, starting with that between *Bedeutung* and *Sinn*, which he dismisses from the opening lines of the *First Investigation* as contrary to the common practice of using one or the other interchangeably (*Logische Untersuchungen*, vol. 2 [Halle: Max Niemeyer, 1913], 53; *Logical Investigations*, trans. J.N. Findlay [London: Routledge & Kegan Paul, 1970], vol. 1, 269). Admittedly, Husserl revives this opposition when he asserts at the end of the same *Investigation* (*Logische Untersuchungen*, vol. 2, § 34, 103; *Logical Investigations*, trans. Findlay, vol. 1, 332) that "If we perform the act {make a statement} and live in it, as it were, we naturally refer to its object and not to its meaning [*signification/Bedeutung*]." It remains nonetheless impossible to align what Husserl calls *Bedeutung* (or *Sinn* indiscriminately) with what Frege called *Sinn*. Signification for Frege is an objective reality, just as it is for Husserl (see the *Fourth Investigation*). However, the former arrives at it by means of an operation (the commutation test) that allows the intervals separating the terms and producing the meaning effect [*effet de sens*] to be determined, while the latter posits signification as a virtual "wanting-to-say" [*vouloir-dire*] that will be actualized and animated by the "life" of a subject in search of intuition. The thought content will be construed in two, completely different, ways. Thus while there may be a superficial analogy to be drawn between the commutational test and the "imaginary variation" that leads to intuition (*Ideen zu einer reinen Phänomenologie und phänomenologischen Philosophie*, *Jahrbuch für Philosophie und phenomenologische Forschung*, vol. 1 (1913), § 70)—since in both cases the methodological act consists in transgressing immediacy—with Frege the result of this act, the *concept*, defines itself only through an identity of the $a = b$ type, whereas on the contrary the Husserlian *essence* is a signification grasped "in person" by a positive intuition of the Ego. At work is a kind of phenomenological reversal of the relation between the content and the operational procedure: evidence is not really the *result* of imaginary variations; instead it is what never ceases to direct the activity of "fiction" through its variations. Like Leibniz, Frege attempts to understand signification in terms of a system, as opposed to Husserl, who does not relinquish the Cartesian problematic of *intuitus*.

One could find the same assumption in the status granted the *I* in the *First Investigation*. For linguistics, the *I* performs the basic function of indicator which, once placed in the system of language [*langue*], refers to the actual speaker: it is therefore a term stripped, strictly speaking, of all signification (*Sinn*), since there exists in the system no *b* for which *I* = *b* would be true. On the other hand, Husserl will insist on speaking of the *meaning* [signification] of the *I* (*Logische Untersuchungen,* vol. 2, 82 ff; *Logical Investigations*, trans. Findlay, vol. 1, 315 ff) like any other deictic (see the *Sixth Investigation*, § 5). He even attempts to define two "meanings . . . built upon one another": an indicating one, residing in the "deictic {*hinweisenden*} intention" in general, and another, indicated meaning, consisting in the perceptual realization of the first meaning. When Husserl comes to qualify his position on the subject (*Logische Untersuchungen,* vol. 2, 21; *Logical Investigations*, trans. Findlay, vol. 2, 685—this is § 5 of the *Sixth Investigation*), he will do away with indicated meaning in these terms: "we must not only draw a general distinction between the perceptual and the significant element in the statement of perception; we must also locate *no part of the meaning* [*signification*] *in the percept itself*." Yet the idea of a *signification of the deictic* remains intact after this purge. What in fact entitles Husserl to use signification and designation interchangeably is his method of constituting evidence: even though one can indeed intuitively think the "content" of *this* or *I* independently of the actual reference (we then find ourselves with the abstract and empty universality Hegel speaks of in the first chapter of the *Phenomenology*), this "content" is not of the same rank as that of a term like *horse* or of a phrase like *let's go,* since these can be replaced by other terms of the system that defines them. For signification, the relevant aspect is not intuition, but substitution (or commutation).

In his remarkable critique of the *First Investigation* (*La voix et le phénomène* [Paris, P.U.F., 1967]), Jacques Derrida, it seems to me, challenges the wrong part of Husserl's analysis of indication. No doubt, as Derrida observes, the idea of "indicated signification" is inconceivable and contrary to the principle of the ideality of meaning [*idéalité du sens*]. But, as we saw, Husserl himself abandons the idea. Furthermore, it does not suffice to justify bringing the deictic signifier back to the level of any other signifier of the system—which is in fact not far from what Husserl does. One had better, after Émile Benveniste (in "La nature des pronoms" [1956], "De la subjectivité dans le langage" [1958], and *Problèmes de linguistique générale* [Paris, Gallimard, 1966]), refer its usage to an assumed exteriority, in this case that of the speaker her- or himself: without this dimension of designation, any deictic remains inconceivable. In other words, the deictic is not merely a value within the system, but an element that from the inside refers to the outside: the deictic is not conceivable *in* the system but *through* it. This difference is of the greatest importance, and does not imply any return to a "metaphysics of presence," as Derrida fears. Frege distinguishes the moon (*Bedeutung*), aimed at through the lens of a telescope, from its image (*Sinn*), situated in this telescope's optical system. The comparison clearly articulates that the moon is no more objective than the image; that the image is no less objective than the moon; and that the only relevant difference lies in the fact that one is inside the (optical and, by analogy, linguistic) system and the other outside of it. With Frege's moon, and Benveniste's deictic, thought eludes the Platonic sun of presence. The designated's *Einseitigkeit* [one-sidedeness] renders all *Erfüllung* [fulfillment] illusory.

The No and the Position of the Object

1. Émile Benveniste, "Remarques sur la fonction du langage dans la découverte freudienne," in *Problèmes de linguistique générale* (Paris, Gallimard, 1966), 85; "Remarks on the Function of Language in Freudian Theory," *Problems in General Linguistics*, trans. Mary Elizabeth Meek (Coral Gables: University of Miami Press, 1971), 73. Freud's text "Die Verneinung" (1925) can be found in Sigmund Freud, *Gesammelte Werke*, vol. 14 (London / Frankfurt am Main: Imago Publishing / S. Fischer Verlag, 1952–), 11–15 [hereafter cited as GW, followed by volume and page number]; and in *The Standard Edition of the Complete Psychological Works of Sigmund Freud*, trans. and ed. James Strachey, with Anna Freud, Alix Strachey, and Alan Tyson, vol. 19 (London: The Hogarth Press, 1953–), 235–239 [hereafter cited as SE, followed by volume and page number]. The French translation by H. Hoesli is published in *Revue française de psychanalyse* 2 (1934): 174–177. For Jean Hyppolite's analysis of the essay, see "Commentaire parlé sur la *Verneinung* de Freud" (1954), *La psychanalyse* 1 (Paris: P.U.F., 1956), and Jacques Lacan, "Introduction et réponse au commentaire de Jean Hyppolite," *La psychanalyse* 1 (Paris: P.U.F., 1956). The same texts by Hyppolite and Lacan can be found in Lacan, *Écrits* (Paris: Seuil, 1966). Paul Ricoeur also provides a commentary of "Die Verneinung" in *De l'interprétation. Essai sur Freud* (Paris: Seuil, 1965), 308–311. A translation of Freud's article appears at the end of the present chapter if only to give the French reader access to a text otherwise impossible to find. [Lyotard's French translation of Freud's "Die Verneinung" has been placed at the end this book as an Appendix. —*Trans.*]
2. GW, vol. 14, 12; SE, vol. 19, 235.
3. [In his introduction, John Mowitt notes that Lyotard translates the title of Freud's essay "Die Verneinung" by "La (dé)négation," while the *Standard Edition* suggests "negation" as the best equivalent for the German term, though it also deems "denial" or "disavowal" acceptable. By adopting the parentheses in the French title, Lyotard is abiding by the *Vocabulaire de la psychanalyse,* which recommends the conflation of *négation* and *dénégation* as a way of covering simultaneously the two meanings of *Verneinung*: negation as grammatical function, and the act of denying or repudiating a statement (Jean Laplanche and Jean-Bertrand Pontalis, *Vocabulaire de la psychanalyse* [Paris: P.U.F., 1967], 113). Yet because Lyotard does not use *(dé)négation* in his own text when referring to *Verneinung*—thereby maintaining the difference between grammatical *négation* and *dénégation* as psychological defense—I translate the latter by "denial" and *négation* by "negation" (reserving "disavowal" for the German term *Verleugnung*, or *déni* in French). —*Trans.*]
4. Benveniste, "Remarques sur la fonction du langage dans la découverte freudienne," 84–85; "Remarks on the Function of Language in Freudian Theory," trans. Meek, 73.

5. Benveniste, "La nature des pronoms," *Problèmes de linguistique générale*, 253 ff; "The Nature of Pronouns," *Problems in General Linguistics*, trans. Meek, 218. See also Benveniste, "Le langage et l'expérience humaine," *Diogène* 51 (1965): 3.
6. Benveniste insists on the property of the genuinely personal pronoun of being without concept and object: "By necessity identical in its form, this experience {that of the speaking subject by being the instance of discourse [*l'instance du discours*]} is not described, it is there, inherent in the form transmitting it. . . . Outside of actual [*effectif*] discourse, the pronoun is nothing but an empty form that can be attached neither to an object nor a concept. It receives its reality and substance from discourse alone" ("Le langage et l'expérience humaine," 4 [translation A.H.]). It seems to me that it would be more accurate to stress the absence of concept than the absence of object. As far as the latter is concerned, one could indeed argue that, strictly speaking, and with the exception of the proper noun, there is never just one object answering to any one term, but essentially several. The use of *I* by different speakers is not, in this respect, any more paradoxical than that of the common "noun." On the contrary, it testifies to the fact that the designation of the instance of discourse is always accompanied by a *reification* of the Self [*Moi*].
7. Ferdinand de Saussure, *Cours de linguistique générale* (Paris: Payot, 1962), 166–168; *Course in General Linguistics*, trans. Roy Harris (London: Duckworth, 1971), 118–119.
8. Immanuel Kant, *Versuch den Begriff der negativen Grössen in die Weltweisheit einzuführen* (Königsberg: Kanter, 1763); *Attempt to Introduce the Concept of Negative Magnitudes into Philosophy,* in *Theoretical Philosophy 1755–1770*, ed. and trans. David Walford and Ralf Meerbote (Cambridge: Cambridge University Press, 1992), 212–216. In keeping with Kant's metaphor, one would say (after Serge Boucheron) that negation, with Hegel, is the facing wind with which the boat contends by zigzagging and tacking in order to reach its destination. With Kant, the negative represses, pushes one to retrace one's steps, makes one regress. One can see how far Freud is from Hegel.
9. Freud writes specifically "die Verneinung ist eine Art, das Verdrängte *zur Kenntnis zu nehmen*" (GW, vol. 14, 12); "Negation is a way *of taking cognizance* of what is repressed" (SE, vol. 19, 235; emphasis J.-F.L.).
10. [Like Mary Lydon, I translate *pulsion*—the accepted French translation of the German *Trieb*—by "drive," except when quoting from the *Standard Edition,* where *Trieb* is translated by "instinct" (see "Fiscourse Digure: The Utopia behind the Scenes of the Phantasy" below, note 2). —*Trans.*]
11. "Die Verneinung," GW, vol. 14, 12; "Negation," SE, vol. 19, 236.
12. "Die Verneinung," GW, vol. 14, 15;"Negation," SE, vol. 19, 239.
13. "Die Verneinung," GW, vol. 14, 13; "Negation," SE, vol. 19, 237.
14. "Die Verneinung," GW, vol. 14, 14; "Negation," SE, vol. 19, 237.
15. Freud, *Three Essays on the Theory of Sexuality* (1905), SE, vol. 7, 222 ff.
16. Freud, *Group Psychology and the Analysis of the Ego* (1921), SE, vol. 18, chap. 7; Freud, *The Ego and the Id* (1923), SE, vol. 19, chap. 3; Freud, *Beyond the Pleasure Principle* (1920), SE, vol. 18, chap. 2. The original version of the latter (*Jenseits des Lustprinzips*) can be found in GW, vol. 13.
17. *Beyond the Pleasure Principle*, SE, vol. 18, 15–17.

18. "Die Verneinung," GW, vol. 14, 15; "Negation," SE, vol. 19, 239. Cf. "Das Unbewusste" (1915), GW, vol. 10, 285–286; "The Unconscious," SE, vol. 14, 186.
19. Benveniste, "Remarques sur la fonction du langage dans la découverte freudienne," 84; "Remarks on the Function of Language in Freudian Theory," trans. Meek, 72–73.
20. Benveniste, "Remarques sur la fonction du langage dans la découverte freudienne," 84; "Remarks on the Function of Language in Freudian Theory," trans. Meek, 73.
21. "Die Verneinung," GW, vol. 14, 15; "Negation," SE, vol. 19, 239.
22. In his *Commentaire*, Hyppolite notices this division of negativity in the course of Freud's reflection: "What, then, does this dissymmetry between affirmation and negation mean? It means that the repressed in its entirety can be recuperated and reused in a kind of suspension, and that, in a way, rather than being subjected to the drives of attraction and expulsion, a margin of thought can occur—an appearance of being in the form of it not being—that is produced with denial [*dénégation*], in other words where the symbol of negation is connected to the concrete attitude of denying [*dénégation*]. . . . It is therefore imperative to separate the drive to destroy and the form of destruction, for otherwise one could not make sense of Freud's argument" ("Commentaire parlé sur la *Verneinung* de Freud," 39–40 [translation A.H.]). As Ricoeur observes, what is surprising (and indeed what is at the very core of Ricoeur's surprise in front of Freud's work) is not that the No of transcendence derives from the No of the drive, but that the latter finds itself represented by the former, given the huge importance that symbolic negation takes on in play, art, and the constitution itself of reality. "This discovery," writes the author of *De l'interprétation*, "is enough to reset in motion the entire analysis of the drive's representatives. The death drive is not closed upon the destructiveness, which is, we said, its clamor; perhaps it opens out onto other aspects of the 'work of the negative,' which remains 'silent' like itself" (Ricoeur, *De l'interprétation*, 311; *Freud and Philosophy: An Essay on Interpretation*, trans. Denis Savage [New Haven, London: Yale University Press, 1970], 317–318 [translation modified A.H.]). It is precisely in the gap between these two No's, in their articulation by *Aufhebung*, that Ricoeur intends to lodge his "spiritual," "dialectical" interpretation of art, culture, and finally religion (*De l'interprétation*, 18 ff).
23. "Die Verneinung," GW, vol. 14, 15; "Negation," SE, vol. 19, 239.
24. "Die Verneinung," GW, vol. 14, 12–13; "Negation," SE, vol. 19, 236.
25. Cf. "Formulierungen über die zwei Prinzipien des psychischen Geschehens" (1911), GW, vol. 8; "Formulations on the Two Principles of Mental Functioning," SE, vol. 12.
26. [See *Plato*, vol. 7, ed. and trans. R.G. Bury (London, New York: William Heinemann; G.P. Putnam's Sons, 1929), 341B–345C (530–542).]

Opposition and Difference

1. Sigmund Freud, "Über die Berechtigung, von der Neurasthenie einen bestimmten Symptomenkomplex als 'Angstneurose' abzutrennen" (1895), in *Gesammelte Werke*, vol. 1 (London/Frankfurt am Main: Imago Publishing/S. Fischer Verlag, 1952–), 318–319 [hereafter cited as GW, followed by volume and page number]; "On the Grounds of Detaching a Particular Syndrome from Neurasthenia under the Description 'Anxiety Neurosis,'" in

The Standard Edition of the Complete Psychological Works of Sigmund Freud, trans. and ed. James Strachey, with Anna Freud, Alix Strachey, and Alan Tyson, vol. 3 (London: The Hogarth Press, 1953–), 93 [hereafter cited as SE, followed by volume and page number].

2. Freud, "Das Unheimliche" (1919), GW, vol. 12, 268; "The Uncanny," SE, vol. 17, 252.
3. There is no emotive body in Merleau-Ponty's phenomenology. Disturbances such as hallucination are only taken as opportunities to confirm the hypothesis of normalcy, which is that of an originary harmony. See in particular Maurice Merleau-Ponty, *Phénoménologie de la perception* (Paris: Gallimard, 1945), 385 ff; *Phenomenology of Perception*, trans. Colin Smith (London, Henley: Routledge & Kegan Paul, 1962), 334 ff.
4. G.W.F. Hegel, *Elements of the Philosophy of Right* (1820), trans. S.W. Dyde (Mineola, N.Y.: Dover, 2005 [1896]), § 302, "Note," 180.
5. Karl Marx, *Kritik des hegelschen Staatsrechts* (1842), in *Marx-Engels Werke* (Berlin: Dietz, 1962), vol. 1, 292; *Critique of Hegel's "Philosophy of Right,"* ed. Joseph O'Malley, trans. Annette Jolin and Joseph O'Malley (Cambridge: Cambridge University Press, 1970), 88.
6. Marx, *Kritik des hegelschen Staatsrechts*, vol. 1, 292; *Critique of Hegel's "Philosophy of Right,"* ed. O'Malley, trans. Jolin and O'Malley, 88. Should we accept this reference to the Shakespearean double stage as Marx uses it here? I have my doubts: the carpenter is Snug *on one stage* and lion *on the other*; redoubled (represented) representation is not an ideology of mediation, for it keeps the two stages apart. What is ideological in Hegel is the fact that middle and extremes are mutually reconciled *on the same stage*. The reader will find at the end of the present book some Shakespearean episodes intended to incite reflection on this reversal.
7. Marx, *Kritik des hegelschen Staatsrechts*, 292; *Critique of Hegel's "Philosophy of Right,"* ed. O'Malley, trans. Jolin and O'Malley, 89; emphasis J.-F.L.
8. [In French in Marx's original: "The extremes come full circle." —*Trans.*]
9. Marx, *Kritik des hegelschen Staatsrechts*, 293; *Critique of Hegel's "Philosophy of Right,"* ed. O'Malley, trans. Jolin and O'Malley, 89.
10. Needless to point out that this *Differenz* is what I refer to here as opposition, and this *Gegensatz* what I aim to define as true difference.
11. Marx, *Kritik des hegelschen Staatsrechts*, 293–294: "Das eine greift über das andre über. Die Stellung ist keine gleiche"; *Critique of Hegel's "Philosophy of Right,"* ed. O'Malley, trans. Jolin and O'Malley, 90.
12. In fact the subject is the relation between the Estates and the power of the crown in relation to legislature.
13. This concept of a difference outside the system should be related to the Freudian notion of differed action. If, for example, the scene of seduction (assuming it exists) takes effect after the fact, as a differed action, this is not because we are still in the gap, but rather because human sex is nonhuman.
14. Ferdinand de Saussure, *Cours de linguistique générale* (Paris: Payot, 1962), quoted in Robert Godel, *Les sources manuscrites du Cours de linguistique générale de Ferdinand de Saussure* (Geneva, Paris: Droz and Minard, 1957), 65 [translation A.H.].
15. Saussure, *Cours*, quoted in Godel, *Les sources manuscrites*, 74 [translation A.H.].
16. Saussure, *Cours de 1910–1911*, quoted in Godel, *Les sources manuscrites*, 92 [translation A.H.].

17. Godel, *Les sources manuscrites,* 197 [translation A.H.].
18. Ibid., 198 [translation A.H.].
19. Roman Jakobson, "The Phonemic and Grammatical Aspects of Language in Their Interrelations," in *Roman Jakobson: Selected Writings,* vol. 2 (The Hague, Paris: Mouton, 1971), 106.
20. Roman Jakobson and Morris Halle, "Phonology and Phonetics," in *Roman Jakobson: Selected Writings,* vol. 1 (The Hague, Paris: Mouton, 1971), 492 ff.
21. Antonin Artaud, *Pour en finir avec le jugement de Dieu* (Paris: K, 1948), 31–32; "To Have Done with the Judgment of God," in *Antonin Artaud: Selected Writings,* ed. Susan Sontag, trans. Helen Weaver (Berkeley, Los Angeles: University of California Press, 1988 [1976]), 566.
22. Artaud, *Pour en finir avec le jugement de Dieu,* 47 [translation A.H.]. [The translation given in the text is only a rough indication of the original, in which Artaud plays on the sound of French: "—a cé tute la question / que Dieu s'en aille ou que Dieu reste / voilà la question qui est posée / Ils dansent la danse de la friction infâme / de la futame avec la fâme et / et de l'union de ron et saun." These lines are from a first draft of *Pour en finir* not translated in the *Selected Writings.* —*Trans.*]
23. Henri Pichette, *Les épiphanies* (Paris: K, 1948), 40. [Modified translation after Geoffrey Bennington, *Lyotard: Writing the Event* (Manchester: Manchester University Press, 1988), 76. —*Trans.*]
24. Claude Lévi-Strauss, *La pensée sauvage* (Paris: Plon, 1962), 120; *The Savage Mind* (London: Weidenfeld and Nicolson, 1966), 91.
25. With the exception, however, of early Hebrew discourse.
26. "The order of chronological succession is absorbed in a timeless matrix-like structure," writes Lévi-Strauss in "La structure et la forme" (*Cahiers de l'I.S.E.A.* 99 [March 1960]: 29 [translation A.H.]). Lévi-Strauss did not always neglect it. The canonical formula of myths that he ventured to lay out in "La structure des mythes" (1955) (in *Anthropologie structurale* [Paris: Plon, 1958], 252) necessarily implies the taking into account of a *form*—a "shutter"-like form with the second panel folding back on the first so as to cancel it. It would take little effort to link the present reflection on difference to Lévi-Strauss's implicit (and unintentional?) formalism. On the subject of form, see Claude Bremond's work on Vladimir Propp in *Communications* 4 (1964): 4–32, and 8 (1966): 60–76.
27. Bremond notes several of these "illogical" moments in Propp's work, generally attributing them to the linguist's coding.
28. I quote from the conclusion of Bremond's study on Propp, "Le message narratif," *Communications* 4 (1964): 31. The schema to which I refer is on the same page.
29. Bremond, "Le message narratif," 25. On *dispositio* see Gérard Genette, *Figures,* vol. 2 (Paris: Seuil, 1969), 23 ff.
30. Bremond, "Le message narratif," 22.
31. See Husserl, *On the Phenomenology of the Consciousness of Internal Time* from 1904–1905, trans. John Barnett Brough (Dordrecht, London: Kluwer Academic, 1990 [1928]), particularly sections 10 and 39; Husserl's *Cartesian Meditations* from 1929, trans. Dorion

Cairns (The Hague: Martinus Nijhoff, 1960), particularly section 18; and the unpublished work by Groupe C quoted by Tran Duc Thao in *Phénoménologie et matérialisme dialectique* (Paris: Minh-Tan, 1951), 139–144.

32. Freud, "Jenseits des Lustprinzips" (1920), GW, vol. 13, 27–28; "Beyond the Pleasure Principle," SE, vol. 18, 28.
33. Hence Tran Duc Thao is right in a sense to compare Husserl's descriptions of time in the unpublished manuscripts with Hegelian dialectics.
34. Freud, "Das Unbewusste" (1915), GW, vol. 10, 286; "The Unconscious," SE, vol. 14, 186–187.
35. GW, vol. 10, 286; SE, vol. 14, 186–187.
36. Freud, "Das Unheimliche" (1919), GW, vol. 12; "The 'Uncanny,' " SE, vol. 17.
37. ". . . dies Ängstliche etwas wiederkehrendes Verdrängtes ist" (GW, vol. 12, 254; SE, vol. 17, 241.)
38. GW, vol. 12, 259; SE, vol. 17, 245.
39. See André Leroi-Gourhan, *Le geste et la parole* (Paris: Albin Michel, 1965), vol. 2, 234 ff; *Gesture and Speech*, trans. Anna Bostock Berger (Cambridge: Massachusetts Institute of Technology, 1993), 384 ff. See also the chapter "Linguistic Sign?" in the present book, note 27.
40. For Pierre Kaufmann, the emotional dispossession that results from the withdrawal of the Other's speech retroactively leads the subject to organize space as if she or he were holding the missing discourse. See in particular Kaufmann's analysis of Vincent van Gogh's pictorial script at the end of *L'expérience émotionnelle de l'espace* (Paris: Vrin, 1967).
41. On this subject, see André Barre's and Albert Flocon's analyses of these corrections in *La perspective curviligne* (Paris: Flammarion, 1968), in particular the first part: "Theoretically the rectangle could not be perceived without distortion unless viewed on the perpendicular axis at the center of its surface and from an infinite distance. This remark implies that theoretically we can never perceive as such either a rectangle or a square or a triangle or any other regular figure except a circle. In fact, and even though it would be geometrically impossible, we have the feeling that we see figures there. Education and habit stimulate the desire to see reality correspond to concepts. Our eye and our brain rectify distortions, to the extent that this can be done without too much violence to verisimilitude, to real space and to the coherence of our spatial logic. In visual perception there is a very complex and flexible play among the object, its retinal image, and its mental representation. Certain compensatory mechanisms intervene and give us a more stable representation of objects in nature than that implied by the laws of geometrical optics. For example, the dimensions of a well-known object seem to us to be changed very little, in spite of relatively important differences in distance. When one looks at one's own hand at 30 cm, then at 60 cm, it appears palpably the same size, even though the angle within which it is perceived is reduced by half" (Flocon and Barre, *Curvilinear Perspective: From Visual Space to the Constructed Image*, trans. Robert Hansen [Berkeley, Los Angeles, London: University of California Press, 1987], 77–78).
42. First, the immobilization of the head: "Let us place ourselves at some distance from the wall, in order to see easily the top and bottom edges of the wall at the same time.

On the right, at infinity, the top edge and the base meet on the horizon; they diverge progressively toward the center but converge again at the extreme left. The curvature of the two lines is undeniable" (Flocon and Barre, *Curvilinear Perspective*, trans. Hansen, 85). Next, the immobilization of the eyes: "For example, in focusing on the center of the wall, we can acknowledge this curvature if, without shifting the eyes, we attend to the top or to the base, or to both at the same time. The results are rather variable depending on the observer and are generally favored by dim light" (Flocon and Barre, *Curvilinear Perspective*, trans. Hansen, 86). Weak lighting favors lateral vision because the responsibility for perception shifts from the cones to the rods, the latter being more sensitive to weak lighting conditions and more evenly distributed on the retina's surface without being concentrated in the foveal zone like the cones. One should draw a connection between this immobilization and René Passeron's comment on the immobility of light in the painter's studio (*L'œuvre picturale et les fonctions de l'apparence* [Paris: Vrin, 1962], 102 ff). After quoting Leonardo and Paillot de Montabert, Passeron writes: "the enemy is the sun. Because it moves. Its light is fickle. All good painters' studios face north. A white and diffuse light comes in—a *clinical* lighting—that allows the other lights to be controlled, those one stores in one's memory, those one inserts in the play of values and colors of the model, those one develops slowly in the experiments of the 'abstract' sketch" [translation A.H.]. I do not believe it is coincidental that a few pages later, on the subject of the painter's attention, Passeron is led to assume that the painter "would possess in the first instance, at the ocular level, a sufficient peripheral vision and, despite a certain fogginess of the edges of the visual field, would be capable of seeing at the same time the central object and the peripheral object" (Passeron, *L'œuvre picturale*, 109 [translation A.H.]). And this other remark, in the same vein: "the painter's proverbial winking in front of objects (just as she or he does in front of the canvas) is intended to erase the details that would divert attention, that would focalize it, and to allow for an attentive grasp of the value relations that constitute the structure of the image in its totality. . . . In the art of seeing there is integration of what is *seen involuntarily* into what is *looked at intentionally*, and the suddenness of this integration can sometimes overwhelm you" (Passeron, *L'œuvre picturale*, 110 [translation A.H.]).

43. "In reality, the field of vision is quite wide. It can span 150° laterally and 170° vertically, and binocular vision can extend laterally to 210°"; the foveal region "is tiny, subtending a visual angle of about 2°. . . . The fovea's 2° field represents approximately a ten-thousandth of the total visual field of the eye" (Flocon and Barre, *Curvilinear Perspective*, trans. Hansen, 81–83). One should add that the periphery has much fewer cones and affords considerably less acuity than the foveal region: by "attributing a value of one to foveal acuity, one finds acuity to be ten times weaker 10° from the center and one hundred times weaker 60° from the center" (Flocon and Barre, *Curvilinear Perspective*, trans. Hansen, 82).

44. See Anton Ehrenzweig, *The Psychoanalysis of Artistic Vision and Hearing: An Introduction to a Theory of Unconscious Perception* (London: Routledge & Kegan Paul, 1953), 193 ff.

45. Georges Braque, *Le jour et la nuit (cahiers 1917–1952)* (Paris: Gallimard, 1952), 38, 21, 23, 30, 33, 38 respectively [translation A.H.].

Veduta on a Fragment of the "History" of Desire

[The ambivalence of the French title—"*Veduta* sur un fragment de l''histoire' du désir"—hinges on the word *histoire*, which may mean "history" as well as "story" or "tale." This ambivalence plays a critical role in a chapter that offers a semblance of a "history" of desire in art and science from the Middle Ages to the Renaissance; but only a semblance, because Lyotard's historical digression is informed (both indebted to and undermined by) an appreciation for the narrative codes of myth and storytelling. To respect this ambivalence between discursive genres, which leaves Lyotard's text prone to the figural play of desire (which in turn may explain why the chapter's numbering is not consecutive), I sometimes resort to *(hi)story* to translate an *histoire* that is at once "story" and "history."

My thanks to Oliver W. Norris, who provided some of the translations from the Latin in this chapter. —*Trans.*]

1. [Although *écriture* would normally translate as "writing," I choose to translate the French term here by "script," since Lyotard frequently refers to a more general system of signification than the purely textual, as when he argues that "in Duccio's work, relief itself is scripted" (*Dans Duccio, le modelé est lui-même écrit*), in other words, that Duccio reduces volume to line. For another instance where script subsumes writing proper, see "It's as if a Line . . . ," Mary Lydon's translation of Lyotard's "On dirait qu'une ligne . . ." (*Contemporary Literature* 29, no. 3 [Fall 1988]: 463) —*Trans.*]
2. I develop these concepts—borrowed from André Lhote—below, with respect to the line.
3. [For the sake of consistency, I follow Mary Lydon's decision to translate *tracé révélateur* by "outline" or "contour," and *tracé régulateur* by "regulating line," each time quoting the French in square brackets. (See "The Line and the Letter" below, note 23, for information on the sources of these expressions in Lhote's *Traité du paysage*.) —*Trans.*]
4. See, for example, Henri Bergson, *Matière et mémoire* (Paris: Alcan, 1889), chap. 2, and *La pensée et le mouvant* (Paris: Alcan, 1934), "Introduction I" (1922).
5. See, for example, Freud, "Formulierungen über die zwei Prinzipien des Psychischen Geschehens" (1911), in *Gesammelte Werke*, vol. 8 (London/Frankfurt am Main: Imago Publishing/S. Fischer Verlag, 1952–) [hereafter cited as GW, followed by volume and page number]; "Formulations on the Two Principles of Mental Functioning," in *The Standard Edition of the Complete Psychological Works of Sigmund Freud*, trans. and ed. James Strachey, with Anna Freud, Alix Strachey, and Alan Tyson, vol. 12 (London: The Hogarth Press, 1953–) [hereafter cited as SE, followed by volume and page number].
6. Claude Lévi-Strauss, "Le Geste d'Asdiwal," *Annuaire de l'École pratique des hautes études* (1958–1959): 1–43.
7. Lévi-Strauss, *La pensée sauvage* (Paris: Plon, 1962), 120 ff.
8. Quoted extensively by Alexandre Koyré in *Études galiléennes* (Paris: Hermann, 1966), 171 ff, 60 ff, respectively.
9. On the opposition between repression and foreclosure, see Jacques Lacan's *Écrits* (Paris: Seuil, 1966). This opposition offers a means of classifying ideologies as either neurotic or psychotic, a subject I will analyze elsewhere.
10. Erwin Panofsky, *Gothic Architecture and Scholasticism* (Latrobe: Arch Abbey Press, 1951); Pierre Kaufmann, *L'expérience émotionnelle de l'espace* (Paris: Vrin, 1967), chap. 3.

11. See Louis Réau, *La miniature* (Melun: Librairie d'Argences, 1947), 11; Gabriele Mandel, *Les manuscrits à peintures* (Paris: Pont-Royal, 1964), 30.
12. In the following terms, which cannot fail to reveal the extent to which they are dictated by discourse's opposition to the figure: "Coeterum in claustris coram legentibus fratribus quid facit illa ridicula monstruositas, mira quaedam deformis formositas ac formosa deformitas? Quid ibi immundae simiae? Quid feri leones? Quid monstruosi centauri, quid semihominis? Quid maculosae tigrides? Quid milites pugnantes? Quid venatores tubicinantes? Videas sub uno capite multa corpora et rursus in uno corpore capita multa. Cernitur hinc in quadrupede cauda serpentis, illinc in pisce caput quadrupedis. . . . Tam multa denique, tam mira diversarum formarum ubique varietas apparet, ut magis legere libeat in marmoribus quam in codicibus, totamque diem occupare singula ista mirando quam in lege Dei meditando" (Apology of William, twelfth abbot of St. Thierry, quoted in Rosario Assunto, *Die Theorie des Schönen im Mittelalter* [Cologne: Du Mont, 1963], 152); [What excuse can there be for these ridiculous monstrosities in the cloisters where the monks do their reading, extraordinary things at once beautiful and ugly? Here we find filthy monkeys and fierce lions, fearful centaurs, harpies, and striped tigers, soldiers at war, and hunters blowing their horns. Here is one head with many bodies, there is one body with many heads. Over there is a beast with a serpent for its tail, a fish with an animal's head. . . . All round there is such an amazing variety of shapes that one could easily prefer to take one's reading from the walls instead of from a book. One could spend the whole day gazing fascinated at these things, one by one, instead of meditating on the law of God] (*Cistercians and Cluniacs: St Bernard's* Apologia *to Abbot William*, trans. Michael Casey [Kalamazoo, Mich.: Cistercian Publications, 1970], 66).
13. Paris, National Library, lat. 8. This is the second Bible of Saint-Martial, from the end of the eleventh century. The Clunisian abbey of Saint Martial was a stop on the road to Compostela. The Limousin school is characterized by rich and heavy decoration, particularly the initials. The second Bible of Saint-Martial, however, is the work of two illuminators, one of whom is "the most remarkable artist of the Southern French School." It is to the latter that the initial under consideration is attributed. See Marie Cordroc'h, *Les trésors de la Bibliothèque nationale*, Manuscript Department, Romanesque period, Southern France (Paris: Publications filmées d'art et d'histoire, 1964), 10–11 and 32–40.
14. Paris, National Library, lat. 254, end of the tenth century. See Cordroc'h, *Les trésors de la Bibliothèque nationale*, 9–10 and 24–28.
15. See *Guide de la peinture (du Mont-Athos)* (Paris: Didron, 1845), passim, particularly 124–128; and Edgar De Bruyne, *Études d'esthétique médiévale* (Bruges: Rijksuniversität te Gent, De tempel, 1946), vol. 1, 284 ff.
16. Wassily Kandinsky, *Über das Geistige in der Kunst* (1911); *Concerning the Spiritual in Art*, trans. M. T. H. Sadler (New York: Dover, 1977), 27–45. It is worth noting that the order Kandinsky proposes is not itself a "natural" one but retains an arbitrary quality: Kandinsky contrasts blue with yellow, not orange, and the latter (the natural complementary of blue) with green.
17. "Since painting," writes De Bruyne (*Études d'esthétique médiévale*, vol. 1, 284–285), "is taken to be a kind of plastic writing, yet one solidly connected to the visible world, we should not be surprised that the signs to which it resorts are often conventional. The

person familiar with the code of traditional figures must be able to recognize instantly the figures presented to her or him. Each character has its own pictorial file: even without a *titulus*, the initiate is capable of identifying it. . . . The features of each saint are set by tradition. The portraits themselves are painted not according to nature, but to pictorial code: one does not 'see' if they look like their model, one 'knows' whom they represent and that suffices" [translation A.H.].

18. When Panofsky reflects on the upheavals affecting the representation of space throughout Western history, he considers the transition from the space of the Carolingian miniature (heir to classical space via Byzantium) to that of Romanesque illuminated manuscripts as a "surface consolidation": the image's frame is heavily outlined, and instead of having the figures scattered across an open space, suggested by barely sketched lines, they are covered by densely pigmented colors. "In short, the ground has congealed into a solid, planar working surface while the design has congealed into a system of two-dimensional area defined by one-dimensional lines." And Panofsky adds that "the 'cartographic' tendency of Romanesque book illumination" will come across in particular through "the transformation of the curves indicating hilly terrain into brightly colored and sharply delineated ribbons." These new objects "have lost all reference to a three-dimensional landscape space and operate as mere partitions" (*Renaissance and Renascences in Western Art* [Stockholm: Almquist & Wiksell, 1960], 131–132). See also Panofsky, "Die Perspektive als symbolische Form," *Vorträge der Bibliothek Warburg* (1924–1925), 260 ff, 292 ff; and Liliane Brion-Guerry, *Cézanne et l'expression de l'espace,* 2nd ed. (Paris: Albin Michel, 1966), 14 ff, 227 ff. The definitive disappearance of the last vestiges of the "open" space inherited from the Hellenistic tradition that still survived in the Carolingian period indicates that the support ceases to be overlooked in a bid to create illusion, but that it is *accepted as support* in the same way that writing does not invest the page upon which it is scripted in order for it to grant the page an apparent depth. The outlining of the figures and the abstraction of the decoration tend toward the same result: the figure closes upon itself to become a quasi-letter, while the decoration sheds its representational function; its value frees itself from the designated, while its signification becomes arbitrary. Panofsky reminds us that even in the Late Gothic the principle of "surface consolidation" is not abandoned.
19. "Libri Carolini," *Patrologia latina*, ed. Jacques-Paul Migne, vol. 98.
20. "Libri Carolini" (col. 1002), *Patrologia latina*, quoted by De Bruyne, *Études d'esthétique médiévale*, vol. 1, 262 [translation O.W.N.].
21. [Translation O.W.N.]
22. Gregory of Nyssa writes, for example, in the panegyric to Saint Theodore: "Having used colors as if in a speaking book, the artist has clearly recounted the martyr's struggle, for mute painting speaks on the wall and is very beneficial" (quoted by De Bruyne, *Études d'esthétique médiévale*, vol. 1, 264 [translation from the French A.H.]). In 1035, the Council of Arras will encourage the painting of church frescoes for the benefit of the illiterate—cf. the chronological tables in Jacques Le Goff, *La civilisation de l'Occident médiéval* (Paris: Arthaud, 1967), 501.
23. De Bruyne, *Études d'esthétique médiévale*, vol. 1, 272 [translation A.H.].
24. Quoted by Assunto, *Die Theorie des Schönen im Mittelalter*, 87, and Plate 24 [translation

from the Latin O.W.N.]. The evangelistary dates from the first quarter of the eleventh century, during the Ottonian period. [The *Majestas Domini* to which Lyotard is referring is an illuminated page in the Hitda Codex depicting Christ enthroned. —*Trans.*]

25. De Bruyne, *Études d'esthétique médiévale*, vol. 1, 278 [translation A.H.].
26. Quoted in De Bruyne, *Études d'esthétique médiévale*, vol. 1, 274.
27. Rabanus Maurus writes to a friend who enjoys illuminated manuscripts and pictures too much: "The letter is of greater value than the deceitful form of the image, for it contributes more to the soul's beauty than the harmony of colors that reveals only the shadow of things. Writing is the perfect and pious measure of salvation. It is of greater worth as far as knowledge of reality is concerned, more useful than anything else; it affords aesthetic taste more immediate satisfaction; for the human senses its meaning is more perfect; and the mind remembers it with greater ease. Literature is at the service of the tongue and the ear, while painting only flatters the gaze and the eye with paltry consolations. . . . Look at those behind the invention and development of these art forms: you will know with certainty with whom you should side. It was Egypt that first outlined the objects' shadow and that, by varying the colors, produced images. 'Egypt' means 'insistent pain'" (Hrabani carmini. Ad Bonosum, carm. 38 [translation from the French A.H.]). Francastel clearly identifies this role of recognition played by the medieval figure under the expression "objective art" (Pierre Francastel, "Espace génétique et espace plastique," *Revue d'esthétique* [1948]; reprinted in *La réalité figurative: Éléments structurels de sociologie de l'art* [Paris: Gonthier, 1965], 145 ff). "A world where movement does not affect volumes and qualities, where objects are truly beings endowed once and for all with complementary and immutable properties. . . . The art of the Middle Ages . . . is an art whose symbolic language relies on a rigid system that elicits moral qualities through specific material attributes" (*La réalité figurative*, 146 [translation A.H.]). Francastel assimilates this art to Aristotelian thought, but concludes somewhat hastily: "The principle of identity *A* is *A* accounts for Saint Anselm as much as Giotto's visual practice" (*La réalité figurative*, 146–147 [translation A.H.]). Neoplatonism is undoubtedly more influential than Aristotelianism, at least until the thirteenth century. See André Grabar, "Plotin et les origines de l'esthétique médiévale," *Cahiers archéologiques* 1 (1945), and André Grabar and Carl Nordenfalk, *Early Medieval Painting from the Fourth to the Eleventh Century* (Lausanne: Skira, 1957).
28. Man paints "sed ad memoriam rerum gestarum et venustatem parietum" [but for the commemoration of events and the beautification of walls] (quoted in De Bruyne, *Études d'esthétique médiévale*, vol. 1, 274 [translation O.W.N.]).
29. John Scotus Erigena (ca. 810–877) translated and interpreted Pseudo-Dionysius the Areopagite's *Corpus* given by the Byzantine Emperor Michael II to Louis the Pious. With Erigena, another Platonism—that of Plotinus and Augustine, the optimistic branch of Platonism—supplants Pythagorean Platonism. See Assunto, *Die Theorie des Schönen im Mittelalter*, 82 ff; and De Bruyne, *Études d'esthétique médiévale*, vol. 1, 339–370.
30. "Opera," *Patrologia latina*, vols. 175–177. See De Bruyne, *Études d'esthétique médiévale*, vol. 2, 203–254; and Roger Baron, *Science et sagesse chez Hugues de Saint-Victor* (Paris: Letielleux, 1957).

31. Since the body is chief among the soul's objects, this agreement first takes shape in the harmony (or music) of the soul and the body, which leads Hugh to develop the thesis of the friendship between mind and flesh, of this friendship's *agreeable* character: "Musica (sive harmonia quae est plurium dissimilium in unum redactorum concordia) inter corpus et animam est illa naturalis amicitia qua anima corpori non corporeis vinculis sed affectibus quibusdam colligatur ad movendum et sensificandum ipsum corpus. Secundum quam *amicitiam* nemo carnem suam odio habuit: musica haec est ut *ametur* caro sed plus spiritus, ut foveatur corpus et non perimatur virtus" ("Didascalicon," book 2, *Patrologia latina*, vol. 176, col. 755 [music (or harmony, which is the congruent unison of many different compositions) between the body and the soul is that innate friendship that binds the soul to the body not by physical chains but out of a sort of desire to move the actual body and endow it with sensation. According to this friendship, nobody hates his own flesh: it is through this music that the flesh is held dear but more so the spirit, that the body is cherished and virtue is not extinguished; translation O.W.N.]). See also "Expositio in Hierarchiam coelestem Sancti Dionysii," *Patrologia latina*, vol. 176, cols. 949–950: "Anima humana quasi de simili ad similia conducta, facile arbitratur visibiles formas invisibilis pulchritudinis imagines esse, illi quod invisibile intus ipsa habet, amica quadam similitudine respondentes eas secundum approbationem et affectum inveniens" [The human soul, as if drawn from like to like, easily considers visible forms to be images of an invisible beauty, finding agreement and pleasure in these forms that correspond, by way of a certain pleasing similitude, to the invisible internal state that the soul itself has; translation O.W.N.].
32. "Hier. Coel.," *Patrologia latina*, vol. 175, col. 949 [translation O.W.N.].
33. "Didasc.," book 7, *Patrologia latina*, vol. 176, col. 82.
34. "Hier. Coel.," *Patrologia latina*, vol. 176, col. 941 [translation O.W.N.].
35. Namely *situs* (beauty of unity within multiplicity), *motus* (simple beauty of what changes place), *species* (visible beauty of things), and *qualitas* (beauty of the other sensoria).
36. "Hier. Coel.," *Patrologia latina*, vol. 176, col. 819; quoted in De Bruyne, *Études d'esthétique médiévale*, vol. 2, 247.
37. "Hier. Coel.," *Patrologia latina*, vol. 176, col. 971; quoted in De Bruyne, *Études d'esthétique médiévale*, vol. 2, 215.
38. "Hier. Coel.," *Patrologia latina*, vol. 176, col. 978; the emphasis is by De Bruyne, who quotes this passage, *Études d'esthétique médiévale*, vol. 2, 21. "Therefore, the more manifestly each drawing demonstrates the truth, the more openly through this dissimilar similitude it proves that it is a drawing and not the truth. And in this, dissimilar similitudes lead our understanding further toward the truth because they do not allow it to dwell on likeness alone"; translation O.W.N.]
39. "Hier. Coel.," book 3, part 2, *Patrologia latina*, vol. 175, col. 987D; quoted by Assunto, "Text-Documente," *Die Theorie des Schönen im Mittelalter*, 157 [translation O.W.N.]. Καλός [*kalos*] is what calls forth (καλεῖν [*kalein*]); see De Bruyne, *Études d'esthétique médiévale*, vol. 2, 217–218.
40. "Didasc.," book 7, *Patrologia latina*, vol. 176, col. 814; quoted in De Bruyne, *Études d'esthétique médiévale*, vol. 2, 209 [translation O.W.N.].
41. "Didasc.," book 7, *Patrologia latina*, vol. 176, col. 790. See De Bruyne, *Études d'esthétique*

médiévale, vol. 2, 208, 313, 343 [translation A.H.]. De Bruyne quotes another comparison of the Scriptures, involving a monument.

42. *Patrologia latina*, vol. 196, col. 96; quoted in De Bruyne, *Études d'esthétique médiévale*, vol. 2, 335 [translation A.H.].

43. "Didasc.," book 7, part 4, *Patrologia latina*, vol. 176; quoted by Assunto, *Die Theorie des Schönen im Mittelalter*, 158 [translation A.H.]. Is it even necessary to alert the reader to this question's proximity with the one informing Claudel's *Art poétique* (Paris: Mercure de France, 1941), particularly with the visible's ambivalence between word and flesh?

44. See Edmund Husserl, "Die Krisis der europäischen Wissenschaften und die phenomenologische Philosophie" (1936), *Gesammelte Werke*, vol. 6 (The Hague: Nijhoff, 1957).

45. I borrow this concept from the advances in stylistics made by the school of generative and transformational grammar. See, for example, the work of James Peter Thorne, more about which below.

46. Statement to be compared to Koyré's, according to which the development of new physics rests on an absence of reference to sensory experience, regardless of what may have been said of Galileo's experimentalism: "Experience, in the sense of raw experience, of observation of a common sense, did not play any role except that of obstacle in the birth of classical science; and the physics of the Paris Nominalists—even Aristotle's—was often much closer to it than Galileo's" (Koyré, *Études galiléennes*, 13; see also Husserl, "Die Krisis der europäischen Wissenschaften und die phenomenologische Philosophie," 153–158 [translation A.H.]). [One can ascertain here the methodology of Bachelard's epistemology.] Raw experience is obviously not identical to the one transcribed in Christian discourse. One cannot, therefore, identify Koyré's observation with what I refer to here as the narrative text's neutralization. Still, Koyré points out that Aristotle's physics, centered on the Cosmos and "the natural place" [*le lieu naturel*], is more consistent with raw experience than Galileo's. For Aristotle's "place" can be taken as the ideological expression of this canon of visual experience, whereby the gaze carves out at the center of the visual field an area in which it lodges what it aims for—which is, in a way, its natural place—and every marginalizing motion constitutes an act of violence against this place. For its part, Christian narrative (like any mythical narrative) tells the story of a similar violence, followed by its neutralization: sin expels mankind from its natural place—a place under the eye of God, at its focal point—and the evangelical message announces and promises the return to this natural place.

47. Hegelian dialectics (at least that of *The Phenomenology of Spirit* and of *The Philosophy of History*) is itself such a story, an ontological narrative discourse based on the stylistic framework of the Christian tale. See, in particular, Hegel's early writings and Jean Hyppolite's essay *Introduction à la philosophie de l'histoire de Hegel* (Paris: Rivière, 1949).

48. See Koyré, "A l'aube de la science classique" (1935–1936) and "Galilée et la loi d'inertie" (1939), in *Études galiléennes*.

49. "Thus we see that the intellectual stance of classical science may be characterized by these two moments that are, in fact, intimately connected: geometrization of space and dissolution of the Cosmos, that is, the disappearance, within scientific reasoning, of any consideration deriving from the Cosmos; and the substitution of the concrete space of

pre-Galilean physics with the abstract space of Euclidean geometry. It is this substitution that made the invention of the law of inertia possible" (Koyré, *Études galiléennes*, 15 [translation A.H.]).

50. Ibid., 171–182.
51. Ibid., 60–79.
52. Ibid., 163.
53. Ibid., 79, 283–290.
54. Ibid., 286.
55. Galileo Galilei, *Dialogo II*, 129; quoted in ibid., 284 [translation A.H.].
56. Galileo, *Dialogo II*, 131; quoted in Koyré, *Études galiléennes*, 286 [translation A.H.].
57. Galileo, *Dialogo II*, 130; quoted in Koyré, *Études galiléennes*, 285 [translation A.H.].
58. Galileo, *Dialogo II*, 131; quoted in Koyré, *Études galiléennes*, 286 [translation A.H.]. Koyré underscores the kinship between what inspires these texts and those of Descartes.
59. Galileo, *Dialogo II*, 132; quoted in Koyré, *Études galiléennes*, 285 [translation A.H.].
60. Koyré stresses that Descartes's thinking (which he credits with the first explicit formulation of the principle of inertia) nevertheless remains much more reliant on the analogical method than Galileo's.
61. Maurice Merleau-Ponty, *L'oeil et l'esprit* (Paris: Gallimard, 1961); "Eye and Mind," trans. Michael B. Smith, in *The Merleau-Ponty Aesthetics Reader*, ed. Galen A. Johnson (Evanston, Ill.: Northwestern University Press, 1993), 121–149.
62. René Descartes, Sixth Discourse, *Dioptrique*, in *Oeuvres*, ed. André Bridoux (Paris: Bibliothèque de la Pléiade, 1946).
63. René Descartes, *Discours de la méthode pour bien conduire sa raison et chercher la vérité dans les sciences*, part 2 (first published in Leyden, 1637).
64. In *L'emploi du temps* (Paris: Minuit, 1956), Michel Butor provides a very beautiful commentary on this grasp of the spatiotemporal difference in the city. Equally close to both texts is the essential *Civilization and Its Discontents* where Freud attempts to convey, by means of the same metaphor, what constitutes the specificity of the space of the unconscious, and which clearly shows that what I call difference is, in the realm of the visible, the indication of the other stage, of the third space. After having described the type of preservation of the past that resists us when we encounter it in historical sites such as Rome, Freud goes on to write: "Now let us, by a flight of imagination, suppose that Rome is not a human habitation but a psychical entity with a similarly long and copious past—an entity, that is to say, in which nothing that has once come into existence will have passed away and all the earlier phases of development continue to exist alongside the latest one. This would mean that in Rome the palaces of the Caesars and the Septizonium of Septimius Severus would still be rising to their old height on the Palatine and that the castle of S. Angelo would still be carrying on its battlements the beautiful statues which graced it until the siege by the Goths, and so on. But more than this. In the place occupied by the Palazzo Caffarelli would once more stand—without the Palazzo having to be removed—the Temple of Jupiter Capitolinus; and this not only in its latest shape, as the Romans of the Empire saw it, but also in its

earliest one, when it still showed Etruscan forms and was ornamented with terracotta antefixes. Where the Coliseum now stands we could at the same time admire Nero's vanished Golden House. On the Piazza of the Pantheon we should find not only the Pantheon of today, as it was bequeathed to us by Hadrian, but, on the same site, the original edifice erected by Agrippa; indeed, the same piece of ground would be supporting the church of Santa Maria sopra Minerva and the ancient temple over which it was built. And the observer would perhaps only have to change (*Änderung*) the direction of his glance or his position in order to call up the one view or the other. There is clearly (*offenbar*) no point (*keinen Sinn*) in spinning our phantasy any further, for it leads to things that are unimaginable and even absurd (*zu Unvorstellbarem, ja zu Absurdem*). If we want to represent historical sequence (*das historische Nacheinander*) in spatial terms we can only do it by juxtaposition in space (*durch ein Nebeneinander im Raum*): the same space cannot have two different contents. Our attempt seems to be an idle game. It has only one justification. It shows us how far we are from mastering (*zu bewältigen*) the characteristics of mental life by representing them in pictorial terms (*durch eine anschauliche Darstellung*)" (*Das Unbehagen in der Kultur* [1930], GW, vol. 14, 427–428; *Civilisation and Its Discontents*, SE, vol. 21, 70–71). I wish to thank Guy Fihman for bringing this text to my attention. One notes that the radical hindrance to *Anschauung*, to the Cartesian *intuitus*, lies in the end in the operations of the unconscious process—condensations and perhaps above all displacements—that ceaselessly shift and blur the object. In this case displacement should be related to the death drive.

65. This is the third "precept" in part 2 of the *Discourse on the Method* (34–35). See Rules Six, Seven, and Ten in Descartes, *Regulae ad directionem ingenii*, and Descartes's letter to Father Mersenne dated 24 December 1640: "it should be noted that in everything I write I do not follow the order of materials [*matières*] but only that of reasons [*raisons*] . . ." [translation A.H.]. This last order is defined as "a facilioribus ad difficiliora" [from the simple to the more complex]; its pertinence is therefore independent of the object, which is provided only by the position of the mind's eye in relation to the field under consideration.

66. ". . . all things, in the sense in which *they can be useful to what we have proposed*—where we are not looking at their isolated natures, but comparing them with one another, *so that some may be known* from others—, can be said to be either 'absolute' or 'relative.' I call 'absolute' whatever contains within itself the pure and simple nature in question, such as all that which is considered, as it were, as independent, a cause, simple, universal, one, equal, similar, straight, or other things of this kind; and, in addition, I call 'absolute' the simplest and easiest thing of all, *in order that we might make use of it* in resolving questions. . . . The secret of the entire art consists in the fact that in all things we should pay careful attention to that which is most absolute. For, *from one point of view,* some things are indeed more absolute than others, yet, from a different point of view, they are more relative. . . . Finally, once again, in order that one better understand that here we are contemplating the series of *things to be known and not the nature of each and every one of them.* . . ." (Rule Six, Descartes, *Regulae ad directionem ingenii*; *Rules for the Direction of the Natural Intelligence*, ed. and trans. George Heffernan [Amsterdam, Atlanta:

Rodopi, 1998], 101, 103; emphasis J.-F.L.). "... individual things, in the order relating to our knowledge of them, have to be considered otherwise than if we were speaking of them in accordance with how they really exist" (Rule Twelve, Descartes, *Regulae ad directionem ingenii*; *Rules*, ed. and trans. Heffernan, 149).

67. In his *Vite* (1550), Vasari says of the *Trinity* that Masaccio painted on the *tramezzo* of Santa Maria Novella (ca. 1425): "But perhaps the most beautiful part of this work, to say nothing of the excellence of the figures, is the coved ceiling, painted in perspective, and divided into square compartments, with a rosette in each compartment; the foreshortening is managed with so much ability, and the whole is so judiciously treated that the surface has all the appearance of being perforated" (*Vasari's Lives of the Artists*, ed. Marilyn Aronberg Lavin, trans. Jonathan Foster [Mineola, N.Y.: Dover Publications, 2005 (1967)], 24–25).
68. See Pierre Francastel, *Peinture et société* (Paris: Gallimard, 1965), chap. 1.
69. Rule Three, Descartes, *Regulae ad directionem ingenii*; *Rules*, ed. and trans. Heffernan, 79.
70. "I call that clear (the knowledge) which is present and manifest to the mind giving attention to it, just as we are said clearly to see objects when, being present to the eye looking on, they stimulate it with sufficient force, and it is disposed to regard them" (Descartes, *The Principles of Philosophy*, part 1, section 45, in *A Discourse on Method*, trans. John Veitch [London, New York: J. M. Dent, E. P. Dutton, 1953 (1912)], 182). It is superfluous to emphasize the recurrence of the theme of *presence*—which is that of the reference to the visible—that runs through all of intuitionism.
71. "But the distinct is that which is so precise and different from all other objects as to comprehend in itself only what appears manifestly to him who considers it as he ought" (Descartes, *The Principles of Philosophy*, part 1, section 45, in *A Discourse on Method*, trans. Veitch, 182).
72. [In the foregoing sentence, "dog" and "God" are in English in the original. —*Trans.*]
73. Descartes, Third Meditation.
74. Descartes, Fourth Discourse, *Dioptrique*, in *Oeuvres*, 203–204; "Descartes' Theory of Vision as Expounded in his *Dioptric*," in *Descartes' Philosophical Writings*, ed. and trans. Norman Kemp Smith (London: Macmillan, 1952), 167.
75. Here is the beginning of this text, where the intention to break from representation and connect with writing is manifest: "We must be careful not to suppose that in order to sense, the mind has to contemplate images which are dispatched by them to the brain, as our philosophers commonly assert; or, at least, we have to conceive the nature of those images in an entirely different manner. For in so far as these philosophers take no account of anything in the images beyond the resemblance they should have to the objects they represent, they are unable to show how they can have been formed by these objects, received by the organs of the external senses, and transmitted by the nerves to the brain. Their only reason in supposing them is that they have observed how our thought can easily be excited by a picture to conceive the object pictured, and that it has therefore seemed to them that in the same way the objects affecting our senses ought to be apprehended by means of certain small pictures which shape themselves in the head. We ought, however, to bear in mind that there are several things besides images

which can excite our thought, as for instance, signs and words, which have no manner of resemblance to the things they signify. And if—making at least possible departure from received opinion—we agree to recognize that the objects which we sense do in fact send these images into the brain, we must at least recognize that none of them . . ." (Descartes, Fourth Discourse, *Dioptrique*, in *Oeuvres*, 203–204; "Descartes' Theory of Vision," ed. and trans. Smith, 167–169).

76. Girard Desargues's, and indirectly Abraham Bosse's, connections to Cartesianism are well known; on this subject see Jurgis Baltrušaitis, *Anamorphoses ou magie artificielle des effets merveilleux* (Paris: Olivier Perrin, 1969), chaps. 4 and 5.
77. 1308–1311, Siena, now at the Museo dell'Opera Metropolitana del Duomo; see Pier Paolo Donati, *La Maestà di Duccio* (Florence: Sadea Sansoni, 1965), in the series "Forma e colore: I grandi cicli dell'arte."
78. 1424–1427, Florence, Church of Santa Maria del Carmine; see *L'opera completa di Masaccio* in the collection "Classici dell'arte" presented by Paolo Volponi, which comes with a valuable critical and philological apparatus by Luciano Berti (Milano: Rizzoli, 1968).
79. See in particular Panofsky's "*I primi Lumi*: Italian Trecento Painting" (in *Renaissance and Renascences*, 114–161) and "Die Perspektive als symbolische Form." The study of these "motifs" corresponds to the history of types developed by Panofsky in *Studies in Iconology: Humanistic Themes in the Art of the Renaissance* (New York: Oxford University Press, 1939), reprinted as chap. 1 of *Meaning in the Visual Arts* (New York: Doubleday, 1955). This study introduces iconographic analysis, an intermediary between the description of the subject itself and the content's (strictly iconological) interpretation. The discussion of the emergence and fate of the *putto* starts on page 145 of *Renaissance and Renascences*.
80. "The classical marbles . . . excited a subtle and pervasive influence upon the formation of the Trecento style, not only in such occidental features as facial types, ornaments and costumes, but also in essence: they helped to infuse into Christian painting some of the substantiality and animal vigor particular to pagan sculpture" (Panofsky, *Renaissance and Renascences*, 153).
81. Ibid., 131–134; this text is quoted in note 18 above.
82. Ibid., 120.
83. Ibid., 119.
84. Ibid., 134–135.
85. Ibid., 136. [In French in the original: "seen through Gothic sensibility" —*Trans.*] Panofsky adds that Duccio, who personally remained beyond the influence of Hellenistic-Roman and primitive Christian art, nevertheless was able to identify and solve the problem of modern space, to the same extent as Cavallini and Giotto (*Renaissance and Renascences*, 137).
86. Ibid., 136.
87. Ibid., 137.
88. Ibid.
89. Pierre Francastel, *La figure et le lieu: L'ordre visuel du Quattrocento* (Paris: Gallimard, 1967), 228–230 and 237 ff.

90. Ibid., 197. The author to whom Francastel's observation is addressed here is John White; see the latter's *The Birth and Rebirth of Pictorial Space* (London: Faber & Faber, 1957), 27–29.
91. Francastel, *Peinture et société*, 85.
92. Francastel, *La figure et le lieu*, 233 ff.
93. Ibid., 234, 234–235 (emphasis Francastel); see below, Plates 10 and 8.
94. In *Brunelleschi* (Milan: Club del libro d'Arte, 1962), Piero Sanpaolesi believes the overall design is due to the architect. Berti (*Masaccio* [Milan: Istituto Editoriale Italiano, 1964]) sees in the stylistic differences between the *Carmine* fresco and the *Trinity* (the first dated 1424–1427, the second 1426–1428) the effect of Brunelleschi's dominance over Donatello in the network of influence exerted upon Masaccio. Refer also to the passage in which Berti quotes Nicholas of Cusa ("Potest igitur homo esse humanus Deus atque Deus humaniter" [It is possible therefore that man is a human God and that God resembles man; translation O.W.N.]) to justify the representation of the divine on a human scale and according to human visual perception ("Catalogo delle opere," *L'opera completa di Masaccio*, 98–99).
95. See the productive comparison Francastel draws between this work and Jan van Eyck's *Virgin and Child in a Church*, now in Berlin (*La figure et le lieu*, 248 ff).
96. See, for example, Gentile da Fabriano's *Adoration of the Magi* (Uffizi, Florence), as well as *The Battle before the Gates of Rome* (Pinacoteca, Turino) by Paolo Uccello's circle, discussed by Francastel in *Peinture et société*, 79. Francastel gives a more detailed account and a more subtle appraisal of the space of Gentile da Fabriano's *Adoration* in "Valeurs socio-psychologiques de l'espace-temps figuratif de la Renaissance," *Année sociologique*, 3rd series (1963) (reprinted in *Études de sociologie de l'art* [Paris: Denoël/Gonthier, 1970], 91–95).
97. See Frederick A. Cooper, "A Reconstruction of Duccio's Maestà," *The Art Bulletin* 47 (June 1965): 155–171. Actually, the reading pattern is a bit more complex than I suggest—more "musical" in the sense of Boethius's aesthetics.
98. This means that the medieval scripting of the figure may strike us—we who have been raised in the tradition of three-dimensional rendering, linear perspective, and uniform light—as the subversion of this tradition. The figural switches sides: it is now the turn of perspectival geometrism to mirror the "distortions" on which our phantasms can feed. But what we are describing here, on the contrary, is medieval abstraction mirroring the thorough deconstruction of perspectival depth. These symmetries are misleading, potentially validating such simplifications as Wilhelm Worringer's opposition between an art of immanence and one of transcendence (*Abstraktion und Einfühlung: Ein Beitrag zur Stilpsychologie* [Munich: Piper, 1908]; *Abstraction and Empathy: A Contribution to the Psychology of Style*, trans. Michael Bullock [Chicago: Ivan R. Dee, 1997]). This opposition is manifested in the following pairs (see in particular the 1959 edition of *Abstraktion und Einfühlung*, 143, 175, 180): *Abstraktion*/*Einfühlung*; monotheism/polytheism; unity/multiplicity; transcendence/immanence; the East/Greece + modern Europe; religion/science; instinct/intellect; fear of the world (*Weltfurcht*) / worldly piety (*Weltfrömmigkeit*). True, as Worringer himself remarked, this dualism represented a step toward greater sophistication with regards to Lipps's "unitary" aesthetics, and more generally to the entire

tradition of Western aesthetics, which "is nothing more than a psychology of the Classical feeling for art" (*Abstraktion und Einfühlung,* 168; *Abstraction and Empathy*, trans. Bullock, 123). True, too, Worringer was careful not to "close the circle again" (*Abstraktion und Einfühlung,* 147; *Abstraction and Empathy*, trans. Bullock, 104), refraining, for example, from presenting Byzantine art as the mere reappearance of the features of Egyptian art after the interruption of Antiquity. Nevertheless, it remains difficult to avoid simplification from the moment one considers abstraction and immanence as contrary impulses (*Dränge*) producing specific forms. In such a perspective, the Irish miniature, Robert Delaunay, and American lyrical abstraction would come under the same category of *Raumscheu* [phobia of space]. But this would be to forget that in the Middle Ages the carelessness toward representation was tied to the plastic signifier's co-option by a linguistic signified (the Scriptures), whereas this is not at all the case for the moderns. This would also be to forget that the latter have no interest in *scripting* the plastic surface, but seek to deconstruct it, that is, free the plastic elements as much as possible in order to present them as immediate signifiers.

The theorizing of the concept of *Abstraktion* (in relation to that of *Einfühlung*, which comes from Lipps) clearly betrays signs of Arthur Schopenhauer's influence—see Worringer, *Abstraktion und Einfühlung,* 52–53; *Abstraction and Empathy*, trans. Bullock, 18. It would be fruitful to compare this influence's importance with the sway it holds in Freud's thought. One thing is immediately apparent: the articulation is not placed in the same way in the two. For Worringer, there are art forms that demonstrate a love of the world and those that demonstrate hatred toward it; art forms suffused with (Schopenhauerian) Will and others where it is repressed. From a Freudian perspective, however, *all art* combines unconscious and preconscious. This is why what I refer to here as *script* [*écriture*], which might seem to be a matter of abstraction, can appear in an art of immanence (of the Renaissance) as much as in an art of transcendence (of the Middle Ages). In this case, "abstraction" has nothing to do with content (with the signified), but with ensnaring the plastic signifier in a web of rules foreign to it. From this angle there is no less abstraction in linear perspective than in Duccio.

On the subject of the representation of concave and convex space by way of conventions entirely independent of the putative height of the beholder's eye, see Panofsky, *Renaissance and Renascences*, 133, and Hans Hahnloser, *Villard de Honnecourt* (Vienna: Schnoll, 1935), Plates 11 and 30a, and the "Commentary," 26 ff, 36 ff, 32, and 211 ff.

99. "Contro ogni legge naturale, più che prospettica" [Against all natural—more than perspectival—rule], as Donati aptly puts it (*La Maestà di Duccio*, vi).

100. In Francastel's inventory of the means by which the earliest generations of Quattrocento painters sought to solve the problem of the creation of the new space, he fails (at least in *Peinture et société*) to draw attention to *The Tribute Money*'s highly idiosyncratic background. This background belongs neither to the solution of segregating planes nor to that of the "Veduta." Masaccio's genius may lie in having dared to paint precisely this background, which is properly speaking phantasmatic for being the deconstruction of all pictorial language, not only in the medieval sense, but in the sense Alberti would later give it.

101. Masolino uses it again in the same cycle of Peter at the Carmine, in the *Raising of Tabitha.* See Francastel, *Peinture et société,* 18 ff, later revised in *La figure et le lieu,* 233.
102. Alessandro Parronchi develops this linear consistency in *Masaccio* (Florence: Sadea-Sansoni, 1966).
103. For the diagram of the panels' disposition on the chapel wall, see Berti, *Masaccio,* 92.
104. Panofsky, *Renaissance and Renascences,* 137.
105. Donati writes that the figures "sono distribuite in un piano prossimo alla superficia del dipinto, mentre gli elementi del fondo vengono qualche volta ribaltati in piani più prossimi all'osservatore di quel che pure indicherebbe la loro posizione in pianta" [are laid out on a plane close to the painting's surface, while the background elements sometimes revert to the fore on planes closer to the beholder than that which their spatial position would otherwise indicate] (*La Maestà di Duccio,* vi [translation A.H.]).
106. Francastel, *La figure et le lieu,* 68 and especially 248: "Tuscan frescoes are meant to be seen rapidly, from afar, as a whole and confronted with the adjacent frescoes, whereas Northern panels are either made to be featured on an altar or contemplated at close range. A similar relation holds between Duccio and Giotto, one that also had momentous consequences. Northern art is intended for meditation; Italian art for evocation. In the latter, optical relations are more readily discernible, though they appeal less to acquired knowledge. They operate more in space than in time." Moreover (*La figure et le lieu,* 236), "Recognition will no longer occur through reference to stories, to information stored in memory, but through the discovery of new optical coordinates that . . . will guide the viewer toward things perceived in a world distinct from the matter of their own thought" [translation A.H.]. The features Francastel identifies here are strictly relevant to the opposition between the two spaces that I have been discussing, except for one: Masaccio's frescoes—precisely because they are to be seen and not read, and because they are inscribed in space rather than in time—*halt* the eye's progress by blocking the quick path of recognition that the letter encourages. (This discrepant feature is amended in *Études de sociologie de l'art,* 54 ff.) Besides this, all the other features refer to the gap between discourse and figure. Francastel does credit Masaccio with the invention of the figure (*La figure et le lieu,* 237), but in the narrow sense of human figure. In fact, Francastel does not acknowledge an opposition between figure and site. (See in particular *La figure et le lieu,* 347–357.) His thesis is that the visual order of the Quattrocento is marked by the appearance of new cultural objects (figures) in pictorial space (*La figure et le lieu,* 75 ff), and above all by the elaboration of a kind of iconic "relay" (*La figure et le lieu,* 88, 347; see also *La réalité figurative*) entirely different from that of the Middle Ages. "The abstract notions of figure and site . . . underscore the ambiguity of these unreal yet concrete figures, and of these purely conventional sites that find themselves simultaneously materialized in a field reduced to the dimensions of a methodically distributed surface, and excluded from this materialization. It is because Masaccio understood this equivocal, artificial, but plausible character of the site and the figure that he may be considered the precursor of a civilization that above all else sought to answer the question of man's place in the universe" (*La figure et le lieu,* 347–348 [translation A.H.]). "Before anyone else, Masaccio, for his part, made visible

the spatial ambiguity of the image, located at once in a fictional space and within the limits of a figurative medium [*support*] endowed with its own dimensions and laws" (*La figure et le lieu*, 345 [translation A.H.]). For it to be possible to make the image's spatial ambiguity visible, it would have had to be invisible before; and if it was invisible before, this is because the image's potential fictive space remained repressed, and because the medieval image functioned as a unit or as a set of graphic units. The spatial ambiguity of Masaccio's imagery is precisely that of figurative representation, implying at the same time a specific treatment of the support (linear perspective, for example) and its penetration (fictional space).

107. See Panofsky, *Renaissance and Renascences*, 133. The narrow space granted the figures, between foreground and background, defines a kind of "paving stone," "a slab of volume."
108. See Francastel, *Peinture et société*, 82.
109. These are the characteristics of "modern" space, according to Panofsky.
110. Panofsky sums up very well this lack of interest for the designated in and of itself—as it *appears*—in relation to the theory of angular perspective ("angle axiom"): "Romanesque and gothic painters—even assuming that they were familiar with scientific optics—had no reason to worry about the angle axiom in the first place because they had learned to think of the painting surface as something impervious and opaque which, for this reason, would not be connected with the theory of sight at all" (*Renaissance and Renascences*, 138).
111. This analysis would deserve comparison with the one Michel Tardy presented at the conference of the French Society of Comparative Literature (*Colloque de la Société française de littérature générale et comparée*, 29 May 1969) under the title "Image et pédagogie." Tardy identified three possible types of referential system for the image: the world, diegesis (narrative), and the phantasy. The medieval iconic system would fall under the diegetic type; that instituted by Masaccio under the phantasmatic. [One has a reason to doubt, however, that diegesis constitutes a reference.]
112. See André Green's introduction to his book *Un œil en trop* (Paris: Minuit, 1969).
113. This is naturally oversimplifying matters: it would take some 150 years for this new physics to free itself from the intermediary, specifically mythical forms that Platonism in particular—the Platonism of the humanists of the Florentine Academy—will invent.
114. Here I am referring to the work of the school of so-called historical psychology. On the nude in the round as a possible model for the "whole" object (as opposed to the "part-object" in Kleinian psychoanalysis), see Adrian Stokes, *Reflections on the Nude* (London: Tavistock, 1967), 3–12.
115. This is exactly the position of discourse one could identify in Thomas More's *Utopia* (1516).
116. Francastel, *Peinture et société*, 43 [translation A.H.].
117. Ibid., 43 [translation A.H.].
118. Ibid., chap. 1.
119. [The French word *scène* has multiple meanings in English—"set" or "setting" (as in "mise-en-scène"), "stage" or "scene"—all of which have to do with dramatic space and spectatorship. In *Discours, figure,* Lyotard seizes on this semantic ambiguity to

encourage slippages between actual, pictorial, and imaginary (phantasmatic) spaces. Thus if in this case I translate *scène* in *une autre scène* by "another scene," the same word becomes "stage" when Lyotard reprises Freud's theatrical metaphors (as in the two "Shakespearean Episodes" in the final chapter of this book). —*Trans.*]

120. Among the earliest "exterior" interiors is the kitchen scene Panofsky notes on the left of *The Last Supper* by the studio of Pietro Lorenzetti (Assisi, Saint Francis, lower church [1320–1330]). Cf. *Renaissance and Renascences,* 143 and Figure 105.
121. See Francastel, *Peinture et société,* 46.
122. Ibid., 43.
123. To which Francastel refers, notably in *La figure et le lieu.*
124. See Panofsky, "Die Perspektive als symbolische Form"; and Brion-Guerry, *Cézanne et l'expression de l'espace.*
125. Ms. *A* (Institut de France) *IV*; see *The Notebooks of Leonardo da Vinci,* vol. 1, ed. Jean Paul Richter (New York: Dover Publications, 1970 [1883]), 53.
126. Leonardo da Vinci, *Notebooks,* ed. Irma A. Richter (Oxford, New York: Oxford University Press, 2008 [1952]), 112.
127. See "Notes on Figures and Plates" below.
128. "This evolution took place in two stages, not one," writes Francastel (*Peinture et société,* 44) [translation A.H.].
129. The art of the religious miniature painting will indeed die out. Cf. Réau, *La miniature.*
130. Leon Battista Alberti, *On Painting,* trans. John R. Spencer (New Haven, London: Yale University Press, 1956), 63. "Tiene in se la pictura forza divina non solo quanto si dice dell'amicitia quale fa li huomini assenti essere presenti ma più i morti dopo molti secoli essere quasi vivi, tale che con molta admiratione del artefice et con molta volupta si riconosco" ("Della pittura di Leone Battista Alberti," ed. by Hubert Janitschek, *Quellenschriften für Kunstgeschichte und Kunsttechnik des Mittelalters und der Renaissance,* vol. 11 [Vienna: Wilhelm Braumüller, 1877], 89). One would be hard pressed to find, at the beginnings of representational painting, a clearer articulation between desire, recognition, and death, as poles around which the pictorial function positions itself. A counterpoint to this text may be found in Edgar Allan Poe's short story "The Oval Portrait," where the painter's act of representing the beloved model causes the latter's death.
131. *Les carnets de Léonard de Vinci* (Paris: Gallimard, 1942), vol. 2, 199 [translation from the French A.H.].
132. "*Perspectiva* ist ein lateinisch Wort, bedeutt eine Durchsehung" (Konrad Lange and Franz L. Fuhse, *Dürers Schriftlicher Nachlass* [Halle: Max Niemeyer, 1893], 319).
133. *Les carnets,* vol. 2, 210; *The Notebooks,* vol. 1, 260.
134. Among numerous other references to mirrors: *Les carnets,* vol. 2, 211; *The Notebooks,* vol. 1, 264.
135. Panofsky, "Die Perspektive als symbolische Form," 260 ff, 292 ff, and 301, note 17. See also *Renaissance and Renascences,* 128.
136. We thus have reason to consider misguided and fruitless any iconographical, iconological, semiological, sociological, or psychoanalytic method that fails to start *by establishing*

precisely the position of the plastic element (line, value, color) *in relation to the screen*. It is in this position, and in this position alone, that the specificity of meaning resides. It makes little sense to apply the same categories to the mosaics in Ravenna and René Magritte's paintings. What is crucial and takes absolute precedence is the nature of the site of inscription. This nature is always in a conceivable relation with the position of the society vis-à-vis itself and the world. To start from the "represented" gaze, as does Jean Paris (in *L'espace et le regard* [Paris: Seuil, 1965]), however sophisticated and accurate the analyses such an approach may yield, is to start from an effect.

The Line and the Letter

1. Hermann Diels and Walther Kranz, *Fragmente der Vorsokratiker* (Berlin: Weidmannsche Verlagsbuchhandlung, 1959), vol. 2, 67 A6, 67 A9, 68 A45 (respectively: Aristotle, *Metaphysics*, A4 985 b 4; *De Generatione et Corruptione*, A1 314 a 21; *Physics*, A5 188 a 22). Vitruvius discusses the same categories in *De architectura*, book 1, vol. 1, chap. 2.
2. See James Février, *Histoire de l'écriture* (Paris: Payot, 1959), notably chap. 6 on the origin of consonantal writing, in particular of archaic Phoenician. See also André Leroi-Gourhan, *Le geste et la parole* (Paris: Albin Michel, 1965), vol. 1, chap. 6, especially 289 ff. It is worth noting in passing the role played, according to scholars, by the rebus in the development of so-called phonetic script. Regarding the appearance of Sumerian-Akkadian script, Février observes: "The rebus leads almost inevitably to phonetic script. Instead of creating for each word a figurative representation, for example drawing a man with a large-brimmed hat and bouffant tie, it is simpler to juxtapose the drawings of a *rat* and a *pine tree*, producing the word 'rapin.' The Sumerians did precisely this . . ." (*Histoire de l'écriture*, 107 [translation A.H.] [When pronounced consecutively, the French words for "rat" and "pine tree"—*rat*, *pin*—produce the sound corresponding to the word *rapin*, meaning an apprentice or second-rate artist donning all the trappings of the Bohemian, complete with large-brimmed hat and bouffant tie. —*Trans.*]; see also Leroi-Gourhan, *Le geste et la parole*, vol. 1, 289). As I will show below, this is only one of the rebus's operations and, significantly, it goes here against the grain of the traditional rebus. Indeed, in an ideographic script this operation allows homophonic correspondences to come to the fore, whereas in the case of alphabetic script the rebus will instead try to *scramble* the inscription's deciphering by *using* existing homophonic elements.
3. André Martinet, *Éléments de linguistique générale* (Paris: Armand Colin, 1966), 1–16, 3–25; *Linguistique synchronique* (Paris: P.U.F., 1965), 31.
4. I adopt Roland Barthes's nomenclature in *Le degré zéro de l'écriture* (Paris: Seuil, 1953).
5. "Just as one speaks only in order to be heard, one writes to convey one's thoughts to readers in an intelligible manner. Roughly the same rules apply to both the written and spoken word. As Diderot argues in the *Encyclopédie*, under 'Punctuation,' the pauses of the voice in speech always correspond to punctuation marks in writing; they also indicate the connection or disjunction of ideas, and stand in for an infinite number of expressions. It follows that it would be equally disadvantageous to omit or misplace *punctuation* signs in written discourse as it would vocal pauses in speech, for both serve

to determine meaning. One could well imagine a sequence of words that, without the help of pauses or characters to indicate them, would only have an uncertain and equivocal meaning [*signification*] and—depending on how these marks were placed—could even lead to contradictory meanings [*sens*]" (Charles-Pierre Girault-Duvivier, *Grammaire des grammaires ou analyse raisonnée des meilleurs traités sur la langue française* [Paris: Janet and Cotelle, 1822], vol. 2, 1007 [translation A.H.]). The latter publication is a compendium of "good" grammatical treatises. Clearly, its author endows punctuation with a signifying function, and the method he employs throughout this chapter (the eleventh) is that of commutation: "To illustrate this we shall submit to our readers several absolutely identical sentences, each one punctuated differently" (Girault-Duvivier, *Grammaire des grammaires*, vol. 2, 1007 [translation A.H.]).

6. Aristotle, *Rhetoric*, book 3, chap. 5.
7. "L'emploi ou le rejet de signes convenus indiquent la prose ou les vers, nommément tout notre art: ceux-ci s'en passent par le privilège d'offrir, sans cet artifice de typographie, le repos vocal qui mesure l'élan; au contraire, chez celle-là, nécessité, tant, que je préfère selon mon goût, sur page blanche, un dessin espacé de virgules ou de points et leurs combinaisons secondaires, imitant, nue, la mélodie—au texte, suggéré avantageusement si, même sublime, il n'était pas ponctué" [The use or rejection of conventional signs indicates either prose or verse, that is, our entire art. Verse can do without such signs thanks to the privilege of offering, without any typographical artifice, the vocal respite that measures the flow. Conversely, prose requires so much of it that I, for one, prefer on the white page a spacious drawing of commas or periods and their secondary combinations, which imitate the melody in pure form, to the text presented to its advantage if, however sublime, it were not punctuated; translation A.H.] (Mallarmé, "Solitude," *Œuvres complètes* [Paris: Gallimard, 1945], 407). Which should be understood: take a text, put it to one side, leaving to the other only bare punctuation: the latter is "preferable" because it yields the *figure* of the text (its "melody"), while its signified remains explicit enough, even without punctuation.
8. Martinet, *Linguistique synchronique*, 20 (from the Greek κενός [*kenos*], meaning empty).
9. Cf. Jérôme Peignot, *De l'écriture à la typographie* (Paris: Gallimard, 1967).
10. The silent reading technique "invented" by Saint Augustine allows the text's understanding to be freed from the figural element that is expressive intonation.
11. The cited texts by Klee are "Die Ausstellung des modernen Bundes im Kunsthaus Zürich," *Die Alpen* (August 1912), Berlin; "Über das Licht," *Der Sturm* (January 1913), Berlin; "Schöpferische Konfession," *Tribüne der Kunst und Zeit* 13 (1920), Berlin; "Wege des Naturstudiums," *Staatliches Bauhaus in Weimar* (Weimar-Munich: Bh Verlag, 1923); "Über die moderne Kunst," Jena Conference (1924); *Pädagogisches Skizzenbuch* (Munich: Langen, 1925) [*Pedagogical Sketchbook*, trans. and introd. Sibyl Mayholy-Nagy (London: Faber and Faber, 1968)]; "Exakter Versuch in Bereich der Kunst," *Bauhaus* 11 (1928), Dessau. Jürg Spiller has done an admirable job collecting and "reworking" these texts in *Das bildnerische Denken* (Basel, Stuttgart: Benno Schwabe, 1956) [*Paul Klee: The Thinking Eye*, ed. Jürg Spiller, trans. Ralph Manheim et al. (London: Percy Lund, Humphries & Co., 1961)]. A fraction of these have been translated into French under

the title *Théorie de l'art moderne* by Pierre-Henri Gonthier (Geneva: Gonthier, 1964). The *Tagebücher von Paul Klee 1898–1918*, edited by Felix Klee (Zurich: Europa, 1957), has been translated by Pierre Klossowski as *Paul Klee: Journal* (Paris: Grasset, 1959) [*The Diaries of Paul Klee, 1898–1918*, ed. Felix Klee, trans. Pierre B. Schneider, R.Y. Zachary, and Max Knight (Berkeley, Los Angeles: University of California Press, 1964)]. Felix Klee collected previously unpublished material in *Paul Klee, Leben und Werk in Dokumenten* (Zurich: Diogenes, 1960), which has been translated into French by Maurice Besset under the title *Paul Klee par lui-même et par son fils Félix Klee* (Paris: Les libraires associés, 1963)—hereafter referred to as *Félix Klee* [Felix Klee, ed., *Paul Klee: His Life and Work in Documents,* trans. Richard and Clara Winston (New York: Braziller, 1962)]. The cited texts by André Lhote are *Traité du paysage* (1939) and *Traité de la figure* (1950), revised and collected in one volume (Paris: Grasset, 1958); *La peinture, le cœur et l'esprit* (1933) and *Parlons peinture* (1937), revised and collected in one volume (Paris: Denoël, 1950); and *Les invariants plastiques* (which includes unpublished texts from 1946 to 1948), ed. Jean Cassou (Paris: Hermann, 1967).

12. Lhote, *Les invariants plastiques*, 91.
13. Ibid. [translation A.H.].
14. *Das bildnerische Denken*, ed. Spiller, 87; *Théorie de l'art moderne*, trans. Gonthier, 20; *Félix Klee*, trans. Besset, 123; *Paul Klee: His Life and Work in Documents*, 171 [translation modified; though he cites both French translations, Lyotard chooses to follow Besset's rather than Gonthier's. Based on the original German edition as well as Lyotard's choice of translation, I cite (and often modify) Richard and Clara Winston's English-language translation. —*Trans.*]
15. Lhote, *Les invariants plastiques*, 112 [translation A.H.].
16. Ibid., 92 ff; cf. *Traité du paysage*, *in fine*.
17. "À la recherche des invariants plastiques" (1946), in *Les invariants plastiques*, 85–118.
18. "Up to the Renaissance, the only dimensions known to the painter were the width and height of his panel, while he would only make spiritual allusions to depth. He did not venture beyond allusion; never does he seek to create a space from scratch" (*Les invariants plastiques*, 92 [translation A.H.]).
19. Lhote, *Traité du paysage,* 44 [translation A.H.].
20. Ibid., 45 [translation A.H.].
21. Ibid. [translation A.H.].
22. Ibid. [translation A.H.].
23. Lhote belonged to the Puteaux group (around the Duchamp-Villon brothers), whose bible was *De divina proportione* by Luca Pacioli, a Neoplatonist known to Leonardo. Lhote exhibited at the *Section d'or* in 1912. At the end of *Traité du paysage*, he cites Matila Ghyka's *Ésthétique des proportions dans la nature et dans les arts* (Paris: Gallimard, 1932). In the same book Lhote admits "not being able to resist" the idea of comparing the "regulating" spiral of a work by Veronese or Rubens to the ("revealing," visible) spiral of an Oceanic shield or even a seashell. See also *Les invariants plastiques*, 117–118, particularly: "In order to rise to the level of divinity it was necessary to shelter the transitory from its endless fluctuations and subject the perishable motifs offered to us by nature

to the invariance of a universal law. Ever since Pythagoras—heir to the engineering science that gave us the pyramids (those epitomes of the world)—one knew that the beauty of the universe is due to the order that brought it into being and that ensured its unwavering march. It was necessary that the painters' reflection converge with that of the philosophers, whose mission it is to provide diverse interpretations of that order" [translation A.H.].

24. "The search for expression goes hand in hand with the will toward abstraction" (Lhote, *Les invariants plastiques*, 93 [translation A.H.]).
25. Lhote, *Traité du paysage*, 53; *Les invariants plastiques*, 92.
26. Lhote, *Les invariants plastiques*, 51–52 [translation A.H.]. This is how, by way of Platonism, Cézanne will end up reintegrated in the Cubist school (see Lhote, *La peinture, le cœur et l'esprit*, 19–29; included in *Les invariants plastiques*, 46–58).
27. Lhote, *Les invariants plastiques*, 51–52 [translation A.H.]. Plato did not even concede that painting could allude to the intelligible; for him the painter is someone who turns away, and draws the spectator away from the contemplation of true reality, and who plunges the eye into the half-light of appearance (such is at least the dominant tenor of *The Republic*). The tradition to which Lhote subscribes is rather that of the "founders" of the High Middle Ages like Boethius or Cassiodorus, for whom strict geometrism is tempered by the legacy of Greco-Latin rhetorics (Quintilian, Fortunatus): "sic pictura, poesis." An affinity substantiated, I believe, by Lhote's preference for Byzantine art: "As long as professors refuse to acknowledge that all has been said, and in the most perfect way possible, by Byzantine illuminators and their spiritual progeny whom we call, disgracefully, the Primitives, and that the excesses of chiaroscuro, perspective, anatomy, and psychology are nothing but superfluous ornaments tacked onto traditional plastic invariants, no teaching will be possible" (*Les invariants plastiques*, 125 [translation A.H.]).
28. Lhote, *Les invariants plastiques*, 110; and "L'art et la bouche," in *Parlons peinture*, 253 [translation A.H.].
29. Lhote, *Les invariants plastiques*, 126 [translation A.H.].
30. Ibid., 127–128 (all emphasis J.-F.L.).
31. Reproduced in Will Grohmann, *Paul Klee* (Paris: Cercle d'Art, 1968), Plate 20, and commentary, 108. See "Notes on Figures and Plates" below.
32. This is how Klee replied to Lothar Schreyer in a discussion that took place in his Bauhaus studio: "I overstep neither the picture's nor the composition's limits. But I do stretch its content by introducing into the picture new subject matter—or rather, not so much new as barely glimpsed subject matter. Obviously this subject matter, like any other, maintains its ties to the natural world. By natural world I am not referring to nature's appearance (as would naturalism) but to the sphere of its possibilities: this content produces images of nature's potentiality. . . . I often say . . . that worlds have come into being and continuously unfold before our eyes—worlds which despite their connection to nature are not visible to everybody, but may in fact only be to children, the mad, and the primitives. I have in mind the realm of the unborn and the already dead which one day might fulfill its promise, but which then again might not—an

intermediate world, an interworld. To my eyes, at least, an interworld; I name it so because I detect its existence between those exterior worlds to which our senses are attuned while at the same time I can introject it enough to be able to project it outside of myself as symbol. It is by following this course that children, the mad, and primitive peoples have remained faithful to—have discovered again—the power of seeing" (Lothar Schreyer, *Souvenirs: Erinnerungen am Sturm und Bauhaus* [Munich: Langen und Müller, 1956], quoted in *Félix Klee*, trans. Besset, 116; *Paul Klee: His Life and Work in Documents*, 183–184 [translation modified —*Trans.*]). This reflection occurs in a passionate and relatively anguished refutation of the function of the imagination in the act of creation: "danger which threatens all of us," "demise of anyone claiming to be an artist," "an alibi for those blind to spiritual realities," "delirium." The importance of this critique will appear shortly, providing the exact context in which to grasp the expression: "to introject [the interworld] enough to be able to project it outside of myself."

33. The same "presentational" function of the phantasm through the trace is thrown into stark relief in Pierre Klossowski's graphite drawings or in Henry Fuseli's oil paintings. André Masson connects the two draughtsmen in his preface to Franco Cagnetta's booklet *De Luxuria spirituali* (Paris: Le cadran solaire, 1967). One would naturally have to add William Blake to this list.
34. *Paul Klee: Journal*, trans. Klossowski, 240; *The Diaries of Paul Klee*, 245 [translation modified —*Trans.*]. See also the previously unpublished short autobiographical text, written ca. 1919, in *Félix Klee*, trans. Besset, 13–16.
35. *Paul Klee: Journal*, trans. Klossowski, 240; *The Diaries of Paul Klee*, 245 [translation modified —*Trans.*].
36. *Paul Klee: Journal*, trans. Klossowski, 17; *The Diaries of Paul Klee*, 10 [translation modified —*Trans.*].
37. *Paul Klee: Journal*, trans. Klossowski, 17; *The Diaries of Paul Klee*, 10 [translation modified —*Trans.*].
38. *Paul Klee: Journal*, trans. Klossowski, 15; *The Diaries of Paul Klee*, 8 [translation modified —*Trans.*].
39. For example, the drawing indexed *Kindheit* 13, dated 1883–1885 (when Klee is between three and five years old), and entitled *Azor Takes Orders from Ms. Frog*. (See "Notes on Figures and Plates" below.) One can see why Klee took issue with those qualifying his drawings as "infantile." A drawing is only infantile when it re-presents, when it shows "man as he is." What interests Klee, however—to present "man as he could be"—requires the exclusion of the tracings found in nature (Jena Conference, *Théorie de l'art moderne*, trans. Gonthier, 31–32; *Das bildnerische Denken*, ed. Spiller, 95). [See also *Félix Klee*, trans. Besset, 130; and *Paul Klee: His Life and Work in Documents*, 178. —*Trans.*]
40. "One night my mother returned from a trip, after an absence of about three weeks; I had long since gone to bed and was supposed to be asleep. I pretended to be, and her homecoming was only celebrated the next morning" (Klee, eight years old) (*Paul Klee: Journal*, trans. Klossowski, 15; *The Diaries of Paul Klee*, 8 [*Tagebücher von Paul Klee*, 16]). This is a direct commentary of the child's game (*fort/da*) as described by Freud in *Beyond the Pleasure Principle*. The lost object is posited as is, in a nocturnal setting.

41. Klee discusses both etchings in very much the same terms I put forward here (*Paul Klee: Journal*, trans. Klossowski, 148–149; *The Diaries of Paul Klee*, 143–144). See "Notes on Figures and Plates" below.
42. See, for example, *Two Men Meet, Each Presuming the Other to Be of Higher Rank*, 1903/5 (*Félix Klee*, trans. Besset, 11); *Lady, Critical of Women's Standards*, 1904/5 (*Félix Klee*, trans. Besset, 33); *Perseus, Wit Has Triumphed over Grief*, 1904/12 (*Félix Klee*, trans. Besset, 12) (Klee discusses *Perseus* in *Paul Klee: Journal*, trans. Klossowski, 166; *The Diaries of Paul Klee*, 160–161); *Comedian*, second version, 1904/14 (Grohmann, *Paul Klee*, Figure 52).
43. *Paul Klee: Journal*, trans. Klossowski, 151; *The Diaries of Paul Klee*, 147 [translation modified —*Trans.*].
44. *Paul Klee: Journal*, trans. Klossowski, 148, 151; *The Diaries of Paul Klee*, 143, 147 [translation modified —*Trans.*].
45. *Paul Klee: Journal*, trans. Klossowski, 152; *The Diaries of Paul Klee*, 147 [translation modified —*Trans.*].
46. Paul Klee was on a first-name basis with his father. In 1902 he notes: "Spiritually, treading along: with every step, more solitary. Differences with my father. The latter younger than I. Amazingly gifted but quick-tempered. Without measure, despite his intellect" (*Paul Klee: Journal*, trans. Klossowski, 128; *The Diaries of Paul Klee*, 119–120 [translation modified —*Trans.*]). Félix reports that his father and grandfather were "like good friends" (*Félix Klee*, trans. Besset, 19; *Paul Klee: His Life and Work in Documents*, 18). This is where the screen-memory intervenes: "For the longest time I placed unconditional faith in my father; he could neither do nor say anything wrong. The only thing I could not suffer from the old man was his mocking. Once, believing myself alone, I fooled around in whimsical mimicry. An unexpected, amused 'pf!' jolted me, hurting my feelings. Even later in life I would occasionally hear such 'pf!'" (*Paul Klee: Journal*, trans. Klossowski, 10; *The Diaries of Paul Klee*, 4 [translation modified —*Trans.*]). Compare this testimony to Klee's remark in the conversation retold by Schreyer: "By the way this interworld is not as wonderful as one might first believe, let alone something sublime. Actually, one often has the impression that one is dealing with cunning spirits. When I mention it I am not taken all that seriously: I am often the butt of quite a lot of irony because of it" (*Félix Klee*, trans. Besset, 117; *Paul Klee: His Life and Work in Documents*, 184 [translation modified —*Trans.*]). A statement dedicated to the experts in sublimation.
47. *Das bildnerische Denken*, ed. Spiller, 86; *Théorie de l'art moderne*, trans. Gonthier, 19, 21. [translation A.H.; see also *Félix Klee*, trans. Besset, 122, 123; and *Paul Klee: His Life and Work in Documents*, 171, 172 —*Trans.*]
48. *Das bildnerische Denken*, ed. Spiller, 90; *Théorie de l'art moderne*, trans. Gonthier, 25 [translation A.H.]; refer to the examples presented in the exhibition catalogue *Bauhaus 1919–1969* (Paris: Musée national d'art moderne / Musée d'art moderne de la Ville de Paris), 2 April–22 June 1969, 63–69; and particularly in *Pädagogisches Skizzenbuch* [*Pedagogical Sketchbook*]. A cursory reading of the opening pages of *Das bildnerische Denken* could lead to a misinterpretation of the logophilic sort, be it Hegelian or prestructuralist: "Der Begriff ohne Gegensatz nicht denkbar. Seine Abhebung um Gegensatz. Der Begriff ohne Gegensatz nicht wirksam. . . . Der Dualismus nicht als solcher behandelt,

sondern in seiner komplementären Einheit" (*Das bildnerische Denken*, 15–16) [A concept is not thinkable without its opposite. The concept stands apart from its opposite. No concept is effective without its opposite. . . . Dualism is treated not as such, but in its unity] (*Paul Klee: The Thinking Eye*, 15, 16; see also *Félix Klee*, trans. Besset, 126). Were it so bold as to take on Klee, the passion for making the figure talk (never more insistent than today, despite Freud's efforts) thankfully would not stand a chance without incurring ridicule.

49. *Paul Klee: Journal*, trans. Klossowski, 297; *The Diaries of Paul Klee*, 310 [translation modified —*Trans.*].
50. "Combined operations and projection in different positions, deviating from pure central perspective. Organic combination of the main forms of perspective: simultaneous interpenetration of space and body, simultaneous inner and outer form. Representation according to essence and appearance. / Points to be considered: simultaneous multi-dimensional phenomena. Multi-dimensional contacts. More complex structures" (*Das bildnerische Denken*, ed. Spiller, 155; *Paul Klee: The Thinking Eye*, 155). This would explain why in *Town Square under Construction* (1923/11) there is "simultaneity of perspectives in plan of picture," and why "front and side view and perspective elements of ground plan" are combined (*Das bildnerische Denken*, 155; *Paul Klee: The Thinking Eye*, 155). Note the use here of the terms *Abweichung* (deviation) and *Verschiebung* (displacement) (*Das bildnerische Denken*, 153; *Paul Klee: The Thinking Eye*, 153).
51. Quoted in Grohmann, *Paul Klee*, 70; all emphases J.-F.L. Klee drew with his left hand and wrote with his right.
52. *Paul Klee: Journal*, trans. Klossowski, 55–57; *The Diaries of Paul Klee*, 55, 53 [translation modified —*Trans.*]. This entry is dated 1901, that is, after Munich and before Italy, when Klee was twenty-one years old.
53. *Paul Klee: Journal*, trans. Klossowski, 141; *The Diaries of Paul Klee*, 135 [translation modified —*Trans.*].
54. *Paul Klee: Journal*, trans. Klossowski, 131; *The Diaries of Paul Klee*, 124 [translation modified —*Trans.*].
55. *Paul Klee: Journal*, trans. Klossowski, 86–87; *The Diaries of Paul Klee*, 85 [translation modified —*Trans.*].
56. *Paul Klee: Journal*, trans. Klossowski, 97–98; *The Diaries of Paul Klee*, 94–95 [translation modified —*Trans.*].
57. (1914). *Paul Klee: Journal*, trans. Klossowski, 298–299; *The Diaries of Paul Klee*, 310, 312 [translation modified —*Trans.*]. "Die Genesis als formale Bewegung ist das Wesentliche am Werk. / Im Anfang das Motiv, Einschaltung der Energie, Sperma. / Werke als Formbildung im materiellen Sinne: urweiblich. / Werke als formbestimmendes Sperma: urmännlich. . . . Formbildung ist energisch abgeschwächt gegenüber Formbestimmung. Letzte Folge beider Arten von Formung ist die Form. Von den Wegen zum Ziel. Von der Handlung zum Perfektum. Vom eigentlich Lebendigen zum Zuständlichen. / Im Anfang die männliche Spezialität des energischen Anstoßes. Dann das fleischliche Waschen des Eies. Oder: zuerst der leuchtende Blitz, dann die regnende Wolke. / Wo ist der Geist am reinsten? Im Anfang" (*Das bildnerische Denken*, ed.

Spiller, 457, 453 [See also *Tagebücher von Paul Klee*, 314]). In Leopold Zahn's book *Paul Klee* (more valuable for the time and place of its publication—Potsdam: Kiepenheimer, 1920—than for its argument, too eager to classify Klee as an abstractionist tempered by personal imagination) I fall upon this quote by Klee, which lends substance to the system of oppositions I am trying to elicit: "The unifying relationship between good and evil gives rise to a moral sphere. Evil does not need to be a victorious and humiliating enemy, but a force that contributes to the constitution of the whole. Co-factor of procreation and evolution (*Mitfaktor der Zeugung und der Entwicklung*). Simultaneous *ur*-masculinity (bad, stimulating, passionate) and *ur*-femininity (good, blossoming, placid) as condition of ethical stability (*eine Gleichzeitigkeit von Urmännlich [böse, erregend, leidenschaftlich] und Urweiblich [gut, wachsend, gelassen] als Zustand ethischer Stabilität*)" (quoted without reference, 25 [translation A.H.]). It is easy enough to see that the phantasm of dialectically reconciling contents feeds off morality; art, on the other hand, only plays off the difference of signifiers.

58. *Das bildnerische Denken*, ed. Spiller, 76; *Théorie de l'art moderne*, trans. Gonthier, 35 [translation A.H.].
59. *Das bildnerische Denken*, ed. Spiller, 103–105; *Théorie de l'art moderne*, trans. Gonthier, 73 [translation A.H.]. Excellent reproductions of selected energetic sketches for the Bauhaus lessons of 14 November 1921 and 30 January 1922 can be found in *Félix Klee*, trans. Besset, 104–106.
60. *Paul Klee: Journal*, trans. Klossowski, 244; *The Diaries of Paul Klee*, 253 [translation modified —*Trans.*].
61. *Paul Klee: Journal*, trans. Klossowski, 299; *The Diaries of Paul Klee*, 312 [translation modified —*Trans.*]. Compare the previously quoted lines with the plant diagram in *Théorie de l'art moderne*, trans. Gonthier, 93. See "Notes on Figures and Plates" below.
62. *Paul Klee: Journal*, trans. Klossowski, 295; *The Diaries of Paul Klee*, 307 [translation modified —*Trans.*].
63. *Paul Klee: Journal*, trans. Klossowski, 230; *The Diaries of Paul Klee*, 232 [translation modified —*Trans.*].
64. *Paul Klee: Journal*, trans. Klossowski, 225–226; *The Diaries of Paul Klee*, 228 [translation modified —*Trans.*].
65. *Paul Klee: Journal*, trans. Klossowski, 224; *The Diaries of Paul Klee*, 226 [translation modified —*Trans.*].
66. *Théorie de l'art moderne*, trans. Gonthier, 42. This passage is missing from *Das bildnerische Denken*, ed. Spiller, 80. Compare it to: "my earthly eye has difficulty distinguishing what lies at hand; it usually overlooks the most beautiful objects. It is thus often said of me: 'You ought to know that he misses the most beautiful things'" ("Autobiographical notes," *Félix Klee*, trans. Besset, 16; *Paul Klee: His Life and Work in Documents*, 16 [translation modified —*Trans.*]).
67. Refer to the conversation in Schreyer's memoirs, quoted above.
68. "From model to matrix!" (*Théorie de l'art moderne*, trans. Gonthier, 30) as a translation of "Vom Vorbildlichen zu Urbildlichen!" (*Das bildnerische Denken*, ed. Spiller, 93). A number of possible combinations are mentioned in the Jena Conference—see, specifically, the passage on "content" or "characteristics of expression" (*Théorie de l'art moderne*, trans.

Gonthier, 25–26; *Das bildnerische Denken*, ed. Spiller, 90–91; and *Paul Klee: His Life and Work in Documents*, 174–175).

69. *Paul Klee: Journal*, trans. Klossowski, 282; *The Diaries of Paul Klee*, 297 [translation modified —*Trans.*]; cf. *Das bildnerische Denken*, ed. Spiller, 518.
70. *Paul Klee: Journal*, trans. Klossowski, 274; *The Diaries of Paul Klee*, 290–291 [translation modified —*Trans.*]; cf. *Das bildnerische Denken*, ed. Spiller, 518.
71. *Das bildnerische Denken*, ed. Spiller, 518; *Paul Klee: Journal*, trans. Klossowski, 270; *The Diaries of Paul Klee*, 287 [translation modified —*Trans.*].
72. *Paul Klee: Journal*, trans. Klossowski, 131; *The Diaries of Paul Klee*, 124 [translation modified —*Trans.*].
73. *Das bildnerische Denken*, ed. Spiller, 109 [translation A.H.]. See "Notes on Figures and Plates" below.
74. *Das bildnerische Denken*, ed. Spiller, 111 [translation A.H.].
75. *Paul Klee: Journal*, trans. Klossowski, 99; *The Diaries of Paul Klee*, 95 [translation modified —*Trans.*].
76. *Paul Klee: Journal*, trans. Klossowski, 103–104 and 101; *The Diaries of Paul Klee*, 99, 98, respectively [translation modified —*Trans.*]; *Das bildnerische Denken*, ed. Spiller, 518: "Möge der Tag des Beweises kommen. Die Gegensätze versöhnen zu können! Die Vielseitigkeit auszusprechen mit einem Wort!! . . . Oh, das überquellende Durcheinander, die Verschiebungen, die blutige Sonne. . . ." (*Tagebücher von Paul Klee*, 105, 107).
77. As opposed to the "regulating" line [*tracé régulateur*], which rationally systematizes the plane. Cf. Lhote, *Traités du paysage et de la figure*, 53.
78. Here the reader will sense that an important piece is missing from our puzzle: an analysis of the Cézannian reversal, along the lines of the methodology we applied to the Renaissance. One would need to emphasize the place from which the *Veduta* was taken; this will be for another time and place. The contrast between Klee and Lhote is of interest only insofar as both, coming out of Cézanne, cultivate the same aesthetic field to which the latter first laid claim.
79. As Klee notes in his *Diaries* in 1909: "Here is for me the master par excellence, much greater even than van Gogh" (*Paul Klee: Journal*, trans. Klossowski, 234; *The Diaries of Paul Klee*, 237 [translation modified —*Trans.*]).
80. Aristotle, *Physics*, book 2, 198b, 17; 199a, 70 [translation A.H. from the French quoted by J.-F.L.: Jean Beaufret, "Phusis et Technè," *Aletheia* 1–2 (January 1964)].
81. To appraise the extent of the *recessus*, compare with *Maiden in a Tree, The Eye of Eros* (1919), and *Fragmenta Veneris* (1938).
82. *Das bildnerische Denken*, ed. Spiller, 454 [translation A.H.].

"The Dream-Work Does Not Think"

1. Sigmund Freud, *Die Traumdeutung*, in *Gesammelte Werke* (Frankfurt am Main: S. Fischer Verlag, 1962–), vols. 2/3, 495 [hereafter cited as GW, followed by volume and page number]; *The Interpretation of Dreams,* in *The Standard Edition of the Complete Psychological Works of Sigmund Freud,* trans. and ed. James Strachey with Anna Freud, Alix Strachey, and Alan Tyson, vol. 5 (London: Hogarth Press, 1953–1974), 491 [hereafter cited as SE, followed by volume and page number.]

2. GW, vols. 2/3, 510; SE, vol. 5, 506.
3. GW, vols. 2/3, 510; SE, vol. 5, 506.
4. GW, vols. 2/3, 510; SE, vol. 5, 506; emphasis in the original.
5. GW, vols. 2/3, 511; SE, vol. 5, 507.
6. GW, vols. 2/3, 511; SE, vol. 5, 507.
7. GW, vols. 2/3, 166; SE, vol. 5, 160.
8. GW, vol. 16, 144; SE, vol. 23, 43.
9. GW, vol. 16, 144: "Es ist bei der Entstellung eines Textes ähnlich wie bei einem Mord. Die Schwierigkeit liegt nicht in der Ausführung der Tat, sondern in der Beseitigung ihrer Spuren. Man möchte dem Worte 'Entstellung' den Doppelsinn verleihen, auf den es Anspruch hat, obwohl es heute keinen Gebrauch davon macht. Es sollte nicht nur bedeuten: in seinen Erscheinung verändern, sondern auch: an eine andere Stelle bringen, anderswohin verschieben. Somit dürfen wir in vielen Fällen von Textentstellung darauf rechnen, das Unterdrückte und Verleugnete doch irgendwo versteckt zu finden, wenn auch abgeändert und aus dem Zusammenhang gerissen. Es wird nur nicht immer leicht sein, es zu erkennen"; SE, vol. 23, 43.
10. GW, vol. 16, 148; SE, vol. 23, 47.
11. GW, vols. 2/3, 510–512; SE, vol. 5, 506–508.
12. GW, vols. 2/3, 302; SE, vol. 4, 296.
13. GW, vols. 2/3, 287; SE, vol. 4, 281.
14. GW, vols. 2/3, 306; SE, vol. 4, 300.
15. GW, vols. 2/3, 301, 309; SE, vol. 5, 294–295, 303.
16. GW, vols. 2/3, 302; SE, vol. 4, 296.
17. The discussion that follows is indebted to the contribution of Claudine Eizykman and Guy Fihman to the seminar on "Travail et langage chez Freud," University of Paris, Nanterre (1968–1969).
18. GW, vols. 2/3, 147–149; SE, vol. 4, 142–144; letter 79 to Wilhelm Fliess, Sigmund Freud, *The Origins of Psycho-Analysis: Letters to Wilhelm Fliess, Drafts and Notes: 1887–1902* (New York: Basic Books, 1954), 238–240.
19. GW, vols. 2/3, 495; SE, vol. 5, 491.
20. See *Neue Folge der Vorlesungen zur Einführung in die Psychoanalyse*, GW, vol. 15, 29; *New Introductory Lectures on Psycho-Analysis,* SE, vol. 22, 28.
21. *Vorlesungen zur Einführung in die Psychoanalyse*, GW, vol. 11, 232; SE, vol. 15, 226. [This volume contains the *Introductory Lectures on Psycho-Analysis (Parts I and II).*]
22. Freud's clearest treatment of this notion occurs in *Über den Traum* (1901), GW, vols. 2/3, 680; *On Dreams*, SE, vol. 5, 667. The relevant paragraph was added, according to Strachey, in 1911: "In the erection of a dream-façade use is not infrequently made of *wishful phantasies which are present in the dream-thoughts in a pre-constructed form,* and are of the same character as the appropriately named 'day-dreams' familiar to us in waking life" (emphasis J.-F.L.). In the same vein, this passage from *The Interpretation of Dreams* may be cited: "a succession of meanings of wish-fulfillments may be superimposed on one another, the bottom one being the fulfillment of a wish dating from earliest childhood" (GW, vols. 2/3, 224; SE, vol. 4, 219). In a report presented to the seminar on "Work and Language in Freud" mentioned above, Françoise Coblence and Sylvie

Dreyfus emphasized the impossibility of putting the different superimposed meanings in the same category. Censorship, which produces interference at the secondary level, must be distinguished from that interference by which desire is primarily led astray.

23. Freud devotes five pages to displacement as against twenty-six to condensation, ninety-five to considerations of representability, and twenty to secondary revision (GW, vols. 2/3, 313, 314; SE, vol. 4, 308).
24. GW, vols. 2/3, 313; SE, vol. 4, 307. This *Textverschiedenheit,* which is true difference, is discussed below in the section *Rebus (Loquitur)* of the chapter "Desire in Discourse."
25. André Breton, *Le surréalisme et la peinture* (Paris: Gallimard, 1965), 270. See "Notes on Figures and Plates" below.
26. GW, vols. 2/3, 350; SE, vol. 5, 344.
27. GW, vols. 2/3, 309; SE, vol. 4, 303.
28. GW, vols. 2/3, 345; SE, vol. 5, 339.
29. GW, vols. 2/3, 345–346; SE, vol. 5, 340.
30. This tendency is clearly expressed by Roland Barthes in *Éléments de Sémiologie* (Paris: Seuil, 1964); *Elements of Semiology,* trans. A. Lavers and C. Smith (New York: Hill & Wang, 1968). See also Algirdas Julien Greimas, *Sémantique structurale* (Paris: Larousse, 1966), 12.
31. Roman Jakobson, *Essais de linguistique générale* (Paris: Minuit, 1963), 43–67; Roman Jakobson and Morris Halle, *Fundamentals of Language* (The Hague: Mouton, 1956), part 2, chaps. 1–4.
32. Quoted in Robert Godel, *Les sources manuscrites du Cours de Linguistique Générale de Ferdinand de Saussure* (Geneva: Droz et Minard, 1957), 237.
33. Quoted in Godel, *Les sources manuscrites*, 240.
34. Jakobson, *Essais de linguistique générale*, 45.
35. Ibid., 61.
36. Ibid., 63, 65.
37. Ibid., 65–66.
38. Ibid., 66, note 1.
39. Jacques Lacan, *Écrits* (Paris: Seuil, 1966), 512; *Écrits: A Selection,* trans. Alan Sheridan (New York: Norton, 1977), 161.
40. Lacan, *Écrits*, 511. At the risk of being pedantic, it should be pointed out that *Verdichtung* is related through *dicht* to the old German *dihan* (like *gedeihen,* to prosper); *Dichtung* comes from the Latin *dictare.* Of course it was simply a pun. But in this case it does not make a philological argument in favor of the classification that Lacan proposes. And in the same vein, *Verdichtung* could hardly be said to "condens[e] in itself the word *Dichtung*. . . ." On the contrary, it combines it with a particle (*Écrits: A Selection*, 160).
41. Lacan, *Écrits*, 507; *Écrits: A Selection*, 156. [The reference is to a poem by Victor Hugo, *"Booz endormi,"* which deals with the encounter between Boaz and Ruth, an episode in the Book of Ruth in the Old Testament. —*Trans. M.L.*]
42. André Breton, *Les manifestes du surréalisme* (Paris: Sagittaire, 1946), 63: "Pour moi la plus forte [image surréaliste] est celle qui présente le degré d'arbitraire le plus élevé, je ne le cache pas."
43. Lacan, *Écrits*, 507; *Écrits: A Selection*, 157.
44. Jakobson, *Essais de linguistique générale*, 61–62.

45. Lacan, *Écrits*, 515; *Écrits: A Selection*, 164.
46. Lacan, *Écrits*, 508; *Écrits: A Selection*, 158. [Translation modified —*Trans. M.L.*]
47. Lacan, *Écrits*, 518; *Écrits: A Selection*, 166.
48. Jakobson, *Essais de linguistique générale*, 47.
49. GW, vols. 2/3, 284; SE, vol. 4, 279.
50. GW, vols. 2/3, 287, 301; SE, vol. 4, 281, 295.
51. GW, vols. 2/3, 301–302; SE, vol. 4, 295–296.
52. GW, vols. 2/3, 309; SE, vol. 4, 303.
53. Lacan, *Écrits*, 511; *Écrits: A Selection*, 160–161.
54. The language of art, speaking as it does with things, making a figure with words, embodies an indissoluble link between discourse and the tangible. Consequently, if the dream is to be placed on the linguistic scale, its position ought not to be at the level of speech operations governing small units, but at the level of stylistics, as Benveniste has pointed out: "It is in style, rather than in language, that we will find a term of comparison with those properties which Freud revealed as descriptive of oneiric 'language'" (Émile Benveniste, *Problèmes de linguistique générale* [Paris: Gallimard, 1966], 86). After some hesitation, Jean Laplanche and Serge Leclaire reached a similar conclusion: "as for the *ontological status* of the unconscious thus constituted, is it necessary to recall that if indeed this status is that of a language, then such a language can in no way be assimilated to our 'verbal' language?" ("L'inconscient: Une Étude psychanalytique," *Les temps modernes* 183 [July 1961]: 118). This last remark still lacks rigor. It is "language of communication" that would be the correct phrase. In verbal language itself there are figures that defy communication and that are the offspring of the unconscious. Freud identified them from the joke (*der Witz*).
55. GW, vols. 2/3, 495; SE, vol. 5, 491.
56. GW, vols. 2/3, 495, 497; SE, vol. 5, 491, 493.
57. GW, vols. 2/3, 503; SE, vol. 5, 499.
58. GW, vols. 2/3, 495; SE, vol. 5, 491.
59. GW, vols. 2/3, 496; SE, vol. 5, 492.
60. GW, vols. 2/3, 505; SE, vol. 5, 500–501.
61. *Fliegende Blätter*, no. 2093 (1885): 78.
62. *Fliegende Blätter*, no. 2034 (1884): 20. The solution to the puzzle is "Nae (Nein), wie dies Ding da schön ist!" (Isn't that thing cute, huh?) The Latin inscription means: "Naevia adorned with reeds."
63. *Fliegende Blätter*, no. 2277 (1899): 100. Solution: "So, g'rad' essen Sie a' Ganserl?!—I' nehm'an Liqueur—es is mir a' net extra." (So, you're eating a little goose just like that?!—Me, I'll have a liqueur, for me it's a lit'l extra.)
64. *Fliegende Blätter*, no. 2241 (1888): 15. Solution: "No, was blas'ma?—Numero Sechs—Hebet a'!" (What shall we play next?—Number six—One, two . . .)
65. *Fliegende Blätter*, no. 2078 (1885): 168. Solution: "Die Anna is da und da Seppei steht a' (auch) d'rob'n, aber er sieht sie net." (Anna is there and Seppei is also standing above, but he doesn't see her.)
66. "Les anagrammes de Ferdinand de Saussure: textes inédits," ed. Jean Starobinski, *Mercure de France* 1204 (February 1964): 243–262.

67. Starobinski, "Les anagrammes de Ferdinand de Saussure," 246.
68. André Leroi-Gourhan, *Le geste et la parole* (Paris: Albin Michel, 1965), especially vol. 1, chap. 6 and vol. 2, chap. 14.
69. GW, vols. 2/3, 504; SE, vol. 5, 500.
70. GW, vols. 2/3, 494; SE, vol. 5, 490.
71. Jean Laplanche and Jean-Bertrand Pontalis, "Fantasme originaire, fantasme des origines, origines du fantasme," *Les temps modernes* 215 (April 1964): 1833–1868.

Desire's Complicity with the Figural

1. [Where French has one word—*désir*—German has, among others, *Wunsch, Begierde,* and *Lust,* and English "desire" and "wish." (See Jean Laplanche and Jean-Bertrand Pontalis, *Vocabulaire de la psychanalyse* [Paris: P.U.F., 1967], 120–122.) The *Standard Edition* translates *Wunsch* by "wish." In *Discours, figure*, however, *désir* often exceeds the aim-driven impulse of Freud's *Wunsch,* coming closer to the more general acceptation of "desire" as a nondirectional or diffuse libidinal force. Hence I frequently translate *désir* by "desire," except when quoting from the *Standard Edition* or in specific expressions—such as "wish-fulfillment" (*accomplissement de désir*). —*Trans.*]
2. Freud will later show, in *Beyond the Pleasure Principle,* that the operation discussed here involves two principles: that of inertia or Nirvana, and that of constancy—Eros finding itself essentially compromised on the one hand by the death drive and on the other by reality.
3. This brief overview corresponds to *Entwurf einer Psychologie* (1895), *Aus den Anfängen der Psychoanalyse,* ed. Marie Bonaparte, Anna Freud, and Ernst Kris (London: Imago Publishing, 1950) (*Project for a Scientific Psychology, The Standard Edition of the Complete Psychological Works of Sigmund Freud,* trans. and ed. James Strachey, with Anna Freud, Alix Strachey, and Alan Tyson, vol. 1 [London: The Hogarth Press, 1953–] [hereafter cited as SE, followed by volume and page number]), and to sections B and C of *Die Traumdeutung* (1900), in *Gesammelte Werke*, vol. vols. 2/3, (London / Frankfurt am Main: Imago Publishing / S. Fischer Verlag, 1952–) [hereafter cited as GW, followed by volume and page number]; *The Interpretation of Dreams,* SE, vol. 5.
4. *Hemmung, Symptom und Angst* (1926), GW, vol. 14, 200; *Inhibitions, Symptoms and Anxiety,* SE, vol. 20, 167.
5. *Entwurf einer Psychologie*, 381; *Project for a Scientific Psychology*, SE, vol. 1, 297. See also *Drei Abhandlungen zur Sexualtheorie* (1905), GW, vol. 5, 33; *Three Essays on the Theory of Sexuality*, SE, vol. 7, 135.
6. *Die Traumdeutung*, GW, vols. 2/3, 604; *The Interpretation of Dreams*, SE, vol. 5, 598.
7. *Anlehnung*. See mainly *Drei Abhandlungen*, GW, vol. 5, 82, 83, 86, 123–130; *Three Essays*, SE, vol. 7, 181–183, 185, 223–229. Laplanche and Pontalis identified the concept—see their definition of *étayage* [anaclisis] in *Vocabulaire de la psychanalyse*, 148–150.
8. See in particular *Die Traumdeutung*, GW, vols. 2/3, chap. 7, part B, 538–555; *The Interpretation of Dreams*, SE, vol. 5, 533–550.
9. *Die Traumdeutung*, GW vols. 2/3, 554; *The Interpretation of Dreams*, SE, vol. 5, 548. The quoted passage was added in 1914.
10. *Die Traumdeutung*, GW, vols. 2/3, 550; *The Interpretation of Dreams*, SE, vol. 5, 543.

11. *Die Traumdeutung*, GW, vols. 2/3, 553; *The Interpretation of Dreams*, SE, vol. 5, 548.
12. "Das Unbewusste" (1915), GW, vol. 10, 294; "The Unconscious," *Papers on Metapsychology*, SE, vol. 14, section 5.
13. "Das Unbewusste," GW, vol. 10, 285, 286. "The Unconscious," SE, vol. 14, 186–188. Similarly, one finds in the *New Introductory Lectures on Psycho-Analysis* (1932) the following remark: "All the linguistic instruments by which we express the subtler relations of thought—the conjunctions and prepositions, the changes in declension and conjugation—are dropped, because there are no means of representing them; just as in a primitive language without any grammar, only the raw material of thought is expressed . . ." (*Neue Folge der Vorlesungen zur Einführung in die Psychoanalyse*, GW, vol. 15, 29; SE, vol. 22, 20.)
14. "Das Unbewusste," GW, vol. 10, 285; "The Unconscious," SE, vol. 14, 186.
15. "Das Unbewusste," GW, vol. 10, 286; "The Unconscious," SE, vol. 14, 187.
16. "Das Unbewusste," GW, vol. 10, 286; "The Unconscious," SE, vol. 14, 187.
17. Mahmoud Sami-Ali, "Préliminaire d'une théorie psychanalytique de l'espace imaginaire," *Revue française de psychanalyse* 33 (January–February 1969): 25–78.
18. Such as Matila Ghyka's reflection in *Le nombre d'or* (Paris: Gallimard, 1931), and Lhote's plastic philosophy.
19. See Anton Ehrenzweig, *The Psychoanalysis of Artistic Vision and Hearing: An Introduction to a Theory of Unconscious Perception* (London: Routledge & Kegan Paul, 1953), 57 ff.
20. In making this claim I distance myself from Italo Tomassoni's phenomenological-existential interpretation of Jackson Pollock's work (cf. *Pollock* [Florence: Sadea, 1968]). André Breton's views strike me as better informed, when he writes about Arshile Gorky, a painter close to Pollock from the very beginning: "I claim that the eye is not *open* so long as it restricts itself to the passive role of mirror, even if the water of this mirror offers some noteworthy particularity: exceptionally clear, or sparkling, or bubbling, or multi-faceted; that this eye seems to me to be no less dead than the eye of slaughtered cattle, unless it shows itself capable of *reflection*,—whether it reflects the object under one or several of its angles, at rest or in motion, whether this object is registered in the waking or oneiric world. The value of the eye lies elsewhere: most artists are still at the stage of turning any which way the face of the watch, without the slightest idea of the *spring* concealed in the opaque casing. / The eye's hairspring. . . . For me, Arshile Gorky is the first painter to whom this secret has revealed itself completely. In the final analysis, the eye simply cannot be reduced to drawing up inventories—like the eye of the bailiff—or to indulging in the illusions of false recognition—like that of the lunatic" (*Le surréalisme et la peinture* [Paris: Gallimard, 1965], 196–197 [translation A.H.]).

    One must pay attention to the totally different functions assumed by a painting presenting the figural-form and one presenting the figural-image. The two spaces are not compatible. The space of Pablo Picasso's drawing remains acceptable, even pleasant: this is imaginary space, no doubt wrested from the silence of the individual psyche and thrust before *our* collective eye. Nonetheless, desire continues to find fulfillment here, because the object (however deconstructed) continues to be offered on the representational stage. Pollock's formal, or rather anti-formal drips, representing the movement of desire itself (and no longer of its hallucinatory object), cannot be cathected by the pleasure principle. Desire has no desire to see itself; it desires its own loss by discharging itself on and in the object. Pollock's space is a space of maximal charge, with no possible loss because there is no objectist or gestaltist way out. From surrealism to postwar American lyrical abstraction, one witnesses precisely the reversal of the figural *image* into figural *form*: deconstructivist activity ceases to target only visible silhouettes and to superimpose visionary outlines; now the space itself of the mise-en-scène, the regulating line [*tracé régulateur*], and the eye's hairspring come under attack. Salvador Dalí embodies the stubborn preservation of scenic space, whereas with Roberto Matta, Gorky, Pollock, the mining and exposure of its underground begin. Breton sensed as much: "Matta pushes the disintegration of external features to far greater lengths.... This is because, for those who can see, all these features are *open*: open not only like Cézanne's apple is to light, but to everything else, including *the other opaque bodies*; because they are constantly on the verge of fusing together, because *only* this fusion produces a key, which is the *only* master key of life.... This is how, too, he never ceases to invite us into a *new space*, in conscious breach with the old, since the latter only makes sense as long as it is distributive of rudimentary and closed bodies" (*Le surréalisme et la peinture*, 192–193 [translation A.H.]).

21. This is the method advocated by Charles Mauron in *Des métaphores obsédantes au mythe personnel* (Paris: Corti, 1963).
22. I do this elsewhere in the present volume.

Desire in Discourse

1. See Roger Martin, "Les idées actuelles sur la structure de la pensée logique," in *Centre International de Synthèse, Notion de structure et structure de la connaissance, XXe Semaine de Synthèse, 18–27 April 1956* (Paris: Albin Michel, 1957); and from the same author, *Logique contemporaine et formalisation* (Paris: P.U.F., 1964). Here again we come across the school of thought that derives from Gottlob Frege, Bertrand Russell, and the Ludwig Wittgenstein of the *Tractatus*. See also Gilles Gaston Granger, *Pensée formelle et sciences de l'homme* (Paris: Aubier, 1965), for example: "Formal thought seems to us to consist essentially ... in the construction of an increasingly precise syntax on the basis of a primitive semantics linking names to still ill-defined things" (40) [translation A.H.].
2. "An artist is originally a man who turns away from reality because he cannot come to terms with the renunciation of instinctual satisfaction which it at first demands, and who allows his erotic and ambitious wishes full play in the life of phantasy. He finds the way back to reality, however, from this world of phantasy by making use of special gifts to mould (*gestaltet*) his phantasies into truths (*Wirklichkeiten*) of a new kind, which are valued by men as precious reflections of reality (*Realität*). Thus in a certain fashion he actually (*wirklich*) becomes the hero, the king, the creator, or the favourite he desired to be, without following the long roundabout path of making real alterations in the external world. But he can only achieve this because other men feel the same dissatisfaction as he does with the renunciation demanded by reality, and because *that dissatisfaction*, which results from the replacement of the pleasure principle by the reality principle, *is*

itself a part of reality" (Freud, "Formulierungen über die zwei Prinzipien des psychischen Geschehens" [1911], in *Gesammelte Werke,* vol. 8, [London / Frankfurt am Main: Imago Publishing / S. Fischer Verlag, 1952–], 230–238 [hereafter cited as GW, followed by volume and page number]; "Formulations on the Two Principles of Mental Functioning," in *The Standard Edition of the Complete Psychological Works of Sigmund Freud,* trans. and ed. James Strachey, with Anna Freud, Alix Strachey, and Alan Tyson, vol. 12 [London: The Hogarth Press, 1953–], 224 [hereafter cited as SE, followed by volume and page number]. Emphasis J.-F.L.).

3. At least on this point there is in fact a surprising unanimity among scholars, even from different schools. Compare for example, on the structuralist side, Roman Jakobson's "Closing Statement: Linguistics and Poetics" in Thomas Albert Sebeok, *Style in Language* (New York, London: John Wiley and Sons; Cambridge, Mass.: Technology Press of Massachusetts Institute of Technology, 1960), or Ivan Fonagy's "Le langage poétique: Forme et fonction," *Diogène* 51 (1965); with, on the generativist side, M.A.K. Halliday, *Descriptive Linguistics in Literary Studies,* English Studies Today, third series (Edinburgh: Edinburgh University Press, 1964), James Peter Thorne, or Henry G. Widdowson (more on the latter below).
4. I speak of "phenomenology" on the basis of the convergence of the analyses of Jean-Paul Sartre, "L'écrivain et sa langue," *Revue d'esthétique* 18, nos. 3–4 (1965); Maurice Merleau-Ponty, "Le langage indirect," in *La prose du monde* (Paris: Gallimard, 1969); and Mikel Dufrenne, *Le poétique* (Paris: P.U.F., 1963); "A priori et philosophie de la nature," *Quaderni della biblioteca filosofica di Torino* 21 (Torino, 1967); *Esthétique et philosophie* (Paris: Klincksieck, 1967).
5. César Chesneau Du Marsais, *Traité des tropes* (1730), second part, article 10 [translation A.H.].
6. The struggle of the grammarian trying to situate figurative construction furnishes (involuntary) evidence that the only relevant feature in this respect is not proper speech but the distortion of what is received by the speaking subjects: figurative construction, argues the grammarian, "deserves its name because it does indeed adopt a figure, a form that differs from that of grammatical construction. In truth, it is accepted in everyday use, but it does not comply with the most acceptable manner of speaking, that is, with the direct and grammatical construction we have just studied. Thus when the order determined by this construction is altered, one speaks of a *figurative,* or better yet, *indirect* and *irregular* construction. Now it may be irregular either by *Ellipsis, Pleonasm, Syllepsis,* or *Inversion*: these are what one calls the four figures of the word" (Charles-Pierre Girault-Duvivier, *Grammaire des grammaires* [Paris: Janet et Cotelle, 1822], vol. 2, 1035 [translation A.H.]). In the "Appendixes" to *Littérature et signification* (Paris: Larousse, 1967), Tzvetan Todorov makes the apposite remarks that the reference to a norm is phantasmatic: the norm of normative grammar is not usage, but the regular, the direct, the straight, etc., which are as many figures. On the other hand, opposing the transgressive to the ordinary figure does not allow poetic language to be distinguished from everyday language. For this I will later suggest another criterion.

   Tradition places the origin of rhetorics in these words of Simonides of Ceos: "Poetry is painting with words." Painting, poetry, and rhetorics are the sites of emergence of the figure that the Pythagorean-Platonic city believes it can eliminate once and for all. In fact, rhetorics and philosophy together belong to the universe of fragmentary discourses engendered by the breakdown of the utterance of *aletheia*. Nevertheless, Platonism grants the figure the function to seduce, that is, to separate the subject from her- or himself and maintain an ally inside the opposite camp. There is a strategy of the figure; this is obviously because it is the cunning of a force: desire.

7. André Breton, *Les manifestes du surréalisme*, followed by *Prolégomènes à un troisième manifeste du surréalisme ou non* (Paris: Sagittaire, 1946), 63; *Manifestoes of Surrealism*, trans. Richard Seaver and Helen Lane (Ann Arbor: University of Michigan Press, 1969), 38.
8. Breton, *Les manifestes du surréalisme*, 65; *Manifestoes of Surrealism*, 39.
9. Here is the same device, this time more pronounced from the fact that the phrases are more common than "rubies of Burgundy wine": "J'étais brun quand je connus Solange. Chacun vantait l'ovale parfait de mon regard" (André Breton, *Poisson soluble*, *Poésie et autre* [Paris: Club du meilleur livre, 1960], 60); "I was tan when I first met Solange. Everyone sang the praises of the perfect oval of the look of my eye" (*Soluble Fish*, *Manifestoes of Surrealism*, 101). Ferdinand Alquié demonstrates how, on a list of definitions, one can obtain the same result by simple *displacement* (*Philosophie du surréalisme* [Paris: Flammarion, 1955], 137–138).
10. Breton, *Les manifestes du surréalisme*, 63; *Manifestoes of Surrealism*, 38.
11. André Breton, "Les mots sans rides," *Poisson soluble*, in *Les pas perdus* (Paris: Gallimard, 1924), 170. Here is another example of this kind of wordplay: "Paroi parée de paresse de paroisse / À charge de revanche et à verge de rechange / Sacre de printemps, crasse de tympan / Daily lady cherche démêlés / avec Daily Mail" (quoted by Hans Richter, *Dada: Art et anti-art* [Brussels: La Connaissance, 1965], 157). [Wall decked in parish sloth / on the condition of payback and with backup rod / Rite of spring, tympanum grime / Daily lady picks a fight / with Daily Mail; translation A.H; for other possible translations see *The Essential Writings of Marcel Duchamp*, ed. Michel Sanouillet and Elmer Peterson (London: Thames and Hudson, 1975) —*Trans.*].
12. Breton, *Les manifestes du surréalisme*, 63–64; *Manifestoes of Surrealism*, 38.
13. "Once he had crossed the bridge, the phantoms came to meet him." This intertitle in F.W. Murnau's film *Nosferatu, eine Symphonie des Grauens* made a lasting impression on the surrealist group. See Pierre Ajame, "Les yeux fertiles" in the special issue of *Europe* devoted to surrealism, 475–476 (November–December 1968), 143; and Alquié, *Philosophie du surréalisme*. The bridge is cited as the essence of the metaphor in Breton's preface to his *Signe ascendant* (Paris: Gallimard, 1968), 10.
14. This is how Freud qualifies the slip of the tongue, and what Ehrenzweig will emphasize. Yvon Belaval's challenge to surrealist spontaneism (cf. "Poésie et psychanalyse," *Cahiers de l'association internationale des études françaises* 7 [June 1955]) raises the issue of the gap between dream and poem, symptom and artwork. Unfortunately, however, Belaval seems eager to come down on the side of the ego: "It is dangerous to repeat 'I is an other' while losing sight of the lesson and teachings of Rimbaud's writings: for the *I* kept crossing out over and over again the *other*'s manuscripts" (Belaval, "Poésie et

psychanalyse," 22). Breton no doubt thought, more accurately, that it was the other who was behind the crossing out, and what the pen was fighting against and had to cross out was the perfectly pre-traced trace, the ego's script. Admittedly, there is also an "instinct of imitation" of the imagination left to its own devices, resulting in the stale repetition of immediate phantasies. But by surrendering to the reality principle, one does not overcome reality, one represses it through a second script.

15. Dufrenne, *Le poétique*, 31 [translation A.H.].
16. Dufrenne goes on: "Expression is in a sense the sensory presence of the signified in the signifier, when the sign awakes in us a feeling similar to that which the object evokes" (ibid., 72 [translation A.H.]). Here *signified* takes the place of *designated*, as is made clear by the previous quote and by the mention of the feeling evoked by the *object* and not by *signification*.
17. Ibid., 72 [translation A.H.].
18. Ibid., 29.
19. Ibid., 30. On this subject, Dufrenne quotes William Empson's *Seven Types of Ambiguity* (London: Chatto & Windus, 1930) and *The Structure of Complex Words* (London: Chatto & Windus, 1951).
20. Dufrenne, *Le poétique*, 33 [translation A.H.].
21. Ibid., 173.
22. Ibid., 155.
23. Ibid., 157 [translation A.H.].
24. The theme of expression plays a central role in Dufrenne's *La phénoménologie de l'expérience esthétique* (Paris: P.U.F., 1953), particularly vol. 1, 173–184 ("signification et expression dans le langage"), 234–243 ("expression et monde"), 397–409 ("de l'expression aux sentiments"), and in vol. 2, 473–480 ("signification et expression"), and 631–644 ("expression et vérité ").
25. Dufrenne concurs; see "L'art est-il langage?" (1966), in *Esthétique et philosophie*, 73–112.
26. Dufrenne, *Le poétique*, chap. 6 and, in particular, 80.
27. Ibid., 82.
28. Louis Aragon, "La rime en 1940," in *Le crève-cœur* (Paris: Gallimard, 1941), 66 [translation A.H.].
29. Benjamin Péret, "Le déshonneur des poètes" (February 1945), reprinted in *Socialisme ou barbarie* 5 (December 1959–February 1960): 29; "The Dishonour of the Poets," trans. James Brook, in *Death to the Pigs: Selected Writings of Benjamin Péret*, ed. and introduced by Rachel Stella (London: Atlas Press, 1988), 204–205.
30. These are the concluding words of Dufrenne's *Le poétique* [translation A.H.].
31. One should emphasize that the material of the rebus belongs to the same corpus that interests the present study. At the end of the nineteenth century, the readers who took delight in deciphering mysterious inscriptions and rebuses were not only Austrian, but European: "The rebus would enjoy considerable popularity (to the point that Rabelais expressed irritation with the fad), peaking at the end of the nineteenth and the beginning of the twentieth century. The Hachette almanac published a serialized version of *Rouletabille* entirely in rebus, and I remember well those dishes at the bottom of which

were reproduced quaint rebuses, which were for my parents a prized ally as I rushed each night, and without the slightest encouragement, to finish my soup in order to discover with joy the enigma hidden under the vermicelli or the tapioca, no matter how many times I had deciphered it before. From 1840 to 1890, and even later, there was not one newspaper that did not publish regularly its own rebus. One finds them in *Le petit journal pour rire*, *Le magazine des demoiselles*, *Le magazine pittoresque*, and *Illusration*. As the editor of an almanac pointed out in 1844: 'Readers of *Illustration* relish its rebuses, which have brought this respectable paper more than twenty-five thousand subscribers'" (Max Favalelli, "Présentation," *Rébus* [Paris: P. Horay, 1964] [translation A.H.]). It was only after the fact that I took notice of this coincidence: it strikes me as indisputable that the passion for the rebus during this period corresponded for the general public to the explorations by Mallarmé, Freud, or Cézanne for the avant-garde. In both cases we find a deconstructive play of linguistic and plastic spaces, as well as a destabilizing of the respective orders governing these spaces, of the scripts. As for the situation Favalelli describes, I let the reader be the judge: the soup placed by the parents between the child and the enigma, the repetition of discovery . . .

32. *Die Traumdeutung*, GW, vols. 2/3, 323; *The Interpretation of Dreams*, SE, vol. 4, 318.
33. *Die Traumdeutung*, GW, vols. 2/3, 319; *The Interpretation of Dreams,* SE, vol. 4, 314.
34. *Die Traumdeutung*, GW, vols. 2/3, 346; *The Interpretation of Dreams,* SE, vol. 5, 341.
35. *Die Traumdeutung*, GW, vols. 2/3, 324; *The Interpretation of Dreams,* SE, vol. 4, 319–320.
36. *Die Traumdeutung*, GW, vols. 2/3, 346–347; *The Interpretation of Dreams,* SE, vol. 5, 341.
37. *Die Traumdeutung*, GW, vols. 2/3, 346; *The Interpretation of Dreams,* SE, vol. 5, 341.
38. *Die Traumdeutung*, GW, vols. 2/3, 283, 284; *The Interpretation of Dreams,* SE, vol. 4, 277–278.
39. Émile Littré, *Dictionnaire de la langue française* (Paris: Hachette, 1874), vol. 4, under *rébus* [translation A.H.].
40. Littré, *Dictionnaire de la langue française* [translation A.H.].
41. A sizeable group (87 examples) may be found among the rebuses collected by Topor and presented by Favalelli in *Rébus.*
42. Favalelli, *Rébus*, 60.
43. If one were to apply the transformational-generative method, one would have the two core sentences: (1) *There is effect, there is cause*, organized according to the relation of dependence: (2) *Thus there is effect, if there is cause*; negative transformation: (3) *Thus there is no effect, if there is no cause*; and final sentence: (4) *There is no effect without a cause.* Sentence (5) *All effects have a cause* must be produced before the negative transformation. On this topic see Noam Chomsky, *Syntactic Structures* (The Hague, Paris: Mouton, 1957), 22, and Nicolas Ruwet, *Introduction à la grammaire générative* (Paris: Plon, 1967), 96.
44. In *Jokes and Their Relation to the Unconscious,* Freud argues that among the joke's techniques, "condensation remains the category to which all the others are subordinated" (*Der Witz und seine Beziehung zum Unbewussten* [1905], GW, vol. 6, 43; *Jokes and Their Relation to the Unconscious,* SE, vol. 8, 42). Now, homophony is a special case of condensation, even, for Freud, an ideal case, because by using the same acoustic material without any alteration that would undermine the rules of discourse, it is proof that double meaning is already present in ordinary language, without it being apparently

necessary to work it over. The joke is, to a much greater extent, subject to preconscious oversight, and closer to ordinary language than the dream. (As Freud observes, this explains why the technique of displacement plays such a minor role for the joke; see *Der Witz und seine Beziehung zum Unbewussten*, GW, vol. 6, 196; *Jokes and Their Relation to the Unconscious*, SE, vol. 8, 172.) The more faithfully wordplay seems to abide by the rules of discourse, the more effective it is: Schleiermacher's pun "Eifersucht ist eine Leidenschaft, die mit Eifer sucht, was Leiden schafft" (Jealousy is a passion that, with a vengeance, seeks what provokes sorrow) is a case in point (quoted by Freud, *Der Witz und seine Beziehung zum Unbewussten*, GW, vol. 6, 35; *Jokes and Their Relation to the Unconscious*, SE, vol. 8, 35).

45. [Pronouncing the letter 'R' in French produces a sound that can be transcribed as *erre* or /ɛr/ (*erres* in plural). —*Trans.*] Lev = lɛv! At the level of the signified, the rebus's function in relation to the pleasure principle could not be more obvious: the one who pays is not the one who caused the damage! As for the cutting-up technique, it is clearly impossible not to associate it with: "Au charmeur des Muses becque- / té, plus prompt à l'estocade, / l'étincelant Henri Becque / rue, et 17, de l'Arcade" [To the seducer of the Muses peck- / ed, quicker to deal the final blow, / the dazzling Henri Becque / Arcade, and 17, street], or "Si vous voulez que je ne meure, / porteurs de dépêche, allez vi- / te où mon ami Montaut demeure, / c'est, je crois, 8, rue Halévy" [If you wish not to see me die, / carriers of dispatch, go quick- / ly to where my friend Montaut lives, / it is, I believe, 8, Halévy Street] (Mallarmé, *Œuvres complètes* [Paris: Gallimard, 1945], 83, 93). Or, at a pinch, and if one is not too averse to ritornello, one could associate the technique with: "Parler d'amour, c'est parler d'elle et parler d'elle / C'est toute la musique et ce sont les jardins / Interdits où Renaud s'est épris d'Armide et l' / Aime sans en rien dire absurde paladin" [To speak of love is to speak of her and to speak of her / is all the music and the forbidden / gardens where Renaud fell in love with Armide and loves / her without declaring his love absurd paladin (Aragon, *Le crève-cœur*, 68); translations A.H.].

46. This use of displacement is what distinguishes, in the first instance, the rebus from the joke, and brings the former closer to the dream.

47. It would be possible to establish the matrix of these combinations.

48. For its part, the joke—unrelated as it is to the image itself—operates mostly by cleansing linguistic units. Because the joke must respect the laws of communication and produce a striking effect, it restricts those operations of displacement that make recognition particularly challenging.

49. It is against this very amalgamation of poetry with image (constant in official and Symbolist poetics) that the Formalists affiliated with the Moscow Circle and the OPOJAZ took a stand. See Viktor Shklovsky, "L'art comme procédé" (1917), in *Théorie de la littérature: textes des formalistes russes*, ed. Tzvetan Todorov (Paris: Seuil, 1965), 76; "Art as Technique," in *Russian Formalist Criticism: Four Essays*, ed. L.T. Lemon and M.J. Reis (Lincoln: University of Nebraska Press, 1965), 3.

50. [A reference to Guillaume Apollinaire's poem "La colombe poignardée et le jet d'eau" in *Calligrammes: Poèmes de la paix et de la guerre (1913–1916)* (Paris: Gallimard, 1925), 77. —*Trans.*]

51. I borrow these expressions from a clarification made by Henry G. Widdowson in "Notes on Stylistics," included in a reader prepared by the Department of Applied Linguistics of Edinburgh University and given to the students enrolled in the 1969 session of the Summer School, entitled *Applied Linguistics in Language Teaching* (document supplied to the author by Andrée Lyotard-May). This problem of extra- and intratextuality led directly to the constitution of the method developed by the Russian Formalists; cf. Lev Yakubinsky, quoted in *Théorie de la littérature,* ed. Todorov, 38 ff and 81 ff. The importance of this problem remains central to their concerns; see Osip Brik, quoted in *Théorie de la littérature,* 153.
52. James Peter Thorne, "Stylistics and Generative Grammars," *Journal of Linguistics*, 1, no. 1 (April 1965).
53. As Dufrenne sometimes suggests. See, for example, "L'art est-il langage?"
54. See Zellig Sabbettai Harris, *Methods in Structural Linguistics* (Chicago: University of Chicago Press, 1951).
55. "The main purpose of constructing a grammar which would provide a satisfactory account of a text like *Anyone lived in a pretty how town* would be to discover how such a grammar differed from a grammar of English. But such a comparison presupposes that both grammars are of the same kind. For example, there would be no point in comparing a transformational grammar of English with a phrase-structure grammar of the text. On a more general level it can be argued that since any adequate grammar of English must contain theoretical terms it follows that, if it is to be of any interest, any grammar of the text must do the same" (Thorne, "Stylistics and Generative Grammars," 53–54).
56. Thorne, "Stylistics and Generative Grammars," 54.
57. *Anyone lived* . . . is a poem by E.E. Cummings, quoted in the section "A Kind of 'Affective Language'" of the present chapter.
58. Thorne, "Stylistics and Generative Grammars," 56–57.
59. Ibid., 55.
60. Freud's use of this method in "Der Moses des Michelangelo" (1914) is well known. [See GW, vol. 10; "The Moses of Michelangelo," SE, vol. 13.]
61. Cf. "Ratschläge für den Arzt bei der psychoanalytischen Behandlung" (1912), GW, vol. 8, 377 ff; "Recommendations to Physicians Practising Psycho-Analysis," SE, vol. 12, 112 ff.
62. Widdowson, "Notes on Stylistics." In what follows, most of the English examples are borrowed from this source; all the others, including the French examples, are my own.
63. This is an obviously impure example that also comprises operations 1.221 (you begin *me* again), 1.222 (I *music* you), and 1.223 (I swim *you* [*je* te *rame*]). [See "Opposition and Difference," note 23 above. —*Trans.*]
64. Translation by Cecil Day Lewis, *The Graveyard by the Sea* (London: Martin Secker & Warburg, 1945), 6.
65. Translation by David Paul, *Paul Valéry: An Anthology*, ed. by James R. Lawler (London, Henley: Routledge & Kegan Paul, 1977), 201.
66. Todorov, "Appendix," *Littérature et signification*, particularly 97–115.
67. Ibid., 107.
68. "Verse is subject not only to the laws of syntax, but also to those of rhythmic syntax, that is, to the syntax that enriches its laws with rhythmic requirements. / In poetry, verse

is the primary word group. In verses, words combine according to the laws of prosaic syntax. / This fact—of the coexistence of the two laws acting upon the same words—is the distinctive characteristic of poetic language. Verse presents us with the results of a combination of words that is at once rhythmical and syntactic" (Brik, "Rythme et syntaxe" [1927], in *Théorie de la littérature,* ed. Todorov, 149 [translation A.H.]).

69. Widdowson, "Notes on Stylistics," 10.
70. An analysis of the phantasy suggests that condensation should be assigned to Eros, and displacement to the death drive.
71. Widdowson himself offers a striking example of this variation, by comparing speech and language [*langue*] deviations in the work of Gerard Manley Hopkins:

(I)	(II)
I. The west which is golden	The west which is dappled with damson
II. The west golden	The west dappled with damson
III. The golden west	(The dappled-with-damson west)

Form III of phrase (II) violates the syntactic rules for generating surface structures.

72. Jean Cohen, *Structure du langage poétique* (Paris: Flammarion, 1966). Also by Cohen see "La comparaison poétique: Essai de systématique," *Langages* 12 (December 1968). This is hardly the place to discuss Cohen's conclusions in detail; the apparent proximity between our respective positions will allow me to bring mine into relief.
73. Cohen, *Structure du langage poétique*, 114 [translation A.H.].
74. Ibid. [translation A.H.].
75. Ibid., 202 [translation A.H.].
76. Ibid., 205. Cohen refers to Dufrenne's *La phénoménologie de l'expérience esthétique*, vol. 2, 544.
77. Take, as an example of a network of equivalence, the synesthesia "bright : dark :: sharp : blunt :: hard : soft :: high : low :: light : heavy," etc. (Roman Jakobson, *Essais de linguistique générale* [Paris: Minuit, 1963], 242). As an example of systems of evaluation, see those which the research on the measurement of meaning attempts to draw out (Charles E. Osgood, George J. Suci, and Percy H. Tannenbaum, *The Measurement of Meaning* [Urbana: University of Illinois Press, 1958]).
78. See Roland Barthes, "Éléments de sémiologie," *Communications* 4 (1964).
79. Cohen, *Structure du langage poétique*, 216. Emphasis J.-F.L [translation A.H.].
80. Ibid., 224 [translation A.H.].
81. See Roland Barthes, "Rhétorique de l'image," *Communications* 4 (1964).
82. Roland Barthes, *Le degré zéro de l'écriture* (Paris: Seuil, 1953).
83. See Claude Lévi-Strauss, *Anthropologie structurale* (Paris: Plon, 1962).
84. The prevalence of metrics over rhythmics is part of this recuperation. In this respect, one should be wary of French cultural tradition: the work of John Donne or Shakespeare is rife with deviations that touch upon the deepest levels of English grammar as well as its semantics.

85. [In English in the original. E. E. Cummings, *50 Poems* (New York: Duell, Sloan and Pearce, 1940 [1939]), 20. —*Trans.*]
86. [Pierre Corneille, *The Cid, Five Classic French Plays*, ed. and trans. Wallace Fowlie (Mineola, N.Y.: Dover Publications, 1997 [1962]), 25. —*Trans.*]
87. See Freud, "Ratschläge für den Arzt bei der psychoanalytischen Behandlung," GW, vol. 8; "Recommendations to Physicians Practising Psycho-Analysis," SE, vol. 12. Moreover, the function of this inter-unconscious communication is not, as in poetry, to make one see, appreciate, accept the offspring of the figure-matrix, but rather to make them understood.
88. See Freud, "Beiträge zur Psychologie des Liebeslebens" (1910, 1912), GW, vol. 8, 85; "Contributions to the Psychology of Love II," SE, vol. 11, 185.
89. "Et c'est toujours le même aveu, la même jeunesse, les mêmes yeux purs, le même geste ingénu des bras autour de mon cou, la même caresse, la même révélation. / Mais ce n'est jamais la même femme. / Les cartes ont dit que je la rencontrerais dans la vie, mais sans la reconnaître" (Paul Éluard, "La dame de carreau," in *Les dessous d'une vie ou la pyramide humaine* [1926], *Choix de poèmes* [Paris: Gallimard, 1941]) [And it is always the same confession, the same youth, the same clear eyes, the same innocent embrace around my neck, the same caress, the same revelation. / But it is never the same woman. / The cards told me I would meet her in life, but without recognizing her —translation A.H.]. Identity of the phantasy, yet indifferent and multiple variety of the "realities": "Toutes le vierges sont différentes. Je rêve toujours d'une vierge" (Éluard, "La dame de carreau") [All virgins are different. I always dream of a virgin—translation A.H.].
90. One could relate this reversing function [*fonction renversante*] to what Boris Tomashevsky called the "denuding of the process" ("Thématique," in *Théorie de la littérature,* ed. Todorov, 300–301). Yet he failed to credit this process with the importance it deserves. Yury Tynyanov comes much closer to what I am trying to argue: "The artistic fact [*Le fait artistique*] does not exist outside the impression of submission, of deformation of all the factors by the constructive factor. (The *coordination* among factors is a negative characteristic of the principle of construction [Viktor Shklovsky].) But if the impression of *interaction* among factors disappears (and it presupposes the necessary presence of *two* elements, subordinating and subordinate), the artistic fact [*le fait artistique*] disappears. Art becomes reflex" ("La notion de construction" [1924], in *Théorie de la littérature,* ed. Todorov, 118 [translation A.H.]). "Any element of prose, once incorporated in the sequence of verse, appears under a different guise, highlighted by its function, thereby generating two different phenomena: this *construction* is the distortion of the unusual object" (Tynyanov, "Le problème de la langue poétique" [1924], in *Théorie de la littérature,* ed. Todorov, 64 [translation A.H.]).
91. This observation does not invalidate in the least the claim that the phantasy can cross the barrier of repression without undergoing any alteration.
92. Terminology borrowed from the Kleinian school.
93. In his *Vorlesungen zur Einführung in die Psychoanalyse* ([1916–1917], GW, vol. 11, 175), Freud compares condensation to this process: "It is possible, naturally, to make a composite structure out of things or places in the same way as out of people, provided that

the various things and places have in common something which is emphasised by the latent dream (*das latente Traum*). The process is like constructing a new and transitory concept which has this common element as its nucleus. The outcome of this superimposing of the separate elements that have been condensed together is as a rule a blurred and vague image, like what happens if you take several photographs on the same plate" ("Introductory Lectures on Psycho-Analysis," SE, vol. 15, 171–172).

94. "Une personnalité toujours nouvelle, toujours différente, l'amour aux sexes confondus dans leur contradiction, surgit sans cesse de la perfection de mes désirs. Toute idée de possession lui est forcément étrangère" (Paul Éluard, *La rose publique* [Paris: Gallimard, 1934]). [An always new personality, always different, love with sexes combined in their contradiction, never ceases to burst forth from the perfection of my desires. By necessity all thought of posession is foreign to it (translation A.H.).]

95. In Cummings's poem quoted above, one finds the same process of condensation of two sentences as in Éluard's poem, through the excision of either the first sentence's predicative nominal group or, alternatively, the second's subject nominal group:

the ocean	wanders the streets
the streets	are so ancient

96. I quote from U.E. Torrigiani's translation in *Les temps modernes* 277–278 (August–September 1969): 314; Lawrence R. Smith, ed., *The New Italian Poetry* (Berkeley, Los Angeles: University of California Press, 1981), 453.

97. Alfredo Giuliani, interview for Südwestrundfunk (6 January 1969), quoted by Torrigiani in "Le groupe dans la littérature italienne contemporaine," *Les temps modernes*, 277–278: 275 [translation A.H.].

98. Umberto Eco, "Poissons rouges et tigres en papier," *Les temps modernes*, 277–278: 289 [translation A.H.]. This issue includes an excellent report on *Gruppo 63* and on the group behind the publication of *Quindici*.

99. *Les temps modernes*, 277–278: 291.

Fiscourse Digure: The Utopia behind the Scenes of the Phantasy

1. This is Freud's metaphor in *Vorlesungen zur Einführung in die Psychoanalyse* (1916–1917 [1915–1917]), in *Gesammelte Werke*, vol. 11 (London / Frankfurt am Main: Imago Publishing / S. Fischer Verlag, 1952–) [hereafter cited as GW, followed by volume and page number]; *Introductory Lectures on Psychoanalysis*, in *The Standard Edition of the Complete Psychological Works of Sigmund Freud*, trans. and ed. James Strachey, with Anna Freud, Alix Strachey, and Alan Tyson, vol. 15 (London: The Hogarth Press, 1953–) [hereafter cited as SE, followed by volume and page number]. See also, as a metaphor for censorship, the insertion within an optical system of a lens with an inadequate refractive index at the end of *The Interpretation of Dreams:* "Everything that can be an object of our internal perception is *virtual,* like the image produced in a telescope by the passage of light-rays. But we are justified in assuming the existence of the systems (which are not in any way physical entities themselves and can never be accessible to our physical perception) like the lenses of a telescope, which cast the image. And if we pursue this analogy, we may compare the censorship between the two systems to the refraction that

takes place when a ray of light passes into a new medium" (*Die Traumdeutung*, GW, vols. 2/3; SE, vol. 5, 611). This is an important text since it shows that repression does not produce contours, but scrambles or layers clichés [in the sense both of photographic negatives and stereotyped phrases —*Trans.*]. Compare with Frege's metaphor.

2. [Except in instances when I am quoting from the Strachey translation, I have opted throughout for "drive" rather than "instinct" as a translation of the French word *pulsion.* Strachey is under heavy fire for the alleged inadequacies of the Standard Edition: see Bruno Bettelheim, *Freud and Man's Soul* (New York: Knopf, 1983), and Samuel Weber, *The Legend of Freud* (Minneapolis: University of Minnesota Press, 1982). Helena Schulz-Keil, however, in a review of the Bettelheim book for *Lacan Study Notes* 1, no. 2 (June 1983), has an interesting discussion of the drive/instinct option, to which I would add the practical comment that "instinct" helpfully yields the adjectival and adverbial forms "instinctual" and "instinctually," whereas fidelity to "drive" has obliged this translator to have recourse to the verb "impel" and the permissible, though rather odd "impulsion." —*Trans.*]
3. ["English lacks a word able to carry the range of meaning in the term *jouissance* which includes enjoyment in the sense of a legal or social possession (enjoy certain rights, enjoy a privilege), pleasure, and crucially, the pleasure of sexual climax," writes Stephen Heath in the Translator's Note to *Image, Music, Text* by Roland Barthes (New York: Hill and Wang, 1977). Since this truth now appears to be universally acknowledged, and the word *jouissance* admitted to the scholarly vocabulary, I have used it throughout. —*Trans.*]
4. "'Ein kind wird geschlagen': Beitrag zur Erkenntnis der Entstehung sexuellen Perversionen," GW, vol. 12, 197–226; "'A Child Is Being Beaten': A Contribution to the Study of the Origin of Sexual Perversions" (1919), SE, vol. 17, 175–205.
5. "Aus der Geschichte einer infantilen Neurose" (1918 [1914]), GW, vol. 12; "From the History of an Infantile Neurosis," SE, vol. 17. The "Wolf Man" case history was published in 1918, the treatment completed in 1914–1915. Perhaps the Wolf Man is the sixth case, or at least one of the six.
6. "'Ein kind wird geschlagen,'" GW, vol. 12, 197; "'A Child Is Being Beaten,'" SE, vol. 17, 179.
7. "'Ein kind wird geschlagen,'" GW, vol. 12, 198; "'A Child Is Being Beaten,'" SE, vol. 17, 181.
8. "'Ein kind wird geschlagen,'" GW, vol. 12, 205; "'A Child Is Being Beaten,'" SE, vol. 17, 186: "I am probably looking on." I am summarizing section III here (GW, vol. 12, 202–205; SE, vol. 17, 183–186). Freud recapitulates this section at the beginning of section VI (GW, vol. 12, 216–217; SE, vol. 17, 195–196).
9. "[B]eating phantasies have a historical development (*Entwicklungsgeschichte*) which is by no means simple, and in the course of which they are changed in most respects (*das meiste an ihnen*) more than once—as regards their relation to the author of the phantasy, and as regards their object (*Objekt*), their content (*Inhalt*) and their significance (*Bedeutung*)" (184). Jacques Nassif suggests for "content": "the clinical manifestation of which the phantasy is merely a symptom"; for "object": "the person, or rather the sex of the subject being beaten in the phantasy"; for "significance": "the connection the subject makes between beating and love or hate" ("Le fantasme dans 'On bat un enfant,'" *Les Cahiers pour l'analyse* 7 [March–April 1967]: 80–81). I am adopting these equivalencies.

10. "'Ein kind wird geschlagen,'" GW, vol. 12, 207; "'A Child Is Being Beaten,'" SE, vol. 17, 187. For those who may be less familiar with Shakespeare than Freud was, here is the witches' prophecy to Banquo (*Macbeth,* 1.3, lines 65 ff): "*1st Witch*: Lesser than Macbeth, and greater.—*2nd Witch*: Not so happy, yet much happier.—*3rd Witch*: Thou shalt get kings, though thou be none."
11. "'Ein kind wird geschlagen,'" GW, vol. 12, 216; "'A Child Is Being Beaten,'" SE, vol. 17, 195.
12. "Einige psychische Folgen des anatomischen Geschlechtsunterschiedes" (1925), GW, vol. 14, 25–26; "Some Psychical Consequences of the Anatomical Distinction between the Sexes," SE, vol. 19, 253–254.
13. "'Ein kind wird geschlagen,'" GW, vol. 12, 214; "'A Child Is Being Beaten,'" SE, vol. 17, 193.
14. "Einige psychische Folgen des anatomischen Geschlechtsunterschiedes," GW, vol. 14, 28; "Some Psychical Consequences of the Anatomical Distinction between the Sexes," SE, vol. 19, 256.
15. "Einige psychische Folgen des anatomischen Geschlechtsunterschiedes," GW, vol. 14, 28; "Some Psychical Consequences of the Anatomical Distinction between the Sexes," SE, vol. 19, 256.
16. "'Ein kind wird geschlagen,'" GW, vol. 12, 211; "'A Child Is Being Beaten,'" SE, vol. 17, 191.
17. This table is derived from a more extensive one drawn up by Guy Fihman and Claudine Eizykman in their report to the seminar "Travail et langage chez Freud," University of Paris, Nanterre (1968–1969).
18. "Triebe und Triebschicksale" (1915), GW, vol. 10, 220; "Instincts and Their Vicissitudes," SE, vol. 14, 127.
19. Freud stresses precisely this ambivalence when he writes, with regard to Phase III: "Its significance lies in the fact that it has taken over the libidinal cathexis of the repressed portion (*Anteil*) and at the same time the sense of guilt which is attached to the content of that portion" ("'Ein kind wird geschlagen,'" GW, vol. 12, 211; "'A Child Is Being Beaten,'" SE, vol. 17, 191).
20. See Jacques Lacan, "The Signification of the Phallus," in *Écrits: A Selection,* trans. Alan Sheridan (New York: Norton, 1977), 281–292. See also "La relation d'objet et les structures freudiennes," *Bulletin de psychologie* 10 (November–December 1956): 426–430.
21. We can go along with Michel Tort ("Le concept freudien de représentant," *Cahiers pour l'analyse* 5 [November–December 1966]: 37–63) when he shows that the ideational representative (*Vorstellungsrepräsentanz*), in contrast to the affect, is an authentically Freudian formulation, located between the region of the drive and that of the psychism, and when he opposes any attempt to make semiology or hermeneutics absorb economics. It would be a different matter, however, to accept his conclusion that *Repräsentanz* is an *ideological* designation for this effectively new formulation; that it leads to psychologism and "psychoanalytic interpretation cannot avoid this step except by viewing the terms 'libidinal' or 'impelled by the drive' as the *structuration* of an object that could be *articulated* in other terms" (63). On the contrary, this inarticulateness is, for Freud, what defines the impossibility of exhausting the unconscious. It is what preserves difference against opposition. It is this very characteristic that Freud will retain by displacing it

under the term death instinct. What Tort would like to uphold, against what he calls ideology, is the ideology of the discursive system as a unified whole made up of fixed oppositions. But the non-theory of the drive in Freud exists in order to preserve a non-place: place of non-signification; of labor (*travail*).

22. "'Ein kind wird geschlagen,'" GW, vol. 12, 208; "'A Child Is Being Beaten,'" SE, vol. 17, 188. Compare with 203–204 where Freud writes: "The motive forces of repression must not be sexualised. Man's archaic heritage forms the nucleus of the unconscious mind and whatever part of that heritage has to be left behind in the advance to later phases of development, because it is unserviceable or incompatible with what is new and harmful to it, falls victim to the process of repression."
23. Lacan emphasizes this necessity in his seminar on object relations; see note 20 in the present chapter.
24. "'Ein kind wird geschlagen,'" GW, vol. 12, 209; "'A Child Is Being Beaten,'" SE, vol. 17, 189–190: "This 'being beaten' is now a convergence of the sense of guilt and sexual love. It is not only the punishment (*die Strafe*) for the forbidden genital relation, but also the regressive substitute for the relation (*der regressive Ersatz für sie*)." After the revision of the diagnosis in 1925, it would be more correct to say, the regressive substitute for penis-envy.
25. "But above all I think I ought to warn you now not to confuse regression with repression. . . . The concept of repression involves no relation to sexuality: I must ask you to take special note of that. It indicates a purely psychological process, which we can characterise still better if we call it a 'topographical' one." (*Vorlesungen zur Einführung in die Psychoanalyse,* GW, vol. 11, 354; *Introductory Lectures on Psychoanalysis*, SE, vol. 16, 341–342.)
26. "Die Verdrängung" (1915), GW, vol. 10, 260; "Repression," SE, vol. 14, 157.
27. I am deliberately avoiding the question of narcissism and autoeroticism here. The masochistic reversal of Phase II seems to present characteristics of what André Green calls double turning around (*le double retournement*) or "décussation" (André Green, "Le narcissisme primaire: Structure ou état, I," *L'inconscient* 1 [January 1967]; II, *L'inconscient* 2 [April 1967]). But here it may only be a case of secondary narcissism. Primary narcissism has already been established for a long time in the cases we are looking at, especially if it is true, as the 1925 hypothesis suggests, that clitoral masturbation already existed in Phase I. It is impossible for us to determine where the initial autoeroticism originates and to verify whether, as Green believes, it is related to "the negative hallucination of the mother that makes representation possible" ("Le narcissisme," II, *L'inconscient* 2, 108–110). But it is certain, on the other hand, that "the double turning around" of the libido on the body constitutes the indispensable mediation between the drive and the constitution of its ideational representatives ("Le narcissisme," II, *L'inconscient* 2, 102 ff). Equally, the constant presence of the imaginary object throughout the various phases of the phantasy seems indeed to bear out Green's conviction that narcissism does not square with a loss of object, but rather with an inhibition in the aim of the drive ("Le narcissisme," I, *L'inconscient* 1, 148–151; "Le narcissisme," II, *L'inconscient* 2, 92–96).
28. Nassif, "Le fantasme dans 'On bat un enfant,'" 84.
29. "Triebe und Triebschicksale," GW, vol. 10, 223–224; "Instincts and Their Vicissitudes," SE, vol. 14, 130–131.

30. *Das Unbehagen in der Kultur* (1930), GW, vol. 14, 427–428; *Civilisation and Its Discontents*, SE, vol. 21, 70–71. See "*Veduta* on a Fragment of the 'Story' of Desire," note 64, above.
31. Freud indirectly gives another description of the unconscious process at the end of the analysis of the "Wolf Man": "I shall now bring together some peculiarities of the patient's mentality which were revealed by the psycho-analytic treatment but were not further elucidated and were accordingly not susceptible to direct influence. Such were his tenacity of fixation, which has already been discussed, his extraordinary propensity to ambivalence, and (as a third trait in a constitution which deserves the name of archaic) his power of maintaining simultaneously (*nebeneinander*) the most various and contradictory libidinal cathexes (*verschiedenartigsten und widersprechendsten*) all of them capable of functioning side by side. His constant wavering (*das beständige Schwanken*) between these (a characteristic which for a long time seemed to block the way to recovery and progress in the treatment) dominated the clinical picture during his adult illness, which I have scarcely been able to touch upon in these pages. This was undoubtedly *a trait belonging to the general character of the unconscious* (*war dies ein Zug aus der Charakteristik des Unbewussten*), which in his case had persisted into processes that had become conscious." The temptation to quote the end of this paragraph is irresistible: "So it was that his mental life impressed one in much the same way as the religion of Ancient Egypt, which is so unintelligible to us because it preserves the earlier stages of its development side by side (*neben*) with the end-products, retains the most ancient gods and their attributes along with the most modern ones, and thus, as it were, spreads out upon a two-dimensional surface what other instances of evolution show us in the solid" ("Aus der Geschichte einer infantilen Neurose" [1918], GW, vol. 12, 154–155; "From the History of an Infantile Neurosis," SE, vol. 17, 118–119—emphasis J.-F.L.)—We should add to the file on *Moses and Monotheism* that Egypt is certainly for Freud, as it was for Baltrušaitis, the place of "aberrations." (See Gilbert Lascault, "L'Egypte des égarements," *Critique* 260 [January 1969].) On the atemporality of the unconscious process, see once again the text of *Jenseits des Lustprinzips* (1920), GW, vol. 13, 27–28; *Beyond the Pleasure Principle*, SE, vol. 18, 27–28, where Freud declares that, "As a result of certain psycho-analytic discoveries, we are to-day in a position to embark on a discussion of the Kantian theorem that time and space are 'necessary forms of thought,'" and proceeds to a "negative description" of the unconscious, which he concludes by attributing our abstract representation time to the "way of working" (*Arbeitsweise*) of the perception-consciousness system.
32. Pseudo-metrics: in a group structure, let e be the element such that a.e = a. Pseudo-metrics of production: a(b.c) = (a.b)c.
33. See "Die Verdrängung" and "Das Unbewusste" (1915), GW, vol. 10; "Repression" and "The Unconscious," SE, vol. 14.
34. See especially "Das Unbewusste" and "Metapsychologische Ergänzung zur Traumlehre" (1917), GW, vol. 10; "The Unconscious" and "A Metapsychological Supplement to the Theory of Dreams," SE, vol. 14.
35. "'Ein kind wird geschlagen,'" GW, vol. 12, 204; "'A Child Is Being Beaten,'" SE, vol. 17, 185.
36. On construction, see "Konstruktionen in der Analyse" (1937), GW, vol. 16; "Constructions

in Analysis" (1937), SE, vol. 23, and Catherine Backès, "Continuité mythique et construction historique," *L'Arc* 34 (1968): 76–86.

37. The statements made by the patient are in italics (the preconscious). Formulae 0.1–0.4 are given by Freud. "'Ein kind wird geschlagen,'" GW, vol. 12, 204, 208; "'A Child Is Being Beaten,'" SE, vol. 17, 185 and 188.
38. See Jean Laplanche and Jean-Bertrand Pontalis, "Fantasme originaire, fantasmes des origines, origines du fantasme," *Les temps modernes* 215 (April 1964): 1833–1868.
39. "'Ein kind wird geschlagen,'" GW, vol. 12, 209; "'A Child Is Being Beaten,'" SE, vol. 17, 189.
40. See Nicolas Ruwet, *Introduction à la grammaire générative* (Paris: Plon, 1967), 252.
41. See especially "Die Verdrängung" (252) and "Das Unbewusste" (274), GW, vol. 10; "Repression" (150) and "The Unconscious" (175), SE, vol. 14.
42. "Die Verkehrung ins Gegenteil" ("Triebe und Triebschicksale," GW, vol. 10, 219); "Reversal into Its Opposite" ("Instincts and Their Vicissitudes," SE, vol. 14, 126).
43. "Die Umkehrung dieses Triumphes: Nein, er liebt dich nicht, denn er schlägt dich." ("'Ein kind wird geschlagen,'" GW, vol. 12, 208); "the reversal of this triumph: 'No, he does not love you, for he is beating you.'" ("'A Child Is Being Beaten,'" SE, vol. 17, 188).
44. In his seminar of 23 January 1956 (*Bulletin de psychologie* 10, 604–605), Lacan equated this experience of being out of circulation with the development of perversion. The latter is not the negative of neurosis, in the sense that it is the result of the straightforward survival of an irreducible partial drive, which may have passed unscathed through the entire Oedipal organization, but the reduction of the whole subjective structure thanks to an intense valorization of the image. The subject steps out of the "intersubjective dialectic" and becomes a "privileged witness and then a sign." It will be the function of the transference, Lacan adds, to rearticulate this "sign" by putting it in its place within the system that governs the relationships between the terms of the drama.—Perhaps this trusts too much the imaginary, for once, and insists too strongly on the off-stage/onstage alternative. The off-stage position (in I and III) in fact marks the place of the subject who is *in* the scene, as the father in I and as a boy in III. That place is certainly not designated by a contour (*tracé révélateur*), but suggested rather by a regulating line (*tracé régulateur*), by the scenography itself, and it is the sadistic component that fixes the scenography within the Oedipal framework.
45. This remark opens the way to reflections about the theater, and more precisely about the specular reversal at the heart of tragedy itself. There are clearly two scenes in *Oedipus Rex* and in *Hamlet* (the Theban/Corinthian scenes in the former, the scenes of Hamlet's family and Polonius's family in the latter) that mirror each other, although in quite different ways. In Sophocles, the Corinthian scene is the one from which truth projects its traces onto the Theban scene. It is the locus of difference, the place of origin of the events. In Shakespeare, Polonius's family is the locus of acting-out that allows Hamlet to persist in and to succumb to misrecognition. See André Green, *Un oeil en trop* (Paris: Minuit, 1969); Octave Mannoni, "Le théâtre du point de vue imaginaire," *La Psychanalyse* 5 (1959); Jean-François Lyotard, "Oedipe juif," *Critique* 277 (June 1970) [the latter translated into English in "Jewish Oedipus," *Genre* 10 (1977): 395–411].

46. *Studien über Hysterie* (1895), GW, vol. 1, 282–283; *Studies on Hysteria,* SE, vol. 2, 160–161. An extraordinary text, which we will analyze elsewhere.
47. See *Die Traumdeutung*, GW, vols. 2/3, chap. 7 (*The Interpretation of Dreams,* chap. 7), the entire section on regression. One of the most formal treatments of this subject is no doubt "Das Ich und das Es" (1923); *The Ego and the Id:* "The study of dreams and of preconscious phantasies as shown in Varendonck's observations can give us an idea of the special character of this visual thinking. We learn that what becomes conscious in it is as a rule only the concrete subject-matter of the thought, and that the relations between the various elements of this subject-matter, which is what specially characterises thoughts, cannot be given visual expression. Thinking in pictures (*das Denken in Bildern*) is, therefore, only a very incomplete form of becoming conscious. In some way too, it stands nearer to unconscious processes than does thinking in words (*das Denken in Worten*), and it is unquestionably older than the latter both ontogenetically and phylogenetically" (GW, vol. 13, 248; SE, vol. 19, 21). In the preface to the English edition of Varendonck's book, *The Psychology of Day-Dreams* (London: Allen and Unwin, 1921), Freud wrote: "I think it is advisable, when establishing a distinction between the different modes of thought-activity, not to utilise the relation to consciousness in the first instance, and to designate the day-dreams, as well as the chains of thought studied by Varendonck, as freely wandering or fantastic thinking, in opposition to intentionally directed reflection" (GW, vol. 13, 440; SE, vol. 8, 272).
48. Laplanche and Pontalis say exactly the same thing in "Fantasme originaire, fantasmes des origines, origines du fantasme."
49. Nassif concluded his examination of a possible "grammar" of this same phantasy in the following terms: "Nothing permits us to say that there is any relationship to be established between the subject, or rather the author of the phantasy, and the grammatical subject of its verbalization (still the child as passive subject), between the subject of the statement and the subject of the enunciation, because in the permutations we have brought to light it is not a question either of metonymic transformations by 'contiguity' or of metaphoric transformations by 'similarity.' That is why we have used the more neutral term 'permutation,' relative to linguistic connotations. And to end the debate without closing it, why not recall (a move that will bring us back to the text) that Freud is not working, in this instance at least, on linguistic 'signifiers' but on 'representations'" ("Le fantasme dans 'On bat un enfant,'" 80).
50. Luce Irigaray, "Du fantasme et du verbe," *L'Arc* 34 (1968), sketches out just such an analysis of "syntactic signification" in which she opposes "to live," for example, to "to absorb" or "to give." Although she tries to show how that meaning of the verb (insofar as it structures the subject) governs the transference, it seems to me that her remarks are inspired by a phenomenological methodology, which significantly limits their relevance. Thus she understands "to desire" as a modalization *(perhaps, doubtless)* and/or a modality *(to want or wish to, to be able to)* of the verb. But Freud says that desire is always assertive, and that it takes no heed of tenses or moods.
51. "Einige psychische Folgen des anatomischen Geschlechtsunterschiedes," GW, vol. 14, 26; "Some Psychical Consequences of the Anatomical Distinction between the Sexes," SE, vol. 19, 254.

52. See Laplanche and Pontalis, "Fantasme originaire, fantasmes des origines, origines du fantasme."

53. I repeat that I am not concerned with the origin of the phantasy. Freud, in the 1919 text, writes: "Es handelt sich vielleicht eher um Erinnerungen an solche Vorgänge, die man angesehen hat, an Wünsche, die bei verschiedenen Anlässen aufgetreten sind, aber *diese Zweifel haben keine Wichtigkeit*" ("'Ein kind wird geschlagen,'" GW, vol. 12, 204); "It is perhaps rather a question of recollections of events which have arisen on various occasions. *But these doubts are of no importance*" ("'A Child Is Being Beaten,'" SE, vol. 17, 185). Emphasis J.-F.L.

54. Serge Leclaire, *Psychanalyser* (Paris: Seuil, 1968), 67. See Freud, "Zur Einführung des Narzissmus," GW, vol., 10, 150; "On Narcissism: An Introduction" (1914), SE, vol. 14, 83. I am following Leclaire's usage here, a usage that will be discussed presently.

55. Leclaire, *Psychanalyser,* 67. One can see how Green's thesis on primary narcissism as a structure might be articulated. Autoeroticism is the application of the erogenous scansion along the objectal axis on the screen of the bodily surface by a rotation of 90 degrees.

56. See especially Leclaire, *Psychanalyser,* 121 ff.

57. Leclaire, *Psychanalyser,* 154.

58. See *Aus den Anfängen der Psychoanalyse*, ed. Marie Bonaparte, Anna Freud, and Ernst Kris (London: Imago, 1950); *The Origins of Psycho-Analysis: Letters to Wilhelm Fliess, Drafts and Notes: 1887–1902* (New York: Basic Books, 1954), Draft D (May 1894), and especially the "first principal thesis" of the "Entwurf einer Psychologie" ("Project for a Scientific Psychology"). For a discussion of this question, see Laplanche and Pontalis, *Vocabulaire de la psychanalyse* (Paris: P.U.F., 1967); *The Language of Psycho-Analysis,* trans. Donald Nicholson-Smith (London: Hogarth Press, 1973), under Principle of Constancy, Principle of Inertia, Nirvana Principle.

59. See, for example, *Die Traumdeutung*, GW, vols. 2/3, chap. 7; *The Interpretation of Dreams,* SE, vol. 5, chap. 7.

60. *Aus den Anfängen der Psychoanalyse*, 381; *The Origins of Psycho-Analysis,* 358.

61. "[T]he binding is a preparatory act which introduces and assures the domination of the pleasure principle" (*Jenseits des Lustprinzips*, GW, vol. 13, 67; *Beyond the Pleasure Principle,* SE, vol. 18, 62).

62. "Das ökonomische Problem des Masochismus" (1924), GW, vol. 13, 373; "The Economic Problem of Masochism," SE, vol. 19, 160. Compare with *Jenseits des Lustprinzips,* GW, vol. 13, 39–40, 53, 60; *Beyond the Pleasure Principle,* SE, vol. 18, 37–38, 49, and 55.

63. *Jenseits des Lustprinzips*, GW, vol. 13, 68–69; *Beyond the Pleasure Principle*, SE, vol. 18, 62–63.

64. Piera Aulagnier advances and maintains the hypothesis that primary masochism is: "the pregnant moment when the Nirvana principle must come to terms with the pleasure principle that regulates psychic energy." She concludes by showing that the phantasy is precisely the "point of convergence" of the two principles: "Primary masochism is the phantasy (and the only one) by means of which the death drive can succumb to the charms of the object and of pleasure, but for all that every phantasy facilitates the manifestation and 'substantification' of desire, it is also the shield that the subject forges to protect himself from being quashed, the instrument for deferring the realization of

desire." ("Remarques sur le masochisme primaire," *L'Arc* 34 [1968]: 54). Note that in the phantasy "A Child Is Being Beaten," Phase II, which is the phase of "return" (regression), is precisely the masochistic phase. But as I have already pointed out in regard to Green's thesis on narcissism, these are only secondary effects. The masochism of Phase II succeeds a sadistic phase. Nonetheless, the conception of the phantasy as a compromise effected between death and pleasure, Nirvana and Constancy remains valuable.

65. "Wir verwunden uns über diese 'ewige Wiederkehr des Gleichen' nur wenig, wenn es sich um ein aktives Verhalten des Betreffenden handelt . . ." (*Jenseits des Lustprinzips*, GW, vol. 13, 21); "This 'perpetual recurrence of the same thing' causes us no astonishment when it relates to active behaviour on the part of the person concerned . . ." (*Beyond the Pleasure Principle,* SE, vol. 18, 22).
66. *Jenseits des Lustprinzips*, GW, vol. 13, 35–37; *Beyond the Pleasure Principle,* SE, vol. 18, 35–36. It is in this passage that Freud speaks of "this compulsion with its hint of possession by some 'daemonic' power" ("den dämonischen Charakter").
67. Nassif hypothesizes a Phase IV: "I am beating the child," which would be another regression. He thinks that Freud's 1925 hypothesis, which suspends the phantasy at castration, justifies this ("Le fantasme dans 'On bat un enfant'").
68. Jean-Bertrand Pontalis, "L'utopie freudienne," *L'Arc* 34 (1968): 14.

Return, Auto-Illustration, Double Reversal

1. May the reader forgive me for referring her or him to the *Note* of clarification (as well as to the bibliography accompanying it, June 1969) concerning the psychoanalytic approach to artworks, which appeared in the general report of UNESCO on the study of literary and artistic expressions. To restrict ourselves to the best-known cases published in France, one will recognize in the premises I put forward those that inform Marie Bonaparte's clinical study of Edgar Allan Poe, as well Charles Mauron's more recent study on Mallarmé—the difference between the two being that, in the first case, the analysis is built on themes identified in the author's life and, in the second, in the work of art.
2. See, for example, "Der Dichter und das Phantasieren" (1908), in *Gesammelte Werke*, vol. 7 (London/Frankfurt am Main: Imago Publishing/S. Fischer Verlag, 1952–) [hereafter cited as GW, followed by volume and page number]; "Formulierungen über die zwei Prinzipen des Psychischen Geschehens" (1911), GW, vol. 8; and *Der Witz und seine Beziehung zum Unbewussten* (1905) GW, vol. 6; respectively, "Creative Writers and Day-Dreaming," in *The Standard Edition of the Complete Psychological Works of Sigmund Freud*, trans. and ed. James Strachey, with Anna Freud, Alix Strachey, and Alan Tyson, vol. 9 (London: The Hogarth Press, 1953–) [hereafter cited as SE, followed by volume and page number]; "Formulations on the Two Principles of Mental Functioning," SE, vol. 12; and *Jokes and Their Relation to the Unconscious* SE, vol. 8.
3. I discuss this opposition on the basis of *Moses and Monotheism* and the point of view of the structure underlying Western ideologies in an essay entitled "Figure forclose" (*L'Écrit du temps* 5 [1984]: 63–105; "Figure Foreclosed," in *The Lyotard Reader*, ed. Andrew Benjamin [Oxford: Basil Blackwell, 1989], 69–110).
4. As Anton Ehrenzweig rightly observes (*The Psychoanalysis of Artistic Vision and Hearing:*

An Introduction to a Theory of Unconscious Perception [London: Routledge & Kegan Paul, 1953], chap. 8: "The Inarticulate ('Baffling') Structure of the Joke"), it is with the joke that Freud comes closest to this formalist conception of art. Needless to specify that the "form" referred to here is taken in its ordinary meaning—as opposed to *content*—and not according to the meaning I have attempted to develop in the present study in contrast to image and matrix.

5. Yet this is the most commonly held thesis. I have already mentioned Yvon Belaval's analysis of André Breton's poetry (see the chapter "Desire in Discourse," note 14), but I could have cited the basic book on the subject—Ernst Kris's *Psychoanalytic Explorations in Art* (New York: International University Press, 1952)—which defends this very thesis ("we are justified in speaking of the ego's control of the primary process" [25]; "the process is dominated by the ego and put to its own purposes—for sublimation in creative activity" [302]), and even, once again, Mauron's psychocritique, no less indebted to this approach.
6. Kris, *Psychoanalytic Explorations in Art*, 25.
7. Charles Mauron, *Des métaphores obsédantes au mythe personnel* (Paris: Corti, 1963), 234.
8. See Maurice Blanchot, "Le regard d'Orphée," *L'espace littéraire* (Paris: Gallimard, 1955). The interpretation of the mythical tale I propose here differs considerably from Blanchot's.
9. See for example Melanie Klein, "Infantile Anxiety Situations Reflected in a Work of Art and in the Creative Impulse" (1929), in *Contributions to Psychoanalysis 1921–1945* (London: Hogarth Press, 1948); and Hanna Segal, "A Psycho-Analytical Approach to Aesthetics" (1952), *International Journal of Psycho-Analysis* 33, no. 1 (1952). These studies represent a notable theoretical improvement on the position of the problem posed in clinical terms ("hysteric," "obsessional," "paranoid," etc., works of art), which seems to be the norm in literary psychiatry.
10. Donald W. Winnicott, "Transitional Objects and Transitional Phenomena. A Study of the First Not-Me Possession," *International Journal of Psycho-Analysis* 34 (1953): 89–97.
11. I owe this term to Pierre Kaufmann, *L'expérience émotionnelle de l'espace* (Paris: Vrin, 1967).
12. Susan Isaacs, "Nature et fonction du phantasme," *La psychanalyse* 5 (1959): 125–182; "The Nature and Function of Phantasy," *International Journal of Psycho-Analysis* 29 (1948): 73–97.
13. This is how I qualify these terms, following Jacques Nassif's definitions, in the section on the phantasy (see "Fiscourse Digure," note 9).
14. Kaufmann (*L'expérience émotionelle de l'espace*, end of chapter 1) argues convincingly that this anxiety—the affect corresponding to dispossession—is the only universal emotion from which all the others (fear, joy, anger, etc.) are constructions in which the mechanism of defense (retroaction) can already be seen taking over.
15. See the special issue of *Réalités* entitled "Introspection de l'Amérique," 197 (June 1962): 76–83. I choose this text because its two versions are readily available to a French audience, and because of its brevity. Of course, it is *Mobile* itself that should have been analyzed (Michel Butor, *Mobile: Étude pour une représentation des États-Unis* [Paris: Gallimard, 1962]).

16. Michel Butor, *Illustrations* (Paris: Gallimard, 1964).
17. Ibid., 91–105.
18. For fear of weighing down this description (and the illustrations), I omit the organization of what the images themselves represent, which is no less meticulous.
19. Butor, *Illustrations*, 101 [translation A.H.]. This same work of concealment through condensation and displacement is brought to bear on the phonic signifier, this time by Henri Pousseur on Butor's text in *Jeu de miroirs de Votre Faust* (LP released by Wergo, 60039, 1967).
20. Guillaume Apollinaire, *Calligrammes: Poèmes de la paix et de la guerre (1913–1916)* (Paris: Gallimard, 1925), 77.
21. Michel Butor, "Le livre comme objet," in *Répertoire II* (Paris: Minuit, 1964), 120 [translation A.H.].
22. Ibid., 119 [translation A.H.].
23. An observation made by Claude Lévi-Strauss regarding the "reading" of myths may help clarify the issue at hand. In essence, what the author of *Anthropologie structurale* ([Paris: Plon, 1958], 234) suggests is that a thousand years from now, scholars, having discovered one of our orchestral scores while having lost the key to its code, will be unable to reconstruct the latter unless they come to understand that the lines on one page are not consecutive, but instead represent as many segments to be performed simultaneously.
24. Butor, "Le livre comme objet."
25. A general matrix of these relations was developed by Boris Eizykman, Guy Fihman, and Corinne Lyotard in the context of the seminar quoted above (see "'The Dream-Work Does Not Think,'" note 17, and "Fiscourse Digure," note 17).
26. Michel Butor, *Les mots dans la peinture* (Paris: Skira, 1969).
27. *El Lissitzky: Maler, Architekt, Typograph, Fotograph: Erinnerungen, Briefe, Schriften*, ed. Sophie Lissitzky-Küppers (Dresden: V.E.B. Verlag der Kunst, 1967).
28. See Bruno Lemenuel, "Espace plastique et espace politique," *Revue d'esthétique* 3–4 (special issue "Art et société," 1970), and the book-object *idiot le piano. Oui, un peu.*
29. To which I should nonetheless add the following fragments by Lissitzky (from *El Lissitzky*, 356–360), which provide ample evidence of his lucidity vis-à-vis our problematic: "The words of the sheet of paper are seen, not heard. One communicates ideas by means of conventional words; by means of letters, the idea must become form (*soll Gestalt werden*).... The design (*Gestaltung*) of the space of the book, through the elements of discourse that obey the rules of typography, must answer to the content's direction- and pressure-related tensions (*den Zug- und Druckspannungen des Inhaltes entsprechen*).... The new book calls for the new scriptor (writer: *Schrift-Steller*). Goose quill and ink bottle are dead.... Language is more than the motion of acoustic waves and a simple means of delivering ideas. Likewise, typography is more than the mere motion of optic waves used to the same end. Typographic intervention goes from passivity, confusion, inarticulateness, to activity and articulateness. The gesture of the living language is recorded ..., typographic expression must achieve through its opticality what the reader's voice and gesture achieve through thought" [translation A.H.]. At this point in his argument, Lissitzky quotes *Gargantua,* chap. 2 ("Les fanfreluches antidotées" [The Antidoted Fanfreluches]),

where Rabelais subjects the beginning of the first five verses to the most astounding typographic contortions. For his part, Butor expresses a similar admiration for the same Rabelais in *Répertoire II.* A careful comparison between Lissitzky's writings (*Topographie der Typographie* [1923], *Typographische Tatsachen* [1925], *Unser Buch* [1926–1927] [All three texts are in *El Lissitzky.* —*Trans.*]) and Butor's (*Le livre comme objet* [1964], *La littérature, l'oreille et l'œil* [in *Répertoire III* (Paris: Minuit, 1968)]) would be worthwhile; it would reveal their common preoccupation with the question of the book as the site of encounter between sensible and sensory, as the *zone of the schema* (in the Kantian sense) or perhaps even *of reconciliation* (in the Hegelian sense).

30. See the last five paragraphs of "Recessus and Hyper-Reflection."

31. The model of the relation between floating and bound does not always follow the description given here, which is based on *Illustrations.* Indeed, there are many others, but this relation always holds. Henri Langlois allowed us to confirm this in reference to cinema: by inviting us—the group of friends whose names dot the notes of the present book, and myself—to present a paper on Georges Méliès at the Cinémathèque française, Langlois gave us the opportunity to discover that the critical and poetic power of this body of work derived from the simultaneous deployment on-screen of, on the one hand, (mechanical and chemical) "special effects" then familiar to audiences of variety shows and science fiction–inspired theater plays, and on the other, specifically cinematic effects achieved thanks to the resources of the camera and the film proper (such as instantaneous substitutions, appearances, and disappearances through stop-motion). The coexistence of techniques affecting "perspective" [*italien*] and filmic space should not be considered only as a compromise and as the source of Méliès's Baroque aesthetic: rather, it is the key to his enduring "freshness" and subversive power.

32. William Shakespeare, *Richard II* (1595–1596), 2.2, lines 16–20. This passage is flagged by Jurgis Baltrušaitis, *Anamorphoses ou magie artificielle des effets merveilleux* (Paris: Olivier Perrin, 1969), 22 and 180, note 46, following a mention of it by Erwin Panofsky in *The Codex Huygens and Leonardo da Vinci's Art Theory* (London: Warburg Institute, 1940), 93, note 1.

33. The "secret portraits" of Charles I are taken from Baltrušaitis's *Anamorphoses.* On Holbein's painting, refer to Baltrušaitis's description in the same book (91–116). Butor also provides a commentary on the work in "Un tableau vu en détail," *Répertoire III*, 33–41.

34. In fact, the geometry of planar anamorphosis consists of inverting the relation between focal point (vanishing point) and distance point: the focal point is placed to the side, where the distance point in legitimate perspective is, and the distance point is situated above it at a distance equal to that between the eye and the focal point. What makes it possible for this planar inversion to reverse the eye's relation to the plastic screen is the painter's attempt to achieve the smallest distance between the two points—bringing the eye ever closer to the painting's surface: displacement by inversion, coupled with condensation. The same inversion governs the mechanics of anamorphosis. This device, with the help of which Emmanuel Maignan painted the large fresco in the cloister of Trinità dei Monti in Rome (1642), is none other than Dürer's small gate used in reverse: the painted surface is no longer that of the gate, as in legitimate perspective, but that of the table (see Baltrušaitis, *Anamorphoses*, 52–58 and 88–90).

35. In a letter to the Florentine painter Cigoli (1559–1613), himself the inventor of a perspectival device, Galileo establishes the same relationship between, on the one hand, the anamorphic figure and the meaning it conceals when seen frontally and, on the other, the phantasmagoria of allegorical poetry and what it signifies (see Panofsky, *Galileo as a Critic of the Arts* [The Hague: Martinus Nijhoff, 1954], 13). Madeleine David compares the formal dualism of the anamorphic figure with the symbol's, in which a signified is produced by an altogether different sign (signified/signifier) (*Le débat sur les écritures et l'hiéroglyphe aux dix-septième et dix-huitième siècles et l'application de la notion de déchiffrement aux écritures mortes* [Paris: SEVPEN, 1969], 141–142; and Baltrušaitis, *Anamorphoses*, chap. 3, and 181, note 94).
36. This is how the dream's façade may come to repeat its core.
37. Freud, "Ratschläge für den Arzt bei der psychoanalytischen Behandlung" (1912), GW, vol. 8, 377; "Recommendations to Physicians Practising Psycho-Analysis," SE, vol. 12, 112.
38. GW, vol. 8, 380; SE, vol. 12, 114.
39. GW, vol. 8, 381; SE, vol. 12, 115.
40. GW, vol. 8, 381; SE, vol. 12, 116. For proof that what Freud calls "interpretation" is indeed this work, we need look no further than to his essay entitled "Psycho-Analysis" written in 1922 (around the time of *The Ego and the Id*) and published in the *Handwörterbuch der Sexualwissenschaft* edited by Max Marcuse in Bonn, where one finds—under the heading "Psycho-Analysis as an Interpretative Art" ("Die Psychoanalyse als Deutungskunst")—the following remark: "Experience soon showed that the attitude {to interpret the hidden meaning in the patient's associations} which the analytic physician could most advantageously adopt was to surrender himself (*sich selbst . . . überlassen*) to his own unconscious mental activity, in a state of *evenly suspended attention*, to avoid so far as possible reflection and the construction of conscious expectations, not to try to fix anything that he heard particularly in his memory, and by these means to catch the drift of the patient's unconscious with his own unconscious." Freud goes on: "It is true that this work of interpretation (*diese Deutungsarbeit*) was not to be brought under strict rules and left a great deal of play to the physician's tact . . ." ("Psychoanalyse," GW, vol. 13, 215; "Psycho-Analysis," SE, vol. 18, 239) These are essential lines, not only because they confirm eleven years later, in the midst of developing the new topography, what Freud was thinking as he was working on his metapsychology, but especially because of the use of the simple word *Arbeit*: interpretation is not discourse, but work, and the precondition for this work is the deconstruction of discourse.
41. Gottlob Frege, "Über Sinn und Bedeutung," *Zeitschrift für Philosophie und philosophische Kritik* 100 (1892): 33; Henry G. Widdowson, "Notes on Stylistics" (1969), 11.
42. "Das Unheimliche" (1919), GW, vol. 12, 259–268; "The Uncanny," SE, vol. 17, 245–252.
43. *Paul Klee: Journal,* trans. Pierre Klossowski (Paris: Grasset, 1959), 224; *The Diaries of Paul Klee, 1898–1918*, ed. Félix Klee, trans. Pierre B. Schneider, R.Y. Zachary, and Max Knight (Berkeley, Los Angeles: University of California Press, 1964), 226; and the passage corresponding to notes 61–65 of "The Line and the Letter."
44. See Ehrenzweig, *The Psychoanalysis of Artistic Vision and Hearing*, chap. 4 ("A dynamic theory of the beauty and ugliness feelings"). In a Kleinian perspective, see also Segal, "A Psycho-Analytical Approach to Aesthetics," 205 ff.

45. [Lyotard is referring to *La vache qui rit*, a popular brand of soft cheese whose circular packaging bears the image of a laughing cow. —*Trans.*]
46. Freud, "Ratschläge für den Arzt bei der psychoanalytischen Behandlung," GW, vol. 8, 380; "Recommendations to Physicians Practising Psycho-Analysis," SE, vol. 12, 114–115.
47. Jean Starobinski, "Hamlet et Freud," preface to the French translation of Ernest Jones, *Hamlet et Œdipe* (1949) (Paris: Gallimard, 1967).
48. However, a note in the Cambridge University Press edition (*New Shakespeare series*, ed. J. Dover Wilson and Sir Arthur Quiller-Couch) specifies that the word is, according to the English philologist C.T. Onions, common in Warwickshire to mean "muffled," wrapped up.
49. [Words in italic are in English in the original. —*Trans.*]
50. [Italicized phrase is in English in the original. —*Trans.*]
51. [*Camouflée* would translate here as "disguised," "concealed." —*Trans.*]
52. [The verb *encanailler* means to slum, to debase oneself. —*Trans.*]

Note to Page 390

1. Heinrich Meng and Ernst L. Freud, eds., *Psycho-Analysis and Faith: The Letters of Sigmund Freud and Oskar Pfister*, trans. Eric Mosbacher (London: Hogarth Press, 1963), 62.

Appendix

1. Le même processus se trouve à la base du processus connu de « l'évocation » (Berufen). « Quelle chance de n'avoir pas eu ma migraine depuis si longtemps ! » Mais c'est le premier avertissement de l'accès, dont on sent déjà l'imminence, auquel pourtant on ne veut pas encore croire. [The same process is at the root of the well-known operation of "evocation" (*Berufen*): "What luck not to have had my migraine for such a long time!" But this is the warning shot of the attack, which we feel to be imminent without, however, wanting to believe in it yet.]
2. Cf. "Triebe und Triebschicksale," GW, vol. 10; "Instincts and Their Vicissitudes," SE, vol. 14.

Plates

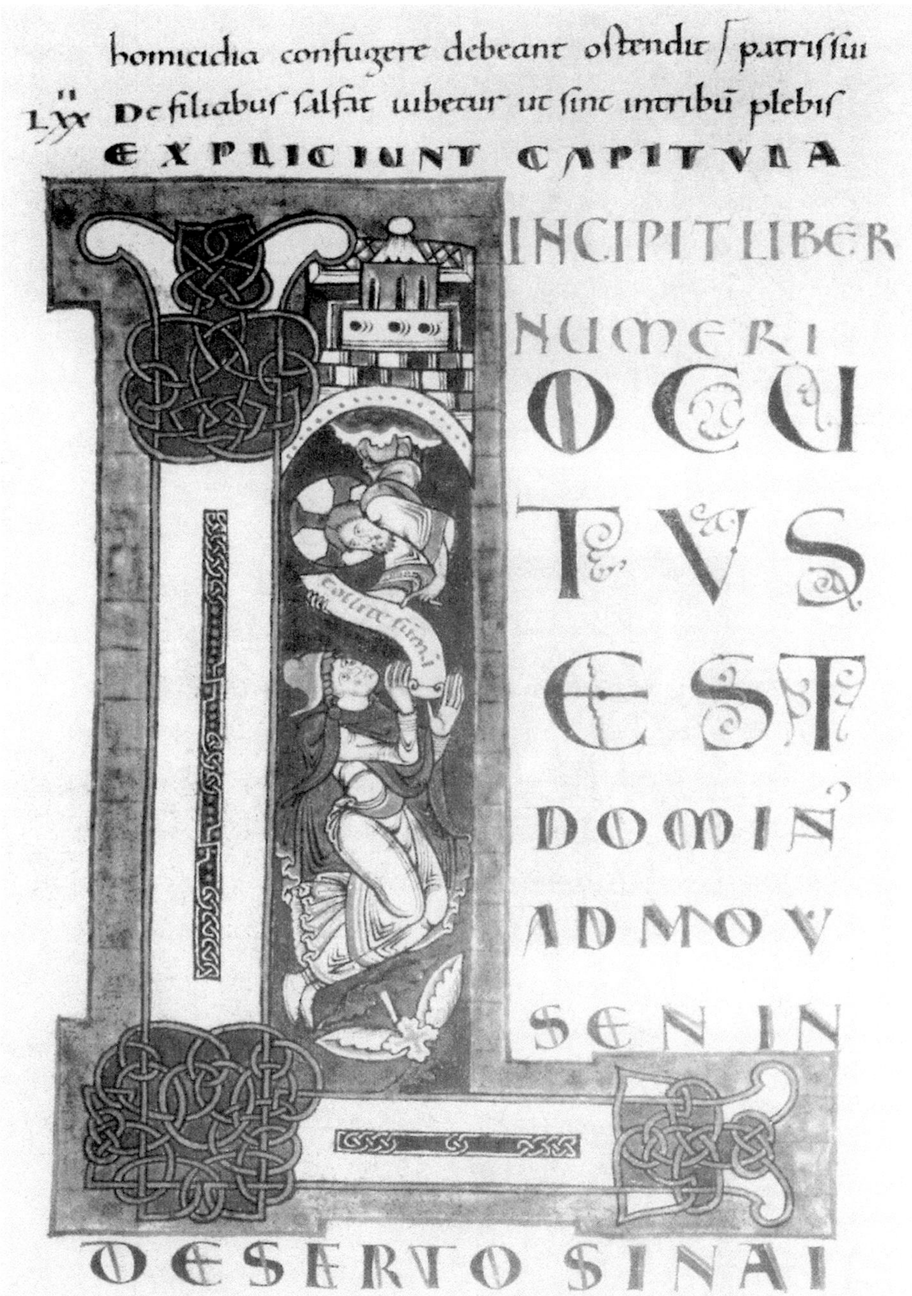

Plate 1. Folio from the beginning of the Book of Numbers, *Bible of Saint-Martial* (Paris: Bibliothèque nationale, ms. lat. 8 [1], f. 52 [image: B.N. A 59/177]), second half of the eleventh century, Limoges.

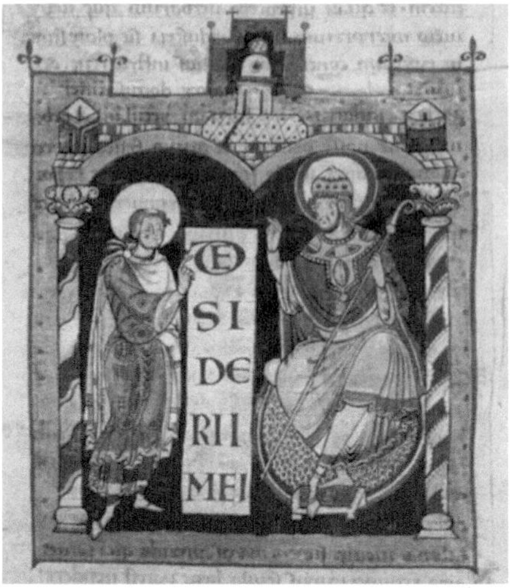

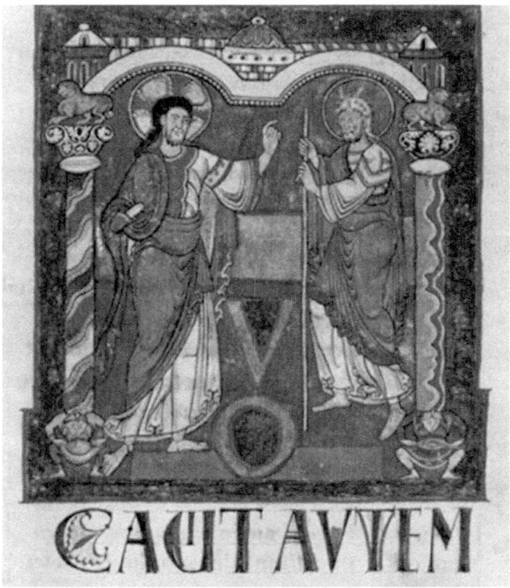

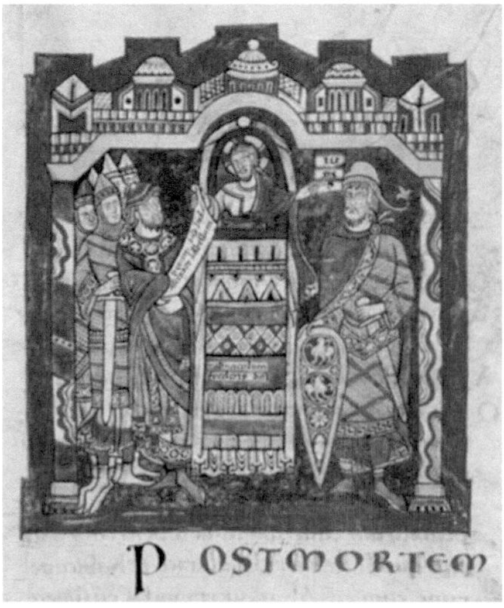

Plate 2a. Folio from the beginning of the preface of Saint Jerome (detail), Book of Genesis, *Bible of Saint-Martial,* f. 4 (image: B.N. A 48/96).

Plate 2b. Folio from the beginning of the Book of Leviticus (detail), *Bible of Saint-Martial,* f. 41 (image: B.N. A 47/258).

Plate 2c. Folio of the beginning of the Book of Judges (detail), *Bible of Saint-Martial,* f. 91 (image: B.N. A 47/259).

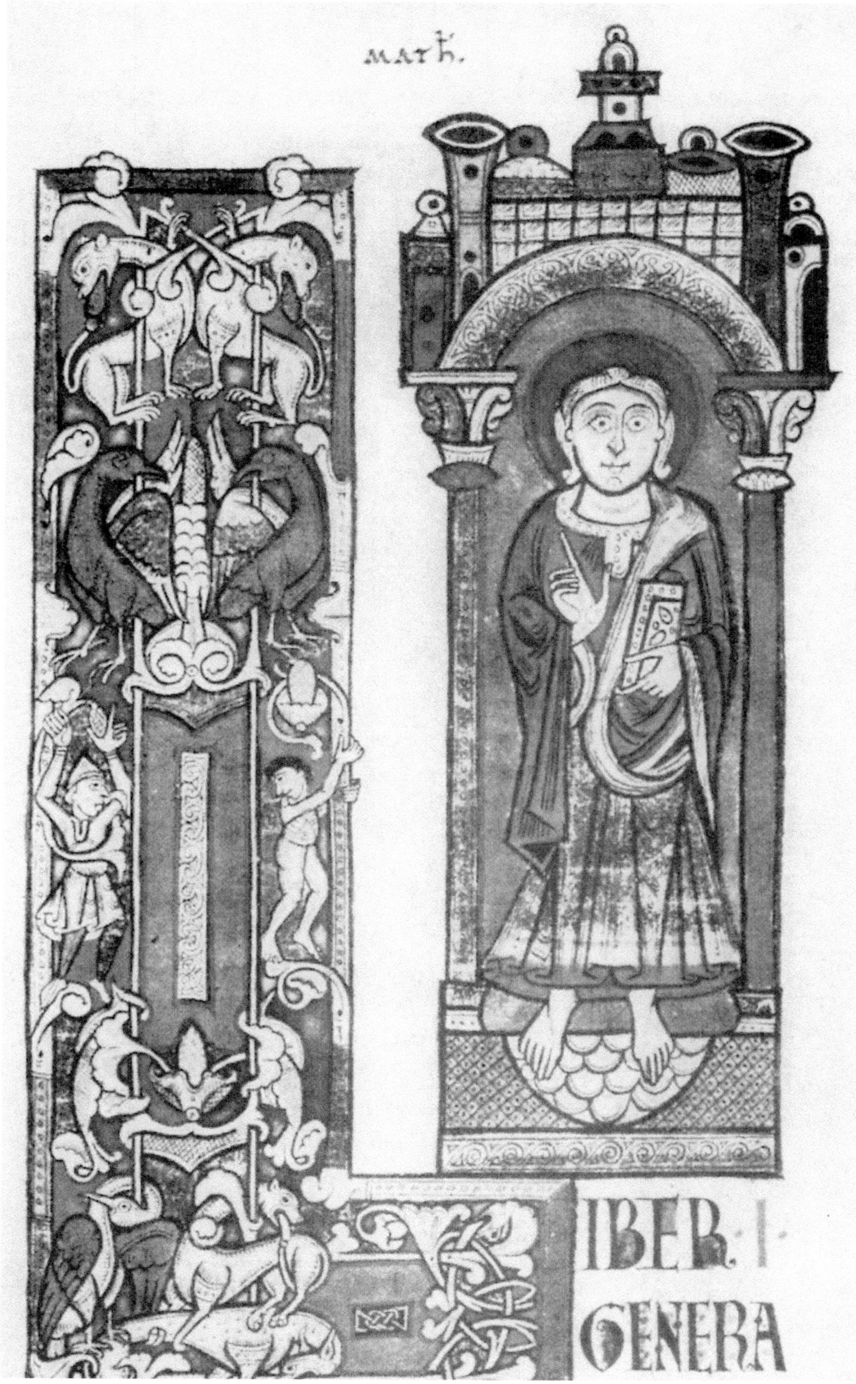

Plate 3. Folio from the beginning of the Gospel according to Saint Matthew (Genealogy of Jesus), New Testament, Moissac (?) (Paris: Bibliothèque nationale, ms. lat. 254, f. 10 [image: B.N. A 48/92]), end of the eleventh century.

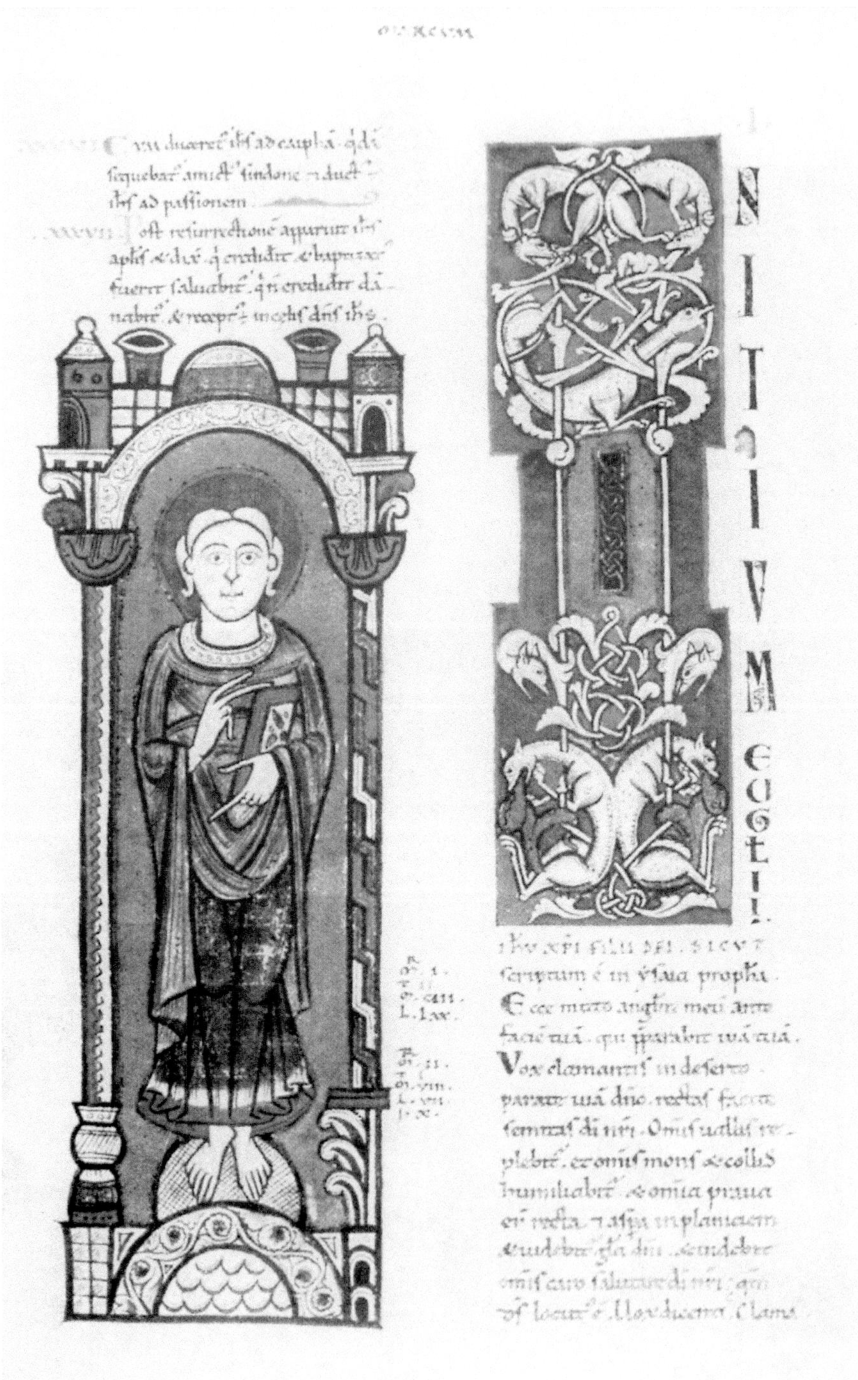

Plate 4. Folio from the beginning of the Gospel according to Saint Mark, New Testament, Moissac (?), f. 32 (image: B.N. A 48/93).

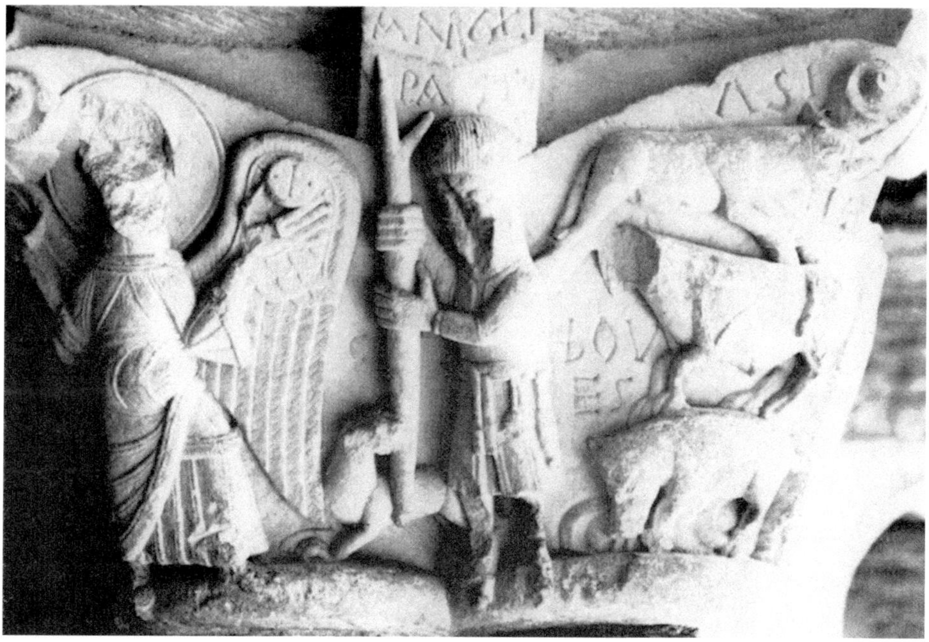

Plate 5. The Annunciation to the Shepherds, capital, cloister of the abbey-church of Saint Peter, Moissac, end of the eleventh century. From Éditions photographiques Auguste Allemand.

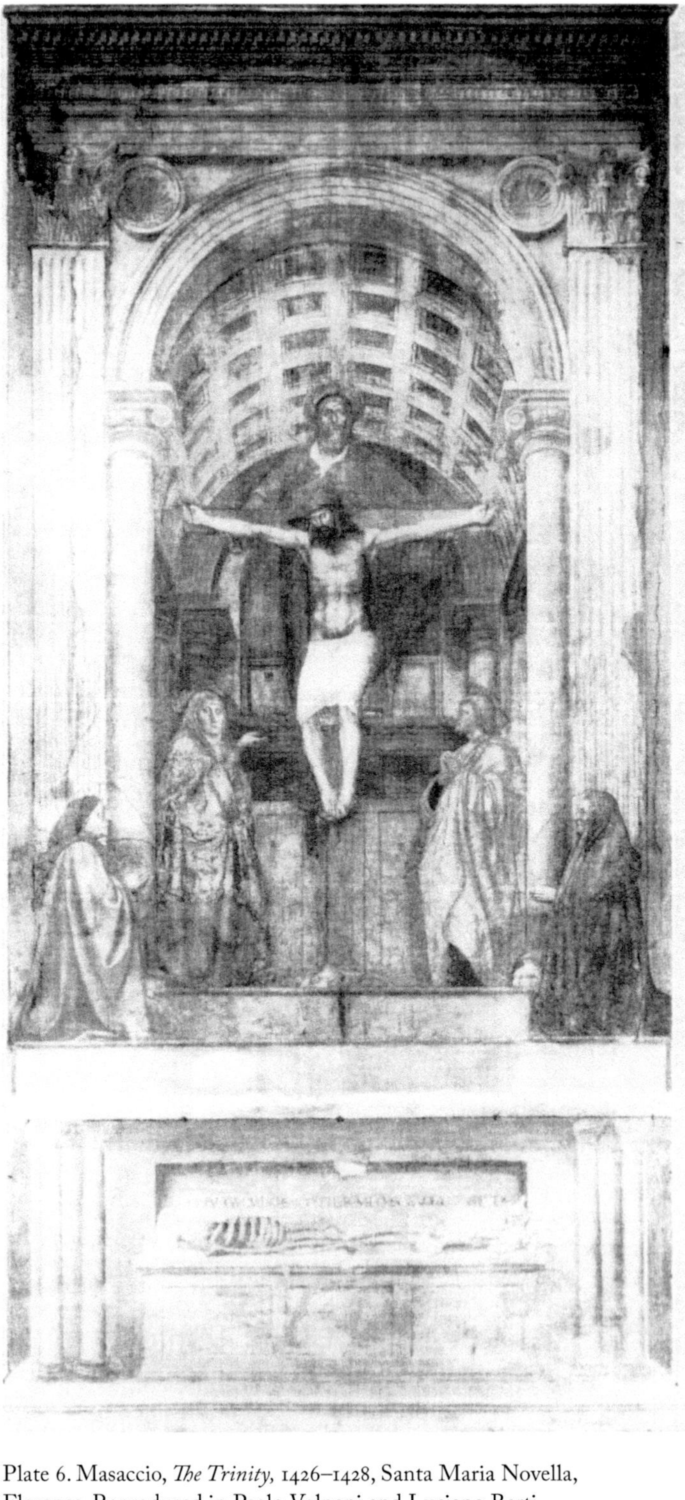

Plate 6. Masaccio, *The Trinity,* 1426–1428, Santa Maria Novella, Florence. Reproduced in Paolo Volponi and Luciano Berti, *L'opera completa di Masaccio* (Milan: Rizzoli, 1968), Plate 27.

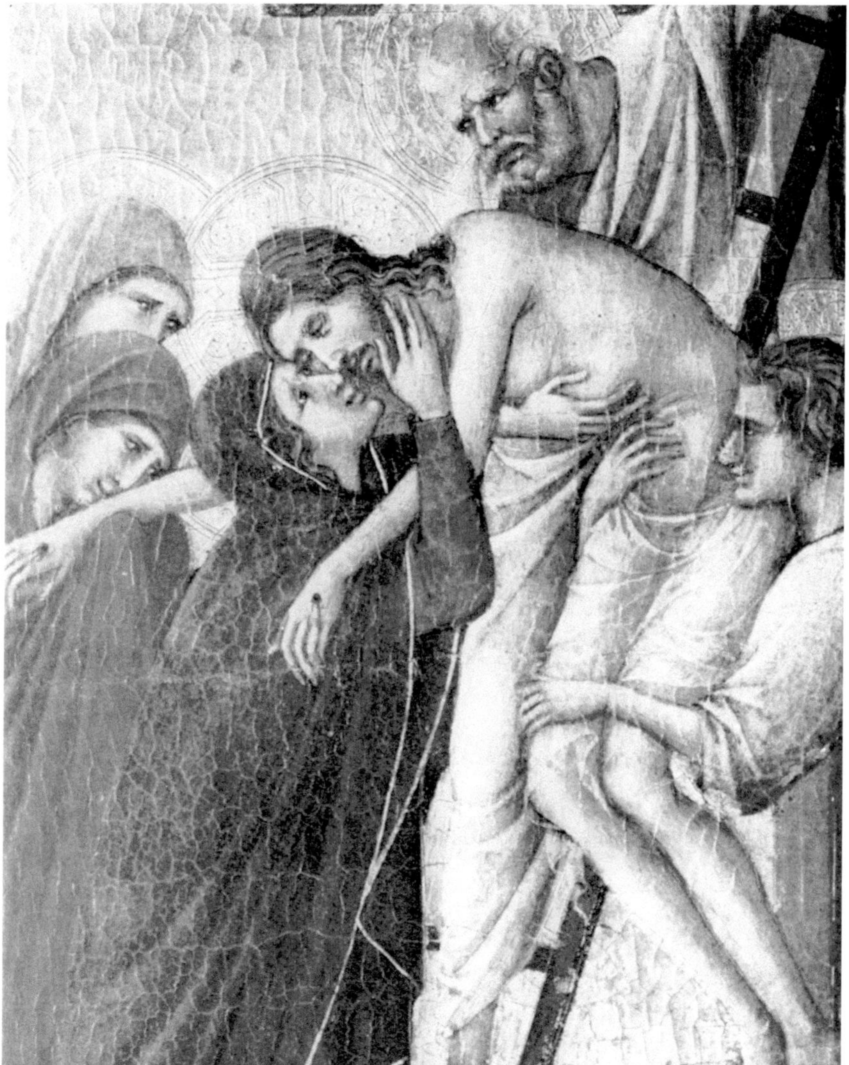

Plate 7. Duccio di Buoninsegna, *Descent from the Cross* (detail), *La Maestà,* 1308–1311, Museo dell'Opera Metropolitana del Duomo, Siena. Reproduced in Pier Paolo Donati, *La Maestà di Duccio* (Florence: Sadea, 1965), Plate 28.

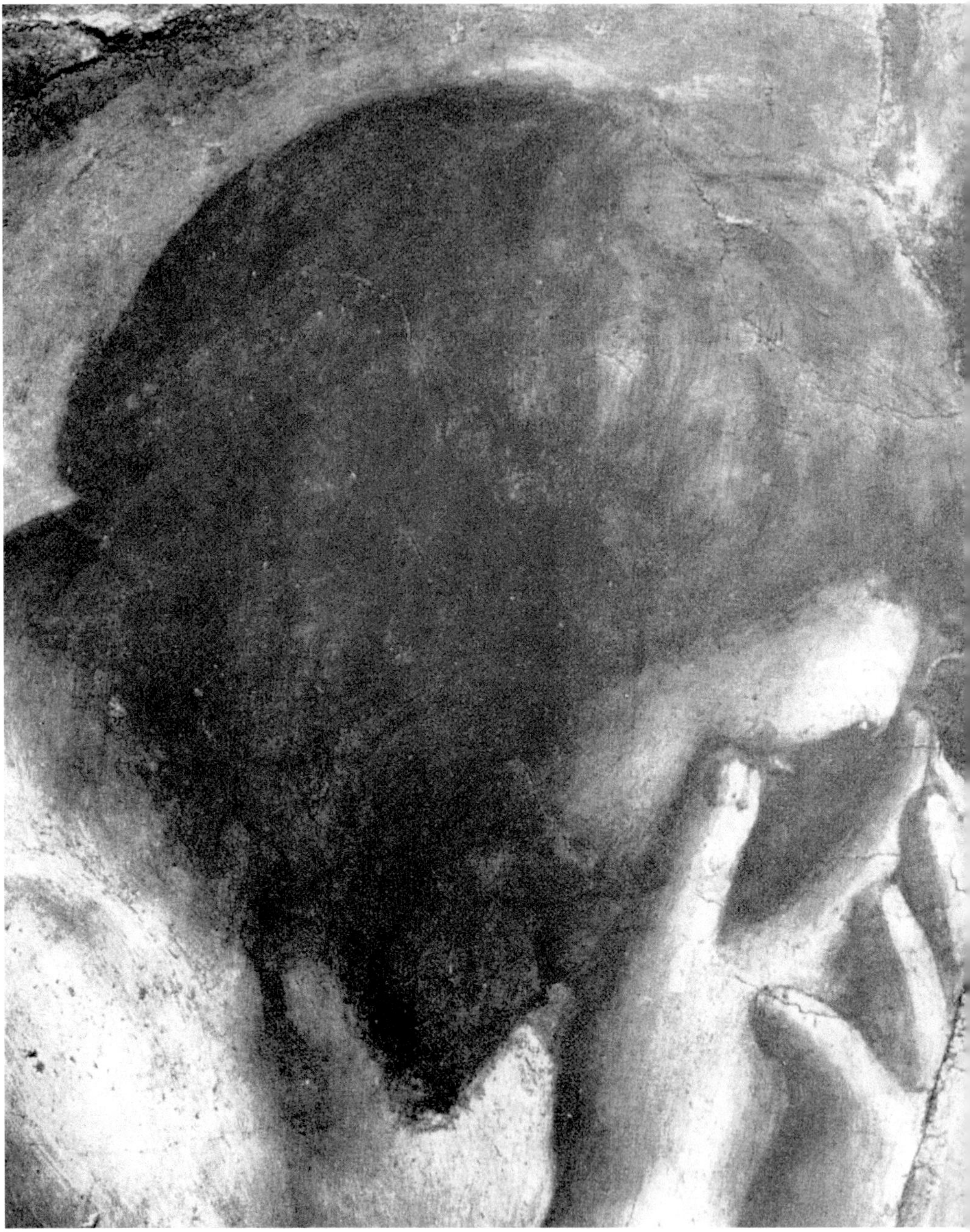

Plate 8. Masaccio, *The Expulsion from the Garden of Eden* (detail), Brancacci Chapel, 1424–1427, Church of Santa Maria del Carmine, Florence. Reproduced in Volponi and Berti, *L'opera completa di Masaccio,* Plates 46–47.

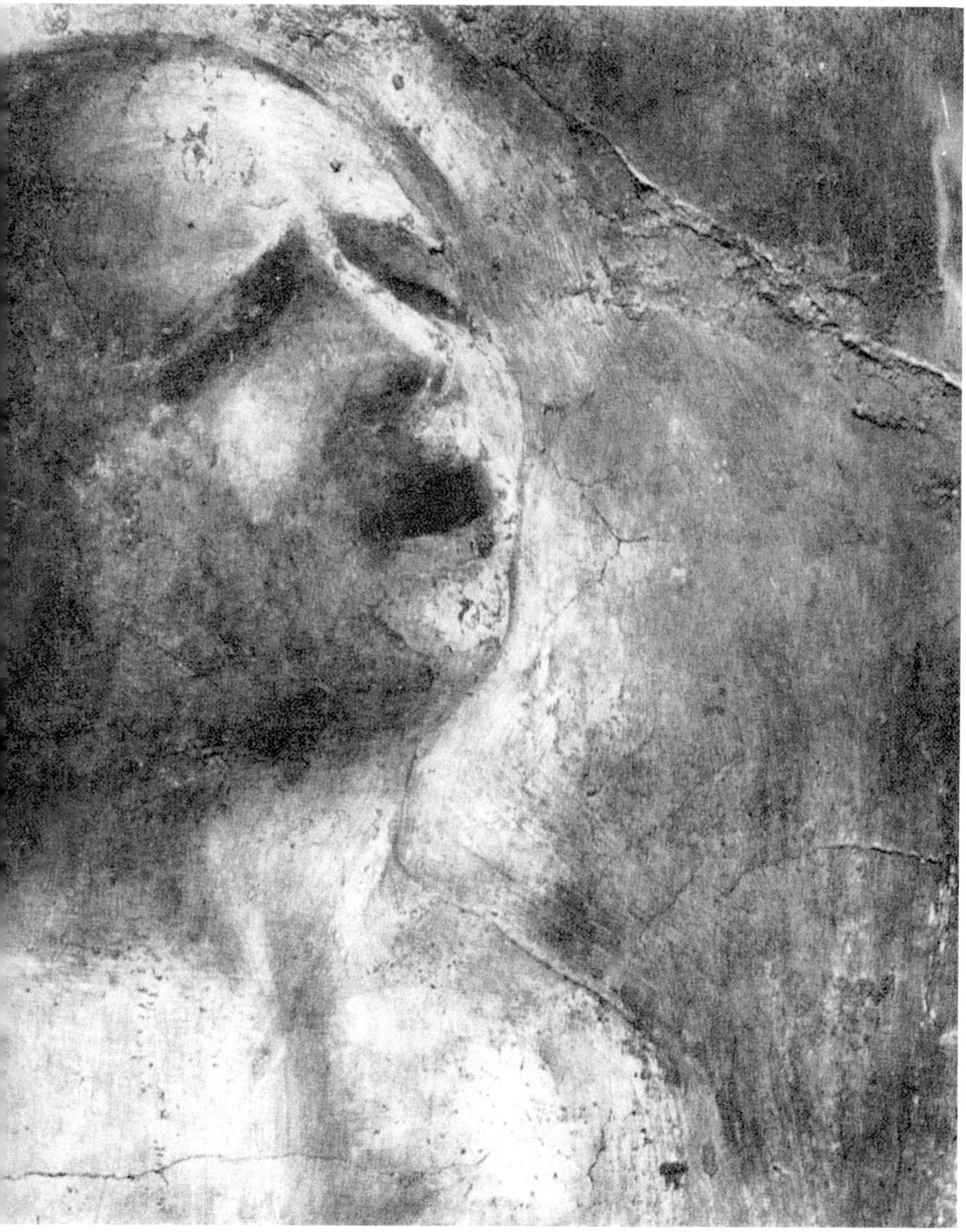

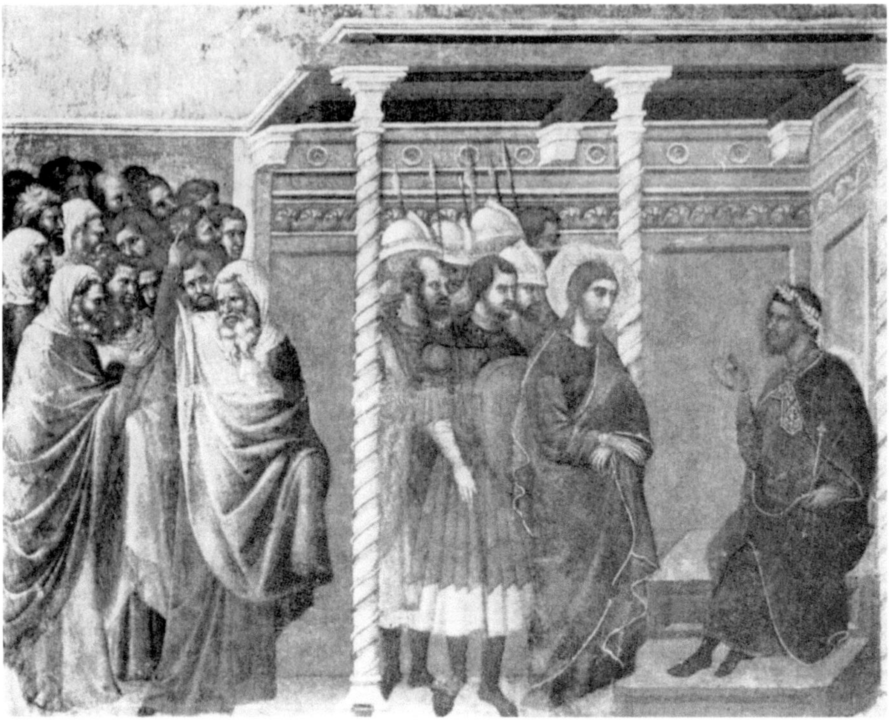

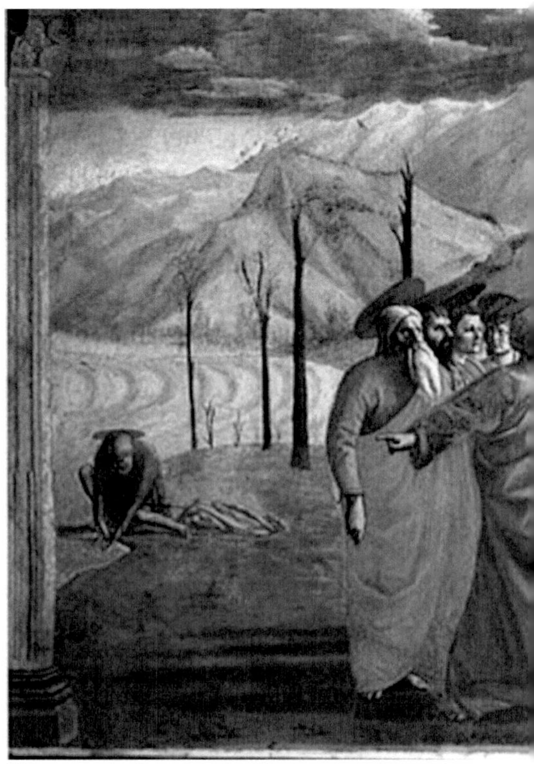

Plate 9. Duccio di Buoninsegna, *Christ before Pilate.* Reproduced in Donati, *La Maestà di Duccio,* Plate 21.

Plate 10. Masaccio, *The Tribute Money,* Brancacci Chapel, 1424–1427. Reproduced in Volponi and Berti, *L'opera completa di Masaccio,* Plates 36–37.

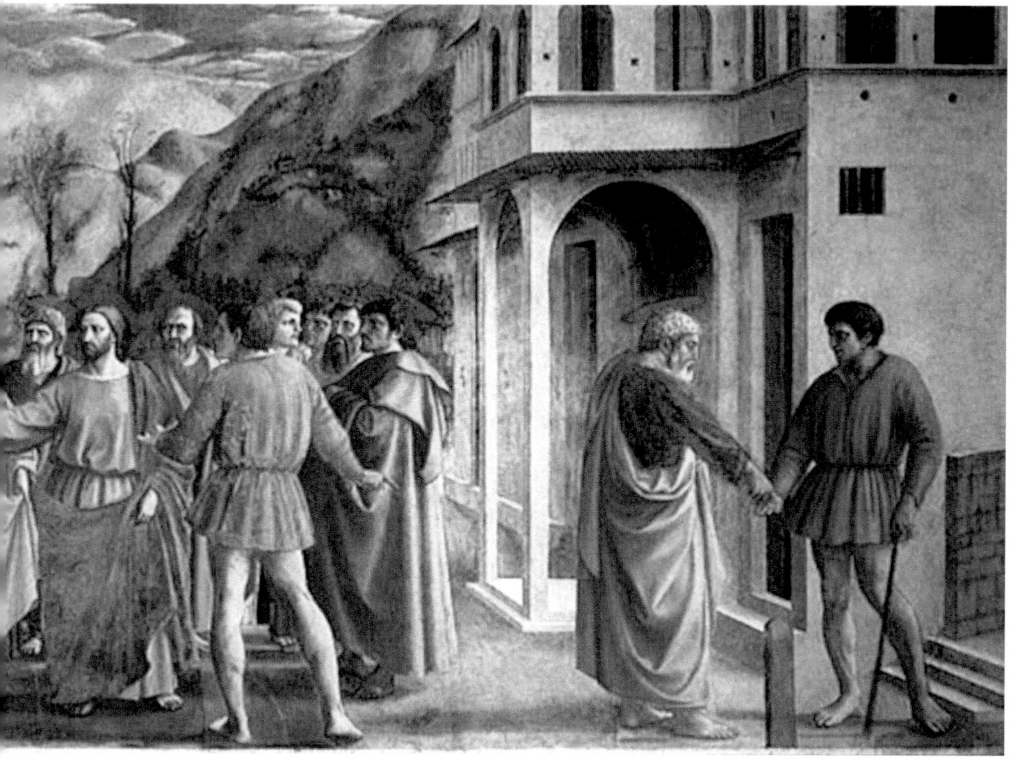

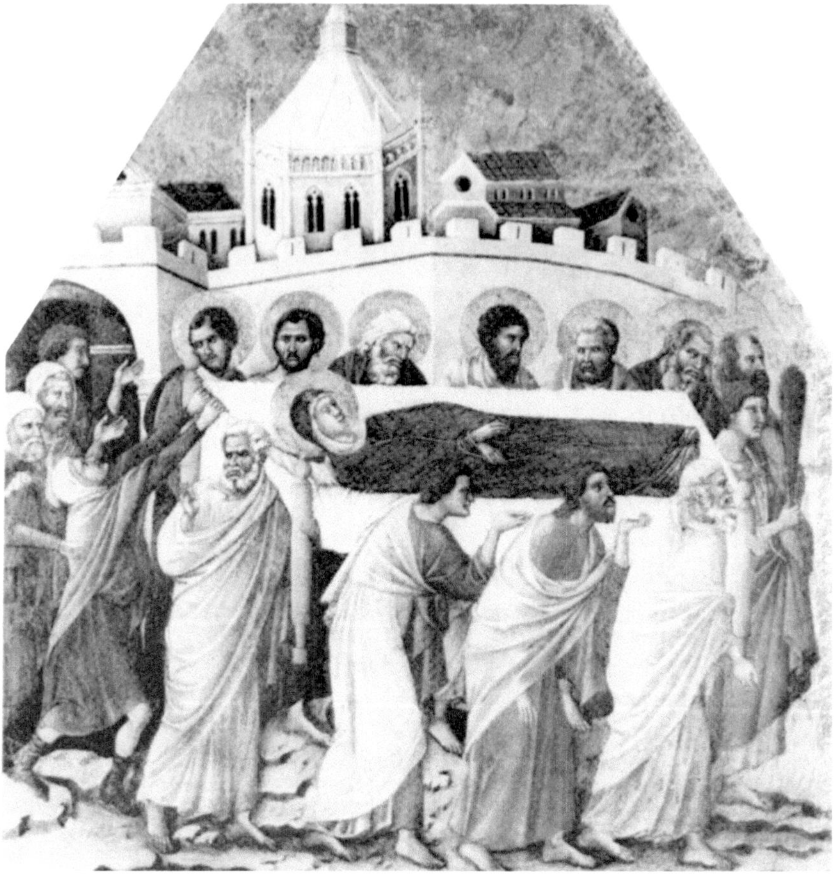

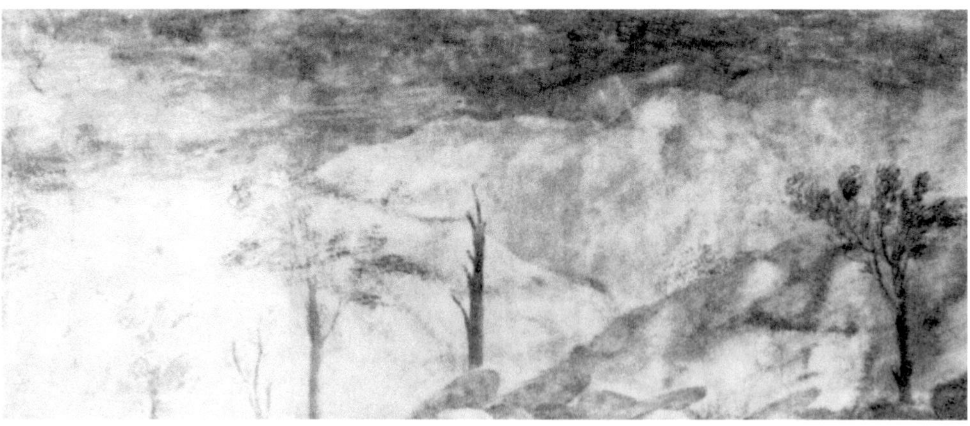

Plate 11a. Duccio di Buoninsegna, *Funeral of the Virgin*, 1308–1311. Reproduced in Donati, *La Maestà di Duccio,* Plate 10.

Plate 11b. Masaccio, *The Tribute Money* (detail), Brancacci Chapel, 1424–1427. Reproduced in Volponi and Berti, *L'opera completa di Masaccio,* Plates 36–37.

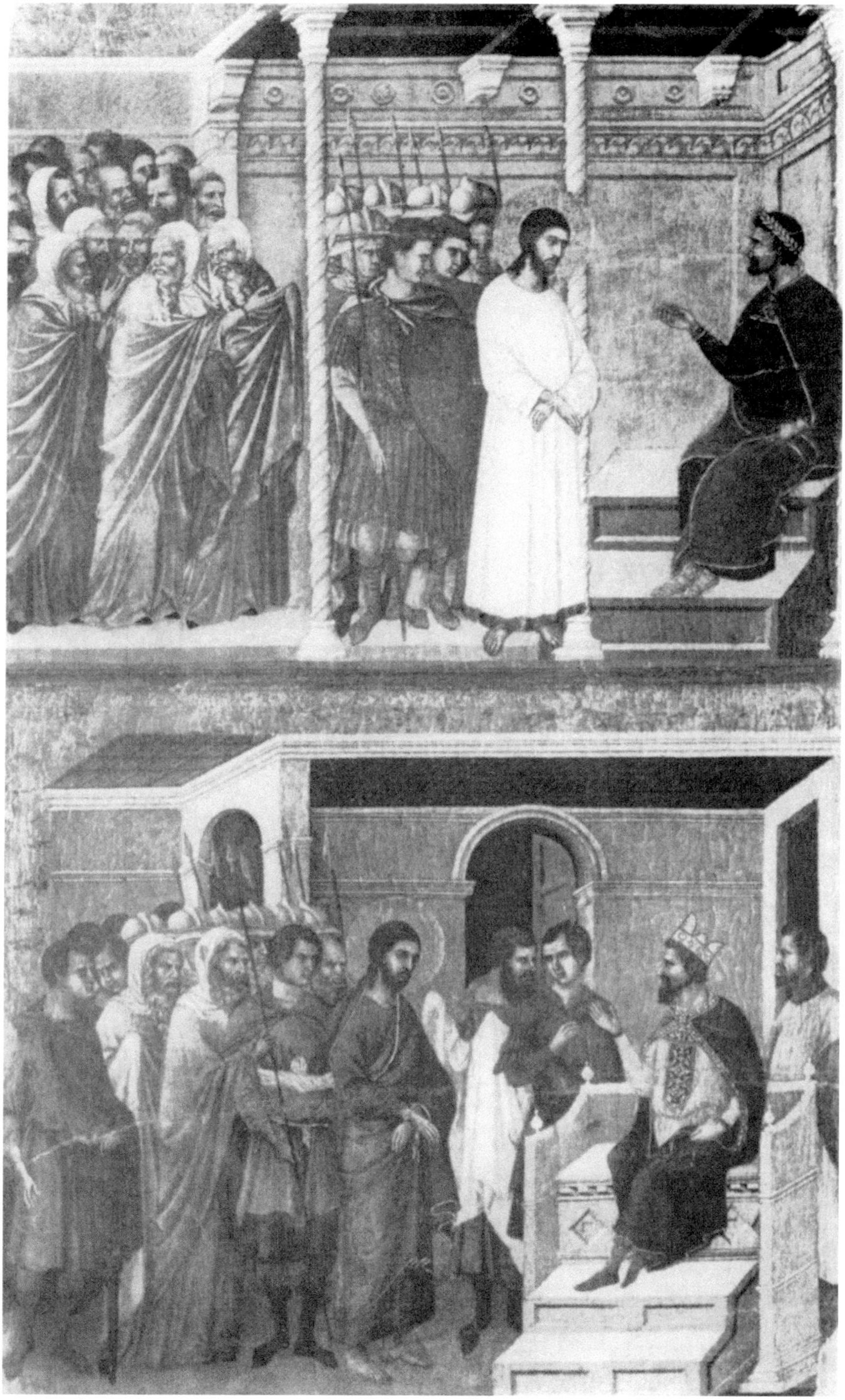

Plate 12. Duccio di Buoninsegna, *Christ before Herod* (below) and *Christ in the Robe before Pilate* (above), 1308–1311. Reproduced in Donati, *La Maestà di Duccio,* Plate 22.

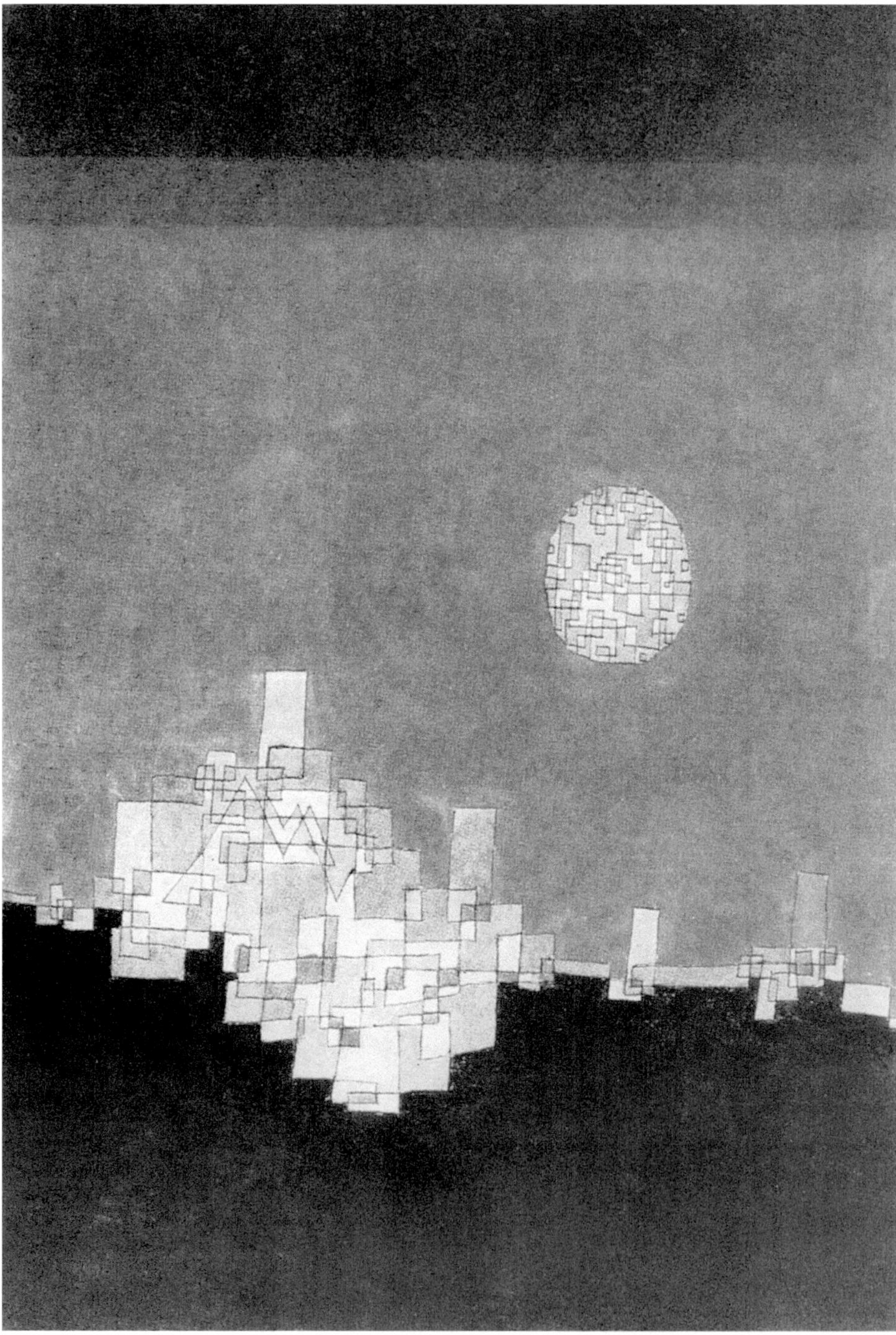

Plate 13. Paul Klee, *Chosen Site*, 1927/x8. Watercolor and ink on paper, 30.5 × 46 cm. Private collection, Munich. Reproduced in Will Grohmann, *Paul Klee* (Paris: Cercle d'art, 1968), Plate 20.

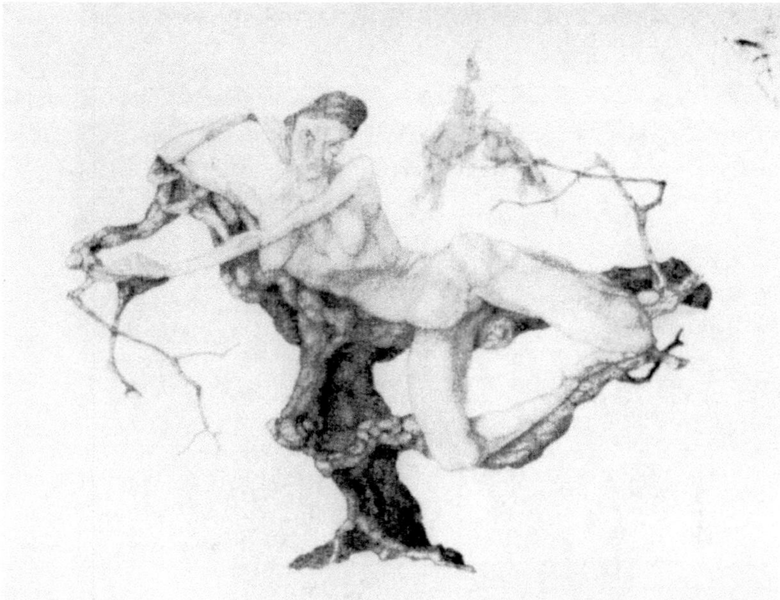

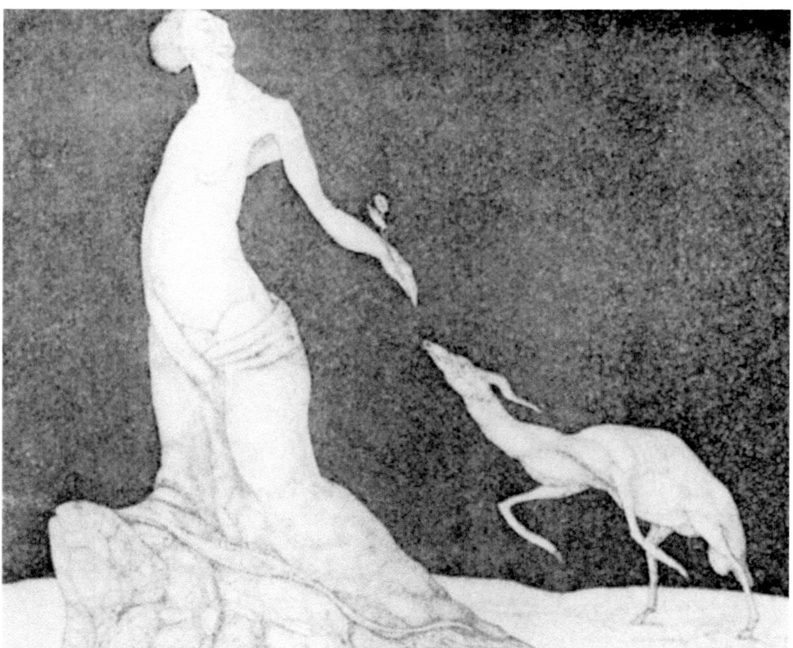

Plate 14a. Paul Klee, *Maiden in a Tree*, 1903/2. Etching, 23.6 × 29.6 cm. Klipstein and Kornfeld, Bern. Reproduced in *Paul Klee par lui-même et par son fils Félix Klee*, 12.

Plate 14b. Paul Klee, *Woman and Beast*, 1903/13. Etching, 19.4 × 22.4 cm. Klipstein and Kornfeld, Bern. Reproduced in *Paul Klee par lui-même et par son fils Félix Klee,* 12.

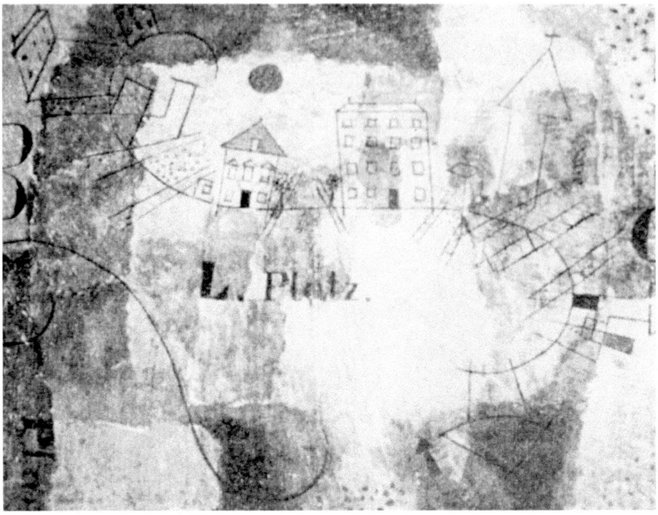

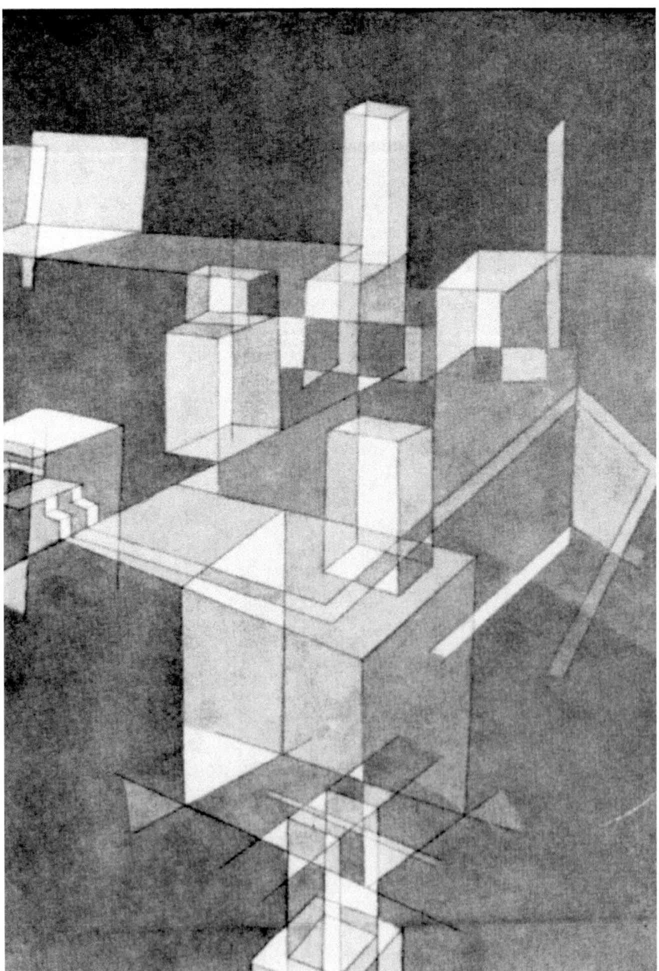

Plate 15a. Paul Klee, *Town Square under Construction*, 1923/11. Watercolor and ink on paper. G. David Tompson, Pittsburgh. Image courtesy of W. Klein, Kunstsammlung Nordrhein-Westphalien, Düsseldorf.

Plate 15b. Paul Klee, *Italian City*, 1928/P 6. Watercolor. Félix Klee, Bern. Reproduced in *Das bildnerische Denken*, 42.

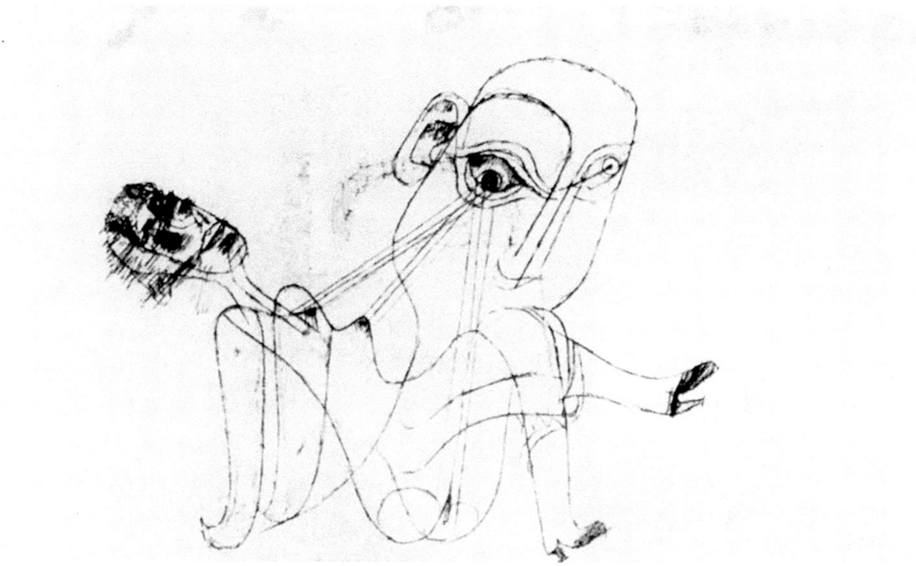

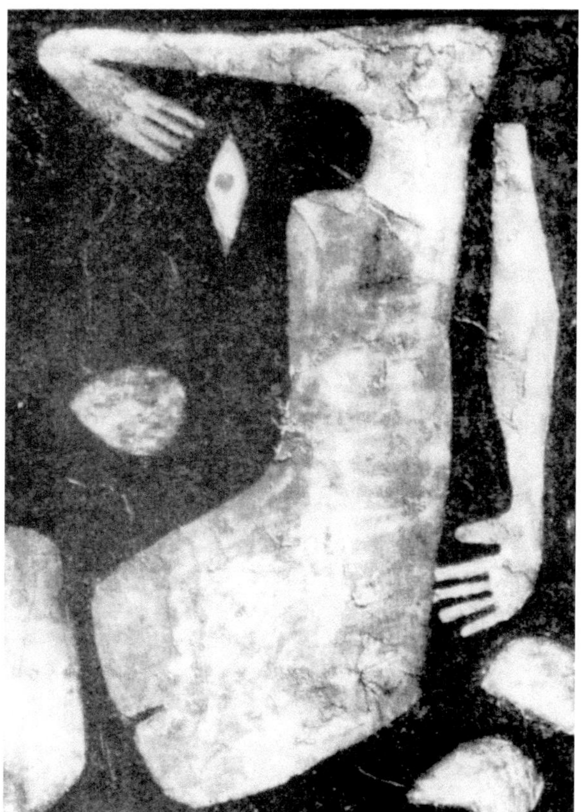

Plate 16a. Paul Klee, *The Eye of Eros*, 1919/53. Ink drawing. Berggruen Gallery. Reproduced in *Paul Klee par lui-même et par son fils Félix Klee*, 77.

Plate 16b. Paul Klee, *Fragmenta Veneris,* 1938/XI. Oil and watercolor on jute canvas primed with plaster. Private collection, Zurich. Reproduced in *Das bildnerische Denken*, 452.

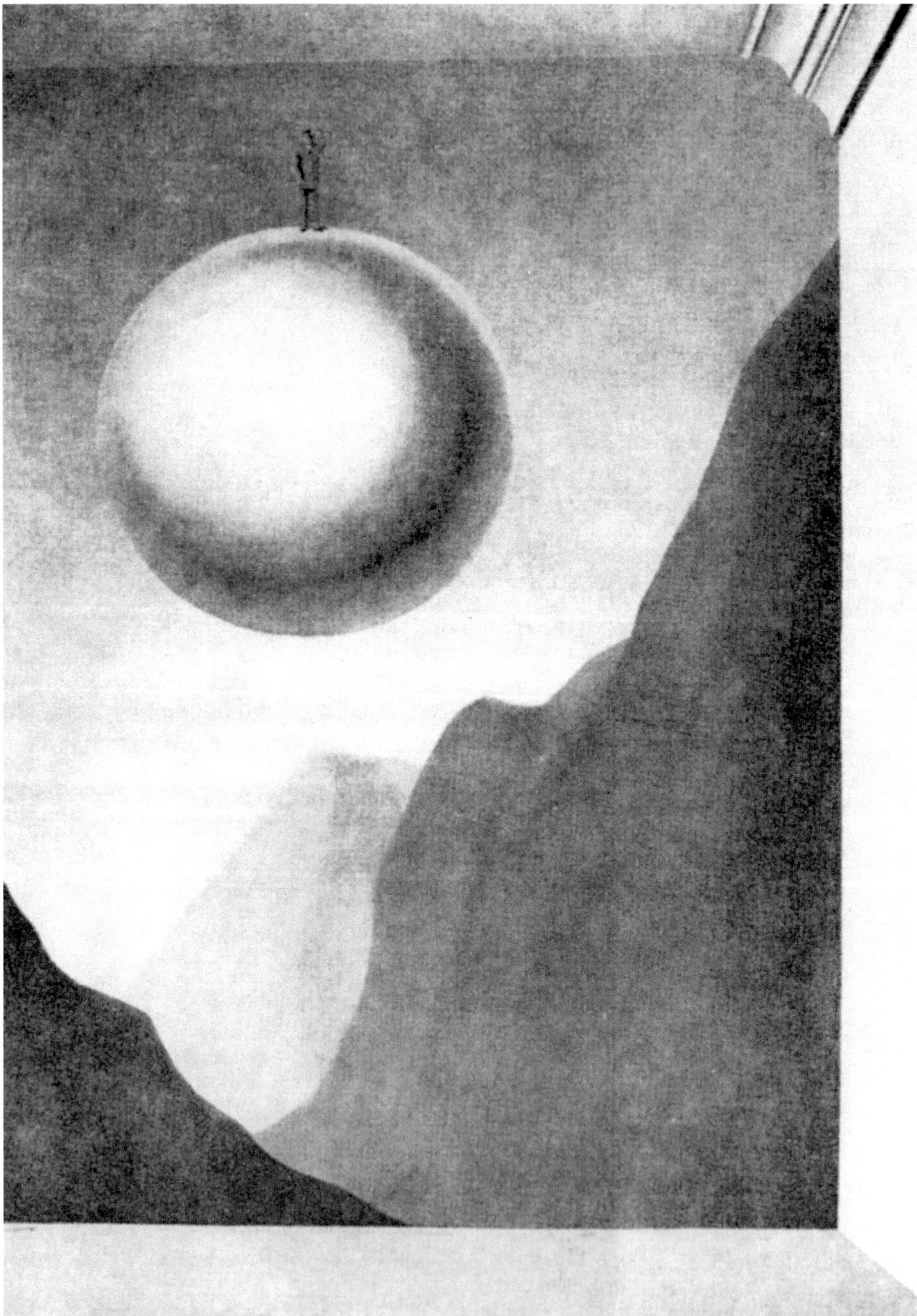

Plate 17. René Magritte, *La reconnaissance infinie,* 1953. Oil on canvas. Reproduced (without indication of origin) in André Breton, *Le surréalisme et la peinture* (Paris: Gallimard, 1965).

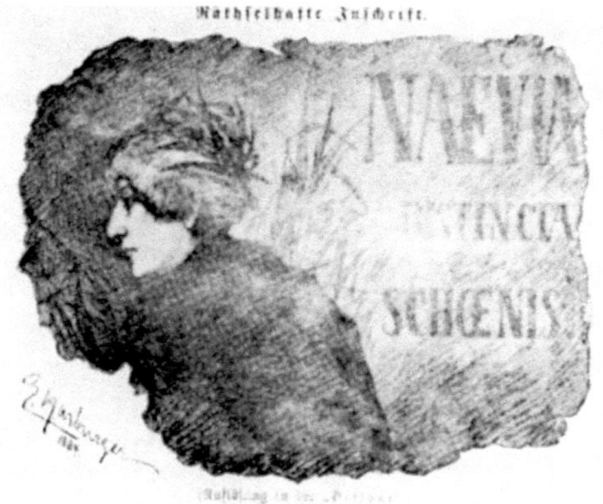

Plate 18a. “Rätselhafte Inschrift,” *Fliegende Blätter* 2034 (1884): 20.

Plate 18b. Saint Gregory, *Commentary on the Book of Job* (frontispiece), Citeaux, Bibliothèque de Dijon, ms. 168, f. 4 v, twelfth century. Courtesy Bibliothèque de Dijon.

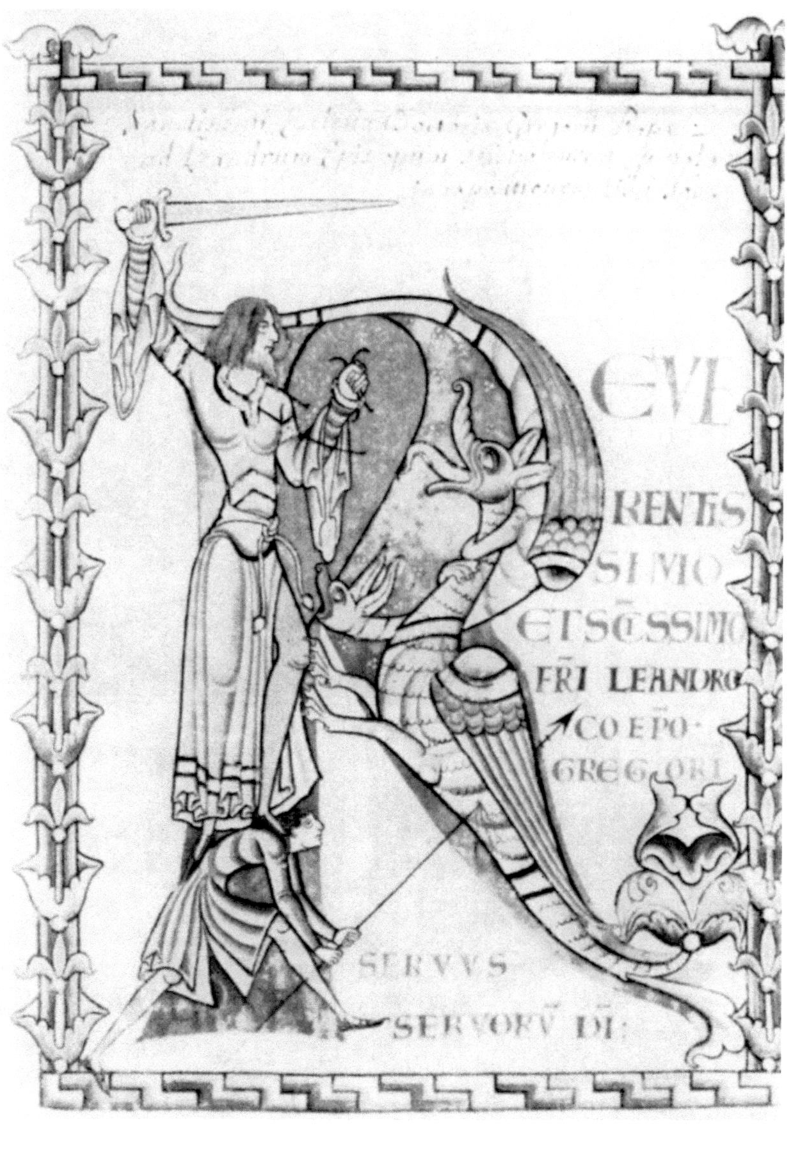

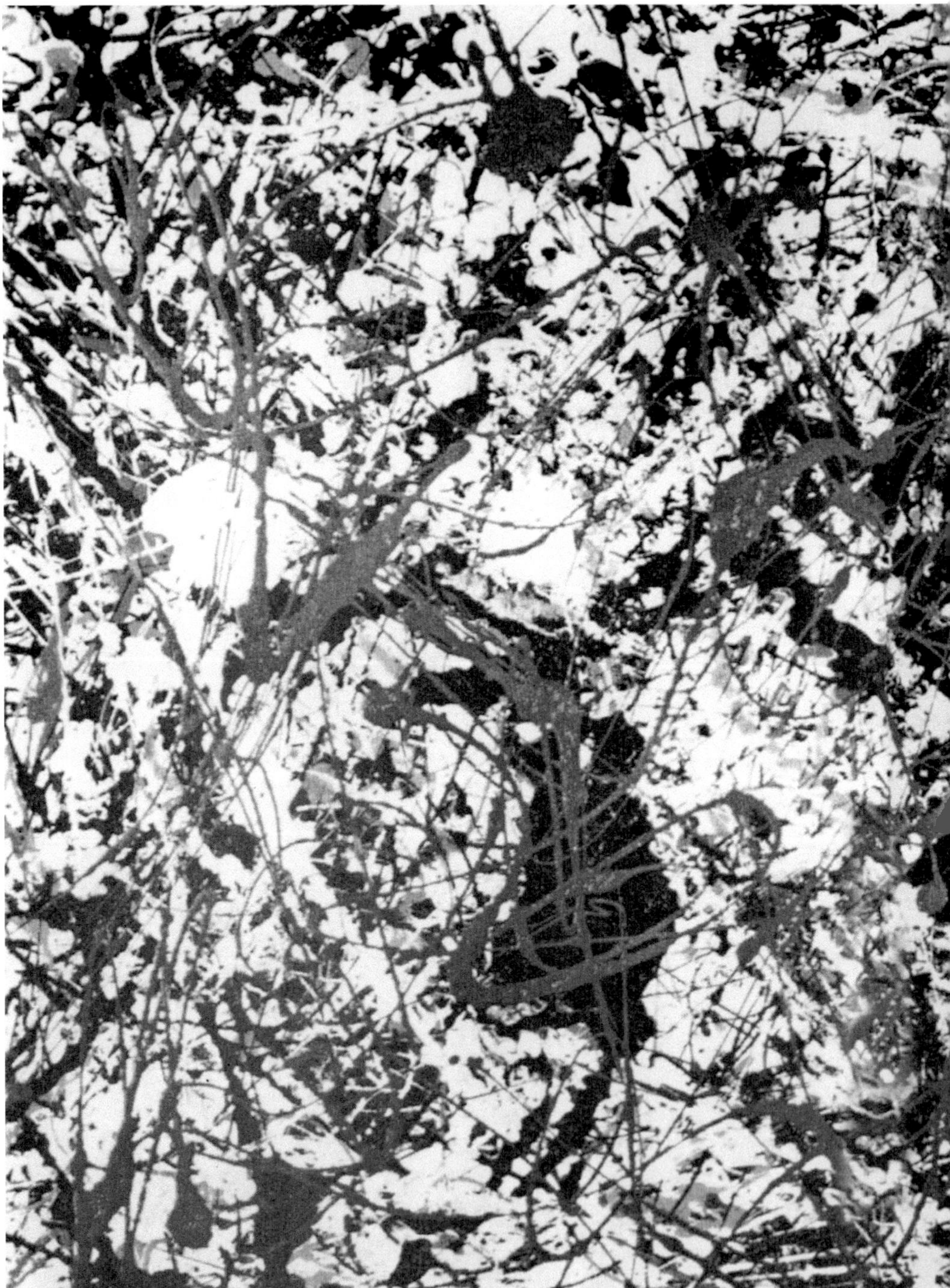

Plate 19. Jackson Pollock, *Painting,* 1948. Oil on paper, 57.3 × 78.1 cm. Paul Facchetti collection, Paris. Reproduced in Italo Tomassoni, *Pollock* (Florence: Sadea, 1968), Plates 44–45.

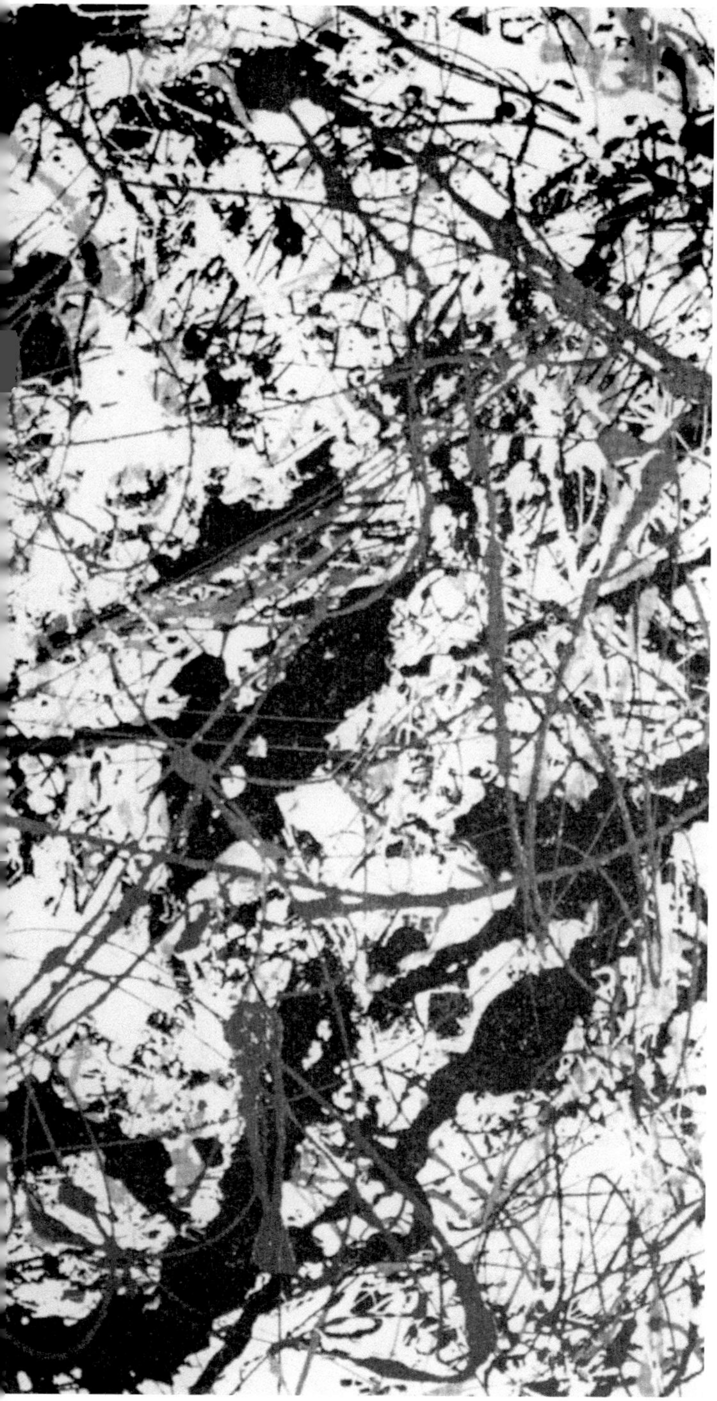

L'APPEL des ROCHEUSES

texte et légendes de Michel Butor

photos d'Ansel Adams et Edward Weston

QUAND les pionniers allant vers l'Ouest et l'or, après des semaines et des semaines dans les plaines et la prairie, apercevaient la grande muraille de rocs, de pics et de forêts, ils savaient qu'au-delà commençaient les déserts, l'immensité menaçante, le pays de l'étonnement, et qu'il faudrait y résister, y subsister pendant des semaines et des semaines avant d'atteindre l'autre grande chaîne, et descendre enfin vers le Pacifique.

Quand l'automobiliste, aujourd'hui, après des heures, des heures, des jours de route droite dans l'interminable ferme du Middle-West, est salué par le monde sauvage, à l'intérieur duquel il lui faudra se faufiler, minuscule et seul, avec précautions, c'est comme une gigantesque respiration qui le saisit, un vent venu du fond des âges, lui, Américain, citoyen d'une nation si rapidement vieillie, se retrouve neuf, au seuil du plus inquiétant des paradis.

Quand l'avion quitte le quadrillage vert dont la régularité s'accentuait de l'Indiana à l'Illinois, de l'Iowa au Nebraska, pour franchir, dans l'État de Colorado, les monts outremer sommés de nacre, et baigner dans la surprenante couleur du sol qui change constamment au-dessous de lui, le jeune voyageur est pris d'un vertige tout autre : en quelques instants, lui semble-t-il, le monde déploie à ses yeux plus de secrets que pendant des années d'études autrefois.

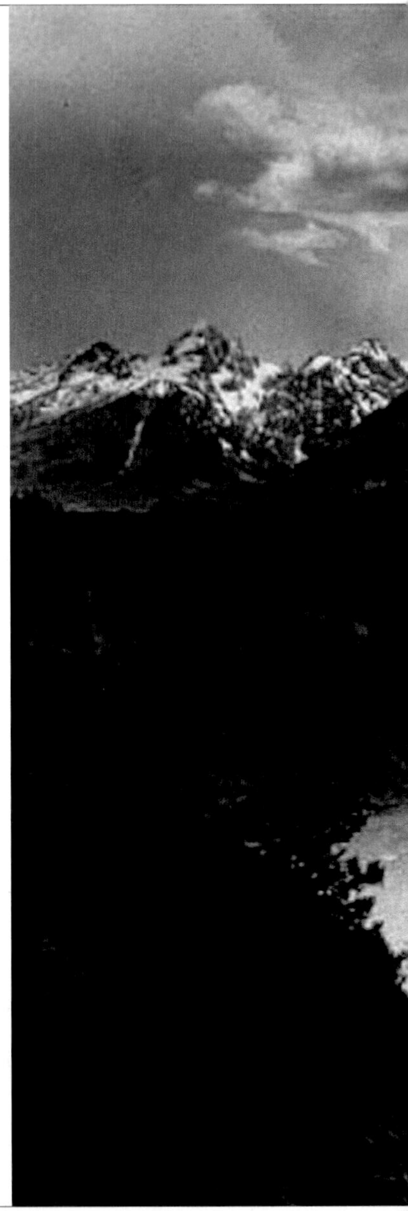

La chaîne des Tétons, ainsi baptisée par des trappeurs français, au-dessus d'une des innombrables rivières nommées Rivière du Serpent. Ces « Alpes d'Amérique », dont le sommet, Grand Téton, dépasse 4 000 m, se dressent presque verticalement au-dessus des lacs d'une haute plaine.

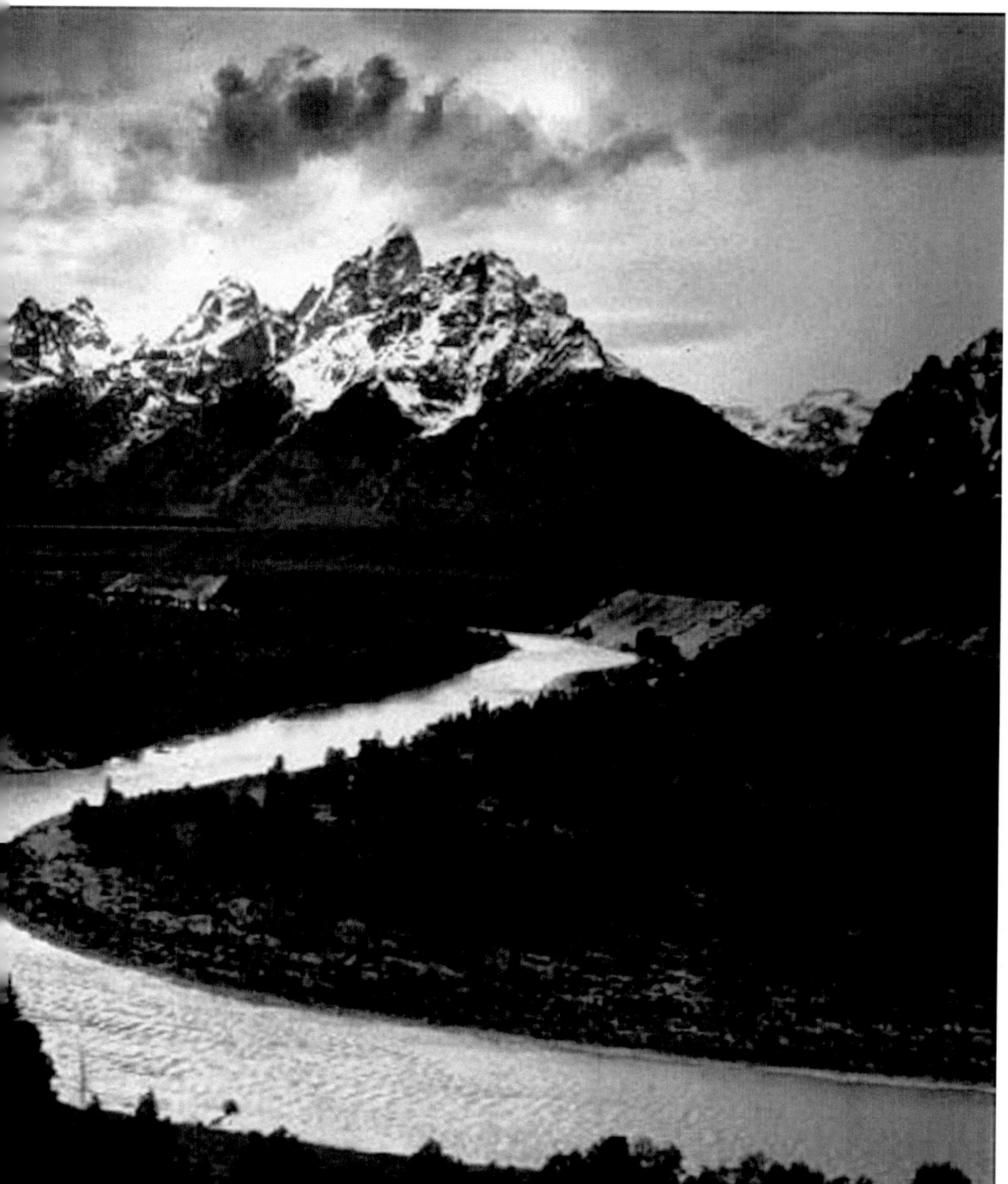

Plate 20. Michel Butor, "L'appel des Rocheuses." Photography by Ansel Adams and Edward Weston. *Réalités* 197 (June 1962): 76–77.

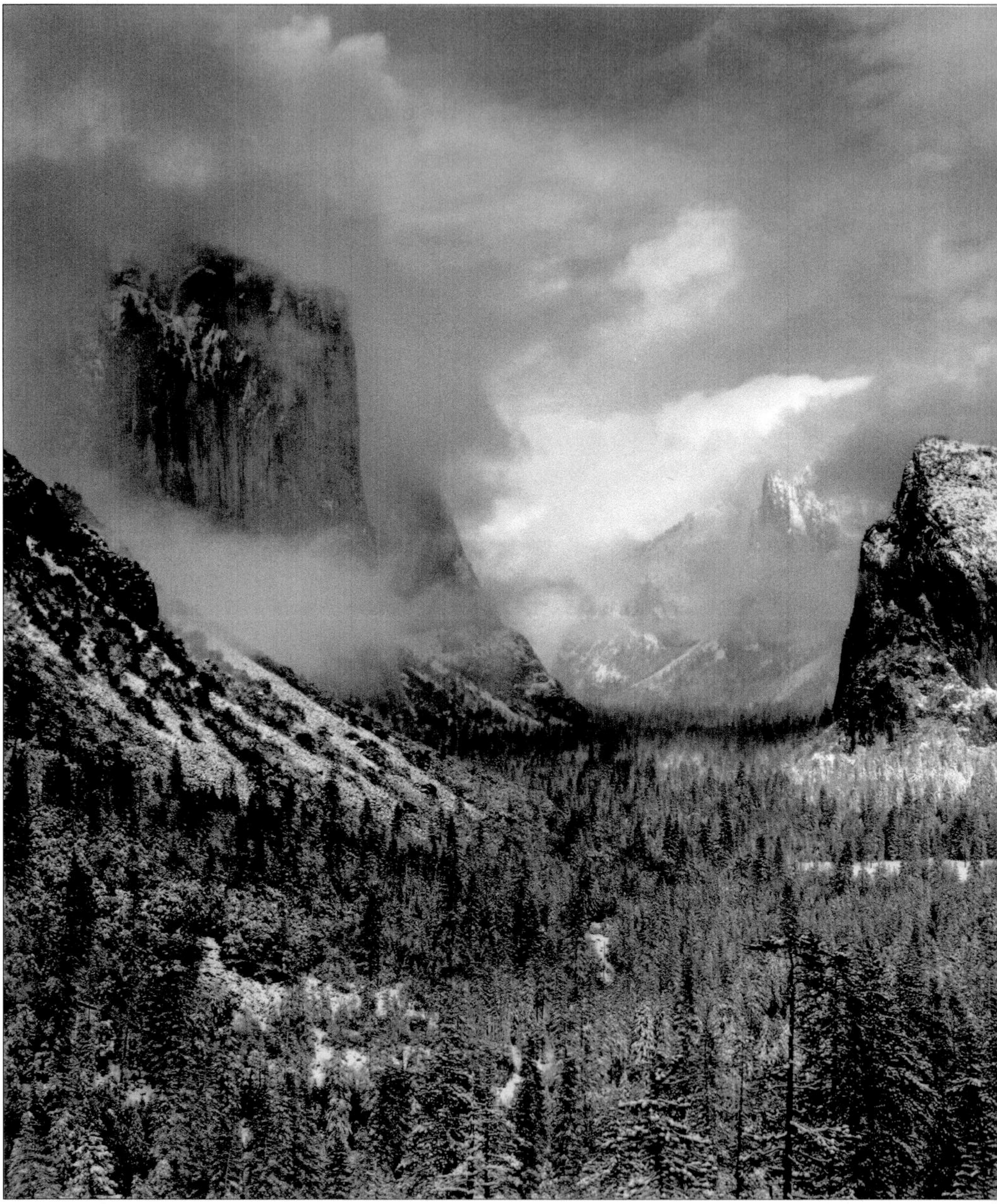

Plate 21. Michel Butor, "L'appel des Rocheuses."
Photography by Ansel Adams and Edward Weston.
Réalités 197 (June 1962): 78–79.

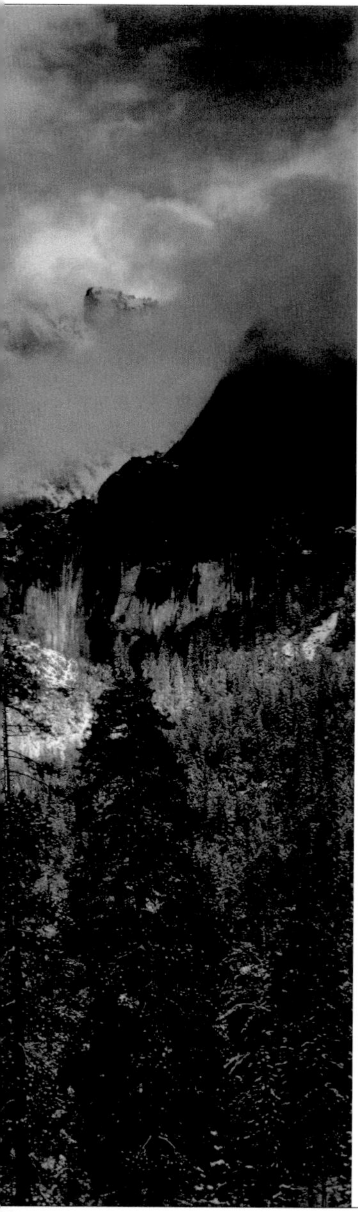

le bruit,
le grondement
répercuté
par les parois taillées
comme à coups
d'énormes couteaux,
le souffle,
la forge
du vent,
l'énorme râle
de la gueule
blanche et bleue,
toutes
les paillettes
de la neige
tombant
d'aiguille en aiguille,
le froissement
de ces rameaux,
mains
gantées de fer,
le grincement des branches
qui se tordent,
se déchirent
et tombent,
déclenchant
un geyser de plumes,
les jets
des chutes
déployant
leurs draperies de giclures,
et le bruit du vent
qui reprend
comme un hurlement.

Le Parc National du Yosemite, dans la Sierra Nevada, Californie, est une énorme région sauvage, dont les parties les plus fameuses et les plus accessibles, par exemple la Yosemite Valley, célèbre par ses chutes d'eau, que l'on voit ici lors d'une tempête d'hiver, attirent, au printemps et en été de véritables hordes de visiteurs venant de la région de San Francisco.

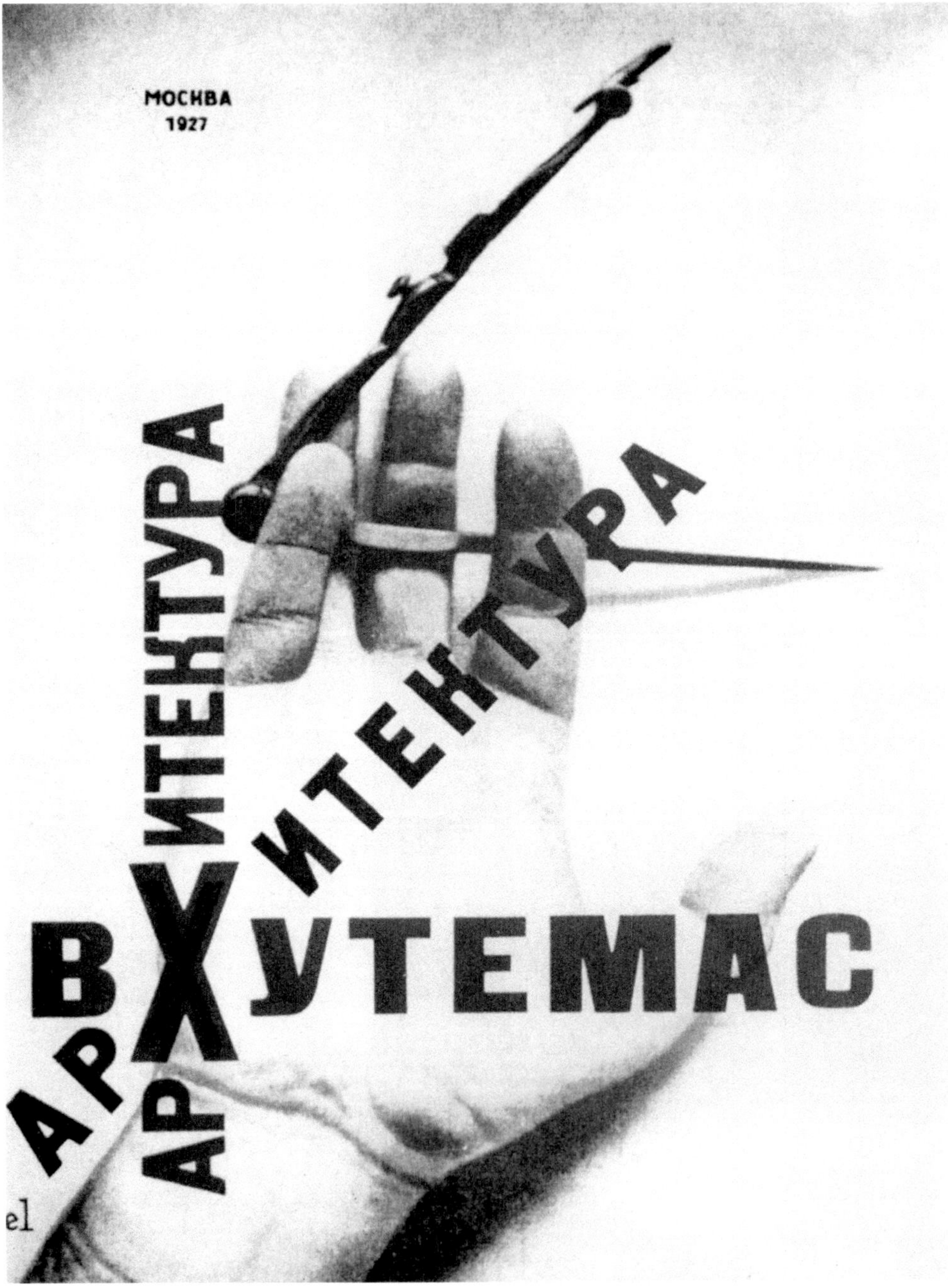

Plate 22. El Lissitzky, cover for the catalogue of the Vkhutemas School, Moscow, 1927. Reproduced in Sophie Lissitzky-Küppers, *El Lissitzky: Maler, Architekt, Typograph, Fotograph: Erinnerungen, Briefe, Schriften* (Dresden: V.E.B. Verlag der Kunst, 1967), Plate 134.

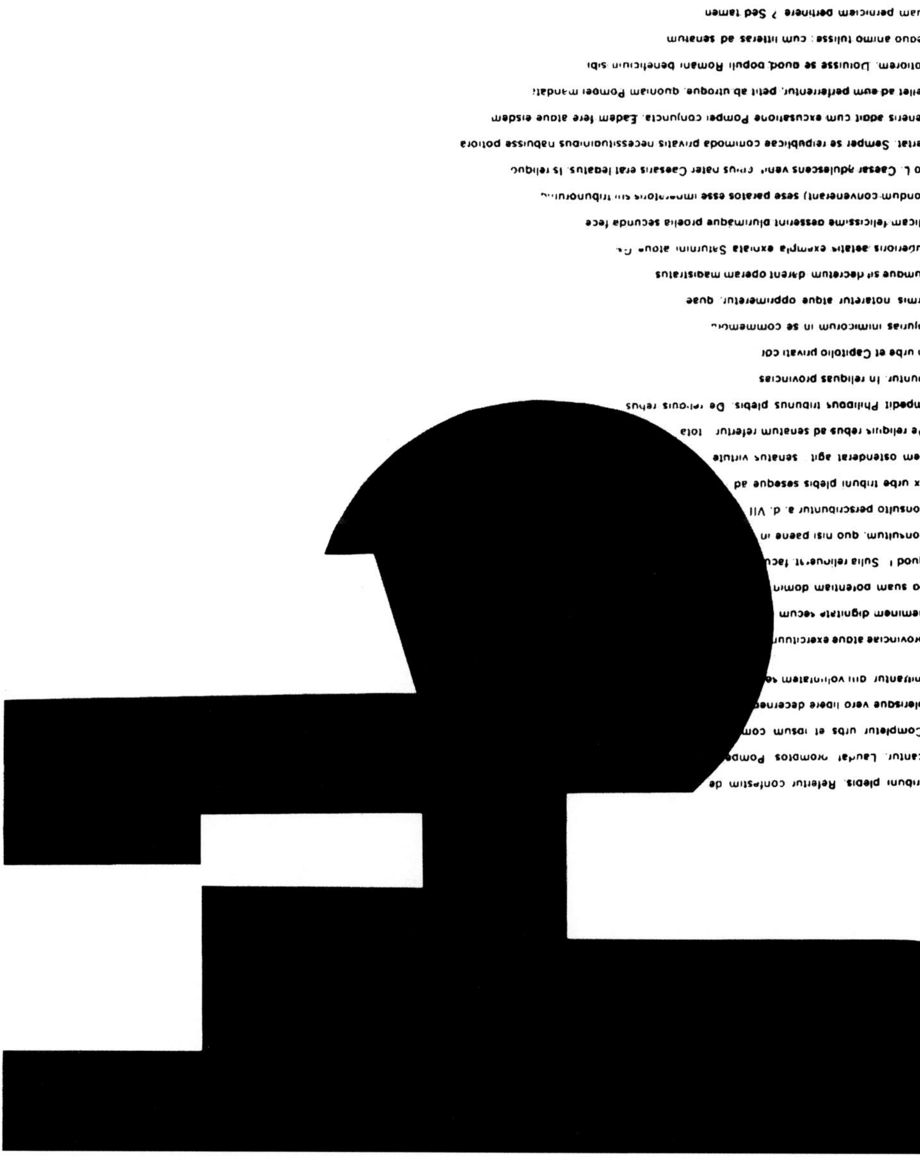

Plate 23. Bruno Lemenuel, *idiot le piano. Oui, un peu,* book-figure (random half-page), 1971. Reproduced by permission of the artist.

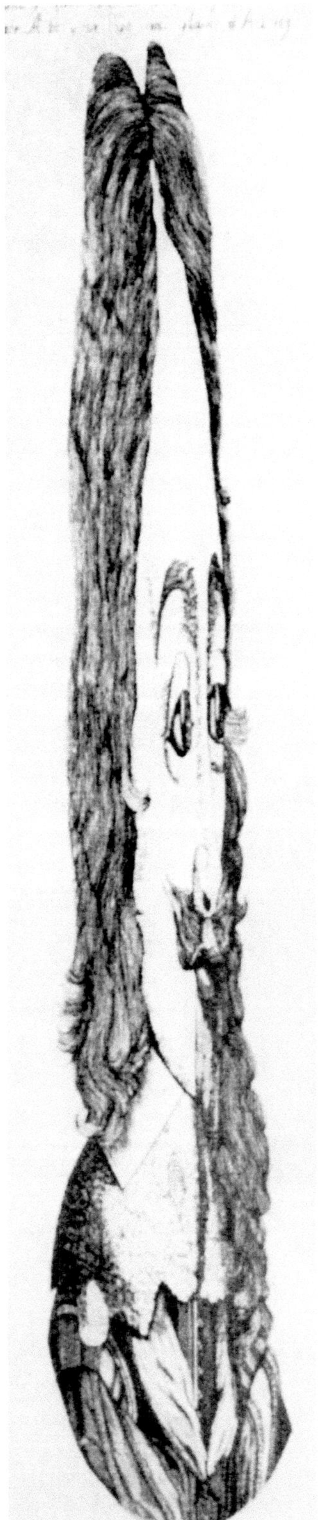

Plate 24a. Anonymous, *Secret Portrait of Charles I,* after 1649. Anthony d'Offay Collection, London. Reproduced in Jurgis Baltrušaitis, *Anamorphoses ou magie artificielle des effets merveilleux* (Paris: Olivier Perrin, 1969).

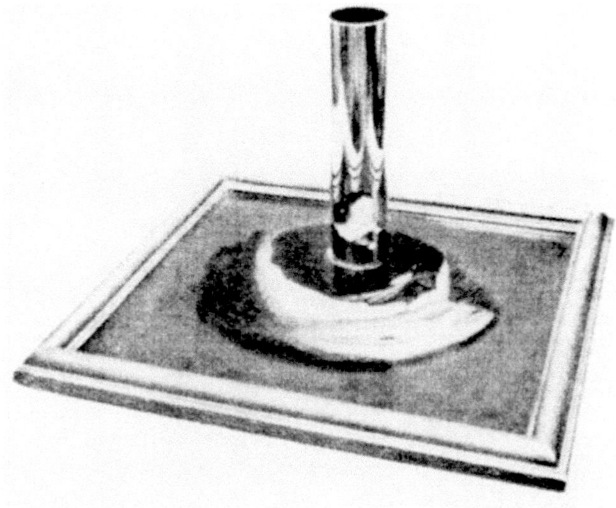

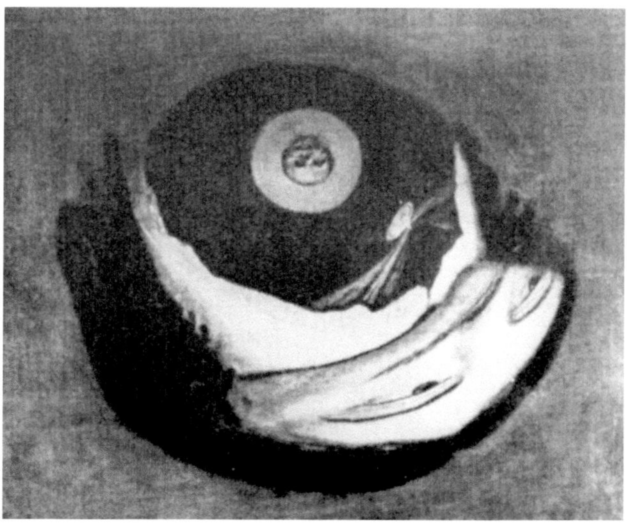

Plate 24b. Anonymous, *Anamorphic Portrait with Mirror of Charles I,* after 1649. Gripsholm Castle Museum, Stockholm. At the center of the work is a representation of a skull. Reproduced in Baltrušaitis, *Anamorphoses ou magie artificielle des effets merveilleux.*

NOTES ON FIGURES AND PLATES

Figures

FIGURE 1. Double-page spread chosen for its syntactical and plastic complexity. At the top of the page, in block italicized letters, the fragment of the statement *Si c'était le Nombre* [If it were the Number], which itself allows for two articulations: (1) *le voile* [the veil of the engagement between the Master and the Ocean] *chancellera, s'affalera, comme si c'était le Nombre* [will falter, collapse, as if it were the Number], and (2) *soucieux, expiatoire et muet rire que si c'était le Nombre, ce serait le Hasard* [anxious, expiatory, and muffled laughter that if it were the Number, it would be Chance]. These two sentences give rise to two different meanings: sentence 1 suggests the hypothesis that the possessor of meaning (the Master holding in his clenched fist the dice whose sum provides the meaning or Notion) will not yield to the blows of the Ocean (of Chance, of mere place) without releasing the dice, and thereby asserting meaning; sentence 2 stresses the fact that, even in this case, even if the work were to be produced, it would remain Chance, illogical [*non-sens*], and this the Master realizes and finds laughable. The segment *c'était le Nombre* appears here, therefore, in a kind of syntactical and semantic *suspension,* to which on the same page the syntagm *le Hasard* puts an end. However, the latter is also indexed at two different points of the discourse: as object of (3) *un coup de dés jamais n'abolira . . .* [a throw of dice never will abolish . . .], and as attribute of (4) *c'était le Nombre, ce serait* [were the Number, it would be . . .]. But this time, in the word's double anchoring, meaning is not thwarted but consolidated, and writing itself inscribes itself on the other space, that of the sea.

After which *choit la plume . . .* [falls the quill . . .], insofar as the signification that it could generate (as the author's pen) is itself no more than the trace of insurmountable confusion, or that the hesitation to throw the dice (which it embodied in the symbolic system of *Un coup de dés*) is trivial.

The commentary on the page's form would not only take time, but actually be interminable. Here I can only indicate the directions that the commentary should take: the nature of the different typographical bodies involved; their coded value in relation to meaning, a value that appears when referring to the other pages; the spatial positioning of the written fragments: here we are no longer in the presence of *blanks* (in plural), as with the intervals between letters in typography, but of *blankness*, of the sea, Chance, in which graphic signifiers are suspended. After italics, roman type will reappear on the following page, in the same body that was used before the *comme si, comme si* [as if, as if] began, and no longer in the future tense (*chancellera, s'affalera* [will falter, collapse]), but in the future anterior (*rien n'aura eu lieu que le lieu* [nothing will have taken place but the place]). Thus on this double-page are intimately combined the discourse's signified (what it says), its reference (what it speaks of, which is nothing but the literary metaphor of what it says), and its signifier (its plastic metaphor). But this combination itself is possible only so long as the signified is the unsignifiable. And it is in fact much more than a combination: it is figural space, already present in the space of the text, that seeps under the graphic signifier and makes it *float*. We are thus dealing with a relation of double reversal: the discourse of signification haunted from within by the deconstructions specific to Mallarmean stylistics, but affected in its exteriority of (graphic) signifier by the same "primary" spatial play.

FIGURE 2. The schematic rendering seeks to bring out the imbrication of the two spaces—figural and textual—in the dropped initial reproduced in Plate 1.

FIGURE 3. At first, thickness or difference is located in the holy Scriptures, whose imagery (in eleventh-century miniature painting, up to and including Duccio's painting) is a plastic signifier constructed analogically with the graphic signifier. With Masaccio, this thickness or difference shifts to the referential pole when desire ceases to *speak the world* through a symbolics (the Scriptures) and must represent a world that can no longer be accounted for by mythical discourse. This rotation defines the two axes between which will take place the deep-seated configurations upholding the major ideologies: to the vertical axis corresponds a type of symbolic ideology in which the designated (exteriority) is established according to an order of meaning (the *dispositio* of myth); to the horizontal axis corresponds a type of ideology of knowledge, where rejection takes on a form such that the object only "presents" itself as unsignified, and where desire sets out in search of signification (scientific discourse). These two axes coincide with the two kinds of representatives acknowledged by Freudian metapsychology (1915): word- and thing-presentations.

See *dispositio, foreclosure, knowledge, symbol, thing-presentation,* and *word-presentation* in the "Index of Concepts and German Expressions."

FIGURE 4. The aim is to produce a trapezoid ABC'D' on the plastic screen V (here seen from the back), such that the eye placed at O sees it *as if* it were a square ABCD placed *at right angles* to the screen, on the ground level where the spectator S is positioned. This *as if* presupposes that the support is treated as a transparent pane of glass: this constitutes the first perspectival rotation. As for the second, it is contained in the act of projection. Although there are several methods of projection, all have indeed a rotation as their precondition: that which allows the distance of the eye to the screen (OP) to be applied onto the latter (dP). The rectangular projection of O onto the screen defines P as the focal or vanishing point, while the projection by 90-degree rotation of the OP segment around P defines d as the distance point. With the first rotation, the screen opens onto a scene; with the second, the screen is treated as an opaque support waiting to be *scripted*, that is, upon which one must produce lines subject to rules and that facilitate recognition. The distance OP is that of designation, whereas the segments PA, dB, RD', which will determine the necessary foreshortening to *re-present* the square ABCD, define the invariable intervals that make possible the recognition of the represented (the scene) at the same time as the misrecognition of the representative (the scenography).

FIGURE 5. This is one of the projective methods. The segments Aa, Ab, etc., drag the eye toward the vanishing point's infinity: these are outlines [*tracés révélateurs*]. The segments Dza, Dyb, etc., will be *erased*: regulating lines [*tracés régulateurs*]. The oblique sometimes acts as if it were inscribed beyond the screen, at other times as if it were inscribed on it (but then it must remain unseen). In the first case, the oblique is a scene or figure-image; in the second, scenography or figure-form. The oblique holds a specific function in the elaboration of the phantasmatic "site": the anamorphosis will be the bringing to the fore of the oblique's illusionistic (scenic) function; the curvature or laterality of Cézannian space will be the bringing to the fore of its regulating (scenographic) function. Viking Eggeling's film *Diagonal Symphony* from 1921 scrutinizes the passage from one function to the other, thanks to movement.

See *anamorphosis*, *curvature*, *figure-form* and *figure-image* in the "Index of Concepts and German Expressions."

FIGURE 6. The distance axiom (Brunelleschi's and that of his successors) can be defined as: an object's apparent size is inversely proportional to its distance to the eye. Objects *a*, *b* being equal, if *a* stands at a distance *d*, and *b* at a distance *2d* from the eye, then *a* will appear twice as big as *b*. According to the angle axiom—which is that of classical optics (Euclid's eighth theorem)—the apparent difference between *a* and *b* will be that of angles α and β, so that *a* will appear smaller than *2b*. In this example we put the finger on the rejection of spatial curvature, of the subject's and the world's immanence in a single symbolic system. This rejection characterizes the classic position of the discursive or plastic signifier.

FIGURE 7. The pencil does not lift from the page: there are only two visible joints, both on Azor's back. The woman's silhouette is rendered with an uninterrupted line. The line's continuity and closure contribute to an impression of a kind of infallibility. The thousands of drawings produced in the final twenty months of Klee's life (between 1939 and 1940) will again betray this unflinching line, as if traced under dictation: the infallibility of the resurgent phantasmatics. Yet, from the beginning to the end, this "inner line" contains a potential critical and ironic power, which the titles reveal. This power is due to the fact that the line's relation to the support never authorizes *Durchsehen*, seeing-through, but instead refers the eye to the form and deformations it undergoes.

FIGURE 8. Although its content is the same, the diagram from *Pädagogisches Skizzenbuch* (Munich: Langen, 1925 [*Pedagogical Sketchbook*, trans. and introd. Sibyl Moholy-Nagy (London: Faber and Faber, 1968)]) reproduced in *Das bildnerische Denken* (ed. Jürg Spiller [Basel-Stuttgart: Benno Schwabe, 1956], 351 [*Paul Klee: The Thinking Eye*, ed. Jürg Spiller, trans. Ralph Manheim et al. (London: Percy Lund, Humphries & Co. Ltd., 1961), 351]) differs plastically from this sketch: in it one recognizes Klee's (left) hand. This diagram is one of the examples given at the Bauhaus, intended to highlight "the fundamental concepts of becoming and the translation of movement into form" (*Das bildnerische Denken*, 293 [*Paul Klee: The Thinking Eye*, 293; translation modified A.H.]), and, more specifically, to reveal particular aspects of these concepts and this formation. "Movement is inherent in all change.

The history of the work as genesis. The function of the work of art. The question of the various real forms of movement and the organic connection between them" (*Das bildnerische Denken*, 343 [*Paul Klee: The Thinking Eye*, 343]). The first example is based on the water mill, the third on the blood's circulation. Klee's initial hypothesis is that of a tripartite organism: active organ, intermediary (*mediale*) organ, and passive organ. One can, he writes, discuss "the concepts active, intermediary, and passive . . . in terms of linguistics: when I say *I drive*, the form is an active one; when I say *I am driven*, it is the linguistic expression of the passive; as for the intermediary form, it would be *I join, I integrate myself with, I ally myself with*" (*Das bildnerische Denken*, 343 [*Paul Klee: The Thinking Eye*, 343; translation modified A.H.]). In the example of the plant, "I. the active impulse is the ground from which the seed grows; relational complex {and not "rational," as the French translation would have it}: humus, seed, nutrition, growth, taking root, produce form I. / II. Having reached the light, the respiratory organs take shape in contact with open air: one, then two small leaves, followed by more leaves, and still more leaves. / III. The flower as outcome, at which point the plant's growth is over" (*Das bildnerische Denken*, 353 [*Paul Klee: The Thinking Eye*, 351; translation modified A.H.]). "What ranking to grant each of these traits? The answer depends on the point of view. In an ideal order, what takes precedence over everything else is the active. In the case of the human being, the impulse toward movement begins in the brain; it is here that thought resides, as father (*als Vater*) of all highly developed activity. From a material point of view, one would need to reverse this order and argue that it is the bone's solid mass that makes movement effective and that deserves pride of place. But it is pointless to try to pit these points of view against each other; what is essential is the organic bond, the result of the interdependence between these three elements" (*Das bildnerische Denken*, 343–344 [*Paul Klee: The Thinking Eye*, 343–344; translation modified A.H.]). Let us draw out from these rather phantasmatic remarks the following points. First, the theme of the work as a corpus that is not so much semiological as energetic, economic in the Freudian sense; second, in this economic corpus, priority given to the *Vater* (which, for the artwork, is drawing), at least from the point of view of causality through ideation, with its own distinctive insignia of *impulse* (*Anstosz*) and darkness; third, the attempt to reconcile active and passive into an organic totality, light and air having color as their equivalent in the plastic artwork; four, this tripartite division should be understood as another version of the double reversal: the *mediale* is the moment when imitative drawing (of the phantasies) is placed upside down and worked over for its own plastic qualities: this is the artist's moment, insofar as the artist is merely the tree trunk through which sap rises—a sap of which the artist is not the author, which is her or his *father*, and whose course the artist must reverse not once, but twice.

FIGURES 9 and 10. This diagram is meant to illustrate the properties of the intermediary (*mediale*) line, which endows the watercolor *Chosen Site* (Plate 13) with its linear energetics. *Calvi (Phantasmatic)* (Figure 9) and *Italian City* (Plate 15b) fall under the same "economic" layout. The line's secret does not lie in its representational power, but in the kind of *charge-discharge* it induces. In this case, the energetic quotient is low, as the line harnesses and tames it into a limited, though perceptible, network. This intermediary character stands in opposition to the active and passive characters, a classification system that should be related to the theory of the artwork's genesis and to that of the double reversal. One should not be surprised to see this *mediale* line recur frequently in the years 1926–1936, when Klee takes regular trips to the Mediterranean (South of France, Corsica, Italy, Egypt, Sicily). The harnessing of active, virile energy in the intermediary drawing goes hand in hand with the receptivity to color and passivity.

See *interworld* in the "Index of Concepts and German Expressions," and Plate 15b.

FIGURE 11. An example of displacement (*Verschiebung*).

See *displacement* in the "Index of Concepts and German Expressions."

FIGURE 12. One of those enigmatic inscriptions Freud uses to explain the process of secondary revision.

See Figures 13 and 14, Plate 18a, and *script (or writing): (pseudography)*, and *secondary revision* in the "Index of Concepts and German Expressions."

FIGURE 13. See Figure 12.

FIGURE 14. See Figure 12.

FIGURE 15. Possibility of incompatibilities, occupation of a single space by several bodies or of the same body by several positions, simultaneity of successiveness, and thus approach toward an a-temporality that will be the time-based equivalent of this "topological" space. Here, however, Picasso's work does not go beyond the deconstruction of silhouettes, of the outline [*tracé révélateur*]. Compare it to the line in Klee's *Town Square under Construction* (Plate 15a), where the incompatibilities belong to different levels, some of which, as in Picasso's drawing, fall under the figure-image (outlines [*traits révélateurs*]), while others fall under the figure-form (regulating lines [*traits régulateurs*]). The *Zwischenwelt* lies beyond the condensation of sketches on the same support, because it lies beyond the sketch. The latter, as in this drawing by Picasso, refers to the *phenomenology* of perception, whereas Klee's drawings and watercolors refer to the *economics* of sensory possibility.

See Plates 15a and 15b.

FIGURES 16–19. See *rebus* in the "Index of Concepts and German Expressions."

FIGURE 20. The double-page spreads are reproduced in facsimile in Figure 21. It is worth comparing Butor's layout with Mallarmé's (Figure 1). No doubt the problems are formulated differently in both cases: Mallarmé figuralizes a graphic signifier, while Butor must on top of this rid his text of its referential value (figure-image). Is this discrepancy responsible for the much more harmonic and much less melodic quality of *Illustrations*? Would the responsibility for this disparity not rest instead on the pictorial spaces taken, implicitly or not, as reference—that of impressionism for Mallarmé, of "abstraction" for Butor? And should we not attribute what one would be tempted to perceive (and critique) as "good form" in the latter to the convergence between specifically typographic requirements and the recognition on behalf of painters, since Delaunay and the Constructivists, of the support's thorough opacity? Such an attribution would do much to clarify the encounter between Butor and Lissitzky on the subject of the book-object.

See Figure 21, and Plates 20 and 21.

FIGURE 21. See Figure 20.

Plates

PLATE 1. See Figure 2.

PLATE 2A. In what space is the beginning of the text *Desiderii mei* inscribed? The complete folio still contains the rest of this text—*desideratas accipi epistolas qui* etc.—written linearly under the painted area in the same body (a mixture of capital and uncial letters: rounded D, E), followed by small Caroline letters. The text *Desiderii mei* appears in a sort of window cut into the image or as a panel placed between the two represented figures. This position implies a kind of equilibrium between textual and figural that is typical of this manuscript: the letter yields to plastic constraints (for example, to the division of the words; the initial uncial of *Desiderii* has been chosen over the capital letter because of its plastic and symbolic power), while the figure-image acts not so much as the text's reference as a seal, emblem, or pictogram that identifies its holy status.

See Plate 1.

PLATE 2B. Moses is called by the Lord. The attention to the integration of the graphic and plastic signifiers clearly comes across in the choice of letters: the initial V of *vocavit autem*, included in the figure-image, is written in capital letters so it can assume a symmetrical and rigid form that this figure requires (just as it does the O). On the contrary, the second V of the same word is written in uncials, which allows for the inclusion of the I for ornamental purposes: textualization of figural space, and figuralization of textual space. However, the intervals between the two operations remain negligible, keeping as they do the perception of the whole within the realm of minimum energetic expenditure, which is the hallmark of textuality.

See Plates 1 and 2a.

PLATE 2C. Here the interpenetration of text and image is slightly different, through the use of the *titulus* (*Judas; tabernaculum foederis domini*, the Ark of the Covenant) and of the scroll (*dixitque dominus: Judas ascendet ad bellum*). The holy text does not encroach on pictorial space, where it is reproduced as a scroll (cf. God's command in Plate 1); the *titulus* clearly subsumes the figures under the category of symbols illustrating a discourse. The entire composition could have been lifted from a fresco. The folio's layout comes close to that of Plate 3.

See Plates 1, 2a, and 2b.

PLATE 3. See Plates 1, 2a, 2b, and 2c.

PLATE 4. Here, even more so than in the previous image (Plate 3), one observes the overlapping of the two spaces: the way in which the image of the Evangelist is rendered is identical to the treatment of the initial I, that is, as "figurative letter," *Bilderschrift,* or hieroglyph, where the line can sometimes take on the role of silhouette of a representational image, sometimes the role of grapheme, and sometimes the role of ornamentation—without providing any plastic feature that would allow one to tell the difference.

See Plate 3.

PLATE 5. Space organized like a pictograph: the semantic units are identified by their reference (angel, shepherd, donkey, ox, dog), without the articulation between the units to form a narrative, which must be done orally. This implies that the figure-images are treated as units of language: recognizable, economical, likely to provoke a very small energetic discharge. The "curvature" (or difference) is evacuated from the image, assigned to the discourse's content as mystery. The captions included in the pictogram are intended to facilitate the scene's recognition by the cleric acting as guide and narrator.

See Plates 1, 2, 3, 4, 7, 9, 11, and 12.

PLATES 6–9. See Sections 3.1 and 4 in "*Veduta* on a Fragment of the 'History' of Desire."

PLATE 10. Exemplary moment of the rotation of the site (or non-site) of difference. The latter remains wedded to the mythical discourse of the Scriptures: just as she or he would before a *Maestà* or a Romanesque fresco, a narrator would have to weave the three episodes together (the exaction of the tribute money, the search for the coin, the guard's payment) into the story which is the Gospel's. The image thus continues to act as support for this story. At the same time, however, the image attracts and fixes upon itself the effects of the opacity. The eye sinks into plastic instability. No longer is difference to be found in the blanks of the signified of a discourse that relies on the depicted episodes; instead it reveals itself as plastic enigma in the depth, lighting effects, and chromatic rhythm, that is, in the *scene* or, to put it yet another way, the separation. Between the energetic charge (anxiety) to which this discovery can give rise, and the discharge of pleasure and recognition afforded by the *reading* of the image according to the New Testament, the equilibrium is shattered in favor of anxiety.

PLATES 11a, 11b, and 12. Duccio follows *to the letter* the Gospel according to Saint Luke, 23:8, where it is said that Herod mockingly makes Jesus wear a white robe before sending him before Pilate. As in several other panels, the story "reads" from bottom to top. It seems difficult to give plastic reasons for this organization; it is more likely due to a requirement of spatial continuity that reinforces the diachronic linearity of the story of the Passion.

PLATE 13. Jürg Spiller's commentary (in *Das bildnerische Denken*, 302) revolves around the question of rhythm and movement; in this text the reader will note with what frequency the terms *Verschiebung* (displacement), *Verdichtung* (condensation), and even *Lockerung* (loosening) occur—the very terms Freud uses to discuss the unconscious process (for example, in *The Ego and the Id*, *Lockerheit*, looseness, qualifies a state of the energy needed for its movement, a state of unbinding).

PLATES 14A and 14B. "*Woman and beast.* . . . The beast in man pursues the woman, who is not entirely unreceptive to this attention. The woman's relationship to animality. Unveiling a bit of the feminine psyche. Recognition of a truth one likes to mask. . . . / *Maiden in a Tree.* Technically more sophisticated, thanks to the deployment of different line intensities. First I etched the tree's outline. Then I tackled the tree's volume and the body's outline, and finally the body's volume and that of the two birds. / The poetic content is, in a way, equivalent to that of *Woman and Beast.* The animals (the two birds) are natural, and *paired.* In her virginity, the woman seeks to achieve individuality, without too much success. Critique of bourgeois society" (*Paul Klee: Journal*, trans. Pierre Klossowski [Paris: Grasset, 1959], 148–149 [*The Diaries of Paul Klee, 1898–1918*, ed. Felix Klee, trans. Pierre B. Schneider, R.Y. Zachary, and Max Knight (Berkeley, Los Angeles: University of California Press, 1964), 143–144; translation modified A.H.]). Klee reworked *Woman and Beast* in November 1903.

PLATE 15A. (1) Note that it is up to the eye to carry out the construction, and not merely the synthesis of objects, as is the case in Picasso's drawing (Figure 15), but that of space itself. Indeed the "square" is presented from the angle of the displacement (*Verschiebung*) of point of view, which is indicated by the large undulatory line upon which the houses and streets are laid out. This line registers on the support the eye's all-encompassing and incomplete movement as it sweeps a space from left to right, top to bottom, back to front—a movement betraying "a trajectory devoid of particular aim," "a restful walk" (*Das bildnerische Denken*, 123 [*Paul Klee: The Thinking Eye*—translation modified A.H.]). The objects are rendered according to these varying vantage points, but in simultaneity. The movement, usually ascribed to the I, to a subject, is here inscribed on a support and transferred on paper. What is inscribed on the latter is no longer only the retinal impression freed from its Euclidian script—that is, the curvature, or sensory thickness, as in Cézanne—but moreover, and at the same time, its architectural rendering (indicated by the word *Plan* written vertically, and more generally by the letters that not only perform a plastic function, but that, thanks to their legibility, make the viewer see that she or he is dealing with a cartographic surface). Such is the *Zwischenstadt.*

(2) "Even from the church tower the activity (*das Treiben*) on the square already looks funny. But imagine how it looks from where I am" (*Das bildnerische Denken*, 153; *Journal: Paul Klee*, trans. Klossowski, 297–298 [*Paul Klee: The Thinking Eye*, 153]). This "from where I am" is the non-site of the primary process. It would not require inordinate amounts of effort to show how what has been called Klee's humor relates to what Freud called the joke (*Witz*). In the former case, it is a question of plastic signifier; in the latter, of the linguistic signifier. But what both have in common is the deviation (*Abweichung*) from the order—perspectival for the plastic line [*le trait plastique*], syntactic and lexical in the case of

wit [*le trait d'esprit*]—to which the signifier that serves as context is subjected. This deviation comes about through a displacement (*Verschiebung*) that triggers a loss of balance, an absence, an anxiety, from which we recover thanks to the closure in secondary signification afforded by the play on words or, in Klee's work, the written title. Here the deviation is not between what is painted and what is scripted, but within painting itself, and it is script that neutralizes it.

See *anamorphosis, curvature, figure-form, figure-image*, and *interworld* in the "Index of Concepts and German Expressions," as well as Figure 15 and Plate 15b.

PLATE 15B. The image brings us back to the question of three-dimensional space. In his notes, Klee divides plastic value in this way: upper part: white, light; lower: dark, black; left: cold; right: warm; and center: gray. Without going further than lines and values, what we have here is an organization in which this energetic code is both respected and neutralized. Oppositions are indeed attenuated at the center, producing gray; but the interplay of the diagonals and the slightly tilted quasi-vertical lines thrusts the whole space toward the upper right-hand corner—an area supposed to be light and warm, yet where the eye encounters only dark values. Conversely, the lower part is treated in such a way as to keep heaviness in check: web of lines, mosaic of light values. Obviously, we find ourselves here with another example of *linear-medial* line, even of *linear-medial* construction (cf. Figures 9 and 10), endowed with a function not so much of reconciliation—however ardently desired such a reconciliation may be, in particular when coming into contact with the Italian city that, for Klee, was Naples from 1906 onward—but of perforation toward an invisible. The cubes are not cubic, since they show irregularities (obliqueness of vertical or horizontal lines, surfaces rendered in reverse perspective), and the play of values everywhere contradicts their consistency as full volumes: it is as if they are lit from within, or from nowhere, and translucent. What is thus offered is neither visual appearance nor architectural organization, but the Italian city as transcendence (trans-disappearing) in immanence (appearing), as interworld in the world, and as invisibility of the *Urbild* (the supporting withdrawn figure) beyond the visibility of the *Vorbild* (the figure in the foreground).

See Figures 9, 10, 15, and Plate 15a.

PLATES 16A and 16B. Compare these two plates with the two engravings from 1903 (Plates 14a and 14b). The line's rotation in relation to the support is that of the subject in relation to desire. In the engravings, we have an illusionistic depth of field and a female body presented in its apparent wholeness. In 1919, the window is broken, the sheet of paper mirrors voyeuristic desire, and this desire is reflected in the paper where it finds solace in irony: such is the function of the joke. In 1938, the I—the assumed subject of desire—has disappeared, as has the scene; what remain, suspended evenly across darkness, are the disconnected fragments of the body in pieces: a libidinal body oblivious to all secondary signification. The following remark by Klee proves that he was aware of the critical importance in the latter image of the figure's relation to the plastic support: "Like the human body, the figure (*Bild*), too, has a skeleton, muscles, skin. One can speak of a distinct anatomy of the figure. A figure whose object is the 'human nude' must be arranged (*gestalten*) not according to human anatomy, but to figural anatomy (*bildanatomisch*)" (1922; quoted in *Das bildnerische Denken*, 449 [*Paul Klee: The Thinking Eye*, 449; translation modified A.H.]).

See Plates 14a and 14b.

PLATE 17. It is not enough to say that the image betrays the word; rather the image casts doubt on the word. There is an element of play in the latter, since by taking it at face value (at its homophonic value) [*au pied de la lettre (au pied des homophonies)*], one arrives at several images. Thus what figurality there is in the word is confirmed by the image. It is precisely through this nonlinguistic polysemy that desire infiltrates discourse; or, to put it another way, it is this very infiltration that cleaves words. Hence Freud's insistence on analyzing the transposition in dream-work of words into images. In *Les mots dans la peinture*, Butor discusses and illustrates this word-image relation in the work of Magritte ([Paris: Skira, 1969], 73–93).

See *figural(ity)* in the "Index of Concepts and German Expressions."

PLATES 18A and 18B. See Figures 12, 13, and 14, and *script (or writing): (pseudography)* and *secondary revision* in the "Index of Concepts and German Expressions."

PLATE 19. I will point out only that Butor dedicated *Mobile* to Pollock. At stake is not the mobility of a subject crossing the field of an experience (be it perceptual, historical, social, or metaphysical), but the simultaneity of events deconstructing recognizable forms, beyond the secondary time and space where the I moves.

PLATES 20 and 21. See *reversal* in the "Index of Concepts and German Expressions."

PLATE 22. The horizontal ("Vkhutemas") and the vertical ("*Arkhitektura*") are printed in red, the diagonal in black; the X is red, overprinted in black. The coordinates are dictated by the revolution; they also form the author's initials; and the plastic rhyme of the compass relies on a play on words: the compass is the architect's tool, but also the sailor's, in both cases allowing one to take a bearing [*faire le point*]. The open hand connotes labor. The whole composition is highly "scripted," leaving little room for the event. At the time, the Vkhutemas School (name composed of the initials of the Russian words for "higher art and technical studios") represents Constructivism's highest point of achievement. Shortly thereafter, Lissitzky will lapse into politically edifying expressions, devoid of all critical reversal. What the eye already detects here is precisely this script: all libidinal energy is channeled into a firmly bound plastic unit; no unexpected slowing down interrupts the energy as it flows along its prescribed path (toward the upper right-hand corner—the area of progress and ideality). Legibility wins the day, at the expense of visibility. The correlation Lissitzky sought (see "Return, Auto-Illustration, Double Reversal," note 29) between the tension (*Spannung*) exerted by the content and that by the signifier results in the restoration of the economic principle.

PLATE 23. "Half-page" because Lemenuel clearly occupies the plastic expanse formed by the two-page spread. And "book-figure" rather than "book-object," since what is put forward in Butor's *Mobile* or *Illustrations* still refers to a state of painting (that of Mondrian, for example), and the graphic signifier's desired *reification* is achieved through a layout determined by an architectural, that is, essentially harmonic plastics (be it a Schönbergian harmony). By contrast, what Lemenuel is after is figurality as energy displacement and production of ephemeral forms. The reversal thus achieved does not operate on the opposition between script and figure-form, but on the deconstruction / construction opposition, the latter affecting the words as well as the plastic signifiers (lines, values). Here for example, not only is the text inverted with regard to the vertical axis of reading (Lissitzky's), but it is, moreover, a pseudography ("mute" text taken from sheets of Letraset lettering). Conversely, it is the black shape, heavily weighed down with passive energy, that occupies the position of a letter, blocking the path of reading with its menacing resistance.

See *curvature* and *script (or writing): (pseudography)* in the "Index of Concepts and German Expressions."

PLATES 24A and 24B. See *anamorphosis, curvature,* and *reversal* in the "Index of Concepts and German Expressions."

BIBLIOGRAPHY

This bibliography reproduces the Works Cited list included in the Klincksieck edition of *Discours, figure* (1971). English translations for many of these sources are provided in the notes of the chapters.

Ajame, P., Les yeux fertiles, *Europe,* 475–476 (nov.–déc. 1968).

Alberti, L.B., *Della pittura,* hrsg von H. Janitschek, in *Quellenschriften für Kunstgeschichte und Kunsttechnik des Mittelalters und der Renaissance,* Bd XI, Wien, Braumüller, 1877.

Alquié, F., *Philosophie du surréalisme,* Paris, Flammarion, 1955.

Apollinaire, G., *Calligrammes,* Paris, Gallimard, 1925.

Aragon, L., *Le crève-cœur,* Paris, Gallimard, 1941.

Arnold, L'univers théâtral d'Antonin Artaud, in *Lettres d'Antonin Artaud à Jean-Louis Barrault,* Paris, Bordas, 1952.

Artaud, A., *Le théâtre et son double, Œuvres complètes,* t. IV, Paris, Gallimard, 1964.

———. *Lettres à Jean-Louis Barrault,* Paris, Bordas, 1952.

———. *Pour en finir avec le jugement de Dieu,* Paris, K. édit., 1948.

Assunto, R., *Die Theorie des Schönen im Mittelalter,* Köln, Du Mont, 1963.

Aulagnier, Piera, Remarques sur le masochisme primaire, *L'arc,* 34 (1968).

Avron, D., Lemenuel, B., Lyotard, J.-F., Espace plastique et espace politique, *Revue d'esthétique,* 3–4, 1970.

Avron, D., Lyotard, J.-F., « A few words to sing » Sequenza III, *Musique en jeu,* 1, 1971.

Backès, Catherine, Continuité mythique et construction historique, *L'arc,* 34, 1968.

Baltrušaitis, J., *Anamorphoses ou magie artificielle des effets merveilleux,* Paris, O. Perrin, 1969.

Baron, R., *Science et sagesse chez Hugues de Saint-Victor,* Paris, Letielleux, 1957.

Barre, A., et Flocon, A., *La perspective curviligne,* Paris, Flammarion, 1968.

Barthes, R., *Le degré zéro de l'écriture,* Paris, Seuil, 1953.

———. Présentation, Recherches sémiologiques, *Communications,* 4, 1964.

———. Rhétorique de l'image, *ibid.*

———. Eléments de sémiologie, *ibid.*

Beaufret, J., Phusis et Technè, *Aletheia,* 1–2, janvier 1964.

Belaval, Y., Poésie et psychanalyse, *Cahiers de l'association internationale des études françaises,* 7, juin 1955.

Benveniste, E., Nature du signe linguistique, *Acta linguistica,* I, 1, 1939 (= *Problèmes de linguistique générale,* chap. IV).

———. Remarques sur la fonction du langage dans la découverte freudienne, *La psychanalyse,* I, 1956 (= *Problèmes . . . ,* chap. VII).

———. La nature des pronoms, in *For Roman Jakobson,* Mouton, La Haye, 1956 (= *Problèmes . . . ,* chap. xx).

———. De la subjectivité dans le langage, *Journal de psychologie,* juillet–septembre 1958 (= *Problèmes . . . ,* chap. xxi).

———. Le langage et l'expérience humaine, *Diogène,* 51, 1965.

———. *Problèmes de linguistique générale,* Paris, Gallimard, 1966.

Bergson, H., *Matière et mémoire,* Paris, Alcan, 1896.

———. *La pensée et le mouvant,* Paris, Alcan, 1934.

Berio, L., *Omaggio a Joyce,* 1959, Philips.

———. *Visage,* 1961, Candide.

———. *Sequenza III,* Harmonia Mundi, 1965.

Berti, L., *Masaccio,* Milan, 1964.

———. en collaboration avec P. Volponi, *Masaccio,* Milan, Rizzoli, 1968.

Blanchot, M., *L'espace littéraire,* Paris, Gallimard, 1955.

Braque, G., *Le jour et la nuit,* Paris, Gallimard, 1952.

Bremond, Cl., Le message narratif, *Communications,* 4, 1964.

Breton, A., *Les manifestes du surréalisme,* Paris, Sagittaire, 1946.

———. *Le surréalisme et la peinture,* Paris, Gallimard, 1965.

Brik, O.M., Rythme et syntaxe, tr. fr. in *Théorie de la littérature,* Paris, Seuil, 1965.

Brion-Guerry, Liliane, *Cézanne et l'expression de l'espace,* Paris, Albin Michel, 1966 (2e éd.).

Bruyne, E. De, *Etudes d'esthétique médiévale,* Rijksuniversität te Gent, Bruges, De tempel, 1946, t. I–III.

Butor, M., Le roman comme recherche (1955), *Répertoire,* Paris, Minuit, 1960.

———. *L'emploi du temps,* Paris, Minuit, 1956.

———. Intervention à Royaumont (1959), *Répertoire, loc. cit.*

———. L'appel des Rocheuses, *Réalités,* 197, juin 1962.

———. *Illustrations,* Paris, Gallimard, 1964.

———. Le livre comme objet, *Répertoire II,* Paris, Minuit, 1964.

———. Livret de *Jeu de miroirs de Votre Faust,* musique de H. Pousseur, Wergo, 1967.

———. Un tableau vu en détail, *Répertoire III,* Paris, Minuit, 1968.

———. *Les mots dans la peinture,* Paris, Skira, 1969.

Cagnetta, F., *De luxuria spirituali,* Paris, Le cadran solaire, 1967.

Chklovski, V., L'art comme procédé (1925), tr. fr. in *Théorie de la littérature,* Paris, Seuil, 1965.

Chomsky, N., *Syntactic Structures,* La Haye-Paris, Mouton, 1957.

Claudel, P., *L'art poétique,* Paris, Mercure de France, 1941.

———. *L'œil écoute,* Paris, Gallimard, 1946.

Cohen, J., *Structure du langage poétique,* Paris, Flammarion, 1966.

———. La comparaison poétique: essai de systématique, *Langages,* 12, décembre 1968.

Cooper, F.A., A reconstruction of Duccio's Maestà, *The Art Bulletin,* XLVII, juin 1965.

Cordroc'h, Marie, *Les trésors de la Bibliothèque nationale,* Département des manuscrits, Epoque romane, France méridionale, Paris, Publications filmées d'art et d'histoire, 1964.

Cummings, E.E., *50 Poems* (1940), tr. fr. in *Cinquante-huit poèmes,* Paris, Bourgois, 1968.

David, M.V., *Le débat sur les écritures et les hiéroglyphes aux dix-septième et dix-huitième siècles,* Paris, 1963.
Davies, G., *Vers une explication rationnelle du Coup de dés.* Essai d'exégèse mallarméenne, Paris, Corti, 1953.
Derrida, J., *De la grammatologie,* Paris, Minuit, 1967.
———. *L'écriture et la différence,* Paris, Seuil, 1967.
———. *La voix et le phénomène,* Paris, P.U.F., 1967.
Détienne, M., *Les maîtres de vérité dans la Grèce archaïque,* Paris, Maspero, 1966.
Diderot, D., *Lettre sur les aveugles* (1749), *Addition à la lettre sur les aveugles* (1782), in *Ecrits philosophiques,* Paris, Pauvert, 1964.
Diels, H., et Kranz, W., *Fragmente der Vorsokratiker,* Berlin, Weidmannsche Verlagsbuchhandlung, 1959, II.
Donati, P., *La Maestà di Duccio,* Sadea, Florence, 1965.
Dubois, J., *Le vocabulaire politique en France de 1868 à 1872,* Paris, Hachette, 1962.
———. Recherches lexicographiques: esquisse d'un dictionnaire structural, *Etudes de linguistique appliquée,* 1962.
Dufrenne, M., *Phénoménologie de l'expérience esthétique,* Paris, P.U.F., 1953, I–II.
———. *Le poétique,* Paris, P.U.F., 1963.
———. L'art est-il langage? (1966), in *Esthétique et philosophie,* Paris, Klincksieck, 1967.
———. La critique littéraire: structure et sens (1967), in *Esthétique et philosophie, loc. cit.*
———. A priori et philosophie de la Nature, *Quaderni della « Biblioteca filosofica di Torino »,* 21, 1967.
Eco, U., Poissons rouges et tigres en papier, *Les temps modernes,* 279, août–septembre 1969.
Ehrenzweig, A., *The Psychoanalysis of Artistic Vision and Hearing, An Introduction to a Theory of Unconscious Perception,* Londres, Routledge & Kegan Paul, 1953.
Eluard, P., *Les dessous d'une vie ou la pyramide humaine* (1926), in *Choix de poèmes,* Paris, Gallimard, 1941.
———. *La rose publique* (1934), *ibid.*
Favalelli, M., *Rébus,* Paris, P. Horay, 1964.
Février, J., *Histoire de l'écriture,* Paris, Payot, 1959.
Fink, E., Concepts thématiques et concepts opératoires (1957), in *Husserl,* Cahiers de Royaumont, Philosophie III, Paris, Minuit, 1959.
Flocon, A., en collaboration avec A. Barre, *La perspective curviligne,* Paris, Flammarion, 1968.
Focillon, H., *La vie des formes,* Paris, P.U.F., 1964.
Fonagy, I., Le langage poétique: forme et fonction, *Diogène,* 51, 1965.
Fraenkel, E., *Les dessins transconscients de St. Mallarmé,* Paris, Nizet, 1960.
Francastel, P., Espace génétique et espace plastique (1948), in *La réalité figurative: Éléments structurels de sociologie de l'art,* Paris, Gonthier, 1965.
———. Valeurs socio-psychologiques de l'espace-temps figuratif de la Renaissance, *Année sociologique,* 3e série, 1963, in *Etudes de sociologie de l'art,* Paris, Denoël-Gonthier, 1970.
———. *Peinture et société,* Paris, Gallimard, 1965.

———. *La figure et le lieu,* Paris, Gallimard, 1967.

Frege, G., Über Sinn und Bedeutung, *Zeitschrift für Philosophie und philosophische Kritik,* 100, 1892.

———. trad. anglaise du précédent: On Sense and Reference, in *Philosophical Writings,* Blackwell, Oxford, 1960.

———. Compte rendu de *Philosophie der Arithmetik* de Husserl, *Zeitschrift für Philosophie und philosophische Kritik,* 108, 1894.

Freud, S., *Aus den Anfängen der Psychoanalyse,* Londres, Imago, 1950; trad. fr., *Naissance de la psychanalyse. Lettres à Fliess, notes et plans,* Paris, P.U.F., 1956.

———. *Studien über Hysterie* (en collaboration avec Breuer) (1895), *Gesammelte Werke,* I.

———. Über die Berechtigung, von der Neurasthenie einen bestimmten Symptomkomplex als « Angstneurose » abzutrennen (1895) GW, I.

———. *Die Traumdeutung* (1900), GW, II/III; tr. fr., *L'interprétation des rêves,* Paris, P.U.F., 1967.

———. *Drei Abhandlungen zur Sexualtheorie* (1905), GW, V; tr. fr., *Trois essais sur la théorie de la sexualité,* Paris, Gallimard, 1962.

———. *Der Witz und seine Beziehung zum Unbewussten* (1905), GW, VI; tr. fr., *Le mot d'esprit et son rapport avec l'inconscient,* Paris, Gallimard, 1953.

———. Der Dichter und das Phantasieren (1908), GW, VII.

———. Formulierungen über die zwei Prinzipien des psychischen Geschehens (1911), GW, VIII.

———. Beiträge zur Psychologie des Liebeslebens (1912), GW, VIII; tr. fr. in *La vie sexuelle,* Paris, P.U.F., 1970.

———. Ratschläge für den Artz bei der psychoanalytischen Behandlung (1912), GW, VIII; tr. fr., Conseils aux médecins sur le traitement psychanalytique, in *De la technique psychanalytique,* Paris, P.U.F., 1953.

———. Zur Einführung des Narzissmus (1914), GW, X; tr. fr., Pour introduire le narcissisme, in *La vie sexuelle, op. cit.*

———. Triebe und Triebschicksale (1915), GW, X; tr. fr., Les pulsions et leurs destins, in *Métapsychologie,* Paris, Gallimard, 1952.

———. Die Verdrängung (1915), *ibid.;* tr. fr., Le refoulement, *ibid.*

———. Das Unbewusste (1915), *ibid.* tr. fr., L'inconscient, *ibid.*

———. *Vorlesungen zur Einführung in die Psychoanalyse* (1916–1917), GW, XI; tr. fr., *Introduction à la psychanalyse,* Paris, Payot, 1945.

———. Metapsychologische Ergänzung zur Traumlehre (1917), GW, X; tr. fr., Complément métapsychologique à la doctrine des rêves, in *Métapsychologie, op. cit.*

———. Aus der Geschichte einer infantilen Neurose (1918), GW, XII; tr. fr., Extrait de l'histoire d'une névrose infantile: l'Homme aux loups, in *Cinq psychanalyses,* Paris, P.U.F., 1954.

———. « Ein Kind wird geschlagen » (1919), GW, XII.

———. Das Unheimliche (1919), GW, XII; tr. fr., L'inquiétante étrangeté in *Essais de psychanalyse appliquée,* Paris, Gallimard, 1933.

———. Jenseits des Lustprinzips (1920), GW, XIII; tr. fr., Au-delà du principe de plaisir, in *Essais de psychanalyse,* Paris, Payot, 1948.

———. Massenpsychologie und Ich-Analyse (1921), *ibid.*; tr. fr., Psychologie collective et analyse du moi, *ibid.*

———. Das Ich und das Es (1923), *ibid.*; tr. fr., Le moi et le Soi, in *Essais de psychanalyse, op. cit.*

———. Introduction to *The Psychology of Day-Dreams,* by J. Varendonck, Allen & Unwin, Londres (1922), GW, XIII.

———. « Psychoanalyse » (1923), GW, XIII.

———. Das ökonomische Problem des Masochismus (1924), GW, XIII.

———. Die Verneinung (1925), GW, XIV.

———. Einige psychische Folgen des anatomischen Geschlechtsunterschieds (1925), GW, XIV; tr. fr., Quelques conséquences psychiques de la différence anatomique des sexes, in *La vie sexuelle,* Paris, P.U.F., 1970.

———. *Hemmung, Symptom und Angst* (1926), GW, XIV; tr. fr., *Inhibition, symptôme et angoisse,* Paris, P.U.F., 1965.

———. *Das Unbehagen in der Kultur* (1930), GW, XIV; tr. fr., *Malaise dans la civilisation,* Paris, Denoël & Steele, 1932.

———. Konstruktionen in der Analyse (1937), GW, XVI.

———. *Der Mann Moses und die monotheistische Religion* (1939), GW, XVI; tr. fr., *Moïse et le monothéisme,* Paris, Gallimard, 1948.

Genette, G., *Figures,* Paris, Seuil, 1966.

———. *Figures* II, Paris, Seuil, 1969.

Ghyka, M., *Proportions dans la nature et dans l'art,* Paris, Gallimard, 1932, I–II.

Girault-Duvivier, Ch.-P., *Grammaire des grammaires,* Paris, Janet et Cotelle, 1822.

Godel, R., *Les sources manuscrites du Cours de linguistique générale de Ferdinand de Saussure,* Genève, Droz et Minard, 1957.

Goldstein, K., Über Farbenamnesie, *Psychologische Forschung,* 1925.

Goldstein, K. et Rosenthal, G., Zur Problem der Wirkung der Farben auf dem Organismus, *Schweizer Archiv für Neurologie und Psychiatrie,* 1930.

Grabar, A., Plotin et les origines de l'esthétique médiévale, *Cahiers archéologiques,* I, 1945.

Grabar, A. et Nordenfalk, G., *Early Medieval Painting from the Fourth to the Eleventh Century,* Lausanne, 1957.

Granger, G.-G., *Pensée formelle et sciences de l'homme,* Paris, Aubier, 1965.

Green, A., Le narcissisme primaire: structure ou état, *L'inconscient,* I et II, 1967.

———. *Un œil en trop,* Paris, Minuit, 1969.

Greimas, A.-J., *Sémantique structurale,* Paris, Larousse, 1966.

Grohmann, W., *Paul Klee,* Paris, Cercle d'Art, 1968.

Hahnloser, L., *Villard de Honnecourt: Kritische Gesamtausgabe des Bauhüttenbuches,* Vienne, Schnoll, 1935.

Halliday, M.A.K., The Linguistic Study of Literary Texts, in *Proceedings of the IX International Congress of Linguists,* Paris-La Haye, Mouton, 1964.

Harris, Z.S., *Methods in Structural Linguistics,* University of Chicago Press, Chicago, 1951.

Hegel, G.W.F., *Phänomenologie des Geistes* (1807), hrsg Hoffmeister, Hambourg, Meiner, 1952.

———. *La phénoménologie de l'esprit,* tr. fr., Paris, Aubier, 1939–1941, I et II.

———. *System der Philosophie* (1817), *Sämtliche Werke,* hrsg Glockner, Stuttgart, Frommann, 1939, t. X.

———. *Principes de la philosophie du droit* (1820), tr. fr., Paris, Gallimard, 1940.

———. *Leçons d'histoire de la philosophie* (1823–1824), tr. fr., Paris, Gallimard, 1954.

———. *Aesthetik* (1818–1829), *Sämtliche Werke, op. cit.,* t. XII–XIV.

Hugues de Saint-Victor, *Opera, Patrologia latina,* Migne édit., Paris, 1844–1855, t. CLXXV–CLXXVII.

Husserl, E., *Logische Untersuchungen* (1900–1901), Halle, Niemeyer, 1913.

———. *Ideen zu einer reinen Phänomenologie und phänomenologischen Philosophie,* I, *Jahrbuch für Philosophie und phänomenologische Forschung,* I, 1913.

———. *Leçons pour une phénoménologie de la conscience intime du temps* (1928), tr. fr., Paris, P.U.F., 1964.

———. *Formale und transzendantale Logik, Jahrbuch . . . , op. cit.,* X., 1929.

———. *Méditations cartésiennes,* Paris, Vrin, 1931.

———. Die Krisis der europäischen Wissenschaften und die transzendantale Phänomenologie, 1, *Philosophia,* Belgrade, 1936.

Hyppolite, J., *Introduction à la Philosophie de l'histoire de Hegel,* Paris, Rivière, 1949.

———. *Logique et existence,* Paris, P.U.F., 1953.

———. Commentaire parlé sur la *Verneinung* de Freud (1954), *La psychanalyse,* 1, Paris, P.U.F., 1965.

Irigaray, Luce, Du fantasme et du verbe, *L'arc,* 34, 1968.

Isaacs, Susan, Nature et fonction du phantasme (1952), tr. fr., *La psychanalyse,* 5, 1959.

Jacob, A., *Temps et langage,* Paris, Colin, 1967.

Jakobson, R., L'aspect phonologique et l'aspect grammatical dans leurs interrelations (1948), in *Essais de linguistique générale,* Paris, Minuit, 1963.

———. Le langage commun des linguistes et des anthropologues (1952), *ibid.*

———. Deux aspects du langage et deux types d'aphasie (1956), *ibid.*

———. Linguistique et poétique (1960), *ibid.*

Jakobson, R. et Halle, M., Phonologie et phonétique (1956), in Jakobson, R., *Essais . . . , op. cit.*

Jones, E., *Hamlet et Œdipe* (1949), tr. fr., Paris, Gallimard, 1967.

Kandinsky, W., *Du spirituel dans l'art, en particulier dans la peinture* (1912), tr. fr., Paris, Denoël-Gonthier, 1969.

———. Séminaire sur la couleur, *Bauhaus,* catalogue de l'exposition aux Musées d'Art moderne, Paris, avril–juin 1969.

Kant, E., *Essai pour introduire en philosophie le concept de grandeur négative* (1763), tr. fr., Paris, Vrin, 1949.

Kaufmann, P., *L'expérience émotionnelle de l'espace,* Paris, Vrin, 1967.

Klee, F., *Paul Klee, Leben und Werk in Dokumenten,* ausgewählt aus den nachgelassenen

Aufzeichnungen und den unveröffentlichten Briefen, Zürich, Diogenes, 1960; tr. fr., *P. Klee par lui-même et par son fils Félix Klee,* Paris, Les libraires associés, 1963.

Klee, P., Über das Licht, *Der Sturm,* Berlin, 1913.

———. Schöpferische Konfession, *Tribüne der Kunst und Zeit,* 13, Berlin, 1920.

———. Wege der Naturstudiums, *Staatliches Bauhaus in Weimar,* Weimar-Münich, Bauhaus Verlag, 1923.

———. Über die moderne Kunst (Conférence d'Iéna), 1924, in Jürg Spiller édit.: P. Klee, *Das bildnerische Denken,* Bâle-Stuttgart, B. Schwabe, 1956.

———. Pädagogisches Skizzenbuch, Münich, Langen, 1925.

———. Exakter Versuch in Bereich der Kunst, *Bauhaus,* 11, Dessau, 1928.

———. *Théorie de l'art moderne,* Genève, Gonthier, 1964.

———. *Tagebücher* (1898–1918), F. Klee édit., Cologne, Dumont-Schauberg, 1956; tr. fr., *Journal,* Paris, Grasset, 1959.

Klein, Melanie, Infantile anxiety situations reflected in a work of art and the creative impulse (1929), in *Contributions to Psycho-Analysis,* Londres, Hogarth Press, 1948.

Koyré, A., *Etudes galiléennes,* Paris, Hermann, 1966.

Kranz, W., v. Diels, H.

Kris, E., *Psychoanalytical Explorations in Art,* New York, International University Press, 1952.

Lacan, J., La relation d'objet et les structures freudiennes (1956–1957), résumés des séminaires, *Bulletin de Psychologie,* X.

———. *Ecrits,* Paris, Seuil, 1966.

Laplanche, J., Interpréter [avec] Freud, *L'arc,* 34, 1968.

Laplanche, J. et Leclaire, S., L'inconscient. Une étude psychanalytique, *Les temps modernes,* 183, juillet 1961.

Laplanche, J. et Pontalis, J.B., Fantasme originaire, fantasme des origines, origines du fantasme, *Les temps modernes,* 215, avril 1964.

———. *Vocabulaire de la psychanalyse,* Paris, P.U.F., 1967.

Lascault, G., L'Egypte des égarements, *Critique,* 260, janvier 1969.

Leclaire, S., en collaboration avec Laplanche, J., L'inconscient. Une étude psychanalytique, *Les temps modernes,* 183, juillet 1961.

———. *Psychanalyser,* Paris, Seuil, 1968.

Le Goff, J., *La Civilisation de l'Occident médiéval,* Paris, Arthaud, 1967.

Lemenuel, B., en collaboration avec Avron, D. et Lyotard, J.-F., Espace plastique et espace politique, *Revue d'esthétique,* 3–4, 1970.

———. *Idiot le piano. Oui, un peu,* livre-figure (à paraître).

Léonard de Vinci, *Les carnets* (édition et traduction Louise Servicen), Paris, Gallimard, 1942.

Lerch, E., Vom Wesen des sprachlichen Zeichens. Zeichen oder Symbol? *Acta linguistica,* I, 3, 1939.

Leroi-Gourhan, A., *Le geste et la parole,* Paris, Albin Michel, 1965, I et II.

Levinas, E., *Totalité et infini,* La Haye, M. Nijhoff, 1961.

———. *Quatre lectures talmudiques,* Paris, Minuit, 1968.

———. Humanisme et anarchie, *Revue internationale de philosophie,* 85–86, 1968.
Lévi-Strauss, Cl., Langage et société (1951), in *Anthropologie structurale,* Paris, Plon, 1958.
———. La notion de structure en ethnologie (1952), *ibid.*
———. La structure des mythes (1955), *ibid.*
———. *La pensée sauvage,* Paris, Plon, 1962.
———. La geste d'Asdiwal, *Annuaire de l'Ecole pratique des Hautes Etudes,* 1958–1959.
———. La structure et la forme. Réflexions sur un ouvrage de Vladimir Propp, *Cahiers de l'Institut de Science économique appliquée,* 99, série M, 7, mars 1960.
Lhote, A., *La peinture, le cœur et l'esprit* (1933), augmenté de *Parlons peinture* (1937), Paris, Denoël, 1950.
———. Traité du paysage (1939), in *Traités du paysage et de la figure,* Paris, Grasset, 1958.
———. *Traité de la figure* (1950), *ibid.*
———. *Les invariants plastiques* (J. Cassou édit.), Paris, Hermann, 1967.
Lissitzky, El, Topographie der Typographie (1923), in Lissitzky-Küppers, S. édit., *El Lissitzky. Maler, Architekt, Typograf, Fotograf. Erinnerungen, Briefe, Schriften,* Dresde, V.E.B. Verlag der Kunst, 1967.
———. Typographische Tatsachen (1925), *ibid.*
———. Unser Buch (1926–1927), *ibid.*
Lissitzky-Küppers, Sophie, v. Lissitzky.
Lyotard, J.-F., Note sur l'approche psychanalytique des expressions littéraires et artistiques, Contribution à un *Rapport international de l'U.N.E.S.C.O.* (exemplaires dactylographiés), juin 1969.
———. A la place de l'homme, l'expression, *Esprit,* juillet–août 1969.
———. La place de l'aliénation dans le retournement marxiste, *Les temps modernes,* 279, août–septembre 1969.
———. Œdipe juif, *Critique,* 277, juin 1970.
———. La théorie, *VH 101,* été 1970.
———. Notes sur la fonction critique de l'œuvre, *Revue d'esthétique,* 3–4, 1970.
———. en collaboration avec Avron, D., et Lemenuel, B., Espace plastique et espace politique, *ibid.*
———. en collaboration avec Avron, D., « A few words to sing » Sequenza III, *Musique en jeu,* 2, 1971.
Lyotard-May, Andrée, A propos du « langage des images », *Revue d'esthétique,* 1, 1969.
Mallarmé, St., *Œuvres complètes,* Paris, Gallimard, 1945.
———. *Un coup de dés jamais n'abolira le hasard,* Paris, Gallimard, 1914.
———. Lettre à Villiers (septembre 1866), *La table ronde,* août 1952.
Mandel, G., *Les manuscrits à peintures,* Paris, Pont-Royal, 1964.
Mannoni, O., Le Théâtre du point de vue imaginaire, *La psychanalyse,* 5, 1959.
Marin, L., Signe et représentation: Philippe de Champaigne et Port-Royal, *Annales. Economies, Sociétés, Civilisations,* juillet 1969.
Martin, R., Les idées actuelles sur la structure de la pensée logique, in *Notion de structure et structure de la connaissance* (XXe semaine de Synthèse, avril 1956), Paris, Albin Michel, 1957.
———. *Logique contemporaine et formalisation,* Paris, P.U.F., 1964.

Martinet, A., La double articulation du langage (1949–1957–1965), in *La linguistique synchronique,* Paris, P.U.F., 1965.

———. *Eléments de linguistique générale* (1960), Paris, Colin, 1966.

———. Le mot, *Diogène,* 51, 1965.

Marx, K., Kritik des hegelschen Staatsrechts (1842), *Marx-Engels Werke,* Berlin, Dietz Verlag, I, 1962.

Mauclair, C., *Mallarmé chez lui,* Paris, Grasset, 1935.

Mauron, Ch., *Des métaphores obsédantes au mythe personnel,* Paris, Corti, 1963.

Merleau-Ponty, M., *Phénoménologie de la perception,* Paris, Gallimard, 1945.

———. Pages d' « Introduction à la prose du monde » (circa 1951), *Revue de Métaphysique et de Morale,* 2, avril–juin 1967.

———. Le langage indirect et les voix du silence, in *Signes,* Paris, Gallimard, 1960.

———. *L'œil et l'esprit* (1961), Paris, Gallimard, 1964.

———. *Le visible et l'invisible,* Paris, Gallimard, 1964.

Mondor, H., *E. Lefébure. Sa vie, ses lettres à Mallarmé,* Paris, Gallimard, 1951.

Mouloud, N., *La peinture et l'espace. Recherche sur les conditions formelles de l'expérience esthétique,* Paris, P.U.F., 1964.

Muche, G., Paul Klee, *Frankfurter Allgemeine Zeitung,* 30 juin 1956.

Nassif, J., Le fantasme dans « On bat un enfant », *Cahiers pour l'analyse,* 7, mars–avril 1967.

Nordenfalk, G., en collaboration avec Grabar, A., *Early Medieval Painting from the Fourth to the Eleventh Century,* Lausanne, 1957.

Ogden, C.K., et Richards, I.A., *The Meaning of Meaning,* Londres, Kegan Paul, 1936.

Ortigues, E., *Le discours et le symbole,* Paris, Aubier, 1964.

Osgood, C.E., Suci, G.J., Tannenbaum, P.H., *The Measurement of Meaning,* Urbana, Illinois, 1957.

Panofsky, E., Die Perspektive als « symbolische Form », *Vorträge der Bibliothek Warburg,* Leipzig-Berlin, 1924–1925.

———. *Studies in Iconology: Humanistic Themes in the Art of the Renaissance,* New York, Oxford University Press, 1939.

———. *The Codex Huygens and Leonardo da Vinci's Art Theory,* Londres, Studies of the Warburg Institute, 1940.

———. *Architecture gothique et pensée scolastique* (1951), tr. fr., Paris, Minuit, 1967.

———. *Galileo as a Critic of the Arts,* La Haye, 1954.

———. *Meaning in the Visual Arts: Papers in and on Art History,* New York, Doubleday and Co., 1955.

———. *Renaissance and Renascences,* Uppsala, Almquist & Wiksells, Boktryckeri Aktiebolag, 1960, I et II.

———. *Essais d'iconologie,* tr. fr., Paris, Gallimard, 1967.

Parain, Br., *Recherches sur la nature et les fonctions du langage,* Paris, Gallimard, 1952.

Paris, J., *L'espace et le regard,* Paris, Seuil, 1965.

Parronchi, A., *Masaccio,* Florence, Sadea-Sansoni, 1966.

Passeron, R., *L'œuvre picturale et les fonctions de l'apparence,* Paris, Vrin, 1962.

Peignot, J., *De l'écriture à la typographie,* Paris, Gallimard, 1967.

Peirce, Ch. S., *Collected Papers* (Hartshorne et Weiss édit.), Cambridge (Mass.), Harvard Univ. Press, 1931–1935, vol. II.

Péret, B., Le déshonneur des poètes (février 1945), in *Socialisme ou Barbarie,* 29, décembre 1959–février 1960.

Pichette, H., *Les épiphanies,* Paris, K. éditeur, 1948.

Poe, E.A., Le portrait ovale (1853), tr. fr. Ch. Baudelaire, in Poe, *Œuvres en prose,* Paris, Gallimard, 1951.

Pontalis, J.B., L'utopie freudienne, *L'arc,* 34, 1965.

———. en collaboration avec Laplanche, J., Fantasme originaire, fantasme des origines, origines du fantasme, *Les temps modernes,* 215, avril 1964.

———. en collaboration avec Laplanche, J., *Vocabulaire de la psychanalyse,* Paris, P.U.F., 1967.

Porta, A., Ouvrir, tr. fr., *Les temps modernes,* 277–278, août–septembre 1969.

Propp, Vl., *Morphology of the Folktale,* Indiana University, Research Center in Anthropology, Folklore and Linguistics, 10, octobre 1958.

Réau, L., *La miniature,* Melun, Librairie d'Argences, 1947.

Richards, I.A., en collaboration avec Ogden, C.K., *The Meaning of Meaning.* Londres, Kegan Paul, 1936.

Richter, H., *Dada-art et anti-art,* Bruxelles, La connaissance, 1965.

Ricoeur, P., *Finitude et culpabilité,* Paris, Aubier, 1960, I et II.

———. *De l'interprétation. Essai sur Freud,* Paris, Seuil, 1965.

———. Cours sur le langage, ex. ronéoté, Nanterre, 1966–1967.

———. La structure, le mot, l'événement, *Esprit,* mai 1967.

Rosolato, G., Le sens des oublis. Une découverte de Freud, *L'arc,* 34, 1968.

Ruwet, N., *Introduction à la grammaire générative,* Paris, Plon, 1967.

Sami-Ali, M., Préliminaire d'une théorie psychanalytique de l'espace imaginaire, *Revue française de psychanalyse,* XXIII, janvier–février 1969.

Sampaolesi, L., *Brunelleschi,* Milan, Club del libro d'arte, 1962.

Sartre, J.-P., L'écrivain et la langue, *Revue d'esthétique,* 3–4, 1965.

Saussure, F. de, *Cours de linguistique générale* (1906–1911), Bally et Séchehaye édit., Paris, Payot, 1962.

———. Les anagrammes, textes inédits publiés par J. Starobinski, *Mercure de France,* 2, 1964.

Schreyer, L., *Souvenirs: Erinnerungen am Sturm und Bauhaus,* Munich, Langen et Müller, 1956.

Segal, Hanna, A Psycho-Analytical Approach to Aesthetics, *International Journal of Psychoanalysis,* XXXIII, 1, 1952.

Starobinski, J., Les anagrammes de Ferdinand de Saussure, *Mercure de France,* 2, 1964.

———. Psychanalyse et critique littéraire, *Preuves,* 181, 1966.

———. Hamlet et Freud, Préface à la tr. fr. de Jones, E., *Hamlet and Œdipus* (1949), Paris, Gallimard, 1967.

Stokes, A., *Reflections on the Nude,* Londres, Tavistock, 1967.

Suci, G.J., en collaboration avec Osgood, C.E., et Tannenbaum, P.H., *The Measurement of Meaning,* Urbana, Illinois, 1957.

Tannenbaum, P.H., en collaboration avec Osgood, C.E., et Suci, G.J., *The Measurement of Meaning,* Urbana, Illinois, 1957.

Thomas, Jacqueline, Phonétique articulatoire, cahier ronéoté, Ecole pratique des Hautes Etudes, 1966–1967.

Thorne, J.P., Stylistics and Generative Grammars, *Journal of Linguistics,* I, 1, 1965.

Todorov, Tz., Les anomalies sémantiques, *Langages,* 1, mars 1966.

———. *Littérature et signification,* Paris, Larousse, 1967.

Tomachevski, B.V., Thématique (1925), tr. fr. in *Théorie de la Littérature,* Paris, Seuil, 1965.

Tomassoni, I., *Pollock,* Florence, Sadea, 1968.

Tomatis, A., *L'oreille et le langage,* Paris, Seuil, 1963.

Torrigiani, U.E., Le groupe dans la littérature italienne contemporaine, *Les temps modernes,* 277–278, août–septembre 1969.

Tort, M., Le concept freudien de représentant, *Cahiers pour l'analyse,* 5, novembre–décembre 1966.

Trân-Dûc Thào, *Phénoménologie et matérialisme dialectique,* Paris, Minh-Tan, 1951.

Trier, J., Das sprachliche Feld. Eine Auseinandersetzung, *Neue Jahrbücher für Wissenschaft und Jugendbildung,* X, 1924.

Troubetzkoy, N.S., *Principes de phonologie* (1939), tr. fr., Paris, Klincksieck, 1964.

Tynianov, J., Le problème de la langue poétique (1924), tr. fr. in *Théorie de la littérature,* Paris, Seuil, 1965.

———. La notion de construction (1924), *ibid.*

Ullmann, St., *The Principles of Semantics,* Oxford-Glasgow, Blackwell-Jackson, 1963.

Valéry, P., *Variété II,* Paris, Gallimard, 1930.

Vasari, G., *Les peintres toscans* (1550), tr. fr. Paris, Hermann, 1966.

Volponi, P., en collaboration avec Berti, L., *Masaccio,* Milan, Rizzoli, 1968.

Widdowson, H.G., Notes on Stylistics, *Applied Linguistics in Language Teaching,* Edinburgh University, Department of Applied Linguistics, cahier ronéoté, 1969.

Winnicott, D.W., Objets transitionnels et phénomènes transitionnels. Etude de la première « not-me possession » (1953), tr. fr. in *La psychanalyse,* 5, 1959.

Zahn, L., *Paul Klee,* Potsdam, Kiepenheimer, 1920.

INDEX OF NAMES

Illustrations are indicated in italic.

Abelard, Peter, 165
Ajame, Pierre, 459n13
Alain, 254
Alberti, Leon Battista, 160, 181, 191, 194, 196, 197, 198, 199, 439n100
Alcuin, 168, 170
Alquié, Ferdinand, 460n9, 460n13
Angelico, Fra, 215
Apollinaire, Guillaume, 310, 311, 370, 462n50
Aragon, Louis, 290, 291, 311, 462n45
Aristotle, 177, 209, 231, 433n46, 443n1
Artaud, Antonin, 88, 139, 414n42
Assunto, Rosario, 429n12, 430–431n24, 431n29, 432n39, 433n43
Augustine, Saint, xi, 148, 431n29, 444n10
Aulagnier, Piera, 473n64
Avron, Dominique, 413n43

Bachelard, Gaston, 290, 434n46
Backès, Catherine, 470–471n36
Baldovinetti, 215
Bally, Charles, 263
Baltrušaitis, Jurgis, 437n76, 470n31, 477nn32–34, 478n35, *Plates 24a–24b*
Baron, Roger, 431n30
Barre, André, 426–427nn41–43
Barthes, Roland, 318, 377, 403n14, 443n4, 453n30, 464n78, 464n81
Baudelaire, Charles, 312
Beaufret, Jean, 231
Belaval, Yvon, 459–460n14, 475n5
Benveniste, Émile, 37, 73, 75–76, 77, 79, 94, 97, 103, 115, 116–118, 123, 125–126, 141–142, 392, 412n18, 420n18, 422n6, 455n54
Bergson, Henri, 55, 161, 429n4
Berio, Luciano, 89
Bernard of Clairvaux, 165, 171
Berti, Luciano, 437n78, 438n94, 440n103, *Plate 6, Plate 8, Plate 10, Plate 11b*
Blake, William, 447n33
Blanchot, Maurice, xviii, 476n8
Boethius, 438n97, 447n27
Bonaparte, Marie, 455n3, 473n58, 474n1
Bosse, Abraham, 437n76
Boucheron, Serge, vii, 399–400n9, 422n8
Braque, Georges, 11, 156
Bremond, Claude, 425nn26–30
Breton, André, 5, 250, 265, 284–286, 325, 453n25, 456–457n20, 460n7, 460n13, 461n14, 476n5, *Plate 17*
Brik, Osip Maksimovich, 464n51, 463–464n68
Brion-Guerry, Liliane, *198,* 430n18, 442n124, 442n127
Brunelleschi, Filippo, 180, 193, 197, 438n94, 483 Figure 6
Bruno, Giordano, 162, 176
Bruyne, Edgar De. *See* De Bruyne, Edgar
Butor, Michel, 78, 361, *363–367,* 369, 371–376, 409n31, 434n64, 477n29, 477n33, 485–486 Figures 20–21, 490 Plate 17, 490 Plates 19–21, 491 Plate 23, *Plates 20–21*

Cagnetta, Franco, 447n33
Caritat, Marie Jean Antoine Nicolas de, marquis de Condorcet, 148

Cassiodorus, 446n27
Cavallini, Pietro, 437n85
Cézanne, Paul, 14, 16–18, 24–25, 54, 69, 155, 159–161, 186, 197, 198, 231, 430n18, 446n26, 451n78, 457n20, 461n31, 488–489 Plate 15a
Chomsky, Noam, 138, 311, 461n43
Claudel, Paul, 3–5, 23, 85, 352, 434n43
Coblence, Françoise, 452–453n22
Cohen, Jean, 315–318
Condorcet. *See* Caritat, Marie Jean Antoine Nicolas de
Cooper, Frederick A., 438n97
Cordroc'h, Marie, 430nn13–14
Corneille, Pierre, 310, 319, 320
Cummings, E. E., 319–320, 463n57, 467n95

Dada, 319, 459n11
Dalí, Salvador, 456–457n20
David, Madeleine V., 478n35
Davies, Gardner, 61, 64, 69, 409n25, 410n35
De Bruyne, Edgar, 429n15, 429–430n17, 431nn29–30, 432–433nn38–41
Delaunay, Robert, 231, 439n98, 485–486 Figure 20
Democritus, 207
Derrida, Jacques, xi–xii, xiv, xviii, xix, 397n7, 405n18, 411n9, 420n18
Desargues, Girard, 437n76
Descartes, René, 16, 176–181, 196, 417n14, 434n58, 434n60, 435n65
Détienne, Marcel, 400n14
Diderot, Denis, 209–210, 417n14, 443n5
Diels, Hermann, 443n1
Donatello, 438n94
Donati, Pier Paolo, 437n77, 439n99, 440n105, *Plate 7, Plate 9, Plate 11a, Plate 12*
Donne, John, 464n84
Dreyfus, Sylvie, 452–453n22
Dubois, Jean, 413n3, 416n6, 418n22
Ducasse, Isodore Lucien. *See* Lautréamont, comte de
Duccio di Buoninsegna, 184–190, 194, 195, 428n1, 437n77, 437n85, 438–439nn97–98, 440–441n106, 482 Figure 3, 487 Plates 11–12, *Plate 7, Plate 9, Plate 11a, Plate 12*
Duchamp, Marcel, 285, 460n11
Duchamp-Villon brothers, 445–446n23
Dufrenne, Mikel, vii, xvi, 15, 287–288, 405n21, 411n15, 412n24, 460n16, 460n19, 460nn24–25, 460n30, 463n53, 464n76
Du Marsais, César Chesneau, 284

Eco, Umberto, 326, 466n98
Ehrenzweig, Anton, xxiii, 427n44, 456n19, 459–460n14, 474–475n4, 478n44
Eizykman, Boris, 476n25
Eizykman, Claudine, 452n17, 468n17
Éluard, Paul, 325, 327, 465n89, 466n95
Emmanuel, Pierre, 291
Empson, William, 460n19
Erigena, John Scotus, 431n29
Euclid, 200, 483 Figure 6, 488–489 Plate 15a

Favalelli, Max, 460–461n31, 461nn41–42
Fechner, Gustav Theodor, 269
Feuerbach, Ludwig Andreas von, xx
Février, James, 443n2
Fihman, Guy, 434–435n64, 452n17, 468n17, 476n25
Fink, Eugen, 418n23
Flaubert, Gustave, 244
Flocon, Albert, 426–427nn41–43
Focillon, Henri, 412n27
Fonagy, Ivan, 458n3
Fortunatus, 446n27
Fraenkel, Ernst, 409–410n34
Francastel, Pierre, 23, 159, 185–186, 194–196, 274, 431n27, 436n68, 438nn95–96, 439n100, 440n101, 440–441n106, 441n108, 442n117, 442nn121–123, 442n128
Frege, Gottlob, 14, 73, 78, 103–114, 118, 125, 159, 279, 280, 383, 401n3, 414n4, 419–421n18, 457n1, 467n1, 478n41
Freud, Sigmund, xii, xiv, xv–xvii, xix, 12–15, 25–26, 53, 56–59, 69, 71, 83, 88, 115–128, 135, 140, 142, 149–151, 159, 161, 230, 233–249,

252–256, 257–259, 264–267, 268–276, 278, 280, 292–298, 303, 309, 321, 328–332, 334–338, 339–344, 346–348, 349–354, 356–359, 381–389, 390, 391–392, 392–396, 404–405n18, 407n12, 421n1, 421n3, 422nn8–9, 423n22, 423–424n1, 428n5, 434n64, 439n98, 442n119, 447n40, 449n48, 452–453nn22–23, 454n54, 455nn1–3, 459–460n14, 461n31, 461–462n44, 463n60, 465nn87–88, 465–466n93, 466–467n1, 468n19, 468–469nn21–22, 470n31, 471n37, 472n47, 472nn49–50, 473nn53–54, 474nn66–67, 474–475n4, 478n40, 479n46

Fuseli, Henry, 447n33

Galileo Galilei, 162, 175–179, 433n46, 478n35

Genette, Gérard, 425n29

Gentile da Fabriano, 438n96

Ghyka, Matila Costiesco, 445–446n23, 456n18

Gide, André, 65, 68, 388

Giotto di Bondone, 184–185, 215, 431n27, 437n85, 440n106

Girault-Duvivier, Charles-Pierre, 443–444n5, 458n6

Giuliani, Alfredo, 467n97

Godel, Robert, 98, 101, 136–137, 416–417nn8–13, 417–418n15, 418n24

Goldstein, Kurt, 412–413n28

Gorky, Arshile, 456–457n20

Grabar, André, 431n27

Granger, Gilles-Gaston, 458n1

Green, André, 441n112, 469n27, 471n45, 473n55, 473–474n64

Gregory of Nyssa, 430n22

Greimas, Algirdas Julien, 453n30

Grohmann, Will, 446–447n31, 448n42, 449n51, *Plate 13*

Hahnloser, Hans, 438–439n98

Halliday, Michael A. K., 458n3

Harris, Zellig Sabbettai, 463n54

Hegel, Georg Wilhelm Friedrich, xv, xvii, xx–xxi, 6, 33–50, 58, 69, 72, 102, 118, 120, 132–134, 148, 253, 289, 301, 317, 392, 397n4, 399n9, 401n5, 401n8, 403nn14–15, 404n18, 407n12, 420n18, 422n8, 424n6, 433n47

Heraclitus, 33, 209

Hitda of Meschede, 169, 431n24

Hjelmslev, Louis, 209

Holbein, Hans (the Younger), 378–379, 477n33

Hölderlin, Friedrich, 384

Horace, 169

Hugh of Saint Victor, 165, 171–174, 183, 432n31

Hugo, Victor, 311, 453n41

Husserl, Edmund, xiv–xv, 15–16, 23, 27, 98, 103, 109, 114, 148–150, 414n4, 419–420n18, 425–426n31, 426n33, 433n44, 433n46

Hyppolite, Jean, xvii–xviii, 41–42, 392, 421n1, 423n22, 432n47

Irigaray, Luce, 472n50

Isaacs, Susan, 359

Jacob, André, 404–405n18

Jakobson, Roman, xvi, 40, 43, 94, 96, 100, 137–138, 245–256, 312, 317, 402n10, 411n20, 413n35, 413n37, 413n38, 418n17, 418n22, 458n3, 464n77

Janitschek, Hubert, 442n130

Jarry, Alfred, 310

Johnson, Samuel, 312

Jones, Ernest, 479n47

Joyce, James, 310, 414n43

Jung, Carl Gustav, 403n14

Kandinsky, Wassily, 168, 413n29, 429n16

Kant, Immanuel, 16, 23, 36, 44–45, 98, 107–108, 120, 134, 237, 289, 422n8

Kaufmann, Pierre, 401n20, 426n40, 475n11, 475n14

Kierkegaard, Søren, 18, 148

Klee, Paul, 9, 13, 159, 213–232, *221, 225, 228, 229,* 310, 325, 348, 383, 400n13,

444–445n11, 446–447n32, 447n34, 447–448nn39–42, 448n46, 448–449n48, 449nn50–52, 449–450n57, 450n59, 450n61, 450–451nn66–68, 451nn78–79, 478n43, 483–485 Figures 7–10, 485 Figure 15, 487–490 Plates 13–16, *Plates 13–16*
Klein, Melanie, 475n9, 478n44
Klossowski, Pierre, 448n33
Koyré, Alexandre, 176, 428n8, 433n46, 433n48, 434n58, 434n60
Kranz, Walther, 444n1
Kris, Ernst, 476n5

Lacan, Jacques, xv–xx, 141, 246, 248, 249–256, 258, 392, 397–398nn6–7, 421n1, 428n9, 453n40, 468n20, 469n23, 471n44
Langlois, Henri, 477n31
Laplanche, Jean, xiii, 267, 391–392, 454n54, 455n1, 455n7, 471n38, 472n48, 473n52, 473n58
Lascault, Gilbert, 470n31
Lautréamont, comte de, 284
Leclaire, Serge, 351–353, 454n54, 473nn54–56
Le Goff, Jacques, 430n22
Leibniz, Gottfried Wilhelm, 111, 114, 420n18
Lemenuel, Bruno, 375, 476n28, 491 Plate 23, *Plate 23*
Leonardo da Vinci, 160, 189, 193, 195, 197, 199, 217, 379, 445–446n23
Lerch, Eugen, 76
Leroi-Gourhan, André, 81, 82, 264, 412n27, 426n39, 443n2
Leucippus, 207
Levinas, Emmanuel, 5, 18, 400n9, 401n21, 405n18
Lévi-Strauss, Claude, 60, 142–143, 318, 406–407n12, 412n25, 425n26, 464n83, 476n23
Lhote, André, 68, 159, 213–220, 225, 230–231, 264, 268, 350, 428n2, 445n11, 445n23, 446n27, 451nn77–78, 456n18
Lipps, Theodor, 438–439n98
Lissitzky, El, 375, 476–477n29, 485–486 Figure 20, 490–491 Plates 22–23, *Plate 22*
Littré, Émile, 296–297, 302
Lorenzetti, Pietro, 184, 442n120
Lyotard, Corinne, 476n25
Lyotard, Jean-François, xi–xxiii, 391–392, 397nn5–6, 398n9, 399n8, 400nn10–11, 413n43, 421n3, 428 translator's note, 428n1, 430–431n24, 441–442n119, 479n45
Lyotard-May, Andrée, 463n51

Magritte, René, 243, 244, 256, 443n136, 490 Plate 17, *Plate 17*
Maignan, Emmanuel, 477n34
Mallarmé, Stéphane, 14, 61–63, 64–65, *66–67*, 68–69, 71, 130, 159, 209, 323, 371, 377, 407n15, 408n25, 408n27, 408–409nn28–29, 409n31, 409–410n34, 410n36, 461n31, 474n1, 485–486 Figure 20
Mandel, Gabriele, 429n11
Manet, Édouard, 186
Manetti, Giannozzo, 193, 197
Mannoni, Octave, 471n45
Mantegna, Andrea, 196
Marin, Louis, 411n5
Martin, Roger, 458n1
Martinet, André, 57, 84, 96, 412n31, 413n6, 414nn1–2, 443n3, 444n8
Marx, Karl, xii, xiv–xvii, xix, xxi–xxiii, 133–135, 392, 425n6
Masaccio, 160, 161, 184–191, 194, 195, 197, 437n67, 437n94, 439n100, 440n103, 440–441n106, 441n111, 482 Figure 3, *Plate 6, Plate 8, Plate 10, Plate 11b*
Masolino da Panicale, 186, 190, 440n101
Masson, André, 447n33
Masson, Loys, 290
Matisse, Henri, 24
Matta, Roberto, 457n20
Mauclair, Camille, 409n29
Mauron, Charles, 321, 357, 360, 457n21, 474n1
Méliès, Georges, 477n31

Merleau-Ponty, Maurice, xiv, xvi, 4, 5, 14–17, 23, 27, 28, 51–58, 65, 73, 74, 76, 132, 153, 178, 399n5, 399n8, 406n3, 407nn8–9, 414–416n5, 425n3, 458n4
Mondor, Henri, 407n16
Mondrian, Piet, 368, 491 Plate 23
More, Thomas, 441n115
Mouloud, Noël, 412–413n28, 413n30
Muche, Georg, 400n13
Münster, school of, 416n6
Murnau, Friedrich Wilhelm, 459n13

Nassif, Jacques, 337, 467n9, 472n49, 474n67, 475n13
Nicholas of Cusa, 438n94
Nietzsche, Friedrich, 11, 13, 69
Nordenfalk, Carl, 431n27

Ogden, Charles Kay, 411n18
Ortigues, Edmond, 73, 410n5
Osgood, Charles E., 464n77

Pacioli, Luca, 445n23
Panofsky, Erwin, 184, 185, 189, *198*, 200, *200*, 428n10, 430n18, 437n79, 437n85, 439n98, 441n107, 441nn109–110, 442n120, 442n124, 477n32, 479n35
Parain, Brice, 401n8
Paris, Jean, 443n136
Parmenides of Elea, 33, 97
Parronchi, Alessandro, 440n102
Passeron, René, 427n42
Peignot, Jérôme, 444n9
Peirce, Charles Sanders, xviii, 73, 94, 403n14, 411n18
Péret, Benjamin, 290–291, 327
Picasso, Pablo, 24–25, 274, *274*, 456n20, 485 Figure 15, 488–489 Plate 15a
Pichette, Henri, 310, 311, 425n23
Plato, 5, 97, 127, 258, 423n26, 446n27
Plekhanov, Georgi, 148
Plotinus, 431n29
Plutarch, 169
Poe, Edgar Allan, xvii–xix, 397n7, 442n130, 475n1
Pollock, Jackson, 275, 456–457n20, 490 Plate 19, *Plate 19*
Pontalis, Jean-Bertrand, 267, 400n16, 455n1, 455n7, 471n38, 472n48, 473n52, 473n58, 474n68
Porta, Antonio, 326
Port-Royal, Logic of, 73
Pousseur, Henri, 476n19
Poussin, Nicolas, 186
Prague School, 90
Pre-Raphaelitism, 160
Prévert, Jacques, 312
Propp, Vladimir, 60, 145, 244, 406–407n12, 425nn26–28
Proust, Marcel, 244
Pythagoras, 170, 446n23

Quintilian, 446n27

Rabanus Maurus (Hraban Maur), 431n27
Rabelais, François, 460–461n31, 477n29
Rameau, Jean-Philippe, 210
Réau, Louis, 429n11, 442n129
Richard of Saint Victor, 173
Richards, Ivor Armstrong, 411n18
Richter, Hans, 459n11
Ricoeur, Paul, 6, 392, 400n9, 414n1, 418n1, 419n17, 421n1, 423n22
Rimbaud, Arthur, 311, 318, 459–460n14
Rodin, Auguste, 281
Rosolato, Guy, 413n41
Rossif, Frédéric, 242, *242*
Roussel, Raymond, 263
Rubens, Peter Paul, 445–446n23
Russell, Bertrand, 457n1
Ruwet, Nicolas, 248, 461n43, 471n40

Sami-Ali, Mahmoud, 456n17
Sanpaolesi, Piero, 438n94
Sartre, Jean-Paul, xiv, xxi, 31, 33, 52, 53, 458n4
Saussure, Ferdinand de, 26, 32, 43, 60, 62,

72, 75, 77–80, 85, 91–96, 98, 100–101, 103, 118, 136–137, 159, 211, 246, 253, 262–263, 400n12, 401n1, 414n4, 417–418n15, 424n14
Schelling, Friedrich Wilhelm Joseph von, 289, 400n9
Schleiermacher, Friedrich, 462n44
Schreyer, Lothar, 446–447n32, 448n46, 450n67
Segal, Hanna, 475n9, 478n44
Shakespeare, William, 310, 377–389, 390, 424n6, 464n84
Shklovsky, Viktor, 462n49, 465n90
Silberer, Herbert, 243, 244, 256
Simonides of Ceos, 169, 458–459n6
Socrates, 11, 127
Sophocles, 194, 471n45
Starobinski, Jean, 263, 387
Stokes, Adrian, 441n114
Suci, George J., 464n77

Tannenbaum, Percy H., 464n77
Tardy, Michel, 441n111
Thomas, Dylan, 311
Thomas, Jacqueline M. C., 414n38
Thorne, James Peter, 305–306, 308, 317, 433n45, 459n3
Todorov, Tzvetan, 312–313, 411n20, 458n6, 463n51
Tomashevsky, Boris, 465n90
Tomassoni, Italo, 456n20, *Plate 19*
Tomatis, Alfred, 413n39
Torrigiani, U. E., 466n96
Tort, Michel, 468–469n21
Tran Duc Thao, xv, xvii, xxii, 397n4, 426n33
Trier, Jost, 90–91, 416n6
Troubetzkoy, Nikolai S., 86, 94
Tynyanov, Yury, 465n90

Uccello, Paolo, 217, 438n96
Ullmann, Stephen, 411n18, 414n4, 417n6

Vachek, Joseph, 91
Valéry, Paul, 61, 65, 312
Van Eyck, Jan, 438n95
Van Gogh, Vincent, 24, 239, 426n40, 451n79
Varendonck, Julien, 472n47
Vasari, Giorgio, 185, 192, 436n67
Verlaine, Paul, 316
Veronese, Paolo, 445n23
Villard de Honnecourt, 439n98
Volponi, Paolo, 437n78, *Plate 6, Plate 8, Plate 10, Plate 11b*
Voltaire (François-Marie Arouet), 220

Wallon, Henri, 403n14
Warner, Lloyd, 142
White, John, 438n90
Widdowson, Henry G., 307, 309, 310–315, 324, 383, 458n3, 463n51, 464n71
Winnicott, Donald Woods, 13, 358
Wittgenstein, Ludwig, 103, 414n4, 457n1
Worringer, Wilhelm, 438–439n98

Yakubinsky, Lev Petrovich, 463n51

Zahn, Leopold, 450n57

INDEX OF CONCEPTS AND GERMAN EXPRESSIONS

affect, 10, 62, 136, 139, 321, 329, 331, 333, 335, 337, 340, 344, 345, 348, 350–355, 360, 369, 385, 394, 409–410n34, 468–469n21, 475n14

anamorphosis: as double reversal, xvi, 378, 379, 380, 477nn32–34, 478n35, 483 Figure 5, 488–489 Plate 15a, 491 Plates 24a–24b; as presence of the figural in the textual, 69, 179, 180, 437n76. *See also* reversal

Andacht, devotion (Hegel), 399–400n9

Anschauung, intuition (Frege), 104, 435n64

arbitrariness: of the linguistic "sign," 42–45, 62–63, 72–73, 79–83, 88, 93, 97, 182, 283, 409–410n34; and reference, 45, 62, 63, 72, 74, 75, 76, 108, 180–182, 190, 205–206, 308, 320, 325, 402–403n13, 406–407n12, 429n16. *See also* designation; sign

articulation, double, 57–58, 83–89, 121, 247, 279–280

atemporality: as irreversible anachrony, 132, 162; of the primary process, 147–152, 271–272, 337–338, 470n31

attention (evenly) suspended, 12, 309, 381–385, 390, 478n40; and recessus, 384–383. *See also* suspended

Aufbau, structure (Goldstein), 55

Aufhebung, dialectical negation (Hegel), 144, 392, 393, 407n12, 423n22

Aufklärer, Enlightenment philosopher, 148

Aufzeigen, to point to/out, to indicate [*désigner*] (Hegel), 36

Augenblick, gaze, glance, 288

Auslassung, omission (Freud), 254–255

Bearbeitung (*sekundäre*), revision (secondary) (Freud), 146, 233, 238, 246, 257–267, 292, 372, 381–382, 453n23, 485 Figure 12, 490 Plates 18a–18b

Bedeutung, quota of affect (Freud), 330–334, 467n9; reference (Frege), 28, 38, 41–42, 103–114, 127, 166, 280, 362, 383, 401n3, 419–420n18

Bejahung, affirmation, to say yes (Freud), 292–293, 396

bezeichnen, to designate [*désigner*] (Frege), 73, 104–107, 280, 402–403n13, 420–421n18

Bildung, culture, education (Hegel), 102

calligramme, 305, 370, 375

castration: as event, 14, 135–136, 144; and fate of the drive, 59, 330–336, 341–342, 345, 349, 474n67; and plastic problem (Klee), 219–232

city (as unconscious space), 179, 229–230, 337, 434–435n64, 458–459n6, 470n31, 489 Plate 15b

comparison, 45–47, 181, 284, 294–296, 306, 420–421n18, 454n54, 463n55. *See also* metaphor

condensation, xvii, 15, 53, 56, 140, 141–142, 146, 224, 278, 297–304, 308–309, 314–315, 321, 322–324, 372, 376, 384–386, 389, 435n64, 464n70, 466n95, 476n19, 485 Figure 15; according to Freud, 238–243, 248, 254–255, 257, 271–272, 344, 453n23, 461–462n44, 465–466n93, 487–488 Plate 13; according to Lacan, 249–255; in myth, 144

connaturality, according to phenomenology, 129–132, 272–274, 287–92, 414–415n5
connotation, 61, 209, 212, 213, 315–322, 324, 362, 370, 472n49
continuity, 15, 59, 75, 182, 208, 288, 289, 309, 315. *See also* variance
corpus, as used in this book, 159–160, 460–461n31
critique, xiii, xvi, xix, xxi, xxii, xxiii, 14, 31, 51, 74, 108, 112, 132, 142, 150, 152, 159, 182, 219–220, 289–291, 318–327, 377, 379–380, 385–386, 410n36
curvature: in anamorphosis, 180, 324, 483 Figure 5, 488–489 Plate 15a, 491 Plates 23–24; as laterality, 15–19, 152–156, 168, 178–180, 188, 215, 426–427nn41–42, 434–436nn64–66, 483 Figures 5–6, 487 Plate 5. *See also* event

Dasein, existence, being-there (Hegel), 40, 131
death (drive), xiv, xvii, xix, 13–14, 121–128, 132, 142, 145, 350–356, 359–361, 384–387, 422n10, 423n22, 434–435n64, 455n2, 464n70, 468n2, 468–469n21, 473–474n64
deconstruction, 12–14, 54–55, 88, 153, 155, 156, 160–161, 210, 232, 275, 276, 292, 296–326, 348, 438–439n98, 439n100, 478n40, 481–482 Figure 1, 485 Figure 15, 491 Plate 23. *See also* recessus
deictics, 33–40, 132: according to Benveniste, 115–117; according to Husserl, 419–421n18; examples of (*see all the terms of this Index as such*). *See also* designation
denial (or disavowal). *See* negation
designation: as decoy for the other space, 121, 129–130, 272–273, 345–348; and expression, 287–292, 340; as indication (*see also* deictics), 33–38; as libidinal distance, 126–128; as meaning in exteriority, 15, 24–27, 39–41, 48, 49, 56–57, 77–78, 80–83, 116–119, 243, 279–280, 282, 301, 412n27; as reference, 50, 68, 72, 73, 93, 94, 97–102, 103–114, 124, 132, 292, 363, 400n10, 420–421n18, 482 Figure 4; and representation, 179–183, 186–187, 190–194, 267; as script in perspectivism, 196–201
Determinierung (*mehrfache*), multiple determination (Freud), 254–255
Deutung, interpretation (Freud), 380–387, 478n40
dialectics, xiv, xvii, xx, xxi, xxii, xxiii, 6, 15, 30–41, 48, 50, 51, 53, 57–59, 69, 97, 101–102, 107–108, 127, 156, 165, 399n9, 398n12, 402n8, 404–405n18, 407n12, 423n22, 471n44; as neutralization of difference in opposition, 101–102, 118–120, 132, 133, 134–136, 142–147, 175–176, 293, 351–353, 357–360, 399–400n9, 401–402n9, 422n8, 426n33, 433n47, 449–450n57
difference, as other of opposition, 3, 7, 9, 13–14, 16, 19, 57, 59, 74, 102, 129–156, 161–164, 166, 170–176, 178, 180, 187, 190–193, 205–210, 216–217, 274, 275, 282, 328, 339, 344, 349–355, 361, 381, 384, 386, 399–400n9, 406–407n12, 417–418n15, 424n10, 424n13, 425n26, 434n64, 453n24, 468–469n21, 471n45, 482 Figure 3, 487 Plate 5, 487 Plate 10
Differenz, opposition (Marx), 133, 424n10
Dingvorstellung, thing-presentation (Freud), 255
discourse: as constant external reference of this book's discourse, it appears on every page; as term endowed in principle with a signification, it presupposes itself in the very act of signifying, thus masking itself on each page; therefore, unindexable.
displacement, 53, 56, 129, 139, 140–142, 146, 206, 209, 224, 232, 255, 271–273, 285, 297–304, 308–309, 314–315, 343, 355, 360, 372, 376, 384, 387–389, 409–410n34, 459n9, 476n19, 477n34, 487–488 Plate 13, 488–489 Plate 15a, 491 Plate 23; according to Freud, 237–238, 241–243, 248, 256,

259, 262, 321–322, 330, 345–346, 352–353, 360, 389, 434–435n64, 449n50, 453n23, 463n44, 462n46, 462n48, 464n70, 485 Figure 11; in this book itself, 13–15, 18–19

dispositio, 142–152, 425n29, 482 Figure 3. *See also* figure-form

dispossession, 18–19, 48, 88, 190–194, 348, 361, 376, 426n40, 475n11, 475n14; and "unsightliness," 383–389

distortion, according to Freud, 15, 123, 128, 141, 219, 235–238, 241, 243, 273, 322, 376, 382, 389, 438–439n98. See also *Entstellung*

Einfühlung, "empathy" (Worringer), 320, 438–439n98

Einseitigkeit, one-sidedness (Frege), 104–105, 421n18

Entstellung, distortion (Freud), 235–241, 359, 376, 395, 452n9

Entzweiung, bifurcation, splitting, 39, 127–128

Erfüllung, fulfillment of (meaning) (Husserl), 421n18

event: castration as, 135–136; linguistic, 19, 32, 74, 140, 141, 324, 376, 414n1, 415n6; as Mallarmean "place," 63–69; in the tale, 146–147, 189; temporal, xi, 148, 151–152, 162, 353, 473n53, 490 Plate 19; as truth, 16–19, 129–132, 164, 178, 179, 194, 278–279, 381, 471n45; as unsightliness, 384; visual, 4, 154–156

expression: as opposed to communication, 10, 42–43, 60, 63, 75–78, 81, 84, 87–89, 90, 163, 166, 168, 170, 173, 208–210, 214–216, 220, 222, 255, 275, 278, 402–403n13, 405n1, 408n25, 412n24, 444n10, 446n24; phantasmatic, as symptom, 122, 199, 218, 245, 294, 321–323, 324, 344, 356–361, 387; as reconciliation, 287–292, 460n16, 460n24; as "representation" according to Frege, 104–105, 105–109, 111, 114; as trace of non-language in language, 8–14, 49–50, 57, 69, 194, 295, 405n21, 415–416n5

exteriority: in Freud, 122–128, 243, 321, 356, 358–359, 392–396; in painting, 153, 166–167, 189–199, 218, 380, 441n111, 442n120, 446–447n32, 482 Figure 3; with regard to language, 5, 7, 8, 10, 34, 36, 41, 42, 45–49, 57, 69, 85, 87, 101, 104, 108, 135, 139, 142, 221, 247, 375, 399–400n9, 403n15, 404n17, 405nn19–20, 419–420n18, 481–482 Figure 1

eye, as anti-discourse, 4–11, 24, 38, 40, 55, 69, 84, 93, 101, 113, 127–128, 129–30, 152–156, 161, 166, 170–173, 178, 182, 185–186, 191, 197, 201, 210, 211–212, 213, 216–218, 221–223, 227, 232, 246, 264–265, 275, 279, 282, 290, 337, 348, 373, 375–377, 379, 380, 389, 404–405n18, 417n14, 426–427n42, 431n27, 440–441n106, 446n27, 450n66, 456–457n20, 477n34, 483 Figure 7, 487 Plate 10, 488–489 Plate 15a, 490 Plate 22

fate of the drive, 334–340, 347, 361

field, 13, 47–48, 90–91, 131, 153–155, 175–179, 187, 224, 406–407n12, 414n4, 490 Plate 19; and gesture, 36, 414–416n5

figurability: according to Freud, 53, 238, 243–246, 256–267, 273; in the rebus, 300–304

figural(-ity): as event, 16–19, 129, 154, 180, 211–213, 233, 241, 267, 268–269, 324, 398 translator's note, 428 translator's note, 438–439n98; as opacity, 7–12, 317; as opposed to figurative, 205, 274–276, 456–457n20, 489–490 Plates 16a–16b; as other of the textual, 8, 46, 47, 48, 50, 57, 60–71, 100, 107, 161–176, 179, 187, 191–195, 199, 205–213, 217, 240, 245, 266, 271, 277–279, 282, 296, 300–305, 308–309, 322, 327–328, 339, 344, 349, 350, 353, 368, 370, 373, 375, 403n15, 408n25, 415–416n5, 444n10, 481–482 Figures 1–2, 485–486 Figure 20, 486 Plates 2a–2b, 490 Plate 17, 491 Plate 23; as strangeness (*das Unheimliche*), 151–152; as truth, 11–16, 160, 183, 230–231, 355, 356, 385, 387; as work (labor), 139–142

figural space. *See* figural(-ity)
figure-form, 49–50, 62–68, 70–71, 142–152, 170, 244–245, 268, 269, 275, 279, 282, 297, 300–302, 320, 324, 328, 343–345, 350–356, 371, 375, 381, 406–407n12, 456–457n20, 474–475n4, 483 Figure 5, 485 Figure 15, 488–489 Plate 15a, 491 Plate 23
figure-image, 49–50, 70–71, 184–199, 218–222, 231, 244–246, 257–267, 268, 269, 274–275, 279, 282, 292, 297, 300–303, 323, 346–348, 357, 358, 368, 370, 374–375, 377–380, 382, 438–439n98, 440–441n106, 456–457n20, 474–475n4, 483 Figure 5, 485 Figure 15, 485–486 Figure 20, 486 Plates 2a–2b, 487 Plate 5, 488–489 Plate 15a
figure-matrix, 15, 75, 128, 163, 227, 241, 244–245, 268–269, 274–276, 279, 282, 286–287, 292, 304, 308, 321, 324, 327–355, 356, 375, 383, 384–386, 406–407n12, 465n87, 475n4
foreclosure: according to Freud and Lacan, 58, 121–128, 161–164, 193–194, 429n9, 482 Figure 3; and denial, 392–396
form. *See* figure-form

Gedanke, thought content (Frege), 105, 107–114
Gegebensein, givenness (Hegel), 104
Gegensatz, difference (Marx), opposition (Freud), 19, 57, 74, 123, 133–135, 148, 162, 163, 166, 205, 339–340, 362, 394–395, 424n10, 468–469n21
Gegenstand, object (Frege), 5, 104
Gestalt(*-ung*), form, formation, configuration, 55, 145, 152–155, 161, 268, 275, 279, 302–304, 350, 384, 415–416nn5–6, 456–457n20
gesture, 5–6, 15–19, 28, 35–39, 54–57, 81–82, 265, 272–273, 282–287, 373, 400n10, 414–416n5, 476–477n29

Hilflosigkeit, helplessness (Freud), 270
hyper-reflection, 51–59, 69–71, 152–154, 292, 378, 405n1

ideology, critique of, which is the aim of this book, 14, 24, 48, 50, 142, 152, 278, 326, 340, 379–380, 386, 424n6, 428n9, 468–469n21, 474n3, 482 Figure 3
image. *See* figure-image
indicator. *See* deictics
intentional negativity, 119, 121. *See also* designation
interiority. *See* exteriority
interworld, 7, 13, 58, 218, 223–232, 290, 348, 385, 446–447n32, 448n46, 484–485 Figures 9–10, 488–489 Plate 15a. *See also* anamorphosis; *Zwischenwelt*

knowledge, 8, 10–13, 17, 18, 27, 49, 50, 62, 69, 102, 103–104, 106, 107–108, 115, 121, 126, 127, 129–132, 141, 163, 164, 175, 180, 193, 194, 213, 215, 216, 277–279, 281, 356, 357, 359, 381–382, 388, 399–400n9, 435–436n66, 436n70, 482 Figure 3. *See also* truth

laterality. *See* curvature
letter: of desire according to Leclaire, 353–356; as opposed to the figure, 60, 63, 64–65, 68, 87, 141, 156, 165–170, 173, 174, 189, 191, 205–213, 221, 237, 238, 242, 243, 256, 282, 285, 295–301, 305, 352, 354, 371, 373, 375, 430n18, 431n27, 440–441n106, 476–477n29, 481–482 Figure 1, 486 Plates 2a–2b, 487 Plate 4, 488–489 Plate 15a; as pseudography, 257–267
listening. *See* reading
Lust-Ich, pleasure-ego (Freud), 123, 394

matrix. *See* figure-matrix
Meinen, immediate aim, meaning (Hegel), 34–35, 38, 401n5, 401–402n9
metaphor: according to Jakobson, xvi, 44, 245–251, 253–254; and comparison, 45–47, 70, 312; and condensation, 252–256; as gesture, 282–287; as Hegelian symbol, 39–47, 134, 253, 403n15

mirror, 27–28, 69–71, 76, 160, 180, 192, 199–200, 279, 285, 323, 373–374, 377, 379, 417n14, 438–439n98, 442n134, 456–457n20, 471n45, 488–490 Plates 16a–16b

Nachfolge, succession in the legal sense (Freud), 122, 396

negation: as denial (or disavowal), xv, xvi, xix, xxiii, 115–120, 149, 293, 398n12, 421n3, 423n22; and destructive drive, xvii, 25, 59, 121–128, 160, 194, 213, 271, 298, 323, 337–338, 341, 391, 397, 422n9, 466–467n1, 470n31, 471n44; as *ekthesis,* designation, reference, 23, 27–28, 34, 48, 51, 64, 73, 109, 123–124, 422n8; as interval (or gap) constitutive of the system, 15, 26, 27, 40, 51, 53, 100, 132, 135, 136, 137, 147, 208, 272, 277, 417–418n15; logical-grammatical, 29, 98, 99, 107, 119, 146, 163, 183, 212, 306, 308, 310, 315, 406–407n12, 461n43, 465n90; as loss (or withdrawal), 58, 360; and representation (Freud), 123–128, 469n27

negativeness [*négatité*], as structural negation, 119, 121, 338–339

Niederschlag, residue, sediment (Freud), 331

opacity: connected to actual reference, 74, 79, 82, 90, 93, 96–102, 137, 163–164, 169, 173–174, 179, 193, 196, 304, 485–486 Figure 20, 487 Plate 10; the figural as, 7–12, 212, 216, 278, 307, 315, 317, 328

opposition, 19, 29, 44, 57, 58, 59, 74, 85, 86, 90–99, 102, 119, 127, 129–156, 161–164, 166, 167–168, 170, 175, 178, 185, 187, 191, 205–212, 214–217, 220–221, 223, 238, 275, 277, 282, 299, 307, 317, 338–339, 344, 349, 350, 351, 352, 361, 373, 374–375, 377, 383, 406n3, 406–407n12, 413n27, 417–418n15, 424n10, 428n9, 429n12, 438–439n98, 449–450n57, 468–469n21. *See also* difference

Phantasie(-ren), phantasy (to phantasize) (Freud), 233, 241–246, 258, 356

phantasy [*fantasme*], 15, 41, 55, 107, 108, 128, 120, 243, 268, 281, 325, 327–355, 356, 358–363, 368, 377, 412n27, 434–435n64, 441n111, 450n57, 457–458n2, 458n6, 460n14, 465n89, 469n27, 473n53, 483–484 Figure 8; as blocking of the death drive, 13, 58, 71, 241, 258, 270, 279, 286, 320–321, 331, 335, 384–387, 452–453n22, 464n70, 465n91, 467n9, 472n47, 472n49, 473–474n64, 474n67; in painting, 190–191, 199, 218–226, 231, 378, 379, 439n100, 447n33

position: according to Marx, 133–136; of discourse, 7, 33, 69, 84, 85, 86, 95, 100, 103, 112, 116, 137, 147–148, 152, 161–164, 170, 175, 177, 193, 251, 278, 279–280, 317, 340, 381, 414n1, 441n115, 454n54; of the line, of the letter, 87, 114, 167, 201, 205–213, 215, 218, 227, 232, 246, 296, 481–482 Figure 1, 491 Plate 23; of the lost object, 120, 121–128, 280–282; of the plastic signifier, 186, 189–201, 275, 358, 378, 380, 381, 383, 442–443n136, 483 Figure 6

Position, position (Kant), 134

presentation. *See* thing-presentation; word-presentation

primary (space, process), xvi, 58, 13–14, 18, 142, 178–179, 187, 219, 232, 235, 239, 240–245, 257, 268–275, 287, 290, 292, 303, 309, 315, 321–322, 324, 328, 357, 381–389, 475n5, 481–482 Figure 1, 488–489 Plate 15a; as atemporality (*see also* atemporality), 147–152, 164, 336–342; as lack of articulation (*see* suspended), 87–89, 350–352

primary space. *See* primary

Raumscheu, dread of space (Worringer), 438–439n98

reading: movement of, and spatial recognition, 13, 152–156, 242; as other of seeing, xxiii, 3–10, 61, 69–71, 108, 141, 160, 168–184, 189, 190, 205–214, 237, 239, 240, 244, 257–267, 282, 304–305, 324–325, 353, 361, 367, 369, 370, 374, 375, 378, 408n27,

429n12, 438n97, 444n10, 460–461n31, 476n23, 487 Plate 10, 491 Plate 23
Real-Ich, reality-ego (Freud), 123, 281, 391
rebus, 56, 59, 243–245, 256, 271, 292–305, 315, 343, 370, 443n2, 460–461n31, 461n41, 462nn45–46, 485 Figures 16–19; this book as, 13
recessus: and anamorphosis, 378–380; and deconstruction, 54–59, 319; and hyper-reflection, 33, 51–71; as other than regression, 71, 359–361, 451n81; as suspended attention, 381–385. *See also* deconstruction
recognition. *See* reading
reconciliation, 6–12, 30–34, 38, 40–42, 47–48, 101, 129–133, 142–148, 175–176, 236, 289–292, 399–400n9, 424n6, 476–477n29, 483–484 Figure 8, 489 Plate 15b; and de-conciliation, 14–19, 57, 58, 127, 132–139, 356–360, 385; as the painter's unfulfilled desire, 226–230, 449–450n57. *See also* connaturality; dialectics
reference. *See* designation
regression, 57, 270–271, 334–336, 338, 384, 469n25, 473–474n64: non-reversible, 355, 357–358, 474n67; and recessus, 71, 358–361; as silence, 343–345, 347–348, 472n47
representation: critique of, xx, xxii, xxiii, 8, 15, 48–49, 130, 160, 182, 205, 216, 220, 226, 231, 323, 324, 372, 378–380, 385–389, 424n6; and the drive (Freud), 58, 125, 219, 230–231, 241, 271, 273, 276, 287, 339–341, 343–344, 345–347, 350–352, 393–395, 442n130, 456–457n20, 460n27, 484–485 Figures 9–10; and negation (Freud), 25, 123, 136, 358; as position of meaning, 4, 77–78, 170, 171, 175, 177–184, 186, 191–208, 300–302, 353, 412n27, 436–437n75, 438–439n98, 440–441n106; as *Vorstellung* (Frege), 78, 104, 105, 361, 367
reversal, 146, 155, 286, 305, 322–326, 344, 349, 356–389, 419–421n18, 456–457n20, 490 Plates 20–21, 491 Plates 23–24; critical, 12, 160, 194, 289, 384–387, 451n78, 490 Plate 22; double, poetic, 224–232, 360–389, 481–482 Figure 1, 483–484 Figure 8, 484–485 Figures 9–10; of the drive, 122, 331, 334–336, 469n27, 471n42, 471n43; and turnaround, 387–389
Rücksicht auf Darstellbarkeit, considerations of figurability (Freud), 238, 243, 244, 255

script (or writing): dream-thoughts as, 236–238; manifest content as false script (pseudography), 258–267, 485 Figure 12, 490 Plates 18a–18b; (rebus), 292–298, 460–461n31, 491 Plate 23; as opposed to figure, 74, 85–89, 141, 152, 160–161, 163–171, 174, 183, 186–189, 206, 217, 219, 231, 243, 276, 302, 317, 324, 358, 362–377, 378–379, 384, 385, 428n1, 430n18, 431n27, 438–439n98, 476–477n29, 488–489 Plate 15a, 490 Plate 22; phantasmatic, 218–224, 386, 447n33, 447n39, 447–448n40, 448n46, 448–449n48, 449n50; as repression of difference, 5, 191–201, 205–218, 438–439n98, 443n2, 459–460n14, 482 Figure 4, 488–489 Plate 15a; as truth of expression, 213–218, 278; as visibility, 61–63, 175, 263–264
secondary revision, 347–353; according to Freud, 146, 233, 238, 239, 257–267, 292, 372, 381, 382, 453n23, 485 Figure 12, 490 Plates 18a–18b
seeing: as other of reading, *see* reading; as other of saying, *see* designation
selection (or commutation), xxii, 28, 36, 38, 40, 60, 70, 77, 80, 99, 108–114, 136–138, 140, 150, 211, 245, 247–249, 254, 266, 296, 310, 312, 382, 414n1, 419–421n18, 443–444n5
Sichtbarmachen, make visible (Klee), 232, 405n20
sign: arbitrariness of the, 62, 63, 72–89; linguistic "sign," xviii, xix, 28, 72–89, 91–102,

103–114, 115–128, 136, 137, 205–213, 246, 248, 251, 253, 256, 263, 273, 278–280, 282, 283, 313, 397n7, 400n10, 410n5, 411n18, 417–418n15, 438–439n98, 443–444n5, 444n7, 471n44; plastic, and discourse, 9, 64, 70, 160, 166, 167, 171–174, 179, 182, 183, 190–192, 196, 199, 214–216, 296, 300, 373, 412n27, 429–430n17, 436–437n75, 460n16, 481–482 Figure 1, 482 Figure 3; plastic, and phantasy, 224–232, 239, 243, 245, 265, 294, 348, 356, 375, 378; and symbol (Hegel, Saussure), 42–51, 75–76, 402–403n13, 403n15, 478n35

signification: as illusion of opacity, 91, 96–102; libidinal "signification" (Freud), 9, 15, 58, 71, 116, 219–220, 234, 266, 329–334, 349–355, 356, 359, 381, 468–469n21, 482 Figure 3; as meaning in interiority, 7, 8, 10, 38, 39–40, 44, 46, 47, 49, 50, 101–102, 279, 402–403n13; as *Sinn* (Frege), 103–114, 419–421n18; as transparency, 9, 77–81, 99, 139, 164, 169, 205–206, 210, 212, 215, 253, 300, 317; as value, 90–98, 256, 417–418n15

Sinn, signification (or sense, meaning) (Frege, Husserl), 38, 40, 41, 44, 103–114, 419–421n18

Stellung, position (Marx), 134, 424n11

Streben (*nach Wahrheit*), striving (for truth) (Frege), 107

support, the sign's or the term's relation to the, 60, 62, 85, 87, 132, 147, 184–185, 189–190, 195–196, 199, 201, 205–206, 214, 215, 230–231, 264, 278, 378–380, 412n27, 430n18, 440–441n106, 482 Figure 4, 483 Figure 7, 485 Figure 15, 485–486 Figure 20, 488–489 Plate 15a

suspended (or floating): attention, evenly, 12, 308–309, 381–385, 390, 479n40; line as object, 196, 212, 219, 489–490 Plates 16a–16b; object, 376–378, 379–381, 478n31; as quantum of anxiety, freely, 129–130; and recessus, 384–386; text, 372–376, 481–482 Figure 1; and unbound (free) energy, 269, 271–272, 274–275. *See also* primary

symbol: according to Hegel, 6, 42–50, 72, 403–404n13, 404–405nn17–18, 482 Figure 3; according to Saussure, 75

term, 29, 30, 31, 38, 43, 44, 46, 47, 58, 60, 68, 72–89, 90, 91–102, 109, 111–114, 116, 118–119, 126–127, 132–139, 140, 144, 150, 151, 155–156, 167, 169, 177, 190–191, 208–209, 240, 246–247, 250–251, 253–254, 272, 277, 280, 284, 287, 302, 304, 312, 314–315, 320, 329, 340, 352, 355, 375, 419–421n18, 422n6

text: false, of the dream, 105, 233, 235–245, 258–267, 268, 295, 452n9; false, of the rebus, 56, 271, 292–298, 300–305, 343, 453n24. *See also* script (or writing)

textual, 3, 4, 6, 50, 59, 60–71, 83, 108, 129, 135, 144, 161, 163, 164, 165–175, 178, 183, 184, 187, 188, 190, 191, 193–199, 205–213, 224, 265, 277–279, 385, 408n25, 409–410n34, 410n36, 428n1, 433n46, 485–486 Figure 20, 486 Plates 2a–2c, 491 Plate 23; as affected by deconstructions, 9, 144, 273, 275, 276, 279–282, 297–300, 305–318, 320, 356, 338–342, 361–377, 463n51, 463n55, 481–482 Figures 1–2. *See also* figural(-ity); script (or writing)

textual space. *See* textual

thing-presentation (Freud), 127, 297–300, 327, 339, 340, 343, 346–349, 482 Figure 3

transformation, of sentences, 138, 142–147, 163, 175, 294–300, 306, 310–315, 324–326, 338–345, 371, 406–407n12, 433n45, 461n43, 463n55

transgression, 16, 51–57, 64, 100, 121, 140, 144, 146–147, 160, 191, 233, 238, 241–242, 250, 268, 272, 274–276, 282, 283, 287, 318–320, 322, 325, 339, 349–355, 356, 360, 383, 387–389, 404–405n18, 406–407n12, 408n27, 419–421n18, 458–459n6

transitional: object, 161, 358–359, 383; this book as (quasi), 13. *See also* interworld truth, xxi, 5, 8, 9, 10–14, 24, 34, 39, 47, 50, 59, 106, 109, 112–114, 129–132, 135, 141, 147, 160, 164, 169, 171–172, 177–178, 183, 196, 226, 231, 265, 277–279, 321, 328, 336, 350, 356–357, 370, 378, 379, 381, 384–385, 388, 399–400n9, 401n6, 419n15, 432n38, 457–458n2, 471n45, 488 Plates 14a–14b. *See also* work (or labor)

übersetzen, to translate (Freud), 294, 296
übertragen, to transpose, to transfer (Freud), 294, 296
Umkehrung, reversal (Freud, Marx), xiv, 335, 424n6, 471n43
unfulfillment, of desire, 69–71, 321–325, 357, 360, 376–389
utopia, 12–14, 349–355, 360. *See also* primary (space, process); suspended (or floating)

value. *See* signification
variance, 27, 28, 29, 54, 57–59, 103–114, 129–138, 141–144, 213–218, 327–334. *See also* continuity
Veduta, 195–196, 439n100, 451n78
Verdichtung, condensation (Freud), 238, 249, 254, 453n40, 487–488 Plate 13
Verkehrung ins Gegenteil, reversal into the opposite (Freud), 335
Verneinung, negation (or denial) (Freud), xvi, xvii, 58, 115–126, 292–293, 391–396, 421n1, 421n3, 422n9, 423n22
Verschiebung, displacement (Freud, Klee), 238, 255, 449n50, 451n76, 452n9, 485 Figure 11, 487–488 Plate 13, 488–489 Plate 15a
visible: as criterion of a classification of figures, 244–245, 268–269, 274–275, 279, 282–283, 457n20; of sight, 9, 49, 54–55, 192, 213, 232, 345–348
Vorstellung, representation (Frege, Freud), 78, 104–108, 367

Wahrheitswert, truth value (Frege), 109
Wahrnehmung, perception, to apprehend truly (Hegel), 39
Wesen, essence, being (Marx), 133
Wissenschaft, knowledge as science (Hegel), 48
word-presentation (Freud), 127, 255, 269, 300–303, 327, 338–346, 482 Figure 3
work (or labor), 12, 31, 60, 83, 98, 100, 404n16, 490 Plate 22; and artwork, xxiii, 8, 9, 46, 62, 71, 77, 139–142, 229–231, 268, 276, 290, 314–315, 324, 326, 346, 361, 368, 370–373, 374, 376, 377, 385–386, 476n19; of the dream, xvi, 71, 77, 232–267, 347, 381, 383, 468–469n21, 470n31, 478n40, 490 Plate 17; of the dream and thought, 144, 233–236, 292–297, 345, 358–359, 461–462n44; of the dream and hyper-reflection, 53; of the rebus, 271, 292–305; of truth, 10–14, 129–132, 147, 160, 164, 277–279, 356–357, 381–382, 385, 388, 423n22. *See also* condensation; displacement; distortion; figurability; reversal; secondary revision
Wunscherfüllung, wish-fulfillment (Freud), 241, 270–271, 281, 453n22, 455n1

Zeigen, to indicate (Hegel), 35, 39, 51, 401n5
Zwischenwelt, interworld (Klee), 226, 383, 485 Figure 15

Jean-François Lyotard (1925–1998) was professor emeritus of philosophy at the University of Paris–VIII (Vincennes, Saint-Denis); a founder and council member of the Collège International de Philosophie in Paris; and the Robert W. Woodruff Professor of French and Philosophy at Emory University in Atlanta, Georgia. He is the author of more than forty books and ninety articles of criticism and philosophy, including *The Postmodern Condition: A Report on Knowledge*; *Postmodern Fables*; *The Differend: Phrases in Dispute*; *Signed, Malraux*; *The Postmodern Explained*; *Political Writings*; *Heidegger and "the jews"*; and *Just Gaming*, all published by the University of Minnesota Press.

Antony Hudek is a research fellow in the UCL Mellon Programme, University College London.

Mary Lydon (1937–2001) was Pickard-Bascom Professor of French at the University of Wisconsin, Madison. Her studies of twentieth-century French literature focus on psychoanalytic, feminist, and poststructuralist theory, and she is the author of *Skirting the Issue: Essays in Literary Theory* and *Perpetuum Mobile: A Study of the Novels and Aesthetics of Michel Butor.*

John Mowitt is professor of English, cultural studies, and comparative literature at the University of Minnesota. He has written numerous books on culture, theory, and politics, including *Re-takes: Postcoloniality and Foreign Film Languages* (Minnesota, 2005). He is coeditor of *The Dreams of Interpretation: A Century down the Royal Road* (Minnesota, 2008) and of the journal *Cultural Critique.*